Sixth Edition

MOSAICS
READING AND WRITING PARAGRAPHS

D0224309

KIM FLACHMANN
California State University, Bakersfield

PEARSON

Boston   Columbus   Indianapolis   New York   San Francisco   Upper Saddle River
Amsterdam   Cape Town   Dubai   London   Madrid   Milan   Munich   Paris   Montréal   Toronto
Delhi   Mexico City   São Paulo   Sydney   Hong Kong   Seoul   Singapore   Taipei   Tokyo

Executive Editor: *Matthew Wright*
Executive Marketing Manager: *Thomas DeMarco*
Executive Digital Producer: *Stefanie A. Snajder*
Senior Supplements Editor: *Donna Campion*
Production Manager: *Savoula Amanatidis*
Project Coordination and Text Design: *Integra-Chicago*
Electronic Page Makeup: *Integra*
Cover Design Manager: *Wendy Ann Fredericks*

Cover Photo: *© Shutterstock*
Photo Research: *Integra*
Senior Manufacturing Buyer: *Roy L. Pickering, Jr.*
Printer and Binder: *R. R. Donnelley and Sons Company–Crawfordsville*
Cover Printer: *Lehigh-Phoenix Color Corporation–Hagerstown*

For permission to use copyrighted material, grateful acknowledgment is made to the copyright holders on pages 678–679, which are hereby made part of this copyright page.

Library of Congress Cataloging-in-Publication Data
Flachmann, Kim.
   Mosaics : reading and writing paragraphs / Kim Flachmann, California State University, Bakersfield.—Sixth edition.
      pages cm
   ISBN-13: 978-0-205-89054-5
   ISBN-10: 0-205-89054-7
1. English language—Paragraphs—Problems, exercises, etc.   2. English language—Rhetoric—Problems, exercises, etc.   I. Title.
   PE1439.F58 2013
   808'.042076—dc23

2013010049

10 9 8 7 6 5 4 3 2 1—DOC—16 15 14 13

PEARSON

www.pearsonhighered.com

Student Edition ISBN-13: 978-0-205-89054-5
Student Edition ISBN-10:   0-205-89054-7
Annotated Instructor's Edition ISBN-13: 978-0-321-89468-7
Annotated Instructor's Edition ISBN-10:   0-321-89468-5

BRIEF CONTENTS

iii

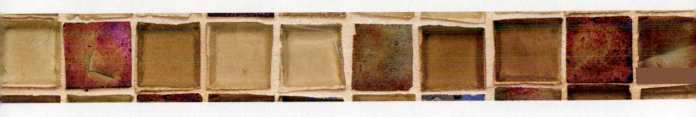

DETAILED CONTENTS

PREFACE

Students have the best chance of succeeding in college if they learn how to respond productively to the varying academic demands made on them throughout the curriculum. One extremely important part of this process is being able to analyze ideas and think critically about issues in many different subject areas. *Mosaics: Reading and Writing Paragraphs* is the second in a series of three books that teach the basic skills essential to all good academic writing. This series illustrates how the companion skills of reading and writing are parts of a larger, interrelated process that moves back and forth through the tasks of prereading and reading, prewriting and writing, and revising and editing. In other words, the *Mosaics* series demonstrates how these skills are integrated at every stage of the communication process in an attempt to help students discover the "mosaics" of their own reading and writing processes.

WHAT'S NEW TO THIS EDITION?

1. The sixth edition of *Mosaics: Reading and Writing Paragraphs* features deeper integration with MyWritingLab:

    -   Students can complete the Writing Prompts in Chapters 6–14 and the Write Your Own activities in Chapters 18–45 of the printed text within the book-specific module in MyWritingLab. These activities are clearly identified in the print text by this new icon:

        ✳ Explore more at **mywritinglab.com**

    -   The eText includes links to pertinent information from Pearson's *What Every Student Should Know About Critical Reading* in Chapter 2 (Reading Critically).

    -   All-new MyWritingLab prompts align with the new MyWritingLab XL platform. In each chapter, references to MyWritingLab appear at strategic points, linking students to more instruction, better practice, and tips for succeeding at each skill.

2. A color-coded system throughout the writing process chapters visually signals different aspects of the reading and writing processes: purple for reading; green for inventing, creating, and composing; blue for revising; and maroon for editing.

3. The supplement package now includes a chapter-by-chapter PowerPoint presentation to accompany each chapter. (See page xvii for more information.)

OVERALL GOAL

Ultimately, each book in the *Mosaics* series portrays writing as a way of thinking and processing information. One by one, these books encourage students to discover how the "mosaics" of their own reading and writing processes work together to form a coherent whole. By demonstrating the interrelationship among thinking, reading, and writing on progressively more difficult levels, these books promise to help prepare your students for success in college throughout the curriculum and in their lives after graduation.

THE *MOSAICS* SERIES

Each of the three books of the *Mosaics* series has a different emphasis. *Reading and Writing Sentences* provides instruction and practice in grammar and usage conventions; *Reading and Writing Paragraphs* highlights the development of paragraphs; and *Reading and Writing Essays* focuses on the composition of complete essays. As they move from personal to more academic writing, the Paragraph and Essay books become gradually more sophisticated in the length and level of their reading selections, the complexity of their writing assignments, the degree of difficulty of their revising and editing strategies, and the content and structure of their student writing samples.

This entire three-book series is based on the following fundamental assumptions:

- Students build confidence in their ability to read and write by reading and writing.
- Students learn best from discovery and experimentation rather than from instruction and abstract discussions.
- Students profit from studying both professional and student writing.
- Students need to discover their personal reading and writing processes.
- Students learn both individually and collaboratively.
- Students benefit most from assignments that actually integrate reading and writing.
- Students learn how to revise by following clear guidelines.
- Students learn grammar and usage rules by editing their own writing.
- Students must be able to transfer their writing skills to all their college courses.
- Students must think critically/analytically to succeed in college.

UNIQUE FEATURES OF THIS BOOK

Mosaics: Reading and Writing Paragraphs teaches and demonstrates the reading–writing connection in the following ways:

- It introduces and demonstrates reading as a process.
- It illustrates all aspects of the writing process through student writing.

- It uses both student and professional paragraphs as models.
- It features culturally diverse, high-interest reading selections.
- It moves students systematically from personal to academic writing.
- It actually develops a student essay from assignment to completed paper.
- It includes a complete, color-coded handbook with exercises.
- It provides a set of Pre- and Post-Unit Tests for each grammar unit.
- It offers worksheets for peer and self-evaluation.

This book teaches a different reading strategy in every chapter of Part II:

- Description   Making Personal Associations
- Narration   Thinking Aloud
- Illustration   Chunking
- Process Analysis   Graphing the Ideas
- Comparison/Contrast   Peer Teaching
- Division/Classification   Summarizing
- Definition   Reacting Critically
- Cause/Effect   Making Connections
- Argument   Recognizing Facts and Opinions
                             Reading with the Author/
                             Against the Author

These strategies are applied to all aspects of the writing process: reading/getting ready to write, reading the prompt, reading another student's paragraph, and reading their own paragraphs.

The innovative lessons of MyWritingLab (www.mywritinglab.com) are strategically integrated into the content of every chapter:

MyWritingLab

- The instruction in each chapter is supplemented by useful suggestions for integrating MyWritingLab into class and/or individual work.
- MyWritingLab Hints appear at strategic points within a given chapter for prewriting, writing, and revising/editing, thereby enabling students to truly benefit from the use of this dynamic online product.
- Each chapter of the *Annotated Instructor's Edition* includes directions for integrating MyWritingLab into a course.
- An informative section with further information on using MyWritingLab with *Mosaics: Reading and Writing Paragraphs* is included in the *Instructor's Resource Manual*.

HOW THIS BOOK WORKS

Mosaics: Reading and Writing Paragraphs teaches students how to read and write critically. For flexibility and easy reference, this book is divided into four parts:

Part I: Reading and Writing for Success in College   All five chapters in Part I demonstrate the cyclical nature of the reading and writing processes. They begin with the logistics of getting ready to read and write and then move systematically through the interlocking stages of the processes by following a student from prereading to rereading and then from prewriting to revising and editing. Part I ends with four review practices that summarize the material and let your students practice what they have learned.

Part II: Reading and Writing Effective Paragraphs   Part II, the heart of the instruction in this text, teaches students how to read and write paragraphs by introducing the rhetorical modes as patterns of development. It moves from personal writing to more academic types of writing: describing, narrating, illustrating, analyzing a process, comparing and contrasting, dividing and classifying, defining, analyzing causes and effects, and arguing. Within each chapter, students learn how to read a professional paragraph critically, write their own paragraphs, and revise and edit another student's paragraph as well as their own. Finally, two professional writing samples are included in each rhetorical mode chapter so students can actually see the features of each strategy at work in different pieces of writing. Each professional essay is preceded by prereading activities and then followed by 10 questions that move students from a literal to an analytical understanding as they consider the essay's content, purpose, audience, and paragraph structure.

Part III: Essays: Paragraphs in Context   The next section of this text helps students move from writing effective paragraphs to writing well-crafted essays. It systematically illustrates the relationship between a paragraph and an essay. Then it explains the essay through both professional and student examples. Part III ends with a series of writing assignments and workshops designed to encourage students to write, revise, and edit an essay and then reflect on their own writing process.

Part IV: The Handbook   Part IV is a complete grammar/usage handbook, including exercises, that covers nine units: The Basics, Sentences, Verbs, Pronouns, Modifiers, Punctuation, Mechanics, Effective Sentences, and Choosing the Right Word. These categories are coordinated with the Editing Checklist that appears periodically throughout this text. Each chapter starts with five self-test questions so students can determine their strengths and weaknesses in a specific area. The chapters provide at least three types of practice after each grammar concept, moving students systematically from identifying grammar concepts to filling in the blanks to writing their own sentences. Each chapter ends with a practical editing workshop that asks students to use the skills they just learned as they work with another student to edit their own writing. Pre- and Post-Unit Tests—including practice with single sentences and paragraphs—are offered for each unit in the *Instructor's Resource Manual*.

APPENDIXES

The appendixes will help students keep track of their progress in the various skills they are learning in this text. References to these appendixes are interspersed throughout the book so students know when to use them as they study the concepts in each chapter:

- Appendix 1: Critical Thinking Log
- Appendix 2A : Your EQ (Editing Quotient)
- Appendix 2B: Editing Quotient Answers
- Appendix 2C: Editing Quotient Error Chart
- Appendix 3: Test Yourself Answers
- Appendix 4: Revising a Paragraph (Forms A and B)
- Appendix 5: Revising an Essay
- Appendix 6: Editing
- Appendix 7: Error Log
- Appendix 8: Spelling Log

ACKNOWLEDGMENTS

I want to acknowledge the support, encouragement, and sound advice of several people who have helped me through the development of the *Mosaics* series. First, Pearson Higher Education has provided guidance and inspiration for this project through the enduring wisdom of Craig Campanella, previous senior acquisitions editor of developmental English, and Matt Wright, current executive editor; the foresight and prudence of Joe Opiela, publisher; the special guidance and leadership of Eric Stano, editor-in-chief of Developmental English; the special creative inspiration of Megan Galvin, senior marketing manager; the unparalleled support of Amanda Dykstra, assistant editor; the exceptional organizational skills of Denise Phillip, production manager; the insight and vision of Marta Tomins and Harriett Prentiss, development editors; the tender loving care of Kristin Jobe, production editor; the hard work and patience of Wesley Hall, permissions editor; the flawless organization of Kristen Pechtol, administrative assistant for Developmental English; and the exceptional leadership of Greg Tobin, President of English, Math, and Student Success. Also, this book would not be a reality without the insightful persistence of Phil Miller, former publisher at Pearson.

I want to give very special thanks to Lauren Martinez, my advisor and source of endless ideas and solutions to problems. I am also grateful to Cheryl Smith for her inspiration and hard work on previous editions and to Rebecca Hewett, Valerie Turner, Li'l Pearl, Lauren Martinez, and Isaac Sanchez for their discipline and hard work—past and present—on the *Instructor's Resource Manuals* for each of the books in the series. Thanks also to Isaac Sanchez, who created a set of PowerPoint slides to accompany this text.

Two more groups of consultants and assistants were inspirational in the development of this particular edition: First, I want to thank Brooke Hughes, Randi Brummett, and Isaac Sanchez for their invaluable expertise and vision in crafting and placing the instructional inserts for MyWritingLab in this edition. Also, I want to express my gratitude to my students, from whom I have learned so much about the writing process, about teaching, and about life itself. Thanks especially to the students who contributed paragraphs and essays to this series: Josh Ellis, Jolene Christie, Mary Minor, Michael Tiede, Juliana Schweiger, and Chris Dison.

In addition, I am especially indebted to the following reviewers who have guided me through the development and revision of this book: Lisa Berman, Miami-Dade Community College; Patrick Haas, Glendale Community College; Jeanne Campanelli, American River College; Dianne Gregory, Cape Cod Community College; Clara Wilson-Cook, Southern University at New Orleans; Thomas Beery, Lima Technical College; Jean Petrolle, Columbia College; David Cratty, Cuyahoga Community College; Allison Travis, Butte State College; Suellen Meyer, Meramec Community College; Jill Lahnstein, Cape Fear Community College; Stanley Coberly, West Virginia State University at Parkersville; Jamie Moore, Scottsdale Community College; Nancy Hellner, Mesa Community College; Ruth Hatcher, Washtenaw Community College; Thurmond Whatley, Aiken Technical College; W. David Hall, Columbus State Community College; Marilyn Coffee, Fort Hays State University; Teriann Gaston, University of Texas at Arlington; Peggy Karsten, Ridgewater College; Nancy Hayward, Indiana University of Pennsylvania; Carol Ann Britt, San Antonio College; Maria C. Villar-Smith, Miami-Dade Community College; Jami L. Huntsinger, University of New Mexico at Valencia Campus; P. Berniece Longmore, Essex County College; Lee Herrick, Fresno City College; Elaine Chakonas, North Eastern Illinois University; Roy Warner, Montana State University; Chris Morelock, Walters State Community College; Carmen Wong, John Tyler Community College; Angela Bartlett, Chaffey College; Sharisse Turner, Tallahassee Community College; Billy Jones, Miami-Dade College; Chrishawn Speller, Seminole Community College; Albert Hernandez, SW Texas College; Greg Zobel, College of the Redwoods; Ben Worth, KCTCS-Bluegrass Community College; Aaron DiFranco, Napa Valley College; Jacinth Thomas, Sacramento City College; Liz Ann Aguilar, San Antonio College; James McCormack, Rochester Community & Technical College; Jessica Carroll, Miami-Dade College; Gloria Browning, Bluegrass Community and Technical College; Lisa Buchanan, Northeast State Community College; Eric R. Fish, Northeast State Community College; and Althea Hunsucker, Richmond Community College.

Finally, I owe a tremendous personal debt to the people who have lived with this project for the past 18 years; they are my closest companions and my best advisers: Michael, Christopher, and Laura Flachmann. I also want to thank one of my newest consultants to the project, Abby Flachmann. To Michael, I owe additional thanks for the valuable support and feedback he has given me through the entire process of creating and revising this series.

Kim Flachmann

SUPPLEMENTS AND ADDITIONAL RESOURCES

Pearson Writing Resources for Instructors and Students

Book-Specific Ancillary Material

Annotated Instructor's Edition for Mosaics: *Reading and Writing Paragraphs*, Sixth Edition

ISBN 0321894685

The *AIE* offers in-text answers, marginal annotations for teaching each chapter, links to the *Instructor's Resource Manual*, and MyWritingLab teaching tips. It is a valuable resource for experienced and first-time instructors alike.

Instructor's Resource Manual for Mosaics: *Reading and Writing Paragraphs*, Sixth Edition

ISBN 0321852370

The material in the *IRM* is designed to save instructors time and provide them with effective options for teaching their writing classes. It offers suggestions for setting up their courses; provides lots of extra practice for students who need it; offers quizzes and grammar tests, including unit tests; furnishes grading rubrics for each rhetorical mode; and supplies answers in case instructors want to print them out and have students grade their own work. This valuable resource is exceptionally useful for adjuncts who might need advice in setting up their initial classes or who might be teaching a variety of writing classes with too many students and not enough time.

PowerPoint Presentations for Mosaics: Reading and Writing Paragraphs, Sixth Edition

ISBN 0321852206

PowerPoint presentations to accompany each chapter consist of classroom-ready lecture outline slides, lecture tips and classroom activities, and review questions. Available for download from the Instructor Resource Center.

Answer Key for Mosaics: Reading and Writing Paragraphs, Sixth Edition

ISBN 0321894677

The Answer Key contains the solutions to the exercises in the student edition of the text. Available for download from the Instructor Resource Center.

À-La-Carte version of Mosaics: Reading and Writing Paragraphs, Sixth Edition

ISBN 0321852192

The À La Carte offers a two-hole punched version of the regular student text at a reduced cost.

Pearson is pleased to offer a variety of support materials to help make teaching writing easier for teachers and to help students excel in their coursework. Many of our student supplements are available free or at a greatly reduced price when packaged with *Mosaics: Reading and Writing Paragraphs*. Visit www.pearsonhighereducation.com, contact your local Pearson sales representative, or review a detailed listing of the full supplements package in the *Instructor's Resource Manual* for more information.

MyWritingLab

Where practice, application, and demonstration meet to improve writing.

MyWritingLab, a complete online learning program, provides additional resources and effective practice exercises for developing writers.

What makes the practice, application, and demonstration in MyWritingLab more effective?

- **Diagnostic Testing**   MyWritingLab's diagnostic Path Builder test comprehensively assesses students' skills in grammar. Students are provided an individualized learning path based on the diagnostic's results, identifying the areas where they most need help.

- **Progressive Learning**   The heart of MyWritingLab is the progressive learning that takes place as students complete the Overview, Animations, Recall, Apply, and Write exercises along with the Posttest within each topic. Students move from preparation (Overview, Animation) to literal comprehension (Recall) to critical understanding (Apply) to the ability to demonstrate a skill in their own writing (Write) to total mastery (Posttest). This progression of critical thinking, not available in any other online resource, enables students to truly master the skills and concepts they need to become successful writers.

- **Online Gradebook**   All student work in MyWritingLab is captured in the Online Gradebook. Instructors can see what and how many topics their students have mastered. They can also view students' individual scores on all assignments throughout MyWritingLab, as well as overviews of student and class performance by module. Students can monitor their progress in new Completed Work pages, which show them their totals, scores, time on task, and the date and time of their work by module. They can also open and review any of their assignments directly from these pages.

- **Enhanced eText**   The *Mosaics: Reading and Writing Paragraphs*, Sixth Edition, eText is accessed through MyWritingLab. Students have the eText at their fingertips while completing the various exercises and activities within MyWritingLab. Students can highlight important material in the eText, tab pages and areas of importance, add notes to any section for reflection and/or further study, and access important content on reading critically.

Reading and Writing for Success in College

"Reading furnishes our minds only with materials and knowledge. It is thinking that makes what we read ours."

—JOHN LOCKE

Part I of *Mosaics* is designed to build your confidence as a reader *and* a writer. In these five chapters, you will discover more about both the reading and writing processes so that you can understand and take control of your unique way of dealing with these skills. As you mold the reading and writing tasks into a series of activities that fit your particular learning style, you will become more aware of your own strengths and weaknesses in communication. You can then use this information to establish your identity in the community of readers and writers throughout college.

1

Reading and Writing as Critical Thinking

Reading and Writing
for Success in College

Critical thinking is the highest form of mental activity that we undertake and a major source of success in college and in life. Thinking critically involves grappling with the ideas, issues, and problems in your immediate environment and in the larger world. It means constantly questioning and analyzing different aspects of life. You can actually learn how to think critically through your reading and writing. But since critical thinking is complex, it requires a great deal of concentration and practice. Once you have a sense of how your mind works at this level, you will be able to think critically whenever you choose.

With some guidance, learning how to read and write according to different rhetorical modes or ways of thinking (such as describing, narrating, or dividing and classifying) can give you the mental workout you need to think critically in much the same way that physical exercise warms you up for various sports. As you move through the chapters in Part II of this text, you will be asked to isolate each rhetorical mode—just as you isolate your abs, thighs, and biceps in a physical workout. Each rhetorical mode offers a slightly different way of observing your surroundings, processing information, and solving problems. So each is really a distinct way of thinking and making sense of the world. Focusing on one rhetorical mode at a time lets you systematically improve your ability to think, read, and write critically.

THE READING PROCESS

The reading process consists of "steps" or "stages" that overlap. But reading, unlike writing, has to occur in a certain order, or you will not be able to understand your material. To get the most out of the process, you have to start at the beginning and read to the end. What you do during the process, however, is what can raise your level of understanding to the analytical or critical level, which is where you want to be to succeed in college and in life after college.

Reading actively (rather than passively) will make you a critical reader. Once you read critically, your writing will rise to a higher level as well. Passive readers open a reading assignment, start at the first page, and read to the end without doing any recognizable activities as they read. Active readers are physically working with their reading material from beginning to end—highlighting it, writing on it, and looping back and forth to re-read passages they don't understand on the first reading. They are making it their own, trying to understand it on a more sophisticated level, and constantly reacting to it as they read. Identifying your own opinions and thoughts in response to your reading material is one of the essential parts of the reading process.

As you work with this process in this textbook, the following graphic might help you understand how various stages of the process can overlap.

activities similar? How are they different? Have each group explain its answer.

INSTRUCTOR'S RESOURCE MANUAL For additional material about teaching the reading process, for journal entries, and for various tests, see the *Instructor's Resource Manual,* Section II, Part I.

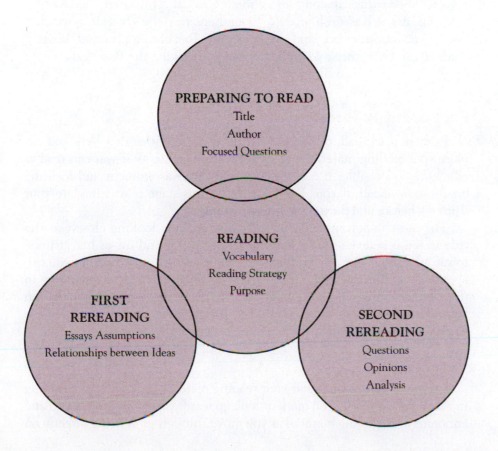

PREPARING TO READ
Title
Author
Focused Questions

READING
Vocabulary
Reading Strategy
Purpose

FIRST REREADING
Essays Assumptions
Relationships between Ideas

SECOND REREADING
Questions
Opinions
Analysis

PRACTICE 1 Answer the following questions.

1. List the three elements of prereading.

   Title, author, focused questions

2. List the three elements of reading.

   Vocabulary, reading strategy, purpose

3. List the two elements of the first rereading.

   Essay's assumptions, relationships between ideas

4. List the three elements of the second rereading.

   Questions, opinions, analysis

Student Comment:
"At first I didn't want to do extra work online, but this topic was really helpful because it told me what questions to ask as I read."

This is a perfect topic to start your class with because it allows your students to think about their own learning. You might suggest that they review this video from time to time as they move through this book.

MyWritingLab **Critical Thinking: Text and Visuals**

To make sure you understand how to think critically about your reading, go to **MyWritingLab.com**, and choose **Critical Thinking: Texts and Visuals** in the **Research** module. From there, read the **Overview**, watch the **Animation** video, and complete the **Recall, Apply,** and **Write** activities. Then check your understanding by taking the **Post-test.**

Preparing to Read

Preparing to read, or **prereading**, refers to activities that help you explore your reading material and its general subject so that you can read as efficiently as possible. It includes surveying your assignment and focusing on the task ahead of you. Your mission at this stage is to stimulate your thinking before and during the act of reading.

The most important tasks at this point include looking closely at the title to see if it reveals any clues about the author and his or her attitude toward the subject of the reading selection, finding out as much as you can about the author (background, profession, biases, etc.), and responding in this textbook to some preliminary questions that will focus your attention before you read. All of these activities will be demonstrated in Chapter 2 as Travis Morehouse approaches a reading assignment.

Reading

Once you have previewed your reading material, you can start **reading** it. As you read, you should mark or look up words you don't understand and annotate your reading material as you move through it. Writing directly on the material itself will keep you engaged in the process. You should also try to figure out the author's primary purpose for writing the selection.

Every chapter in Part II of this book will focus on a different reading strategy. These strategies can be applied to any reading material and are especially useful in helping you become an active reader. Once you learn different strategies that will improve your reading comprehension, you can choose your favorites to use in other courses.

First Rereading

Most students don't want to read their assignments more than once, but the second and third readings are the ones that teach you how to read critically. Only after the **first rereading** can you hope to understand your reading material more completely. This second reading allows you to get to the assumptions that lie behind the words on the page, identify any confusion you might have, and see relationships between ideas that you didn't notice in the first reading.

With this reading, you are closer to critical reading, but you are not there yet. This reading helps you dig more deeply into what the author is saying and prepares you to go one step further when you read an essay for the third time. Once again, the mechanics of this reading will be demonstrated by Travis Morehouse in Chapter 2 as he records his reactions to the reading material.

Second Rereading

Now read the material one more time slowly and carefully to locate any remaining confusion, discover your opinions, and analyze the author's argument. This analytical or critical reading is the highest level of comprehension and should be your goal with each essay that you approach in this book. To achieve this level of understanding, you must actually wrestle with the subject matter—ask questions, make associations of your own, and draw conclusions that capture your personal reaction to the reading material.

This reading requires the most energy on your part because you have to produce the questions and argue with the essay as it moves from point to point. Although this **second rereading** takes the most energy, it is also the most rewarding because your mind gets to exercise and grapple with ideas on a level that helps you understand both your reading and writing assignments more completely. Ultimately, this level of reading will raise your grades in all subjects.

Reading as a Cycle

Once you start reading and understand where you are headed, you can loop in and out of these "stages" in any order—just as you do in writing. You may look up a word, argue with an idea in the first paragraph, and go back over a paragraph for a second reading—all in the first few minutes of an essay. Although you may never approach any two reading projects in the same way, the chapters in Part I will help you discover your personal reading process and guide you toward a comfortable ritual as a reader.

PRACTICE 2 Answer the following questions.

1. When does the reading process start?

   The reading process begins the minute you get a reading assignment.

   _____

2. Explain "preparing to read" or "prereading" in your own words.

   Prereading allows you to explore a reading selection and its general subject matter, in

   particular the title, author, and questions connected with the selection.

3. Describe your reading environment.

   Answers will vary.

   _____

4. What does "reading" consist of?

   Reading includes understanding vocabulary, using a reading strategy that makes you

   an active reader, and discovering the author's purpose for writing the selection.

5. What does rereading accomplish?

   Rereading lets you understand your reading material at a deeper level and finally be

   able to argue with and analyze the material.

TEACHING THE WRITING
PROCESS
Ask your students to bring
in a visual representation
of their writing process.
Like the visual of the
reading process, it can
be anything—cut-up
magazines, something with
props, a drawing—that
conveys how they go
through this process. Once
again, be careful not to

THE WRITING PROCESS

The writing process begins the minute you get a writing assignment—whether you are writing a book, an essay, or a single paragraph. It involves all the activities you do, from choosing a topic to turning in a final draft. During this time, you will be thinking about your topic on both a subconscious and conscious level. Whether you are washing your car, reading in the library, preparing a meal, or writing a draft of your paper, you are going through your writing process. The main parts of the process are pictured here and then explained one by one. This design shows how the stages of the writing process can overlap.

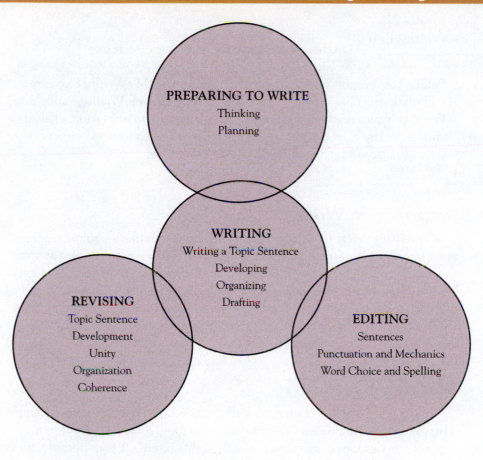

PRACTICE 3 Answer the following questions.

1. List the two elements of preparing to write.
   Thinking and planning

2. List the four elements of writing.
   Writing a topic sentence, developing ideas, organizing thoughts, drafting

3. List the five elements of revising.
   Topic sentence, development, unity, organization, coherence

4. List the three elements of editing.
   Sentences, punctuation and mechanics, word choice and spelling

MyWritingLab | ## Understanding the Writing Process

Before you go any further in this chapter, go to **MyWritingLab.com**, and click on **The Writing Process** in **The Craft of Writing** module. For this topic, read the **Overview**, watch the two **Animation** videos, and complete the **Recall, Apply,** and **Write** activities. Then check your understanding by taking the **Post-test.**

Preparing to Write

Prewriting refers to all activities that help you explore a subject, generate ideas about it, settle on a specific topic, establish a purpose, and analyze the audience for your essay. In Chapter 3, you will learn different strategies for accomplishing these goals before you actually begin to write a draft of your paragraph or essay. Your mission at this stage is to stimulate your thinking before and during the act of writing. Every time you think of a new idea during the writing process, you are prewriting.

Writing

When you have lots of ideas to work with, you are ready to start **writing.** This "stage" of the process involves writing a topic sentence, developing or expanding your ideas, organizing your thoughts to reflect your purpose, and writing a first draft. To begin your draft, you may want to spread out your class notes, your journal entries, or various other prewriting notes so that you can start to put your ideas together into coherent sentences. This is the time to keep your thoughts flowing without worrying about grammar, punctuation, mechanics, or spelling.

Revising

As you may already suspect, the process of writing is not finished with your first draft. You should always revise your work to make it stronger and better. **Revising** involves rethinking your content and organization so that your writing says exactly what you want it to. (Editing, the last step, focuses on correcting grammar and spelling.) Your main goal in revising is to make sure that the purpose of your essay is clear to your audience and that your main ideas are supported with details and examples. In addition, you should check that your organization is logical.

Editing

The final step in the writing process is **editing.** In this stage, you should read your paragraph or essay slowly and carefully to make sure no errors in grammar, punctuation, mechanics, or spelling have slipped into your draft. Such errors can distract your reader from the message you are trying to communicate or can cause communication to break down altogether. Editing gives you the chance to clean up your draft so that your writing is clear and precise.

Writing as a Cycle

Even though we talk about the stages of writing, it is actually a cyclical process, which means that at any point you may loop in and out of other stages. Once you start on a writing project, the stages of writing do not have to occur in any specific order. You may change a word (revise) in the very first sentence you write and then think of another detail (prewrite) you can add to your opening sentence and next cross out and rewrite a misspelled word (edit)—all in the first two minutes of writing. Although you may approach every writing project in a different way, we hope that as you move through Part I, you will establish a personal routine writing process and start to get comfortable as a writer working within that structure.

PRACTICE 4 Answer the following questions.

1. Explain prewriting in your own words.

   Prewriting includes exploring a subject, generating ideas, choosing a topic, establish-

   ing a purpose, and analyzing the audience.

2. Describe your writing environment.

   Answers will vary.

3. What does "writing" consist of?

   Writing involves writing a topic sentence, developing ideas, organizing thoughts, and

   writing a first draft.

4. What is the difference between revising and editing?

   Revising involves content and organization; editing deals with grammar, punctuation,

   mechanics, and spelling.

GETTING READY TO READ AND WRITE

Whether you read email messages, your favorite magazine, or a contract you received in the mail, you are a reader. Conversely, whether you are making a grocery list, emailing a friend, doing your history assignment, or writing a report for your manager, you are part of a community of writers. In fact, you *are* a writer.

As you face more complex reading and writing tasks in college, you need to understand the sequence of activities that make up the reading and writing processes. Learning to use these processes so the work you produce is the best you are capable of is what this book is all about.

Before you actually begin to read or write, a wise move is to get your surroundings ready. Preparing your surroundings involves setting aside a time and place to do your work, gathering supplies, and establishing a routine that fits comfortably into your life.

1. **Set aside a special time for reading and writing, and plan to do nothing else during that time.** The dog's bath can wait until tomorrow, the kitchen appliances don't have to be scrubbed today, drawers can be cleaned and organized some other time, and the dirt on the car won't turn to concrete overnight. When you first get a reading or writing assignment, a little procrastination is natural. The trick is to know when to quit procrastinating and get down to work.

2. **Find a comfortable place with few distractions.** In her famous essay *A Room of One's Own*, Virginia Woolf claims that all writers have a basic need for space, privacy, and time. You need to set up a place of your own that suits your needs as a reader and writer. It should be a place where you are not distracted or interrupted. Some people work best sitting in a straight chair at a desk while others write in a big armchair or on a bed. The particular place doesn't matter, as long as you feel comfortable studying there.

Even if you are lucky enough to have a private study area, you may find that you still need to make some adjustments. For example, you might want to turn off the ringer on your phone during the time you spend on your assignments. Or you may discover that listening to your favorite music helps you shut out noise from other parts of the house but doesn't distract you in the way talk shows on TV might. One student may write sitting in bed with her legs crossed, wearing jeans and a T-shirt; another may read sprawling on the floor in pajamas. The point is this: Whatever your choices, you need to set up a working environment that is comfortable for you.

3. **Gather your supplies before you begin to study.** Who knows what great idea might escape while you search for a computer or a pen that

works! Some students use a legal pad and a pencil to take notes on their reading or start a writing task while others go straight to their computers. One of the main advantages of working on a computer is that once you type in your ideas, changing them or moving them around is easy. As a result, you are more likely to revise when you work on a computer, and, therefore, you will probably turn in a better paper. Whatever equipment you choose, make sure it is ready at the time you have set aside to write.

4. **Think of yourself as a reader and a writer.** Once you have a time and place for studying and all the supplies you need, you are ready to discover your own reading and writing processes. Understanding your unique habits and rituals is extremely important to your growth as a writer. So in the course of recognizing yourself as a reader and writer, take a moment now to record some of your own preferences when you undertake these tasks.

PRACTICE 5 Explain the rituals you instinctively follow as you prepare to study. Where do you read? Where do you write? At what time of day do you produce your best work? Do you like noise? Quiet? What other details describe your study environment? What equipment do you use when you read? When you write? *Answers will vary.*

KEEPING A JOURNAL

The word *journal* means "a place for daily writing." Your journal is a place for you to record ideas, snatches of conversation, dreams, descriptions of people, pictures of places or objects—whatever catches your attention.

To help improve your life as a reader and writer, you will find a personal journal extremely valuable. As with any skill, the more you practice, the more you will improve. In addition, your journal is a collection of thoughts and topics for your writing assignments. In other words, your journal is a place to both generate and retrieve your ideas. Finally, writing can help you solve problems. Writing in your journal can help you discover what you think and feel about specific issues as well as think through important choices you have to make.

You can use this textbook to help you establish the habit of journal writing. For example, in your journal you might answer the questions that accompany the instruction and readings in Part II of this text, the guidelines for writing an essay in Part III, and the writing exercises in the Handbook (Part IV). You might also want to use your journal for prewriting or generating ideas on a specific topic. Keeping track of your journal is much easier than collecting assorted scraps of paper when you need them.

steps they go through when studying for an exam. (For example, how many times do they review a concept?) Have them find on the Web stories about other study routines. Then, have students compare the process of studying to the reading and writing processes. How are the two cyclical natures both similar and different? Have each group explain its answer.

INSTRUCTOR'S RESOURCE MANUAL For additional material about teaching reading and writing as critical thinking, for journal entries, and for various tests, see the *Instructor's Resource Manual*, Section II, Part I.

Making at least one section of your journal private is also a good idea. Sometimes when you think on paper or let your imagination loose, you don't want to share the results with anyone, but those notes can be very important in finding a subject to write about or in developing a topic.

If you use a notebook for your journal, take some time to pick a size and color you really like. Some people choose spiral-bound notebooks while others prefer cloth-bound books or loose-leaf binders. You might even want a notebook divided into sections so that different types of entries can have their own location. The choice is yours—unless your instructor specifies a particular journal. Just remember that a journal should be a notebook you enjoy writing in and carrying with you.

On the other hand, your journal might be electronic. However, unless you have a laptop, you won't have your journal with you all the time. As a result, you need to schedule time to write at your computer every day. Also be sure to back up computer journal entries on a travel drive and save your work fairly often so you don't lose anything in a power failure. You may also want to print hard copies of your journal entries to take with you to class.

Everyone's journal entries will be different and will often depend on the instructor's objectives in a particular course. But some basic advice applies to all entries, whether you keep your journal on paper or on a computer.

1. Date your entries. (Jotting down the time is also useful so you can see when your best ideas occur.)

2. Record anything that comes to your mind, and follow your thoughts wherever they take you (unless your instructor gives you different directions).

3. Download or tape anything into your journal that stimulates your thinking or writing—cartoons, ads, podcasts, poems, videos, blogs, pictures, advice columns, podcasts, YouTube extracts, or other sources.

4. Think of your journal as someone to talk to—a friend who will keep your cherished ideas safe and sound and won't talk back or argue with you.

PRACTICE 6 Begin your own journal.

1. Buy a notebook that you like, and write in it.

2. Record at least two journal entries on your computer.

3. Which type of journal do you prefer—paper or electronic? Write an entry explaining your preference. *Answers will vary.*

Reading Critically

✳─[**Explore** more at **mywritinglab.com**

Reading critically is the source of all successful college work. But only after much practice that includes time and reflection will your mind be engaged so you can read critically and be productive students and citizens in a very fast-moving world. Reading critically will affect every aspect of your life in and out of college in a positive way—especially your writing ability.

This chapter demonstrates various activities readers use as they read. As you work through the chapter, you will see how Travis Morehouse uses each strategy on a paragraph and then have a chance to try out the technique yourself. Consider keeping your responses to these activities in a journal you can refer to throughout the course.

PREPARING TO READ

Activities that take place before you actually start reading are labeled **prereading** or **preparing to read.** More specifically, prereading consists of the following tasks:

- Survey and analyze the title
- Find out what you can about the author
- Focus your attention on the subject of the reading selection

---

MyWritingLab | **Preparing to Read**

To learn how to preview your reading material, click on the **Study Skills Learning Path** in **MyWritingLab.com,** and choose **Concentrating When You Read and Study.** From there, watch the **Overview** video, and follow the links for tips on creating an appropriate learning space

---

TEACHING READING CRITICALLY
Reading a book online is quite a different experience than reading it in the traditional way. Ask your students to find a novel they want to read online. They can start at bibliomania.com. Then they can choose any type of book they want and see what it is like to read online by downloading the book.

TEACHING ON THE WEB
Discussion Topic: Divide students into groups of three or four, and have them discuss how electronic devices have changed the way they read. How much reading do they do electronically in a day? How much reading do they do with actual books? How do they integrate reading and electronics into their lives?

Student Comment:
"When I read, I have a hard time focusing. The interactive activity in this topic showed me how to preview a work in order to prepare my mind for reading."

When discussing
Concentrating When

and improving your concentration when you read. When you feel you have mastered the fundamentals, click on the **Interactive Activity** to practice previewing a text. Once you complete these activities, check your understanding through the **Self-Check**.

Title: Micanopy

Travis learned that the paragraph he was assigned is from an essay entitled "Micanopy." Travis doesn't know what that word means, so he looks it up and discovers it is not in the dictionary. Then he looks on the Internet and finds out it is the name of a small town (population about 600) in northern Florida, just south of Jacksonville. So Travis is expecting the author to be characterizing some aspects of the town.

Author: Bailey White

Travis then learns that the author's name is Bailey White, but he doesn't even know if this is a male or a female. So he does a Google search for the name and finds the following biography:[1]

> White was born in 1950 in Thomasville, Georgia. White still lives in the same house in which she grew up, on one of the large tracts of virgin longleaf pine woods. Her father, Robb White, was a fiction writer and later a television and movie script writer. Her mother, Rosalie White, was a farmer, and worked for many years as the executive director of the local Red Cross Chapter. She has one brother, who is a carpenter and boat builder, and one sister, who is a bureaucrat. White graduated from Florida State University in 1973, and has taken a break from teaching first grade to pursue writing full-time.
>
> White is the author of *Sleeping at the Starlite Motel, Mama Makes Up Her Mind,* and *Quite a Year for Plums.* Her commentaries can be heard on NPR's award-winning newsmagazine *All Things Considered.*

Focusing Your Attention

In this book, a set of questions is furnished to help you focus your attention on the material you are about to read. Without this book, you should try to generate your own questions (about the author, about the

---

[1]©2004, NPR®, used with the permission of NPR. Any unauthorized duplication is strictly prohibited. [Source: http://www.npr.org/templates/story/stroy.php?storyId=2101366]

subject matter, about the title) so that you start your reading actively rather than passively.

Here are some questions to focus your attention on the Bailey White paragraph. Writing your thoughts to these questions in a journal is the most beneficial approach to this exercise. Travis recorded his personal reactions to these questions before he started reading the essay.

1. What sights, sounds, smells, tastes, and textures are you aware of on a daily basis? Do these sensory signals have any special meaning for you?

2. In the paragraph you are about to read, the writer describes one of her favorite places so vividly it feels as if we are there. What are some of your favorite places? What details do you remember about these places?

READING

As you approach a reading task, you should plan to **read** it three times if you want to understand it critically. To get to the deeper levels of meaning, you need to work through literal and interpretive comprehension first.

As you read, you are making meaning out of a text that someone else has written. You must work in partnership with the author and his or her words to make sense of the material. Usually this does not happen in one reading. In like manner, when someone reads your writing, he or she must work with your words on the page to figure out what you are saying and what your words are implying.

Expanding Your Vocabulary ✳ Explore more at **mywritinglab.com**

The first task you should undertake in your reading is to get the gist of the selection and look up vocabulary words you don't understand. In this book, difficult vocabulary words are identified and defined for you. You should keep this list handy and add other words to it as you read.

If you actually want to increase your vocabulary and take these words with you into your own speaking and writing, you should highlight the words, compose your own lists, create index cards—interact with the text in some way that will make the words your own. In this text, a specific task is suggested in each vocabulary section so you can try a few different activities and then choose those that work best for you.

Here is a list of difficult words you need to know for the first reading of "Micanopy." Circle those that are new for you and start a vocabulary log of your own in your journal.

Micanopy: small town in northern Florida

wisteria: a climbing plant with blue, pink, or white flowers

stealthily: quietly

Using a Reading Strategy   ✳ ⎡Explore more at mywritinglab.com

As you work through the material in Part II, you will be prompted to use a reading strategy with each reading assignment. Here are the ten reading strategies we introduce in this book:

Making Personal Associations

We all naturally make personal associations with our reading. However, one person's associations are usually quite different from those of someone else. Recording the associations you make with a reading selection lets you "own" the ideas. It allows you to connect the author's ideas to your own experiences. To perform this strategy, make notes in the margin that relate some of your specific memories to the details in the reading. Be prepared to explain the connection between your notes and the facts in the selection.

Travis's Personal Associations   Travis read the following paragraph by Bailey White. He was fascinated by the level of detail in this small paragraph and jotted a couple notes to himself in the margins as he read.

Wow! She must really like this place!

But the reason <u>I drive the two hundred miles year after year</u> is the bookstore. The building is tall, a beautiful pink brick. The sign says,

O. Brisky

Books

Old Used Rare

Bought and Sold

<u>Out of Print Search Service</u>

Even before you go inside, <u>you can smell the old, used, and rare books.</u> On sunny days, Mr. Brisky arranges a collection of books on a table on the sidewalk. There are books in the windows and stacks of books on the floor just inside the entrance. From an open back door the misty green light of (Micanopy) shines into the dust. <u>Tendrils of wisteria</u> have crept in through the doorway and are stealthily making their way toward the religion and philosophy section.

I can always smell old books.

Name of town?

What is this— plants?

Your Personal Associations   Read Bailey White's paragraph, and add your own notes to Travis's comments in the margins.

Thinking Aloud

As we read and interpret an author's words, we absorb them on a literal level, add to them any implications the author suggests, think about how the ideas relate to one another, and keep the process going until the entire reading selection makes sense. These focused thoughts are what help us process the author's writing. On another level, however, we may stray from the essay in a wide variety of ways—thinking about chores we need to do, calls we forgot to return, and plans we are looking forward to on the weekend. These random ideas are only loosely related to the reading. As you might suspect, focused reading is more productive than random reading, but you can teach yourself to apply your stray ideas to a better understanding of the material. To do this strategy, stop and "think aloud" about what is on your mind as you read. Point out confusing passages, connections you make, specific questions you have, related information you know, and personal experiences you associate with the text. In this way, you can hear what your mind does (both focused and randomly) as you read.

Travis's Think Aloud   Travis read Bailey White's paragraph and recorded his thoughts in brackets as accurately as possible so we could see how his mind worked as he read this passage.

> But the reason I drive the two hundred miles year after year *[I don't think I drive that much for any reason all year long]* is the bookstore. *[Really? What could be so great about a bookstore? Sounds like more school work to me.]* The building is tall, a beautiful pink brick. *[Oh wow! That was the color of the brick on the boardwalk at Pismo Beach. What a great weekend! And the....]* The sign says,
>
>
>
> O. Brisky
> Books
> Old Used Rare
> Bought and Sold
> Out of Print Search Service *[This could be useful]*
>
>
>
> Even before you go inside, you can smell the old, used, and rare books. *[I feel like I'm in this bookstore. It makes me think of my Grandma's house.]* On sunny days, Mr. Brisky arranges a collection of books on a table on the sidewalk *[a boardwalk of books!]*. There are books in the windows and stacks of books on the floor just inside the entrance. From an open back door the misty green light of Micanopy *[I'd love to go to Florida—maybe to see/smell this bookstore]* shines into the dust *[makes me think of a puddle of water]*. Tendrils of wisteria have crept in through the doorway and are stealthily making their way *[like invaders—Twilight Zone stuff]* toward the religion and philosophy section.

Your Think Aloud   Read Bailey White's essay, and put your own thoughts in brackets as you read.

Chunking

Reading critically means looking closely at the selection to discover what its purpose is and how it is structured to make its point. To understand how a reading selection works, circle the main idea. Then draw horizontal lines throughout the selection to separate the various topics that support the main idea. These lines may or may not coincide with paragraph breaks in an essay. Finally, in the margins, label the topics of each "chunk." Be prepared to explain the divisions you made.

Travis's Chunking   Travis marked the following chunks in the White paragraph and labeled them in the margin.

Entrance	But the reason I drive the two hundred miles year after year is the bookstore. The building is tall, a beautiful pink brick. The sign says,

O. Brisky

Books

Old Used Rare

Bought and Sold

Out of Print Search Service

Smell	Even before you go inside, you can smell the old, used, and rare books./On sunny days, Mr. Brisky arranges
Sight	a collection of books on a table on the sidewalk. There are books in the windows and stacks of books on the floor just inside the entrance. From an open back door the misty green light of Micanopy shines into the dust./Tendrils of
Crawling plants	wisteria have crept in through the doorway and are stealthily making their way toward the religion and philosophy section.

Your Chunking   Divide and label the chunks you see in Bailey White's paragraph.

Graphing the Ideas

To understand their reading material and see how it works, students often find that making drawings of its ideas and details is much more effective than outlining. Graphic organizers, or concept maps, let you literally "draw" the relationship of ideas to one another. Figuring out what framework to use for this exercise is part of the process. You can make up a drawing of your own or do a Web search for "graphic organizers" to see some different options. Be prepared to explain your drawing.

Travis's Graphic   Travis created the following framework for the White paragraph.

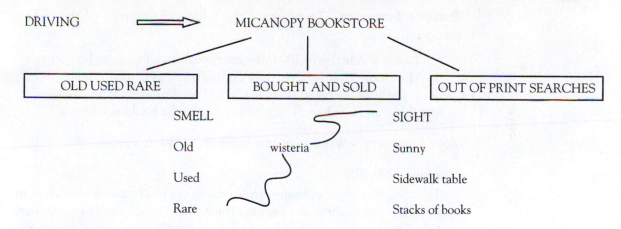

Your Graphic Draw your own picture of the structure of White's paragraph.

Peer Teaching

Teaching something to your peers is an excellent way to test your understanding. To practice this technique, the class must first divide a reading selection into parts. The class members should then form groups representing each of these sections and choose one of the topics/sections. After identifying the main ideas, the details, and their relationships to one another, each group should teach its section to the rest of the class.

Travis's Peer Teaching Travis chooses the following section to teach with his group.

> On sunny days, Mr. Brisky arranges a collection of books on a table on the sidewalk. There are books in the windows and stacks of books on the floor just inside the entrance. From an open back door the misty green light of Micanopy shines into the dust.

The group first asks the class members to think about a bookstore they have visited. Then they ask the class members to list the sights they can remember from that bookstore. Finally, Travis and his group ask the class to list the sights that White talks about in this portion of her paragraph.

Your Peer Teaching Form a group, and teach another portion of the paragraph to the rest of your class.

Summarizing

As you read more difficult selections, the ability to summarize is essential. A summary features the main ideas of a selection in a coherent paragraph. First, identify the main ideas in your reading; then fold them into a paragraph with logical transitions so your sentences flow from one to another. After you write your summary, draft three questions for discussion.

Travis's Summary   Travis wrote the following summary of the White paragraph.

> Bailey White drives 200 miles every year to her favorite bookstore in Micanopy, Florida, that buys and sells old and used books. The store smells of old books that are stacked on the sidewalk and all over the floors and windowsills. Crawling among the books is wisteria.

Your Summary   Write your own summary of White's paragraph.

Reacting Critically

Forming your own opinions and coming up with meaningful ideas in response to your reading are very important parts of the reading process that you need to learn how to produce. As you read a selection, record your notes on a separate piece of paper. First, draw a vertical line down the center of your paper. Then, as you read, write the author's main ideas on the left and your reactions to those ideas on the right side of the page. Be prepared to explain the connection between your notes and the material in the reading.

Travis's Critical Reactions   Here are Travis's critical notes on the paragraph by Bailey White.

White's Main Ideas	My Reactions
White drove 200 miles to this bookstore.	That's a long way to drive to a bookstore.
The bookstore was in Micanopy.	I found out Micanopy is in Florida.
The bookstore smelled like old books.	That's a distinctive smell that anyone can recognize.
Books were stacked everywhere.	I can tell the character of the bookstore and the bookstore owner from this detail.
A wisteria plant was crawling around the bookstore.	This living plant is a nice contrast to the nonliving books in the bookstore.

Your Critical Reactions   Create your own list of main ideas from the paragraph, and add your critical reactions to them.

Making Connections

Separating causes from effects is an important part of understanding a cause/effect paragraph. After a first reading of a cause/effect paragraph, divide a sheet of paper into two parts with a vertical line. Then as you read the selection for a second time, record the causes in the left column and the results on the right. Draw lines from each cause to its related effect (if applicable). Be prepared to explain the connection between your lists and the details in the essay.

Travis's Connections   Travis generated the following lists using this strategy.

First List	Related Ideas
Smell of books ——————	old, used, rare
Stacks of books ——————	on floor, on windowsills, on sidewalk, at entrance
Sights ——————	pink brick, green light, books, dust, wisteria
Living things ——————	wisteria plant

Your Connections   Generate your own lists from White's paragraph.

Recognizing Facts and Opinions

Reading an argument critically calls for very high-level skills. You need to understand your reading on a literal level, know the difference between opinions and facts, and come up with your own thoughts on the topic by challenging the author's ideas. To do this, highlight facts in one color and the author's opinions in another color. This activity works very well with the next strategy.

Travis's Highlighting   Travis highlighted the facts in White's paragraph in yellow and the author's opinions in green.

But the reason I drive the two hundred miles year after year is   x the bookstore. The building is tall, a beautiful pink brick. The sign says,

> O. Brisky
> Books
> Old Used Rare
> Bought and Sold
> Out of Print Search Service

Even before you go inside, you can smell the old, used, and rare books. On sunny days, Mr. Brisky arranges a collection of books on a table on the sidewalk. There are books in the windows and stacks of books on the floor just inside the entrance. From an open back door the misty green light of Micanopy shines into the dust. Tendrils of wisteria have crept in through the doorway and are stealthily making their way toward the religion and philosophy section.

Your Highlighting Do you disagree with any of Travis's highlighting? Explain your answer.

Reading with the Author/Against the Author*

This approach is a very advanced form of reading. It asks you to consciously figure out which ideas you agree with and which you disagree with. By doing this, you force yourself to form your own reactions and opinions. From the previous highlighting exercise, put an X by any facts or opinions that you do not agree with or that you want to question in some way. Then record your own thoughts and opinions on a separate sheet of paper. Be prepared to explain any marks you made on the paragraph.

Travis's Response

I put an X by the bookstore because, as much as I love to read, I can't imagine driving 200 miles to a bookstore. There would have to be something very special about the store. I can imagine the sights and smells, but gas prices now would discourage me from that trip.

Your Response Write your own response to your highlighting.

MyWritingLab   **How to Read Critically**

To make sure you understand how to read critically, click on the **Study Skills Learning Path** in **MyWritingLab.com,** and choose **Getting the Most from Your Reading**. From there, watch the **Overview** video, and follow the links for tips on preparing to read and annotating reading material. When you feel you have mastered the fundamentals, click on the **Interactive Activity** to practice annotating a text. Once you complete these activities, check your mastery through the **Self-Check**.

PRACTICE 1 Now that you have been introduced to several prereading strategies, which is your favorite? Why do you like it best? *Answers will vary.*

PRACTICE 2 Using two reading strategies on one reading assignment is often a good idea. What is your second favorite reading strategy? Why do you like this strategy? *Answers will vary.*

*This strategy is most effective with an argument rather than a description, like White's paragraph.

FIRST REREADING

Your **first rereading** should now focus on raising your level of thinking, which means trying to reach a deeper understanding of the words and sentences in the paragraph or essay. Looking again at the reading material with an inquiring mind is the heart of this stage.

This book provides questions on increasingly more difficult levels to help you accomplish this goal. But without this assistance, you need to ask your own questions as you read. Focusing on questions that wonder "why" or "how" something happened will move you to these higher levels.

Travis's First Rereading   As Travis read White's essay a second time, he saw several details he had not seen earlier. He made more notes on the essay and then answered the following questions provided in the text. His answers appear after each question.

Thinking Critically About Content

1. How do you know that White really enjoyed visiting Brisky's bookstore?

   Driving "two hundred miles year after year" shows the reader that she really appreciates this bookstore.

2. How can plants invade the bookstore?

   It seems that the wisteria in particular has "crept through the doorway" and is now literally growing into different areas of the store.

3. What details from the paragraph work together to make the bookstore real for you?

   I can see the stacks of books all over this store—on a table on the sidewalk, in the windows, on the floor. Those details remind me of a bookstore I visited long ago on a family trip with my parents in Cedar City, Utah.

Thinking Critically About Purpose and Audience

4. What do you think White's purpose is in this paragraph?

   I think White is trying to share her love of this bookstore with us so we see it the same way she does.

5. What type of audience do you think would most understand and appreciate this paragraph?

   Anyone can appreciate this paragraph, but it might be especially appealing to

   people who like books and bookstores.

6. Why do you think White included the entire bookstore sign in her paragraph?

   Reading the sign word for word makes us feel like we are really there with the

   author. It also slows us down, like we are entering the bookstore.

Thinking Critically About Paragraphs

7. What is the paragraph's main idea?

   The main idea is that White loves to visit this particular bookstore.

8. Does White give you enough examples to understand her feelings about this bookstore? Explain your answer.

   Yes, she does. Of the five senses, she covers sight, smell, and touch, so readers

   can feel as if they are appreciating the bookstore with her.

9. Does the paragraph move smoothly from one sentence to the next? If so, how does the author accomplish this?

   The paragraph moves very smoothly because of transitions White uses to connect

   her sentences.

10. Think of a favorite place of yours. What purpose does this place serve for you?

    I have a favorite place high above the city that I retreat to when I need to think

    clearly and solve problems.

Your First Rereading   Read the excerpt from "Micanopy" a second time, and take more notes about assumptions and relationships between ideas, writing them in the margins as you read. Then, in your journal, generate two "why" or "how" questions about ideas in this paragraph. Exchange questions with a classmate, and answer each other's questions in your journal.

SECOND REREADING

This **final reading** is the real test of your understanding. It has the potential to raise your grades in all subjects if you complete it for each of your reading assignments. It involves understanding the author's ideas as you also form your own opinions and analyze your thoughts.

To accomplish this reading, you should identify any remaining confusion you might have and ask more questions that go beyond the words on the page. Then answer these questions in writing. You should also bring your own opinions to the surface. Write them down as they occur to you. Finally, analyze your thoughts so that you end with some form of self-evaluation.

Travis's Second Rereading   Travis took the following notes in his journal as he read White's essay for the third time. He asked himself some questions, answered those questions as best he could, recorded his opinions as they occurred to him, and analyzed his thoughts along the way.

> I really liked Bailey White's description of the bookstore. The first sentence shows how much she likes this place. She gives so many examples about why she drives 200 miles just to go to this bookstore. I don't really have a place that I would drive that far to see. I wish I did! I wouldn't say a bookstore or library is my favorite place. I get too bored looking at so many books, but I do like feeling alone in such a big place. I guess my favorite place would just be out of the house. Far, far away where no one can find me. I love to be by myself, even though most of my friends don't understand this.

Your Second Rereading   Take notes in your journal as you read White's essay for the third time. Ask yourself more "how" and "why" questions, answer those questions, record your opinions, and analyze your thoughts as they occur.

WHAT EVERY STUDENT SHOULD KNOW ABOUT CRITICAL READING   ✳—[**Explore** more at **mywritinglab.com**

What Every Student Should Know About Critical Reading is a free Pearson supplement that defines critical reading; reinforces some key reading strategies; discusses inferences, main ideas, and details; and explains argument and bias. Ultimately, it will help increase your understanding of all your course materials. For your free copy, go to the *Mosaics: Reading and Writing Paragraphs* eText in MyWritingLab, and click on any of the "Explore More at MyWritingLab.com" icons in Chapter 3. *What Every Student Should Know About Critical Reading* is also available in print (ISBN: 0-205-86992-0).

3

Writing Critically

Writing critically involves going through the entire writing process with the intention of analyzing all aspects of your subject matter. As you learned in Chapter 1, this process consists of a number of identifiable stages that overlap in several unique ways. In this chapter, we will go through the writing process, following Travis Morehouse's response to the following writing assignment or "prompt." You will also be working on this assignment over the next few chapters. By the end of Chapter 5, you will have a feel for the entire writing process, which is essential to strengthening your identity as a writer.

| **Writing Prompt** |  **Complete** this **Writing Prompt** at **mywritinglab.com** |

Think about a favorite place that you visit frequently. It could be somewhere that is peaceful, beautiful, or busy. It could be a restaurant, a park, or a place of employment or worship. Then describe this location to someone who has never been there. Explain the sights, sounds, tastes, smells, and textures that attract you to this spot.

TEACHING PREPARING
TO WRITE
Give students a topic—
such as magazines, music,
or the Internet—and have
them practice each of the
prewriting strategies. Once
students discover which
prewriting strategy they
are most comfortable with,
have them use this strategy
for future paragraphs.

PREPARING TO WRITE

Many students are surprised that a number of steps in the writing process occur before the actual act of putting words on paper. These steps fall into the general category of **prewriting** or **preparing to write.** Prewriting activities help us do the following tasks:

- Explore a subject
- Generate ideas about a subject
- Choose a topic
- Establish a purpose
- Analyze the audience

The activities in this chapter are divided into two categories: thinking and planning. Thinking involves exploring a subject and generating ideas on that subject; planning focuses on choosing a topic, establishing a purpose, and analyzing the audience. Let's begin this chapter by looking at tasks many writers use to stimulate their thinking as they approach a writing assignment. You will get a chance to try each of these. Consider keeping your responses to these activities in a journal you can refer to throughout the course.

| MyWritingLab | ## Understanding Prewriting |

Before you move on, let's make sure you understand all the important elements of prewriting. Go to **MyWritingLab.com**, and click on **Prewriting** in **The Craft of Writing** module. From there, read the **Overview,** watch the six **Animation** videos, and complete the **Recall, Apply,** and **Write** activities. Then check your understanding of this material by taking the **Post-test.**

Thinking

Thinking is always the initial stage of any writing project. It's a time to explore your topic and let your mind run freely over the material you have to work with. We'll explore five activities that promise to stimulate your best thoughts: freewriting, brainstorming, clustering, questioning, and discussing. You will see how Travis Morehouse uses each strategy and then have a chance to try out the technique yourself.

Freewriting

Writing about anything that comes to your mind is freewriting. You should write without stopping for 5 to 10 minutes. Do not worry about grammar or spelling. If you get stuck, repeat an idea or start rhyming words. The mere act of writing makes writers think of other ideas. So just keep writing.

Travis's Freewriting   Travis had trouble freewriting, but he followed directions and just started in.

Here I am in English class, and we're supposed to be freewriting. But I don't know what to write about—my mind is a complete blank. Blank blank blankety blank. I could write about my car. It's been burning oil like crazy. Wherever I drive, there's a trail of blue smoke. I have to put in a quart of oil every week or two! But I don't want to take it in because I don't have the money to get it fixed. The rest of my tuition payment is due. I need money coming in, not going out. But if I don't get my car fixed, I'm not going to be able to get to school. That would not be good. School ends up being an escape for me—from my family, from my friends, from my teachers. It's where my dreams are. I don't know what these dreams are yet, but I think they're at school. For the first time in my life I actually like school. Who would have thought?

Focused freewriting is the same procedure focused on a specific topic—either one your instructor gives you or one you choose. It is a systematic way of turning thoughts and impressions into words.

Travis's Focused Freewriting

Travis produced the following focused freewriting in his journal. He is trying to get his mind ready to write about his favorite place.

> I don't know what I consider to be my favorite place. I usually just get in my car and drive when I want to get away from things. I guess I can consider that ridge I sometimes go to as my favorite place. I do end up driving there when I just feel like I want to leave everything behind. I like how I can see the city and the river from up high. I especially like to be there during sunsets because it is always so beautiful. I feel a peace that I can't seem to describe. Although no one would really understand anyway.

Your Freewriting

To start preparing for your own paragraph, try a focused freewriting assignment by writing in your journal about some of your favorite places.

Brainstorming

Like freewriting, brainstorming draws on free association—one thought naturally leads to another. But brainstorming is usually done in list form. You can brainstorm by yourself, with a friend, or with a group. Regardless of the method, list whatever comes into your mind on a topic—ideas, thoughts, examples, facts. As with freewriting, don't worry about grammar or spelling.

Travis's Brainstorming

Here is Travis's brainstorming on his favorite place:

> the ridge—high above the city
> can see the city
> the river—always has boats
> sometimes I can see cars

the sunsets are really beautiful

the city lights always look cool when it gets dark

sometimes it can get really cold at night

it's peaceful

I can be alone

I can think out my problems

Your Brainstorming Brainstorm in your journal about a favorite place or several favorite places.

Clustering

Clustering is like brainstorming, but it has the advantage of showing how your thoughts are related. To cluster, take a sheet of blank paper, write a key word or phrase in the center of the page, and draw a circle around it. Next, write down and circle any related ideas that come to mind. As you add ideas, draw lines to the thoughts they are related to. Try to keep going for two or three minutes. When you finish, you'll have a map of your ideas that can help you find your way to a good paragraph.

Travis's Cluster Here is Travis's cluster:

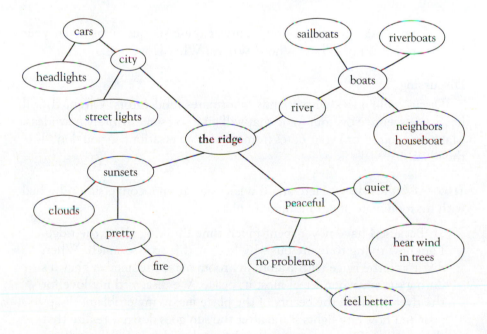

Your Cluster Write "favorite place" in the middle of a piece of paper, circle it, and draw a cluster of your own personal associations with these words.

Questioning

Journalists use the questions known as the "five *W*s and one *H*"—Who? What? When? Where? Why? and How?—to check that they've included all the necessary information in a news story. You can use these same questions to generate ideas on a writing topic.

Travis's Questions   Here is how Travis used questioning to generate ideas on his topic:

Who?	I most enjoy being by myself up here, but I sometimes bring my friend Carlos because he thinks it's cool too.
What?	My favorite place that is really quiet and peaceful, the ridge that sits high above the city.
When?	My absolute favorite time to be here is when the sun goes down. The sun looks like it's on fire before it finally sets.
Where?	The ridge that's high above the city.
Why?	I can think up here. The beautiful sunset and the city and river help me clear my mind so I can solve problems.
How?	Just watching the boats and looking at the view make me feel better.

Your Questions   In your journal, answer these six questions about your favorite place: Who? What? When? Where? Why? How?

Discussing

Discuss your ideas with friends, classmates, and tutors. Often, they'll have a perspective on your topic that will give you some entirely new ideas. Make sure you record your notes from these conversations so you don't lose the ideas.

Travis's Discussion   Here are Travis's notes from a conversation he had with his roommate about his favorite place:

> Because I have never spent much time thinking about the ridge, I am now trying to figure out why I enjoy this spot so much. When discussing the ridge with Ralph, my roommate, I remember that it's during sunsets when I feel most at peace. We discussed my love for the river and how the beauty of the place makes my problems disappear and how city lights shine after the sun goes down. I realize that this spot means more to me than I first thought. I want to tell my classmates about this place without sounding sentimental; I'm afraid that people will think I am too sensitive.

Your Discussion   Discuss your favorite place with someone, and record notes from your conversation in your journal.

PRACTICE 1   Now that you have been introduced to several prewriting strategies, which is your favorite? Why do you like it best?

PRACTICE 2   Using two prewriting strategies on one assignment is often a good idea. What is your second favorite prewriting strategy? Why do you like this strategy?

Planning

In this course, you'll be writing paragraphs—single paragraphs at first and paragraphs in essays later. A paragraph is a group of sentences on a single topic. The first line of each paragraph is indented to show that a new topic or subtopic is starting. Although paragraphs vary in length, typical paragraphs in student themes usually range from 50 to 250 words, averaging about 100 words.

Writing a paragraph takes planning. You need to make certain decisions about your subject, your purpose for writing, and your audience before you actually write so the task of writing is as smooth and stress-free as possible.

- **What is your subject (person, event, object, idea, etc.)?** A paragraph focuses on a single topic and includes related thoughts and details. Your first decision, therefore, is about your *subject:* What are you going to write about? Sometimes your topic is given to you—for example, when your sociology instructor assigns a paper on drug abuse among teenagers. But other times, you choose your own topic. In such cases, choosing a subject that interests you is the best strategy. You will have more to say, and you will enjoy writing much more if you find your topic appealing.

- **What is your purpose?** Your *purpose* is your reason for writing a paragraph. Your purpose could be to explore your feelings on a topic (*to do personal writing*), to tell a friend about something funny that happened to you (*to entertain*), to explain something or share information (*to inform*), or to convince others of your position on a controversial issue (*to persuade*). Whatever your purpose, deciding on it in advance makes writing your paragraph much easier.

- **Who is your audience?** Your *audience* consists of the people for whom your message is intended. The more you know about your audience, the more likely you are to accomplish your purpose. The audience for your writing in college is usually your instructor, who represents what is called a "general audience"—people with an average amount of knowledge on most subjects. A general audience is the group to aim for in all your writing unless you are given other directions.

PRACTICE 3 Identify the subject, purpose, and audience of each of the following paragraphs.

1. At the heart of *America's Promise* are five basic promises made to every child in America. To point kids in the right direction, to help them grow up strong and ready to take their place as successful adults, these five promises must be fulfilled for all youth: (1) an ongoing relationship with a caring adult—parent, mentor, tutor, or coach; (2) a safe place with structured activities during non-school hours; (3) a healthy start; (4) a marketable skill through effective education; and (5) a chance to give back through community service. (COLIN POWELL, "A Promise to Our Youth")

   Subject: *America's promises to children*

   Purpose: *to inform*

   Audience: *parents and children*

2. My best friend just got arrested for rioting. Until yesterday, she was a great student with an unblemished record, and now she will be spending school time in court trying to keep out of jail. I don't know why she did it; she says she got caught up in the energy of the crowd. That just sounds like an excuse to me. She knew she was doing something wrong, she knew she was hurting business owners, and she did it anyway. I know she'll be punished for what she did and that will be humiliating enough, but I don't think she realizes her parents, friends, and teachers will now see her as someone who has the potential for getting into trouble. (STUDENT WRITER)

   Subject: *trouble with the law*

   Purpose: *to inform*

   Audience: *young adults*

3. If you're a man, at some point a woman will ask you how she looks. "How do I look?" she'll ask. You must be careful how you answer this question. The best technique is to form an honest yet sensitive opinion, then collapse on the floor with some kind of fatal seizure. Trust me. This is the easiest way out, because you will never come up with the right answer. (DAVE BARRY, "The Ugly Truth About Beauty")

   Subject: *women's appearance*

   Purpose: *to inform or to entertain*

   Audience: *men*

4. The press is about finding the truth and telling it to the people. In pursuit of that, I am making a case for the broadest possible freedom

of the press. However, with that great gift comes great responsibility. The press—print and electronic—has the power to inform, but that implies the power to distort. The press can lead our society toward a more mature and discriminating understanding of the process by which we choose our leaders, make our rules, and construct our values, or it can encourage people to despise our systems and avoid participating in them. The press can teach our children a taste for violence, encourage a fascination with perversity and inflicted pain, or it can show them a beauty they have not known. The press can make us wiser, fuller, surer, and sweeter than we are. (MARIO CUOMO, "Freedom of the Press Must Be Unlimited")

Subject: *freedom of the press*
Purpose: *to inform or to persuade*
Audience: *general*

5. My friends say that when I get in my car, I become blind to my surroundings. I have driven next to friends and not seen them, have been waiting at stop lights next to friends and not noticed them, and have passed friends on a small two-lane road and not known it. I tell them it's because I am very engrossed in my driving; I take driving a vehicle very seriously. Actually, though, I am usually daydreaming about where I wish I could be going. (STUDENT WRITER)

Subject: *driving alertness*
Purpose: *to inform*
Audience: *general*

Travis's Plans Travis made the following decisions before beginning to write about his favorite place:

Subject: The peacefulness of the ridge
Purpose: Personal—to reflect on the characteristics of my favorite place
Audience: General—I want people who read this to imagine a similar place where they can think about their problems

Your Plans Identify the subject, purpose, and audience of the paragraph you will write on your favorite place.

Subject: _____

Purpose: _____

Audience: _____

WRITING

Writing is made up of several steps that lead you to your first draft. At this point, you have chosen a topic (a favorite place) and worked through various prewriting techniques with that subject. You have generated a number of ideas that you can use in a paragraph and decided on a subject, purpose, and audience. In this chapter, you will first learn how to write a topic sentence. Next, you will add some specific, concrete details to your notes from your prewriting activities and choose a method of organization for your paragraph. Finally, you will write the first draft of your paragraph, which you will then revise and edit in Chapters 4 and 5. Again, you will be writing alongside Travis as he goes through the writing process with you.

Writing a Topic Sentence

The decisions you made earlier in this chapter about subject, purpose, and audience will lead you to your topic sentence. The **topic sentence** of a paragraph is its controlling idea. A typical paragraph consists of a topic sentence and details that expand on the topic sentence. Although a topic sentence can appear as the first or last sentence of its paragraph, it functions best as the first sentence. Beginning a paragraph with the topic sentence gives direction to the paragraph and provides a kind of road map for the reader.

A topic sentence has two parts—a topic and a statement about that topic. The topic should be limited enough that it can be developed in the space of a paragraph.

Topic	Limited Topic	Statement
Writing	In-class writing	is difficult but is good practice for a job.
Voting	Voting in the United States	is a right of citizenship.
Sports	Participation in sports	makes people well rounded.
Anger	Road rage	seems to me like a waste of energy.

MyWritingLab

Understanding Topic Sentences

To make sure you have a solid understanding of the fundamentals of topic sentences, go to **MyWritingLab.com,** and find **The Topic Sentence** in **The Craft of Writing Module.** For this topic, read the

Overview, watch the **Animation** video, and complete the **Recall, Apply,** and **Write** activities. Then check your understanding of this topic by taking the **Post-test.**

This topic ends up being difficult for students for two reasons: First, many of the answers are similar, which forces students to analyze their answers; and second, students learn that a topic sentence can appear in different places within a paragraph.

PRACTICE 4 Limit the following topics. Then develop them into statements that could be topic sentences. *Answers will vary.*

Topic	Limited Topic	Statement
1. Weekends	_____	_____
2. Work	_____	_____
3. Restaurants	_____	_____
4. Reading	_____	_____
5. Winter	_____	_____

PRACTICE 5 Complete the following topic sentences. Make sure they are general enough to be developed into a paragraph but not too broad. *Answers will vary.*

1. Automobile accidents _____

2. _____ is my favorite movie.

3. Smoking _____.

4. Teen pregnancies _____

5. _____ must be brought under control in the United States.

PRACTICE 6 Write topic sentences for the following paragraphs.

1. *My dog, Rusty, is my best friend.* _____

When I come home from school, Rusty is always the first one to greet me. He usually jumps on me and knocks me down, but I am used to this. After we wrestle on the ground, he follows me to my room and sits by my feet while I do homework. Every once in a while he'll nudge my hand so I will pet him. When I go to bed, Rusty always sleeps with me at night, which is nice because I can snuggle up to his fur and know that I am safe.

2. *Becoming a certified scuba diver is difficult.*

First, you must undergo an intensive scuba diving class that includes a lot of reading and calculating. Next, you must practice scuba skills in a pool so you can learn how to react if, for instance, your breathing regulator comes out of your mouth underwater. Then you have four checkout dives in the ocean. Finally, after six weeks of preparation, you'll be a certified scuba diver.

3. *I know exactly what my future home will look like.*

It will be two stories and will be painted blue. Inside it will have at least four bedrooms and an office for me to work. It will have a grand kitchen and enough room to entertain all my friends and co-workers. A pool would be nice, with a lush backyard for my dogs to get lost in. And I hope that it will be close to my mom and dad's house.

Travis's Topic Sentence   Travis writes a topic sentence that he thinks represents his whole paragraph. It introduces a ridge in his hometown.

Limited Topic	Statement
A high, wooded ridge	overlooks my hometown.

Your Topic Sentence   Write a topic sentence here that can serve as the controlling idea for your paragraph.

Topic Limited	Statement
_____	_____

Developing

After you have written a topic sentence, you are ready to develop the specific details that will make up the bulk of your paragraph. Later in this text, you will learn about different methods of developing your ideas, such as describing, using examples, comparing and contrasting, and defining. For now, we are simply going to practice generating concrete supporting details and examples that are directly related to a specific topic. Concrete words refer to anything you can see, hear, touch, smell, or taste, like *trees, boats, water, friends, fire alarm,* and *fresh bread.* They make writing come alive because they help us picture what the writer is discussing.

MyWritingLab   Understanding Development

To make sure you understand how to develop your body paragraphs, go to **MyWritingLab.com,** and choose **Developing and Organizing a Paragraph** in **The Craft of Writing** module. Next, read the **Overview,** watch the three **Animation** videos, and complete the **Recall, Apply,** and **Write** activities. Finally, check your understanding of this material by taking the **Post-test.**

Student Comment:
"My teachers would always tell me to develop my paragraphs, so I used to just add a few sentences at the end of the paragraph. I know now how to make my paragraphs longer without copping out."

This topic can be confusing to students because it expects them to know the difference between an explanation, an example, and a reason. Because many students see these items as similar, you might want to go over these terms in class before your students complete the MyWritingLab exercises.

PRACTICE 7 For each of the following topic sentences, list five details and/or examples to develop them. *Answers will vary.*

1. If I win the lottery, I will be the envy of all my friends.

_____

_____

_____

_____

_____

2. People can't always count on their relatives.

_____

_____

_____

_____

_____

3. My favorite pastime is fun as well as challenging.

_____

_____

_____

_____

_____

4. Palm readers must lead interesting lives.

_____

_____

_____

_____

_____

5. People living in big cities hardly ever get bored.

_____

_____

_____

_____

_____

Travis's Development   To come up with concrete details and examples that would support his topic sentence, Travis goes back to the questions he used during his planning stage (five Ws and one H) and adds these details.

Who?	I like to be by myself
What?	rowboats, sailboats, motorboats, freight liners
	I like the sailboats best because I love to sail
	car lights outlining the streets in the distance
When?	sunset—pink and purple
	light at dusk; moonlight
	headlights streaming through the darkness
Where?	outside the city
	above the city
	people in the city don't know I am watching
Why?	the scent of honeysuckle on a hot summer day
	the smell of the earth
	birds building nests, scolding other birds to keep them away
	traffic noises, wind, rain, thunder, lightning
	problems fade away
How?	peaceful, quiet
	I can think out my problems

Your Development Choose one of the prewriting activities you learned earlier in this chapter, and use it to generate more specific details and examples about your topic sentence.

Organizing

At this point, you are moving along quite well in the writing process. You chose a topic for your paragraph (your favorite place). You have generated some ideas; determined your subject, purpose, and audience; and written your topic sentence. You have also thought of details, examples, and facts to develop your topic sentence. Now you are ready to organize your ideas. What should come first? What next? Would one way of organizing your ideas accomplish your purpose better than another?

Most paragraphs are organized in one of five ways:

1. General to particular
2. Particular to general
3. Chronologically (by time)
4. Spatially (by physical arrangement)
5. From one extreme to another

Let's look at these methods of organization one by one.

General to Particular

The most common method of organizing details in a paragraph is to begin with a general statement and then offer particular details to prove or explain that topic sentence. The general-to-particular paragraph looks like this, although the number of details will vary:

Topic Sentence
  Detail
  Detail
  Detail

Here is a paragraph organized from general to particular:

Over the past two years, I have become an adventurous person because of my friend Taylor. <u>When</u> I met Taylor, she had just signed up for a rock-climbing class, and it sounded so interesting that I joined too. We loved climbing the amazingly tall rocks so much that we decided to try skydiving. <u>Next</u> we both jumped out of a plane attached to a qualified instructor; it was incredible. <u>In fact</u>, we've been back four times. <u>Now</u> we are trying our hands at exploring the ocean and are in the middle of scuba-diving lessons. By the time we are certified, we'll be off on a two-week vacation to South America, where we can participate in all three exciting sports.

This paragraph moves from the general idea of being adventurous to the specific examples of rock climbing, skydiving, and scuba diving. Notice how the underlined transitions move the paragraph from one idea to the next.

PRACTICE 8 Turn to the essay "What Is Poverty?" on page 267, and find two paragraphs organized from general to particular.   *paragraphs 1–6, 8–12, 14*

PRACTICE 9 Write a paragraph organized from general to particular that begins with this sentence: "Several people I know have broken bad habits."

Particular to General

Occasionally, the reverse order of particular to general is the most effective way to organize a paragraph. In this case, examples or details start the paragraph and lead up to the topic sentence, which appears at the end of the paragraph. This type of organization is particularly effective if you suspect that your reader might not agree with the final point you are going to make or you need to lead your reader to your opinion slowly and carefully. A particular-to-general paragraph looks like this, although the number of details may vary:

> Detail
> Detail
> Detail
> Topic Sentence

Here is an example of particular-to-general organization:

> Two sunny-side-up eggs, the whites rimmed with ruffled edges, lay in the middle of the plate. Specks of red pimento and green pepper peeked out of a heap of perfectly diced hash brown potatoes. <u>Alongside</u> lay strips of crispy, crinkly, maple-flavored bacon. A tall glass of ice-cold orange juice stood to my left. A big mug of steaming coffee was at my right. <u>Then</u> the biggest blueberry muffin in the universe was delivered straight from the oven, its aroma curling up to my nose. I broke it open and spread it with real butter. Nobody makes breakfast like my mom!

This paragraph starts with specific details about the writer's breakfast and ends with the topic sentence ("Nobody makes breakfast like my mom!"). Again, notice how the transitions move the paragraph along.

PRACTICE 10 Turn to the essay "Eleven" on page 122, and find one paragraph in the first half of the essay that demonstrates particular-to-general organization. *paragraph 3*

PRACTICE 11 Write a paragraph organized from particular to general that ends with this sentence: "Some people put their free time to good use."

Chronological Order

When you organize details chronologically in a paragraph, you are arranging them according to the passage of time—in other words, in the order in which they occurred. Most of the time when you tell a story or explain how to do something, you use chronological order. Paragraphs organized chronologically use such signal words as *first, then, next,* and *finally.*

Topic Sentence
    First
    Then
    Next
    Finally

Here is an example of a paragraph organized in chronological order:

    Paper training is an easy way to housebreak a puppy. <u>First</u>, locate a box that is low enough for the puppy to climb in and out of easily. <u>Then</u> line the box with newspapers and place it in an area that is always available to the puppy. <u>Next</u>, place the puppy in the box at regular intervals. <u>As soon as</u> the puppy begins to understand what is required, scold him or her for making mistakes. <u>Finally</u>, praise the puppy when he or she uses the box properly, and you will soon have a well-trained puppy.

This paragraph is chronological because it explains how to housebreak a puppy according to a time sequence and uses transitions such as *first, then, next, as soon as,* and *finally.*

PRACTICE 12 Turn to the essay "Life Sentences" on page 294, and find two paragraphs organized chronologically. *paragraphs 6, 11, 12*

PRACTICE 13 Write a topic sentence for the following group of sentences. Then organize the sentences into a paragraph using chronological order. Add words, phrases, or sentences as necessary to smooth out the paragraph.

Topic Sentence: _Making your own candles is easy._

_2_ Add the color of your choice to the melted wax.

_4_ Drop a wick in the melted wax.

_1_ First, melt some paraffin in a saucepan.

_5_ Put the mold in the refrigerator overnight. (This way, the wax will contract and will be easy to get out of the mold the next day.)

_6_ Finally, take the candle out of the mold and admire your creation.

_3_ Pour the melted wax in a candle mold of any shape.

Spatial Order

Another method of arranging details is by their relationship to each other in space. You might describe someone's outfit, for example, _from head to toe_ or recount your summer travels across the country _from the east coast to the west coast_. Beginning at one point and moving detail by detail around a specific area is the simplest way of organizing by space. This method uses signal words such as _here, there, next, across,_ and _beyond_ to help the reader move through the paragraph smoothly and efficiently.

> Topic Sentence
>> Here
>> There
>> Next
>> Across
>> Beyond

Here is an example of a paragraph that uses spatial organization:

> The prison was ringing with angry men wanting attention. <u>In the first cell</u> was a small, prickly man who was yelling the loudest. He was banging a cup on the bars to signal that he needed something to drink. <u>The next cell</u> held two men who were trying to get their energy up to yell but couldn't seem to make their vocal cords work. The guard was grateful for this small favor. <u>Across the room</u>, a ferocious-looking man waving a newspaper was in the third cell. He was citing a passage from the paper and demanding his rights. <u>Opposite the first cell</u> was a generally quiet man who was reciting the names of people. All the prisoners in this particular block were gearing up for quite a day.

This paragraph is arranged spatially because it moves around the prison, using such words as _in the first cell, the next cell, across the room,_ and _opposite the first cell._

PRACTICE 14 Turn to the essay "Magpies" on page 93, and find one paragraph in the first half of the essay that uses spatial organization. *paragraphs 6, 7, 8, 9*

PRACTICE 15 Write a topic sentence for the following group of sentences. Then organize the sentences into a paragraph in spatial order. Add words, phrases, or sentences as necessary to smooth out the paragraph.

Topic Sentence: *I have decided to rearrange my room.*

3 Actually, the plant should separate the bed from the door.

1 I'll begin by putting my bed against the west wall in the north corner of the room.

2 I would like my floor plant to be next to the head of my bed.

6 My bureau fits perfectly in the southeast corner of the room.

4 The desk will be best in the southwest corner of the room where the window is.

7 The entire east wall is covered with closets.

5 My bookcase will go between the bed and the desk (on the west wall).

From One Extreme to Another

Sometimes the best way to organize a paragraph is from one extreme to another: from most important to least important, from most troublesome to least troublesome, from least serious to most serious, from most humorous to least humorous, and so on. Use whatever extremes make sense for your topic. For example, you might describe the courses you are taking this term from most important to least important in terms of a career. On returning from a trip, you might talk about the places you visited from least interesting to most interesting. Arranging your ideas from one extreme to another has one distinct advantage over the other four approaches—it is the most flexible. When no other method of organization works, you can always organize details from one extreme to the other. Words such as *most*, *next most*, *somewhat*, and *least* signal transitions in this type of paragraph.

Topic Sentence
   Most
   Next most
   Somewhat
   Least

Here is an example of organization that moves from one extreme to the other:

> I like some of my extracurricular activities better than others. My <u>favorite</u> is dance. I take classes in jazz, tap, and ballet, and I'm anxious to get home on the days I go to the dance studio. My <u>next favorite</u> activity is track. During track season, my schedule is tight, but I really look forward to working out every day. Although no one would believe it, my <u>next favorite</u> activity is shopping for school supplies. I love going to the big office supply stores and getting lost for 30 minutes or so. It is really like going into another world. When I emerge, I have some supplies that will make my life as a student easier. My <u>least favorite</u> activity is work. I work part time delivering food for a restaurant at night. No matter when I deliver the food, it is too late or too cold or too hot. No one is satisfied. That is why this is my <u>least favorite</u> task.

This paragraph moves from most to least favorite extracurricular activities with the help of such words as *favorite*, *next favorite*, and *least favorite*.

PRACTICE 16 Turn to the essay "Why Men Fail" on page 211, and find one paragraph that is organized from one extreme to the other.   *paragraphs 5, 7*

PRACTICE 17 Write a topic sentence for the following group of sentences. Then arrange these sentences in a paragraph from one extreme to another. Add words, phrases, and sentences as necessary to smooth out the paragraph. Also, label your system of classification: from most _____ to least _____ or from least _____ to _____ most. *Answers will vary.*

Topic Sentence: *Life at college is much more difficult than I thought it would be.*

I am failing math.

I still do not understand when to use semicolons in my writing.

My English instructor says my style of writing is loose.

I am barely passing music theory.

I have cut my philosophy class twice.

My tennis coach is mad at me.

I have not talked to my family in two weeks.

I have more homework than I could do in my lifetime.

I hardly ever have time to sleep.

Travis's Organization   Travis decides to organize his paragraph from one extreme to another—from his most favorite view to his least favorite view on the ridge. He first wants to introduce the ridge that sits over his hometown. Then he plans to describe his favorite views from this isolated place (the river with its boats, the beautiful sunset, and finally the city at night). He thinks the following order might work. He lists as many concrete details as he can under each view.

General: A high, wooded ridge is in my hometown.

Most Favorite View: I love the river.

Specific Details: I like the sailboats because I love to sail.

I like to see different kinds of boats— rowboats, sailboats, motorboats, freight liners.

Next Favorite View: sunset—beautiful

Specific Details: at dusk; moonlight

clouds from pink to purple to red

sun like fire

Third Favorite View: I like seeing the whole city.

Specific Details: headlights streaming through the darkness, lighting the streets

traffic noises, wind, rain, thunder, lightning

Fourth Favorite: I like to be by myself.

Specific Details: peaceful, quiet

I can think out my problems.

problems fade away.

Does the method of organization that Travis has chosen suit his topic? Would any other method of organization work as well?

Your Organization   What method of organization will work best for your ideas about your favorite place? Why do you think this method will be best?

Drafting

Drafting is putting your thoughts on paper. Having completed lots of prewriting and writing activities, you're ready to compose a working draft of your paragraph in complete sentences—no more lists and circles. The prewriting phase of this process has helped you generate lots of ideas, observations, and details for your paragraph. If you let these notes lead you to related ideas, you will have plenty of material to work with. At this stage, don't worry too much about grammar or spelling; you'll deal with those particulars when you edit your writing.

Travis's First Draft   Here is Travis's first draft, the result of his thinking, planning, developing, and organizing. (We'll look at editing errors at the next stage.)

A high, wooded ridge overlooks my hometown. I can sit up there and see the river, the sunset, and the city. The sun shines like fire, and then the sun is gone behind the ridge. I love the river best, I can always see the river. I watch different kinds of boats on the river. I see rowboats, sailboats, motorboats, and freight liners. I have always liked to sail. My next favorite view is the sunset. Some nights the sunset is really beautiful. There are huge clouds when the sun goes down behind them. When it gets dark. I can see the headlights of the cars moving through the city streets. I bet people don't realize they're being watched. The headlights follow the street lights. When I am up high above the city, I get lost in my dreams. All my troubles melt away. I just look around this place, think about this place's beauty, and feel good—automatically.

Your First Draft   Write a draft of your thoughts on your favorite place.

_____

_____

_____

_____

_____

_____

_____

_____

_____

_____

MyWritingLab   **Helpful Hints**

Need more ideas to fill out your first draft? Generate more details through prewriting; visit **Prewriting** in **The Craft of Writing** module in **MyWritingLab** to find out how.

Revising

As you know, the writing process does not end with your first draft. **Revising** means "seeing again," and that is exactly what you should do when you revise—see your writing again from as many different angles as possible. More specifically, revising your writing means working with it so that it says exactly what you mean in the most effective way. Revision involves both *content* (what you are trying to say) and *form* (how you deliver your message). Revising content means working with your words until they express your ideas as accurately and completely as possible. Revising form consists of working with the organization of your writing.

When you revise, you should look closely at five basic elements of your paragraph, listed in the following checklist.

MyWritingLab Understanding Revising

To make sure you thoroughly understand the revision process, go to **MyWritingLab.com,** and click on **Revising the Paragraph** in **The Craft of Writing** module. Next, read the **Overview,** watch the **Animation** videos that walk you through the specifics of revising your paragraph, and then complete the **Recall, Apply,** and **Write** activities. Finally, check your understanding of this material by taking the **Post-test.**

Student Comment:
"I never fully understood revising and editing until **MyWritingLab** helped show me. Now, I'm a revising and editing machine!"

Have students refer to the Revising Checklists in *Mosaics* for help as they complete the MyWritingLab topics. In these checklists, they will find information to help refine their writing process and complete the exercises.

Revising Checklist

TOPIC SENTENCE

✔ Does the topic sentence convey the paragraph's controlling idea?

✔ Does the topic sentence appear as the first or last sentence of the paragraph?

TEACHING REVISING
Divide students into groups of three or four, and have them exchange papers. Have the first student read his or her paper aloud while the other students listen and take notes so they can make revision suggestions based on the Revising Checklist. When the reader finishes, have each listener offer suggestions. Make sure the reader does not talk or try to clarify any points during this interchange. After all suggestions have been relayed, have the next writer read his or her paper, and so on. Spend only 10 minutes per paper.

TEACHING ON THE WEB
Discussion Topic: Divide students into groups of three or four, and have them discuss how the Internet can be a tool for revision. What types of Web sites will help students get revising feedback for their papers? How else can the Internet help?

INSTRUCTOR'S RESOURCE MANUAL
For additional material about teaching revising, for journal entries, and for various tests, see the *Instructor's Resource Manual,* Section II, Part I.

DEVELOPMENT

✔ Does the paragraph contain *specific* details that support the topic sentence?

✔ Does the paragraph include *enough* details to explain the topic sentence fully?

UNITY

✔ Do all the sentences in the paragraph support the topic sentence?

ORGANIZATION

✔ Is the paragraph organized logically?

COHERENCE

✔ Do the sentences move smoothly and logically from one to the next?

Let's look at these revision strategies one by one as they were outlined as part of the writing process in Chapter 3.

Revising Your Topic Sentence

As you learned in Chapter 3, every successful paragraph has a topic sentence that states the paragraph's main idea. This sentence is extremely important because it gives the paragraph direction. Following are some specific guidelines from the Revising Checklist for making your topic sentence as effective as possible.

TOPIC SENTENCE

✔ Does the topic sentence convey the paragraph's controlling idea?

✔ Does the topic sentence appear as the first or last sentence of the paragraph?

As you also learned from Chapter 3, a topic sentence consists of both a limited topic and a statement about that topic. Generally, the topic sentence is the first sentence in a paragraph, but occasionally it is the last sentence, as in particular-to-general order.

PRACTICE 1 Revise the underlined topic sentences so that they introduce all the details and ideas in their paragraphs.

1. <u>I have many friends</u>. I know that if I talk to Sean about a problem, he won't repeat it to anyone. He's also great to talk to because he never really tells me what I should do. Instead, he gives me what he thinks are all of my options and then helps me decide what to do. Karen, on the other hand, is a wonderful person, and I love to spend time with her. But I know she has trouble keeping a secret. She is great to talk to about small problems (things I don't care if anyone else knows about), but not the big problems. These friends mean a lot to me.

Revised Topic Sentence: *Sean and Karen are two of my very different friends.*

2. I really enjoy watching suspense films because I am constantly afraid of what may happen next. Then I like the action movies. These are great because they move so fast and they usually have the best special effects. I hate it when they throw in love stories, though. This just takes away from the real action. My least favorite are the romantic love stories. I can't stand to watch people for over two hours going through near-misses or traumatic problems. I know they are going to end up together in the end, so spare me the time to get there! <u>Overall, going to movies is a lot of fun.</u>

Revised Topic Sentence: *I love movies, but some types are definitely better than others.*

3. <u>Buying a car is not an enjoyable experience.</u> First, the buyers have to decide on whether they want a new car or a used car. Some people want a new car because they know they won't have to worry about it breaking down for a while and they would have a longer warranty. Others want the price break a used car brings, but they don't know the people selling the cars, and they are afraid of getting ripped off. A good compromise might be to buy a used car from a reputable car dealership. This way the buyer gets the best of both worlds.

Revised Topic Sentence: *The decision of whether to buy a new car or a used car is complex.*

PRACTICE 2 Write a topic sentence for each of the following paragraphs.

1. *Before every test, I go through the same study ritual.*

   I always have to put my sweats on and tie back my hair. I then sit on the couch and watch TV, all the while looking at my study guide and feeling guilty that I'm not putting more energy into it. After about a half hour, I realize I am going to get a bad grade on my test if I keep up this behavior, so I turn the TV off, get comfortable, and start studying hard. If I go through this routine, then I know I will have a good study session and will get a good grade on a test.

2. *My Aunt Rita hates camping trips.*

   Yet she goes with us every year. She complains about sleeping in a tent, cooking over an open fire, and not having a clean bathroom for a week. Aunt Rita always ends up having fun, but she hates to do so much extra work. We love to joke with her and tease her about being a "city slicker."

Every year she says she will never go camping again, but we always make sure she comes along. I guess this has turned into a family ritual, and I'm glad. I always enjoy her company—especially when she complains.

3. *My roommate is a slob.* _____

Even though my roommate has her own room, she leaves clothes all over the place. I've found jeans on the couch, sweaters in the kitchen, and underwear in the bathroom. I once peeked into her room, which was so cluttered I couldn't even see her carpet. When she cooks, she leaves pots, pans, and dishes (all dirty and caked with food) all over the place.

Travis's Revision   When Travis looks back at his topic sentence in Chapter 3, he realizes it does not accurately introduce what he talks about in his paragraph. His topic sentence tells readers only that a ridge overlooks his hometown, not that this ridge is his favorite place:

> **Topic Sentence:**   A high, wooded ridge overlooks my hometown.

He decides to expand his topic sentence so that it more accurately introduces the details that will follow in his paragraph:

> **Revised Topic Sentence:**   A high, wooded ridge **that** overlooks my hometown **is my favorite place.**

He feels that this topic sentence introduces his favorite place and will let him talk about the river, the sunset, and the city.

Your Revision   With these guidelines in mind, revise your topic sentence.

Your Topic Sentence: _____

Your Revised Topic Sentence: _____

_____

_____

Revising Your Development

Details are the building blocks for constructing a paragraph. This section will guide you through the process of developing paragraphs, starting with the questions here from the Revising Checklist.

DEVELOPMENT

✔ Does the paragraph contain *specific* details that support the topic sentence?

✔ Does the paragraph include *enough* details to explain the topic sentence fully?

The details in your paragraph should be as specific as possible, and you should provide enough details to support your topic sentence. If you keep both of these guidelines in mind, you will develop your paragraphs specifically and adequately.

Specific Details Can you recognize those details that are more specific than other details? This is a major part of development. Look at the following details, and see how they move from general to specific and from abstract to concrete. As you learned in Chapter 3, concrete words refer to items you can see, hear, touch, smell, or taste—as opposed to abstract words that refer to ideas and concepts, like *hunger* and *happiness*.

transportation (general, abstract)
  vehicle
    car
      Dodge
        Dodge Durango
          red Dodge Durango
            red Dodge Durango
            with four-wheel drive
            and black interior
            (specific, concrete)

nutrition (general, abstract)
  food
    meat
      beef
        tri-tip
          tri-tip marinated in sauce
            tri-tip marinated in
            Aunt Bertha's homemade
            barbecue sauce
            (specific, concrete)

PRACTICE 3 Underline the most specific word or phrase in each group.

1. street, small road, Westwind Avenue, city, neighborhood

2. household, chores, weekend, dirty rag, employment

3. grade point average, science major, science class, sulfuric acid, academic units

4. landscaping, address, roses, garden, city planning

5. mountains, a state, beach resorts, Dave's Run, a ski resort in Mammoth

PRACTICE 4 Fill in the blanks so that each sequence moves from the general and abstract to the specific and concrete. *Answers will vary.*

1. homework _____
   _____
   _____

2. _____
   dog _____
   _____
   _____

3. trouble _____
   _____
   _____
   _____

4. _____
   _____
   _____
   state championship _____

5. _____
   _____
   piano _____
   _____

Travis's Revision   When Travis looks at his first draft, he realizes that he can make his details much more specific and concrete. Here are three sentences that he revises (with concrete details in bold type):

Revised: I can sit up there and see the river **with its many ripples,** the **colorful** sunset, and the city **with lots of tall buildings.**

Revised: There are huge clouds **that change from pink to purple to red** when the sun goes down behind them.

Revised: ~~All my troubles~~ **Homework and family problems** melt away.

Enough Details In addition to providing specific, concrete details, you need to furnish enough details to support the main idea of each paragraph. Without enough details, the main idea of a paragraph will not be adequately developed and may be misunderstood.

PRACTICE 5 List three details that could support each of the following sentences.   *Answers will vary.*

1. Some people have funny hobbies.

   _____

   _____

   _____

2. The campus health center is a friendly place.

   _____

   _____

   _____

3. My favorite food is Italian.

   _____

   _____

   _____

4. My paycheck never lasts as long as it should.

   _____

   _____

   _____

5. Exercising is important for people of all ages.

   _____

   _____

   _____

PRACTICE 6 Develop the following topic sentences with enough specific details.   *Answers will vary.*

1. Advertising surrounds us every day all day long.

   _____

   _____

   _____

2. The cost of living affects salaries.

_____

_____

_____

3. Severe mood changes are a sign of depression.

_____

_____

_____

4. Most people use their sense of right and wrong to make major decisions.

_____

_____

_____

5. College life can be frustrating.

_____

_____

_____

Travis's Revision   Travis's paragraph also needs not only *more specific* details but also *more* details to help it communicate its message. Travis accomplishes this by adding more details about the river, the sunset, the city, and his feelings. He talks about how the street lights guide the cars; he explains that the boats look like toys; he compares the colors in the clouds to a kaleidoscope and a color wheel; and he talks about time stopping when he is on the ridge.

General statement   A high, wooded ridge **that** overlooks my hometown **is my favorite place.** I can sit up there and see the river **with its many ripples,** the **colorful** sunset, and the city **with lots of tall buildings.** The sun   Specific details
shines like fire, and then the sun is gone behind the ridge. I love the river best, I can always see the river. I watch different kinds of boats on the river. I see rowboats, sailboats, motorboats, and freight liners. **The boats look like toys because I am up so high.**   Specific comparison
I have always liked to sail. My next favorite view is the sunset. Some nights the sunset is really beautiful. There are huge clouds **that change from pink to**

Specific details

purple to red when the sun goes down behind them. **Sometimes I think of a kaleidoscope, and other times I think of a color wheel that spins in slow motion.** When it gets dark. I can see the headlights of the cars moving through the city streets. I bet people don't realize they're being watched. The **bright** headlights follow the street lights **as if the street lights are showing the cars where to go.** When I am up high above the city, I get lost in my dreams, **and time doesn't exist. Homework and family problems** melt away. I just look around this place, think about this place's beauty, and feel good—automatically.

(margin right) Concrete details

(margin right) Specific comparison

(margin right) Concrete details

(margin left) Specific details

Your Revision   Add more details to your paragraph, making your explanations and descriptions as concrete and specific as possible.

Revising for Unity

A paragraph has unity when it discusses the one idea that is introduced in the topic sentence. Starting with questions from the Revising Checklist, this section will help you make sure your paragraphs have unity.

UNITY

✔ Do all the sentences in the paragraph support the topic sentence?

All sentences in a paragraph should expand on the topic sentence and relate to it in some way. Information not about the main idea is considered irrelevant and does not belong in the paragraph.

PRACTICE 7 Cross out the three irrelevant sentences in the following paragraph.

Reading helps bring back memories from our own lives. I never liked to read until I had Ms. Fischer. If we are reading about the thrill of McGwire's record in home runs, we might remember a great sports event in our lives. ~~I never liked sports, but my mom made me play soccer.~~ If we are reading about Jules Verne traveling around the world, memories of our favorite trips might come to the surface of our minds. ~~I liked Europe, but all I wanted to do was go home. I was also missing my girlfriend.~~ Reading is a wonderful way to lose ourselves in the lives of others while reliving some important moments in our own lives.

PRACTICE 8 Cross out the three irrelevant sentences in the following paragraph.

Your body has a three-stage reaction to stress: (1) alarm, (2) resistance, and (3) exhaustion. In the alarm stage, your body recognizes the presence of stress and, through a release of hormones from the endocrine glands, prepares for fight or flight. ~~I've been there; I have felt the fight feeling before~~. In the resistance stage, your body repairs any damage caused by the stress. ~~Repairing must be difficult for the body, but it has to be done~~. If the stress does not go away, however, the body cannot repair the damage and must remain alert. This plunges you into the third stage—exhaustion. If this state continues long enough, you may develop one of the diseases of stress. ~~I'll bet these diseases are difficult to diagnose and cure, but I don't know for sure~~. The best idea would be to learn how to deal with stress of all kinds and use it to your benefit.

Travis's Revision   Travis sees now that some of his sentences do not fit into his paragraph. In his case, the comments about his love for sailing and about people not knowing they are being watched do not support his topic sentence, the first sentence in his paragraph. When Travis drops these details, the revised paragraph looks like this:

A high, wooded ridge that overlooks my hometown is my favorite place. I can sit up there and see the river with its many ripples, the colorful sunset, and the city with lots of tall buildings. The sun shines like fire, and then the sun is gone behind the ridge. I love the river best, I can always see the river. I watch different kinds of boats on the river. I see rowboats, sailboats, motorboats, and freight liners. The boats look like toys because I am up so high. ~~I have always liked to sail.~~ My next favorite view is the sunset. Some nights the sunset is really beautiful. There are huge clouds that change from pink to purple to red when the sun goes down behind them. Sometimes I think of a kaleidoscope, and other times I think of a color wheel that spins in slow motion. When it gets dark. I can see the headlights of the cars moving through the city streets. ~~I bet people don't realize they're being watched.~~ The bright headlights follow the street lights as if the street lights are showing the cars where to go. When I am up high above the city, I get lost in my dreams, and time doesn't exist. Homework and family problems melt away. I just look around this place, think about this place's beauty, and feel good—automatically.

Your Revision   Read your paragraph carefully, and cross out any irrelevant sentences or ideas.

Revising Your Organization

Organization refers to the order of the details in a paragraph. Following the guidelines in this section, beginning with the question below from the Revising Checklist will help you revise the organization of the details in your paragraph.

ORGANIZATION

✔ Is the paragraph organized logically?

In Chapter 3, you learned five ways to organize your paragraphs:

1. General to particular
2. Particular to general
3. Chronologically (by time)
4. Spatially (by physical arrangement)
5. From one extreme to another

You might want to review pages 39–46 for an explanation of each of these methods.

The method you choose depends to a great extent on your topic and your purpose. What are you trying to accomplish? What order will help you deliver your message as effectively and efficiently as possible?

PRACTICE 9 Reorganize the following sentences so that they are in logical order. Then identify your method of organization.

5 This is convenient because it's at the beginning of the Riverwalk.

9 Hours later, I walk back to my car and think of the day I can return.

4 I always eat at my favorite Mexican restaurant first.

1 Whenever I visit San Antonio, my hometown, I always go to the Riverwalk.

7 I usually end my journey near a road that will lead me to the Alamo.

2 I always park at the end with the newest hotels and mall.

6 I then walk down the paths, stopping in all of the unique shops.

8 I always stop here because it is a wonderful historical monument.

3 This way I can spend hours just walking along the beautiful paths and stopping in my favorite places.

Method of Organization: *Chronological*

PRACTICE 10 Reorganize the sentences in the following paragraph so that they are in logical order. Then label your method of organization.

³I know that I have about three feet when I get out of bed before I run into the dresser.²It is especially bad at night, when I don't have my contacts in and I have to get from my bed to the bathroom.¹My sight is so bad that I can't even see three feet in front of me without my contacts.⁵From the doorway, I then go left and walk three steps to the bathroom.⁴From the dresser, if I turn right, I have to walk five steps to get to the doorway of my room.⁶If I reverse my steps and count backward, I can usually make it to and from the bathroom without breaking a toe or crashing into a wall.

Method of Organization: *Spatial*

Travis's Revision In Chapter 3, Travis decided that the best way to organize his paragraph was from most favorite to least favorite. But now he needs to make sure that every detail is in the right place. He notices a sentence about the sunset that is out of order, so he moves the sentence to the part of the paragraph that focuses on the sunset.

A high, wooded ridge that overlooks my hometown is my favorite place. I can sit up there and see the river with its many ripples, the colorful sunset, and the city with lots of tall buildings. ~~The sun shines like fire, and then the sun is gone behind the ridge.~~ I love the river best, I can always see the river. I watch different kinds of boats on the river. I see rowboats, sailboats, motorboats, and freight liners. The boats look like toys because I am up so high. My next favorite view is the sunset. Some nights the sunset is really beautiful. There are huge clouds that change from pink to purple to red when the sun goes down behind them. Sometimes I think of a kaleidoscope, and other times I think of a color wheel that spins in slow motion. **The sun shines like fire, and then the sun is gone behind the ridge.** When it gets dark. I can see the headlights of the cars moving through the city streets. The bright headlights follow the street lights as if the street lights are showing the cars where to go. When I am up high above the city, I get lost in my dreams, and time doesn't exist. Homework and family problems melt away. I just look around this place, think about this place's beauty, and feel good—automatically.

Your Revision Double-check the method of organization you chose in Chapter 3, and make sure each of your details is in its proper place.

Revising for Coherence

A paragraph is coherent when its parts *cohere*, or stick together. The questions here from the Revising Checklist will be your focus in this section as you revise your writing for coherence.

COHERENCE

✔ Do the sentences in the paragraph move smoothly and logically from one to the next?

A coherent paragraph is smooth, not choppy, and readers move logically from one thought to the next, seeing a clear relationship between the ideas. Here are four different strategies that writers use to help readers follow their train of thought: *transitions, repeated words, synonyms,* and *pronouns.*

Transitions *Transitional words and phrases* are like bridges or links between thoughts. They show your readers how one idea is related to another or when you are moving to a new point. Good use of transitions makes your writing smooth rather than choppy.

Choppy: I watch different kinds of boats on the river. I see rowboats, sailboats, motorboats, and freight liners.

Smooth: I watch different kinds of boats on the river. **For instance,** I see rowboats, sailboats, motorboats, and freight liners.

Transitions have very specific meanings, so you should take care to use the ones that fit the logic of your sentences.

Confusing: I watch different kinds of boats on the water. **Besides,** I see rowboats, sailboats, motorboats, and freight liners.

Here is a list of some common transitional words and phrases that will make your writing more coherent. They are classified by meaning.

Some Common Transitions

Addition:	*again, and, and then, also, besides, finally, first, further, furthermore, in addition, last, likewise, moreover, next, nor, second, third, too*
Comparison:	*in like manner, likewise, similarly*
Contrast:	*after all, and yet, at the same time, but, however, in contrast, nevertheless, on the contrary, on the other hand, otherwise, still, yet*

Emphasis:	*actually, after all, essentially, in any event, indeed, in fact, of course, to tell the truth*
Example:	*for example, for instance, in this case*
Place:	*adjacent to, beyond, here, near, nearby, opposite, there*
Purpose:	*for this purpose, to this end, with this objective*
Result:	*accordingly, as a result, consequently, hence, so, then, therefore, thus*
Summary:	*as I have said, in brief, in other words, in short, in sum, on the whole, that is, to conclude, to sum up, to summarize*
Time:	*after a few days, afterward, at length, (at) other times, immediately, in the meantime, later, meanwhile, now, sometimes, soon, still, then*

See pages 372–374 in the Handbook (Part IV) for more information on transitions.

PRACTICE 11 Fill in the blanks in the following paragraph with logical transitions. *Answers may vary.*

People should spay or neuter their animals so that we don't end up with kittens and puppies that no one wants. *For example* , a family might have a male cat that they let roam the neighborhood, and this cat might get a female cat pregnant. *Then* who will care for the new kittens? Some people give them away or take them to a neighborhood SPCA. Some people, *on the other hand* , just let the kittens roam free, hoping someone will take care of them. This irresponsible action causes more problems, *however* .

PRACTICE 12 Rewrite the following paragraph, adding at least three transitions to make it more coherent. *Answers will vary.*

Growing up, my brother, sister, and I always looked forward to the summer Saturdays that our dad took us water-skiing. We often prepared the night before for our outing the next day. We would get our day-bags packed and our clothes ready to put on. We would pack a lunch big enough for all of us. We would make sure we had plenty of sodas for the entire day. We loved spending the whole day with him. We hated that time went so fast. When he would drop us back at home, we would anxiously wait for the next Saturday to come.

Repeated Words *Repeating key words* also helps bind the sentences of a paragraph together and guide readers through its ideas. At the same time, too much repetition becomes boring.

Effective Repetition: Sometimes **I think of** a kaleidoscope, and other times **I think of** a color wheel that spins in slow motion.

PRACTICE 13 Underline the four effective repeated words in the following paragraph.

I worked in a law firm during my first summer break from college because I wanted to discover if a legal career was really for me. The law firm I worked in was very large, and many of the lawyers specialized in criminal law. I learned quite a lot about tricky defense strategies at this law firm, and I decided that if I did pursue a law degree, I would become a prosecutor, not a defender. Actually working in a law firm was a great way to learn more about the legal profession.

PRACTICE 14 Add five repeated words where appropriate to clarify and smooth out the following paragraph.

My friend Manuel is a TV addict. He watches it for over 10 hours
TV

every day, and he never gets his homework finished. He doesn't un-

derstand that his instructors won't let him turn in his work late, so he
TV   TV
watches it whenever he's home. The shows he watches on it are usually

pretty boring; they don't require thought when he watches them. But
TV
he loves to sit there and watch it anyway. I hope he'll learn soon that
TV
watching it instead of doing other things can only lead to nowhere.

Synonyms Next, using *synonyms* can link your sentences and help you avoid needless repetition. Synonyms are words with identical or similar meanings. They can add variety and interest to your writing. A thesaurus, or book of synonyms, can help you locate the best replacements for specific words.

In the following example from Travis's paragraph, Travis uses *town* in place of one of his references to *city*.

Original Reference: When I am up high above the **city,** I get lost in my dreams, and time doesn't exist.

Synonym: When I am up high above the **town,** I get lost in my dreams, and time doesn't exist.

PRACTICE 15 Underline at least four synonyms that refer to cooking in the following paragraph.

I have loved to cook since I was 12 years old. My mother taught me everything I know. I especially love to cook for my dad because he is what we call "cooking challenged." When he cooks, he thinks microwaving is the only way to go, and even then he overcooks or burns the food. He kids me for cooking from scratch and using traditional methods because he firmly believes there's only one way to cook. I broil; he microwaves. I roast; he microwaves. I barbecue; he microwaves. But he always praises me for my culinary ability because in the end, he knows I will someday be a famous chef.

PRACTICE 16 Replace two references to *professor* with synonyms in the following paragraph.   *Answers will vary.*

I have discovered that one key to making good grades is to get a good professor. A good professor can encourage me to do my best and can make learning fun. I find that I do better for professors who don't just lecture the entire time but let us interact with one another in some way. Professors with a sense of humor also encourage me to perform better. They actually make me look forward to coming to their classes. The good professors simply help me earn a good grade.

Pronouns The final way to link your sentences is with *pronouns*. When appropriate, you can replace specific words with pronouns. Not only do pronouns link your ideas, but they also keep your writing moving at a fairly fast pace.

Travis uses a pronoun to get rid of a repetition of the word *boats*.

Repetition: I watch different kinds of boats on the river. For instance, I see rowboats, sailboats, motorboats, and freight liners. **The boats** look like toys because I am up so high.

Pronoun: I watch different kinds of boats on the river. For instance, I see rowboats, sailboats, motorboats, and freight liners. ~~The boats~~ They look like toys because I am up so high.

For more information on pronouns, see pages 365–367 in the Handbook (Part IV).

PRACTICE 17 Underline the 14 pronouns in the following paragraph.

When I was preparing for my wedding, I relied a lot on my best friend, Tanya. She helped me pick out my dress, decide on the flowers, and book the banquet hall. They all were the perfect choices for me. Tanya worked in a craft store, so she was able to help me decorate the hall for a reasonably cheap price. Throwing a wedding is a huge event, and Tanya was a great friend throughout the process. I couldn't have done it without her.

PRACTICE 18 Add five pronouns where appropriate in the following paragraph.

Tom, Sandy, and I have been friends for life. Tom, Sandy, and I *We*
met in third grade when we all tried to survive the neighborhood
bully on our walks home. Tom, Sandy, and I *We* went through high
school together and are now attending the same college. Tom, Sandy, *Our*
and my college is two hours from our hometown. So, Tom, Sandy, *We*
and I share an apartment. Our apartment is very nice, and our apart- *it*
ment is always clean. I hope that Tom, Sandy, and I *we* will always
remain good friends.

Travis's Revision   When Travis checks his paragraph for coherence, he decides his writing can use some improvement. So he makes the following revisions that help bind his sentences together and show the relationships between his ideas.

Here is Travis's paragraph with transitions, repeated words, synonyms, and pronouns highlighted.

	A high, wooded ridge that overlooks my hometown is	
	my favorite place. I can sit up **there on the ridge** and see	repetition
	the river with its many ripples, the colorful sunset, and the	
	city with lots of tall buildings. I love the river best, I can	
repetition	always see **~~the river~~ it from the ridge.** I watch different	pronoun
transition	kinds of boats on the **~~river~~ water. For instance,** I see row-	synonym
pronoun	boats, sailboats, motorboats, and freight liners. **~~The boats~~**	
	They look like toys because I am up so high. My next	
repetition	favorite view is **the sunset.** Some nights **the sunset** is re-	
	ally beautiful. There are huge clouds that change from pink	
	to purple to red when the sun goes down behind them.	
transition	**Sometimes I think of** a kaleidoscope, and **other times I**	
	think of a color wheel that spins in slow motion. The sun	
pronoun	shines like fire, and then **~~the sun~~ it** is gone behind the	repetition
	ridge. **Finally,** when it gets dark. I can see the headlights	transition
	of the cars moving through the city streets. The bright	
	headlights follow the street lights as if the street lights are	
repetition	showing the cars where to go. When I am up **~~high~~ on the**	
	ridge above the **~~city~~ town,** I get lost in my dreams, and	synonym
transition	time doesn't exist. **On the whole,** homework and family	
	problems melt away. I just look around this place, think	
	about **~~this place's~~ its** beauty, and feel good—automatically.	pronoun

Transitions In addition to *for instance*, *sometimes*, and *other times*, Travis added two more transitions to his paragraph. What are they?

finally, on the whole

List the meaning of all five transitions in Travis's paragraph:

1. Transition: *for instance* Meaning: *example*
2. Transition: *sometimes* Meaning: *time*
3. Transition: *other times* Meaning: *time*
4. Transition: *finally* Meaning: *addition*
5. Transition: *on the whole* Meaning: *summary*

Repeated Words When Travis checked his paragraph for repeated key words, he thought he needed to refer directly to the ridge more often, so he revised some of his sentences. How many new references to the ridge did he add?

three

Synonyms When Travis looked at his paragraph again, he found another opportunity to use a synonym to link his ideas more clearly. Besides the addition of *town* for *city*, what other synonym does Travis use in his revision?

_____ *water* _____ for _____ *river* _____

Pronouns Finally, in addition to substituting *they* for *boats*, Travis found three more places to use pronouns to bind his paragraph together. Where are these places in his paragraph?

_____ *it* _____ for _____ *the river* _____

_____ *it* _____ for _____ *the sun* _____

_____ *its* _____ for _____ *this place's* _____

Your Revision   Now it's time to make your paragraph more coherent.

Transitions Check the transitions in your paragraph. Do you use enough transitions so that your paragraph moves smoothly and logically from one idea to the next? Do you use your transitions correctly?

Repeated Words Look at your paragraph to see when you might want to repeat a key word. Then revise your paragraph accordingly.

Synonyms Look for places in your paragraph where you might add synonyms to link your sentences. Use a thesaurus in book form or on your computer if you need help.

Pronouns Check your paragraph for opportunities to use pronouns. Add appropriate pronouns.

MyWritingLab **Helpful Hints**

- **Is your topic sentence as effective as it can be?** Topic sentences are the controlling ideas of your paragraph. If you need help with these important sentences, see **The Topic Sentence** in **The Craft of Writing** module in **MyWritingLab**.
- **Did you make the best choice for organizing your ideas?** Get help finding an organization that is perfect for your paragraph by going to **Developing and Organizing a Paragraph** in **The Craft of Writing** module in **MyWritingLab**. Good organization ensures that your audience can follow your reasoning.

Travis's Revised Paragraph   After revising his topic sentence, his development, his unity, his organization, and his coherence, Travis produced the following revised paragraph. All of his revisions are in bold type.

A high, wooded ridge **that** overlooks my hometown **is my favorite place.** I can sit up ~~there~~ **on the ridge** and see the river **with its many ripples,** the **colorful** sunset, and the city **with lots of tall buildings.** ~~The sun shines like fire, and then the sun is gone behind the ridge.~~ I love the river best, I can always see ~~the river~~ **it** from the ridge. I watch different kinds of boats on the ~~river~~ **water. For instance,** I see rowboats, sailboats, motorboats, and freight liners. ~~The boats~~ **They** look like toys because I am up so high. ~~I have always liked to sail.~~ My next favorite view is the sunset. Some nights the sunset is really beautiful. There are huge clouds **that change from pink to purple to red** when the sun goes down behind them. **Sometimes I think of a kaleidoscope, and other times I think of a color wheel that spins in slow motion. The sun shines like fire, and then** ~~the sun~~ **it** is gone **behind the ridge. Finally,** when it gets dark. I can see the headlights of the cars moving through the city streets. ~~I bet people don't realize they're being watched.~~ The **bright** headlights follow the street lights **as if the street lights are showing the cars where to go.** When I am up ~~high~~ **on the ridge** above the ~~city~~ **town,** I get lost in my dreams, **and time doesn't exist. On the whole,** ~~All my troubles~~ **homework and family problems** melt away. I just look around this place, think about ~~this place's~~ **its** beauty, and feel good—automatically.

Your Revised Paragraph   Now that you have applied all the revision strategies to your own writing, write your revised paragraph here.

_____

_____

_____

_____

_____

_____

_____

_____

_____

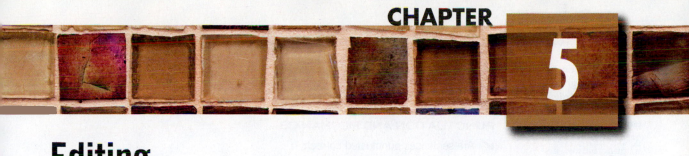

Editing

After you have revised your paragraph, you are ready to edit it. **Editing** involves checking your grammar, punctuation, mechanics, word choice, and spelling to be sure your writing is free of errors. These five features of writing are as important to communicating clearly as well-chosen details. They help your reader navigate through your writing. Nothing confuses readers more than editing errors, which attract the readers' attention and can seriously distract from what you are saying.

For easy reference, we have divided the editing strategies into three large categories in the following checklist: sentences, punctuation and mechanics, and word choice and spelling. This checklist doesn't cover all the grammar and usage problems you may find in your writing, but it focuses on some of the most common mistakes college students make.

MyWritingLab **Understanding Editing**

Remembering that editing and revising are different can be challenging. To test your understanding of the difference between them, go to **MyWritingLab.com,** and click on **Editing the Paragraph** in **The Craft of Writing** module. For this topic, read the **Overview,** watch the two **Animation** videos, and complete the **Recall, Apply,** and **Write** activities. Then check your mastery of this material by taking the **Post-test.**

Editing Checklist

SENTENCES

✔ Does each sentence have a main subject and verb?

✔ Do all subjects and verbs agree?

Student Comment:
"I not only learned a lot from this explanation, but I went back and checked out the video about editing when I was writing my other papers—not even just for English!"

Have the students refer to the Editing Checklists in *Mosaics* for help as they complete the MyWritingLab topics. In these checklists, they will find information to help refine their writing process and complete the exercises.

TEACHING EDITING
Divide students into six groups, and designate

✔ Do all pronouns agree with their nouns?

✔ Are modifiers as close as possible to the words they modify?

PUNCTUATION AND MECHANICS

✔ Are sentences punctuated correctly?

✔ Are words capitalized properly?

WORD CHOICE AND SPELLING

✔ Are words used correctly?

✔ Are words spelled correctly?

Editing is a two-part job: First, you must locate the errors. Then you must know how to correct them.

Finding Your Errors

Since you can't correct errors until you find them, a major part of editing is proofreading. *Proofreading* is reading to catch grammar, punctuation, mechanics, word choice, and spelling errors. If you do not proofread carefully, you will not be able to make the changes that will improve your writing.

One good idea is to read your paragraphs backward, starting with the last sentence first, so you can concentrate on your sentences. Another technique is to keep an error log in which you list the mistakes you make most often. An Error Log form is provided for you in Appendix 6. To use this log in proofreading, read your paper for one type of error at a time. For example, if you often write fragments, you should read your paper once just to catch fragments. Then read it again to find a second type of error. Asking a friend or tutor to read your writing is always a good idea because you might be missing some errors in your writing that another reader will see. When others read your writing, they might want to use the editing symbols on the inside back cover of this textbook to label your errors. You can also use the grammar- or spell-checker on your computer, which will point out possible grammar or spelling errors and make suggestions for correcting them.

MyWritingLab **Helpful Hints**

- **Confused about when to revise and edit?** Revising and editing are crucial parts of the writing process. To make sure you understand where they fit in the writing process, see **The Writing Process** in **The Craft of Writing** module in **MyWritingLab.**

- **Not sure what to look for when you edit?** Each writer has a unique set of grammar errors that occur in his or her writing; these common errors are your "editing quotient." For more help with grammar and mechanics, go to the **Basic Grammar** module in **MyWritingLab.**

PRACTICE 1 **Finding Your EQ** Find your Editing Quotient (EQ) by taking the EQ Test on pages 661–663 (Appendix 2A). This test will help you learn what errors you have the most trouble identifying when you proofread.

PRACTICE 2 **Scoring Your EQ** Score your EQ Test by using the answer key that follows the test (Appendix 2B).

PRACTICE 3 **Analyzing Your EQ** Circle the errors you missed on the EQ Test, and chart them in Appendix 2C. Do they fall into any clear categories?

Correcting Your Errors

After you find your errors, you need to correct them. To guide you through this phase, a complete handbook is provided in Part IV of this text, along with a list of correction symbols (on the inside back cover) that your instructor might use on your papers.

As you proofread, you should record in your Error Log the corrections you make in your writing. This log can then help you get control of these errors. If you record your corrections each time you find errors, you will learn the pattern of your mistakes and eventually be able to master the grammar concepts that are confusing to you.

Finally, you should use the Editing Checklist at the beginning of this chapter to help you edit your writing. As you attempt to answer each one of the questions on this checklist, look up the grammar items in Part IV and make your corrections.

PRACTICE 4 **Using the Handbook** Using the Handbook in Part IV, list the page number where you can look up each type of error listed below. This activity will help you start to use the Handbook as a reference guide.

abbreviation   page _____

capitalization   page _____

comma   page _____

confused word   page _____

end punctuation   page _____

fragment	page _____
modifier	page _____
number	page _____
pronoun agreement	page _____
run-together sentences	page _____
spelling	page _____
subject-verb agreement	page _____
verb form	page _____

PRACTICE 5 Using the Error Log and the Spelling Log Turn to Appendixes 7 and 8, and start an Error Log and a Spelling Log of your own with the errors you didn't recognize in Practice 1. For each error, write out the mistake, the Handbook reference, and your correction.

PRACTICE 6 Using the Editing Checklist Use the Editing Checklist at the beginning of this chapter to edit two of the paragraphs from the EQ Test on pages 661–663. Rewrite the entire paragraphs.

Travis's Editing   When Travis proofreads his paper for grammar, punctuation, mechanics, word choice, and spelling, he finds two errors that he looks up in Part IV and corrects. The first error is a comma splice:

> **Run-Together:**   I love the river best, I can always see it from
> the ridge.

Travis realizes that this sentence has too many subjects and verbs without any linking words or end punctuation between them. He looks up "fused sentences and comma splices" on page 410 of Part IV and corrects the error by putting a comma and a coordinating conjunction (*and*) between the two sentences.

> **Correction:**   I love the river best, **and** I can always see it from
> the ridge.

He also finds a sentence that doesn't sound complete—it is not a sentence but a fragment:

> **Fragment:**   Finally, when it gets dark.

When he looks up the problem in Part IV (page 396), he learns that a fragment is easily corrected by connecting it to another sentence.

> **Correction:**   Finally, when it gets dark/, I can see the headlights of
> the cars below me moving through the city streets.

Travis's Edited Draft   Both of these errors are corrected here in Travis's edited draft.

A high, wooded ridge that overlooks my hometown is my favorite place. I can sit up on the ridge and see the river with its many ripples, the colorful sunset, and the city with lots of tall buildings. I love the river best, **and** I can always see it from the ridge. I watch different kinds of boats on the water. For instance, I see rowboats, sailboats, motorboats, and freight liners. They look like toys because I am up so high. My next favorite view is the sunset. Some nights the sunset is really beautiful. There are huge clouds that change from pink to purple to red when the sun goes down behind them. Sometimes I think of a kaleidoscope, and other times I think of a color wheel that spins in slow motion. The sun shines like fire, and then it is gone behind the ridge. Finally, when it gets dark**/,** I can see the headlights of the cars moving through the city streets. The bright headlights follow the street lights as if the street lights are showing the cars where to go. When I am up on the ridge above the town, I get lost in my dreams, and time doesn't exist. On the whole, homework and family problems melt away. I just look around this place, think about its beauty, and feel good—automatically.

Your Editing   Proofread your paragraph carefully to find errors. Then use at least two of the methods from this chapter to help you correct any errors you made in your paragraph. Record your errors and their corrections here.

_____

_____

_____

_____

Your Edited Draft   Now write out a corrected draft of your paragraph.

_____

_____

_____

_____

_____

_____

_____

_____

_____

_____

_____

Review of the Reading and Writing Processes

The **reading process** is a series of tasks that involve prereading, reading, first rereading, and second rereading.

- **Preparing to Read** involves thinking about the title, the author, and some focused questions.

- **Reading** includes focusing on vocabulary, learning a reading strategy, and understanding the author's purpose.

- **First Rereading** consists of understanding an essay's assumptions and relationships between ideas.

- **Second Rereading** consists of writing questions, forming opinions, and analyzing.

The **writing process** is a series of cyclical tasks that involves prewriting, writing, revising, and editing.

- **Preparing to Write** consists of _thinking_ about a topic and _planning_ your paragraph.
  Thinking: Exploring a subject and generating ideas through freewriting, brainstorming, clustering, questioning, or discussing.
  Planning: Choosing a topic, establishing a purpose, analyzing the audience.
- **Writing** includes writing a topic sentence, developing your ideas, organizing your thoughts, and drafting a paragraph.
  Writing a topic sentence: A limited topic and a statement about that topic.
  Developing: Making details more specific; adding details and examples.
  Organizing: General to particular, particular to general, chronological, spatial, one extreme to another.
  Drafting: Writing a first draft.

- **Revising** means "seeing again" and working with development, unity, organization, and coherence.
- **Editing** involves proofreading and correcting your grammar, punctuation, mechanics, word choice, and spelling errors.

REVIEW PRACTICE 1 Answer the following questions to review the material in Part I.

1. What are the four main parts of the reading process?
   Prereading, reading, first rereading, and second rereading

2. What are the four main parts of the writing process?
   Prewriting, writing, revising, and editing

3. What is your favorite reading strategy? Why is it your favorite?
   Answers will vary.

4. What is your favorite prewriting activity? Why is it your favorite?
   Answers will vary.

5. What individual activities do you find yourself doing to get started on a reading project?
   Answers will vary.

6. What individual activities do you find yourself doing to get started on a writing project?
   Answers will vary.

7. Where do you usually do your academic reading? Why do you choose this place?
   Answers will vary.

8. Where do you usually do your academic writing? Do you write your first draft on a computer? What time of day do you do your best writing?

Answers will vary.

9. What are the five main methods of organization?

General to particular, particular to general, chronological, spatial, and from one extreme to another

10. What is the difference between revising and editing?

Revising involves content (development, unity, organization, coherence); editing deals with form (grammar, punctuation, mechanics, word choice, and spelling).

11. What are the three main categories of editing?

The three main categories are sentences, punctuation and mechanics, and word choice and spelling.

12. Do you try to get someone to read your writing before you turn it in? Explain your answer.

Answers will vary.

REVIEW PRACTICE 2 Develop each of the following topics into topic sentences, limiting them as much as possible. Then, by following the guidelines furnished in Part I, develop one topic sentence into a paragraph. *Answers will vary.*

1. My English class
2. National politics
3. My favorite pastime
4. Families
5. On the way to school

6. When students relax
7. My dream job
8. The best stereo system
9. What supervisors should never do
10. The clothes I wear to school

REVIEW PRACTICE 3 Revise the paragraph you wrote for Review Practice 2, using the checklist on pages 47–48 *Answers will vary.*

REVIEW PRACTICE 4 Edit the paragraph you wrote for Review Practice 2, using the checklist on pages 67–68 *Answers will vary.*

Reading and Writing Effective Paragraphs

"Learn as much by writing as by reading."

—LORD ACTON

Part II of *Mosaics* will help you read and then write effective paragraphs. Each chapter features one rhetorical strategy as a pattern for processing information. These nine chapters will teach you how to use each rhetorical mode to understand and communicate ideas. First, each chapter provides you with specific guidelines for prewriting in a particular mode, which always includes reading. Then the chapter guides you through the writing process in each mode. Next, you work systematically on revising and editing—first with a student paragraph, then with your own writing. Students can often see problems in other students' writing more easily than they can in their own, so you will apply each chapter's guidelines to someone else's writing before working with your own paragraph in a particular mode. Finally, the chapter introduces two essays written by professional writers. The questions framing these selections will help you process the content of the essays critically so you will ultimately be prepared to write a well-developed essay of your own at the end of each chapter. Throughout this section of the text, you will see how reading and writing complement each other in the process of communication.

6

Describing

TEACHING DESCRIPTION
Begin by asking students
what kind of animal they
would *create* if they had
the power to do so. Prompt
students by asking them
questions that cover all five
senses:

Sight: How many arms and
legs does your animal have?

Sound: What kind of noise
does it make?

Touch: What outer
covering does it have—fur?
feathers? hard shell?

Taste: What does it eat?

Smell: What does its
environment smell like?

Once students have
answered these questions,
have them write an
organized paragraph about
their animal (5–8 minutes).

Then have each
student switch papers
with another student and
draw that person's animal
on the basis of his or her
paragraph (5–10 minutes).
Make sure they do not
talk or get clarification.
(Providing colored markers
is a nice touch.)

After everyone is
finished, have students
return the paragraphs and

"You can observe a lot just by watching."

—YOGI BERRA

We all use description every day of our lives when we tell others about

- The noisy home we grew up in;
- The worn-leather smell of our favorite baseball glove;
- The sour taste of a lemon;
- The smoothness of a snake's skin;
- The beauty of a special sunset;
- A sudden clap of thunder in the middle of a quiet night.

Whatever you do, description is a large part of your daily thought and language. Your friends might ask what kind of smartphone you just bought; your parents may want to know what your duties will be in your new job; your supervisor might need a description of the project you just completed. You really can't communicate effectively without being able to describe people, places, objects, and activities for different audiences.

Description paints a picture in words to help a reader visualize something you have seen or heard or done. Writing about some early memories, Mike Rose describes "a peculiar mix" of elements in his life. Notice all the vivid details in the paragraph.

I have many particular memories of this time, but in general these early years seem a peculiar mix of physical warmth and barrenness: a gnarled lemon tree, thin rugs, a dirt alley, concrete in the sun. My uncles visited a few times, and we went to the beach or to orange groves. The return home, however, left the waves and spray, the thick leaves, and split pulp far in the distance. I was aware of my parents watching their money and got the sense from their conversations that things could quickly take a turn for the worse. I started taping pennies to the bottom of a shelf in the kitchen.

You will refer to this example again when you are learning the guidelines for writing a good description paragraph.

| MyWritingLab | ## Understanding Description |

To make sure you understand describing, go to **MyWritingLab.com**, and click on **Describing** in the **Paragraph Development** module. At this point, read the **Overview,** watch the **Animation** video, and complete the **Recall, Apply,** and **Write** activities. Then check your mastery of this material by taking the **Post-test.**

PREPARING TO WRITE A DESCRIPTION PARAGRAPH

If you learn how to read a description paragraph critically, these skills will naturally transfer to your writing. But you need to be conscious of the process you use to understand your reading so you can use it just as effectively in your writing. Reading and writing critically will enhance your ability to succeed in college and to perform many other tasks in all facets of life.

To begin with, you need to learn how to read critically. Let's look closely at a description paragraph. First, you will apply a specific reading strategy to the paragraph. Next, you will answer some questions about the paragraph in an attempt to discover how it functions. With a detailed understanding of your reading, you will have more tools at your disposal as you write.

For more detailed information on "personal associations," see page 16 in Chapter 2.

READING CRITICALLY
Making Personal Associations with a Professional Paragraph

We all naturally make personal associations with our reading. However, one person's associations are usually quite different from those of someone else. Recording the associations you make with a reading selection lets you "own" the ideas. It allows you to connect the author's thoughts to your own experiences. As you read the following paragraph, make at least two notes in the margins that relate some of your specific memories to the information in the paragraph. Be prepared to explain the connection between your notes and the facts in the paragraph.

Reading Strategy

Reading a Description Paragraph

In an autobiographical essay, Joseph Bruchac talks about growing up as a mixture of Native American, Slovak, and French. Accepting his ethnic identity was a big step he had to take in order to be at peace with himself as a person. As you read this paragraph, make your personal notes in the margin. Then answer the questions after the reading to discover how the paragraph works.

What do I look like? The features of my face are big: a beaked nose, lips that are too sensitive, and sand-brown eyes and dark eyebrows that lift one at a time like the wings of a bird, a low forehead that looks higher because of receding brown hair, an Adam's apple like a broken bone, two ears that were normal before wrestling flattened one of them. Unlike my grandfather's, my skin is not brown throughout the seasons but sallow in the winter months, though it tans dark and quickly when the sun's warmth returns. It is, as you might gather, a face I did not used to love. Today I look at it in the mirror and say, Bruchac, you're ugly and I like you. The face nods back at me, and we laugh together.

Discovering How This Paragraph Works

To help you discover the elements that make this an effective description paragraph so you can use them in your own writing, answer the following questions in as much detail as possible.

1. The entire paragraph creates a certain mood. What is this general impression that Bruchac communicates?

   acceptance

2. In this particular passage, Bruchac describes his face mainly through the sense of seeing, with a few references to touching and hearing. List at least one example of each of these senses in this paragraph.

Seeing: *beaked nose, sensitive lips, sand-brown eyes, dark eyebrows, flattened*

ear, brown hair, Adam's apple, low forehead, receding brown hair, etc.

Touching: *sun's warmth*

Hearing: *say, laugh*

3. Bruchac works hard in this paragraph to *show* rather than *tell* us what he looks like. He tells us that the features of his face are "big" and then tries to prove it by supplying specific details. What three details go beyond telling to *show* us his face is "big"? *Answers may vary.*

a beaked nose

lips that are too sensitive

a low forehead that looks higher because of receding brown hair

4. What does Bruchac compare to the wings of a bird? To a broken bone? These comparisons are called *similes* (comparisons between two unlike items using *like* or *as*). How do they *show* rather than tell?

He compares dark eyebrows that lift one at a time to the wings of a bird

and an Adam's apple to a broken bone.

These comparisons show rather than tell by helping us picture his features.

5. Look back at Chapter 3 to review the five ways of organizing ideas in a paragraph. Which method does Bruchac use to organize the details in his paragraph? List some of his details in the order they appear. Then identify his method of organization: general to particular, particular to general, spatial, chronological, or one extreme to another. *Details will vary.*

beaked nose   *low forehead...*

sensitive lips   *two ears...*

sand-brown eyes   *skin is not brown...*

dark eyebrows...   *tans dark and quickly*

Method of organization: *Particular to general (specific features to whole face)*

WRITING A DESCRIPTION PARAGRAPH

Now that you have read and studied a paragraph, you will be writing one of your own. This section will help you generate a rough draft that you will then revise and edit in the third section of this chapter. It will guide you through a careful reading of the writing assignment, give you several ways to generate ideas, and finally furnish you with concrete guidelines for writing an effective description paragraph. We encourage you to write notes and lists throughout this section so you can use them when you write a draft of your paragraph at the end of this section.

 Reading Strategy

Reading the Prompt

The very first step in writing a good paragraph is making sure you understand the writing assignment or "prompt." An assignment attempts to "prompt" you to respond to a specific issue or question. The more clearly you understand the prompt, the better paragraph or essay you will create. Applying the chapter reading strategy to your writing assignment is a good way to accomplish this goal.

READING CRITICALLY
Making Personal Associations with the Prompt

Add your personal associations to the writing prompt below. What ideas come to mind as you read this prompt? Write as many personal notes as you can in the margins of this assignment. Then underline the directions for completing this assignment. Finally, start a conversation with the assignment by responding to the questions at the beginning of the prompt.

Writing Prompt

Complete this **Writing Prompt** at **mywritinglab.com**

What are some of your most vivid memories from childhood? Do any of them form a single impression when you think about them? Write a paragraph describing your clearest recollection. Explain your experience through as many senses as possible, following the guidelines below for developing a description paragraph.

PREWRITING EXERCISE
Brainstorm vivid memories in class to help students consider possible topics.

Thinking About the Prompt

Before you focus on a specific topic, you should generate as many ideas as you can so you have several to choose from. List some memorable experiences you have from your childhood. Why do you remember these experiences? Did any of them form an impression on you worth writing about? Choose one of these experiences, and use one or more of the prewriting techniques you learned in Chapter 3 to generate and record as many thoughts as possible about it.

Guidelines for Writing a Description Paragraph

Describing is a very natural process that we all do simply and freely without any complex directions. But have you noticed that some people seem to describe events and objects more clearly than other people do? When they tell you what they saw or did, you feel as though you were there too. You can improve your description skills by following a few simple guidelines. As we go through these features of a good description paragraph, we will refer to the paragraph you read at the beginning of the chapter by Mike Rose.

1. **Decide on a dominant impression—the feeling or mood you are trying to communicate.** Do you want your reader to feel sorry for you, to sense the excitement of an amazing fireworks display, or to share your disappointment in a bad restaurant? Choosing a dominant impression will give your description focus and unity. You can't possibly write down everything you observe about a person, place, incident, or object. The result would be a long, confusing, and probably boring list. But if you first decide on a dominant impression for your description, you can then choose which details will best convey that impression.

   In the Reading: The dominant impression Rose conveys about his childhood is its strange mix of "warmth and barrenness [emptiness]." This dominant impression gives his paragraph focus and helps him choose the details that will communicate this feeling most effectively.

   In Your Writing: What dominant impression do you want to communicate in your paragraph? Can you put it in a sentence?

2. **Draw on your five senses to write a good description.** If you use all your senses, your readers will be able to see, hear, smell, taste, or touch what you are describing as if they were there with you having the same experience. The more senses you draw on, the more interesting your description will be.

   In the Reading: Look again at Rose's description. He uses his sense of touch when he talks about "physical warmth and barrenness" and refers to "concrete in the sun." He draws on sight when he mentions "a gnarled lemon tree, thin rugs, a dirt alley." "The waves and spray, the thick leaves, and split pulp" also draw on our senses of touch and sight. His paragraph is vivid because of all the specific sensory details he furnishes.

   In Your Writing: Which senses will your paragraph cover? Do your prewriting notes have ideas that refer to all the senses? Which of your details draw on sight, sound, touch, smell, and taste? Label the items on your list by senses so you know what you have covered so far. Can you add more details at this point that refer to some of the senses you don't include?

3. **When you describe, try to *show* rather than *tell* your readers what you want them to know.** You can tell someone you bought a "great new car." But if you say you bought a "sleek, new black Blazer with four-wheel drive, a tan interior, custom wheels, and an awesome stereo," you're *showing* your readers why you are so excited about your purchase.

   In the Reading: If Rose had simply stopped after stating his dominant impression (that he felt a combination of physical warmth and barrenness in his early childhood), he would be *telling* his readers how he felt. Instead, he *shows* them: The sensory details he cites demonstrate his main point, and the statement "I started taping pennies to the bottom of a shelf in the kitchen" shows us that the feeling of "barrenness" had even seeped into the family finances.

   In Your Writing: How can you show rather than just tell in your paragraph? What other details or information would show your reader exactly what your experience was like? Add these details to your prewriting list at this point.

4. **Organize your description so that your readers can easily follow it.** Most descriptions are organized from general to particular (from main idea to details), from particular to general (from details to main idea), or spatially (from top to bottom, left to right, inside to outside, and so on). These patterns are all easy for readers to follow.

   In the Reading: Mike Rose organizes his paragraph from general to particular. He starts with the main idea that his childhood was a mixture of "physical warmth and barrenness" and then explains this idea with specific details of both the love and good times (warmth) along with the poverty and insecurity (barrenness) he experienced. In his paragraph, the idea of "warmth" is represented by references to "concrete in the sun," his uncle's visits, trips to the beach, outings to the orange groves, and home. He characterizes the barrenness of his childhood with such details as "a gnarled lemon tree, thin rugs, a dirty alley"; "parents watching their money"; and "pennies under the kitchen counter." The choice and order of these details make Rose's topic sentence come alive.

   In Your Writing: Review these three patterns of organization in Chapter 3, and then look at the details and examples on your prewriting list. How should you organize these items to communicate the impression you have in mind? List the material you have to work with so far in a few different ways. What organization pattern does each list follow? Which is the best order to create your general impression?

Writing a Draft of Your Paragraph

Now is the time to collect all your personal associations, your notes, your prewriting exercises, and your lists as you generate the first draft of your paragraph. You might want to review the professional paragraphs, the writing assignment, and the chapter guidelines to help you write a draft of your paragraph. At this point, don't think about revising or editing; just get a rough draft of your ideas down on paper in response to the writing prompt.

MyWritingLab **Helpful Hints**

- **Having trouble getting started?** We have the solution. **Prewriting** in **The Craft of Writing** module in **MyWriting Lab** will give you lots of creative ways to approach your topic.
- **Need help with your dominant impression?** Creating a strong topic sentence is important in any paragraph because it provides a focus. If you need help writing yours, check out the video and activities for **The Topic Sentence** in **The Craft of Writing.**

REVISING AND EDITING

You are now ready to learn how to revise and edit. This section will guide you through the process of revising and editing description paragraphs in reference to two writing samples: another student's paragraph and your own paragraph. Finding strengths and weaknesses in another person's writing is often much easier than evaluating your own, so you will be reviewing the chapter guidelines by revising and editing another student's writing before applying the same guidelines to your own writing.

REVISING AND EDITING OPTIONS
Consider teaching revising and editing in a class discussion, in small groups, or in pairs.

Reading a Student Paragraph

At this point, we will once again use our chapter reading strategy. Here is a descriptive paragraph written by Joe Simmons, a college student. In it, he describes his dorm room as his favorite place.

Reading Strategy

READING CRITICALLY
Making Personal Associations
with the Student Essay

As you read Joe's draft, write your personal associations in the margins of his paragraph, paying special attention to the dominant impression he creates and the senses he uses to trigger that impression.

CLASS ACTIVITY
Put a sentence on the board that *tells* the reader information, and have students, as a class, offer suggestions to change it to *show* the reader that information. For example, change "The car went down the street" to

"The dark green Honda glided down the brightly lit street under a canopy of trees."

¹I started college. ²I decided to redecorate my room. ³It is now one of my favorite places in the world. ⁴But it used to remind me of a damp cave with no light. ⁵The room had no personality at all. ⁶Now the walls is loaded with posters of my favorite mottoes. ⁷And musical groups. ⁸The bed came from Goodwill Industries and is made of black wrought iron. ⁹The space at an angle to my bed is a window covered by some wild curtains of blue, green, silver, and lavender that my grandma made. ¹⁰My antique desk with a roll-top is against the wall opposite my bed the top of it is always buried with everything but school work. ¹¹Some incense sits on a small table next to my door. ¹²My door is usually closed so I can get some peace and quiet. ¹³I love the silent times behind my door. ¹⁴When no one can get to me.

Revising and Editing the Student Paragraph

This paragraph is Joe's first draft, which now needs to be revised and edited. First, apply the Revising Checklist to the content of Joe's draft. When you are satisfied that his ideas are fully developed and well organized, use the Editing Checklist to correct his grammar and mechanics errors. Answer the questions, and complete the tasks in each category. Then write your suggested changes directly on Joe's draft.

REVISING STRATEGIES
This chapter focuses on the following revising elements:

Topic sentence
Development

Revising the Student Paragraph

TOPIC SENTENCE

✔ Does the topic sentence convey the paragraph's controlling idea?

✔ Does the topic sentence appear as the first or last sentence of the paragraph?

1. What dominant impression does Joe communicate in his paragraph?
    security, comfort
    _____

2. Put brackets around Joe's topic sentence. Does it convey Joe's dominant impression?
    [I started college.] No
    _____

3. Rewrite it if necessary to introduce all the ideas in Joe's paragraph.
    One possibility: When I started college, I decided to redecorate my room.
    _____

DEVELOPMENT

✔ Does the paragraph contain *specific* details that support the topic sentence?

✔ Does the paragraph include *enough* details to fully explain the topic sentence?

1. Does the paragraph draw on all five senses? Record three details from Joe's paragraph that come from three different senses. Label each example with the sense related to it.

Sense	Detail
Seeing	*Answers will vary.*
Touching	*damp cave*
Hearing	*silent times*

2. Does Joe's paragraph *show* rather than *tell* readers what they need to know?

   Yes

   Give three examples.

   Answers will vary.

3. Add another detail to Joe's paragraph.

4. Add one simile to Joe's paragraph. (Reminder: A simile is a comparison between two unlike items using *like* or *as:* My _____ looked like _____.)

UNITY

✔ Do all the sentences in the paragraph support the topic sentence?

1. Read each of Joe's sentences with his topic sentence (revised, if necessary) in mind.

2. Drop or rewrite any of his sentences that are not directly related to his topic sentence.   *All are relevant.*

ORGANIZATION

✔ Is the paragraph organized logically?

1. Read Joe's paragraph again to see if all the sentences are arranged logically.

2. List some of his details in the order they appear. Then identify his method of organization: general to particular, particular to general, or spatial.   *Details may vary.*

posters	*antique desk*
bed from Goodwill Industries	*incense next to the door*
a window covered by some wild curtains	*closed door*

Method of organization: *Spatial*

COHERENCE

✔ Do the sentences move smoothly and logically from one to the next?

For a list of transitions, see page 59–60.

1. Circle three transitions Joe uses.   *Answers will vary.*

2. Explain how one of these transitions makes Joe's paragraph easier to read.
   Answers will vary.
   _____

   _____

 Now rewrite Joe's paragraph with your revisions.

EDITING STRATEGIES
This chapter focuses on the following editing problems:

Fragments
Run-togethers
Subject-verb agreement

Editing the Student Paragraph

SENTENCES

Subjects and Verbs

✔ Does each sentence have a main subject and verb?

For help with subjects and verbs, see Chapter 20.

1. Underline the subjects once and verbs twice in your revision of Joe's paragraph. Remember that sentences can have more than one subject-verb set.

2. Does each of the sentences have at least one subject and verb that can stand alone?   *Sentence 7 in the original paragraph has no verb.*

For help with fragments, see Chapter 21.

3. Did you find and correct Joe's two fragments? If not, find and correct them now.   *Sentences 7 and 14*

For help with run-togethers, see Chapter 22.

4. Did you find and correct Joe's run-together sentence? If not, find and correct it now.   *Sentence 10*

Subject-Verb Agreement

✔ Do all subjects and verbs agree?

For help with subject-verb agreement, see Chapter 25.

1. Read aloud the subjects and verbs you underlined in your revision of Joe's paragraph.

2. Did you find and correct the subject and verb that do not agree? If not, find and correct them now.   *Sentence 6*

Pronoun Agreement

✔ Do all pronouns agree with their nouns?

For help with pronoun agreement, see Chapter 29.

1. Find any pronouns in your revision of Joe's paragraph that do not agree with their nouns.   *All pronouns in the original paragraph agree with their nouns.*

2. Correct any pronouns that do not agree with their nouns.

Modifier Errors

✔ Are modifiers as close as possible to the words they modify?

1. Find any modifiers in your revision of Joe's paragraph that are not as close as possible to the words they modify. *There are no modifier errors in the original paragraph.*

2. Rewrite sentences if necessary so that modifiers are as close as possible to the words they modify.

For help with modifier errors, see Chapter 32.

PUNCTUATION AND MECHANICS

Punctuation

✔ Are sentences punctuated correctly?

1. Read your revision of Joe's paragraph for any errors in punctuation.

2. Find the two fragments and one run-together sentence you revised, and make sure they are punctuated correctly.

For help with punctuation, see Chapters 33–37.

Mechanics

✔ Are words capitalized properly?

1. Read your revision of Joe's paragraph for any errors in capitalization. *All capitals are correct in the original paragraph.*

2. Be sure to check Joe's capitalization in the fragments and run-together sentence you revised.

For help with capitalization, see Chapter 38.

WORD CHOICE AND SPELLING

Word Choice

✔ Are words used correctly?

1. Find any words used incorrectly in your revision of Joe's paragraph. *All words are used correctly in the original paragraph.*

2. Correct any errors you find.

For help with confused words, see Chapter 44.

Spelling

✔ Are words spelled correctly?

1. Use spell-check and a dictionary to check the spelling in your revision of Joe's paragraph. *All words are spelled correctly in the original paragraph.*

2. Correct any misspelled words.

For help with spelling, see Chapter 45.

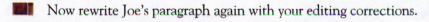

 Now rewrite Joe's paragraph again with your editing corrections.

Reading Your Own Description Paragraph

Reading Strategy

Returning to the description paragraph you wrote earlier in this chapter, you are now ready to revise and edit your own writing. You will first read your paragraph with the same reading strategy you have applied to other reading tasks in this chapter so you can look at it as your reader might.

READING CRITICALLY
Making Personal Associations
with Your Own Paragraph

Just as you made personal associations with your reading to help you understand what the author was saying, annotate your own writing with personal associations and sensory details that occur to you as you read. Then consider adding some of these notes to your paragraph to help your readers understand your experience as if they were there.

Revising and Editing Your Own Paragraph

The checklists here will help you apply what you have learned in this chapter to your own paragraph. Work first with the content, making sure your thoughts are fully developed and organized effectively before you find and correct your grammar and usage errors.

For Revising Peer Evaluation Forms, go to Appendix 4.

Revising Your Own Paragraph

TOPIC SENTENCE

☐ Does the topic sentence convey the paragraph's controlling idea?

☐ Does the topic sentence appear as the first or last sentence of the paragraph?

1. What dominant impression are you trying to communicate in your paragraph?

   _____

2. Put brackets around your topic sentence. Does it convey your dominant impression?

   _____

3. How can you change your topic sentence if necessary to introduce all the ideas in your paragraph?

   _____

DEVELOPMENT

☐ Does the paragraph contain *specific* details that support the topic sentence?

☐ Does the paragraph include *enough* details to fully explain the topic sentence?

1. Does your paragraph draw on all five senses? Record three details from your paragraph that draw on three different senses. Label each example with the sense it draws on.

Sense   Detail

_____   _____

_____   _____

_____   _____

2. Does your paragraph *show* rather than *tell* readers what they need to know? Give three examples.

_____

_____

_____

3. Add another detail to your paragraph.

4. Add one comparison or simile to your paragraph. (Reminder: A simile is a comparison between two unlike items using *like* or *as*.)

UNITY

☐ Do all the sentences in the paragraph support the topic sentence?

1. Read each of your sentences with your topic sentence in mind.

2. Drop or rewrite any sentences that are not directly related to your topic sentence.

ORGANIZATION

☐ Is the paragraph organized logically?

1. Read your paragraph again to see if all the sentences are arranged logically.

2. List some of your details in the order they appear. Then identify your method of organization: general to particular, particular to general, or spatial.

_____

_____

_____

_____

Method of organization: _____

COHERENCE

☐ Do the sentences move smoothly and logically from one to the next?

1. Circle three transitions you used.

For a list of transitions, see pages 59–60.

2. Explain how one of these transitions makes your paragraph easier to read.

_____

Now rewrite your paragraph with your revisions.

For Editing Peer Evaluation Forms, go to Appendix 6.

Editing Your Own Paragraph

SENTENCES

Subjects and Verbs

☐ Does each sentence have a main subject and verb?

For help with subjects and verbs, see Chapter 20.

1. Underline the subjects once and verbs twice in your revised paragraph. Remember that sentences can have more than one subject-verb set.

2. Does each of your sentences have at least one subject and verb that can stand alone?

_____

For help with fragments, see Chapter 21.

For help with run-togethers, see Chapter 22.

3. Correct any fragments you have written.

4. Correct any run-together sentences you have written.

Subject-Verb Agreement

☐ Do all subjects and verbs agree?

For help with subject-verb agreement, see Chapter 25.

1. Read aloud the subjects and verbs you underlined in your revised paragraph.

2. Correct any subjects and verbs that do not agree.

Pronoun Agreement

☐ Do all pronouns agree with their nouns?

For help with pronoun agreement, see Chapter 29.

1. Find any pronouns in your revised paragraph that do not agree with their nouns.

2. Correct any pronouns that do not agree with their nouns.

Modifier Errors

☐ Are modifiers as close as possible to the words they modify?

For help with modifier errors, see Chapter 32.

1. Find any modifiers in your revised paragraph that are not as close as possible to the words they modify.

2. Rewrite sentences if necessary so that your modifiers are as close as possible to the words they modify.

PUNCTUATION AND MECHANICS

Punctuation

☐ Are sentences punctuated correctly?

1. Read your revised paragraph for any errors in punctuation.

2. Make sure any fragments and run-together sentences you revised are punctuated properly.

For help with punctuation, see Chapters 33–37.

Mechanics

☐ Are words capitalized properly?

1. Read your revised paragraph for any errors in capitalization.

2. Be sure to check your capitalization in any fragments or run-together sentences you revised.

For help with capitalization, see Chapter 38.

WORD CHOICE AND SPELLING

Word Choice

☐ Are words used correctly?

1. Find any words used incorrectly in your revised paragraph.

2. Correct any errors you find.

For help with confused words, see Chapter 44.

Spelling

☐ Are words spelled correctly?

1. Use spell-check and a dictionary to check your spelling.

2. Correct any misspelled words.

For help with spelling, see Chapter 45.

To make a personal log of your grammar/usage errors, go to Appendix 7.

To make a personal log of your spelling errors, go to Appendix 8.

Now rewrite your paragraph again with your editing corrections.

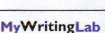 **More Helpful Hints**

- **Do you need some reminders about revising?** Description paragraphs require excellent organization and structure, so you need to pay special attention to these features as you revise. Go to **Revising the Paragraph** in **The Craft of Writing** module in **MyWritingLab** for some helpful guidelines.

- **Searching for the right words for your description?** To be effective, a description paragraph requires many well-chosen adjectives and adverbs. Before you write, you can practice using these descriptive words when you go to **Adjectives and Adverbs** in the **Basic Grammar** module in **MyWritingLab.**

PRACTICING DESCRIPTION: FROM READING TO WRITING

This final section lets you practice the reading and writing skills you learned in this chapter. It includes two reading selections and several writing assignments on "your reading" and "your world." The section then offers guidance in peer evaluation and reflection, ending with suggestions about how to lead your instructor through your writing in ways that will benefit both of you.

Reading Strategy

Reading Workshop

Here are two essays that demonstrate the guidelines you studied in this chapter: In the excerpt from *The Joy Luck Club* by Amy Tan, entitled "Magpies," a young girl observes the sights, sounds, smells, textures, and tastes she encounters when she arrives at her new home. The second selection, an essay called "Life with Father" by Itabari Njeri, considers the right of human beings to die a natural death. As you read, notice how the writers pull you into each experience through sensory details.

MAGPIES
by Amy Tan

SUMMARY
Vivid illustrations help a young girl describe the new, lavish home she will share with her mother and new stepfather in China.

READABILITY
(Flesch-Kincaid grade level) 7.8

INSTRUCTOR'S RESOURCE MANUAL
For additional teaching strategies, for journal entries, for vocabulary and reading quizzes, and for more writing assignments, see the *Instructor's Resource Manual*, Section II, Part II.

Focusing Your Attention

1. Think of a place you are very familiar with: your room, your home, your school, your place of employment, a garden, a restaurant. Then make a list of the sights, sounds, textures, smells, and tastes that come to mind as you think of that place.

2. In the excerpt you are about to read, a young girl recounts the many sights, sounds, smells, textures, and tastes she encountered when she first arrived at her new home. Think of an occasion when you entered a place for the first time. What sights, sounds, textures, smells, and tastes made the strongest impressions on you?

Expanding Your Vocabulary

The following words are important to your understanding of this essay. Highlight them throughout the essay before you begin to read. Then refer to this list as you get to these words in the essay.

British Concession: areas the Chinese allowed the British to occupy (paragraph 1)

concubines: women who were part of a man's household and were expected to fulfill his needs (paragraph 14)

mourning: representing grief over a person's death (paragraph 17)

READING CRITICALLY
Making Personal Associations with Your Reading

As you learned in this chapter, practice making connections with your reading by writing personal associations in the margins of this essay. Jot down anything that comes to mind. These notes will put your individual stamp on the essay with a set of memories that only you can recall. They will also help you understand the essay on an analytical level. Share your notes with one of your classmates.

MAGPIES[1]
by Amy Tan

I knew from the beginning our new home would not be an ordinary house. My mother had told me we would live in the household of Wu Tsing, who was a very rich merchant. She said this man owned many carpet factories and lived in a mansion located in the British Concession of Tientsin, the best section of the city where Chinese people could live. We lived not too far from Paima Di, Racehorse Street, where only Westerners could live. And we were also close to little shops that sold only one kind of thing: only tea, or only fabric, or only soap.   1

The house, she said, was foreign-built; Wu Tsing liked foreign things because foreigners had made him rich. And I concluded that was why my mother had to wear foreign-style clothes, in the manner of newly rich Chinese people who liked to display their wealth on the outside. And even though I knew all this before I arrived, I was still amazed at what I saw.   2

The front of the house had a Chinese stone gate, rounded at the top, with big black lacquer doors and a threshold you had to step over. Within the gates I saw the courtyard, and I was surprised. There were no willows or sweet-smelling cassia trees, no garden pavilions, no benches sitting by a pond, no tubs of fish. Instead, there were long rows of bushes on both sides of a wide brick walkway, and to each side of those bushes was a big lawn area with fountains. And as we walked down the walkway and got closer to the house, I saw this house had been built in the Western style. It was three stories high, of mortar and stone, with long metal balconies on each floor and chimneys at every corner.   3

When we arrived, a young servant woman ran out and greeted my mother with cries of joy. She had a high scratchy voice: "Oh Taitai, you've already arrived! How   4

---

[1] Amy Tan, "Magpies," from *The Joy Luck Club* by Amy Tan, copyright © 1989 by Amy Tan. Used by permission of G.P. Putnam's Sons, a division of Penguin Group (USA) Inc.

can this be?" This was Yan Chang, my mother's personal maid, and she knew how to fuss over my mother just the right amount. She had called my mother Taitai, the simple honorable title of Wife, as if my mother were the first wife, the only wife.

5   Yan Chang called loudly to other servants to take our luggage, called another servant to bring tea and draw a hot bath. And then she hastily explained that Second Wife had told everyone not to expect us for another week at least. "What a shame! No one to greet you! Second Wife, the others, gone to Peking to visit her relatives. Your daughter, so pretty, your same look. She's so shy, eh? First Wife, her daughters…gone on a pilgrimage to another Buddhist temple. Last week, a cousin's uncle, just a little crazy, came to visit, turned out not to be a cousin, not an uncle, who knows who he was."

6   As soon as we walked into that big house, I became lost with too many things to see: a curved staircase that wound up and up, a ceiling with faces in every corner, then hallways twisting and turning into one room then another. To my right was a large room, larger than I had ever seen, and it was filled with stiff teakwood furniture: sofas and tables and chairs. And at the other end of this long, long room, I could see doors leading into more rooms, more furniture, then more doors. To my left was a darker room, another sitting room, this one filled with foreign furniture: dark green leather sofas, paintings with hunting dogs, armchairs, and mahogany desks. And as I glanced in these rooms, I would see different people, and Yan Chang would explain: "This young lady, she is Second Wife's servant. That one, she is nobody, just the daughter of cook's helper. This man takes care of the garden."

7   And then we were walking up the staircase. We came to the top of the stairs, and I found myself in another large sitting room. We walked to the left, down a hall, past one room, and then stepped into another. "This is your mother's room," Yan Chang told me proudly. "This is where you will sleep."

8   And the first thing I saw, the only thing I could see at first, was a magnificent bed. It was heavy and light at the same time: soft rose silk and heavy, dark, shiny wood carved all around with dragons. Four posts held up a silk canopy, and at each post dangled large silk ties holding back curtains. The bed sat on four squat lion's paws, as if the weight of it had crushed the lion underneath. Yan Chang showed me how to use a small step stool to climb onto the bed. And when I tumbled onto the silk coverings, I laughed to discover a soft mattress that was ten times the thickness of my bed in Ningpo.

9   Sitting in this bed, I admired everything as if I were a princess. This room had a glass door that led to a balcony. In front of the window door was a round table of the same wood as the bed. It too sat on carved lion's legs and was surrounded by four chairs. A servant had already put tea and sweet cakes on the table and was now lighting the houlu, a small stove for burning coal.

10   It was not that my uncle's house in Ningpo had been poor. He was actually quite well-to-do. But this house in Tientsin was amazing. And I thought to myself, My uncle was wrong. There was no shame in my mother's marrying Wu Tsing.

11   While thinking this, I was startled by a sudden clang! clang! clang! followed by music. On the wall opposite the bed was a big wooden clock with a forest and bears carved into it. The door on the clock had burst open, and a tiny room full of people was coming out. There was a bearded man in a pointed cap seated at a table. He was

---

ANSWERS TO QUESTIONS

Thinking Critically About Content

1. Here are some examples:

Seeing:

"was still amazed at what I saw" (para. 2)

"big black lacquer doors…had to step over" (para. 3)

"Within the gates I saw the courtyard" (para. 3)

"There were long rows of bushes on both sides of a wide brick walkway, and to each side of those bushes was a big lawn area with fountains" (para. 3)

bending his head over and over again to drink soup, but his beard would dip in the bowl first and stop him. A girl in a white scarf and blue dress was standing next to the table, and she was bending over and over again to give the man more of this soup. And next to the man and girl was another girl with a skirt and short jacket. She was swinging her arm back and forth, playing violin music. She always played the same dark song. I can still hear it in my head after these many years—ni-ah! nah! nah! nah! nah-ni-nah!

12   This was a wonderful clock to see, but after I heard it that first hour, then the next, and then always, this clock became an extravagant nuisance. I could not sleep for many nights. And later, I found I had an ability: To not listen to something meaningless calling to me.

13   I was so happy those first few nights, in this amusing house, sleeping in the big soft bed with my mother. I would lie in this comfortable bed, thinking about my uncle's house in Ningpo, realizing how unhappy I had been, feeling sorry for my little brother. But most of my thoughts flew to all the new things to see and do in this house.

14   I watched hot water pouring out of pipes not just in the kitchen but also into washbasins and bathtubs on all three floors of the house. I saw chamber pots that flushed clean without servants having to empty them. I saw rooms as fancy as my mother's. Yan Chang explained which ones belonged to First Wife and the other concubines, who were called Second Wife and Third Wife. And some rooms belonged to no one. "They are for guests," said Yan Chang.

15   On the third floor were rooms for only the men servants, said Yan Chang, and one of the rooms even had a door to a cabinet that was really a secret hiding place from sea pirates.

16   Thinking back, I find it hard to remember everything that was in that house; too many good things all seem the same after a while. I tired of anything that was not a novelty. "Oh, this," I said when Yan Chang brought me the same sweet meats as the day before. "I've tasted this already."

17   My mother seemed to regain her pleasant nature. She put her old clothes back on, long Chinese gowns and skirts now with white mourning bands sewn at the bottoms. During the day, she pointed to strange and funny things, naming them for me: bidet, Brownie camera, salad fork, napkin. In the evening, when there was nothing to do, we talked about the servants: who was clever, who was diligent, who was loyal. We gossiped as we cooked small eggs and sweet potatoes on top of the houlu just to enjoy their smell. And at night, my mother would again tell me stories as I lay in her arms falling asleep.

18   If I look upon my whole life, I cannot think of another time when I felt more comfortable: when I had no worries, fears, or desires, when my life seemed as soft and lovely as lying inside a cocoon of rose silk.

Thinking Critically About Content

1. List two details from this essay for each of the five senses: seeing, hearing, touching, smelling, and tasting. How do these details *show* rather than tell the readers the narrator's impressions of her new house?

Hearing:
> "high scratchy voice" (para. 4)
> "clang! clang! clang!" (para. 11)
> "ni-ah! nah! nah! nah! nah-ni-nah!" (para. 11)

Touching:
> "draw a hot bath" (para. 5)
> "stiff teakwood furniture" (para. 6)
> "soft rose silk" (para. 8)

Smelling:
> "sweet-smelling cassia trees" (para. 3)
> "just to enjoy their smell" (para. 17)

Tasting:
> "tea and sweet cakes" (para. 9)
> "sweet meats" (para. 16)
> "small eggs and sweet potatoes" (para. 17)

2. The main character is enchanted with her home because everything she encounters is new to her. The novelty of her surroundings eventually wears off.

3. The narrator is so comfortable in these surroundings because everything is provided for her in her new life, but she also remains a part of her old heritage.

Thinking Critically About Purpose and Audience

4. The dominant impression in the

beginning of the essay is one of wonder and excitement. Later this excitement turns to ordinariness.

5. All readers can enjoy this essay because it is filled with vivid details that they can identify as the author becomes accustomed to her surroundings.

6. Answers will vary.

Thinking Critically About Paragraphs

7. Paragraph 12 is unified because every sentence in it focuses on the idea of Tan becoming used to her surroundings.

8. Paragraph 17 is organized from general to particular.

9. Answers will vary.

10. Answers will vary.

To keep track of your critical thinking progress, go to Appendix 1.

2. In one or more complete sentences, state the main character's point of view.

3. What does the narrator mean when she says, "If I look upon my whole life, I cannot think of another time when I felt more comfortable: when I had no worries, fears, or desires, when my life seemed as soft and lovely as lying inside a cocoon of rose silk" (paragraph 18)? Why do you think she is so comfortable in these surroundings?

Thinking Critically About Purpose and Audience

4. What dominant impression does the writer create in this description? How does this impression change throughout the essay?

5. Do you think readers who have never been to China can appreciate and enjoy this essay? Explain your answer.

6. What specific observations are most interesting to you? Why? In what ways do these observations help you imagine the entire scene?

Thinking Critically About Paragraphs

7. If a paragraph is unified, all of its sentences are related to one central idea. Based on this explanation, is paragraph 12 unified? Explain your answer.

8. Look closely at paragraph 17, and explain how it is organized. (Refer to Part I for information on organization.)

9. Choose one body paragraph, and decide if it has enough details. What is the most interesting detail in the paragraph?

10. Write a paragraph describing the inner feelings of the main character when she finally settles into her new home.

LIFE WITH FATHER
by Itabari Njeri

SUMMARY
Memories of her father in their Harlem apartment reminds this author of the fear and loathing she had for her father that were occasionally broken by tender moments.

READABILITY
(Flesch-Kincaid grade level) 10.8

Focusing Your Attention

1. Do you consider yourself close to all members of your family? Which ones are you closest to? What is your relationship with your father?

2. The essay you are about to read describes the unsettling relationship the author had with her alcoholic father with vivid details of what it was like to live with him.

Expanding Your Vocabulary

The following words are important to your understanding of this essay. Highlight them throughout the essay before you begin to read. Then refer to this list as you get to these words in the essay.

apocryphal: fictional (paragraph 5)

exemplified: shown (paragraph 5)

cryptically: briefly (paragraph 9)

unpleasantries: difficulties (paragraph 9)

affiliations: connections (paragraph 11)

compelled: forced (paragraph 15)

confirmation: acceptance (paragraph 15)

debunks: exposes (paragraph 16)

resonant: echoing (paragraph 17)

rational: reasonable (paragraph 17)

cosmos: world (paragraph 17)

disavow: not allow (paragraph 23)

vulnerability: weakness (paragraph 23)

Ralph Ellison: American novelist (1914–1994)

Paul Robeson: American singer, actor, and political activist (1898–1976)

Richard Wright: American writer (1908–1960)

unreconciled: unresolved (paragraph 25)

approbation: approval (paragraph 25)

Morpheus: one of the children of Sleep in Greek mythology (paragraph 26)

INSTRUCTOR'S RESOURCE MANUAL
For additional teaching strategies, for journal entries, for vocabulary and reading quizzes, and for more writing assignments, see the *Instructor's Resource Manual*, Section II, Part II.

READING CRITICALLY
Making Personal Associations as You Read

As you did with the previous essay, write any personal associations you make with this essay in the margins as you read. This process will give you some good insights into the author's approach to her topic and into her methods of developing her ideas. Write down anything at all that occurs to you. Then share your notes with one of your classmates.

LIFE WITH FATHER[2]
by Itabari Njeri

1   Daddy wore boxer shorts when he worked; that's all. He'd sit for hours reading and writing at a long, rectangular table covered with neat stacks of *I.F. Stone's Weekly, The Nation, The New Republic,* and the handwritten pages of his book in progress, *The Tolono Station and Beyond.* A Mott's applesauce jar filled with Teacher's scotch was a constant, and his own forerunner of today's wine coolers was the ever-present chaser: ginger ale and Manischewitz Concord grape wine in a tall, green iced-tea glass.

2   As he sat there, his beer belly weighing down the waistband of his shorts, I'd watch. I don't know if he ever saw me. I hid from him at right angles. From the bend of the hallway, at the end of a long, dark, L-shaped corridor in our Harlem apartment, it was at least thirty feet to the living room where my father worked, framed by the doorway. I sat cross-legged on the cold linoleum floor and inspected his seated, six-foot-plus figure through a telescope formed by my forefinger and thumb: bare feet in thonged sandals, long hairy legs that rose toward the notorious shorts (I hated those shorts, wouldn't bring my girlfriends home because of those shorts), breasts that could fill a B cup, and a long neck on which a balding head rested. Viewed in isolation, I thought perhaps I'd see him clearer, know him better.

3   Daddy was a philosopher, a Marxist historian, an exceptional teacher, and a fine tenor. He had a good enough voice to be as great a concert artist as John McCormack, one of his favorites. The obstacles to that career couldn't have been much greater than the ones he actually overcame.

4   The state of Georgia, where my father grew up, established its version of the literacy test in 1908, the year he was born. If you substituted Georgia for Mississippi in the story that Lerone Bennett Jr. relates in *Before the Mayflower: A History of Black America,* the main character could easily have been my father: A black teacher, a graduate of Eton and Harvard, presents himself to a Mississippi registrar. The teacher is told to read the state constitution and several books. He does. The registrar produces a passage in Greek, which the teacher reads. Then another in Latin. Then other passages in French, German, and Spanish, all of which the teacher reads. The registrar finally holds up a page of Chinese characters and asks: "What does this mean?" The teacher replies: "It means you don't want me to vote."

5   Apocryphal, perhaps, but the tale exemplified enough collective experience that I heard my father tell virtually the same story about a former Morehouse College classmate to a buddy over the phone one afternoon. At the punchline, he fell into a fit of laughter, chuckling hard into a balled fist he held at his mouth. Finally, he said, "Fred, I'll have to call you back," then fell back on the bed, in his boxer shorts, laughing at the ceiling.

---

[2] Itabari Njeri, "Life with Father," from *Every Goodbye Ain't Gone* by Itabari Njeri. Originally published in *Harper's Magazine,* January 1990.

He claimed he burst out laughing like this once in a class at Harvard. A law professor, discussing some constitutional issue in class, singled out my father and said, "In this matter, regarding men of your race—". 6

"Which race is that?" my father boomed, cutting him off, "the 50 yard or the 100?" But it seemed to me he always related that particular tale with a sneer on his lips. 7

He'd been at Harvard studying law on a postdoctoral scholarship from 1942 to 1943. After receiving his Ph.D. in philosophy from the University of Toronto ten years earlier, he had headed toward the dust bowls others were escaping in the mid-1930s and became the editor of a black newspaper, the *Oklahoma Eagle,* in Tulsa. He eventually returned to academia and by 1949 was the head of the philosophy department at Morgan State University in Baltimore. That's where he met my mother, a nurse many years his junior. 8

My mother—who commits nothing to paper, speaks of the past cryptically, and believes all unpleasantries are best kept under a rug—once leaked the fact that she and my father took me to a parade in Brooklyn when I was about three. We were standing near the arch at Grand Army Plaza when he suddenly hauled off and punched her in the mouth, with me in her arms. My mother, a very gentle and naive woman, said the whole thing left her in a state of shock. My father had never been violent before. 9

They separated, and I seldom saw my father again until my parents reunited when I was seven. We moved into my father's six-room apartment on 129th Street, between Convent Avenue and St. Nicholas Terrace. It was certainly far more spacious than the apartment I'd lived in with my mother on St. James Place in Brooklyn. The immediate neighborhood was an attractive, hilly section of Harlem, just a few blocks from City College. All things considered, I hated it. More precisely, I hated my father, so I hated it all. 10

Because of his past leftist political affiliations, Daddy had lost his government and university jobs. Now, out of necessity but also desire, he decided to devote his time to teaching younger people. He wanted to reach them at a stage in their lives when he felt he could make a difference. He joined the faculty of a Jersey City high school and began teaching journalism, history, and English. He also taught English at night to foreign-born students at City College. His students, I came to learn, loved him; his daughter found it hard to. I made the mistake of calling him Pop—once. He said, "Don't ever call me that again. If you don't like calling me Daddy, you can call me Dr. Moreland." 11

Once, my mother deserted me, leaving me alone with him. She went to Atlanta for several weeks with my baby brother to tend my ailing Grandma Hattie, my father's mother. Since I hadn't known this man most of my seven years on the planet, and didn't like him much now that I did, I asked him if I could stay around the corner with a family friend, Aunt Pearl. "If she asks you to stay, fine. But don't ask her," he told me. Naturally I asked her. 12

When he asked me if I had asked her, I hesitated. But I was not a child inclined to lie. So I said, "I don't want to lie. I asked her." I got a beating for that, a brutal beating with a belt that left welts and bruises on my legs for months. 13

ANSWERS TO
QUESTIONS

**Thinking Critically
About Content**

1. He was a teacher
   and a writer.

2. Here are some
   examples:

Sight:

   "boxer shorts"
   (para. 1)

   "a long, rectangular
   table" (para. 1)

   "I examined his
   face" (para. 26)

Sound:

   "burst out laughing"
   (para. 6)

   "released a long and
   resonant 'Yesssss'"
   (para. 10)

   "I heard the clink
   of a metal spoon
   against a glass
   as he sang"
   (para. 19)

Touch:

   "punched [my
   mother] in the
   mouth" (para. 9)

14   My father felt children should be hit for any infraction. Further, they should be seen and not heard, speak only when spoken to, etc. From the day he hit me, the latter became my philosophy, too. I never consciously decided to stop speaking to my father, but for the next ten years, I rarely initiated a conversation with him. Later he would tell me, "You were a very strange child."

15   But if I would not accept him as a father, my curiosity would not let me deny him as a teacher. One day, a question about the nature of truth compelled a thaw in my emotional cold war—nothing less could have. Truth changes, a classmate in the seventh grade had insisted that day. It is constant, I argued, and went to my father for confirmation.

16   People's perceptions change, I explained. New information debunks the lies of the past, but the truth was always there. And I told my father what I had told my mostly white classmates in a Bronx junior high school at the height of the civil rights movement: Black people were always human beings worthy of the same rights other Americans enjoyed, but it took hundreds of years of a slave system that dehumanized the master as well as the slave and a social revolution before most white Americans would accept that truth.

17   My father turned from his worktable, took off his glasses, with their broken right temple piece, and released a long and resonant "Yesssss." And then he spoke to me of a rational cosmos and what Lincoln had to do with Plato. When our philosophical discussion ended, we each went to our separate corners.

18   My father had a beaten, black upright piano in the parlor, badly out of tune. But its bench was a treasure of ancient sheet music: Vincent Youman's "Through the Years," with a picture of Gladys Swarthout on the frayed cover. And I loved the chord changes to "Spring Is Here."

19   I ventured from the sanctuary of my blue-walled room one summer afternoon, walking down the long hallway toward the kitchen, then stopped abruptly. I heard my father in the kitchen several feet away; he was making an ice-cream soda, something as forbidden to him as alcohol since he was a diabetic. I heard the clink of a metal spoon against a glass as he sang, "For I lately took a notion for to cross the briny ocean, and I'm off to Philadelphia in the morning." It was an Irish folk song made famous by John McCormack. I backed up. Too late. He danced across the kitchen threshold in his boxer shorts, stopped when he spotted me in the shadows, then shook his head. He smiled, lifted one leg and both arms in a Jackie Gleason "and away we go" motion, then slid off.

20   Minutes later he called me. "Jill the Pill, you know this song!" I knew all the songs and wrote down the words to "Moon River" for him. Then he asked me to sing it. I was always ready to sing, even for my father.

21   He sat on the edge of his bed with the lyrics in his hand as I sang. When I finished the phrase "We're after the same rainbow's end, waitin' round the bend, my huckleberry friend," my daddy looked at me and said what others would tell me years later but with far less poetry: "My girl, you have the celestial vibration." And then he asked me to sing it again and told me it was "wonderful." Then I left him.

22   For days, maybe weeks, a tense calm would reign in the apartment. Then, without warning, the hall would fill with harsh voices. My father stood in the narrow, shadowy space hitting my mother. "Put it down," he yelled. "Put it down or I'll . . ."

My mother had picked up a lamp in a lame effort to ward off his blows. His shouting had awakened me. I'd been sick in bed with the flu and a high fever. When he saw me open my bedroom door he yelled, "Get back in your room." I did, my body overtaken by tremors and the image of my mother branded on my eyeballs. I swore that I would never let anyone do that to me or to anyone else I had the power to help. I had no power to help my mother. It was an oath with terrible consequences, one I'd have to disavow to permit myself the vulnerability of being human.

I know my father's fury was fueled by his sense of insignificance. He felt himself to be an intellectual giant boxed in by mental midgets. Unlike Ralph Ellison, Paul Robeson, or Richard Wright°—all contemporaries and acquaintances of my father's—he was never acknowledged by the dominant culture whose recognition he sought. He could be found, Ellison once told me, pontificating in Harlem barbershops, elucidating the dialogues of Plato for a captive audience of draped men, held prone, each with a straight-edge razor pressed against his cheek.

My father's unreconciled identities—the classic schizophrenia of being black and an American, the contradictions of internalizing whole the cultural values of a society that sees you, when it sees you at all, as life in one of its lower forms—stoked his alcoholism. And since my father at once critiqued the society that denied him and longed for its approbation he lived with the pain-filled consciousness of one who knows he is a joke. I think sometimes he laughed the hardest, so often did I stumble upon him alone, chuckling into his balled fist at some silent, invisible comedian.

When his drunken rages ended, he slept for days, spread out on the bed wearing only his boxer shorts. I watched him on those days too daring to come closer, safe with the knowledge that Morpheus° held him. I examined his face, wondering who he was and why he was. As I watched, he'd lift his head off the pillow then fall back muttering: "Truth and justice will prevail."

Thinking Critically About Content

1. What did Njeri's father do for a living?

2. Find at least one detail for each of the five senses (sight, sound, touch, taste, smell) that describes Njeri's father. Does the author draw on any one sense more than the others?

3. Why does Njeri dislike her father? Why do his students like him?

Thinking Critically About Purpose and Audience

4. What dominant impression does Njeri create in this essay?

5. Who do you think is Njeri's primary audience?

6. What were your expectations when you read the title? Did the essay match those expectations?

---

23 "I got a beating [from my father]" (para. 13)

Taste:
"ice cream soda" (para. 19)
"alcohol" (para. 19)

Smell:
none

24 She relies most on sight and sound in this essay.

3. Njeri doesn't like her father because he beats her and her mother and because he is emotionally abusive to her.

25 His students probably don't see this behavior.

Thinking Critically About Purpose and Audience

4. Njeri creates a feeling of helplessness and despair to help her readers feel what it is like to live in an abusive situation.

26

5. Njeri's primary audience is a general audience; anyone can understand and identify with the contents of this essay.

6. Answers will vary.

Thinking Critically About Paragraphs

7. The topic sentence is "I know my father's fury was fueled by his sense of insignificance." All of the sentences relate to this sentence because they all are examples that lead to this feeling.

8. Some transitions in paragraph 11 are "because," "and," "now," and "if." They help the paragraph progress smoothly because they move the reader from idea to idea.

9. Paragraph 2 is organized spatially.

10. Answers will vary.

To keep track of your critical thinking progress, go to Appendix 1.

ADDITIONAL WRITING TOPIC
Let your students expand the paragraphs they wrote on page 82 into well-developed essays.

TEACHING ON THE WEB
Discussion Topic: The Internet has become indispensable in today's society. Put students in groups of three or four, and have them discuss how they think the Internet has affected the way people experience life and whether they think people are more or less aware of their surroundings because of the Internet. Have one person from each group report the group's conclusions to the class.

TEACHING ON THE WEB
Links: Have students link to world-renowned museums and view famous pieces of art. How do some of these masterpieces convey the five senses?

Possible sites:

Metropolitan Museum of Art, New York, metmuseum.org

Thinking Critically About Paragraphs

7. What is the topic sentence of paragraph 24? Do all the sentences in that paragraph relate to its topic sentence? Explain your answer.

8. If a paragraph is coherent, it is considered logical and easy to read. Often, well-chosen transitions help a writer achieve coherence. (Refer to pages 59–60 for a list of transitions.) Underline three transitions Njeri uses in paragraph 11. How do these words help this paragraph read smoothly? Explain your answer.

9. How are the details organized in paragraph 5? (See Part I for more information on organization.)

10. Write a paragraph describing what you think the secret to longevity is.

Writing Workshop

This final section gives you the opportunity to apply what you have learned in this chapter to another writing assignment. This time, we provide you with the guidelines only and let you go through your own writing process with occasional feedback from your peers. Refer to sections of the chapter as necessary until the process of producing a description paragraph becomes automatic for you.

Guidelines for Writing a Description Paragraph

1. Decide on a dominant impression—the feeling or mood you are trying to communicate.
2. Draw on your five senses to write a good description.
3. When you describe, try to *show* rather than *tell* your readers what you want them to know.
4. Organize your description so that your readers can easily follow it.

Writing About Your Reading

1. In the first selection, Amy Tan draws on impressions from all the senses to show how her main character observes her new home. Think of a place that is very important to you, a place that is a part of your life now or that was a part of your life in the past. Write a description of that place, drawing on as many of the senses as possible—seeing, hearing, touching, smelling, and tasting—so that your readers can experience this place the way you did.

2. How healthy are you? Write a description of the foods you eat and the exercise you get in a normal week. In what ways are you taking good care of yourself so that you have a chance for a long, healthy life?

3. What do you think are the most important features of a good description? Why are they important? What effect do they have on you?

Writing About Your World

Russell Illig/Getty Images

1. Place yourself in the scene above, and describe it in as much detail as possible. Imagine that you can see, hear, smell, taste, and touch everything in this picture. What are your sensations? How do you feel? Before you begin to write, decide what dominant impression you want to convey. Then choose your details carefully.

2. Starting college is an important decision for students and everyone associated with them—parents, children, friends, relatives, even the household pets. Describe a person who was helpful with your decision to go to college. Be sure to decide on a dominant impression before you begin to write.

3. You have been asked to write a short statement for your psychology class on the study environment that is best for you. Describe this environment. Where do you study? What sounds do you hear? What do you eat or drink as you study? What do you wear? Help your readers picture your study environment so that they feel they are actually there. Be sure you decide on a dominant impression before you begin to write.

4. Create your own description assignment (with the help of your instructor), and write a response to it.

Louvre Museum, Paris, louvre.fr
National Gallery, London, nationalgallery.org.uk

TEACHING ON THE WEB
Research: Have students search various Web sites to find one that incorporates all five senses. How difficult was it to find a site? How are all the senses represented?

Revising

Small Group Activity (5–10 minutes per writer) Working in groups of three or four, read your description papers to each other. Those listening should record their reactions on a copy of the Revising Peer Evaluation Forms in Appendix 4. After your group goes through this process, give your evaluation forms to the appropriate writers so that each writer has two or three peer comment sheets for revising.

Paired Activity (5 minutes per writer) Using the completed Peer Evaluation Forms, work in pairs to decide what you should revise. If time allows, rewrite some of your sentences, and have your partner check them.

Individual Activity Rewrite your paper, using the revising feedback you received from other students.

Editing

Paired Activity (5–10 minutes per writer) Swap papers with a classmate, and use the Editing Peer Evaluation Form in Appendix 6 to identify as many grammar, punctuation, mechanics, and spelling errors as you can. If time allows, correct some of your errors, and have your partner check them. Record your grammar, punctuation, and mechanics errors in the Error Log (Appendix 7) and your spelling errors in the Spelling Log (Appendix 8).

Individual Activity Rewrite your paper again, using the editing feedback you received from other students.

Reflecting on Your Writing   When you have completed your own paragraph, answer these six questions:

1. What was most difficult about this assignment?

2. What was easiest?

3. What did you learn about description by completing this assignment?

4. What do you think are the strengths of your description? Place a wavy line by the parts of your paragraph that you feel are very good.

5. What are the weaknesses, if any, of your paper? Place an X by the parts of your paragraph you would like help with. Write any questions you have in the margins.

6. What did you learn from this assignment about your own writing process—about preparing to write, about writing the first draft, about revising, and about editing?

Narrating

"One must be drenched in words, literally soaked in them, to have the right ones form themselves into the proper pattern at the right moment.**"**

—HART CRANE

Although you may not realize it, you are already very good at narrating. Think of the times you told someone about something that happened to you:

- The traffic jam on the way to school today;
- The conversation you had at the gym last night;
- The funny experience at the mall;
- Your favorite vacation as a child.

Narrating is storytelling. Whenever you tell someone about something that happened to you—your senior prom, a job interview, an argument with a friend, a terrific (or terrible) date—you are narrating. We probably rely more on narration than on any other rhetorical mode. Even jokes depend on our ability to tell a story.

Narration is a powerful way of focusing other people's attention on the thoughts you want to share with them. Because narration is often based on personal experience, it also teaches us about life. As an example, Russell Baker, a newspaper writer and the author of an award-winning autobiography entitled *Growing Up*, recalls the "sweet times" in his house when he was a young child.

> The summer I was four years old my mother bought me my first book and started to teach me to read. One night at bedtime she and my father stretched out on the blanket for sleep, but before dousing the lamp my father wanted to see how I was progressing with the written word.

TEACHING NARRATION Prior to class, cut out unbelievable/absurd tabloid headings, and paste them onto a poster board.

Divide students into small groups, and have each group choose a headline to write about. Remind them to use the five Ws and one H to get started.

Before students begin, explain that they should take turns writing the story: The first student writes the first paragraph, the second student writes the second paragraph, the third student writes the third paragraph, and so on. They should write the thesis statement together so that it resembles the tabloid headline.

Have students develop a plot and characters, use dialogue, establish a setting, and devise a resolution to the conflict. Give students the majority of class time to draft the story, and then let them revise together. The different student voices will take the story in unpredictable directions. Then revising will teach students about voice, coherence, unity, organization, and audience.

You might create a contest out of the assignment and have other instructors read and select a winner from all the essays submitted.

They placed me between them with the open book. I knew a few words, but under pressure to perform forgot everything. It was beginner material: "cat," "rat," "boy," "girl," "the." I didn't recognize a word.

My mother was disappointed that I could do nothing but stare stupidly at the printed page. My father saved my pride. "Have a little patience with him," he said. Taking the book in hand, he moved me close against him and rubbed his cheek against mine. "Now," he said, pointing to a word, "you know that word, don't you?"

I did indeed. "The," I said.

"You're a smart boy. I bet you know this one too."

"Boy," I said.

When I read most of the sentence without too much help, he said to my mother, "You're doing good with him. Maybe we ought to send him to college." Pleased, my mother reached across me and kissed him on the cheek. Smiling down at me, he said, "You want to go to college?" They both laughed a little at this. Maybe he liked the extravagance of the idea as much as she did. Then he turned off the kerosene lamp. That night they let me sleep between them.

You will refer to these paragraphs again when you are learning the guidelines for writing a good narration paragraph.

Just as students need to know the rhetorical modes before getting into the **MyWritingLab** exercises for Part II, be sure your students are also familiar with the methods of organization. All the material from **MyWritingLab** covered in Part II of *Mosaics* asks at least one question about how the paragraph(s) are organized.

MyWritingLab   ## Understanding Narration

To make sure you understand the concepts in the narration chapter, go to **MyWritingLab.com,** and click on **Narrating** in the **Paragraph Development** module. For this topic, read the **Overview,** watch the **Animation** video, and complete the **Recall, Apply,** and **Write** activities. Then check your understanding by taking the **Post-test.**

PREPARING TO WRITE A NARRATION PARAGRAPH

Learning how to read narration paragraphs critically gives you insight into the writing process in this particular rhetorical mode. Narration represents a way of thinking that you need to master so that you can use it in both your reading and writing. Approaching narration critically helps you raise your level of communication and function more successfully in college and in life. If you learn how to work with the author of a narration paragraph to understand how he or she makes meaning, your insights will transfer naturally to your writing so that you will also be improving your writing ability.

Reading critically is the first step to writing critically. So let's look closely at a narration paragraph. First, you will apply a reading strategy to the paragraph. Then, you will respond to the questions that follow the paragraph in an attempt to discover how it functions. With a thorough understanding of your reading, you will have more strategies to work with in your writing.

READING CRITICALLY
Thinking Aloud As You Read
a Professional Paragraph

For more detailed information on "think alouds," see pages 16–17 in Chapter 2.

As we read and interpret an author's words, we absorb them on a literal level, add to them any implications the author suggests, think about how the ideas relate to one another, and keep the process going until the entire selection makes sense. These focused thoughts are what help us process an author's writing. On another level, however, we also may stray from the reading in a variety of ways—thinking about chores we need to do, calls we forgot to return, and plans we are looking forward to on the weekend. These random ideas are only loosely related to the reading. As you might suspect, **focused reading** is more productive than **random reading,** but you can teach yourself to apply your stray ideas to a better understanding of the material. As you read this next selection, stop and "think aloud" about what is on your mind throughout the paragraph. Point out places that are confusing to you, connections you make, specific questions you have, related information you know, and personal experiences you associate with the paragraph. In this way, you are coming to terms with what your mind actually does (both focused and randomly) as you read.

Reading a Narration Paragraph

Reading
Strategy

This paragraph is from a book titled *Deaf in America: Voices from a Culture*. It was written by Bernard Bragg, a deaf man. In it, Bragg recalls his thoughts and feelings as a young child left alone at a residential school for deaf students. Include your thoughts as you read the paragraph aloud. Then answer the questions that follow.

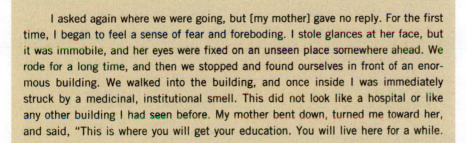

I asked again where we were going, but [my mother] gave no reply. For the first time, I began to feel a sense of fear and foreboding. I stole glances at her face, but it was immobile, and her eyes were fixed on an unseen place somewhere ahead. We rode for a long time, and then we stopped and found ourselves in front of an enormous building. We walked into the building, and once inside I was immediately struck by a medicinal, institutional smell. This did not look like a hospital or like any other building I had seen before. My mother bent down, turned me toward her, and said, "This is where you will get your education. You will live here for a while.

Don't worry. I will see you again later." Then she couldn't seem to say any more. She hugged me quickly, gave me a kiss, and then, inexplicably, left.

Discovering How This Paragraph Works

To help you discover the elements that make this an effective narration paragraph so you can use them in your own writing, answer the following questions in as much detail as possible.

1. The main point of this paragraph is not as obvious as the main point of the previous example; nevertheless, all the details support one main idea. What is that idea?

   The writer is afraid of being abandoned.

2. Bragg covers all the journalist's questions. Record at least one detail he uses in response to each question.

   Who is involved in the paragraph? *his mom and he*

   What is the paragraph about? *being abandoned*

   When did the story take place? *in his childhood*

   Where did the story take place? *a home for deaf children*

   Why did this story take place? *because he was deaf*

   How did the story unfold? *his mom left him with no warning*

3. Bragg uses vivid descriptive details to develop his brief story. In your opinion, which two details are most vivid? Why are they vivid?

   Answer will vary.

   _____

   _____

4. How does Bragg organize the details in this paragraph? List some of his details in the order they appear. Then identify his method of organization. *Details will vary.*

   sense of fear and foreboding   *medicinal, institutional smell*

   stole glances at her face   *did not look like a hospital*

   face was immobile   *mother bent down*

   here yes were fixed . . .   *she couldn't seem to say . . .*

   enormous building   *she hugged me . . . and left*

Method of organization: *Chronological*

WRITING A NARRATION PARAGRAPH

Now that you have read and studied a narration paragraph, you will be writing one of your own. This section will help you generate a rough draft that you will then revise and edit in the third section of this chapter. It will guide you through a careful reading of the writing assignment, give you several ways to generate ideas, and finally furnish you with concrete guidelines for writing an effective narrative paragraph. We encourage you to write notes and lists throughout this section so you can use them when you write a draft of your paragraph at the end of this section.

Reading the Prompt

The very first step in writing a good paragraph is making sure you understand the writing assignment or "prompt." An assignment attempts to "prompt" you to respond to a specific issue or question. The more clearly you understand the prompt, the better paragraph or essay you will create. Applying the chapter reading strategy to your writing assignment is a good way to accomplish this goal.

READING CRITICALLY
Thinking Aloud As You Read the Prompt

As you read this prompt, stop and "think aloud" about what is on your mind. Point out places that are confusing to you, connections you can make, specific questions you have, related information you know, and personal experiences you associate with the prompt. In this way, you are hearing (and letting others hear) what your mind does (both focused and randomly) as you read. Then, underline the key words in this assignment. Finally, start a conversation with the assignment by responding to the questions at the beginning of the prompt.

Writing Prompt   ⚙ ─[**Complete** this **Writing Prompt** at **mywritinglab.com**

What are some events in your life that have taught you important lessons? Does one event stand out in your mind? What lesson did it teach you? Write a paragraph telling the students in your class about this event. Make sure your story has a point and follows a time sequence.

Thinking About the Prompt

Before you focus on a specific topic, you should generate as many ideas as you can so you have several to choose from. List some memorable events you have experienced. Why do you remember these events? Can you think

PREWRITING EXERCISE
Have students ask questions (using the five Ws and one H) about one event that taught them a lesson in life.

of an event that taught you something important about life? What was the event? What did you learn? Use one or more of the prewriting techniques you learned in Chapter 3 to generate and record as many thoughts as possible about this event.

Guidelines for Writing a Narration Paragraph

1. **Make sure your story has a point.** Before you begin to write, decide what the main point of your story is. What is your purpose for writing the narrative? We have all heard stories that seem to go on forever with no apparent point. Such unfocused narratives become boring very quickly.

   In the Reading: In the excerpt by R ussell Baker, the author captures the pride he and his parents felt as he showed off his new reading skills. All the details in the story build up to this main point.

   In Your Writing: Now think about the paragraph you are going to write. What do you think its focus should be? What will be its main point? Make any notes to yourself that will remind you of your decisions here.

2. **Use the five Ws and one H to construct your story.** The five Ws and one H are the questions *Who? What? When? Where? Why?* and *How?* These are the questions journalists use to make sure they cover all the basic information in a news story. Though you may not be a journalist, these questions can help you come up with details and ideas for a well-developed narrative paragraph.

   In the Reading: When you review Baker's story, you can see that he might have used the reporter's questions to guide his writing: Who is present? What is each person doing? When is this scene taking place? Where are they? Why is Baker proud of himself? How do we know this was a memorable event for Baker? Baker covers the answers to all these questions in this brief narrative.

   In Your Writing: Jot down your answers to the following questions in reference to the paragraph you will write.

   Who? _____

   What? _____

   When? _____

   Where? _____

   Why? _____

   How? _____

3. **Use vivid descriptive details to develop your story.** The more specific your details, the more vivid your story becomes because your readers will actually be able to picture the scenes. These descriptive details should fill in the ideas you generated with the six journalistic questions.

In the Reading: Look again at Baker's story. From this narrative, we know that Baker is four years old; we know it is bedtime; we know Baker is between his parents in bed; we know he is reading his first book, which is full of words like *cat*, *rat*, *boy*, *girl*, and *the*; we know his father encouraged him by rubbing his cheek against Baker's; we know Baker finally read the words *the* and *boy*; we know his parents were pleased enough to let him sleep between them that night. These descriptive details help readers participate in Baker's narrative.

In Your Writing: Look back at your prewriting notes, and see if you have enough details to make your paragraph interesting and lively. Add any other details that come to your mind at this point.

4. **Organize your narration so that your readers can easily follow it.** Most narratives are organized chronologically, according to a time sequence. Begin your paragraph with a topic sentence, and then arrange your details in the order they happened: First this happened, then that, and next something else. Help your reader follow your narrative by using good transitions—words like *first*, *second*, *then*, *next*, and *finally*. Good transitions also make your narrative smooth rather than choppy. To write a narration paragraph, you simply tell a story with a point to it. It doesn't have to be a heart-stopping adventure or a romantic episode with a happy ending. Just draw on what you know, as the quotation that opened this chapter suggests. Choose an event that matters to you, and give your readers a sense of that event's significance. Here are some guidelines to help you make your narrative interesting. As we go through these features of a good narration paragraph, we will refer to the paragraph you read at the beginning of the chapter by Russell Baker.

In the Reading: Russell Baker organizes his narrative chronologically. It moves through time from one incident to the next. Baker begins by explaining that his mom was teaching him how to read when he was four years old, continues by relating how he was going to show his father his progress, and finishes by implying how happy he was that his parents were so proud of him. Because it follows a single time sequence and does not jump around, this paragraph is easy to follow.

In Your Writing: Review chronological organization in Chapter 3, and then look at your prewriting list of details and examples. How should you organize the details in your story to make your point as effectively as possible? Rewrite your list of details a few different ways to help you make your decision.

Writing a Draft of Your Paragraph

Now is the time to collect all your notes, your prewriting exercises, and your lists so you can generate the first draft of your paragraph. You might want to review the professional essay, the writing assignment, and

aspects of the story did they find most enjoyable? Why?

Interpersonal
Have students choose their favorite villain from a popular movie. Then have them act out a scene from the movie to see if other students can guess who the villain might be.

Naturalist
Ask students to go outdoors to a secluded brook, park, or trail. Have them imagine what could have happened at this spot 100 years ago. What story did they envision while reflecting on this place?

INSTRUCTOR'S RESOURCE MANUAL
For additional material about teaching narration, for journal entries, and for various tests, see the *Instructor's Resource Manual*, Section II, Part II.

the chapter guidelines to help you write a draft of your paragraph. At this point, don't think about revising or editing; just get a rough draft of your ideas down on paper in response to the writing prompt.

MyWritingLab **Helpful Hints**

- **Having trouble developing your ideas?** Developing your thoughts with specific examples helps your readers fully understand what you want to say. For help with this, go to **Developing and Organizing a Paragraph** in **The Craft of Writing** module in **MyWritingLab.**
- **Trying to make your point clear to the reader?** Narration paragraphs often rely on good description of the subjects being discussed. For help with description, visit **Describing** in the **Paragraph Development** module in **MyWritingLab.**

REVISING AND EDITING
OPTIONS
Consider teaching revising and editing in a class discussion, in small groups, or in pairs.

REVISING AND EDITING

You are now ready to learn how to revise and edit. This section will guide you through the process of revising and editing narration paragraphs in reference to two writing samples: another student's paragraph and your own paragraph. Finding strengths and weaknesses in another person's writing is often much easier than evaluating your own, so you will be reviewing the chapter guidelines by revising and editing another student's writing before applying the same guidelines to your own writing.

 Reading Strategy

Reading a Student Paragraph

Following is a narrative paragraph written by a student named Robert Martinez. As you read his paragraph, try to figure out his main point.

CLASS ACTIVITY
Provide students with an essay that is missing part of the five Ws and one H and has few descriptive details. In groups of three or four, have students fill in the gaps to make the story more vivid and interesting.

READING CRITICALLY
Thinking Aloud As You Read the Student Paragraph

As you read Robert's paragraph, stop and "think aloud," saying what is on your mind. Point out places that are confusing to you, connections you make, specific questions you have, related information you know, and personal experiences you associate with the ideas in the paragraph.

¹We started our vacation early in the morning fishing for bass. ²We had gone to the lake so many times with our dads, and now we were there all by ourselves. ³Boy, this was a great feeling? ⁴We settled back. ⁵And waited for those nibbles on my line. ⁶The first sign of trouble came when the conservation officer's boat started heading toward us. ⁷Suddenly, I remembered fishing licenses, a detail our dads always took care of for us. ⁸We were worried, but we didn't think that anything really bad would happen. ⁹Except for once when I got caught cheating on a science test, I had never been in trouble before. ¹⁰But we have several friends who get in trouble all the time. ¹¹The conservation officer looked serious. ¹²Can you imagine our surprise when he told us we really were in trouble. ¹³We were under arrest. ¹⁴Suddenly, we weren't so excited about being on our own.

Revising and Editing the Student Paragraph

This paragraph is Robert's first draft, which now needs to be revised and edited. First, apply the following Revising Checklist to the content of Robert's draft. When you are satisfied that his ideas are fully developed and well organized, use the Editing Checklist to correct his grammar and mechanics errors. Answer the questions, and complete the tasks in each category. Then write your suggested changes directly on Robert's draft.

Revising the Student Paragraph

TOPIC SENTENCE

✔ Does the topic sentence convey the paragraph's controlling idea?

✔ Does the topic sentence appear as the first or last sentence of the paragraph?

1. What is Robert's main point in his paragraph?

   He was not completely prepared for his first fishing trip without parents.

2. Put brackets around Robert's topic sentence. Does it convey Robert's main point?

   [We started our vacation early in the morning fishing for bass.] No

3. Rewrite it if necessary to introduce all the ideas in his paragraph.

   One possibility: Our first fishing trip on our own started out smoothly but had a

   surprise ending.

REVISING STRATEGIES
This chapter focuses on the following revising elements:
Topic sentence
Development
Unity

DEVELOPMENT

✔ Does the paragraph contain *specific* details that support the topic sentence?

✔ Does the paragraph include *enough* details to explain the topic sentence fully?

1. Does the paragraph answer all the journalist's questions? Record at least one detail Robert uses in response to each question.   *Answers may vary.*

    Who? *Robert and his friend(s)*

    What? *fishing trip*

    When? *on vacation*

    Where? *a lake*

    Why? *to take a fishing trip without parents*

    How? *venturing out on their own*

2. Add two new details to Robert's paragraph that support his main idea.

UNITY

✔ Do all the sentences in the paragraph support the topic sentence?

1. Read each of Robert's sentences with his topic sentence (revised, if necessary) in mind.

2. Cross out the two sentences that are not directly related to Robert's topic sentence.   *Sentences 9 and 10*

ORGANIZATION

✔ Is the paragraph organized logically?

1. Read Robert's paragraph again to see if all the sentences are arranged logically.

2. List the word clues in Robert's paragraph that tell you how it is organized. Then identify his method of organization.   *Answers may vary.*

    We started in the morning   *The first sign of trouble*

    We settled back   *Suddenly I remembered*

Method of organization: *Chronological*

COHERENCE

✔ Do the sentences move smoothly and logically from one to the next?

1. Circle two words or phrases Robert repeats.   *Answers will vary.*

2. Explain how one of these words or phrases makes Robert's paragraph easier to read.

   Answers will vary.

   _____

   _____

 Now rewrite Robert's paragraph with your revisions.

Editing the Student Paragraph

EDITING STRATEGIES
This chapter focuses on the following editing problems:

Fragments

Pronoun agreement

End punctuation

SENTENCES

Subjects and Verbs

✔ Does each sentence have a main subject and verb?

1. Underline the subjects once and verbs twice in your revision of Robert's paragraph. Remember that sentences can have more than one subject-verb set.

   For help with subjects and verbs, see Chapter 20.

2. Does each of the sentences have at least one subject and verb that can stand alone?

   Sentence 5 in the original paragraph has no subject.

3. Did you find and correct Robert's fragment? If not, find and correct it now.   *Sentence 5*

   For help with fragments, see Chapter 21.

Subject-Verb Agreement

✔ Do all subjects and verbs agree?

1. Read aloud the subjects and verbs you underlined in your revision of Robert's paragraph.

   For help with subject-verb agreement, see Chapter 25.

2. Correct any subjects and verbs that do not agree.   *All subjects and verbs agree in the original paragraph.*

Pronoun Agreement

✔ Do all pronouns agree with their nouns?

1. Find any pronouns in your revision of Robert's paragraph that do not agree with their nouns.   *Sentences 5 and 7*

   For help with pronoun agreement, see Chapter 29.

2. Did you find and correct the two pronouns that do not agree with their nouns? If not, find and correct them now.

Modifier Errors

✔ Are modifiers as close as possible to the words they modify?

For help with modifier errors, see Chapter 32.

1. Find any modifiers in your revision of Robert's paragraph that are not as close as possible to the words they modify. *There are no modifier errors in the original paragraph.*

2. Rewrite sentences if necessary so that modifiers are as close as possible to the words they modify.

PUNCTUATION AND MECHANICS

Punctuation

✔ Are sentences punctuated correctly?

For help with punctuation, see Chapters 33–37.

1. Read your revision of Robert's paragraph for any errors in punctuation.

2. Find the fragment you revised, and make sure it is punctuated correctly.

3. Did you find and correct his other two punctuation errors? If not, find and correct them now. *Sentence 3, exclamation point; sentence 12, question mark*

Mechanics

✔ Are words capitalized properly?

For help with capitalization, see Chapter 38.

1. Read your revision of Robert's paragraph for any errors in capitalization. *All capitals are correct in the original paragraph.*
2. Be sure to check Robert's capitalization in the fragment you revised.

WORD CHOICE AND SPELLING

Word Choice

✔ Are words used correctly?

For help with confused words, see Chapter 44.

1. Find any words used incorrectly in your revision of Robert's paragraph. *All words are used correctly in the original paragraph.*
2. Correct any errors you find.

Spelling

✔ Are words spelled correctly?

For help with spelling, see Chapter 45.

1. Use spell-check and a dictionary to check the spelling in your revision of Robert's paragraph. *All words are spelled correctly in the original paragraph.*

2. Correct any misspelled words.

Now rewrite Robert's paragraph again with your editing corrections.

Reading Your Own Narration Paragraph

Returning to the narration paragraph you wrote earlier in this chapter, you are now ready to revise and edit your own writing. You will first read your paragraph with the same reading strategy you have applied to other reading tasks in this chapter so you can look at it as your reader might.

READING CRITICALLY
Thinking Aloud As You Read Your Own Paragraph

As you begin to rework your paragraph, use the same technique you did in your reading. "Think aloud" as you read your own writing, saying what is on your mind as if you are the reader. Point out places that are confusing, connections that you make, specific questions you have, related information you know, and personal experiences you associate with the paragraph. Be aware of what your mind is doing (both focused and randomly) as you read.

Revising and Editing Your Own Paragraph

 Reading Strategy

The checklists here will help you apply what you have learned in this chapter to your own paragraph. Work first with the content, making sure your thoughts are fully developed and organized effectively before you find and correct your grammar and usage errors.

Revising Your Own Paragraph

For Revising Peer Evaluation Forms, go to Appendix 4.

TOPIC SENTENCE

☐ Does the topic sentence convey the paragraph's controlling idea?

☐ Does the topic sentence appear as the first or last sentence of the paragraph?

1. What is the main point you are trying to make in your paragraph?

   _____

2. Put brackets around your topic sentence. Does it convey your main idea?

   _____

3. How can you change your topic sentence if necessary to introduce all the ideas in your paragraph?

   _____

DEVELOPMENT

✔ Does the paragraph contain *specific* details that support the topic sentence?

✔ Does the paragraph include *enough* details to explain the topic sentence fully?

1. Does your paragraph answer all the journalist's questions? Record at least one detail you use in response to each question.

   Who? _____

   What? _____

   When? _____

   Where? _____

   Why? _____

   How? _____

2. Add two new details to your paragraph that support your main idea.

UNITY

☐ Do all the sentences in the paragraph support the topic sentence?

1. Read each of your sentences with your topic sentence (revised, if necessary) in mind.

2. Drop or rewrite any sentences that are not directly related to your topic sentence.

ORGANIZATION

☐ Is the paragraph organized logically?

1. Read your paragraph again to see if all the sentences are arranged logically.

2. List the word clues in your paragraph that tell you how it is organized. Then identify your method of organization.

   _____

   _____

Method of organization: _____

COHERENCE

☐ Do the sentences move smoothly and logically from one to the next?

1. Circle two words or phrases you repeat.

2. Explain how one of these words or phrases makes your paragraph easier to read.

   _____

   _____

Now rewrite your paragraph with your revisions.

Editing Your Own Paragraph

For Editing Peer Evaluation Forms, go to Appendix 6.

SENTENCES

Subjects and Verbs

☐ Does each sentence have a main subject and verb?

1. Underline the subjects once and verbs twice in your revised paragraph. Remember that sentences can have more than one subject-verb set.

For help with subjects and verbs, see Chapter 20.

2. Does each of your sentences have at least one subject and one verb that can stand alone?

3. Correct any fragments you have written.

4. Correct any run-together sentences you have written.

For help with fragments, see Chapter 21.
For help with run-togethers, see Chapter 22.

Subject-Verb Agreement

☐ Do all subjects and verbs agree?

1. Read aloud the subjects and verbs you underlined in your revised paragraph.

For help with subject-verb agreement, see Chapter 25.

2. Correct any subjects and verbs that do not agree.

Pronoun Agreement

☐ Do all pronouns agree with their nouns?

1. Find any pronouns in your revised paragraph that do not agree with their nouns.

For help with pronoun agreement, see Chapter 29.

2. Correct any pronouns that do not agree with their nouns.

Modifier Errors

☐ Are modifiers as close as possible to the words they modify?

1. Find any modifiers in your revised paragraph that are not as close as possible to the words they modify.

For help with modifier errors, see Chapter 32.

2. Rewrite sentences if necessary so that your modifiers are as close as possible to the words they modify.

PUNCTUATION AND MECHANICS

Punctuation

☐ Are sentences punctuated correctly?

1. Read your revised paragraph for any errors in punctuation.

For help with punctuation, see Chapters 33–37.

2. Make sure any fragments and run-together sentences you revised are punctuated correctly.

Mechanics

☐ Are words capitalized properly?

For help with capitalization, see Chapter 38.

1. Read your revised paragraph for any errors in capitalization.

2. Be sure to check your capitalization in any fragments or run-together sentences you revised.

WORD CHOICE AND SPELLING

Word Choice

☐ Are words used correctly?

For help with confused words, see Chapter 44.

1. Find any words used incorrectly in your revised paragraph.

2. Correct any errors you find.

Spelling

☐ Are words spelled correctly?

For help with spelling, see Chapter 45.

To make a personal log of your grammar/usage errors, go to Appendix 7.

To make a personal log of your spelling errors, go to Appendix 8.

1. Use spell-check and a dictionary to check the spelling in your revised paragraph.

2. Correct any misspelled words.

Now rewrite your paragraph again with your editing corrections.

MyWritingLab More Helpful Hints

- **Do you need some reminders about revising?** Narration paragraphs require a strong point of view and voice. So you need to pay special attention to these as you revise. Go to **Revising the Paragraph** in **The Craft of Writing** module in **MyWritingLab** for some helpful guidelines.

- **Are you having trouble explaining the action in your narration paragraph?** To create a good story, you need to rely on strong verbs. Review your paragraphs to make sure your verbs capture what you are trying to communicate. Go to **Subjects and Verbs** in the **Basic Grammar** module in **MyWritingLab** for some guidance and practice in creating strong verbs.

PRACTICING NARRATION: FROM READING TO WRITING

This final section lets you practice the reading and writing skills you learned in this chapter. It includes two reading selections and several writing assignments on "your reading" and "your world." The section then offers guidance in peer evaluation and reflection, ending with suggestions about how to lead your instructor through your writing in ways that will benefit both of you.

Reading Workshop

Reading Strategy

Here are two narrative essays that follow the guidelines you studied in this chapter. In "Eleven," Sandra Cisneros recalls the humiliation she suffered in front of her classmates as a result of an insensitive teacher. In the second selection, "Choosing the Path with Honor," Michael Arredondo tells a moving story about his education. As you read, notice how the writers cover the journalistic questions and use vivid descriptive details to pull you into their narratives, making the significance of the essays all the more meaningful.

ELEVEN
by Sandra Cisneros

Focusing Your Attention

1. Can you recall a time when you felt embarrassed in front of your classmates? What details do you recall?

2. In the story you are about to read, "Eleven" refers to the age of the main character in the story. Try to remember what your life was like when you were 11 years old; you would have been in fifth or sixth grade. Were you particularly sensitive about your looks? Did you worry about what your friends thought of you or whether or not you were popular? Have you become more or less self-conscious about these issues as you have gotten older?

Expanding Your Vocabulary

The following word is important to your understanding of this story. Start a vocabulary log of your own by recording any words you don't understand as you read. When you finish reading the essay, write down what you think the words mean. Then check your definitions in the dictionary.

rattling: moving around and making noise (paragraph 5)

SUMMARY
An 11-year-old girl relates how a teacher and a misidentified sweater ruined her 11th birthday.

READABILITY
(Flesch-Kincaid grade level)
6.8

INSTRUCTOR'S RESOURCE MANUAL
For additional teaching strategies, for journal entries, for vocabulary and reading quizzes, and for more writing assignments, see the *Instructor's Resource Manual,* Section II, Part II.

READING CRITICALLY
Thinking Aloud As You Read

As you learned at the beginning of this chapter, "think aloud" as you read. Interject personal references and focused ideas into your oral reading of the essay. The clearer you make your connections, the more deeply you will understand the essay. Read the essay at least two times. Discuss with a classmate the types of ideas you had as you read (focused or random). Which one of you did more focused reading?

ELEVEN[1]
by Sandra Cisneros

1   What they don't understand about birthdays and what they never tell you is that when you're eleven, you're also ten, and nine, and eight, and seven, and six, and five, and four, and three, and two, and one. And when you wake up on your eleventh birthday, you expect to feel eleven, but you don't. You open your eyes and everything's just like yesterday, only it's today. And you don't feel eleven at all. You feel like you're still ten. And you are—underneath the year that makes you eleven.

2   Like some days you might say something stupid, and that's the part of you that's still ten. Or maybe some days you might need to sit on your mama's lap because you're scared, and that's the part of you that's five. And maybe one day when you're all grown up, maybe you will need to cry like if you're three, and that's okay. That's what I tell Mama when she's sad and needs to cry. Maybe she's feeling three.

3   Because the way you grow old is kind of like an onion or like the rings inside a tree trunk or like my little wooden dolls that fit one inside the other, each year inside the next one. That's how being eleven years old is.

4   You don't feel eleven. Not right away. It takes a few days, weeks even, sometimes even months before you say Eleven when they ask you. And you don't feel smart eleven, not until you're almost twelve. That's the way it is.

5   Only today I wish I didn't have only eleven years rattling inside me like pennies in a tin Band-Aid box. Today I wish I was one hundred and two instead of eleven because if I was one hundred and two I'd have known what to say when Mrs. Price put

_____

[1] "Eleven" by Sandra Cisneros. From *Woman Hollering Creek.* © 1991 by Sandra Cisneros. Published by Vintage Books, a division of Random House, Inc., and originally in hardcover by Random House Inc. By permission of Susan Bergholz Literary Services, New York, NY and Lamy, NM. All rights reserved.

the red sweater on my desk. I would've known how to tell her it wasn't mine instead of just sitting there with that look on my face and nothing coming out of my mouth.

"Whose is this?" Mrs. Price says, and she holds the red sweater up in the air for all the class to see. "Whose? It's been sitting in the coatroom for a month."

6

"Not mine," says everybody. "Not me."

7

"It has to belong to somebody," Mrs. Price keeps saying, but nobody can remember. It's an ugly sweater with red plastic buttons and a collar and sleeves all stretched out like you could use it for a jump rope. It's maybe a thousand years old, and even if it belonged to me I wouldn't say so.

8

Maybe because I'm skinny, maybe because she doesn't like me, that stupid Sylvia Saldívar says, "I think it belongs to Rachel." An ugly sweater like that, all raggedy and old, but Mrs. Price believes her. Mrs. Price takes the sweater and puts it right on my desk, but when I open my mouth nothing comes out.

"That's not, I don't, you're not...Not mine," I finally say in a little voice that was maybe me when I was four.

"Of course it's yours," Mrs. Price says. "I remember you wearing it once." Because she's older and the teacher, she's right and I'm not.

Not mine, not mine, not mine, but Mrs. Price is already turning to page thirty-two, and math problem number four. I don't know why, but all of a sudden I'm feeling sick inside, like the part of me that's three wants to come out of my eyes, only I squeeze them shut tight and bite down on my teeth real hard and try to remember today I am eleven, eleven. Mama is making a cake for me for tonight, and when Papa comes home everybody will sing Happy birthday, happy birthday to you.

But when the sick feeling goes away and I open my eyes, the red sweater's still sitting there like a big red mountain. I move the red sweater to the corner of my desk with my ruler. I move my pencil and books and eraser as far from it as possible. I even move my chair a little to the right. Not mine, not mine, not mine.

In my head I'm thinking how long till lunchtime, how long till I can take the red sweater and throw it over the schoolyard fence, or leave it hanging on a parking meter, or bunch it up into a little ball and toss it in the alley. Except when math period ends Mrs. Price says loud and in front of everybody, "Now, Rachel, that's enough," because she sees I've shoved the red sweater to the tippy-tip corner of my desk and it's hanging all over the edge like a waterfall, but I don't care.

"Rachel," Mrs. Price says. She says it like she's getting mad. "You put that sweater on right now and no more nonsense."

"But it's not—"

"Now!" Mrs. Price says.

This is when I wish I wasn't eleven, because all the years inside of me—ten, nine, eight, seven, six, five, four, three, two, and one—are pushing at the back of my eyes when I put one arm through one sleeve of the sweater that smells like cottage cheese, and then the other arm through the other and stand there with my arms apart like if the sweater hurts me and it does, all itchy and full of germs that aren't even mine.

That's when everything I've been holding in since this morning, since when Mrs. Price put the sweater on my desk, finally lets go, and all of a sudden I'm crying in front of everybody. I wish I was invisible but I'm not. I'm eleven and it's my birthday today

9

10

11

12

13

14

15

16

17

18

19

when Rachel says, "Because she's older and the teacher, she's right and I'm not."

Thinking Critically About Purpose and Audience

4. Cisneros's purpose is to entertain readers and bring them back to a time in their childhood when even the smallest problem seemed too overwhelming to fix.

5. Anyone can enjoy this essay, but perhaps young adults will find it most enlightening.

6. The audience does feel Rachel's pain and hurt because Cisneros is able to transport the reader into Rachel's head. Allowing readers to hear Rachel's voice lets them experience what she is feeling.

Thinking Critically About Paragraphs

7. If Rachel were an adult, readers would not be experiencing the event right along with her, and to recall this event as an adult would take away the intensity of what Rachel was feeling in the heat of the moment.

8. Here are some examples:

"you will need to cry like if you're three" (para. 2)

"it's hanging over the edge like

---

and I'm crying like I'm three in front of everybody. I put my head down on the desk and bury my face in my stupid clown-sweater arms. My face all hot and spit coming out of my mouth because I can't stop the little animal noises from coming out of me, until there aren't any more tears left in my eyes, and it's just my body shaking like when you have the hiccups, and my whole head hurts like when you drink milk too fast.

20   But the worst part is right before the bell rings for lunch. That stupid Phyllis Lopez, who is even dumber than Sylvia Saldívar, says she remembers the red sweater is hers! I take it off right away and give it to her, only Mrs. Price pretends like everything's okay.

21   Today I'm eleven. There's a cake Mama's making for tonight, and when Papa comes home from work we'll eat it. There'll be candles and presents and everybody will sing Happy birthday, happy birthday to you, Rachel, only it's too late.

22   I'm eleven today. I'm eleven, ten, nine, eight, seven, six, five, four, three, two, and one, but I wish I was one hundred and two. I wish I was anything but eleven, because I want today to be far away already, far away like a runaway balloon, like a tiny *o* in the sky, so tiny-tiny you have to close your eyes to see it.

Thinking Critically About Content

1. Why do you think Cisneros pays such close attention to Rachel's age and to the fact that it is her birthday?

2. What does Rachel mean when she says that although there will be a cake and candles and presents and singing that evening at her home, "it's too late" (paragraph 21)?

3. What details does Cisneros use to show that Rachel is far more sensitive and intelligent than her teacher, Mrs. Price, thinks she is?

Thinking Critically About Purpose and Audience

4. What do you think Cisneros's purpose is in this essay? Explain your answer.

5. What type of audience do you think would most understand and appreciate this recollection?

6. Does the writer succeed in making the audience feel the pain and hurt of an 11-year-old? How does she accomplish this?

Thinking Critically About Paragraphs

7. In this story, Cisneros adopts the point of view of an 11-year-old girl, using the language, thought processes, and behavior of a child that age. Paragraph 19 is an especially good example of the author's point of view in this essay. How would this paragraph be different if it were told by Rachel as an adult remembering the incident?

8. In this essay, Cisneros uses several comparisons called *similes*. A simile uses "like" or "as" in a comparison between two unlike items. These

comparisons help us understand an item the author is trying to explain. Here are some examples:

> Because the way you grow old is kind of like an onion or like the rings inside a tree trunk or like my little wooden dolls that fit one inside the other, each year inside the next one. That's how being eleven years old is. (paragraph 3)

Find two more similes, and explain why they are effective.

9. Record three specific details from paragraph 9. What do they add to the paragraph?

10. Rachel feels terribly frustrated because her teacher simply does not understand the significance of making Rachel claim ownership for the ugly red sweater. Pretend you are Mrs. Price, and rewrite this event from her point of view, portraying her frustration over Rachel's behavior.

"a waterfall" (para. 14)

"I want to be far away already, far like a runaway balloon, like a tiny o in the sky" (para. 22)

Similes are effective because they make an observation more vivid.

9. Answers will vary.
10. Answers will vary.

To keep track of your critical thinking progress, go to Appendix 1.

CHOOSING THE PATH WITH HONOR
by Michael Arredondo

Focusing Your Attention

1. Have you ever wanted something you couldn't have? What was it? Why couldn't you have it?

2. This narrative is about a person who, since he was six years old, had a dream he didn't know if he could achieve. Have you ever had a dream that seemed impossible? What have you done to keep that dream alive?

Expanding Your Vocabulary

The following words are important to your understanding of this essay. Start a vocabulary log of your own by recording any words you don't understand as you read. When you finish reading the essay, write down what you think the words mean. Then check your definitions in the dictionary.

ruptured: burst (paragraph 1)

fragmented: broken into pieces (paragraph 2)

deployed: sent off (paragraph 15)

fibrilators: medical tools that help control an abnormal heartbeat (paragraph 17)

ablation: process of melting away (paragraph 17)

empowering: enabling (paragraph 23)

predominantly: mainly (paragraph 27)

SUMMARY
A Native American explains his quest for an education against great odds.

READABILITY
(Flesch-Kincaid grade level)
7.5

INSTRUCTOR'S RESOURCE MANUAL
For additional teaching strategies, for journal entries, for vocabulary and reading quizzes, and for more writing assignments, see the *Instructor's Resource Manual,* Section II, Part II.

READING CRITICALLY
Thinking Aloud As You Read

As you did with the previous essay, "think aloud" as you read this essay by Michael Arredondo. This process will give you some good insights into the author's approach to his topic. Write down any new ideas you discover. As you continue to read critically, you will deepen your understanding of this essay. Read the essay at least two times. Discuss with a classmate the types of ideas you had as you read (focused or random). Which one of you did more focused reading?

CHOOSING THE PATH WITH HONOR[2]
by Michael Arredondo

1   I get my Shawnee blood from my mother's side of the family. Her father was Shawnee, and her mother was Turtle Mountain Chippewa. My father's family is from Mexico. My great, great grandfather, David Dushane, was chief of the Eastern Shawnee in the 1940s, who died in 1976 of a ruptured appendix. The Shawnee were involuntarily placed in Oklahoma. But of course we were promised the land would always be ours and it would never be owned by whites.

2   As we all know, in 1907 Oklahoma, land of the Red people, home of the Red people, became the 46th state. The Shawnee were fragmented into three tribes—the Loyal, the Absentee, and the Eastern extreme.

3   We have about 1,000 tribal members, and if my math is correct, it's only two to three percent that are fluent in our language. There is no way to learn our language unless you go home. There is no other way to learn the language. You have to go home and attend language class on Wednesday nights. Being a student here at Cornell, it is just impossible for me to be in Oklahoma on Wednesday nights. I understand the elders reasoning for doing that. However, it is a difficult thing to accept.

4   The Shawnee never received a reservation. Instead, we received offers to buy tracts of land for individual ownership.

5   I have two older sisters, and my father took a look at the poverty, high unemployment, poor health, and the welfare system and said, "I cannot raise my family here. I need to go where I can do the best for them." So he moved us to Albuquerque, New Mexico. You know, they say if you don't like Mexicans and you don't like Indians, don't go to Albuquerque.

---

[2] Michael Arredondo, "Choosing the Path with Honor," *Native Americans*, vol. 19, no. 3–4 (Fall–Winter 2002). Reprinted by permission of the author.

So we fit right in there, and that is where we grew up. My mom's parents were also there. My grandfather sat me down as he would from time to time and told me about all the bad things I would hear about being Native.

As my life unfolded, I saw that it was indeed true. I did hear those things. In paralleling Sitting Bull's words, in his time, he told me that I had been born into a white man's world and that I would be walking on a white man's road.

He said, "You should acquire the white man's medicine and his skills and his planning, and you bring them back to us. We will be waiting for you."

I have been trying my whole life to get to college. It has been quite a long road. I learned about college while watching TV. I caught about the last five minutes of a TV program, and I went and found my mom after it was over, and I asked her what an Ivory Leaf school was.

She was chuckling for about as long as you are, and she told me that it was a school that you could go to if you had a lot of money. I asked her if we had enough.

She looked at me, and she said, "It might be a little while." So this college thing sounded pretty good, and if I was going to go, I was definitely going to go to the best, because that was what the TV program said.

So I went out, and I got all the jobs a little kid can get at that age. I raked leaves and picked up old cans and that sort of thing. They were all too happy to pay me to do odd jobs to contribute to my Ivory Leaf school fund. After some time, I put all this money together and took it to my mom, and I asked her if I had enough yet to go to the best school.

She didn't bother to count it. She only looked at me, and she said, "You know, it might be a while." So this continued for some time, but I noticed that a very indirect and subtle message began to appear. Over time as I got older, it came to be a very direct message. I was told by various people in the school system that certain programs, institutions, and educational opportunities weren't for me. Weren't for Indians. Weren't for people of color. And that perhaps I should make other plans.

So I quit talking about it so much, and by the time I got to high school, I quit talking about it altogether. In four years of high school, I did not have one teacher, one administrator, one coach, one advisor, one counselor ask me if I wanted to go to college. Not one.

So after high school, I joined the U.S. Navy to get the G.I. bill so I could go to college, because I knew my parents couldn't help me. Shortly thereafter I was deployed to the Gulf War. Being medical personnel in the Gulf on the USS *Iwo Jima* put me in a pretty bad position. We had what was termed the worst accident in the history of the Gulf War. I had never seen and I hope I never see again bodies that were burned that bad, beyond recognition. Using their dental records to identify their remains, preparing them to be shipped back home, I could only stop and think, this is not what I had in mind. I just wanted to get money to go to school.

But you know what they say, join the service, see the world, get money for your education. When I got back from the Gulf, I applied and was accepted to the cardiovascular school of medicine in Bethesda, Maryland. To give you a very brief idea of what a cardiovascular technologist does, we function in place of a physician's assistant to the cardiologist. We scrub in with the physician at the table in the OR. We are a cross between a physician's assistant and first assistant in the operating room.

Along with the doctor, we know all the procedures that clear out the blockages in the heart. We know how to program and implant internal fibrillators that will restore an abnormal heartbeat. We know how to map the electricity inside the heart, find the abnormal pathways, and fry them out with radio frequency ablation to restore normal rhythms.

I really love what I do, what I have been doing for ten years already. When I got out of the Navy five years ago, I was 26. I had to stop and think, do I still want to be assisting physicians in ten years? In ten years, I could be a physician.

So I had three goals ahead of me. I needed to get out of debt. I am a skydiver. I have been skydiving for six years now, and I stopped counting jumps at 200, which is a whole other story. But I had to master a significant amount of debt. I needed to get in school, because as we all know, being outside of the school system and getting to the point where you are sitting down in the classroom and taking classes can be quite a hurdle.

I also wanted to find a way to finance my education and cost of living. I looked around for about six months. I found a job in Seattle, and I moved up there. In a year, I pounded down about $17 grand worth of debt, and I got into school.

I reduced my hours to part-time at work, which in my field is about 30 hours a week. And while taking chemistry, calculus, physics, organic chemistry, biology, and all those sorts of classes, I found that it was becoming just too much, the stress of my work and my classes.

So I wrote a letter to the richest man in the world, explaining my plight to accomplish my third goal. The richest man in the world wrote me back and said, I understand your situation. I understand what you have been up against. I understand that not very many people have given you a chance. I'll take a chance on you.

It's really been quite a thing to think that somebody that I don't even know has decided to back me like that. For every semester that I successfully complete, along my pathway, I get funding from the Bill and Linda Gates Foundation, and it covers my tuition, my books and my fees, cost of living, groceries and electricity bill, food plan. It's really quite a deal. It is one of the most empowering things that has ever happened to me.

So, this last spring, a letter came in the mail from an Ivory Leaf school.

I opened that letter up, and it told me that the dream that I had inside for 25 years, the dream of a six-year-old child, had finally come true.

This past summer, I sold most of what I owned and loaded the rest in a U-Haul and took six days to drive out here to Cornell, to finish my pre-med requirements. I am here at Cornell.

The Native students here, we face our own issues. We wonder if we got accepted for our blood. I've talked with other Native people, not here at Cornell, that feel perhaps we have sold out, come to a predominantly white institution, that what we need is to attend our own schools and tribal colleges.

When you look at all the physicians in the United States, divide them up by race, and point to all of them that are Indian, it's one tenth of one one-hundredth.

When you look at all of the applicants in the Cornell pre-med pool every year, out of everybody that applies to medical school from Cornell University every year, on the average 81 percent get in. Those are huge numbers when you compare that to other institutions.

I came here to increase my chances, to take the road that gives me the best chance to accomplish my dream. Unfortunately the reality is that if I blow my grades, I blow my ride. It's that simple.

I imagine with my heritage I could just as well work for indigenous people from Mexico. But I wasn't nurtured that way. I know that in the end, when I stand before the Creator and look him in the eye, I know that I have chosen the more narrow, more difficult path, but one with great honor.

That will be my message to those that are yet to come, not to be self-serving. To pick that most difficult path, to come back and serve your own, to be proud of who you are, be proud of being Indian and where you come from. To be humble before the Creator, to listen to the children, for they will be sitting where you sit and I will sit. They'll be the only ones.

29

30

31

"I did not have one teacher, one administrator, one coach, one advisor, one counselor, ask me if I wanted to go to college" (para. 14)

"Using their dental records to identify their remains, preparing them to be shipped back home" (para. 15)

"I had to master a significant amount of debt" (para. 19)

"I found that it was becoming just too much, the stress of my work and my classes" (para. 21)

Thinking Critically About Content

1. What race is the author? When do we learn this fact?

2. What is the author's dream for his future?

3. According to Arredondo, what was "one of the most empowering things that has ever happened to me" (paragraph 23)?

Thinking Critically About Purpose and Audience

4. Explain your understanding of this essay's title.

5. Who do you think is Arredondo's primary audience?

6. Arredondo uses a very informal tone in this essay, which makes the readers feel he is actually talking to us. Do you feel this is an effective way to get his message across? Explain your answer.

Thinking Critically About Paragraphs

7. Find four details in Arredondo's essay that help us understand the difficult time the author had getting to college.

8. How does Arredondo organize his details in paragraph 22? Is this an effective order for this paragraph?

9. Why does Arredondo focus on children in his final paragraph? Is this an effective ending to his essay?

10. Write a paragraph describing what you think Arredondo's mother was thinking the first time he asked her about college.

8. The author organized paragraph 22 chronologically. It is effective because it outlines how Arredondo got his funding for college.

9. Arredondo focuses on children in the last paragraph because he believes the future is in their hands and they need to be encouraged to follow their dreams in a way that he was not. It is effective because he leaves them with a clear message.

10. Answers will vary.

To keep track of your critical thinking progress, go to Appendix 1.

Writing Workshop

This final section gives you the opportunity to apply what you have learned in this chapter to another writing assignment. This time, we provide you with the guidelines only and let you go through your own writing process with occasional feedback from your peers. Refer to sections of the chapter as necessary until the process of producing a paragraph becomes automatic for you.

 Guidelines for Writing a Narration Paragraph

1. Make sure your story has a point.
2. Use the five *W*s and one *H* to construct your story.
3. Use vivid descriptive details to develop your story.
4. Organize your essay so readers can easily follow it.

Writing About Your Reading

1. If being eleven, according to Cisneros, is also being ten, nine, eight, seven, six, and so on, what is being twenty? thirty? Choose an age older than eleven, and write a narrative to explain it to other students in your class.

2. How clear are your goals? Arredondo set his career objectives at six years old and then worked twenty-five years just to get into pre-med school. What are your main goals in life? How do you plan to reach them? Explain your goals for the future.

3. What do you think are the most important features of a good story? Why are they important? What effect do they have on you?

Writing About Your World

1. Place yourself in the photo on the next page, and write a narrative about what is happening. How did you get here? Why are you here? Where are you going? Be sure to decide on a main point before you begin to write.

2. We have all had experiences that began as carefree adventures and ended up as misadventures. Imagine that a national magazine is asking for honest stories about experiences that turned bad unexpectedly. The winning story will be published, and the author will win $200. You decide to enter the competition. The directions are to explain an experience in such a way that you reveal your feelings about this activity. Be sure to decide on a main point before you begin to write.

Rafael Macia/Science Source

3. Your high school's alumni newsletter has asked you to explain an episode that influenced the values you hold today. Recall an event that influenced the kind of person you are today. First, identify one of your core values, such as honesty, hard work, a strong sense of responsibility, independence, or patience. Then think back to what happened to give you this particular value, and write a paragraph telling the story about that value. The purpose of this narrative is to give current high school students some sense of how values might form in their own lives. Where can they look? How do values develop? Be sure to decide on a main point before you begin to write.

4. Create your own narration assignment (with the help of your instructor), and write a response to it.

Revising

Small Group Activity (5–10 minutes per writer) Working in groups of three or four, read your narration papers to each other. Those listening should record their reactions on a copy of the Revising Peer Evaluation Forms in Appendix 4. After your group goes through this process, give your evaluation forms to the appropriate writers so that each writer has two or three peer comment sheets for revising.

Paired Activity (5 minutes per writer) Using the completed Peer Evaluation Forms, work in pairs to decide what you should revise. If time allows, rewrite some of your sentences, and have your partner check them.

Individual Activity Rewrite your paper, using the revising feedback you received from other students.

Editing

Paired Activity (5–10 minutes per writer) Swap papers with a classmate, and use Editing Peer Evaluation Form in Appendix 6 to identify as many grammar, punctuation, mechanics, and spelling errors as you can. If time allows, correct some of your errors, and have your partner check them. Record your grammar, punctuation, and mechanics errors in the Error Log (Appendix 7) and your spelling errors in the Spelling Log (Appendix 8).

Reflecting on Your Writing   When you have completed your own paragraph, answer these six questions:

1. What was most difficult about this assignment?

2. What was easiest?

3. What did you learn about narration by completing this assignment?

4. What do you think are the strengths of your narration? Place a wavy line by the parts of your paragraph that you feel are very good.

5. What are the weaknesses, if any, of your paper? Place an X by the parts of your paragraph you would like help with. Write any questions you have in the margins.

6. What did you learn from this assignment about your own writing process—about preparing to write, about writing the first draft, about revising, and about editing?

Illustrating

*"*Writing, when properly managed, is but a different name for conversation.*"*

—LAWRENCE STERNE

Think of the many times you have said to someone, "What do you mean? Can you give me an example?" We use examples every day to make a point.

- **Point:** We spend a lot of money on medical research in the United States;
- **Example:** Nationally, we spend over $1 billion a year on cancer research;
- **Point:** San Francisco is an exciting city;
- **Example:** Crossing the Golden Gate Bridge is a thrill, and the people and cable cars are always in motion.

Illustrating is simply giving examples to make a point. In other words, examples, or illustrations, are specific instances that explain a general statement. Examples come very naturally in daily conversation. You might say, for instance, that professional athletes train hard and long to maintain their skills and then give a couple of examples to prove your point: Peyton Manning spends three hours a day practicing football with his team; Maria Sharapova trains three to four hours a day all year long; and Kobe Bryant does fitness training for two hours a day, seven days a week during the basketball off-season.

You can draw examples from your experience, your observations, and your reading. Well-chosen examples supply concrete detail to support abstract ideas such as courage, embarrassment, understanding, love, and boredom. For example, you can *tell* your reader that you were bored ("I was bored"), or you can *show* how bored you were by giving an example ("I was so bored

TEACHING ILLUSTRATION
Bring a selection of popular magazines to class. Divide the students into four groups, and distribute the magazines evenly. Provide each group with a different topic, such as these:

The media are responsible for many teen eating disorders.

The media are not necessarily concerned with presenting the truth.

The media often present women in a poor light.

The media are overly concerned with sex.

Have each group find four or five examples of its topic in the magazines to present to the class. Also have students find two examples that don't quite fit into their category. After 15 minutes, have each group present about 10 examples

133

for their topic (including the two that don't fit). Have the other groups try to determine which two examples don't fit.

To include a demonstration on thesis, have each group turn its topic into a good thesis statement (for example, *Because of the way they portray celebrities, the media are responsible for many teens' eating disorders*), and then show students how much easier it is to find examples for a focused thesis than it is for a vague thesis.

that I read the cereal box"). Similarly, you can make a generalization ("I like sweets") more interesting by furnishing specifics ("I love chocolate").

For his article "It's Such a Pleasure to Learn," Wallace Terry interviewed a 100-year-old man named John Morton-Finney. In his topic sentence, Terry uses the general term *special* to describe Morton-Finney. In the rest of the paragraph, he uses specific examples to support this claim.

> John Morton-Finney is a very special old man. Born the son of a former slave, he served in World War I, became fluent in six foreign languages, earned 11 degrees, taught school until he was 81, and still practices law. His thirst for learning has never abated. In his 60s, he started college all over again, earning his fourth bachelor's degree at 75. Today he attends law-school seminars with the wide-eyed eagerness of a freshman.

You will refer to this passage again when you are learning the guidelines for writing a good illustration paragraph.

Student Comment:
"This topic was really hard until I read the book and did the boxes. Doing the work together helped me really understand the topics better."

Be sure to explain concrete examples to your students before they begin working on this topic in the program.

MyWritingLab · **Understanding Illustration**

To test your knowledge of illustrating, go to **MyWritingLab.com,** and click on **Illustrating** in the **Paragraph Development** module. Then, read the **Overview** and watch the **Animation** video on illustration paragraphs. When you feel you have mastered this method of thinking, complete the **Recall, Apply,** and **Write** activities. Finally, check your understanding by taking the **Post-test.**

PREPARING TO WRITE AN ILLUSTRATION PARAGRAPH

Reading and writing are actually two halves of a whole process. For example, if you can see how a writer is accomplishing his or her purpose in a particular rhetorical mode, you will be more likely to use that same strategy effectively in your own writing. Being able to use these strategies critically or analytically is especially important for success in college and in life beyond college. This section will guide you to higher levels of thinking as you learn to use illustration.

Discovering how an illustration paragraph works is essential to writing a good illustration paragraph. Let's look closely at an illustration paragraph. First, you will apply a specific reading strategy to the paragraph. Next, you will answer some questions about the paragraph in an attempt to discover how it functions. If you read the paragraph thoughtfully, you will understand more accurately how to write an illustration paragraph of your own.

For more detailed information on "chunking," see page 18 in Chapter 2.

READING CRITICALLY
Chunking a Professional Paragraph

Reading an illustration passage critically means looking closely at it to discover its purpose and then analyzing each example the author uses to prove his or her point. To understand how this paragraph works, circle the main idea or topic sentence. Then draw horizontal lines throughout the paragraph to separate the various examples the author uses to support her main idea. Finally, in the margins, give each example a name or label that makes sense to you. Be prepared to explain the divisions you make.

Reading an Illustration Paragraph

This sample paragraph, from "A Century of Women" by Lynn Peters Alder, uses examples to prove its point. As you read this paragraph, use the strategy explained in the Reading Critically box to help you understand how this paragraph works. Then respond to the questions after the paragraph.

Reading Strategy

What a century [the 20th twentieth century was] for women. In countries around the world, women have overturned several millennia's worth of second-class citizenship to participate at nearly all levels of society. We have won the right to vote, own property, make our own decisions about sexual orientation, marriage, motherhood, and custody of our children. Should we choose to marry, we can keep our own names and legal identities. We can pursue higher education, have our own credit, earn and control our own money. We have access to most jobs, are rapidly establishing our own businesses, and are being elected to political office in ever-increasing numbers. We have established our right to sexual pleasure and reproductive freedom.

Discovering How This Paragraph Works

To help you discover the elements that make this an effective illustration paragraph so you can use them in your own writing, answer the following questions in as much detail as possible.

1. What main idea do you think Alder is trying to communicate?

   Women's rights have dramatically improved over the past century.

2. Alder groups her examples in five different sentences. How does each sentence illustrate her main idea?

"won the right" *Shows how women have more control over their lives*

"choose to marry" *Gives examples of choices women can make regarding marriage*

money *Suggests that women can make decisions about their own money and education*

jobs *Talks about new access women have in the job market*

sexual freedom *Reminds us of the sexual freedom women now have*

3. Does Alder use enough examples to make her point? Explain your answer.
Answers will vary.

4. How does Alder organize her examples: chronologically or spatially? Do you think this method is the best choice? Why or why not?
Chronologically

Answers will vary beyond this.

WRITING AN ILLUSTRATION PARAGRAPH

Now that you have read and studied an illustration paragraph, you will be writing one of your own. This section will help you generate a rough draft that you will then revise and edit in the third section of this chapter. It will guide you through a careful reading of the writing assignment, give you several ways to generate ideas, and finally furnish you with concrete guidelines for writing an effective illustration paragraph. We encourage you to write notes and lists throughout this section so you can use them when you write a draft of your paragraph at the end of this section.

Reading Strategy

Reading the Prompt

The very first step in writing any good paragraph is making sure you understand the writing assignment or "prompt." An assignment attempts to "prompt" you to respond to a specific issue or question. The more clearly you understand the prompt, the better paragraph or essay you will create. Applying the chapter reading strategy to your writing assignment is a good way to accomplish this goal.

READING CRITICALLY
Chunking the Prompt

As you read this prompt, draw horizontal lines to separate the various parts of this assignment, and use the margins to label the parts you have created. These will be very small sections because the assignment is short, but this activity will help you dissect the prompt so you understand it as thoroughly as possible. Then underline the directions that are essential for completing this assignment. Finally, start thinking about the prompt by responding to the questions within the assignment.

Writing Prompt   ⚙️━[**Complete** this **Writing Prompt** at **mywritinglab.com**

Who is a very special person in your life? Why is this person so special? Write a paragraph that starts with a general statement about your special person and includes specific examples to support your claim. Make sure your paragraph has a point.

Thinking About the Prompt

Before you focus on a specific topic, you should generate as many ideas as you can so you have several to choose from. List as many special people as you can think of. Why are these people special? List other memories about these people next to their names. Do any of them stand out from the others? Choose one person for your paragraph, and use one or more of the prewriting techniques you learned in Chapter 3 to generate and record as many thoughts as possible about this person.

PREWRITING EXERCISE
Have students write a short journal entry about a special person in their lives. What makes this person so special?

Guidelines for Writing an Illustration Paragraph

To write an illustration paragraph, you use examples to support a point you want to make. Although good examples come in a variety of forms, they often draw on description. For example, if you say that someone is a good cook, you might give the following examples, all of which draw on description: His chicken pot pie has huge chunks of chicken and carrots and the flakiest crust ever; he makes a really crunchy cole slaw; and the sweet, nutty smell of his cinnamon rolls makes you want to eat breakfast three times a day. Furnishing examples usually just means following your instincts, but the guidelines here will help you write a paragraph that uses examples in clear and interesting ways, with reference to the sample paragraph by Wallace Terry at the beginning of this chapter.

1. **State your main point in your first sentence.** Before you begin to write, think about the main point you want to make. Then choose your words

TEACHING TIPS
The following eight teaching tips are based on Howard Gardner's list of multiple intelligences:

Verbal/Linguistic
Have students each create a list of every example they can think of on a topic of their choice (for example, how violence on TV affects children). How many can they generate?

Musical/Rhythmic
Choose a word such as *loss* or *happiness,* and have students find examples of this term in at

least three different pieces of music.

Logical/Mathematical

Provide students with a list of examples that fall into at least two categories. Have students sort the examples to determine which go with which topic. Include examples that don't fit either topic.

Visual/Spatial

Provide each student with an art book, and assign a topic such as *dancing*. Then have students find examples from many different time periods of paintings or sculptures that illustrate the topic.

Bodily/Kinesthetic

Divide students into groups of three, and send them on a pseudo scavenger hunt around your campus to find examples of items that relate to technology. The students should list the items and their locations. The group that brings back the longest list wins.

Intrapersonal

Have students reflect on the times when they think best. What examples can help them prove their point?

Interpersonal

Have a small group of students think of a current issue on your campus. How does the group think the issue should be resolved? Have the students provide as many examples as possible to help illustrate their views.

Naturalist

Have students each recall times they have spent outdoors and determine how they feel being out in

as carefully as possible to express that idea as the topic sentence of your paragraph. This should be your first sentence. In the rest of your paragraph, you will explain this main point through the examples you furnish.

In the Reading: In the sample paragraph at the beginning of this chapter, Terry expresses his main point in his first sentence: *John Morton-Finney is a very special old man.* He introduces this idea as the focus of the paragraph and then sets out to expand on it.

In Your Writing: Make sure the paragraph you write in response to the Terry paragraph states your main point in the first sentence. Write a tentative first sentence for your paragraph that captures the main idea you want to make. Then, revise it as you develop your paragraph.

2. **Choose examples that focus on the point you want to make.** The examples serve as your explanation of the paragraph's main point. They help you prove that your main point is true, and they should all be directly related to your main point. As in a well-written descriptive paragraph, good examples *show* rather than *tell* the readers what the author is trying to say.

In the Reading: In his paragraph, Terry provides examples from Morton-Finney's life that *show* why he is special. All of the examples in the paragraph focus on this single point: Morton-Finney's specialness. This clear focus makes this paragraph coherent and unified.

In Your Writing: Look at the examples in your prewriting notes, and check those that support the point you want to make. Cross out those that are not related to your main idea.

3. **Use a sufficient number of examples to make your point.** How many examples is enough? That depends on the point you are trying to make. Usually, two or three short examples are sufficient, although sometimes one extended example is the best choice.

In the Reading: Wallace Terry offers eight examples to demonstrate how special Morton-Finney's life really was: son of a slave, World War I veteran, six foreign languages, 11 degrees, teacher until 81, law practice, fourth bachelor's degree at 75, law seminars. He wants to make sure his readers have no doubts whatsoever about the truth of his main point.

In Your Writing: Do you have enough examples on your prewriting list to develop a good paragraph? If not, add some additional illustrations to your list that will help prove your point. It is always better to provide too many rather than too few examples.

4. **Organize your illustrations so that your readers can easily follow along.** Most illustration paragraphs are organized from general to particular—in other words, a general statement is followed by examples. The examples should also be organized in some logical way—chronologically, spatially, or by extremes (most to least or least to most).

In the Reading: Terry organizes his paragraph from general to particular and presents two different sets of examples chronologically. The first six examples name some extraordinary feats in Morton-Finney's life: son of a slave, World War I, six languages, 11 degrees, teaching until 81, practicing law at age 100. Two more chronological examples demonstrate his thirst for learning: his fourth bachelor's degree at age 75 and his law seminars. Terry's method of organizing these illustrations allows us to easily follow his train of thought.

In Your Writing: How should you organize your examples? Put your details in the order you think will most effectively accomplish your purpose. Is this the most effective method of organization to prove your main point? Move the items around until you are satisfied with their order.

Writing a Draft of Your Paragraph

Now is the time to collect all your notes, your prewriting exercises, and your lists as you generate the first draft of your paragraph. You might want to review the professional essay, the writing assignment, and the chapter guidelines to help you write a draft of your paragraph. At this point, don't think about revising or editing; just get a rough draft of your ideas down on paper in response to the writing prompt.

> **MyWritingLab** | **Helpful Hints**
>
> - **Not sure what to do next?** Writing can be confusing if you don't know what to do next; we can help. **The Writing Process** in **The Craft of Writing** module in **MyWritingLab** will give you some ideas for getting started and keeping the writing process going.
> - **Not sure if all your paragraphs have topic sentences?** Topic sentences are the controlling ideas of your paragraphs. If you need help with these important sentences, see **Topic Sentences** in **The Craft Writing** module in **MyWritingLab.**

REVISING AND EDITING

You are now ready to learn how to revise and edit. This section will guide you through the process of revising and editing illustration paragraphs in reference to two writing samples: another student's paragraph and your own paragraph. Finding strengths and weaknesses in another person's writing is often much easier than evaluating your own, so you will be reviewing the chapter guidelines by revising and editing another student's writing before applying the same guidelines to your own writing.

nature. Have them provide several examples that illustrate why they feel the way they do.

INSTRUCTOR'S RESOURCE MANUAL For additional material about teaching illustration, for journal entries, and for various tests, see the *Instructor's Resource Manual,* Section II, Part II.

REVISING AND EDITING OPTIONS Consider teaching revising and editing in a class discussion, in small groups, or in pairs.

Reading
Strategy

Reading a Student Paragraph

Following is a paragraph written by Amanda Bliss, a freshman in college. As you read her paragraph, apply the chapter reading strategy, and try to figure out Amanda's main point.

CLASS ACTIVITY
Write a topic on the board, and have students provide examples that support the topic. Have the class fill the board with many ideas; then determine which examples would work best if you were going to write an illustration paragraph.

READING CRITICALLY
Chunking the Student Essay

As you read this draft of Amanda's paragraph, circle the main idea and then draw horizontal lines throughout the paragraph to separate the various examples Amanda uses to support her main idea. Then write yourself notes in the margins to show how each example relates to the main idea. Be prepared to explain the divisions you make.

[1]When I was growing up I never understood the holidays. [2]My mom always wanted everyone to get along all year long. [3]The tension begins about a week before Thanksgiving she starts bringing a ton of strange foods into the house. [4]We had evergreen wreaths on every door, evergreen candle holders, evergreen tablecloths with matching napkins, and evergreen baskets with pine cones. [5]At about the same time the strange foods come into the house, she decides that every room in the house needs decorations of some sort. [6]One year their was so much stuff that smelled like cinnamon in our house that I dreamed to often about working in a spice factory. [7]During another year, Mom decided that are entire house should smell like evergreen, and look like a pine forest. [8]Mom had finally gone off the deep end, who is usually a stable person.

Revising and Editing the Student Paragraph

This paragraph is Amanda's first draft, which now needs to be revised and edited. First, apply the following Revising Checklist to the content of Amanda's draft. When you are satisfied that her ideas are fully developed and well organized, use the Editing Checklist to correct her grammar and mechanics errors. Answer the questions, and complete the tasks in each category. Then write your suggested changes directly on Amanda's draft.

REVISING STRATEGIES
This chapter focuses on the following revising elements:

Topic sentence
Development
Unity
Organization

Revising the Student Paragraph

TOPIC SENTENCE

✔ Does the topic sentence convey the paragraph's controlling idea?

✔ Does the topic sentence appear as the first or last sentence of the paragraph?

1. What is Amanda's main idea in this paragraph?

   Holidays were a hassle when she was growing up.

2. Put brackets around Amanda's topic sentence. Does it convey Amanda's main idea?

   [When I was growing up I never understood the holidays.] No

3. Rewrite it if necessary to introduce all the ideas in her paragraph.

   One possibility: When I was growing up, holidays at our house were difficult.

DEVELOPMENT

✔ Does the paragraph contain *specific* details that support the topic sentence?

✔ Does the paragraph include *enough* details to explain the topic sentence fully?

1. Are Amanda's examples specific enough?

   Answers will vary.

   Add another more specific detail to an example in her paragraph.

2. Does she give enough examples to make her point?

   Answers will vary.

   Add at least one new example to Amanda's paragraph to strengthen her topic sentence.

UNITY

✔ Do all the sentences in the paragraph support the topic sentence?

1. Read each of Amanda's sentences with her topic sentence (revised, if necessary) in mind.

2. Cross out the one sentence that is not directly related to Amanda's topic sentence.   *Sentence 2*

ORGANIZATION

✔ Is the paragraph organized logically?

1. Read Amanda's paragraph again to see if all the sentences are arranged logically.

2. List some of her examples in the order they appear. Then identify her method of organization.   *Details will vary.*

evergreen wreaths on every door

evergreen candle holders

evergreen tablecloths with matching napkins

evergreen baskets with pine cones

working in a spice factory

look like a pine forest

Method of organization: *General to particular*

3. Move the one sentence that is out of place in Amanda's paragraph.
   Move sentence 4 after sentence 7

COHERENCE

✔ Do the sentences move smoothly and logically from one to the next?

For a list of transitions, see pages 59–60.

1. Circle three transitions, repetitions, synonyms, or pronouns Amanda uses.

For a list of pronouns, see page 365.

2. Explain how one of these makes Amanda's paragraph easier to read.
   Answers will vary.

 Now rewrite Amanda's paragraph with your revisions.

EDITING STRATEGIES
This chapter focuses on the following editing problems:

Run-togethers

Modifier errors

Commas

Confused words

For help with subjects and verbs, see Chapter 20.

Editing the Student Paragraph

SENTENCES

Subjects and Verbs

✔ Does each sentence have a main subject and verb?

1. Underline the subjects once and verbs twice in your revision of Amanda's paragraph. Remember that sentences can have more than one subject-verb set.

2. Does each of the sentences have at least one subject and verb that can stand alone?
   Yes in the original paragraph.

For help with run-togethers, see Chapter 22.

3. Did you find and correct Amanda's run-together sentence? If not, find and correct it now.   *Sentence 3.*

Subject-Verb Agreement

✔ Do all subjects and verbs agree?

1. Read aloud the subjects and verbs you underlined in your revision of Amanda's paragraph.

   For help with subject-verb agreement, see Chapter 25.

2. Correct any subjects and verbs that do not agree. *All subjects and verbs agree in the original paragraph.*

Pronoun Agreement
✔ Do all pronouns agree with their nouns?

1. Find any pronouns in your revision of Amanda's paragraph that do not agree with their nouns. *All pronouns agree with their nouns in the original paragraph.*

   For help with pronoun agreement, see Chapter 29.

2. Correct any pronouns that do not agree with their nouns.

Modifier Errors
✔ Are modifiers as close as possible to the words they modify?

1. Find any modifiers in your revision of Amanda's paragraph that are not as close as possible to the words they modify. *"who is usually a stable person" (sentence 8)*

   For help with modifier errors, see Chapter 32.

2. Did you find and correct her misplaced modifier? If not, find and correct it now. *Move "who is usually a stable person" next to "Mom."*

PUNCTUATION AND MECHANICS

Punctuation
✔ Are sentences punctuated correctly?

1. Read your revision of Amanda's paragraph for any errors in punctuation.

   For help with punctuation, see Chapters 33–37.

2. Find the run-together sentence you revised, and make sure it is punctuated correctly.

3. Did you find and correct her two comma errors? If not, find and correct them now. *Sentences 1 and 7*

Mechanics
✔ Are words capitalized properly?

1. Read your revision of Amanda's paragraph for any errors in capitalization. *All capitals are correct in the original paragraph.*

   For help with capitalization, see Chapter 38.

2. Be sure to check Amanda's capitalization in the run-together sentence you revised.

WORD CHOICE AND SPELLING

Word Choice
✔ Are words used correctly?

1. Find any words used incorrectly in your revision of Amanda's paragraph. *their (sentence 6), to (sentence 6), are (sentence 7)*

   For help with confused words, see Chapter 44.

2. Did you find and correct her three confused words? If not, find and correct them now. *their/there, to/too, are/our*

Spelling

✔ Are words spelled correctly?

For help with spelling, see Chapter 45.

1. Use spell-check and a dictionary to check the spelling in your revision of Amanda's paragraph.   *All words are spelled correctly in the original paragraph.*

2. Correct any misspelled words.

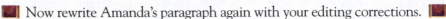

 Now rewrite Amanda's paragraph again with your editing corrections.

 Reading Strategy

Reading Your Own Illustration Paragraph

Returning to the illustration paragraph you wrote earlier in this chapter, you are ready to revise and edit your own writing. You will first read your paragraph with the same reading strategy you have applied to other reading tasks in this chapter so you can look at it as your reader might.

READING CRITICALLY
Chunking Your Own Paragraph

As you begin to rework your own paragraph, apply the same reading strategy to it that you have used throughout this chapter. Circle your main idea; then draw horizontal lines between the examples you use to support your main idea. As you label these examples in the margin, decide whether they are the best choices to prove your point. Should you change any of them? Should you explain any of them further?

Revising and Editing Your Own Paragraph

The checklists here will help you apply what you learned in this chapter to your own paragraph. Consider your content, especially your development and organization, before you find and correct your grammar and usage errors.

For Revising Peer Evaluation Forms, go to Appendix 4.

Revising Your Own Paragraph

TOPIC SENTENCE

☐ Does the topic sentence convey the paragraph's controlling idea?

☐ Does the topic sentence appear as the first or last sentence of the paragraph?

1. What is the main point you are trying to communicate in your paragraph?

2. Put brackets around your topic sentence. Does it convey your main idea?

_____

3. How can you change your topic sentence if necessary to introduce all the ideas in your paragraph?

_____

DEVELOPMENT

☐ Does the paragraph contain *specific* details that support the topic sentence?

☐ Does the paragraph include *enough* details to explain the topic sentence fully?

1. Are your examples specific enough?

_____

Add another more specific detail to an example in your paragraph.

2. Do you give enough examples to make your point?

_____

Add at least one new example to your paragraph to strengthen your topic sentence.

UNITY

☐ Do all the sentences in the paragraph support the topic sentence?

1. Read each of your sentences with your topic sentence in mind.

2. Drop or rewrite any sentences that are not directly related to your topic sentence.

ORGANIZATION

☐ Is the paragraph organized logically?

1. Read your paragraph again to see if all the sentences are arranged logically.

2. List some of your examples in the order they appear. Then identify your method of organization.

_____

_____

_____

_____

Method of organization: _____

COHERENCE

☐ Do the sentences move smoothly and logically from one to the next?

For a list of transitions, see pages 59–60.

For a list of pronouns, see page 365.

1. Circle three transitions, repetitions, synonyms, or pronouns you use.

2. Explain how one of these makes your paragraph easier to read.

_____

_____

Now rewrite your paragraph with your revisions.

For Editing Peer Evaluation Forms, go to Appendix 6.

Editing Your Own Paragraph

SENTENCES

Subjects and Verbs

☐ Does each sentence have a main subject and verb?

For help with subjects and verbs, see Chapter 20.

1. Underline the subjects once and verbs twice in your revised paragraph. Remember that sentences can have more than one subject-verb set.

2. Does each of your sentences have at least one subject and verb that can stand alone?

_____

For help with fragments, see Chapter 21.

For help with run-togethers, see Chapter 22.

3. Correct any fragments you have written.

4. Correct any run-together sentences you have written.

Subject-Verb Agreement

☐ Do all subjects and verbs agree?

For help with subject-verb agreement, see Chapter 25.

1. Read aloud the subjects and verbs you underlined in your revised paragraph.

2. Correct any subjects and verbs that do not agree.

Pronoun Agreement

☐ Do all pronouns agree with their nouns?

For help with pronoun agreement, see Chapter 29.

1. Find any pronouns in your revised paragraph that do not agree with their nouns.

2. Correct any pronouns that do not agree with their nouns.

Modifier Errors

☐ Are modifiers as close as possible to the words they modify?

For help with modifier errors, see Chapter 32.

1. Find any modifiers in your revised paragraph that are not as close as possible to the words they modify.

2. Rewrite sentences if necessary so that your modifiers are as close as possible to the words they modify.

PUNCTUATION AND MECHANICS

Punctuation

☐ Are sentences punctuated correctly?

1. Read your revised paragraph for any errors in punctuation.

2. Make sure any fragments and run-together sentences you revised are punctuated correctly.

For help with punctuation, see Chapters 33–37.

Mechanics

☐ Are words capitalized properly?

1. Read your revised paragraph for any errors in capitalization.

2. Be sure to check your capitalization in any fragments and run-together sentences you revised.

For help with capitalization, see Chapter 38.

WORD CHOICE AND SPELLING

Word Choice

☐ Are words used correctly?

1. Find any words used incorrectly in your revised paragraph.

2. Correct any errors you find.

For help with confused words, see Chapter 44.

Spelling

☐ Are words spelled correctly?

1. Use spell-check and a dictionary to check the spelling in your revised paragraph.

2. Correct any misspelled words.

For help with spelling, see Chapter 45.

To make a personal log of your grammar/usage errors, go to Appendix 7.

Now rewrite your paragraph with your editing corrections.

To make a personal log of your spelling errors, go to Appendix 8.

MyWritingLab   More Helpful Hints

- **Do you need some reminders about revising?** Illustrating paragraphs require specific examples and clarity to help readers understand your paragraph. So you need to pay special attention to examples and clarity as you revise. Go to **Revising the Paragraph** in **The Craft of Writing** module in **MyWritingLab** for some helpful guidelines.

- **Do you have more questions about pronouns?** All the pronouns you use and the words they refer to (their antecedents) must agree in number. This can sometimes be tricky, so be sure to check out **Pronoun-Antecedent Agreement** in the **Sentence Skills** module in **MyWritingLab** for a complete explanation.

PRACTICING ILLUSTRATION: FROM READING TO WRITING

This final section lets you practice the reading and writing skills you learned in this chapter. It includes two reading selections and several writing assignments on "your reading" and "your world." The section then offers guidance in peer evaluation and reflection, ending with suggestions about how to lead your instructor through your writing in ways that will benefit both of you.

 Reading Strategy

Reading Workshop

In this section, are two essays that use examples to make their points. The first essay, "Mute in an English-Only World," written by Chang-Rae Lee, uses examples to show her mother's painful adjustment to the English language. In the second essay, "Walk On By," Brent Staples uses some examples from his own experience to send a warning to kids in gangs. As you read, notice how both writers use examples to support and advance their ideas.

MUTE IN AN ENGLISH-ONLY WORLD
by Chang-Rae Lee

SUMMARY
In this essay, Chang-Rae Lee explains her mother's plight with English when she moved to the United States.

READABILITY
(Flesch-Kincaid grade level) 9.0

INSTRUCTOR'S RESOURCE MANUAL
For additional teaching strategies, for journal entries, for vocabulary and reading quizzes, and for more writing assignments, see the *Instructor's Resource Manual*, Section II, Part II.

Focusing Your Attention

1. Can you think of a time in your life when you had trouble adjusting to a new situation? How did you handle it?

2. The essay you are about to read explains through well-chosen examples how it feels to live in a country where you don't understand the language. Have you ever had this experience? If so, how did you feel? if not, how do you think you would feel?

Expanding Your Vocabulary

The following words are important to your understanding of this essay. Organize this list into two columns—words you know and words you don't know. Write the definitions of the words you don't know over the words in the essay.

proliferation: rapid increase (paragraph 1)

vital: important (paragraph 1)

exclusionary: something that excludes others (paragraph 2)

aping: mimicking like an ape (paragraph 5)

sundry: of various kinds (paragraph 7)

harrowing: causing distress (paragraph 8)

deft: quick and skilled (paragraph 8)

READING CRITICALLY
Chunking Your Reading

As you learned earlier, circle the main idea of the following essay, and then separate each example with horizontal lines. Label the examples in the margin. Then share your marks with a classmate, justifying each of your decisions.

MUTE IN AN ENGLISH-ONLY WORLD[1]
by Chang-Rae Lee

1. When I read of the troubles in Palisades Park, New Jersey, over the proliferation of Korean-language signs along its main commercial strip, I unexpectedly sympathized with the frustrations, resentments, and fears of the longtime residents. They clearly felt alienated and even unwelcome in a vital part of their community. The town, like seven others in New Jersey, has passed laws requiring that half of any commercial sign in a foreign language be in English.

2. Now I certainly would never tolerate any exclusionary ideas about who could rightfully settle and belong in the town. But having been raised in a Korean immigrant family, I saw every day the exacting price and power of language, especially with my mother, who was an outsider in an English-only world. In the first years we lived in America, my mother could speak only the most basic English, and she often encountered great difficulty whenever she went out.

3. We lived in New Rochelle, New York, in the early seventies, and most of the local businesses were run by the descendants of immigrants who, generations ago, had come to the suburbs from New York City. Proudly dotting Main Street and North Avenue were Italian pastry and cheese shops, Jewish tailors and cleaners, and Polish and German butchers and bakers. If my mother's marketing couldn't wait until the weekend, when my father had free time, she would often hold off until I came home from school to buy the groceries.

4   Though I was only six or seven years old, she insisted that I go out shopping with her and my younger sister. I mostly loathed the task, partly because it meant I couldn't spend the afternoon off playing catch with my friends but also because I knew our errands would inevitably lead to an awkward scene and that I would have to speak up to help my mother.

5   I was just learning the language myself, but I was a quick study, as children are with new tongues. I had spent kindergarten in almost complete silence, hearing only the high nasality of my teacher and comprehending little but the cranky wails and cries of my classmates. But soon, seemingly mere months later, I had already become a terrible ham and mimic, and I would crack up my father with impressions of teachers, his friends, and even himself. My mother scolded me for aping his speech, and the one time I attempted to make light of hers I rated a roundhouse smack on my bottom.

6   For her, the English language was not very funny. It usually meant trouble and a good dose of shame and sometimes real hurt. Although she had a good reading knowledge of the language from university classes in South Korea, she had never practiced actual conversation. So in America she used English flash cards and phrase books and watched television with us kids. And she faithfully carried a pocket workbook illustrated with stick-figure people and compound sentences to be filled in.

7   But none of it seemed to do her much good. Staying mostly at home to care for us, she didn't have many chances to try out sundry words and phrases. When she did, say, at the window of the post office, her readied speech would stall, freeze, sometimes altogether collapse.

8   One day was unusually harrowing. We ventured downtown in the new Ford Country Squire my father had bought her, an enormous station wagon that seemed as long—and deft—as an ocean liner. We were shopping for a special meal for guests visiting that weekend, and my mother had heard that a particular butcher carried fresh oxtails, which she needed for a traditional soup.

9   We'd never been inside the shop, but my mother would pause before its window, which was always lined with whole hams, crown roasts, and ropes of plump handmade sausages. She greatly esteemed the bounty with her eyes, and my sister and I did also, but despite our desirous cries she'd turn us away and instead buy the packaged links at the Finast supermarket, where she felt comfortable looking them over and could easily spot the price—and, of course, not have to talk.

10   But that day she was resolved. The butcher store was crowded, and as we stepped inside, the door jingled a welcome. No one seemed to notice. We waited for some time, and people who entered after us were now being served. Finally an old woman nudged my mother and waved a little ticket, which we hadn't taken. We patiently waited again, until one of the beefy men behind the glass display hollered our number.

11   My mother pulled us forward and began searching the cases, but the oxtails were nowhere to be found. The man, his big arms crossed, sharply said, "Come on, lady, whaddya want?" This unnerved her, and she somehow blurted the Korean word for oxtail, *soggori.*

The butcher looked as if my mother had put something sour in his mouth, and he glanced back at the lighted board and called the next number.

Before I knew it, she had rushed us outside and back in the wagon, which she had double-parked because of the crowd. She was furious, almost vibrating with fear and grief, and I could see she was about to cry.

She wanted to go back inside, but now the driver of the car we were blocking wanted to pull out. She was shooing us away. My mother, who had just earned her driver's license, started furiously working the pedals. But in her haste she must have flooded the engine, for it wouldn't turn over. The driver started honking, and then another car began honking as well, and soon it seemed the entire street was shrieking at us.

In the following years, my mother grew steadily more comfortable with English. In Korean she could be fiery, stern, deeply funny, and ironic; in English just slightly less so. If she was never quite fluent, she gained enough confidence to make herself clearly known to anyone, and particularly to me.

Five years ago she died of cancer, and some months after we buried her I found myself in the driveway of my father's house, washing her sedan. I liked taking care of her things; it made me feel close to her. While I was cleaning out the glove compartment, I found her pocket English workbook, the one with the silly illustrations. I hadn't seen it in nearly twenty years. The yellowed pages were brittle and dog-eared. She had fashioned a plain paper wrapping for it, and I wondered whether she meant to protect the book or hide it.

I don't doubt that she would have appreciated doing the family shopping on the new Broad Avenue of Palisades Park. But I like to think, too, that she would have understood those who now complain about the Korean-only signs.

I wonder what these same people would have done if they had seen my mother studying her English workbook—or lost in a store. Would they have nodded gently at her? Would they have lent a kind word?

Thinking Critically About Content

1. What examples from the essay illustrate the mother's discomfort with the English language during her first few years in America?

2. How does the author's mother learn to speak English?

3. Why is the English workbook an important part of this story?

Thinking Critically About Purpose and Audience

4. Why do you think the author wrote this essay?

5. What type of audience do you think would most understand and appreciate this essay?

6. Are you one of the people who would criticize foreign signs in your community?

12
13
14
15
16
17
18

Thinking Critically About Content

4. The author wanted to demonstrate her mother's struggle to learn the English language and the difficulty foreign citizens have adjusting to social constructs in America.

5. Americans who have experienced this adjustment and socialization process either coming from another country or going to a foreign country would be most likely to appreciate this essay, but all readers can understand it and identify with it in some way.

6. Answers will vary.

Thinking Critically About Content

7. The shift to the present tense in paragraph 17 represents the author's move back to the present in real time. She concludes the essay with some questions that still pertain to American immigrants and their struggle to adjust to a new language and culture.

8. Paragraph 9 is unified because sentence 1 is the topic sentence, and all the sentences after it support it by showing the mother's excitement and apprehension at the butcher's.

9. The paragraph is organized from general (doing chores) to particular (her mother's English workbook) to create sympathy for the mother in her struggle with the English language. Answers beyond this will vary.

10. Answers will vary.

To keep track of your critical thinking progress, go to Appendix 1.

Thinking Critically About Paragraphs

7. The author writes this essay predominantly in the past tense until paragraph 17 when she shifts to the present. What does this shift represent in the essay?

8. Look closely at paragraph 9. Is it unified? Do the examples the author uses in this paragraph support its topic sentence? Explain your answer.

9. How does the writer organize her details in paragraph 16? Is this an effective order?

10. Write a paragraph introducing a difficult adjustment you have made in your life.

WALK ON BY
by Brent Staples

SUMMARY
In this essay, Staples illustrates how people react to him, a black man, when they walk by him on the streets late at night.

READABILITY
(Flesch-Kincaid grade level) 8.5

INSTRUCTOR'S RESOURCE MANUAL
For additional teaching strategies, for journal entries, for vocabulary and reading quizzes, and for more writing assignments, see the *Instructor's Resource Manual*, Section II, Part II.

Focusing Your Attention

1. Do you intimidate people with any of your behavior? Are you intimidated by anyone in particular?

2. The essay you are about to read discusses the image of African American males as criminals or suspects. It is written by someone who doesn't deserve this reputation. Have you ever been blamed for something you didn't do? What were you blamed for? Why were you blamed?

Expanding Your Vocabulary

The following words are important to your understanding of this essay. Organize this list into two columns—words you know and words you don't know. Write the definitions of the words you don't know over the words in the essay.

affluent: wealthy (paragraph 1)

impoverished: poor (paragraph 1)

uninflammatory: giving no cause for concern (paragraph 1)

billowing: waving (paragraph 1)

menacingly: dangerously (paragraph 1)

unwieldy: large, unmanageable (paragraph 2)

insomnia: sleeplessness (paragraph 2)

wayfarers: wanderers, travelers (paragraph 2)

accomplice: associate, helper (paragraph 2)

tyranny: cruelty (paragraph 2)

errant: out of place (paragraph 2)

crowd cover: presence of large numbers of people (paragraph 4)

SoHo: a neighborhood of Manhattan, south of Houston Street (paragraph 4)

taut: strained, intense (paragraph 4)

ruthless: cruel (paragraph 5)

extols: praises (paragraph 5)

panhandlers: beggars (paragraph 5)

warrenlike: crowded (paragraph 6)

bandolier style: over one shoulder (paragraph 6)

lethality: deadliness (paragraph 7)

flailings: flinging one's arms in the air (paragraph 8)

mark: victim (paragraph 8)

cowered: cringed (paragraph 8)

valiant: brave, courageous (paragraph 8)

bravado: false bravery (paragraph 9)

perilous: dangerous (paragraph 10)

proprietor: owner (paragraph 11)

skittish: easily frightened (paragraph 13)

congenial: friendly (paragraph 13)

constitutionals: walks (paragraph 14)

Beethoven: 1770–1827, a German composer (paragraph 14)

Vivaldi: 1678–1741, an Italian composer (paragraph 14)

READING CRITICALLY
Chunking Your Reading

Once again, circle the thesis of the following essay, and draw horizontal lines in the essay to show the different examples the author has chosen to support his thesis. Label the examples in the margins. Then compare your marks with those of a classmate, and justify your divisions to each other.

WALK ON BY[2]
by Brent Staples

1   My first victim was a woman—white, well dressed, probably in her early twenties. I came upon her late one evening on a deserted street in Hyde Park, a relatively affluent neighborhood in an otherwise mean, impoverished section of Chicago. As I swung onto the avenue behind her, there seemed to be a discreet, uninflammatory distance between us. Not so. She cast back a worried glance. To her, the youngish black man—a broad six feet two inches with a beard and billowing hair, both hands shoved into the pockets of a bulky military jacket—seemed menacingly close. After a few more quick glimpses, she picked up her pace and was soon running in earnest. Within seconds she disappeared into a cross street.

2   That was more than a decade ago. I was 22 years old, a graduate student newly arrived at the University of Chicago. It was in the echo of that terrified woman's footfalls that I first began to know the unwieldy inheritance I'd come into—the ability to alter public space in ugly ways. It was clear that she thought herself the quarry of a mugger, a rapist, or worse. Suffering a bout of insomnia, however, I was stalking sleep, not defenseless wayfarers. As a softy who is scarcely able to take a knife to a raw chicken—let alone hold it to a person's throat—I was surprised, embarrassed, and dismayed all at once. Her flight made me feel like an accomplice in tyranny. It also made it clear that I was indistinguishable from the muggers who occasionally seeped into the area from the surrounding ghetto. That first encounter, and those that followed, signified that a vast, unnerving gulf lay between nighttime pedestrians—particularly women—and me. And I soon gathered that being perceived as dangerous is a hazard in itself. I only needed to turn a corner into a dicey situation, or crowd some frightened, armed person in a foyer somewhere, or make an errant move after being pulled over by a policeman. Where fear and weapons meet—and they often do in urban America is always the possibility of death.

3   In the first year, my first away from my hometown, I was to become thoroughly familiar with the language of fear. At dark, shadowy intersections in Chicago, I could cross in front of a car stopped at a traffic light and elicit the *thunk, thunk, thunk, thunk* of the driver—black, white, male, or female—hammering down the door locks. On less traveled streets after dark, I grew accustomed to but never comfortable with people who crossed to the other side of the street rather than pass me. Then there were the standard unpleasantries with police, doormen, bouncers, cab drivers, and others whose business it is to screen out troublesome individuals *before* there is any nastiness.

4   I moved to New York nearly two years ago, and I have remained an avid night walker. In central Manhattan, the near-constant crowd cover minimized tense one-on-one street encounters. Elsewhere—visiting friends in SoHo, where sidewalks are narrow and tightly spaced, buildings shut out the sky—things can get very taut indeed.

---

[2] Brent Staples, "Walk On By." *Ms.* magazine (1986). Reprinted by permission of the author.

Black men have a firm place in New York mugging literature. Norman Podhoretz in his famed (or infamous) 1963 essay, "My Negro Problem—and Ours," recalls growing up in terror of black males; they "were tougher than we were, more ruthless," he writes—and as an adult on the Upper West Side of Manhattan, he continues, he cannot constrain his nervousness when he meets black men on certain streets. Similarly, a decade later, the essayist and novelist Edward Hoagland extols a New York where once "Negro bitterness bore down mainly on other Negroes." Where some see mere panhandlers, Hoagland sees "a mugger who is clearly screwing up his nerve to do more than just *ask* for money." But Hoagland has "the New Yorker's quick-hunch posture for broken-field maneuvering," and the bad guy swerves away.

I often witness that "hunch posture" from women after dark on the warrenlike streets of Brooklyn where I live. They seem to set their faces on neutral and, with their purse straps strung across their chests bandolier style, they forge ahead as though bracing themselves against being tackled. I understand, of course, that the danger they perceive is not a hallucination. Women are particularly vulnerable to street violence, and young black males are drastically overrepresented among the perpetrators of that violence. Yet these truths are no solace against the kind of alienation that comes of being ever the suspect, against being set apart, a fearsome entity with whom pedestrians avoid making eye contact.

It is not altogether clear to me how I reached the ripe old age of 22 without being conscious of the lethality nighttime pedestrians attributed to me. Perhaps it was because in Chester, Pennsylvania, the small, angry industrial town where I came of age in the 1960s, I was scarcely noticeable against a backdrop of gang warfare, street knifings, and murders. I grew up one of the good boys, had perhaps a half-dozen fist fights. In retrospect, my shyness of combat has clear sources.

Many things go into the making of a young thug. One of those things is the consummation of the male romance with the power to intimidate. An infant discovers that random flailings send the baby bottle flying out of the crib and crashing to the floor. Delighted, the joyful babe repeats those motions again and again, seeking to duplicate the feat. Just so, I recall the points at which some of my boyhood friends were finally seduced by the perception of themselves as tough guys. When a mark cowered and surrendered his money without resistance, myth and reality merged—and paid off. It is, after all, only manly to embrace the power to frighten and intimidate. We, as men, are not supposed to give an inch of our lane on the highway; we are to seize the fighter's edge in work and in play and even in love; we are to be valiant in the face of hostile forces.

Unfortunately, poor and powerless young men seem to take all this nonsense literally. As a boy, I saw countless tough guys locked away; I have since buried several. They were babies, really—a teenage cousin, a brother of 22, a childhood friend in his mid-twenties—all gone down in episodes of bravado played out in the streets. I came to doubt the virtues of intimidation early on. I chose, perhaps even unconsciously, to remain a shadow—timid, but a survivor.

The fearsomeness mistakenly attributed to me in public places often has a perilous flavor. The most frightening of these confusions occurred in the late 1970s and early 1980s when I worked as a journalist in Chicago. One day, rushing into the

5

6

7

8

9

10

reputation when he was 22 years old and was walking alone on the streets of Chicago. A woman was frightened of him because he was black and the street was deserted.

3. Staples thinks young thugs are foolish. In the last two sentences of the paragraph, he sarcastically talks about how men feel the need to intimidate others.

Thinking Critically About Purpose and Audience

4. Staples wants readers to understand that not all African Americans are out to harm people, but he understands why people might be afraid.

5. Staples's primary audience is general.

6. Answers will vary.

Thinking Critically About Paragraphs

7. "In the first year, my first away from my hometown, I was to become thoroughly familiar with the language of fear" (sentence 1) is the topic sentence of paragraph 7. All the sentences in this paragraph support his topic sentence because they demonstrate the fear Staples describes.

8. He is implying that he is a criminal of

office of a magazine I was writing for with a deadline story in hand, I was mistaken for a burglar. The office manager called security and, with an ad hoc posse, pursued me through the labyrinthine halls, nearly to my editor's door. I had no way of proving who I was. I could only move briskly toward the company of someone who knew me.

11   Another time I was on assignment for a local paper and killing time before an interview. I entered a jewelry store on the city's affluent Near North Side. The proprietor excused herself and returned with an enormous red Doberman pinscher straining at the end of a leash. She stood, the dog extended toward me, silent to my questions, her eyes bulging nearly out of her head. I took a cursory look around, nodded, and bade her good night. Relatively speaking, however, I never fared as badly as another black male journalist. He went to nearby Waukegan, Illinois, a couple of summers ago to work on a story about a murderer who was born there. Mistaking the reporter for the killer, police hauled him from his car at gunpoint and but for his press credentials would probably have tried to book him. Such episodes are not uncommon. Black men trade tales like this all the time.

12   In "My Negro Problem—and Ours," Podhoretz writes that the hatred he feels for blacks makes itself known to him through a variety of avenues—one being his discomfort with that "special brand of paranoid touchiness" to which he says blacks are prone. No doubt he is speaking here of black men. In time, I learned to smother the rage I felt at so often being taken for a criminal. Not to do so would surely have led to madness—via that special "paranoid touchiness" that so annoyed Podhoretz at the time he wrote the essay.

13   I began to take precautions to make myself less threatening. I move about with care, particularly late in the evening. I give a wide berth to nervous people on subway platforms during the wee hours, particularly when I have exchanged business clothes for jeans. If I happen to be entering a building behind some people who appear skittish, I may walk by, letting them clear the lobby before I return, so as not to seem to be following them. I have been calm and extremely congenial on those rare occasions when I've been pulled over by the police.

14   And on late-evening constitutionals along streets less traveled by, I employ what has proved to be an excellent tension-reducing measure: I whistle melodies from Beethoven and Vivaldi and the more popular classical composers. Even steely New Yorkers hunching toward nighttime destinations seem to relax, and occasionally they even join in the tune. Virtually everybody seems to sense that a mugger wouldn't be warbling bright, sunny selections from Vivaldi's *Four Seasons.* It is my equivalent of the cowbell that hikers wear when they know they are in bear country.

Thinking Critically About Content

1. According to Staples, what reputation do African American men have?

2. When did the author become aware of this reputation?

3. What is Staples's opinion of "young thugs" (paragraph 8)? How did you come to this conclusion?

Thinking Critically About Purpose and Audience

4. What do you think Staples's purpose is in this essay?

5. Who do you think is Staples's primary audience?

6. Which of Staples's examples convince you that people are sometimes intimidated by African American men?

Thinking Critically About Paragraphs

7. What is the topic sentence of paragraph 3? Do all the sentences in that paragraph support that topic sentence? Explain your answer.

8. Staples begins his essay with the words "My first victim." What is he implying by these words? Is this an effective beginning? Explain your answer.

9. What is the organization of paragraph 9? Is this an effective order for these details? Explain your answer.

10. Write a paragraph using examples to explain one of your opinions about society today.

some sort. This is an effective beginning because readers wonder what Staples is talking about, which makes them want to read the rest of the essay.

9. Paragraph 9 is organized from general to particular. It is effective because readers want to understand more details about the topic sentence.

10. Answers will vary.

To keep track of your critical thinking progress, go to Appendix 1.

Writing Workshop

This final section gives you the opportunity to apply what you have learned in this chapter to another writing assignment. This time, we provide you with the guidelines only and let you go through your own writing process with occasional feedback from your peers. Refer to sections of the chapter as necessary until the process of producing a paragraph becomes automatic for you.

Guidelines for Writing an Illustration Paragraph

1. State your main point in your first sentence.
2. Choose examples that focus on the point you want to make.
3. Use a sufficient number of examples to make your point.
4. Organize your illustration so that your readers can easily follow along.

Writing About Your Reading

1. Contemporary American society rewards compulsive, fast-moving people. But some people just can't keep up for any number of reasons. Have you ever felt the way Lee says her mother feels in her essay? Discuss any similarities you see between yourself and Lee's mother.

ADDITIONAL WRITING TOPIC
Have your students expand the paragraphs they wrote on page 139 into well-developed essays.

TEACHING ON THE WEB
Discussion Topic: Divide students into groups of three or four, and have them discuss the many ways in which the Internet can help them succeed in college. Have them list specific examples and then share the examples with the other groups.

TEACHING ON THE WEB
Links: Find Web sites that use examples. How do these examples help Internet users understand the purpose of the Web site? Here are some possible sites:

Matrix of Examples WebQuests, webquest.org

Web site Authors,
authorsguild.org/news/
member_websites/a.html
Resume-Resource, resume-
resource.com

TEACHING ON THE WEB
Research: Give your
students a controversial
topic to research on the
Web (for example, funding
for the space program
or the value of bilingual
education), and have them
locate as many Web sites
as possible that advocate
either the pro or con side
of the issue. How do these
Web sites collectively show
students the usefulness of
illustration?

2. What are some of the main dangers on the streets in your hometown? What characterizes these dangers? How do you deal with them?

3. What do you think writers should consider first when choosing examples to support a topic sentence? Why are these criteria most important when working with examples?

Writing About Your World

Grant Taylor/Getty Images

1. Identify one of the themes in this collage. Then explain what you think the collection of pictures says about this theme.

2. Share with your classmates one of your opinions about the United States government, and use examples to explain it.

3. Use examples or illustrations to explain your observations on the increased interest in fitness among Americans.

4. Create your own illustration assignment (with the help of your instructor), and write a response to it.

Revising

Small Group Activity (5–10 minutes per writer) Working in groups of three or four, read your illustration papers to each other. Those listening should record their reactions on a copy of the Revising Peer Evaluation Forms in Appendix 4. After your group goes through this process, give your evaluation forms to the appropriate writers so that each writer has two or three peer comment sheets for revising.

Paired Activity (5 minutes per writer) Using the completed Peer Evaluation Forms, work in pairs to decide what you should revise. If time allows, rewrite some of your sentences, and have your partner check them.

Individual Activity Rewrite your paper, using the revising feedback you received from other students.

Editing

Paired Activity (5–10 minutes per writer) Swap papers with a classmate, and use Editing Peer Evaluation Form in Appendix 6 to identify as many grammar, punctuation, mechanics, and spelling errors as you can. If time allows, correct some of your errors, and have your partner check them. Record your grammar, punctuation, and mechanics errors in the Error Log (Appendix 7) and your spelling errors in the Spelling Log (Appendix 8).

Individual Activity Rewrite your paper again, using the editing feedback you received from other students.

Reflecting on Your Writing When you have completed your own paragraph, answer these six questions:

1. What was most difficult about this assignment?

2. What was easiest?

3. What did you learn about illustration by completing this assignment?

4. What do you think are the strengths of your illustration? Place a wavy line by the parts of your paragraph that you feel are very good.

5. What are the weaknesses, if any, of your paper? Place an X by the parts of your paragraph you would like help with. Write any questions you have in the margins.

6. What did you learn from this assignment about your own writing process—about preparing to write, about writing the first draft, about revising, and about editing?

9

Analyzing a Process

"Either write something worth reading or do something worth writing."

—BENJAMIN FRANKLIN

TEACHING PROCESS
ANALYSIS
Bring in a 5- to 10-minute
clip from a cooking show
that explains how to cook
a somewhat complicated
dish. Show the clip without
explaining what the
students will have to do.

After the clip has been
shown once, have students
write down the ingredients
and the exact recipe for
the dish they just watched
being made. Ask them
to explain the steps in
the correct order and to
be thorough and precise.
Don't let them look at
other students' lists.

After 8 to 10 minutes,
show the clip again. This
time, have the students
compare their directions
and see what steps they
omitted or put out of
order. Ask the students
how many of them got
everything exactly correct
(some will say they did),

Just visit any bookstore to find out how much we depend on process analysis in our daily lives. Books with such titles as the following have been on the best-seller lists for years.

- *How to Dress for Success;*
- *I Dare You! How to Stay Young Forever;*
- *How the West Was Won;*
- *Why We Love: The Nature and Chemistry of Romantic Love;*
- *How to Win Friends and Influence People;*
- *How to Make $1,000,000 in the Stock Market Automatically!*

When we **analyze a process,** we explain how to do something or how something happened. Process analysis involves explaining an activity or event according to what comes first, second, and so forth. Think about how often you try to do this. If you want to teach someone how to snowboard, if someone wants to know what caused John F. Kennedy Jr.'s plane to crash, if you're late for a class or for your job, if someone doesn't understand how a car engine works, what is the first thing you say? "Let me explain."

In "Playing to Win: Do You Think Like a Champ?" Coach Mike Shanahan of Super Bowl fame explains how to be a winner—on the field and in life. In other words, the author is analyzing a process. You have been reading how-to process analysis all your life in the form of instruction manuals, recipes, and directions for assembling products. In this paragraph, Shanahan provides an excellent example of how-to analysis.

> It's easy to become a winner if you're simply willing to learn from those who have been winners themselves. Find out who has had the most success at what they do. Watch their technique. Observe their methods. Study their behavior. By finding the best people in your industry, you'll learn what their routines are, the mistakes they made along the way, and the various scenarios they're forced to confront on a day-to-day basis. Then not only can you imitate their habits, but you can also imitate their results. It can be that easy.

You will refer to this sample again when you are learning the guidelines for writing a good process analysis paragraph.

MyWritingLab

Understanding Process Analysis

As you begin this chapter, let's make sure you understand all the important concepts connected with analyzing a process. First, go to **MyWritingLab.com,** and click on **Process** in the **Paragraph Development** module. Next, read the **Overview,** watch the **Animation** video, and complete the **Recall, Apply,** and **Write** activities. Finally, check your understanding of process analysis by taking the **Post-test.**

and explain to them how much we all take process analysis for granted. You can repeat the process with a history clip if you want to demonstrate both types of process analysis, but be sure to show the clips back to back, before revealing the assignment, so that students don't anticipate listing the steps.

Student Comment: "I like that when I mess up on a quiz I have the chance to re-take it and learn from my mistakes."

Now is the time to cover transitions with your students before they work on this topic.

PREPARING TO WRITE A PROCESS ANALYSIS PARAGRAPH

Reading process analysis essays critically involves understanding the steps of a process or sequence of an event and then going further to evaluate the steps or sequence. Are these steps the best way to create the final product or carry out the event? Would the results have been different with another approach? Dealing with this line of inquiry in both reading and writing will raise your level of thinking in all that you do.

First of all, you need to learn how to read critically. Having examined the "how-to-do-something" process analysis in the Shanahan paragraph, we're now going to look at another type of process analysis—how something works. First, you will apply a specific reading strategy to the paragraph. Next, you will answer some questions about the paragraph in an attempt to discover how it functions. With a clear understanding of your reading, you will understand more precisely how to write a process analysis paragraph.

For more detailed information on graphing ideas, see pages 18–19 in Chapter 2.

READING CRITICALLY
Graphing a Professional Paragraph

To understand their reading material and see how it works, students often find that making drawings of its ideas and details is much more effective than outlining. Graphic organizers, or concept maps, let you literally "draw" the relationship of ideas to one another. Figuring out what framework to use for this exercise is part of the process. You can make up a drawing of your own or do a Web search for "graphic organizers" to see some different options. For the following paragraph, show the relationship of the ideas to one another in a graphic form that makes sense to you. Be prepared to explain your drawings.

Reading Strategy

Reading a Process Analysis Paragraph

The example from eHow.com explains how the scheduling feature works on Facebook and Twitter. Draw a picture of the ideas in the paragraph, and see if you can understand the details well enough to explain the process to someone else. Then respond to the questions after the paragraph.

> If you use a Facebook Page to promote your business or band, you'll find scheduling is built right in. When you enter a new status or choose to upload a photo or video on a page you own, you see a clock icon below and to the left of the text box. Click it, and then choose the year, month, hour and minute you want the post to appear. Click "Schedule" to schedule your post. To view your scheduled posts, click the "Edit Page" button at the top of your page and choose "Use Activity Log."

Discovering How This Paragraph Works

To help you discover the elements that make this an effective process analysis paragraph so you can use them in your own writing, answer the following questions in as much detail as possible.

1. What process does this paragraph explain? Which sentence gives you this information?

   The first sentence tells us that this paragraph is about scheduling on a Facebook

   page.

2. Explain the process in your own words.

   Answers will vary.

   _____

   _____

3. If you don't understand the process, what else do you need to know?

   Answers will vary.

   _____

   _____

4. Is the information about this process in chronological order? What word clues tell you the author's method of organization?

   The words When and then highlight the chronological order.

   _____

   _____

WRITING A PROCESS ANALYSIS PARAGRAPH

Now that you have read and studied a process analysis paragraph, you will be writing one of your own. This section will help you generate a rough draft that you will then revise and edit in the third section of this chapter. It will guide you through a careful reading of the writing assignment, give you several ways to generate ideas, and finally furnish you with concrete guidelines for writing an effective process analysis paragraph. We encourage you to write notes and lists throughout this section so you can use them when you write a draft of your paragraph at the end of this section.

Reading the Prompt

The very first step in writing any good paragraph is making sure you understand the writing assignment or "prompt." An assignment attempts to "prompt" you to respond to a specific issue or question. The more clearly you understand the prompt, the better paragraph or essay you will create. Applying the chapter reading strategy to your writing assignment is a good way to accomplish this goal.

 Reading Strategy

READING CRITICALLY
Graphing the Prompt

Draw your version of the following writing prompt. What tasks do you need to complete? In what order will you address them? How are these tasks related to one another? In this case, you are not graphing the ideas for your paragraph, but the jobs you need to complete for the assignment. You can make up a drawing of your own or do a Web search for "graphic organizers" to see some options. Then, underline the key words in your drawing for completing this assignment.

Writing Prompt

 **Complete** this **Writing Prompt** at **mywritinglab.com**

Think of an activity that you enjoy or that you do well. Consider all the steps involved in this activity. Then write directions for someone else to follow. Some possible topics are how to change a tire, make a bed, get money from an ATM, keep a young child entertained, play pickup basketball, make chocolate chip cookies, change the oil in a car, relax after a stressful day, plan a surprise party, give a manicure, or cheer up a friend.

Thinking About the Prompt

What activities do you know well? Make a list of these activities. Which of these activities can you analyze? In what areas can you give people advice? Choose one of these activities to focus on in your paragraph, and use one or more of the prewriting strategies you learned in Chapter 3 to generate and record ideas about it.

Guidelines for Writing a Process Analysis Paragraph

Most process analysis essays fall into one of two categories. The first type tells *how to do something*, such as become a winner (Shanahan), change a tire, write an essay, or download an app. The second type clarifies *how something happened* or *how something works*, such as how scheduling works on Facebook, how Post-it Notes were created, how the Civil War started, how Bill Gates became a billionaire, how glasnost changed the Soviet Union, or how the heart pumps blood.

Explaining a process is often much easier in speech than in writing. Think about the last time you gave someone directions to get someplace. Your listener probably interrupted a couple of times to ask a question or clarify what you meant. ("If I pass Randall Road, have I gone too far?") Or perhaps you saw a confused look on the person's face, so you knew you had to re-explain or add information. ("Don't worry, you can count stoplights. Elm Street is the fifth stoplight.") In a conversation, you can rely not only on your words to communicate but also on the tone of your voice, the expression on your face, and the movements of your hands and body.

When you write, however, you don't have face-to-face contact, so your listener can't ask what you mean, and you don't have the chance to add information or clear up confusion along the way. You must therefore furnish all the steps in the exact order in which they must occur. Your job will be much easier if you follow the guidelines listed here. We will also refer to the paragraph by Mike Shanahan at the beginning of the chapter.

1. **State in the topic sentence what the reader should be able to do or understand by the end of the paragraph.** The topic sentence should give your readers a road map for what's to follow. They need to know where they're headed from the beginning of the paragraph. For example, a person giving directions might start by saying, "It's easy to get to Jeff's house from here." That introduces the task. You also want to try to make your topic sentence as interesting as possible. Look at the difference in these topic sentences for a paragraph about making a cup of coffee:

Topic Sentence 1: I am going to tell you how to make a really good cup of coffee.

Topic Sentence 2: Everyone can make coffee, but I have a secret for making the best cup of coffee you will ever taste.

In the Reading: Mike Shanahan's topic sentence says exactly what the readers will learn when they read his paragraph—how to become a winner. The rest of his paragraph explains how to achieve a winning edge.

In Your Writing: For the paragraph you are about to write, draft a clear topic sentence that tells the readers what they will be able to do or understand by the end of the paragraph. Make any changes in this sentence to clarify your statement as you develop your paragraph.

2. **Explain the rest of the process in the remainder of the paragraph.** By the end of a how-to paragraph, your reader should be able to perform the activity you are analyzing. In the how-something-works paragraph, the reader should be able to operate the device being discussed. And in the how-something-happened paragraph, the reader should understand more about a particular event.

The success of a process analysis paragraph depends to a great extent on how well you know your audience. Since you are giving them complete directions, you need to understand how much they already know about a process. Knowing your audience also helps you decide how much detail you need to include and which terms to define.

In the Reading: Shanahan's paragraph tells us how to be a winner in four easy steps:

a. Find out who has had the most success at what they do.

b. Watch their technique.

Logical/Mathematical

Have students list the steps people need to take to save a computer file to a disk. Suggest that the final draft of an important paper is on the disk and that one error would wipe it out. Have one person read the list while another demonstrates it.

Visual/Spatial

Have students watch a documentary to determine how something happened. How well did the documentary account for everything that occurred? Do students feel any gaps were present in the film?

Bodily/Kinesthetic

Put students in pairs, and blindfold one of the two. Have the blindfolded student tell the other student how to get from point A to point B while the other student follows the directions. Make sure students know that if, for instance, the blindfolded student gives the direction to walk through a doorway without saying to open the door, the other student cannot progress beyond the closed door. When the blindfolded student thinks the instructions are completed, have him or her remove the mask to discover where the fellow student actually ended up.

Intrapersonal

Have students think of the process they typically go through before they write a paper. Does this ritual ever change? What steps may be different from assignment to assignment?

Interpersonal

Divide students into groups of three or four. Have them list the steps to

c. Observe their methods.

d. Study their behavior.

He even tells us the results we can expect after following these steps.

In Your Writing: In preparation for your paragraph, list all the steps involved in doing the activity you have chosen to explain. You can explain how to do something, how something works, or how something happened. Following your topic sentence, prepare to take your readers step by step through the activity you have chosen to explain. In outlining your points, make sure you don't skip any necessary information.

3. **Organize your material in chronological order.** Your readers need to know what happens first, second, and so on in order to perform a task or understand a device or an event. This is why transitions such as *first*, *second*, and *then* are very common in process paragraphs. Most process analysis paragraphs are organized chronologically (according to a time sequence), with the explanation starting at one point and progressing step by step through the process, directions, or event.

Explaining every step of a process is very important. Suppose, for example, that you see these directions for preparing a frozen pizza:

> Preheat the oven to 425 degrees. If you like a crisp crust, put the pizza directly on the oven rack. If you prefer a soft crust, put the pizza on a cookie sheet. Bake for 20 minutes. Remove from the oven and enjoy.

Do you have all the information you need here to prepare a frozen pizza? What about the paper and the cardboard that just caught fire in the oven? The step after "Preheat the oven" should be "Remove all paper and cardboard from the pizza."

In the Reading: The guidelines in Shanahan's paragraph are in a loose chronological order. They move from identifying winners to studying their behavior. Shanahan uses no transitions with his guidelines. He simply writes them as commands. Near the end of his paragraph, he uses the word *then* to lead his readers into the final two sentences.

In Your Writing: Now put the items on your list in chronological order. Revise your list if any items are out of order, and add necessary information that will make your list clearer.

Writing a Draft of Your Paragraph

Now is the time to collect all your notes, your prewriting exercises, and your lists as you generate the first draft of your paragraph. You might want to review the professional essay, the writing assignment, and the chapter guidelines to help you write a draft of your paragraph. At this point, don't think about revising or editing; just get a rough draft of your ideas down on paper in response to the writing prompt.

MyWritingLab **Helpful Hints**

- **Can't figure out where to start?** Just coming up with ideas so you can start your paragraph is sometimes the most difficult task of all. **Prewriting** in **The Craft of Writing** module in **MyWritingLab** will give you several creative ways to approach your subject.
- **Having trouble developing your ideas?** Developing your ideas with specific examples helps your readers fully understand what you want to say. For help with this, go to **Developing and Organizing a Paragraph** in **The Craft of Writing** module in **MyWritingLab.**

REVISING AND EDITING

You are now ready to learn how to revise and edit. This section will guide you through the process of revising and editing process analysis paragraphs in reference to two writing samples: another student's paragraph and your own paragraph. Finding strengths and weaknesses in another person's writing is often much easier than evaluating your own, so you will be reviewing the chapter guidelines by revising and editing another student's writing before applying the same guidelines to your own writing.

Reading a Student Paragraph

At this point, we will once again use our chapter reading strategy. Following is a process analysis paragraph written by Victor Cantanzaro, a student. As you read it, notice when his paragraph tells you what he is explaining.

READING CRITICALLY
Graphing the Student Paragraph

See if you can follow Victor's steps as you read his first draft by making drawings of his ideas and details. After you read the paragraph, show the relationship of his ideas to one another in a coherent graphic form that makes sense to you. Be prepared to explain your drawing.

REVISING AND EDITING OPTIONS
Consider teaching revising and editing in a class discussion, in small groups, or in pairs.

Reading Strategy

CLASS ACTIVITY
On the board or overhead projector, show a how-to paragraph filled with jargon or technical terms. Ask the class to determine what is wrong with the paragraph.

Remind students to remember their audience and to be sure that their words are clear; for example, they should be careful not to tell a beginner scuba diver to "slowly ascend for the mandatory decompression safety stop." In this case, it's a matter of life and death.

¹You will be surprised to find out how furniture goes from the store to your door. ²First of all, most furniture stores hire independent trucking agencies to deliver their orders. ³These delivery services have to schedule their days very tightly so they can get as much furniture delivered per day as possible. ⁴Customers don't understand this idea. ⁵They go on errands and make life very difficult for the delivery service. ⁶Why can't they wait patiently for their furniture when they know it's coming? ⁷Then the driver's deliver the furniture in the order set by the computer. ⁸The drivers from the delivery service has to pick up the furniture at the furniture stores in reverse order so that the pieces of furniture they're going to deliver first is at the end of the truck. ⁹The drivers always call the customers once the days schedule is set. ¹⁰The weather outlook is a major part of packing the truck, because the furniture has to be covered with plastic, foam, or paper. ¹¹Depending on the conditions outside. ¹²The worst situation is customers who decide when the delivery truck arrives. ¹³That they don't want the furniture after all.

Revising and Editing the Student Paragraph

This paragraph is Victor's first draft, which now needs to be revised and edited. First, apply the following Revising Checklist to the content of Victor's draft. When you are satisfied that his ideas are fully developed and well organized, use the Editing Checklist to correct his grammar and mechanics errors. Answer the questions, and complete the tasks in each category. Then write your suggested changes directly on Victor's draft.

REVISING STRATEGIES
This chapter focuses on the following revising elements:

Topic sentence
Development
Unity
Organization
Coherence

Revising the Student Paragraph

TOPIC SENTENCE

✔ Does the topic sentence convey the paragraph's controlling idea?

✔ Does the topic sentence appear as the first or last sentence of the paragraph?

1. What is Victor's purpose in this paragraph?

   To explain how furniture is delivered to customers

2. Put brackets around Victor's topic sentence. Does it state his purpose?

   [You will be surprised to find out how furniture goes from the store to your door.] It could be clearer.

3. Write an alternate topic sentence.

   One possibility: Furniture delivery has to follow strict guidelines to work smoothly.

DEVELOPMENT

✔ Does the paragraph contain *specific* details that support the topic sentence?

✔ Does the paragraph include *enough* details to explain the topic sentence fully?

1. Do Victor's details explain the process of delivering furniture step by step?

   Yes

2. Where do you need more information?

   Answers will vary.

3. What new details can you add to Victor's paragraph to make his steps clearer?

   Answers will vary.

UNITY

✔ Do all the sentences in the paragraph support the topic sentence?

1. Read each of Victor's sentences with his topic sentence (revised, if necessary) in mind.

2. Cross out the three sentences that are not directly related to Victor's topic sentence.   *Sentences 4, 5, and 6*

ORGANIZATION

✔ Is the paragraph organized logically?

1. Read Victor's paragraph again to see if all the sentences are arranged logically.

2. List the general steps covered in this paragraph.

   independent trucks hired   *drivers deliver in order*

   drivers call customers   *weather determines packing*

   pick up in reverse order   *difficult customers cause problems*

3. Circle in item 2 the one step that is out of order.   *Drivers deliver in order.*

4. Renumber the sentences in chronological order.

COHERENCE

✔ Do the sentences move smoothly and logically from one to the next?

1. Circle three transitions Victor uses.   *Sentence 7 goes after sentence 11.*

For a list of transitions, see pages 59–60.

2. Explain how one of these transitions makes Victor's paragraph easier to read.

Answers will vary.

 Now rewrite Victor's paragraph with your revisions.

EDITING STRATEGIES
This chapter focuses on the following editing problems:
Fragments
Subject-verb agreement
Apostrophes (contractions)

Editing the Student Paragraph

SENTENCES

Subjects and Verbs

✔ Does each sentence have a main subject and verb?

For help with subjects and verbs, see Chapter 20.

1. Underline the subjects once and verbs twice in your revision of Victor's paragraph. Remember that sentences can have more than one subject-verb set.

2. Does each of Victor's sentences have at least one subject and verb that can stand alone?

No, not in the original paragraph.

For help with fragments, see Chapter 21.

3. Did you find and correct the two fragments in Victor's first draft? If not, find and correct them now. *Sentences 11 and 13*

Subject-Verb Agreement

✔ Do all subjects and verbs agree?

For help with subject-verb agreement, see Chapter 25.

1. Read aloud the subjects and verbs you underlined in your revision of Victor's paragraph.

2. Did you find and correct the two subjects and verbs that do not agree? If not, find and correct them now. *The drivers/has, the pieces/is (sentence 8)*

Pronoun Agreement

✔ Do all pronouns agree with their nouns?

For help with pronoun agreement, see Chapter 29.

1. Find any pronouns in your revision of Victor's paragraph that do not agree with their nouns. *All pronouns agree with their nouns in the original paragraph.*

2. Correct any pronouns that do not agree with their nouns.

Modifier Errors

✔ Are modifiers as close as possible to the words they modify?

1. Find any modifiers in your revision of Victor's paragraph that are not as close as possible to the words they modify. *There are no modifier errors in the original paragraph.*

2. Rewrite sentences if necessary so that the modifiers are as close as possible to the words they modify.

PUNCTUATION AND MECHANICS

Punctuation

✔ Are sentences punctuated correctly?

1. Read your revision of Victor's paragraph for any errors in punctuation.

2. Find the two fragments you revised, and make sure they are punctuated correctly.

3. Did you find and correct Victor's two apostrophe errors? If not, find and correct them now. *driver's (sentence 7), days (sentence 9)*

For help with punctuation, see Chapters 33–37.

Mechanics

✔ Are words capitalized properly?

1. Read your revision of Victor's paragraph for any errors in capitalization. *All capitals are correct in the original paragraph.*
2. Be sure to check Victor's capitalization in the fragments you revised.

For help with capitalization, see Chapter 38.

WORD CHOICE AND SPELLING

Word Choice

✔ Are words used correctly?

1. Find any words used incorrectly in your revision of Victor's paragraph. *All words are used correctly in the original paragraph.*
2. Correct any errors you find.

For help with confused words, see Chapter 44.

Spelling

✔ Are words spelled correctly?

1. Use spell-check and a dictionary to check the spelling in your revision of Victor's paragraph. *All words are spelled correctly in the original paragraph.*

2. Correct any misspelled words.

For help with spelling, see Chapter 45.

Now rewrite Victor's paragraph again with your editing corrections.

Reading Your Own Process Analysis Paragraph

Reading Strategy

Returning to the process analysis paragraph you wrote earlier in this chapter, you are now going to revise and edit your own writing. You will first read your paragraph with the same reading strategy you have applied to other reading tasks in this chapter so you can look at it as your reader might.

READING CRITICALLY
Graphing Your Own Paragraph

As you set out to revise and edit your own paragraph, apply to your writing the strategy you learned in this chapter for critical reading. Draw a picture of the relationship of your ideas to one another. In this way, you can check for logic and organization and make any changes that you think are necessary at this time.

Revising and Editing Your Own Paragraph

The checklists here will help you apply what you have learned in this chapter to your writing. First, revise your content so your thoughts are fully developed and effectively organized. Then turn to your grammar and usage.

For Revising Peer Evaluation Forms, go to Appendix 4.

Revising Your Own Paragraph

TOPIC SENTENCE

☐ Does the topic sentence convey the paragraph's controlling idea?

☐ Does the topic sentence appear as the first or last sentence of the paragraph?

1. What is your purpose in this paragraph?

   _____

2. Put brackets around your topic sentence. Does it state your purpose?

   _____

3. How can you change it if necessary to introduce all the stages of the activity you are analyzing?

   _____

DEVELOPMENT

☐ Does the paragraph contain *specific* details that support the topic sentence?

☐ Does the paragraph include *enough* details to explain the topic sentence fully?

1. Do the details in your paragraph explain step by step the activity you are discussing?

   _____

2. Where do you need more information?

_____

3. What details can you add to your paragraph to make your analysis clearer?

_____

UNITY

☐ Do all the sentences in the paragraph support the topic sentence?

1. Read each of your sentences with your topic sentence in mind.

2. Drop or rewrite any sentences that are not directly related to your topic sentence.

ORGANIZATION

☐ Is the paragraph organized logically?

1. Read your paragraph again to see if all the sentences are arranged in chronological order.

2. What word clues help your readers move logically through your paragraph?

COHERENCE

☐ Do the sentences move smoothly and logically from one to the next?

1. Circle three transitions you used.

2. Explain how one of these transitions makes your paragraph easier to read.

For a list of transitions, see pages 59–60.

_____

3. Add another transition to your paragraph to make it read more smoothly.

 Now rewrite your paragraph with your revisions.

Editing Your Own Paragraph

For Editing Peer Evaluation Forms, go to Appendix 6.

SENTENCES

Subjects and Verbs

☐ Does each sentence have a main subject and verb?

1. Underline the subjects once and verbs twice in your revised paragraph. Remember that sentences can have more than one subject-verb set.

For help with subjects and verbs, see Chapter 20.

2. Does each of your sentences have at least one subject and verb that can stand alone?

_____

For help with fragments, see Chapter 21.

For help with run-togethers, see Chapter 22.

3. Correct any fragments you have written.

4. Correct any run-together sentences you have written.

Subject-Verb Agreement

☐ Do all subjects and verbs agree?

For help with subject-verb agreement, see Chapter 25.

1. Read aloud the subjects and verbs you underlined in your revised paragraph.

2. Correct any subjects and verbs that do not agree.

Pronoun Agreement

☐ Do all pronouns agree with their nouns?

For help with pronoun agreement, see Chapter 29.

1. Find any pronouns in your revised paragraph that do not agree with their nouns.

2. Correct any pronouns that do not agree with their nouns.

Modifier Errors

✔ Are modifiers as close as possible to the words they modify?

For help with modifier errors, see Chapter 32.

1. Find any modifiers in your revised paragraph that are not as close as possible to the words they modify.

2. Rewrite sentences if necessary so that your modifiers are as close as possible to the words they modify.

PUNCTUATION AND MECHANICS

Punctuation

✔ Are sentences punctuated correctly?

For help with punctuation, see Chapters 33–37.

1. Read your revised paragraph for any errors in punctuation.

2. Make sure any fragments and run-together sentences you revised are punctuated correctly.

Mechanics

☐ Are words capitalized properly?

For help with capitalization, see Chapter 38.

1. Read your revised paragraph for any errors in capitalization.

2. Be sure to check your capitalization in any fragments or run-together sentences you revised.

WORD CHOICE AND SPELLING

Word Choice

✔ Are words used correctly?

1. Find any words used incorrectly in your revised paragraph.

2. Correct the errors you find.

For help with confused words, see Chapter 44.

Spelling

✔ Are words spelled correctly?

1. Use spell-check and a dictionary to check the spelling in your revised paragraph.

2. Correct any misspelled words.

For help with spelling, see Chapter 45

To make a personal log of your grammar/usage errors, go to Appendix 7.

 Now rewrite your paragraph again with your editing corrections.

To make a personal log of your spelling errors, go to Appendix 8.

 **More Helpful Hints**

- **Do you need some reminders about revising?** Process analysis paragraphs require strong transitions and excellent organization, so you need to pay special attention to these elements as you revise. Go to **Revising the Paragraph** in **The Craft of Writing** module in **MyWritingLab** for some helpful guidelines.

- **Need help finding words to explain your process?** An effective process analysis paragraph needs many carefully selected adverbs to explain to your reader *how, when, where, how often,* and *to what extent* your process works. Before you write, you can practice using these words when you go to **Adjectives and Adverbs** in the **Basic Grammar** module in **MyWritingLab.**

PRACTICING PROCESS ANALYSIS: FROM READING TO WRITING

This final section lets you practice the reading and writing skills you learned in this chapter. It includes two reading selections and several writing assignments on "your reading" and "your world." The section then offers guidance in peer evaluation and reflection, ending with suggestions about how to lead your instructor through your writing in ways that will benefit both of you.

Reading Workshop

The following essays explain different events or processes; in other words, they tell you how to do something or how something happened the way it did. The first, "Getting Out of Debt (and Staying Out)" by Julia Bourland, offers practical suggestions for getting and staying out of debt. It demonstrates how to do something. "Coming Over," by Russell Freedman, explains what people had to go through at Ellis Island to immigrate to the United States around the turn of the twentieth century. It demonstrates the how-something-happened process analysis. As you read, notice how the writers explain every step of the process carefully and completely.

GETTING OUT OF DEBT (AND STAYING OUT)
by Julia Bourland

SUMMARY
In this essay, Bourland explains how to avoid debt altogether or how to get out of debt and stay out.

READABILITY
(Flesch-Kincaid grade level)
10.5

INSTRUCTOR'S RESOURCE MANUAL
For additional teaching strategies, for journal entries, for vocabulary and reading quizzes, and for more writing assignments, see the *Instructor's Resource Manual*, Section II, Part II.

Focusing Your Attention

1. Think of a time when you had to explain to someone how to do something. Was it an easy or a difficult task? Did the person understand you? Was the person able to follow your directions?

2. In the process analysis essay you are about to read, the writer tells us how to manage money and control debt. Do you manage your money efficiently? Have you ever been in debt? Do you know how to avoid debt?

Expanding Your Vocabulary

The following words are important to your understanding of this essay. As you read, circle any words you don't know beyond this list. Then break into groups, and help each other figure out the meanings of these unknown words.

assumption: a claim (paragraph 1)

incurred: gained (paragraph 1)

deferring: putting off (paragraph 2)

vulnerable: capable of being hurt (paragraph 5)

meager: small (paragraph 8)

insatiable: unsatisfied (paragraph 8)

conscientious: careful (paragraph 8)

inundated: swamped (paragraph 8)

gingerly: with caution (paragraph 8)

diligent: hardworking (paragraph 9)

accrue: gain (paragraph 10)

amassed: gathered (paragraph 10)

uber-exorbitant: very extreme (paragraph 15)

READING CRITICALLY
Graphing Your Reading

As you learned at the beginning of this chapter, practice drawing graphic organizers for the ideas in this essay. Exchange "pictures" with someone in your class, and write a brief statement of what your classmate's drawing communicates to you.

GETTING OUT OF DEBT (AND STAYING OUT)[1]
by Julia Bourland

I'm going to make the bold assumption that you have incurred a little debt during your great entrance into adulthood, from either student loans, devilish credit cards, or that car loan you recently signed with its 36 easy installment payments. If you haven't tasted debt, you are abnormally perfect and un-American and can just skip on down to the next section on retirement planning and chill out until the rest of us catch up with you.

Some debt, such as student loans, is money well borrowed and an investment in your future. Because of their relatively low interest rates, manageable (though seemingly eternal) repayment plans, and reasonable deferment options, student loans should not be the source of midnight panic attacks during your second semester of senior year, even if you've incurred thousands and thousands of dollars to fund your education and still don't have a job that suggests that all the debt was worth it. If you haven't graduated yet, toward the end of your final semester, your college student loan officer will give you all the dirty details of your repayment schedule (hopefully armed with ample tissue for the tears that are certain to flood your contacts), as well as tell you how to defer paying back your loans if you aren't employed by the time your repayment grace period is up, as was my case. The cheery thing I discovered about deferring repayment is that the groovy government actually paid the interest I owed during my six-month deferment. That's not the case with all student loans, but you'll find that out when you start reading the fine print.

If you're like me, you may have several loans to repay. Again, you probably got (or will get) the skinny from your financial aid administrator at college, but in case he or she is on drugs, I'll summarize. There are a few consolidation plans that can make the whole process of paying back your loans less horrifying. Consolidating means that you will be able to merge all of your loans into one giant superloan that offers a low interest rate, as well as various options for shortening or lengthening your repayment schedule (which will increase or decrease the amount you owe each month, thereby

1

2

3

[1] Julia Bourland, "Getting Out of Debt (and Staying Out)" from *The Go-Girl Guide*, pp. 302–309. Copyright © 2000 by Julia Bourland. Reprinted by permission of The McGraw-Hill Companies, Inc.

increasing or decreasing the amount of interest you ultimately end up paying). But the best reason to consolidate your loans is that you will receive only one bill every month, which means you have to think and stress about all the student loan money you owe only once every 30 days! I highly recommend consolidation, if only for that.

4   If you have several loans from one financial institution, contact your lender directly about its consolidation options, or try these two programs: Federal Direct Consolidation Loan Program (800–557–7392; www.ed.gov/directloan) and Student Loan Marketing Association (a.k.a. Sallie Mae) Smart Loan Account (800–524–9100; www.salliemae.com).

5   Student loans are much less threatening and guilt-provoking than credit card debt, to which we 20-somethings are painfully vulnerable. There are so many things we want and need. Credit card companies seize upon our vulnerability, especially during college, sending us application after application with such enticing incentives as a *free water bottle, a two-pound bag of M&Ms, a 10% discount on first purchases, free checks* to spend anywhere we please, our very own *head shot* on the card, a *4.9% introductory interest rate,* and *bonus airline miles.* My first advice on the whole matter of credit card debt is to avoid it like the devil! I know many honest, smart girls who've become submerged in debt through the seductive power of plastic.

6   Our society once thrived without credit, so it *is* possible to stay out of debt as we begin our adult lives. But since you will probably experiment with credit despite the danger, memorize these eight guidelines compliments of those who've battled the plastic demons:

1. No Department Store Credit Cards

7   In-store credit usually carries a much higher interest rate than credit cards issued by banks. If you don't pay your debt back right away, what you buy is going to cost you much more than you bargained for. The only exception is if you have money to pay off your debt as soon as the bill arrives, and signing up for a card gives you a substantial discount on your first purchase. In these cases, get the card (and discount), pay your bill in full, and immediately cancel the card and shred it into a million pieces, lest you be tempted to use it again without the discount and money to pay for it. Note: If the discount isn't more than $10 or $20, don't even bother, because when you sign on, you'll probably get put on some annoying direct-mail list that will be sold to a bunch of trashy companies who will send you junk mail every single day.

2. One Card Only

8   The fewer little plastic rectangles you have, the less you'll be tempted to live beyond your meager means (and the fewer hysteria-provoking bills you'll receive). Ideally, you should use your card only for items that you know you can pay off with your next paycheck or for unavoidable emergencies, like getting new brakes for your clunker or fillings for your insatiable sweet tooth. The ideal cards have fixed annual percentage rates ranging from 9 to 12 percent, or less if you can find them, no annual fee, and a grace period that doesn't start charging interest on what you buy until the bill's due date. If you are a conscientious customer, you will be inundated with appealing offers for new cards boasting Platinum status and $25,000 credit lines.

ANSWERS TO
QUESTIONS

**Thinking Critically
About Content**

1. Bourland believes
    that student
    loan debts are
    worthwhile.

2. Here are Bourland's
    eight guidelines for
    avoiding credit card
    debt:

    1. No Department
        Store Credit
        Cards

        These have high
        interest rates
        and are only
        worthwhile if
        your discount is
        over $20.

    2. One Card Only

        Use one card
        for emergencies
        only.

    3. Use Your ATM
        Credit/Debit
        Card Instead

When you receive these, gingerly toss them into the recycling bin. Opening them will only lead you into trouble. There is one exception to this rule, but I'll get to that when we talk about transferring balances. First, a few more basic tips.

3. Use Your ATM Credit/Debit Card Instead

If you're diligent about balancing your checkbook, there's no reason to fear the credit card capabilities of your ATM card, which most banks are offering these days. Keep the receipt for whatever you purchase with your card as you would had you withdrawn money from the bank, and record the amount in your checkbook ledger as you would a check. Your debit card is just as convenient as a credit card, but your purchase won't accrue interest, which will save you money. Definitely use your debit card instead of a real credit card when grocery shopping or buying little things at the pharmacy, unless you like the idea of paying 18 percent interest on cereal and tampons. Trust your elders: the interest on all the little things makes them as costly as a raging girl's night out.

4. Pay Back as Much as You Can, as Soon as You Can

If we take the *minimum* payment request on our monthly statements to heart, we may not pay off our account in full until we qualify for social security. That's because interest continues to accrue on our balance each month. If we don't pay off everything we owe, the remainder plus the interest we've amassed will be charged interest the following month and the month after that, which means our balance continues to grow at the speed of our card's annual percentage rate (APR) despite the fact that we pay our minimum due every month and have hidden our credit card in the closet under five shoe boxes. That's how credit card companies make so much money and why we should avoid getting into debt in every humanly possible (but legal) way.

If you have debt from several sources, pay back whatever has higher interest rates first—usually your credit cards—then tackle the typically lower-rated student loan and car loan debts. If your credit card debt is spiraling out of control, you could refinance your student or car loans so that you will owe less on them each month, using the extra money to pay off your credit cards. Then, when your costlier debts have been paid off (and cards dumped in the nearest incinerator), you can designate all your funds to paying back your temporarily neglected student and car loans as quickly as you can.

5. Trash Those Credit Card Checks That Come with Your Statement, and Shun Cash Advances from the ATM

Both checks and cash advances will cost you dearly, since many card companies tack on an additional finance charge to your bill when you use them, plus impose an interest rate for the amount you borrow that's much higher than the rate you have for normal purchases. That means that if you withdraw $100 from your card at a bank or ATM or use one of those checks for your rent, you'll be paying back your credit card company a lot more than the amount you borrowed.

6. Switch to a Card with a Lower Interest Rate

I said earlier that you should throw away offers for additional credit cards, and that is a good rule unless you are carrying a balance on a card (or cards) with an

9

10

11

12

13

This card is used like a credit card, but the money is taken out of your checking account instead. Remember to keep receipts and balance your checkbook!

4. Pay Back as Much as You Can, as Soon as You Can

By your paying only the minimum each month, interest keeps adding up onto your bill. Also, pay off higher-interest cards first.

5. Trash Those Credit Card Checks That Come with Your Statement, and Shun Cash Advances from the ATM

If you take out cash advances from the ATM or use credit card checks, interest is added. Therefore, you are paying more than you originally took.

6. Switch to a Card with a Lower Interest Rate

Try to move your balance to a card with a lower interest rate so that you can cancel your higher-interest card.

7. Apply for a Secured Credit Card if Your Credit Is Screwed
   You can give an issuer a sum of money to get a credit card that gives you a specific amount of money to spend. This way you can prove your worthiness and raise your credit rating.

8. Check Your Credit Report
   You can check your credit report online or by phone for a minimal amount of money. This is important in case there are errors that must be fixed.

3. You can check your credit rating out on the phone or online through Experian, Equifax, or Trans Union.

Thinking Critically About Purpose and Audience

4. Bourland's purpose is to inform people about credit card debt and the measures they can take to avoid it.

5. Bourland's primary audience is young people just beginning to establish credit. Debt plays a big role in these people's lives in the form of school loan debt, first credit

---

outrageous interest rate, say more than 12 percent. In that case, it's a good financial move to transfer your balance(s) to one card with the lowest rate you can find. Some offer temporary introductory interest rates as low as 2.9 percent on all transferred balances; when you apply, make sure you note the expiration date for those low rates on your calendar, and have another card offer lined up and ready to take on the load when the time comes. I know this sounds tedious, but careful organization and diligence will save you money as you attempt to pay the whole balance off.

14   If you play credit card musical chairs, keep three things in mind. First, some balance transfer offers have associated fees or finance charges that aren't exactly highlighted in their promotions. Always inquire about transfer fees, and try to talk them out of it; many issuers are willing to waive the fees upon request. Second, even after you transfer your balance in full, the account remains open. To close it, you must officially cancel. The issuing bank won't automatically cancel a zero-balance account, so if you don't, your access to that credit line will remain on your credit report. That could be problematic later on when you're applying for a mortgage and have thousands of dollars worth of potential debt in your financial profile—something that makes lenders skittish. The other reason to cancel is to avoid the temptation to start using that clean slate of credit that your old card suddenly presents. And the third caveat: When you transfer your balance, do not use this new card to purchase new things. Declare it a debt repayment card only, and stick that shiny piece of plastic in the file where you keep your monthly statements. Here's why:

15   When you charge new items on a card that has adopted old debt, many card issuers apply a different (and uber-exorbitant) interest rate to those new purchases. The higher interest rate will remain on the amount of your new purchases until your entire debt has been repaid. Therefore, when you are trying to pay off a large debt, you should try to have two credit cards—one with a very low balance-transfer interest rate for your main debt and another with a reasonable interest rate on new purchases that you will use for emergencies only, since you are, after all, trying to get out of the hole, not rack up new debt. A good resource for finding low-rate, no-fee cards is a company called CardWeb.com, Inc., which publishes a newsletter called CardTrak that lists these desirable cards. You can access the newsletter and other credit card consumer information on its website (www.cardweb.com) or by calling (800) 344–7714.

7. Apply for a Secured Credit Card If Your Credit Is Screwed

16   If you have damaged your credit rating by defaulting on a loan or debt, your main priority (besides coming up with a repayment plan that suits all your creditors) is to rebuild your credit. Secured credit cards can help. You give the issuer a certain sum of money up front, which is kept in an account for you as a security deposit. Depending on the terms of your agreement, you can then charge a specified amount on that card. Once you've proved that you can repay your debts in this secured way, you may be offered a new card with real credit that doesn't require you to put up money ahead of time. CardWeb.com, Inc. (cited in the previous entry) can provide a list of secured credit cards as well as low-rate, no-fee cards.

17   If you are in a bad situation and creditors are calling you about monster debt that you can't currently pay off, don't pack up and move to North Dakota, thinking creditors

won't be able to find you—they will. A couple of nonprofit credit counseling organizations can help with debt-repayment planning assistance: Consumer Credit Counseling Services, associated with the National Foundation for Consumer Credit (800–388–2227; www.nfcc.org), and Debt Counselors of America (800–698–5182; www.dca.org).

8. Check Your Credit Report

I've already expounded on why a clean credit report is so important, so I won't beat that dead horse, but I will add that it's wise to check up on your report every now and then to make sure there are no surprises (or mistakes) that need mending. There are three agencies that compile credit reports, and they all get their information separately, so what one company says is part of your credit history may differ from what another company includes. You can get copies of your credit report from each company for $8 or less, depending on your state of residence. If you have had bad credit in the past but believe you've been exonerated (usually after seven years), you should make sure all three companies are showing you in the proper light.

The agencies keeping tabs are Experian (formerly TRW) (888–397–3742; www.experian.com/ecommerce/consumercredit.html); and Equifax (800–685–1111; www.econsumer.equifax.com).

Thinking Critically About Content

1. According to Bourland, what types of debt are worthwhile?

2. What are Bourland's eight guidelines for avoiding credit card debt? Summarize each guideline.

3. How can you check your credit rating?

Thinking Critically About Purpose and Audience

4. What do you think Bourland's purpose is in writing this essay?

5. Who do you think is Bourland's primary audience? Does debt play any part in their lives?

6. Which of Bourland's guidelines are most likely to help you now and in the future? Explain your answer.

Thinking Critically About Paragraphs

7. Summarize Bourland's essay. Make sure you cover all her main points.

8. Choose a paragraph from this essay, and explain why it is well developed.

9. How is the information in paragraph 3 organized? Why is this an effective order for this topic?

10. Write a paragraph trying to convince a bill collector that you will pay a specific overdue bill next month.

---

cards, car payments, and so on.

6. Answers will vary.

Thinking Critically About Paragraphs

7. Bourland discusses how to avoid and get out of debt. She begins by speaking about student loans and how they are "good" loans because they are investments in the future. Then she discusses her eight guidelines for staying out of debt. The eight points include tips such as keeping one credit card for emergencies only, using ATM Debit/Credit cards instead of a credit card, making larger monthly payments, as well as checking your credit report regularly. By following her eight steps, people can learn about and avoid debt.

8. Answers will vary.

9. Paragraph 3 is organized from general to particular. This is effective because Bourland is helping her readers understand consolidation with more specific details as the paragraph develops.

10. Answers will vary.

To keep track of your critical thinking progress, go to Appendix 1.

18

19

COMING OVER
by Russell Freedman

SUMMARY
Freedman depicts what immigrants encountered when they came to the United States around the turn of the twentieth century.

READABILITY
(Flesch-Kincaid grade level) 6.7

INSTRUCTOR'S RESOURCE MANUAL
For additional teaching strategies, for journal entries, for vocabulary and reading quizzes, and for more writing assignments, see the *Instructor's Resource Manual,* Section II, Part II.

Focusing Your Attention

1. If you could immigrate to another country, which one would you go to and why?

2. The following essay chronicles the experiences of Europeans trying to immigrate into the United States around 1900. Do you know any recent immigrants to the United States? What did they do to get into the United States? Was it a traumatic experience for them?

Expanding Your Vocabulary

The following words are important to your understanding of this essay. As you read, circle any words you don't know beyond this list. Then break into groups, and help each other figure out the meanings of these unknown words.

impoverished: poor (paragraph 1)

fervent: intense (paragraph 1)

narrows: a strait connecting two bodies of water (paragraph 6)

jabbered conversation: rapid talk that can't be understood (paragraph 6)

din: continuous noise (paragraph 6)

flustered: confused (paragraph 13)

indomitable: unable to be conquered (paragraph 15)

READING CRITICALLY
Graphing Your Reading

As you did with the previous essay, draw a graphic organizer for the ideas in the following essay. Make the drawing so accurate that someone could look at it and understand the basic concepts in the essay. Compare your drawing with someone else's in your class, and write a brief statement about the reading from your partner's graphic organizer.

COMING OVER[2]
by Russell Freedman

In the years around the turn of the [twentieth] century, immigration to America reached an all-time high. Between 1880 and 1920, 23 million immigrants arrived in the United States. They came mainly from countries of Europe, especially from impoverished towns and villages in southern and eastern Europe. The one thing they had in common was a fervent belief that in America life would be better.

1

Most of these immigrants were poor. Somehow they managed to scrape together enough money to pay for their passage to America. Many immigrant families arrived penniless. Others had to make the journey in stages. Often the father came first, found work, and sent for his family later. Immigrants usually crossed the Atlantic as steerage passengers. Reached by steep, slippery stairways, the steerage lay deep down in the hold of the ship. It was occupied by passengers paying the lowest fare.

2

Men, women, and children were packed into dark, foul-smelling compartments. They slept in narrow bunks stacked three high. They had no showers, no lounges, and no dining rooms. Food served from huge kettles was dished into dinner pails provided by the steamship company. Because steerage conditions were crowded and uncomfortable, passengers spent as much time as possible up on deck.

3

The voyage was an ordeal, but it was worth it. They were on their way to America.

4

The great majority of immigrants landed in New York City at America's busiest port. They never forgot their first glimpse of the Statue of Liberty.

5

Edward Corsi, who later became United States Commissioner of Immigration, was a 10-year-old Italian immigrant when he sailed into New York harbor in 1907:

6

> My first impression of the New World will always remain etched in my memory, particularly that hazy October morning when I first saw Ellis Island. The steamer *Florida,* fourteen days out of Naples, filled to capacity with 1600 natives of Italy, had weathered one of the worst storms in our captain's memory; and glad we were, both children and grown-ups, to leave the open sea and come at last through the Narrows into the Bay.
>
> My mother, my stepfather, my brother, Giuseppe, and my two sisters, Liberta and Helvetia, all of us together, happy that we had come through the storm safely, clustered on the foredeck for fear of separation and looked with wonder on this miraculous land of our dreams.

---

[2] From *Immigrant Kids* by Russell Freedman, copyright © 1980 by Russell Freedman. Used by permission of Dutton Children's Books, A Division of Penguin Young Readers Group, A Member of Penguin Group (USA) Inc., 345 Hudson Street, New York, NY 10014. All rights reserved.

Giuseppe and I held tightly to Stepfather's hands, while Liberta and Helvetia clung to Mother. Passengers all about us were crowding against the rail. Jabbered conversation, sharp cries, laughs and cheers—a steadily rising din filled the air. Mothers and fathers lifted up babies so that they too could see, off to the left, the Statue of Liberty....

Finally the *Florida* veered to the left, turning northward into the Hudson River, and now the incredible buildings of lower Manhattan came very close to us.

The officers of the ship...went striding up and down the decks shouting orders and directions and driving the immigrants before them. Scowling and gesturing, they pushed and pulled the passengers, herding us into separate groups as though we were animals. A few moments later we came to our dock, and the long journey was over.

7   But the journey was not yet over. Before they could be admitted to the United States, immigrants had to pass through Ellis Island, which became the nation's chief immigrant processing center in 1892. There they would be questioned and examined. Those who could not pass all the exams would be detained; some would be sent back to Europe. And so their arrival in America was filled with great anxiety. Among the immigrants, Ellis Island was known as "Heartbreak Island."

8   When their ship docked at a Hudson River pier, the immigrants had numbered identity tags pinned to their clothing. Then they were herded onto special ferryboats that carried them to Ellis Island. Officials hurried them along, shouting "Quick! Run! Hurry!" in half a dozen languages.

9   Filing into an enormous inspection hall, the immigrants formed long lines separated by iron railings that made the hall look like a great maze.

10   Now the examinations began. First, the immigrants were examined by two doctors of the United States Health Service. One doctor looked for physical and mental abnormalities. When a case aroused suspicion, the immigrant received a chalk mark on the right shoulder for further inspection: L for lameness, H for heart, X for mental defects, and so on.

11   The second doctor watched for contagious and infectious diseases. He looked especially for infections of the scalp and at the eyelids for symptoms of trachoma, a blinding disease. Since trachoma caused more than half of all medical detentions, this doctor was greatly feared. He stood directly in the immigrant's path. With a swift movement, he would grab the immigrant's eyelid, pull it up, and peer beneath it. If all was well, the immigrant was passed on.

12   Those who failed to get past both doctors had to undergo a more thorough medical exam. The others moved on to the registration clerk, who questioned them with the aid of an interpreter: What is your name? Your nationality? Your occupation? Can you read and write? Have you ever been in prison? How much money do you have with you? Where are you going?

13   Some immigrants were so flustered that they could not answer. They were allowed to sit and rest and try again.

14   About one immigrant out of every five or six was detained for additional examinations or questioning.

The writer Angelo Pellegrini has recalled his own family's detention at Ellis Island:

> We lived there for three days—Mother and we five children, the youngest of whom was three years old. Because of the rigorous physical examination that we had to submit to, particularly of the eyes, there was this terrible anxiety that one of us might be rejected. And if one of us was, what would the rest of the family do? My sister was indeed momentarily rejected; she had been so ill and had cried so much that her eyes were absolutely bloodshot, and Mother was told, "Well, we can't let her in." But fortunately, Mother was an indomitable spirit and finally made them understand that if her child had a few hours' rest and a little bite to eat, she would be all right. In the end we did get through.

Most immigrants passed through Ellis Island in about one day. Carrying all their worldly possessions, they left the examination hall and waited on the dock for the ferry that would take them to Manhattan, a mile away. Some of them still faced journeys overland before they reached their final destination. Others would head directly for the teeming immigrant neighborhoods of New York City.

Thinking Critically About Content

1. What common belief did the American immigrants share?

2. Make a chart of the stages of the immigration process in 1900, starting with receiving identity tags.

3. Why were families who wanted to move to the United States so anxious when they reached Ellis Island?

Thinking Critically About Purpose and Audience

4. What do you think is the purpose of this essay?

5. Who would be most interested in this essay?

6. Does the excerpt by Edward Corsi (paragraph 6) capture the excitement the new immigrants probably felt when they saw Ellis Island for the first time?

Thinking Critically About Paragraphs

7. Why do you think Freedman includes the paragraph written by Angelo Pellegrini (paragraph 15)? Do the details in this paragraph support its topic sentence? Explain your answer.

8. This essay has a number of well-chosen transitions in every paragraph to help move the readers through the author's ideas. Look closely at

15 3. They were afraid they would be rejected by one of the processes and would have to return to their country.

Thinking Critically About Purpose and Audience

4. The purpose of this essay is to inform readers of the hardships immigrants had to endure to enter the country.

16

5. A general audience would be interested in this essay, particularly readers who are descendents of immigrants.

6. Corsi's excerpt captures the excitement because he illustrates how happy and anxious they became at their first glimpses of Manhattan.

Thinking Critically About Paragraphs

7. Freedman includes the Pellegrini paragraph to give readers a firsthand account of the fear immigrants felt about passing the examinations. The details in this paragraph about his sister being temporarily rejected support its topic sentence.

8. Transitions include *Now, First,* and *When a case aroused suspicion.*

9. The topic sentence is "But the journey was not yet over." The remaining sentences support this sentence because they outline the rest of the process to get to Manhattan.

10. Answers will vary.

To keep track of your critical thinking progress, go to Appendix 1.

ADDITIONAL WRITING TOPIC
Let your students expand the paragraphs they wrote on page 166 into well-developed essays.

TEACHING ON THE WEB
Discussion Topic:
Divide students into groups of three or four, and have them discuss what life was like before the Internet. How did people formerly find maps, recipes, or general directions to make something work? How has the Internet revolutionized us in this way?

TEACHING ON THE WEB
Links: Have students find links to Web sites that sell how-to books and books about history. What three titles in each category sound most interesting to them?

Possible sites:

Amazon, amazon.com

Barnes & Noble, barnesandnoble.com

Waldenbooks, powells.com

paragraph 10, and underline three transition words or phrases. (Refer to pages 59–60 for information on transitions.)

9. What is the topic sentence of paragraph 7? Do all the sentences in that paragraph support this topic sentence? Explain your answer.

10. Pretend (if necessary) you and your family came to the United States from another country. Write a paragraph explaining the process you went through to get admitted to the country. If any members of your family actually went through the immigration process to be allowed into the United States, you might want to talk to them before you write.

Writing Workshop

This final section gives you the opportunity to apply what you have learned in this chapter to another writing assignment. This time, we provide you with the guidelines only and let you go through your own writing process with occasional feedback from your peers. Refer to sections of the chapter as necessary until the process of producing a paragraph becomes automatic for you.

 Guidelines for Writing a Process Analysis Paragraph

1. State in the topic sentence what the reader should be able to do or understand by the end of the paragraph.
2. Explain the rest of the process in the remainder of the paragraph.
3. Organize your material in chronological order.

Writing About Your Reading

1. In the first essay, Julia Bourland discusses debt as a normal part of life. Have you ever thought of debt in this way? Explain a process from your experience that is another normal part of life.

2. Think of something in life that you want as much as the Europeans described in Freedman's essay wanted to come to the United States. Then explain your plan for achieving this goal or accomplishing this mission you have set for yourself.

3. Which type of process analysis do you find more interesting—how-to essays or background explanations? Explain your answer.

Writing About Your World

Blend Images/Alamy

TEACHING ON THE WEB
Research: Have students
find Web sites that explain
how something happened.
Have them determine
whether all the steps are
present or if any were left
out. Ask them then to
explain how important each
step was to the process
analysis they found.

1. Place yourself in the photo above, and write a process analysis paragraph explaining the background, an event leading up to the picture, or
   an activity in the photograph. Be sure your explanation covers all steps
   or stages of the process you are discussing. Be sure that your topic sentence tells what the reader should know by the end of the paragraph.

2. Tell your classmates about a sport or hobby that you enjoy. Include
   what it takes to get started in this activity and what the satisfactions
   are. For example, how would a person get started playing the guitar, collecting stamps, or snowboarding? And what could it lead to?

3. Your college newspaper is running a special edition on study habits, and
   the editor has asked you to write an article explaining how you manage
   all the demands on your time, including studying, socializing, working,
   and keeping family obligations. Prepare your explanation for the next
   edition of the paper.

4. Create your own process analysis assignment (with the help of your instructor), and write a response to it.

Revising

Small Group Activity (5–10 minutes per writer) Working in groups
of three or four, read your process analysis papers to each other. Those
listening should record their reactions on a copy of the Revising Peer
Evaluation Forms in Appendix 4. After your group goes through this
process, give your evaluation forms to the appropriate writers so that
each writer has two or three peer comment sheets for revising.

Paired Activity (5 minutes per writer) Using the completed Peer Evaluation Forms as guides, work in pairs to decide what you should revise. If time allows, rewrite some of your sentences, and have your partner check them.

Individual Activity Rewrite your paper, using the revising feedback you received from other students.

Editing

Paired Activity (5–10 minutes per writer) Swap papers with a classmate, and use the Editing Peer Evaluation Form in Appendix 6 to identify as many grammar, punctuation, mechanics, and spelling errors as you can. If time allows, correct some of your errors, and have your partner check them. Record your grammar, punctuation, and mechanics errors in the Error Log (Appendix 7) and your spelling errors in the Spelling Log (Appendix 8).

Individual Activity Rewrite your paper again using the editing feedback you received from other students.

Reflecting on Your Writing   When you have completed your own paragraph, answer these six questions:

1. What was most difficult about this assignment?

2. What was easiest?

3. What did you learn about process analysis by completing this assignment?

4. What do you think are the strengths of your process analysis? Place a wavy line by the parts of your paragraph that you feel are very good.

5. What are the weaknesses, if any, of your paper? Place an X by the parts of your paragraph you would like help with. Write any questions you have in the margins.

6. What did you learn from this assignment about your own writing process—about preparing to write, about writing the first draft, about revising, and about editing?

Comparing and Contrasting

"Writing is a way of talking without being interrupted."

—JULES RENARD

We rely on comparison and contrast to make many decisions—both big and small—that affect our lives every day:

- What to have for breakfast;
- Where to go on vacation;
- Which college to attend;
- Whom to marry.

Actually, you are comparing and contrasting constantly. In fact, comparison and contrast are at the heart of our competitive society. When we are children, we compare our toys with our friends' toys and what we wear with how the in-group dresses. As we grow up, we learn that colleges award scholarships and coaches put together athletic teams by comparing our abilities with other students' abilities. Even after college, comparison and contrast are essential elements in our social and professional lives.

Comparison and contrast allow us to understand one subject by putting it next to another. **Comparing** involves discovering similarities; **contrasting** is based on finding differences. But comparison and contrast are generally considered part of the same process. As a result, the word *compare* is often used to refer to both techniques.

TEACHING COMPARISON AND CONTRAST
Divide students into four groups. Pass out to each group two pictures of artwork that are similar (possible pairs include Picasso's *Three Dancers* and Degas's *Prima Ballerina,* Monet's *River* and Cezanne's *L'Estaque,* El Greco's *Toledo in a Storm* and Curry's *Line Storm,* and Picasso's *Young Girl at the Mirror* and Whistler's *Little White Girl*).

Tell students to find the five most obvious similarities or differences (for example, Picasso's abstract art versus Degas's impressionistic work). Then have students find the 10 least obvious similarities and differences (for example, the walls running through both El Greco and Curry).

Allow approximately 15 minutes. Have a spokesperson for the group present both the obvious and less obvious comparisons and contrasts to the other groups.

When students finish their presentations, have a class discussion about how relatively easy it is to do this exercise because they can *see* the similarities and differences, even though some took longer to spot than others. Then discuss the correlation to writing: When writing comparison and contrast, students should be sure to look for what is obvious and what is not so obvious and then compare and contrast in a logical manner.

In the following paragraph, Shannon Brownlee uses humor to compare and contrast the behavior of preteens and teenagers. As you read, see if you can figure out Brownlee's purpose.

> One day, your child is a beautiful, charming 12-year-old, a kid who pops out of bed full of good cheer, clears the table without being asked, and brings home good grades from school. The next day, your child bursts into tears when you ask for the salt and listens to electronic music at maximum volume for hours on end. Chores? Forget it. Homework? There's little time, after talking to friends on the phone for five hours every night. Mornings? Your bluebird of happiness is flown, replaced by a groaning lump that can scarcely be roused for school. In short, your home is now inhabited by a teenager.

You will refer to this example again when you are learning the guidelines for writing a good comparison/contrast paragraph.

Student Comment: "Even though I 'exhausted' all my tries for this module four times, I wasn't frustrated with the program. It was patient in explaining the information to me, and I finally mastered it!"

For their work in this chapter, let your students know that different labels are sometimes used to describe the AAA, BBB method of organizing comparison/contrast paragraphs: "block style," "topic-by-topic," and "subject-by-subject."

MyWritingLab   ## Understanding Comparison/Contrast

To check your understanding of comparison and contrast, go to **MyWritingLab.com,** and click on **Comparing and Contrasting** in the **Paragraph Development** module. For this topic, read the **Overview,** watch the **Animation** video, and then complete the **Recall, Apply,** and **Write** activities. Finally, to check your mastery of this material, take the **Post-test.**

PREPARING TO WRITE A COMPARISON/CONTRAST PARAGRAPH

Looking closely at how a comparison/contrast paragraph works will improve your reading comprehension and transfer over time to your writing. Like two parts of a circle, the reading and writing processes function together and, as you learn how they operate, will serve you well in your college courses and in life.

To begin with, you need to learn how to read critically. Looking closely at a comparison/contrast example will help you understand your options for developing this type of paragraph. As you read, first you will apply a specific reading strategy to the paragraph. Then you will answer some questions about the paragraph to discover how it functions. With a detailed understanding of your reading, you will have more tools at your disposal in your writing.

For more detailed information on "peer teaching," see page 19 in Chapter 2.

READING CRITICALLY
Peer Teaching a Professional Paragraph

Teaching something to your peers is an excellent way to check your understanding. To practice this technique, the class must first divide the reading into parts—either by theme or by sentence count. The class members should then form groups representing each of these sections and choose one of the topics or sections. After identifying the main idea, the details, and their relationship to one another, each group teaches its material to the rest of the class. This strategy is called "peer teaching."

Reading a Comparison/Contrast Paragraph

 Reading Strategy

This paragraph, by Deborah Tannen, compares and contrasts the behavior of groups of boys and girls when they are young. Divide into two groups (one for each paragraph), and use peer teaching to explain each paragraph to the other group. Then work together to answer the questions that follow the paragraph.

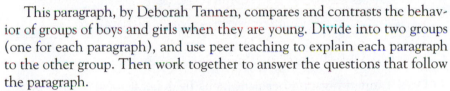

Anthropologists Daniel Maltz and Ruth Borker point out that boys and girls socialize differently. Little girls tend to play in small groups or, even more common, in pairs. Their social life usually centers around a best friend, and friendships are made, maintained, and broken by talk—especially "secrets." If a little girl tells her friend's secret to another little girl, she may find herself with a new best friend. The secrets themselves may or may not be important, but the fact of telling them is all-important. It's hard for newcomers to get into these tight groups, but anyone who is admitted is treated as an equal. Girls like to play cooperatively; if they can't cooperate, the group breaks up.

Little boys tend to play in larger groups, often outdoors, and they spend more time doing things than talking. It's easy for boys to get into the group, but not everyone is accepted as an equal. Once in the group, boys must jockey for their status in it. One of the most important ways they do this is through talk: verbal display such as telling stories and jokes, challenging and sidetracking the verbal displays of other boys, and withstanding other boys' challenges in order to maintain their own story—and status. Their talk is often competitive talk about who is best at what.

Discovering How This Paragraph Works

To help you discover the elements that make this an effective comparison/contrast paragraph so you can use them in your own writing, answer the following questions in as much detail as possible.

1. Although this excerpt is two paragraphs, they share a single topic sentence. What is their topic sentence?

   Boys and girls socialize differently.

2. What exactly is Tannen comparing or contrasting in this paragraph? List some of her main points under the topics below.

Girls	Boys
play in small groups or pairs	*play in larger groups, usually*
	outdoors
focus on best friend	*do things rather than talk*
can make and break friendships	*have open groups and unequal*
with secrets	*status*
socialize in tight groups and	*talk about competition*
have equal status	

3. Does Tannen organize her paragraphs by general topics or by specific points of comparison?

   By general topics

WRITING A COMPARISON/CONTRAST PARAGRAPH

Now that you have read and studied a comparison/contrast paragraph, you will be writing one of your own. This section will help you generate a rough draft that you will then revise and edit in the third section of this chapter. It will guide you through a careful reading of the writing assignment, give you several ways to generate ideas, and finally furnish you with concrete guidelines for writing an effective comparison/contrast paragraph. We encourage you to write notes and lists throughout this section so you can use them when you write a draft of your paragraph at the end of this section.

Reading Strategy

Reading the Prompt

The very first step in writing a good paragraph is making sure you understand the writing assignment or "prompt." An assignment attempts to "prompt" you to respond to a specific issue or question. The more clearly you understand the prompt, the better paragraph or essay you will create. Applying the chapter reading strategy to your writing assignment is a good way to accomplish this goal.

READING CRITICALLY
Peer Teaching the Prompt

Divide the writing assignment that follows into parts. Then assign a group of students to each part of the assignment you created. (This assignment would fall easily into three pieces.) Then each group should brainstorm and discuss the different ways to interpret and respond to their section of the prompt. After this discussion, a spokesperson from each group should summarize the group's discussion for the entire class. Everyone will benefit from understanding the various perspectives they now have on the details of this assignment and their relationship to one another. Write notes in the margins of the assignment as each group presents its findings.

Writing Prompt

⚙️ **Complete** this **Writing Prompt** at **mywritinglab.com**

Think of two individuals you know, such as two friends, two dates, two grandmothers, or two coworkers. How are they similar? How are they different? Write a paragraph comparing or contrasting these two people.

Thinking About the Prompt

Before you focus on a specific topic, you should generate as many ideas as you can so you have several to choose from. List some individuals that you might compare and contrast in your paragraph. Check the pairs that would be the best possibilities for producing a good comparison/contrast paragraph. Why are these pairs the best candidates for your paragraph? Choose one pair, and use one or more of the prewriting techniques you learned in Chapter 3 to generate and record as many thoughts as possible about these individuals.

PREWRITING EXERCISE
Create a cluster with the class's suggestions that compares and contrasts high school and college life. Show the class how clustering can work for this rhetorical mode.

Guidelines for Writing a Comparison/Contrast Paragraph

To write a good comparison/contrast paragraph, you need to focus on items that will lead to a specific point. The following guidelines will help you write a comparison/contrast paragraph. They refer to Brownlee's paragraph at the beginning of this chapter as an example.

1. **Decide what point you want to make with your comparison, and state it in your topic sentence.** All good comparisons have a point. You might be using comparison and contrast to reveal a team's strengths

TEACHING TIPS
The following eight teaching tips are based on Howard Gardner's list of multiple intelligences:

Verbal/Linguistic
Write a few sentences with approximately the same meaning but with variations in key words. For example, write the following three sentences:

My overworked girlfriend is frightened for her health, so she has decided to slow down.

My compulsive wife is afraid of heart disease, so she is resorting to group therapy.

My frantic old lady is about to expire, so she'd better regroup.

Have students compare and contrast the different meanings of these sentences. What are the connotations of each sentence? Could they all be said about the same type of woman under similar circumstances? What type of person is most likely to speak each sentence?

Musical/Rhythmic

Have students compare the same song or piece of music recorded by two separate artists. Have them compare and contrast the two and explain which version they prefer.

Logical/Mathematical

Provide students with prints from Escher that depict many different features at once. Have students compare and contrast the inconsistencies in each print against the others. Which one do they prefer?

Visual/Spatial

Have students visit a museum (in person or online) to look at various art periods. Have them compare and contrast the artwork in different periods to determine their favorite era. What made them ultimately choose this time period?

Bodily/Kinesthetic

Have students ride (or imagine riding) a bicycle for one mile and then ride

and weaknesses. Or you might be trying to find the best stereo system or the most durable camera. Whatever your purpose, the items you are comparing or contrasting should be stated clearly in your topic sentence along with your main point.

In the Reading: In Shannon Brownlee's paragraph, the author explains the normal transition from preteen to teenager by comparing the pleasant preteen behavior with that of the difficult teenager. The author saves her main idea for the last sentence, which ties together the entire paragraph.

In Your Writing: Think about the paragraph you are about to write, and draft a tentative topic sentence. Does this topic sentence include your main point and the topics you are comparing? What is your main point?

2. **Choose items to compare and contrast that will make your point most effectively.** To write a successful comparison, you should choose items from the same category. For example, you can compare two movies to make a point, but it would be difficult to compare a movie with a swimming pool and come to any sensible conclusion.

In the Reading: When you choose two items to compare, you might want to brainstorm a list of similarities and differences to see what patterns emerge. A common characteristic in this list will give your paragraph a focus. Brownlee's brainstorming might have looked something like the following:

Preteenager	Teenager
cheerful	sullen
communicates with parents	avoids parents, talks with friends
loves school	hates school, won't do homework
no emotional problems	bursts into tears without warning
responsible at home	avoids chores at home
looks forward to getting up	hates to get out of bed

In Your Writing: Now look at your prewriting notes, and add the features you are going to compare. Are the items you intend to compare from the same category? Is your list of features balanced, with the same number of details from each item? Should any other items be on the list? Should any items be deleted? Work on your list until you feel it is focused and complete.

3. **Organize your paragraph either by topics or by points of comparison.** When you are ready to write, you have to decide whether to organize your ideas by general topics or by specific points of comparison. Both methods are effective.

In the Reading: Brownlee's paragraph is organized by general topics—preteens and teens. First she talks about topic A, preteens; then she deals with topic B, teens. The result is a paragraph with the pattern AAAA, BBBB:

Topic by Topic

A	Preteen Emotions
A	Preteen Chores
A	Preteen Homework
A	Preteen Mornings
B	Teen Emotions
B	Teen Chores
B	Teen Homework
B	Teen Mornings

Brownlee could just as easily have organized her paragraph by specific points of comparison—emotions, chores, homework, and mornings. In this case, her outline would fall into the pattern AB, AB, AB, AB:

Point by Point

Emotions	A	Preteen Emotions
	B	Teen Emotions
Chores	A	Preteen Chores
	B	Teen Chores
Homework	A	Preteen Homework
	B	Teen Homework
Mornings	A	Preteen Mornings
	B	Teen Mornings

Notice that the same four qualities are covered in both the topical pattern (AAAA, BBBB) and the point-by-point pattern (AB, AB, AB, AB). If you mention one topic for one group, you should mention it for the other group. Also, in both patterns, the qualities should always be discussed in the same order. If emotions are first for one topic, they should be first for the second topic as well. Following the same order makes your comparison easy for your reader to follow.

In Your Writing: How do you plan to organize the details in your paragraph? Will they be grouped by general topics or specific points?

(or imagine riding) an indoor bike for one mile. How are these two relatively identical forms of exercise both similar and different?

Intrapersonal
Have students keep a journal for three days on a computer and for three days in a binder. Then ask if the choice of medium had any effect on their journal entries. Which medium did students prefer?

Interpersonal
Have students watch two different versions of a movie (for example, the two versions of *Freaky Friday, Dial M for Murder/A Perfect Murder*, or the two versions of *Ocean's Eleven*). Have them compare and contrast the two versions to determine which they think is the better film.

Naturalist
Have students think of their two favorite outdoor activities. If they had to choose one over the other, which one would they choose and why?

INSTRUCTOR'S RESOURCE MANUAL
For additional material about teaching comparison/contrast, for journal entries, and for various tests, see the *Instructor's Resource Manual*, Section II, Part II.

Which is the most effective order for what you are trying to accomplish? Revise your paragraph one more time, if necessary, so that its organization supports its purpose.

Writing a Draft of Your Paragraph

Now is the time to collect all your personal associations, notes, prewriting exercises, and lists as you generate the first draft of your paragraph. You might want to review the professional essay, the writing assignment, and the chapter guidelines to help you write a draft of your paragraph. At this point, don't think about revising or editing; just get a rough draft of your ideas down on paper in response to the writing prompt.

MyWritingLab **Helpful Hints**

- **Do you remember all the elements of the writing process?** You can review **The Writing Process** in **The Craft of Writing** module in **MyWritingLab.** This topic provides an overview of the process and explains how it can help you create a coherent paragraph.
- **Can't think of any examples for your paragraph?** Providing enough examples for the topic you're writing about is important because you want to prove your point to your reader. Go to **Illustrating** in the **Paragraph Development** module in **MyWritingLab** to help you learn how to come up with more examples.

REVISING AND EDITING OPTIONS
Consider teaching revising and editing in a class discussion, in small groups, or in pairs.

REVISING AND EDITING

You are now ready to learn how to revise and edit. This section will guide you through the process of revising and editing comparison/contrast paragraphs in reference to two writing samples: another student's paragraph and your own paragraph. Finding strengths and weaknesses in another person's writing is often much easier than evaluating your own, so you will be reviewing the chapter guidelines by revising and editing another student's writing before applying the same guidelines to your own writing.

Reading Strategy

Reading a Student Paragraph

Following is a comparison/contrast paragraph written by Nathalie Johnson, a college student. Her comparison identifies some real differences between two teachers. As you read, use peer teaching to make sure this comparison is clear to you.

READING CRITICALLY
Peer Teaching the Student Paragraph

Read Nathalie's paragraph, focusing on her purpose. Then think about how you will present her main point to your class in a creative way. Think of an approach to this task that no one else will pursue. You might also present your peer teaching ideas to each other in groups and then prepare a group presentation for the class. Take notes on the highlights of these presentations from your classmates. This strategy makes sure you understand the content of a paragraph well enough to present it to others. Write some notes to yourself in the margins before you discuss the paragraph as a class.

CLASS ACTIVITY
Ask the students to think of every instance they compared or contrasted during the past week. Write their examples on the board, trying to fill all available space. Prompt them when necessary. After the board is relatively full, point out that comparison and contrast are instinctive and will not be difficult to transfer into words.

[1]Ms. Tramel, my art teacher, and Mr. Morgan, my physics teacher, have two different approaches to their students. [2]Students eventually find out that even though Mr. Morgan doesn't smile much, he cares more about the students than they initially think he does. [3]When a student first meets Ms. Tramel, they think she is an easy teacher because she is so friendly. [4]Ms. Tramel encourages students to work hard on their own Mr. Morgan helps students study by giving them study questions and working with them outside of class. [5]I couldn't believe I got an A from Mr. Morgan. [6]He always helped me outside of class. [7]They both like their students a lot; however, Mr. Morgan doesn't smile as much as Ms. Tramel. [8]A student learns very quickly that both of these teachers will be there for them no matter what; even though the teachers express themselves in different ways.

Revising and Editing the Student Paragraph

This paragraph is Nathalie's first draft, which now needs to be revised and edited. First, apply the Revising Checklist that follows to the content of Nathalie's draft. When you are satisfied that her ideas are fully developed and well organized, use the Editing Checklist to correct her grammar and mechanics errors. Answer the questions, and complete the tasks in each category. Then write your suggested changes directly on Nathalie's draft.

Revising the Student Paragraph

TOPIC SENTENCE

✔ Does the topic sentence convey the paragraph's controlling idea?

✔ Does the topic sentence appear as the first or last sentence of the paragraph?

REVISING STRATEGIES
This chapter focuses on the following revising elements:
Topic sentence
Development
Unity

Organization
Coherence

1. What is the main point of Nathalie's paragraph?

   Teachers teach differently.

2. Put brackets around Nathalie's topic sentence. Does it introduce her main point?

   [Ms. Tramel, my art teacher, and Mr. Morgan, my physics teacher, have two different

   approaches to their students.] Not effectively

3. Write an alternate topic sentence.

   One possibility: Ms. Tramel, my art teacher, and Mr. Morgan, my physics teacher,

   approach their students differently but get similar results.

DEVELOPMENT

✔ Does the paragraph contain *specific* details that support the topic sentence?

✔ Does the paragraph include *enough* details to explain the topic sentence fully?

1. Does Nathalie compare the same qualities in both teachers?

   Yes

2. Where do you need more information?

   Answers will vary.

3. What specific details can you add to Nathalie's paragraph to make her comparison more effective?

   Answers will vary.

UNITY

✔ Do all the sentences in the paragraph support the topic sentence?

1. Read each of Nathalie's sentences with her topic sentence (revised, if necessary) in mind.

2. Cross out the two sentences that are not directly related to Nathalie's topic sentence.   *Sentences 5 and 6*

ORGANIZATION

✔ Is the paragraph organized logically?

1. Read Nathalie's paragraph again to see if all the sentences are arranged logically.

2. List some of the points Nathalie compares and contrasts in her paragraph in the order they appear.

Ms. Tramel	Mr. Morgan
first seems easy because she's	*doesn't smile much but cares*
so friendly	*about students*
encourages students to work on	*gives study questions, works with*
their own	*students outside class*
smiles more than Mr. Morgan	*doesn't smile much*
likes her students	*likes his students*

3. Is the paragraph organized by general topics or by specific points of comparison?

   By specific points of comparison

4. Move the one sentence that is out of order.   *Move sentence 2 after sentence 7.*

COHERENCE

✔ Do the sentences move smoothly and logically from one to the next?

1. Circle all of Nathalie's references to *teacher* or *teachers*.

2. Change two of these words to synonyms.

   Students might use mentors, instructors, or faculty as synonyms.

Editing the Student Paragraph

SENTENCES

Subjects and Verbs

✔ Does each sentence have a main subject and verb?

EDITING STRATEGIES
This chapter focuses on the following editing problems:

Run-togethers
Pronoun agreement
Semicolons

1. Underline Nathalie's subjects once and verbs twice. Remember that sentences can have more than one subject-verb set.

   For help with subjects and verbs, see Chapter 20.

2. Does each of Nathalie's sentences have at least one subject and verb that can stand alone?

   Yes, in the original paragraph

3. Did you find and correct Nathalie's run-together sentence? If not, find and correct it now.   *Sentence 4*

   For help with run-togethers, see Chapter 22.

Subject-Verb Agreement

✔ Do all subjects and verbs agree?

For help with subject-verb agreement, see Chapter 25.

1. Read aloud the subjects and verbs you underlined in your revision of Nathalie's paragraph.

2. Correct any subjects and verbs that do not agree. *All subjects and verbs agree in the original paragraph.*

Pronoun Agreement

✔ Do all pronouns agree with their nouns?

For help with pronoun agreement, see Chapter 29.

1. Find any pronouns in your revision of Nathalie's paragraph that do not agree with their nouns. *a student/they (sentence 3), a student/them (sentence 8)*

2. Did you find and correct the two pronouns that do not agree with their nouns? If not, find and correct them now. *a student/he or she, students/they; a student/him or her, students/them*

Modifier Errors

☐ Are modifiers as close as possible to the words they modify?

For help with modifier errors, see Chapter 32.

1. Find any modifiers in your revision of Nathalie's paragraph that are not as close as possible to the words they modify. *There are no modifier errors in the original paragraph.*

2. Rewrite sentences if necessary so that modifiers are as close as possible to the words they modify.

PUNCTUATION AND MECHANICS

Punctuation

☐ Are sentences punctuated correctly?

For help with punctuation, see Chapters 33–37.

1. Read your revision of Nathalie's paragraph for any errors in punctuation.

2. Find the run-together sentence you revised, and make sure it is punctuated correctly.

3. Did you find and correct Nathalie's semicolon error? If not, find and correct it now. *Sentence 8*

Mechanics

☐ Are words capitalized properly?

For help with capitalization, see Chapter 38.

1. Read your revision of Nathalie's paragraph for any errors in capitalization. *All capitals are correct in the original paragraph.*

2. Be sure to check Nathalie's capitalization in the run-together sentence you revised.

WORD CHOICE AND SPELLING

Word Choice

☐ Are words used correctly?

For help with confused words, see Chapter 44.

1. Find any words used incorrectly in your revision of Nathalie's paragraph. *All words are used correctly in the original paragraph.*

2. Correct any errors you find.

Spelling

☐ Are words spelled correctly?

1. Use spell-check and a dictionary to check the spelling in your revision of Nathalie's paragraph. *All words are spelled correctly in the original paragraph.*

2. Correct any misspelled words.

For help with spelling, see Chapter 45.

 Now rewrite Nathalie's paragraph again with your editing corrections.

Reading Your Own Comparison/ Contrast Paragraph

Reading Strategy

Returning to the comparison/contrast paragraph you wrote earlier in this chapter, revise and edit your own writing. You will first read your paragraph with the same reading strategy you have applied to other reading tasks in this chapter so you can look at it as your reader might.

READING CRITICALLY
Peer Teaching Your Own Paragraph

Once you have a draft, apply the chapter reading technique to your own writing. Divide yourselves into groups of three or four, swap paragraphs, and then "teach" someone else's paragraph to the group. Summarize the writer's main point, and then briefly explain the details and their relationship to the paragraph's main idea. Point out gaps and problems as you move from person to person.

Revising and Editing Your Own Paragraph

The checklists here will help you apply what you have learned in this chapter to your paragraph. First, consider your content, including development and organization. Then find and correct your grammar and usage errors.

Revising Your Own Paragraph

For Revising Peer Evaluation Forms, go to Appendix 4.

TOPIC SENTENCE

☐ Does the topic sentence convey the paragraph's controlling idea?

☐ Does the topic sentence appear as the first or last sentence of the paragraph?

1. What main point are you trying to make in your paragraph?

   _____

2. Put brackets around your topic sentence. Does it introduce your main point and your topics?

   _____

3. How can you change it if necessary to introduce your main point and your topics?

   _____

DEVELOPMENT

☐ Does the paragraph contain *specific* details that support the topic sentence?

☐ Does the paragraph include *enough* details to explain the topic sentence fully?

1. Do you cover the same characteristics of both topics?

   _____

2. Where do you need more information?

   _____

3. What specific details can you add to your paragraph to make your comparison more effective?

   _____

UNITY

☐ Do all the sentences in the paragraph support the topic sentence?

1. Read each of your sentences with your topic sentence in mind.

2. Drop or rewrite any sentences that are not directly related to your topic sentence.

ORGANIZATION

☐ Is the paragraph organized logically?

1. Is your paragraph organized by topics or by points of comparison?

   _____

2. Is the order you chose the most effective approach to your subject?

   _____

COHERENCE

☐ Do the sentences move smoothly and logically from one to the next?

1. Circle any words you repeat.

2. Should any of them be replaced with pronouns or synonyms?

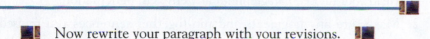 Now rewrite your paragraph with your revisions.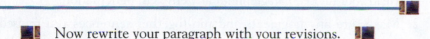

Editing Your Own Paragraph

For Editing Peer Evaluation Forms, go to Appendix 6.

SENTENCES

Subjects and Verbs

☐ Does each sentence have a main subject and verb?

1. Underline the subjects once and verbs twice in your revised paragraph. Remember that sentences can have more than one subject-verb set.

For help with subjects and verbs, see Chapter 20.

2. Does each of your sentences have at least one subject and verb that can stand alone?

3. Correct any fragments you have written.

4. Correct any run-together sentences you have written.

For help with fragments, see Chapter 21.

For help with run-togethers, see Chapter 22.

Subject-Verb Agreement

☐ Do all subjects and verbs agree?

1. Read aloud the subjects and verbs you underlined in your revised paragraph.

For help with subject-verb agreement, see Chapter 25.

2. Correct any subjects and verbs that do not agree.

Pronoun Agreement

☐ Do all pronouns agree with their nouns?

1. Find any pronouns in your revised paragraph that do not agree with their nouns.

For help with pronoun agreement, see Chapter 29.

2. Correct any pronouns that do not agree with their nouns.

Modifier Errors

☐ Are modifiers as close as possible to the words they modify?

1. Find any modifiers in your revised paragraph that are not as close as possible to the words they modify.

For help with modifier errors, see Chapter 32.

2. Rewrite sentences if necessary so that your modifiers are as close as possible to the words they modify.

PUNCTUATION AND MECHANICS

Punctuation
☐ Are sentences punctuated correctly?

For help with punctuation, see Chapters 33–37.

1. Read your revised paragraph for any errors in punctuation.
2. Make sure any fragments and run-together sentences you revised are punctuated correctly.

Mechanics
☐ Are words capitalized properly?

For help with capitalization, see Chapter 38.

1. Read your revised paragraph for any errors in capitalization.
2. Be sure to check your capitalization in any fragments or run-together sentences you revised.

WORD CHOICE AND SPELLING

Word Choice
☐ Are words used correctly?

For help with confused words, see Chapter 44.

1. Find any words used incorrectly in your revised paragraph.
2. Correct any errors you find.

Spelling
☐ Are words spelled correctly?

For help with spelling, see Chapter 45.

To make a personal log of your grammar/usage errors, go to Appendix 7.

1. Use spell-check and a dictionary to check your spelling.
2. Correct any misspelled words.

To make a personal log of your spelling errors, go to Appendix 8.

Now rewrite your paragraph again with your editing corrections.

MyWritingLab **More Helpful Hints**

- **Do you need some reminders about revising?** Comparison/contrast paragraphs require well-developed ideas and good sentence unity, so you need to pay special attention to these features as you revise. Go to **Revising the Paragraph** in **The Craft of Writing** module in **MyWritingLab** to get some help with these aspects of revising.

- **Do you sometimes get confused by *then* and *than*?** *Then* is used to show time passing. *Than* marks a comparison and is often used in comparison/contrast writing. For more help with *then/than* and other commonly confused words, see **Easily Confused Words** in the **Usage and Style** module in **MyWritingLab.**

PRACTICING COMPARISON/CONTRAST: FROM READING TO WRITING

This final section lets you practice the reading and writing skills you learned in this chapter. It includes two reading selections and several writing assignments on "your reading" and "your world." The section then offers guidance in peer evaluation and reflection, ending with suggestions about how to lead your instructor through your writing in ways that will benefit both of you.

Reading Workshop

Reading Strategy

The following essays show how comparison and contrast work in a complete essay. The first, "The Barrio" by Ernesto Galarza, is from his book *Barrio Boy*, which traces Galarza's move from Tepic, Mexico, to California. The second essay, "Why Men Fail" by David Brooks, compares and contrasts the performance of males and females in society today. As you read, notice how the writers make their points through well-thought-out, detailed comparisons and contrasts.

THE BARRIO
by Ernesto Galarza

Focusing Your Attention

1. Have you ever watched someone merge two cultures or tried to blend two cultures yourself? What are the advantages of merging cultures? What are the disadvantages?

2. In the essay you are about to read, the writer compares and contrasts various characteristics of American and Latin American life from the perspective of someone who has come to America for the first time. What do you think are some of the differences between these two cultures? Some of the similarities?

Expanding Your Vocabulary

The following words are important to your understanding of this essay. Start a vocabulary log of your own by recording any words you don't understand as you read. When you finish reading the essay, write down what you think the words mean. Then check your definitions in the dictionary.

barrio: Spanish-speaking neighborhood (title)

mercados: marketplaces (paragraph 1)

chiquihuite: basket (paragraph 1)

pilón: sugar candy (paragraph 1)

Mazatlán: a city in Mexico (paragraph 1)

SUMMARY
Galarza describes the Mexican culture surrounded by American customs in the Sacramento *barrio* by comparing it to life in Mazatlán.

READABILITY
(Flesch-Kincaid grade level)
10.1

INSTRUCTOR'S RESOURCE MANUAL
For additional teaching strategies, for journal entries, for vocabulary and reading quizzes, and for more writing assignments, see the *Instructor's Resource Manual,* Section II, Part II.

Judases: images of the disciple who betrayed Jesus (paragraph 2)

Holy Week: the week leading up to Easter (paragraph 2)

promenades: parades (paragraph 2)

plaza: public square (paragraph 2)

cathedral: large church (paragraph 2)

Palacio de Gobierno: town hall (paragraph 2)

vecindades: close-knit neighborhoods (paragraph 3)

mirth: fun, laughter (paragraph 4)

boisterous: noisy (paragraph 4)

compadre: godfather (paragraph 5)

comadre: godmother (paragraph 5)

cherubs: angels depicted as babies with wings (paragraph 5)

mica: a mineral (paragraph 5)

atole: a drink (paragraph 5)

corridos: songs (paragraph 5)

paddy wagon: police van (paragraph 6)

IOUs: debts (paragraph 8)

pochos: Mexicans living in the United States who grew up in the United States (paragraph 9)

chicanos: Mexicans living in the United States who grew up in Mexico (paragraph 9)

READING CRITICALLY
Peer Teaching Your Reading

As you learned at the beginning of this chapter, practice peer teaching by dividing the following essay into logical pieces and teaching it to each other. You could divide the essay into topics (Mexican and American) or sections (a certain number of paragraphs). Once you decide on the divisions, break the class up into just as many groups. Study your material as deeply as you can in the time allowed. Then teach it to the rest of the class.

THE BARRIO[1]
by Ernesto Galarza

We found the Americans as strange in their customs as they probably found us. Immediately we discovered that there were no *mercados* and that when shopping you did not put the groceries in a *chiquihuite*. Instead, everything was in cans or in cardboard boxes, or each item was put in a brown paper bag. There were neighborhood grocery stores at the corners and some big ones uptown, but no *mercado*. The grocers did not give children a *pilón,* and they did not stand at the door and coax you to come in and buy, as they did in Mazatlán. The fruits and vegetables were displayed on counters instead of being piled up on the floor. The stores smelled of fly spray and oiled floors, not of fresh pineapple and limes.

Neither was there a plaza, only parks which had no bandstands, no concerts every Thursday, no Judases exploding on Holy Week, and no promenades of boys going one way and girls the other. There were no parks in the *barrio,* and the ones uptown were cold and rainy in winter, and in summer there was no place to sit except on the grass. When there were celebrations, nobody set off rockets in the parks, much less on the street in front of your house to announce to the neighborhood that a wedding or a baptism was taking place. Sacramento did not have a *mercado* and a plaza with the cathedral to one side and the Palacio de Gobierno on another to make it obvious that there and nowhere else was the center of the town.

It was just as puzzling that the Americans did not live in *vecindades,* like our block on Leandro Valle. Even in the alleys, where people knew one another better, the houses were fenced apart, without central courts to wash clothes, talk, and play with the other children. Like the city, the Sacramento *barrio* did not have a place which was the middle of things for everyone.

In more personal ways, we had to get used to the Americans. They did not listen if you did not speak loudly, as they always did. In the Mexican style, people would know that you were enjoying their jokes tremendously if you merely smiled and shook a little, as if you were trying to swallow your mirth. In the American style, there was little difference between a laugh and a roar, and until you got used to them you could hardly tell whether the boisterous Americans were roaring mad or roaring happy.

The older people of the *barrio,* except in those things which they had to do like the Americans because they had no choice, remained Mexican. Their language at home was Spanish. They were continuously taking up collections to pay somebody's funeral expenses or to help someone who had had a serious accident. Cards were sent to you to attend a burial where you would throw a handful of dirt on top of the coffin and listen to tearful speeches at the graveside. At every baptism, a new *compadre* and a new *comadre* joined the family circle. New Year greeting cards were exchanged, showing angels and cherubs in bright colors sprinkled with grains of mica so that they glistened like gold dust. At the family parties, the huge pot of steaming tamales was still the center of attention, the *atole* served on the side with chunks of brown sugar for sucking and crunching. If the party lasted long enough, someone produced a guitar; the men took over and the singing of *corridos* began.

6   In the *barrio* there were no individuals who had official titles or who were otherwise recognized by everybody as important people. The reason must have been that there was no place in the public business of the city of Sacramento for the Mexican immigrants. We only rented a corner of the city and as long as we paid the rent on time everything else was decided at City Hall or the County Court House, where Mexicans went only when they were in trouble. Nobody from the *barrio* ever ran for mayor or city councilman. For us, the most important public officials were the policemen who walked their beats, stopped fights, and hauled drunks to jail in a paddy wagon we called *La Julia.*

7   The one institution we had that gave the *colonia* some kind of image was the *Comisión Honorífica,* a committee picked by the Mexican Consul in San Francisco to organize the celebration of the *Cinco de Mayo* and the Sixteenth of September, the anniversaries of the battle of Puebla and the beginning of our War of Independence. These were the two events which stirred everyone in the *barrio,* for what we were celebrating was not only the heroes of Mexico but also the feeling that we were still Mexicans ourselves. On these occasions, there was a dance preceded by speeches and a concert. For both the *cinco* and the sixteenth, queens were elected to preside over the ceremonies.

8   Between celebrations, neither the politicians uptown nor the *Comisión Honorífica* attended to the daily needs of the *barrio.* This was done by volunteers—the ones who knew enough English to interpret in court, on a visit to the doctor, a call at the county hospital, and who could help make out a postal money order. By the time I had finished the third grade at the Lincoln School, I was one of these volunteers. My services were not professional, but they were free, except for the IOU's I accumulated from families who always thanked me with "God will pay you for it."

9   My clients were not *pochos,* Mexicans who had grown up in California, probably had even been born in the United States. They had learned to speak English of sorts and could still speak Spanish, also of sorts. They knew much more about the Americans than we did and much less about us. The *chicanos* and the *pochos* had certain feelings about one another. Concerning the *pochos,* the *chicanos* suspected that they considered themselves too good for the *barrio* but were not, for some reason, good enough for the Americans. Toward the *chicanos,* the *pochos* acted superior, amused at our confusions but not especially interested in explaining them to us. In our family, when I forgot my manners, my mother would ask me if I was turning *pochito.*

10 Turning *pocho* was a half-step toward turning American. And America was all around us, in and out of the *barrio.* Abruptly we had to forget the ways of shopping in a *mercado* and learn those of shopping in a corner grocery or in a department store. The Americans paid no attention to the Sixteenth of September, but they made a great commotion about the Fourth of July. In Mazatlán, Don Salvador had told us, saluting and marching as he talked to our class, that the *Cinco de Mayo* was the most glorious date in human history. The Americans had not even heard about it.

ANSWERS TO QUESTIONS

Thinking Critically About Content

1. Answers will vary.
2. Answers will vary.
3. He is referring to a Mexican term, *pocho,* which is a Mexican "who had grown up in California" (para. 9), and he means that becoming a *pocho* was to give up part of the Mexican heritage to be Americanized.

Thinking Critically About Purpose and Audience

4. Galarza's purpose is to show his readers how life differs in Mazatlán and Sacramento and why he prefers the Mexican way of living.
5. Galarza's primary audience is Americans.
6. Galarza calls his essay "The Barrio" because he wants readers to understand that it is not

Thinking Critically About Content

1. Explain three differences between American and Latin American customs.

2. What difference between these customs is most interesting to you? Why?

3. What does Galarza mean when he says, "Turning *pocho* was a half-step toward turning American" (paragraph 10)?

Thinking Critically About Purpose and Audience

4. What is Galarza's purpose in writing this essay?

5. Who do you think is his primary audience?

6. Why does Galarza call his essay "The Barrio"? What is his point of view toward the *barrio*?

Thinking Critically About Paragraphs

7. Explain how the topic sentence works in paragraph 4. Does it supply the controlling idea for the entire paragraph?

8. Choose a paragraph from this essay, and underline all of its transitional words and phrases. Do these transitions help move the reader through the paragraph? Explain your answer. (Refer to pages 59–60 for information on transitions.)

9. Galarza sprinkles Spanish words throughout his essay. What effect does the addition of Spanish words have on the essay?

10. Write a paragraph responding to some of Galarza's observations. What are some of his confusions?

as nice a place to live as his neighborhood in Mazatlán. His point of view toward the *barrio* is that he wishes it could be more like life in Mexico.

Thinking Critically About Paragraphs

7. The topic sentence works by providing the controlling idea that Galarza had to get used to Americans on a personal level, and all the supporting sentences illustrate this point.

8. Answers will vary.

9. The inclusion of Spanish words throughout the essay helps merge the Mexican and American cultures, illustrating what is happening in his actual life.

10. Answers will vary.

To keep track of your critical thinking progress, go to Appendix 1.

WHY MEN FAIL
by David Brooks

Focusing Your Attention

1. What differences between males and females do you find most obvious?

2. In the essay you are about to read, the author explains why females succeed in the world today at a higher rate than males. What evidence of this observation do you see in your immediate environment?

Expanding Your Vocabulary

The following words are important to your understanding of this essay. Start a vocabulary log of your own by recording any words you

SUMMARY
In this essay, Brooks cites some of the ways in which females are bypassing males in the world of work today, along with some of the results that are occurring.

READABILITY
(Flesch-Kincaid grade level)
8.8

INSTRUCTOR'S
RESOURCE MANUAL
For additional teaching
strategies, for journal
entries, for vocabulary and
reading quizzes, and for
more writing assignments,
see the *Instructor's
Resource Manual,*
Section II, Part II.

don't understand as you read. When you finish reading the essay, write down what you think the words mean. Then check your definitions in the dictionary.

median: average (paragraph 4)

dominate: control (paragraph 5)

neurological: related to the nervous system (paragraph 6)

genetic: hereditary (paragraph 6)

posits: proposes (paragraph 7)

adaptability: flexibility (paragraph 7)

mores: traditions (paragraph 7)

innate: inborn (paragraph 8)

immune to: unaffected by (paragraph 9)

pioneering: trying out (paragraph 10)

resiliently: easily (paragraph 11)

adhered to: followed (paragraph 13)

ideologies: beliefs (paragraph 13)

preconceptions: expectations (paragraph 13)

Achilles: Greek hero in the Trojan War (paragraph 14)

imposing: forcing (paragraph 14)

Odysseus: Greek hero known for his resourcefulness (paragraph 14)

sojourner: traveler (paragraph 14)

READING CRITICALLY
Peer Teaching Your Reading

As you did with the previous reading, divide the following reading into logical pieces and teach it to each other in class. You could divide the essay into topics (males and females) or sections (a certain number of paragraphs). Once you decide on the divisions, break the class up into just as many groups. Study your material as deeply as you can in the time allowed. Then teach it to the rest of the class.

WHY MEN FAIL[2]
by David Brooks

1   You're probably aware of the basic trends. The financial rewards to education have increased over the past few decades, but men failed to get the memo.

2   In elementary and high school, male academic performance is lagging. Boys earn three-quarters of the D's and F's. By college, men are clearly behind. Only 40 percent of bachelor's degrees go to men, along with 40 percent of master's degrees.

3   Thanks to their lower skills, men are dropping out of the labor force. In 1954, 96 percent of the American men between the ages of 25 and 54 worked. Today, that number is down to 80 percent. In Friday's jobs report, male labor force participation reached an all-time low.

4   Millions of men are collecting disability. Even many of those who do have a job are doing poorly. According to Michael Greenstone of the Hamilton Project, annual earnings for median prime-age males have dropped by 28 percent over the past 40 years.

5   Men still dominate the tippy-top of the corporate ladder because many women take time off to raise children, but women lead or are gaining nearly everywhere else. Women in their 20s outearn men in their 20s. Twelve out of the 15 fastest-growing professions are dominated by women.

6   Over the years, many of us have embraced a certain theory to explain men's economic decline. It is that the information-age economy rewards traits that, for neurological and cultural reasons, women are more likely to possess. To succeed today, you have to be able to sit still and focus attention in school at an early age. You have to be emotionally sensitive and aware of context. You have to communicate smoothly. For genetic and cultural reasons, many men stink at these tasks.

7   But, in her fascinating new book, "The End of Men," Hanna Rosin posits a different theory. It has to do with adaptability. Women, Rosin argues, are like immigrants who have moved to a new country. They see a new social context, and they flexibly adapt to new circumstances. Men are like immigrants who have physically moved to a new country but who have kept their minds in the old one. They speak the old language. They follow the old mores. Men are more likely to be rigid; women are more fluid.

8   This theory has less to do with innate traits and more to do with social position. When there's big social change, the people who were on the top of the old order are bound to cling to the old ways. The people who were on the bottom are bound to experience a burst of energy. They're going to explore their new surroundings more enthusiastically.

---

[2] http://www.nytimes.com/2012/09/11/opinion/brooks-why-men-fail.html?ref=davidbrooks&pagewanted=print

ANSWERS TO QUESTIONS

Thinking Critically About Content

1. Brooks compares the ways men and women have adapted to the current economy, citing evidence that suggests that women have adapted more effectively to recent economic and cultural changes.

2. Answers will vary.

3. Brooks means that men must adapt

to the economic
changes in the
world. He compares
men to Odysseus
from Greek my-
thology, who had
to adjust to the
changes in his
homeland of Ithaca
upon his return
from a twenty-year
journey.

**Thinking Critically
About Purpose and
Audience**

4. Brooks's purpose
is to explain to the
readers what men
must do to suc-
ceed in the work
world by comparing
the recent suc-
cess of women to
the recent failures
of men.

5. The target audience
is young adult men
entering the work
world.

6. Answers will vary.

**Thinking Critically
About Paragraphs**

7. Brooks cites the
findings of a study
by the National
Federation of
Independent
Business that show
that women are
more likely than
men to experience
financial success af-
ter getting divorces
and entering new
workplaces.

8. The sentences
develop the control-
ling idea in the topic
sentence, explaining
how working-class
women in Alabama
are exploring new

9   Rosin reports from working-class Alabama. The women she meets are flooding into new jobs and new opportunities—going back to college, pursuing new careers. The men are waiting around for the jobs that left and are never coming back. They are strangely immune to new options. In the Auburn-Opelika region, the median female income is 140 percent of the median male income.

10   Rosin also reports from college campuses where women are pioneering new social arrangements. The usual story is that men are exploiting the new campus hookup culture in order to get plenty of sex without romantic commitments. Rosin argues that, in fact, women support the hookup culture. It allows them to have sex and fun without any time-consuming distractions from their careers. Like new immigrants, women are desperate to rise, and they embrace social and sexual rules that give them the freedom to focus on their professional lives.

11   Rosin is not saying that women are winners in a global gender war or that they are doing super simply because men are doing worse. She's just saying women are adapting to today's economy more flexibly and resiliently than men. There's a lot of evidence to support her case.

12   A study by the National Federation of Independent Business found that small businesses owned by women outperformed male-owned small businesses during the last recession. In finance, women who switch firms are more likely to see their performance improve, whereas men are more likely to see theirs decline. There's even evidence that women are better able to adjust to divorce. Today, more women than men see their incomes rise by 25 percent after a marital breakup.

13   Forty years ago, men and women adhered to certain ideologies, what it meant to be a man or a woman. Young women today, Rosin argues, are more like clean slates, having abandoned both feminist and prefeminist preconceptions. Men still adhere to the masculinity rules, which limits their vision and their movement.

14   If she's right, then men will have to be less like Achilles, imposing their will on the world, and more like Odysseus, the crafty, many-sided sojourner. They'll have to acknowledge that they are strangers in a strange land.

Thinking Critically About Content

1. What is the main idea that David Brooks presents in this essay?

2. Do you see any evidence of Brooks's points about men and women in your community?

3. What do you think Brooks means when he says, "They'll have to acknowledge that they are strangers in a strange land" (paragraph 14)?

Thinking Critically About Purpose and Audience

4. Why do you think Brooks wrote this essay?

5. Who would be most interested in this essay?

6. How does this essay make you feel about men and women in general?

Thinking Critically About Paragraphs

7. What examples does Brooks use in paragraph 12 to explain his topic sentence? Do these examples get his point across in this paragraph?

8. If a paragraph is unified, all of its sentences refer to the idea expressed in the topic sentence. In paragraph 9, three sentences follow the topic sentence. How do these three sentences relate to the paragraph's topic sentence?

9. Brooks begins his essay with a direct statement to his readers: "You're probably aware of the basic trends." Is this an effective beginning for this essay? Explain your answer.

10. Write a paragraph exploring another comparison or contrast about men and women.

Writing Workshop

This final section gives you the opportunity to apply what you have learned in this chapter to another writing assignment. This time, we provide you with the guidelines only and let you go through your own writing process with occasional feedback from your peers. Refer to sections of the chapter as necessary until the process of producing a paragraph becomes automatic for you.

Guidelines for Writing a Comparison/ Contrast Paragraph

1. State the point you want to make with your comparison in your topic sentence.
2. Choose items to compare and contrast that will make your point most effectively.
3. Organize your paragraph either by topics or by points of comparison.

Writing About Your Reading

1. In the first essay, Ernesto Galarza talks about the differences he sees on a daily basis between two cultures. Compare and contrast your family's rituals and practices with those of another family.

2. Expand the comparison you wrote in response to question 10 after David Brooks's essay.

3. What process do you have to go through to come up with an interesting comparison or contrast? How is it different from the process you go through for other rhetorical modes?

job openings while men are limiting their opportunities.

9. The statement acknowledges the readers' awareness of the economic challenges that men face, but it also suggests that the readers may not be able to explain the current situation.

10. Answers will vary.

To keep track of your critical thinking progress, go to Appendix 1.

ADDITIONAL WRITING TOPIC
Let your students expand the paragraphs they wrote on page 196 into well-developed essays.

TEACHING ON THE WEB
Discussion Topic: Divide students into groups of three or four. Ask them to compare and contrast email and regular mail. In what circumstances is one better than the other? What are the disadvantages of both?

TEACHING ON THE WEB
Links: Provide students with a topic, and have them link to three Web sites that deal with that topic. How are these sites similar in their treatment of the topic? How are they different? Possible sites for the topic *sports:*
National Basketball Association, nba.com
National Football League, nfl.com
Professional Golf Association, pga.com

TEACHING ON THE WEB
Research: Have students find Web sites that sell the same type of products. How are these sites similar, and how are they different? Which product would students buy based on the Web sites? How did comparison and contrast help them come to this decision?

Writing About Your World

Bill Bachmann/PhotoEdit and Evans/Three Lions/Getty Images

1. Explain the similarities and differences in these pictures. How can one place be so different and yet the same?

2. Discuss the similarities and differences between your high school life and your college life. Are your classes more difficult? Do you still hang out with your friends from high school? Are you treated differently by your parents, school officials, or old classmates? Have your expectations of yourself changed? Do you now have to juggle school and work?

3. You have been hired by your local newspaper to compare and contrast various aspects of daily life. For example, you might compare two musical groups, good drivers and bad drivers, two malls, or two kinds of pets. Decide on the point you want to make before you begin writing.

4. Create your own comparison/contrast assignment (with the help of your instructor), and write a response to it.

Revising

Small Group Activity (5–10 minutes per writer) Working in groups of three or four, read your comparison/contrast papers to each other. Those listening should record their reactions on a copy of the Revising Peer Evaluation Forms in Appendix 4. After your group goes through this process, give your evaluation forms to the appropriate writers so that each writer has two or three peer comment sheets for revising.

Paired Activity (5 minutes per writer) Using the completed Peer Evaluation Forms, work in pairs to decide what you should revise. If time allows, rewrite some of your sentences, and have your partner check them.

Individual Activity Rewrite your paper, using the revising feedback you received from other students.

Editing

Paired Activity (5–10 minutes per writer) Swap papers with a classmate, and use the Editing Peer Evaluation Form in Appendix 6 to identify as many grammar, punctuation, mechanics, and spelling errors as you can. If time allows, correct some of your errors, and have your partner check them. Record your grammar, punctuation, and mechanics errors in the Error Log (Appendix 7) and your spelling errors in the Spelling Log (Appendix 8).

Individual Activity Rewrite your paper again using the editing feedback you received from other students.

Reflecting on Your Writing When you have completed your own paragraph, answer these six questions:

1. What was most difficult about this assignment?

2. What was easiest?

3. What did you learn about comparison/contrast by completing this assignment?

4. What do you think are the strengths of your comparison/contrast? Place a wavy line by the parts of your paragraph that you feel are very good.

5. What are the weaknesses, if any, of your paper? Place an X by the parts of your paragraph you would like help with. Write any questions you have in the margins.

6. What did you learn from this assignment about your own writing process—about preparing to write, about writing the first draft, about revising, and about editing?

11

Dividing and Classifying

"The most valuable of all talents is that of never using two words when one will do."

—THOMAS JEFFERSON

Dividing and classifying play important roles in our daily lives. Think of how we all organize our environment:

- Our coursework is separated into different binders and notebooks;
- The names in our address book are divided alphabetically;
- Our shirts, socks, and sweaters all get their own bureau drawers;
- Our garden supplies and household tools have separate locations in the garage.

In fact, division and classification come so naturally to us that we sometimes aren't even aware we are using them. Imagine going to a grocery store that doesn't group its merchandise logically: Dairy products wouldn't be together; salad dressings might be randomly scattered throughout the store; some breakfast foods could be in the deli section—and who knows where the rest might be? The result would be total chaos, and finding what you were looking for would be frustrating and time consuming.

Dividing and classifying are actually mirror images of each other. **Dividing** is sorting into smaller categories, and **classifying** is grouping into larger categories. Division moves from one category to many, while classifying moves in the opposite direction, from many categories to one. For example, the general category of food can be divided or sorted into soups, salads, dairy products, beef, chicken, and so on. In like manner, soups, salads, dairy products, beef, and chicken can be grouped into the single category of food. To classify, you need to find the common trait that all the items share.

Here is a paragraph from *Entrepreneur* magazine that is based on division and classification. Written by Debra Phillips, the essay, "Tween Beat," puts the youngest consumers into three categories to discuss their buying power. Notice how division and classification work together in this paragraph.

In his widely hailed research on child-age consumers, author and Texas A&M University marketing professor James McNeal points out that there's not one but three different children's markets. First and foremost, there's the market created by kids' direct spending. Second, there's the market stemming from kids' influence over their family's purchases. Finally, there's the market of the future—that is, courting kids to eventually become loyal adult consumers. With so much at stake, it's easy to see why so many eyes are on the tween-age kids of the baby boomers. They are the present; they are also the future.

You will refer to this passage again when you are learning the guidelines for writing a good division/classification paragraph.

MyWritingLab   Understanding Division/Classification

To make sure you have a good understanding of dividing and classifying, go to **MyWritingLab.com,** and click on **Division/Classification** in the **Paragraph Development** module. At this point, read the **Overview,** watch the **Animation** video, and complete the **Recall, Apply,** and **Write** activities. Then check your understanding of this topic by taking the **Post-test.**

PREPARING TO WRITE A DIVISION/CLASSIFICATION PARAGRAPH

Learning how to read division/classification paragraphs critically will help you become a better writer. As you see how a paragraph is constructed and how a topic is developed in this mode, you will be able to apply what you discover to your own writing. Reading and writing in any mode are demanding, but they are both necessary for success in college and in life.

To begin with, you need to learn how to read this type of paragraph critically. An example will help you understand more clearly the choices you have to make when you write division/classification paragraphs. As you read, you will apply a specific reading strategy to the passage. Then, you will answer some questions about the paragraph in an attempt to discover

Then put one group's smaller categories on the board (division), and have the class as a whole put them into larger categories (classification). In this way, students can understand the dual functions of this mode.

Student Comment:
"I admit it. I'm a crammer. I memorize information before a test, and I don't remember anything 10 minutes later. **MyWritingLab** doesn't make me feel the pressure to memorize the info. I can 'cheat' at any time and watch the video."

Students often find this topic difficult because it requires more critical and analytical thinking than some of the other modes. Before having students work on this topic in **MyWritingLab,** consider having a class discussion about dividing and classifying before students go to **MyWritingLab.**

how it functions. With a complete understanding of your reading, you will have more features to choose from in your own writing.

For more detailed information on summarizing, see pages 19–20 in Chapter 2.

READING CRITICALLY
Summarizing a Professional Paragraph

As you read more difficult selections, the ability to summarize is essential. A summary features the main ideas of a selection in a coherent paragraph. First, identify the main ideas in your reading; then fold them into a paragraph with logical transitions so your sentences flow from one to another. After you write a summary of the following selection, draft one question for discussion that comes from your summary.

Reading Strategy

Reading a Division/Classification Paragraph

In this sample paragraph, author Sarah Hodgson divides dogs' personalities into five categories and explains each. As you read it, locate her five categories. Then write a summary and a discussion question based on your understanding of the paragraph. Finally answer the questions after the paragraph.

Some people may think that only humans have a real personality. Anyone who has ever had a dog knows better. Dogs, like us, have their own personalities. Some are extremely funny. I call this rowdy bunch *The Comedians.* They can be frustrating as heck, constantly dancing on the edge of good behavior. But in your most serious or sad moments, they'll make you laugh. Then we have *The Eager Beavers,* the dogs many of us dream of. They'll do anything that warrants approval. Sounds fantastic, but they'll be bad, too, if that gets attention, so even the Eager Beavers can find themselves on the "B" list if their owners aren't careful. There are also *The Sweet Peas* of the planet, quiet souls who prefer the sidelines over the spotlight. Taking the sweet thing a step too far are those dogs who are *Truly Timid.* Almost anything will freak them out. Poor creatures, they require a lot of understanding. And then there is *The Boss.* This fellow thinks a little too highly of himself. He needs lots of training to tame his egotism. Take a look at where your dog fits in, because like us, they all learn differently!

Discovering How This Paragraph Works

To help you recognize the elements that make this an effective division/classification paragraph so you can use them in your own writing, answer the following questions in as much detail as possible.

1. This paragraph doesn't simply classify the personalities of dogs for its own sake. It has a broader message. What is Hodgson's general purpose in this paragraph?

   Dogs have personalities that can be classified, much like humans.

2. Does this paragraph use both division and classification?

   Yes

   When does Hodgson move from one to many (division)? From many to one (classification)?

   Division: *Dogs can be divided into five types.*

   Classification: *Many dogs fit into each category.*

3. Different methods of organization work well with different topics. How is this paragraph organized? (See Chapter 3 for more information on organization.)

   From one extreme to another—from funny to serious

WRITING A DIVISION/CLASSIFICATION PARAGRAPH

Now that you have read and studied a division/classification paragraph, you will be writing one of your own. This section will help you generate a rough draft that you will then revise and edit in the third section of this chapter. It will guide you through a careful reading of the writing assignment, give you several ways to generate ideas, and finally furnish you with concrete guidelines for writing an effective division/classification paragraph. We encourage you to write notes and lists throughout this section so you can use them when you write a draft of your paragraph at the end of this section.

Reading the Prompt

Reading Strategy

The first step in writing a good paragraph is making sure you understand the writing assignment or "prompt." An assignment attempts to "prompt" you to respond to a specific issue or question. The more clearly you understand the prompt, the better paper you will create. Applying the chapter reading strategy to your writing assignment is a good way to accomplish this goal.

READING CRITICALLY
Summarizing the Prompt

Put the following writing assignment in your own words. What are the main tasks of this prompt? How are they related to one another? Write out your understanding of the prompt; then exchange papers with two other classmates so you can read other versions of the assignment. Finally, revise your statement to include anything you learned from the statements you read.

Writing Prompt    **Complete** this **Writing Prompt** at **mywritinglab.com**

We all have lots of friends, and we naturally divide them into categories, whether we realize it or not. We have close friends, acquaintances, out-of-town friends, etc. What categories do your friends fall into? Write a paragraph that introduces your categories and then explains why specific friends fit into each category. The guidelines below will help you get started on your paragraph.

PREWRITING EXERCISE
Put students into pairs, and have them discuss the different categories their friends might fall into. Then have the class discuss some of these categories.

Thinking About the Prompt

Before you focus on a specific topic, you should generate as many ideas as you can so you have several to choose from. List the names of as many friends as you can think of. Next, put these names in groups according to how you think about them. Finally, label the groups based on the type of friendship you have with the names in the group. Use one or more of the prewriting techniques you learned in Chapter 3 to generate and record as many thoughts as possible about your categories.

TEACHING TIPS
The following eight teaching tips are based on Howard Gardner's list of multiple intelligences:

Verbal/Linguistic
Provide students with four very limited categories, and ask them to determine how many classifications the categories can fall into. For example, show students how "8-lb. 6-oz., 21-in. baby girl" might fall into the classifications *family, children, siblings,*

Guidelines for Writing a Division/Classification Paragraph

To write a division/classification paragraph, keep in mind that the same items can be divided and classified many different ways. No two kitchens are exactly alike, and your friends probably don't organize their closets the same way you do. Methods of organizing schoolwork also vary from person to person. Similarly, in writing, you can divide and classify a topic differently, but following the guidelines listed here will help you create an effective division/classification paragraph. The paragraph at the beginning of this chapter by Debra Phillips serves as an example.

1. **Decide on your purpose for writing, and include it in your topic sentence.** Dividing and classifying are not very interesting in themselves

unless you are trying to make a point. In other words, division and classification should be the means of communicating a coherent message. This message is the heart of your topic sentence.

In the Reading: In Debra Phillips's paragraph on "tweens," for example, Phillips uses division and classification to show that the younger generation affects the economy more than most people realize. She does so by using James McNeal's division of child consumers into three categories—direct spending, influences on family buying, and future consumers.

In Your Writing: In response to your writing assignment, what will be the purpose of your paragraph? Draft a tentative topic sentence that clearly states your purpose. You will then revise your topic sentence as you develop the details of your paragraph.

2. **Divide your topic into categories (division); explain each category with details and examples (classification).** Since division and classification are so closely related, you will often use both of them in a single paragraph. In fact, each one actually helps explain the other. When you choose examples, remember that they must share a common trait. You should not, for instance, classify cars on the basis of safety features and use air bags, antilock brakes, and leather seats as your examples because leather seats have nothing to do with safety.

In the Reading: In her paragraph, Debra Phillips uses a combination of division and classification. She establishes three categories for her topic (division) and then explains how children fit into these categories (classification). All the examples share a common trait—they all refer to types of buying markets.

In Your Writing: Do your examples on your prewriting list share a common trait? Do they explain your purpose? Adjust your categories and/or lists of examples so they will support your main point.

3. **Organize your categories so that they help you communicate your message clearly.** Being logical is really the only requirement for organizing a division/classification paragraph. You want to move smoothly from one category to another with transitions that help your readers understand your reasoning.

In the Reading: The paragraph on child consumers is organized according to the degree of influence children have on the buying market. Phillips's first category is a small market of children's direct purchases. This market is certainly not as large as the group of children who influence their parents' purchases. Finally, in the future, when these children are grown, they will have enormous buying power of their own. So Phillips's categories move from small to large and from present to future.

population, budget, and so on.

Musical/Rhythmic

Have students divide *contemporary music* into categories and subcategories. How can these categories help someone understand the music of today?

Logical/Mathematical

Provide students with an abundance of related words that can be divided into three levels of specificity. Then have students figure out the main category, subdivisions that stem from this main category, and sub-subdivisions that stem from the subcategories. For example, use *university* as one level; *College of Arts, College of Business,* and *College of Sciences* as a second level; and *English, sociology, history, finance, accounting, management, mathematics, biology,* and *psychology* as a third level.

Visual/Spatial

Bring a good selection of magazines to class. Have students divide the magazines into logical categories. How many categories can students generate? How many magazines fit into more than one category?

Bodily/Kinesthetic

Blindfold students, one at a time, and ask them to identify the categories of obvious objects you place in their hands. For example, you might have an orange, a pencil, an apple, a banana, a paper clip, and a stapler for students to identify as either *fruit* or *office supplies.*

Intrapersonal

Have students classify the way they spend their time on any given day. If *work,* school, and *family* are classifications they use, have them further divide their day to determine how they spend their time.

Interpersonal

Have students classify the different groups of people they deal with in a typical day. How many categories do the people fall into?

Naturalist

Have students find as many types of trees and flowers as possible on your campus. How many varieties are there? Can they be classified or divided into other groups?

INSTRUCTOR'S RESOURCE MANUAL For additional material about teaching division/ classification, for journal entries, and for various tests, see the *Instructor's Resource Manual,* Section II, Part II.

In Your Writing: How will you organize the points you want to make? Which type of friends will you talk about first? Which will be second and third? Think through your method of organization before you write a draft of your paragraph.

Writing a Draft of Your Paragraph

Now is the time to collect all your summaries, your notes, your prewriting exercises, and your lists as you generate the first draft of your paragraph. You might want to review the professional essay, the writing assignment, and the chapter guidelines to help you write a draft of your paragraph. At this point, don't think about revising or editing; just get a rough draft of your ideas down on paper in response to the writing prompt.

MyWritingLab **Helpful Hints**

- **Trying to make your point clear to the reader?** Division and classification paragraphs often rely on good description of the subjects discussed. For help with description, visit **Describing** in the **Paragraph Development** module in **MyWritingLab.**
- **Not sure if your paragraph has a topic sentence?** Topic sentences are the controlling ideas of your paragraphs. If you need assistance with these important sentences, see **Topic Sentences** in **The Craft of Writing** module in **MyWritingLab.**

REVISING AND EDITING OPTIONS Consider teaching revising and editing in a class discussion, in small groups, or in pairs.

REVISING AND EDITING

You are now ready to learn how to revise and edit. This section will guide you through the process of revising and editing division/classification paragraphs in reference to two writing samples: another student's paragraph and your own paragraph. Finding strengths and weaknesses in another person's writing is often much easier than evaluating your own, so you will be reviewing the chapter guidelines by revising and editing another student's writing before applying the same guidelines to your own writing.

Reading Strategy

Reading a Student Paragraph

Here is a division/classification paragraph written by LaKesha Montgomery. Her paragraph focuses on the different types of interior decorators she has come across in her experience. Can you figure out when she is using division and when she is using classification?

READING CRITICALLY
Summarizing the Student Paragraph

On your first reading of LaKesha's paragraph, underline her main point. During your second reading, note in the margins the ideas that support her main idea. Then write a summary in a coherent paragraph of your own words with logical transitions so your sentences flow from one another. Finally, draft one question for discussion that comes from your summary.

CLASS ACTIVITY
Have the students in your class agree on several types of friends, dividing this general topic into categories. Then discuss how, when the process of division is reversed, all the categories or divisions they created make up the larger classification of friends.

[1]I learned that interior decorators really fall into three different categories. [2]I also found out that they work hard after decorating my new apartment. [3]First is an interior decorator who specializes in residences. [4]This person has to work closely with people and try to get into there lifestyles. [5]So that he or she can help the customer make decisions. [6]The next type of interior decorator sells estate furniture. [7]He or she works in an upscale store called a gallery. [8]His or her main responsibility is to acquire all kinds of merchandise from estate sales and than sell it to those people who our interested in these more valuable pieces. [9]I certainly wasn't in this category. [10]I don't even know how I learned about this type of interior decorator. [11]Some interior decorators specialize in office décor. [12]They enjoy working with exotic schemes. [13]And making peoples stark office space come alive.

Revising and Editing the Student Paragraph

This paragraph is LaKesha's first draft, which now needs to be revised and edited. First, apply the following Revising Checklist to the content of LaKesha's draft. When you are satisfied that her ideas are fully developed and well organized, use the Editing Checklist to correct her grammar and mechanics errors. Answer the questions, and complete the tasks in each category. Then write your suggested changes directly on LaKesha's draft.

Revising the Student Paragraph

TOPIC SENTENCE

✔ Does the topic sentence convey the paragraph's controlling idea?

✔ Does the topic sentence appear as the first or last sentence of the paragraph?

REVISING STRATEGIES
This chapter focuses on the following revising elements:
Topic sentence
Development
Unity

Organization
Coherence

1. What general message is LaKesha trying to communicate in this paragraph?

   There are three types of interior decorators.

2. Put brackets around LaKesha's topic sentence. Does it capture her main point?

   [I learned that interior decorators really fall into three different categories.]

   Almost

3. Expand LaKesha's topic sentence.

   One possibility: Interior decorators fall into three categories based on different

   responsibilities.

DEVELOPMENT

✔ Does the paragraph contain *specific* details that support the topic sentence?

✔ Does the paragraph include *enough* details to explain the topic sentence fully?

1. Do the details in the paragraph describe all three types of interior decorators?

   Yes

2. Where do you need more information?

   Answers will vary.

3. Add a closing sentence to LaKesha's paragraph.

   Answers will vary.

UNITY

✔ Do all the sentences in the paragraph support the topic sentence?

1. Read each of LaKesha's sentences with her topic sentence (revised, if necessary) in mind.

2. Cross out the two sentences that are not directly related to LaKesha's topic sentence.   *Sentences 9 and 10*

ORGANIZATION

✔ Is the paragraph organized logically?

1. Read LaKesha's paragraph again to see if all the sentences are arranged logically.

2. List the main categories LaKesha explains in this paragraph.

   residence décor

   estate furniture

   office décor

3. Move the one category that seems to be out of order.   *Switch categories 2 and 3.*

4. Identify LaKesha's method of organization:

   From one extreme to another

COHERENCE

✔ Do the sentences move smoothly and logically from one to the next?

1. Circle three transitions, repetitions, synonyms, or pronouns LaKesha uses.   *Answers will vary.*

   For a list of transitions, see pages 59–60.

2. Explain how one of these makes LaKesha's paragraph easier to read.
   Answers will vary.

   For a list of pronouns, see page 365.

   Now rewrite LaKesha's paragraph with your revisions.

Editing the Student Paragraph

EDITING STRATEGIES
This chapter focuses on the following editing problems:

Fragments
Modifier errors
Apostrophes (possession)
Confused words

SENTENCES

Subjects and Verbs

✔ Does each sentence have a main subject and verb?

1. Underline the subjects once and verbs twice in your revision of LaKesha's paragraph. Remember that sentences can have more than one subject-verb set.

   For help with subjects and verbs, see Chapter 20.

2. Does each of the sentences have at least one subject and verb that can stand alone?
   No

3. Did you find and correct LaKesha's two fragments? If not, find and correct them now.   *Sentences 5 and 13*

   For help with fragments, see Chapter 21.

Subject-Verb Agreement

✔ Do all subjects and verbs agree?

For help with subject-verb agreement, see Chapter 25.

1. Read aloud the subjects and verbs you underlined in your revision of LaKesha's paragraph.

2. Correct any subjects and verbs that do not agree. *All subjects agree with their verbs in the original paragraph.*

Pronoun Agreement

✔ Do all pronouns agree with their nouns?

For help with pronoun agreement, see Chapter 29.

1. Find any pronouns in your revision of LaKesha's paragraph that do not agree with their nouns. *All pronouns agree with their nouns in the original paragraph.*
2. Correct any pronouns that do not agree with their nouns.

Modifier Errors

✔ Are modifiers as close as possible to the words they modify?

For help with modifier errors, see Chapter 32.

1. Find any modifiers in your revision of LaKesha's paragraph that are not as close as possible to the words they modify. *"After decorating my apartment" (sentence 2)*
2. Did you find and correct LaKesha's one modifier error? If not, find and correct it now.

PUNCTUATION AND MECHANICS

Punctuation

✔ Are sentences punctuated correctly?

For help with punctuation, see Chapters 33–37.

1. Read your revision of LaKesha's paragraph for any errors in punctuation.

2. Find the two fragments you revised, and make sure they are punctuated correctly.

3. Did you find and correct the apostrophe error in LaKesha's paragraph? If not, find and correct it now. *"peoples" (sentence 13)*

Mechanics

✔ Are words capitalized properly?

For help with capitalization, see Chapter 38.

1. Read your revision of LaKesha's paragraph for any errors in capitalization. *All capitals are correct in the original paragraph.*
2. Be sure to check LaKesha's capitalization in the fragments you revised.

WORD CHOICE AND SPELLING

Word Choice

✔ Are words used correctly?

For help with confused words, see Chapter 44.

1. Find any words used incorrectly in your revision of LaKesha's paragraph. *there (sentence 4), than (sentence 8), our (sentence 8)*
2. Did you find and correct her three confused words? If not, find and correct them now. *their, then, are*

Spelling

✔ Are words spelled correctly?

1. Use spell-check and a dictionary to check the spelling in your revision of LaKesha's paragraph. *All words are spelled correctly in the original paragraph.*

For help with spelling, see Chapter 45.

2. Correct any misspelled words.

 Now rewrite LaKesha's paragraph again with your editing corrections.

Reading Your Own Division/Classification Paragraph

 Reading Strategy

Returning to the division/classification paragraph you wrote earlier in this chapter, revise and edit your own writing. First, you will be applying to your essay the same reading strategy you have been practicing throughout this chapter. Treating your essay as a reading selection that you are trying to understand and respond to will help you revise and edit your own work with some distance on it.

READING CRITICALLY
Summarizing Your Own Paragraph

Now write a summary of your own paragraph. See if all your ideas are clear and easy to identify. Make sure the connections between the points in your summary are logical and understandable. Are these connections also clear in your paragraph itself? Change any elements of your paragraph that will make your main idea clearer and more logical to your readers.

Revising and Editing Your Own Paragraph

The checklists here will help you apply what you have learned in this chapter to your paragraph. Work first with the content, making sure your thoughts are fully developed and effectively organized.

Revising Your Own Paragraph

For Revising Peer Evaluation Forms, go to Appendix 4.

TOPIC SENTENCE

☐ Does the topic sentence convey the paragraph's controlling idea?

☐ Does the topic sentence appear as the first or last sentence of the paragraph?

1. What is the main point or general message in your paragraph?

   _____

2. Put brackets around your topic sentence. Does it capture your main point?

   _____

3. How can you change it if necessary to introduce all the ideas in your paragraph?

   _____

DEVELOPMENT

☐ Does the paragraph contain *specific* details that support the topic sentence?

☐ Does the paragraph include *enough* details to explain the topic sentence fully?

1. Does your paragraph use both division and classification? Where does it divide? Where does it classify?

   Dividing   **Classifying**

   _____   _____

   _____   _____

   _____   _____

2. Add any categories or details that will make your paragraph clearer.

UNITY

☐ Do all the sentences in the paragraph support the topic sentence?

1. Read each of your sentences with your topic sentence in mind.

2. Drop or rewrite any sentences that are not directly related to your topic sentence.

ORGANIZATION

☐ Is the paragraph organized logically?

1. Read your paragraph again to see if all the sentences are arranged logically.

2. List some of your examples in the order they appear. Then identify your method of organization.

   _____   _____

   _____   _____

   _____   _____

Method of organization: _____

COHERENCE

☐ Do the sentences move smoothly and logically from one to the next?

1. Circle three transitions, repetitions, synonyms, or pronouns you use.
2. Explain how one of these makes your paragraph easier to read.

_____

_____

For a list of transitions, see pages 59–60.

For a list of pronouns, see page 365.

 Now rewrite your paragraph with your revisions.

Editing Your Own Paragraph

For Editing Peer Evaluation Forms, go to Appendix 6.

SENTENCES

Subjects and Verbs

☐ Does each sentence have a main subject and verb?

1. Underline the subjects once and verbs twice in your revised paragraph. Remember that sentences can have more than one subject-verb set.
2. Does each of your sentences have at least one subject and verb that can stand alone?

_____

3. Correct any fragments you have written.
4. Correct any run-together sentences you have written.

For help with subjects and verbs, see Chapter 20.

For help with fragments, see Chapter 21.

For help with run-togethers, see Chapter 22.

Subject-Verb Agreement

☐ Do all subjects and verbs agree?

1. Read aloud the subjects and verbs you underlined in your revised paragraph.
2. Correct any subjects and verbs that do not agree.

For help with subject-verb agreement, see Chapter 25.

Pronoun Agreement

☐ Do all pronouns agree with their nouns?

1. Find any pronouns in your revised paragraph that do not agree with their nouns.
2. Correct any pronouns that do not agree with their nouns.

For help with pronoun agreement, see Chapter 29.

Modifier Errors

☐ Are modifiers as close as possible to the words they modify?

For help with modifier errors, see Chapter 32.

1. Find any modifiers in your revised paragraph that are not as close as possible to the words they modify.

2. Rewrite sentences if necessary so that your modifiers are as close as possible to the words they modify.

PUNCTUATION AND MECHANICS

Punctuation

☐ Are sentences punctuated correctly?

For help with punctuation, see Chapters 33–37.

1. Read your revised paragraph for any errors in punctuation.

2. Make sure any fragments and run-together sentences you revised are punctuated correctly.

Mechanics

☐ Are words capitalized properly?

For help with capitalization, see Chapter 38.

1. Read your revised paragraph for any errors in capitalization.

2. Be sure to check your capitalization in any fragments or run-together sentences you revised.

WORD CHOICE AND SPELLING

Word Choice

☐ Are words used correctly?

For help with confused words, see Chapter 44.

1. Find any words used incorrectly in your revised paragraph.

2. Correct any errors you find.

Spelling

☐ Are words spelled correctly?

For help with spelling, see Chapter 45.

1. Use spell-check and a dictionary to check your spelling.

2. Correct any misspelled words.

To make a personal log of your grammar/usage errors, go to Appendix 7.

To make a personal log of your spelling errors, go to Appendix 8.

 Now rewrite your paragraph again with your editing corrections.

MyWritingLab **More Helpful Hints**

- **Do you need some reminders about revising?** Division/classification paragraphs require good coherence and logical transitions. So you need to pay special attention to these features as you revise. Go to **Revising**

Your Paragraph in **The Craft of Writing** module in **MyWritingLab** to get some help with the revising process

- **Are you looking for a way to make your paragraph more interesting to read?** See **Varying Sentence Structure** in the **Usage and Style** module in **MyWritingLab.** By changing the order of the items in your sentences, you can keep your readers interested and communicate your ideas more effectively.

PRACTICING DIVISION/CLASSIFICATION: FROM READING TO WRITING

This final section lets you practice the reading and writing skills you learned in this chapter. It includes two reading selections and several writing assignments on "your reading" and "your world." The section then offers guidance in peer evaluation and reflection, ending with suggestions about how to lead your instructor through your writing in ways that will benefit both of you.

Reading Workshop

Reading Strategy

Here are two essays that follow the guidelines you have studied in this chapter. "Rapport: How to Ignite It" by Camille Lavington divides and classifies personality types by communication styles, and "The Ways We Lie" by Stephanie Ericsson divides and classifies the various lies we tell. As you read, notice how the writers use these rhetorical modes to make their points.

RAPPORT: HOW TO IGNITE IT
by Camille Lavington

Focusing Your Attention

1. Do you get along easily with others? Do you like different types of people?

2. The essay you are about to read classifies the different personality traits in people. What are your dominant personality traits? What impression do you usually make on people? How do you know you make this particular impression?

Expanding Your Vocabulary

The following words are important to your understanding of this essay. Organize this list into two columns—words you know and words

INSTRUCTOR'S
RESOURCE MANUAL
For additional teaching
strategies, for journal
entries, for vocabulary and
reading quizzes, and for
more writing assignments,
see the *Instructor's
Resource Manual,*
Section II, Part II.

you don't know. Write the definitions of the words you don't know above their words in the essay.

rapport: chemistry between people (title)

reticent: reserved, shy (paragraph 2)

Henry Kissinger: U.S. secretary of state during the Nixon administration (paragraph 2)

out of sync: out of step, out of alignment (paragraph 2)

persona: image, public identity (paragraph 2)

affinity: liking, attraction (paragraph 4)

endowed: gifted (paragraph 4)

remedied: fixed, corrected (paragraph 6)

hyperactive: energetic (paragraph 9)

intrusive: pushy (paragraph 9)

paradoxically: surprisingly, contrary to what was expected (paragraph 9)

reservoir: supply (paragraph 9)

eliciting: bringing forth, drawing out (paragraph 13)

vogue: trend, fad, style (paragraph 13)

osmosis: effortless learning, absorption (paragraph 17)

ESP: intuition, insight (paragraph 17)

cosmic: coming from the universe (paragraph 17)

charismatic: charming (paragraph 17)

nonconformity: difference from the norm (paragraph 17)

prudent: cautious (paragraph 21)

affluent: wealthy (paragraph 22)

monster: huge (paragraph 23)

superiority complex: the feeling that one is more important than other people (paragraph 23)

frivolities: matters of little importance (paragraph 23)

cerebral: intellectual (paragraph 24)

stick-in-the-mud: an old-fashioned or unprogressive person (paragraph 24)

from the heart: based on emotion (paragraph 25)

from the gut: based on intuition or insight rather than reason (paragraph 25)

empathetic: kindly, sensitive to the feelings of others (paragraph 25)

modified: adapted, changed (paragraph 25)

got strokes: was praised or rewarded (paragraph 25)

spontaneous: impulsive (paragraph 26)

all is not hearts and flowers: the situation is not entirely positive (paragraph 26)

psychoanalyze: try to explain the thoughts and emotions of others (paragraph 26)

benchmarks: criteria, milestones, points of reference (paragraph 29)

READING CRITICALLY
Summarizing Your Reading

As you learned at the beginning of this chapter, practice your summary skills on the following essay. Then work with someone in the class, and write a single paragraph that represents both of your summaries.

RAPPORT: HOW TO IGNITE IT[1]
by Camille Lavington

It happens in a flash, based entirely on surface cues, but people use first impressions to make sometimes irreversible judgments.

So don't be reticent about the talent you've been given. It's your obligation to share it with the world, and your personality is the driving force behind your talent. As Henry Kissinger once said, history is fueled not by impersonal forces, but by personalities. If yours is out of sync, it may need some work. That doesn't mean adopting a phony persona; it simply means adjusting your communicating style in order to relate better to others.

[1] From *You've Only Got Three Seconds* by Camille Lavington and Stephanie Losee, copyright © 1997 by Camille Lavington and Stephanie Losee. Used by permission of Doubleday, a division of Random House, Inc.

3   Understanding your own personality makes it easier to spot someone with whom you'd like to connect. There are simple signs that signal personality types, and you can recognize them—even in strangers.

4   We are all a combination of many personality traits, but most people have a stronger affinity for one. Or you may be one of those rarely gifted individuals who are *evenly* endowed in *every* style.

5   **Introverts** are deep thinkers who prefer time alone to read, or stare at their computer screens, or gaze into outer space. They strive for, and appreciate, excellence. Ironically, introverts often have meaningful friendships. These are their positive qualities. But, as with all personality types, there are negative aspects: Introverts have a tendency to be suspicious and worried. Introverts can also be intellectual snobs who are unaccepting of others and perfectionists to a fault. They may be self-centered and have friends who are jealous of them.

6   Much of introversion is caused by shyness and lack of experience. Of all the personality traits, I think that introversion is the one characteristic that most needs to be remedied. Why? Introversion borders on selfishness. By hanging back during interactions with others, introverts are protecting themselves. A conversation is like a canoe that requires the exertion of both participants to keep moving forward; an introvert isn't engaging his paddle. It's everyone's job to contribute to relationships and to make others comfortable.

7   **Extroverts** aren't perfect, but society tends to reward their behavior. They have many good qualities, including their friendliness and magnetism. Energetic and sparkling, they inspire others. They like people, variety, and action. Extroverts like to chat a lot. They get their energy from other people.

8   You won't see an extrovert going to the movies alone, eating dinner alone, taking a vacation alone. Extroverts are born leaders. It should come as no surprise that most CEOs and politicians are extroverts.

9   Still, extroverts can be hyperactive and intrusive. They need to be the center of attention at all times, and they have a habit of boasting. They're looking for a vote of confidence from the outside, even if they have to solicit it. Paradoxically, this is sometimes because they don't tap into their own reservoir of strength and thus haven't learned their own value.

10   The easiest way to achieve rapport with others is to remember that time together is either a learning or an entertaining experience. With this attitude, you'll always be eager to draw people into any dialogue by inviting them to add a comment or an opinion—rather than draining other people's energy by dominating or shortchanging the conversation.

11   Lock two extroverts in a room, and each will complain that the other is a poor conversationalist. (An extrovert thinks a good conversationalist is someone who is interested in what *he* has to say.)

12   **Sensers** are just-the-facts people, and they get that way by using their objective senses, rather than their intuition, to gather information. A senser relies on his eyes and ears for clues. Practical and bottom-line oriented, sensers are doers who want action and want it now. They are competitive and highly organized, and they set high standards for themselves.

Sensers are master manipulators who have a talent for eliciting the response they want from people; many actors, comedians, and salespeople are sensers for just that reason. Sensers prefer to wear comfortable clothing, but peer pressure means so much to them that they will give in to the current vogue and wear what people they admire are wearing.

13

On the negative side, sensers can be self-involved, arrogant, and status-seeking. They tend to act first and think later. Also, they can be domineering and lacking in trust.

14

Sometimes you will be thrown off by a senser's easygoing manner because of his sense of humor, but don't waste his time. Get to the point quickly; remember that he's action-oriented and looking for short-term personal gain. If you have no previous knowledge about his temperament, take a look around for clues. A senser decorates his walls and bookshelves with personal trophies and memorabilia that remind him of his conquests.

15

You will lose points if you ever try to upstage a senser. This type, of all the others, wants to be the center of interest, as indicated by all of the personal trophies on his walls.

16

Intuitors make up a scant 10% of the population. So you're dealing with a rare bird. Albert Einstein is the classic intuitor—a genius who didn't speak until he was six years old. Intuitors gather information through a sort of osmosis, absorbing ESP signals and cosmic energy. Creative, imaginative, and original, they are driven by inspiration and a powerful intellect. Intuitors see the big picture in spite of a tenuous grasp of the details. Intuitors can be quite charismatic, although they tend to be unaware of their effect on people. They are also magnets to each other—finding their counterparts in the arts, sciences, wherever. Their nonconformity makes them dress in unusual combinations. In fact, they'll wear anything.

17

On the other hand, intuitors can drive others to madness. At times they're unrealistic and impractical. They're allergic to focusing on details. Fantasy-bound, they can be long on vision and short on action.

18

To approach an intuitor, spark her curiosity. When picking the brain of an intuitor, ask her to problem-solve without following any rules. You want to hear her unedited ideas.

19

If you're trying to impress an intuitor, don't waste time. You'll lose her attention if you give her a lot of background. Instead, respect her right-brain ability to jump to the heart of the matter in a flash.

20

Thinkers are the mainstay of society. They make life better because of their strong work ethic and high standards. Deliberate, prudent, and objective thinkers dwell in the world of rationality and analysis. Thinkers like to sleep on it. Many are effective communicators, possibly because they consider carefully before they speak. They make good jurors, who wait until closing arguments are concluded before weighing the evidence carefully. Their checkbooks are balanced.

21

Thinkers tend to like tailored, conservative clothing. If they're affluent, they have a tie that shows they met the rigid qualifications for entry to a top-ranked school. Teaching is a profession often favored by thinkers.

22

Thinkers can get trapped in their love of analysis, becoming over cautious and indecisive. They can be frustrating in a relationship by being too rigid, impersonal,

23

and unemotional. Some of them walk around with monster superiority complexes, trying at every turn to prove they're smarter than others. Some don't care how they look, because they're trying to send a message: *I have too big a brain to concern myself with frivolities like appearance.* But they're not out to hurt anyone; they forget their own feelings as well as the feelings of others. Thinkers often forget to stop and smell the roses.

These cerebral types can sound like sticks-in-the-mud, but don't take them lightly. Some of the finest minds in the world fall into this category. Put this trait together with extroversion and you've got one remarkable leader.

Feelers operate from the heart and the gut. They're warm and always observing interactions among people and interpreting them: *Why didn't she invite me to that meeting? Was that look he gave me a sign of disapproval?* Feelers read between the lines. They are nurturing and empathetic. Their need for an emotional response can have an odd side effect: Whatever childhood behavior got attention from their parents is the one they'll pursue in a modified form as adults—so a feeler child who got strokes for bringing home straight A's will turn into a feeler adult who works overtime at the office.

Feelers are not trendsetters; they are more comfortable in the mainstream, following traditional values. They like colorful clothes that reflect their emotions. They are loyal, spontaneous, and persuasive. But all is not hearts and flowers. Feelers overreact and get defensive if things don't go their way. Their need to psychoanalyze everyone gets them into trouble as they over-personalize every interaction, stirring up conflict. Some are guilt-ridden, ruled by thoughts of what they've done wrong.

Judges aren't any more judgmental than the rest of us. Any personality type can be judgmental.

If you are a judge, you like to think you have some control over life. Judges are structured and organized; they want to finish things and move along. They set standards for themselves and for others and follow them. Judges are surprised every time someone fails to live up to his or her agreement, as if that were unusual. Judges set goals and meet them—thriving on the resulting sense of closure.

Dealing with a judge is simple: Make a commitment, and live up to it. Set goals, and use benchmarks to measure your performance by objective standards. Fail to meet a judge's expectations of you, and you'll travel a rocky road.

Perceivers are always receptive to more information or stimulation before acting. They take each day as it comes and don't kick themselves for letting chores slide into tomorrow. Perceivers generally grew up in either an unstructured environment or a very structured one against which they rebel as adults. These people can be very kind to others because they're kind to themselves. They don't become angry because you're late or take offense if you ask them a personal question. They see life as a process. A lot of artistic people fall into this category.

Pressure tactics just don't work with perceivers, but perceivers are so easy to be around that they are certainly worth rewarding with a little patience.

Once you've discovered what makes the other person tick—which traits are getting in the way of good communication between the two of you—then you have to decide what to do with that information.

24

25

26

27

28

29

30

31

32

Thinking Critically About Content

1. What are the eight different personality types Lavington outlines in her essay?

2. Are these personality traits evenly distributed in you, or is one dominant? Explain your answer.

3. Do you agree with Lavington when she says, "Don't be reticent about the talent you've been given. It's your obligation to share it with the world" (paragraph 2)?

Thinking Critically About Purpose and Audience

4. What do you think Lavington's purpose is in this essay?

5. Who do you think is her primary audience?

6. When did you last make an important judgment based on a first impression of someone? Was your impression fairly accurate?

Thinking Critically About Paragraphs

7. Explain how the topic sentence works in paragraph 7. Does it supply the controlling idea for the entire paragraph? Are the other sentences in this paragraph related to the topic sentence?

8. Why do you think Lavington discusses these personality types in this particular order? What is her rationale for moving from one type to the next?

9. How does Lavington start her essay? Is it effective?

10. Write an alternative conclusion to Lavington's essay.

8. Lavington groups the categories together according to opposites (introverts/extroverts, sensers/intuitors, and so on) to help readers see these different traits. Someone could conceivably be an extrovert, a senser, a thinker, and a perceiver all at the same time. Her rationale for moving from type to type is to enhance our understanding of our fellow humans.

9. Lavington begins her essay by talking about first impressions and the reasons people make snap judgments. She then suggests that if we understood personality traits, we would be better equipped to project good first impressions.

10. Answers will vary.

To keep track of your critical thinking progress, go to Appendix 1.

THE WAYS WE LIE
by Stephanie Ericsson

Focusing Your Attention

1. Do you find that you don't tell the truth in every situation? When do you stretch the truth? Why do you stretch the truth?

2. In the essay you are about to read, the author categorizes the different types of lies we tell every day. These categories will help you realize how often we all lie. How often do you lie or stretch the truth in a typical day? What are the consequences of these lies? Explain your answer.

Expanding Your Vocabulary

The following words are important to your understanding of this essay. Organize this list into two columns—words you know and words

SUMMARY
This essay classifies the different types of lies we tell on a daily basis to avoid the consequences of the truth.

READABILITY
(Flesch-Kincaid grade level) 8.3

INSTRUCTOR'S RESOURCE MANUAL
For additional teaching strategies, for journal

entries, for vocabulary and reading quizzes, and for more writing assignments, see the *Instructor's Resource Manual,* Section II, Part II.

you don't know. Write the definitions of the words you don't know above their words in the essay.

haggard: looking unwell or tired (paragraph 2)

merit: worth or value (paragraph 4)

penance: punishment for wrongdoing (paragraph 6)

façades: deceptive outer appearance (paragraph 10)

plethora: an excessive amount (paragraph 11)

recklessly: lacking concern for consequences (paragraph 12)

blatant: openly unashamed (paragraph 14)

deflectors: people who cause deviation (paragraph 16)

culprit: someone or something that is responsible for a negative outcome (paragraph 16)

rabbinical: relating to Rabbis or Jewish teachings (paragraph 18)

renegade: someone who defies set principles (paragraph 19)

obliterated: destroyed (paragraph 22)

invulnerability: incapable of being harmed (paragraph 25)

schizophrenics: people having a mental disorder involving hallucinations (paragraph 30)

catatonia: immobility (paragraph 30)

gamut: the complete range of something (paragraph 31)

READING CRITICALLY
Summarizing Your Reading

Once again, write a summary of the following essay, and exchange it with another person in your class. Then combine your two summaries into one summary that accurately represents the main ideas in this essay.

THE WAYS WE LIE[2]
by Stephanie Ericsson

The bank called today and I told them my deposit was in the mail, even though I hadn't written a check yet. It'd been a rough day. The baby I'm pregnant with decided to do aerobics on my lungs for two hours, our three-year-old daughter painted the living-room couch with lipstick, the IRS put me on hold for an hour, and I was late to a business meeting because I was tired.   1

I told my client that traffic had been bad. When my partner came home, his haggard face told me his day hadn't gone any better than mine, so when he asked, "How was your day?" I said, "Oh, fine," knowing that one more straw might break his back. A friend called and wanted to take me to lunch. I said I was busy. Four lies in the course of a day, none of which I felt the least bit guilty about.   2

We lie. We all do. We exaggerate, we minimize, we avoid confrontation, we spare people's feelings, we conveniently forget, we keep secrets, we justify lying to the big-guy institutions. Like most people, I indulge in small falsehoods and still think of myself as an honest person. Sure I lie, but it doesn't hurt anything. Or does it?   3

I once tried going a whole week without telling a lie, and it was paralyzing. I discovered that telling the truth all the time is nearly impossible. It means living with some serious consequences: The bank charges me $60 in overdraft fees, my partner keels over when I tell him about my travails, my client fires me for telling her I didn't feel like being on time, and my friend takes it personally when I say I'm not hungry. There must be some merit to lying.   4

But if I justify lying, what makes me any different from slick politicians or the corporate robbers who raided the S&L industry? Saying it's okay to lie one way and not another is hedging. I cannot seem to escape the voice deep inside me that tells me: When someone lies, someone loses.   5

What far-reaching consequences will I, or others, pay as a result of my lie? Will someone's trust be destroyed? Will someone else pay *my* penance because I ducked out? We must consider the *meaning of our actions.* Deception, lies, capital crimes, and misdemeanors all carry meanings. *Webster's* definition of *lie* is specific: 6

1. a false statement or action especially made with the intent to deceive;
2. anything that gives or is meant to give a false impression.

A definition like this implies that there are many, many ways to tell a lie. Here are just a few.   7

---

[2] Stephanie Ericsson, "The Ways We Lie." Copyright © 1992 by Stephanie Ericsson. Originally published by *The Utne Reader*. Reprinted by the permission of Dunham Literary, Inc. as agents for the author.

The White Lie

A man who won't lie to a woman has very little consideration for her feelings.

—Bergen Evens

8   The white lie assumes that the truth will cause more damage than a simple, harmless untruth. Telling a friend he looks great when he looks like hell can be based on a decision that the friend needs a compliment more than a frank opinion. But, in effect, it is the liar deciding what is best for the lied to. Ultimately, it is a vote of no confidence. It is an act of subtle arrogance for anyone to decide what is best for someone else.

9   Yet not all circumstances are quite so cut-and-dried. Take, for instance, the sergeant in Vietnam who knew one of his men was killed in action but listed him as missing so that the man's family would receive indefinite compensation instead of the lump-sum pittance the military gives widows and children. His intent was honorable. Yet for 20 years this family kept their hopes alive, unable to move on to a new life.

Façade

Et tu, Brute?

—Caesar

10   We all put up façades to one degree or another. When I put on a suit to go to see a client, I feel as though I am putting on another face, obeying the expectation that serious businesspeople wear suits rather than sweatpants. But I'm a writer. Normally, I get up, get the kids off to school, and sit at my computer in my pajamas until four in the afternoon. When I answer the phone, the caller thinks I'm wearing a suit (though the UPS man knows better).

11   But façades can be destructive because they are used to seduce others into an illusion. For instance, I recently realized that a former friend was a liar. He presented himself with all the right looks and the right words and offered lots of new consciousness theories, fabulous books to read, and fascinating insights. Then I did some business with him, and the time came for him to pay me. He turned out to be all talk and no walk. I heard a plethora of reasonable excuses, including in-depth descriptions of the big break around the corner. In six months of work, I saw less than a hundred bucks. When I confronted him, he raised both eyebrows and tried to convince me that I'd heard him wrong, that he'd made no commitment to me. A simple investigation into his past revealed a crowded graveyard of disenchanted former friends.

Ignoring the Plain Facts

Well, you must understand that Father Porter is only human.

—A Massachusetts Priest

12   In the '60s, the Catholic Church in Massachusetts began hearing complaints that Father James Porter was sexually molesting children. Rather than relieving him of his duties, the ecclesiastical authorities simply moved him from one parish to another between 1960 and 1967, actually providing him with a fresh supply of unsuspecting families and innocent children to abuse. After treatment in 1967 for

pedophilia, he went back to work, this time in Minnesota. The new diocese was aware of Father Porter's obsession with children, but they needed priests and recklessly believed treatment had cured him. More children were abused until he was relieved of his duties a year later: By his own admission, Porter may have abused as many as a hundred children.

Ignoring the facts may not in and of itself be a form of lying, but consider the context of this situation. If a lie is *a false action done with the intent to deceive*, then the Catholic Church's conscious covering for Porter created irreparable consequences. The church became a co-perpetrator with Porter. 13

Deflecting

When you have no basis for an argument, abuse the plaintiff.

—Cicero

I've discovered that I can keep anyone from seeing the true me by being selectively blatant. I set a precedent of being up-front about intimate issues, but I never bring up the things I truly want to hide; I just let people assume I'm revealing everything. It's an effective way of hiding. 14

Any good liar knows that the way to perpetuate an untruth is to deflect attention from it. When Clarence Thomas exploded with accusations that the Senate hearings were a "high-tech lynching," he simply switched the focus from a highly charged subject to a radioactive subject. Rather than defending himself, he took the offensive and accused the country of racism. It was a brilliant maneuver. Racism is now politically incorrect in official circles—unlike sexual harassment, which still rewards those who can get away with it. 15

Some of the most skilled deflectors are passive-aggressive people who, when accused of inappropriate behavior, refuse to respond to the accusations. This you-don't-exist stance infuriates the accuser, who, understandably, screams something obscene out of frustration. The trap is sprung and the act of deflection successful because now the passive-aggressive person can indignantly say, "Who can talk to someone as unreasonable as you?" The real issue is forgotten and the sins of the original victim become the focus. Feeling guilty of name-calling, the victim is fully tamed and crawls into a hole, ashamed. I have watched this fighting technique work thousands of times in disputes between men and women, and what I've learned is that the real culprit is not necessarily the one who swears the loudest. 16

Omission

The cruelest lies are often told in silence.

—R. L. Stevenson

Omission involves telling most of the truth minus one or two key facts whose absence changes the story completely. You break a pair of glasses that are guaranteed under normal use and get a new pair, without mentioning that the first pair broke during a rowdy game of basketball. Who hasn't tried something like that? But what about omission of information that could make a difference in how a person lives his or her life? 17

18   For instance, one day I found out that rabbinical legends tell of another woman in the Garden of Eden before Eve. I was stunned. The omission of the Sumerian goddess Lilith from Genesis—as well as her demonization by ancient misogynists as an embodiment of female evil—felt like spiritual robbery. I felt like I'd just found out my mother was really my stepmother. To take seriously the tradition that Adam was created out of the same mud as his equal counterpart, Lilith, redefines all of Judeo-Christian history.

19   Some renegade Catholic feminists introduced me to a view of Lilith that had been suppressed during the many centuries when this strong goddess was seen only as a spirit of evil. Lilith was a proud goddess who defied Adam's need to control her, attempted negotiations, and, when this failed, said adios and left the Garden of Eden.

20   This omission of Lilith from the Bible was a patriarchal strategy to keep women weak. Omitting the strong-woman archetype of Lilith from Western religions and starting the story with Eve the Rib has helped keep Christian and Jewish women believing they were the lesser sex for thousands of years.

Stereotypes and Cliches

Where opinion does not exist, the status quo becomes stereotyped, and all originality is discouraged.

—Bertrand Russell

21   Stereotype and cliché serve a purpose as a form of shorthand. Our need for vast amounts of information in nanoseconds has made the stereotype vital to modern communication. Unfortunately, it often shuts down original thinking, giving those hungry for the truth a candy bar of misinformation instead of a balanced meal. The stereotype explains a situation with just enough truth to seem unquestionable.

22   All the "isms"—racism, sexism, ageism, et al.—are founded on and fueled by the stereotype and the clichés, which are lies of exaggeration, omission, and ignorance. They are always dangerous. They take a single tree and make it a landscape. They destroy curiosity. They close minds and separate people. The single mother on welfare is assumed to be cheating. Any black male could tell you how much of his identity is obliterated daily by stereotypes. Fat people, ugly people, beautiful people, old people, large-breasted women, short men, the mentally ill, and the homeless all could tell you how much more they are like us than we want to think. I once admitted to a group of people that I had a mouth like a truck driver. Much to my surprise, a man stood up and said. "I'm a truck driver, and I never cuss." Needless to say, I was humbled.

Groupthink

Who is more foolish, the child afraid of the dark or the man afraid of the light?

—Maurice Freehill

23   Irving Janis, in *Victims of Group Think,* defines this sort of lie as a psychological phenomenon within decision-making groups in which loyalty to the group has become more important than any other value, with the result that dissent and the appraisal of alternatives are suppressed. If you've ever worked on a committee or in a corporation, you've encountered groupthink. It requires a combination of other forms of lying-ignoring facts, selective memory, omission, and denial, to name a few.

The textbook example of groupthink came on December 7, 1941. From as early as the fall of 1941, the warnings came in, one after another, that Japan was preparing for a massive military operation. The navy command in Hawaii assumed Pearl Harbor was invulnerable—the Japanese weren't stupid enough to attack the United States' most important base. On the other hand, racist stereotypes said the Japanese weren't smart enough to invent a torpedo effective in less than 60 feet of water (the fleet was docked in 30 feet); after all, US technology hadn't been able to do it. 24

On Friday, December 5, normal weekend leave was granted to all the commanders at Pearl Harbor, even though the Japanese consulate in Hawaii was busy burning papers. Within the tight, good-ole-boy cohesiveness of the US command in Hawaii, the myth of invulnerability stayed well entrenched. No one in the group considered the alternatives. The rest is history. 25

Out-And-Out Lies

The only form of lying that is beyond reproach is lying for its own sake.

—Oscar Wilde

Of all the ways to lie, I like this one the best, probably because I get tired of trying to figure out the real meanings behind things. At least I can trust the bald-faced lie. I once asked my five-year-old nephew, "Who broke the fence?" (I had seen him do it.) He answered, "The murderers." Who could argue? 26

At least when this sort of lie is told it can be easily confronted. As the person who is lied to, I know where I stand. The bald-faced lie doesn't toy with my perceptions—it argues with them. It doesn't try to refashion reality; it tries to refute it. *Read my lips.* . . . No sleight of hand. No guessing. If this were the only form of lying, there would be no such things as floating anxiety or the adult-children-of-alcoholics movement. 27

Dismissal

Pay no attention to that man behind the curtain!
I am the Great Oz!

—The Wizard of Oz

Dismissal is perhaps the slipperiest of all lies. Dismissing feelings, perceptions, or even the raw facts of a situation ranks as a kind of lie that can do as much damage to a person as any other kind of lie. 28

The roots of many mental disorders can be traced back to the dismissal of reality. Imagine that a person is told from the time she is a tot that her perceptions are inaccurate. *"Mommy, I'm scared."* "No you're not, darling." *"I don't like that man next door. He makes me feel icky."* "Johnny, that's a terrible thing to say. Of course you like him. You go over there right now and be nice to him." 29

I've often mused over the idea that madness is actually a sane reaction to an insane world. Psychologist R. D. Laing supports this hypothesis in *Sanity, Madness and the Family,* an account of his investigation into the families of schizophrenics. The common thread that ran through all of the families he studied was a deliberate, staunch dismissal of the patient's perceptions from a very early age. Each of the 30

31

**Thinking Critically
About Content**

1. Ericsson suggests
that we lie to avoid
certain conse-
quences (para. 4).

2. The white lie,
façade, ignoring
the plain facts,
deflecting, omis-
sions, stereotypes
and clichés, group-
think, out-and-out
Lies, dismissal, and
delusion

3. Ericsson states that
telling the truth is
"almost impossible"
because we don't
want to live with
the consequences.

**Thinking Critically
About Purpose and
Audience**

4. Ericsson wrote the
essay to explore
lies that are used to
influence situations
and events in life.

5. The essay interests
every individual.
As Ericsson writes,
"We lie. We all do."
(para. 4).

6. Answers will vary.

**Thinking Critically
About Paragraphs**

7. Two examples
Ericsson cites to
explain omission are
about an individual
who receives a new
pair of glasses for a
broken pair

patients started out with an accurate grasp of reality, which, through meticulous and methodical dismissal, was demolished until the only reality the patient could trust was catatonia.

Dismissal runs the gamut. Mild dismissal can be quite handy for forgiving the foibles of others in our day-to-day lives. Toddlers who have just learned to manipulate their parents' attention sometimes are dismissed out of necessity. Absolute attention from the parents would require so much energy that no one would get to eat dinner. But we must be careful and attentive about how far we take our "necessary" dismissals. Dismissal is a dangerous tool, because it's nothing less than a lie.

Delusion

We lie loudest when we lie to ourselves.

—Eric Hoffer

32   I could write the book on this one. Delusion, a cousin of dismissal, is the tendency to see excuses as facts. It's a powerful lying tool because it filters out information that contradicts what we want to believe. Alcoholics who believe that the problems in their lives are legitimate reasons for drinking rather than results of the drinking offer the classic example of deluded thinking. Delusion uses the mind's ability to see things in myriad ways to support what it wants to be the truth.

33   But delusion is also a survival mechanism we all use. If we were to fully contemplate the consequences of our stockpiles of nuclear weapons or global warming, we could hardly function on a day-to-day level. We don't want to incorporate that much reality into our lives because to do so would be paralyzing.

34   Delusion acts as an adhesive to keep the status quo intact. It shamelessly employs dismissal, omission, and amnesia, among other sorts of lies. Its most cunning defense is that it cannot see itself.

The liar's Punishment [...] is that he cannot believe anyone else.

—George Bernard Shaw

35   These are only a few of the ways we lie or are lied to. As I said earlier, it's not easy to entirely eliminate lies from our lives. No matter how pious we may try to be, we will still embellish, hedge, and omit to lubricate the daily machinery of living. But there is a world of difference between telling functional lies and living a lie. Martin Buber once said, "The lie is the spirit committing treason against itself." Our acceptance of lies becomes a cultural cancer that eventually shrouds and reorders reality until moral garbage becomes as invisible to us as water is to a fish.

36   How much do we tolerate before we become sick and tired of being sick and tired? When will we stand up and declare our *right* to trust? When do we stop accepting that the real truth is in the fine print? Whose lips do we read this year when we vote for president? When will we stop being so reticent about making judgments? When do we stop turning over our personal power and responsibility to liars?

37   Maybe if I don't tell the bank the check's in the mail I'll be less tolerant of the lies told me every day. A country song I once heard said it all for me: "You've got to stand for something, or you'll fall for anything."

Thinking Critically About Content

1. According to Ericsson, why do we all lie?

2. What are the 10 types of lies the author delineates?

3. Why does Ericsson claim that telling the truth all the time is "almost impossible" (paragraph 4)?

Thinking Critically About Purpose and Audience

4. Why do you think Ericsson wrote this essay?

5. Who would be most interested in this essay?

6. Which of these types of lies do you tell most often? Why do you resort to them?

Thinking Critically About Paragraphs

7. What examples does Ericsson use to explain the category of "Omission" (paragraphs 17–20)? Add one more example to this list.

8. Underline two transitions in paragraphs 8 and 9. Then explain how they make the discussion of white lies smooth and coherent. (Refer to pages 59–60 for more information on transitions.)

9. Choose one paragraph, and decide whether or not it has enough details. Explain your answer.

10. Write an alternate introduction to Ericsson's essay.

Writing Workshop

This final section gives you the opportunity to apply what you have learned in this chapter to another writing assignment. This time, we provide you with the guidelines only and let you go through your own writing process with occasional feedback from your peers. Refer to sections of the chapter as necessary until the process of producing a paragraph becomes automatic for you.

Guidelines for Writing a Division/Classification Paragraph

1. Decide on your overall purpose for writing, and state it in your topic sentence.
2. Divide your topic into categories (division); explain each category with details and examples (classification).
3. Organize your categories so that they help you communicate your message clearly.

guaranteed under normal circumstances and does not mention that they were broken during a basketball game and about the Samarian goddess Lilith, omitted from Genesis to keep women weak and believing that they are the lesser sex. Beyond this, answers will vary.

8. Transitions in paragraphs 8 and 9 include *but, ultimately, yet, for instance, but.* The transitions provide a logical bridge that moves the reader from one example to the next.

9. Answers will vary.

10. Answers will vary.

To keep track of your critical thinking progress, go to Appendix 1.

ADDITIONAL WRITING TOPIC
Ask your students to expand the paragraph they wrote on page 222 into well-developed essays.

TEACHING ON THE WEB
Discussion Topic: Divide students into groups of three or four, and have them discuss how Web sites use division and classification. How do the various links demonstrate this mode? In what other ways are division and classification present?

TEACHING ON THE WEB
Links: Provide students with a topic, and have them link to Web sites that will divide the topic into

categories. What are the
different divisions that Web
sites make? Which Web site
is easiest to follow?

Possible sites for the topic
television:

ABC (American
Broadcasting Corporation),
abc.com

CBS (Columbia Broadcast
System), cbs.com

NBC (National
Broadcasting Corporation),
nbc.com

TEACHING ON THE WEB
Research: Have students
go to educational or
government Web sites
to determine how those
sites use division and
classification. Then have
students do the same with a
commercial Web site. How
do these Web sites use
division and classification
differently? How do
division and classification
help sell the products from
a commercial site?

Writing About Your Reading

1. In the first essay, Camille Lavington divides and classifies the personality types she sees in the human race. Using her essay as a reference, explain what category you fit into and why you fit there.

2. Using Stephanie Ericsson's categories, divide the lies you tell in a typical week of your life into categories. Then explain each category.

3. How do division and classification work together? Refer to one of the essays in this chapter to respond to this question.

Writing About Your World

Rudi Von Briel/PhotoEdit

1. Place yourself in the picture above, and tell someone who isn't looking at the picture about the different types of products you see as you move through the outdoor market. In other words, use division and classification to describe the market.

2. Think of the many occasions in your life that require different types of clothes. For example, you would never wear to a funeral what you wear to the beach. Group the routine events in your life, and explain how various clothes in your wardrobe are appropriate for specific types of events.

3. Think of the various jobs you will be qualified for when you finish college. Classify these jobs into a few categories, and explain your interest in each category.

4. Create your own division/classification assignment (with the help of your instructor), and write a response to it.

Revising

Small Group Activity (5–10 minutes per writer) Working in groups of three or four, read your division/classification papers to each other. Those listening should record their reactions on a copy of the Revising Peer Evaluation Forms in Appendix 4. After your group goes through this process, give your evaluation forms to the appropriate writers so that each writer has two or three peer comment sheets for revising.

Paired Activity (5 minutes per writer) Using the completed Peer Evaluation Forms, work in pairs to decide what you should revise. If time allows, rewrite some of your sentences, and have your partner check them.

Individual Activity Rewrite your paper, using the revising feedback you received from other students.

Editing

Paired Activity (5–10 minutes per writer) Swap papers with a classmate, and use the Editing Peer Evaluation Form in Appendix 6 to identify as many grammar, punctuation, mechanics, and spelling errors as you can. If time allows, correct some of your errors, and have your partner check them. Record your grammar, punctuation, and mechanics errors in the Error Log (Appendix 7) and your spelling errors in the Spelling Log (Appendix 8).

Individual Activity Rewrite your paper again, using the editing feedback you received from other students.

Reflecting on Your Writing When you have completed your own paragraph, answer these six questions:

1. What was most difficult about this assignment?

2. What was easiest?

3. What did you learn about division/classification by completing this assignment?

4. What do you think are the strengths of your division/classification? Place a wavy line by the parts of your paragraph that you feel are very good.

5. What are the weaknesses, if any, of your paper? Place an X by the parts of your paragraph you would like help with. Write any questions you have in the margins.

6. What did you learn from this assignment about your own writing process—about preparing to write, about writing the first draft, about revising, and about editing?

12

Defining

"Words are the tools with which we work.... Everything depends on our understanding of them."

—FELIX FRANKFURTER

Part of our daily communication process is asking people for clarification and definitions.

- "What do you mean by that?"
- "Can you clarify 'unfair'?"
- "Can you explain what you mean by 'hyper'?"
- "Can someone tell me what HTML is?"

Definitions keep the world running efficiently. Whenever we communicate—in spoken or written form—we use words we all understand. If we did not work from a set of shared definitions, we would not be able to communicate at all. We use definitions to explain concrete references (crayfish, DVD, laser beam), to identify places and events (Grand Canyon, Empire State Building, Cinco de Mayo celebration), and to discuss complex ideas (democracy, ambition, happiness).

Definition is the process of explaining a word, an object, or an idea in such a way that the audience knows as precisely as possible what you mean. A good definition of a word, for example, focuses on the special qualities of the word that set it apart from similar words. In the following paragraph, Mary Pipher defines the concept of family. She uses humorous, realistic examples to explain the responsibilities and rewards of being part of a family. See if you can pick out the main points of her definition.

> Families are the people for whom it matters if you have a cold, are feuding with your mate, or are training a new puppy. Family members use magnets to fasten the newspaper clippings about your bowling team on the refrigerator door. They save your drawings and homemade

pottery. They like to hear stories about when you were young. They'll help you can tomatoes or change the oil in your car. They're the people who will come visit you in the hospital, will talk to you when you call with "a dark night of the soul," and will loan you money to pay the rent if you lose your job. Whether or not they are biologically related to each other, the people who do these things are family.

You will refer to this example again when you are learning the guidelines for writing a good definition paragraph.

MyWritingLab ## Understanding Definition

How well do you understand defining? Test your knowledge by going to **MyWritingLab.com** and clicking on **Definition** in the **Paragraph Development** module. For this topic, read the **Overview,** watch the **Animation** video, and check your level of understanding by completing the **Recall, Apply,** and **Write** activities. Then check your mastery by taking the **Post-test.**

Student Comment:
"This explanation in **MyWriting-Lab** was very helpful, and I enjoyed it."

Have your students print the paragraphs in the Apply exercise. This way, they can fully annotate the paragraphs as they answer the questions.

PREPARING TO WRITE A DEFINITION PARAGRAPH

Reading definition paragraphs critically will help you write effective definitions. Once you understand how a paragraph is constructed when you read it, you will be able to apply that information to your writing. Like two halves of the same circle, these two skills will enhance your ability to perform a variety of other tasks in many other aspects of life.

To begin with, you need to learn how to read definition paragraphs critically. An example will help you understand more clearly how good definition paragraphs work. As you read, you will apply a specific reading strategy to the passage. Then, you will answer some questions about the paragraph in an attempt to discover how it functions. With a complete understanding of your reading, you will have more tools to work with in your own writing.

READING CRITICALLY
Reacting Critically to a Professional Paragraph

For more detailed information on reacting critically, see page 20 in Chapter 2.

Forming your own opinions and coming up with meaningful ideas in response to your reading are very important parts of the reading process that you need to learn how to do. As you read the following paragraph, record your notes on a separate piece of paper. First, draw a vertical line down the center of your paper. Then, as you read, write the authors' main ideas on the left and your reactions to those ideas on the right side of the paper. Be prepared to explain the connection between your notes and the material in the paragraph.

Reading Strategy

Reading a Definition Paragraph

The sample paragraph defines *the cloud*, as it relates to technology. It is from "What Is the Cloud?" by Rama Ramaswami and Dian Schaffhauser. As you read, take the time to record the authors' points in one column and your reactions to those points in another column. Then answer the questions after the paragraph.

The easiest way to understand the cloud is to think of it as a utility, like electricity. When you plug a device into a wall outlet, electricity flows. You didn't generate the electricity yourself. In fact, you probably have no idea where the electricity was generated. It's just there when you want it. All you care about is that your device works. Cloud computing works on the same principle. Through an Internet connection (the equivalent of an electrical outlet), you can access whatever applications, files, or data you have opted to store in the cloud—anytime, anywhere, from any device. How it gets to you and where it's stored are not your concern.

Discovering How This Paragraph Works

To help you recognize the elements that make this an effective definition essay so you can use them in your own writing, answer the following questions in as much detail as possible.

1. What is this paragraph defining?

   "The cloud"
   _____

2. Does this author rely on a synonym, a category, or a negation at the beginning of this paragraph? Explain your answer.

   A category—a utility
   _____

   _____

3. What examples does Feld use to develop his definition? List some here.

   These authors use electricity as an example to define the cloud, including plugging a

   device into an outlet.
   _____

   _____

4. How does Feld organize the information in his paragraph: general to particular, particular to general, or chronologically?

Particular to general

Explain your answer.

The authors move from the specific example of electricity to the more general

concept of the Internet to explain the cloud.

WRITING A DEFINITION PARAGRAPH

Now that you have read and studied a definition paragraph, you will be writing one of your own. This section will help you generate a rough draft that you will then revise and edit in the third section of this chapter. It will guide you through a careful reading of the writing assignment, give you several ways to generate ideas, and finally furnish you with concrete guidelines for writing an effective definition paragraph. We encourage you to write notes and lists throughout this section so you can use them when you write a draft of your paragraph at the end of this section.

Reading the Prompt

The very first step in writing a good paragraph is making sure you understand the writing assignment or "prompt." An assignment attempts to "prompt" you to respond to a specific issue or question. The more clearly you understand the prompt, the better paragraph or essay you will create. Applying the chapter reading strategy to your writing assignment is a good way to accomplish this goal.

READING CRITICALLY
Reacting Critically to the Prompt

After you read the following prompt, draw a vertical line down the center of a sheet of paper. Record the tasks of the assignment on the left and your ideas about those tasks on the right. Write as many notes as you can about each task. Then underline the key words in the left column for completing the assignment.

Writing Prompt  **Complete** this **Writing Prompt** at **mywritinglab.com**

Everyone has a personal definition of the word *student*. What is your definition of this word? Explain it in a paragraph. Use the following guidelines to help you develop a draft.

Thinking About the Prompt

Before you focus on a specific topic, you should generate as many ideas as you can so you have several to choose from. List all the associations you have with the word *student*. How did you develop these associations? Do any of these ideas form a pattern that you could use as a focus for your paragraph? Use one or more of the prewriting techniques you learned in Chapter 3 to generate and record as many ideas as possible about this word.

Guidelines for Writing a Definition Paragraph

Definitions vary in length from short summaries (such as dictionary entries) to longer, extended pieces (such as essays and whole books written on complex concepts like *courage*). In addition, definitions can be objective and factual (as in a textbook) or subjective (combined with personal opinion). Whether short or long, objective or subjective, a good definition meets certain basic requirements. The following guidelines, using Mary Pipher's paragraph at the beginning of this chapter as an example, will help you write an effective definition paragraph.

1. **State your purpose in your topic sentence.** Sometimes a definition is used by itself (as in a classified ad for a job opening). More often, definitions are used in other types of writing, such as process analysis, comparison/contrast, and division/classification. In any case, the topic sentence in a definition paragraph should state your purpose as clearly as possible.

   In the Reading: In Mary Pipher's paragraph, the author lays out her purpose right away in her topic sentence: "Families are the people for whom it matters if you have a cold, are feuding with your mate, or are training a new puppy." She explains this definition in the rest of her paragraph.

   In Your Writing: In the paragraph you are going to write, what will be your purpose? Write yourself some notes that might develop into a clear topic sentence. Draft a tentative topic sentence if you are ready to do so.

2. **Decide how you want to define your term or idea.** Definitions are the building blocks of communication. Therefore, you want to be sure your audience understands how you're using certain words and key terms. Consider your audience, and define the term in a way your readers will understand. The three possibilities are by synonym, by category, or by negation.

   By synonym: The simplest way to define a word or term is to provide a synonym, or word that has a similar meaning. This synonym should be easier to understand than the word being defined. For example, "A *democracy* is a *free society*."

   By category: Defining by category is a two-step process. First, you put the word you are defining into a specific class or category: "A *democracy* is a form of government." Then you need to state how the word is different from other words in that category: "A *democracy* is a form of government based on individual freedom that is developed *by* the people and *for* the people."

By negation: When you define a word by negation, you say what the word is *not* before stating what it is. For example, "A *democracy* is not a socialist form of government. Rather, it is based on freedom and independence."

In the Reading: In her paragraph, Pipher uses the second method to define her term. First, she puts the term *family* in the category of *people*. Then she explains how members of a family are different from other people. Your family cares "if you have a cold, are feuding with your mate, or are training a new puppy."

In Your Writing: List all the ideas related to the word *student* that will help you make your point. With this list in front of you, which approach outlined above would be the best one for your definition? Is this the best method to use to achieve your purpose? Would another strategy be more effective? More interesting? Clearer?

3. **Use examples to expand on your definition.** These examples should show your word in action. Concrete examples are an option for accomplishing this task.

   In the Reading: In Pipher's paragraph, the author uses examples to expand on her definition of the word *family*. Every example is concrete, appealing to one of the five senses, and action oriented.

   > Family members use magnets to fasten the newspaper clippings about your bowling team on the refrigerator door.
   >
   > They save your drawings and homemade pottery.
   >
   > They like to hear stories about when you were young.
   >
   > They'll help you can tomatoes or change the oil in your car.
   >
   > They're the people who will come visit you in the hospital, will talk to you when you call with "a dark night of the soul," and will loan you money to pay the rent if you lose your job.

   By the end of the paragraph, you have a very clear sense of what family means to Mary Pipher.

   In Your Writing: Do you have enough ideas on your list for your definition? Take some time to brainstorm and list a few more details that come to mind. Think of your topic from as many different perspectives as possible.

4. **Organize your examples to communicate your definition as clearly as possible.** Your examples should progress in some logical order—from

students play charades and try to guess the definitions of the words. Be sure to provide words that can be acted out (such as *veterinarian* or *friend*).

Intrapersonal

Provide students with the words *noisy* and *quiet,* and ask them to make lists of numerous synonyms for each. How many words on their lists are positive words? Negative? Which list has more positive words? Why do they think this is the case?

Interpersonal

Put students into groups of three or four. Have each student think of a place he or she loves to go and then give a one-sentence definition of the place without actually naming it. Can the members of the group determine where this place is?

Naturalist

Have students recall one of their favorite outdoor activities and provide a definition of it that would make other students want to try it. Which part of the students' definition most entices someone to try the activity?

INSTRUCTOR'S RESOURCE MANUAL For additional material about teaching definition, for journal entries, and for various tests, see the *Instructor's Resource Manual,* Section II, Part II.

most serious to least serious, from least important to most important, chronologically, or spatially. What's important is that they move in some recognizable way from one to the next.

In the Reading: In her paragraph, Pipher arranges her examples from least crucial (putting your bowling score on the refrigerator) to most crucial (loaning you money when you lose your job). Pipher's method of organization is subtle but important to the flow of the paragraph.

In Your Writing: How will you organize the details in your paragraph? What order would be most effective to get your main point across to the readers? Choose a method of organization from those listed in this guideline.

Writing a Draft of Your Paragraph

Now is the time to collect all your associations, your notes, your prewriting exercises, and your lists as you generate the first draft of your paragraph. You might want to review the professional essay, the writing assignment, and the chapter guidelines to help you write a draft of your paragraph. At this point, don't think about revising or editing; just get a rough draft of your ideas down on paper in response to the writing prompt.

MyWritingLab **Helpful Hints**

- **Want to make sure everyone will understand what you mean?** Try using several approaches to your topic. Through examples, for instance, you can create a clear picture for your reader. See **Illustrating** in the **Paragraph Development** module in **MyWritingLab** for more help.
- **Have you forgotten the elements of the writing process?** You can review **The Writing Process** in **The Craft of Writing** module in **MyWritingLab.** This topic provides an overview of the process and explains how it can help you create a coherent paragraph.

REVISING AND EDITING
OPTIONS
Consider teaching revising and editing in a class discussion, in small groups, or in pairs.

REVISING AND EDITING

You are now ready to learn how to revise and edit. This section will guide you through the process of revising and editing definition paragraphs in reference to two writing samples: another student's paragraph and your own paragraph. Finding strengths and weaknesses in another person's writing is often much easier than evaluating your own, so you will be reviewing the chapter guidelines by revising and editing another student's writing before applying the same guidelines to your own writing.

Reading a Student Paragraph

Here is a definition paragraph written by Inez Morales. Her paragraph defines *success*. After you read her definition, see if you can restate her definition in your own words.

READING CRITICALLY
Reacting Critically to the Student Paragraph

As you read Inez's paragraph, record your notes on a separate piece of paper. First, draw a vertical line down the center of the paper. Then, write Inez's main ideas on the left and your reactions to those ideas on the right side of the page. Be prepared to explain the connection between your notes and the statements in the paragraph.

[1]To me, success is having an education, a decent job, and a happy, healthy family. [2]In order to be successful in life people must first get a college degree. [3]This education will prepare them for whatever situation in life that may come up. [4]I believe that having professional jobs like doctors, lawyers, and teachers help show a level of success. [5]When people work in professional jobs, they has the ability to build bigger homes, and buy better cars. [6]They are able to travel to different parts of the world with their families. [7]Many of my friends whose parents have professional jobs don't enjoy traveling. [8]They also don't have large families. [9]The last element of success are having a happy and healthy family. [10]Without an education, people will not be qualified for well-paying jobs. [11]I believe this is the formula for making it if people have all three of these in their lives, then they have success.

Revising and Editing the Student Paragraph

This paragraph is Inez's first draft, which now needs to be revised and edited. First, apply the following Revising Checklist to the content of Inez's draft. When you are satisfied that her ideas are fully developed and well organized, use the Editing Checklist to correct her grammar and mechanics errors. Answer the questions, and complete the tasks in each category. Then write your suggested changes directly on Inez's draft.

Revising the Student Paragraph

TOPIC SENTENCE

✔ Does the topic sentence convey the paragraph's controlling idea?

✔ Does the topic sentence appear as the first or last sentence of the paragraph?

1. What is Inez defining?

   The word "success"

2. Put brackets around Inez's topic sentence. Does it explain what she is defining?

   [To me, success is having an education, a decent job, and a happy, healthy family.]

   Yes

3. Make sure it introduces all the ideas in Inez's paragraph.

DEVELOPMENT

✔ Does the paragraph contain *specific* details that support the topic sentence?

✔ Does the paragraph include *enough* details to fully explain the topic sentence?

1. Do the details in the paragraph define success?

   Yes

2. Does Inez rely on synonyms, categories, or negation to develop her definition?

   Categories

3. Where do you need more information?

   Answers will vary.

4. Add at least one other detail to Inez's paragraph.

UNITY

✔ Do all the sentences in the paragraph support the topic sentence?

1. Read each of Inez's sentences with her topic sentence (revised, if necessary) in mind.

2. Cross out the two sentences that are not directly related to Inez's topic sentence.   *Sentences 7 and 8*

ORGANIZATION

✔ Is the paragraph organized logically?

1. Read Inez's paragraph again to see if all the sentences are arranged logically.

2. List some of the examples in Inez's paragraph in the order they appear.

   Need college degree

   Professional jobs lead to better life

   Have a happy and healthy family

3. Move the one example that seems to be out of order.   *Move sentence 10 before sentence 4.*

4. Identify Inez's method of organization:

Chronological

COHERENCE

✔ Do the sentences move smoothly and logically from one to the next?

1. Circle three transitions Inez uses.

2. Add another transition to Inez's paragraph, and explain how it makes her paragraph easier to read.

   Answers may vary.

For a list of transitions, see pages 59–60.

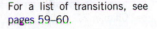

 Now rewrite Inez's paragraph with your revisions.

Editing the Student Paragraph

SENTENCES

Subjects and Verbs

✔ Does each sentence have a main subject and verb?

1. Underline the subjects once and verbs twice in your revision of Inez's paragraph. Remember that sentences can have more than one subject-verb set.

2. Does each of the sentences have at least one subject and verb that can stand alone?

   Yes, in the original paragraph

3. Did you find and correct Inez's run-together sentence? If not, find and correct it now.   *Sentence 11*

Subject-Verb Agreement?

✔ Do all subjects and verbs agree?

1. Read aloud the subjects and verbs you underlined in your revision of Inez's paragraph.

2. Did you find and correct the three subjects and verbs that don't agree? If not, find and correct them now.   *having/help (sentences 4), they/has (sentence 5), and element/are (sentence 9)*

Pronoun Agreement

✔ Do all pronouns agree with their nouns?

EDITING STRATEGIES
This chapter focuses on the following editing problems:

Run-togethers
Subject-verb agreement
Commas

For help with subjects and verbs, see Chapter 20.

For help with run-togethers, see Chapter 22.

For help with subject-verb agreement, see Chapter 25.

For help with pronoun agreement, see Chapter 29.

1. Find any pronouns in your revision of Inez's paragraph that do not agree with their nouns. *All pronouns agree with their nouns in the original paragraph.*

2. Correct any pronouns that do not agree with their nouns.

Modifier Errors

✔ Are modifiers as close as possible to the words they modify?

For help with modifier errors, see Chapter 32.

1. Find any modifiers in your revision of Inez's paragraph that are not as close as possible to the words they modify. *There are no modifier errors in the original paragraph.*

2. Rewrite sentences if necessary so that the modifiers are as close as possible to the words they modify.

PUNCTUATION AND MECHANICS

Punctuation

✔ Are sentences punctuated correctly?

For help with punctuation, see Chapters 33–37.

1. Read your revision of Inez's paragraph for any errors in punctuation.

2. Find the run-together sentence you revised, and make sure it is punctuated correctly.

3. Did you find and correct the two comma errors in Inez's paragraph? If not, find and correct them now. *Sentences 2 and 5*

Mechanics

✔ Are words capitalized properly?

For help with capitalization, see Chapter 38.

1. Read your revision of Inez's paragraph for any errors in capitalization. *All capitals are correct in the original paragraph.*

2. Be sure to check Inez's capitalization in the run-together sentence you revised.

WORD CHOICE AND SPELLING

Word Choice

✔ Are words used correctly?

For help with confused words, see Chapter 44.

1. Find any words used incorrectly in your revision of Inez's paragraph. *All words are used correctly in the original paragraph.*

2. Correct any errors you find.

Spelling

✔ Are words spelled correctly?

For help with spelling, see Chapter 45.

1. Use spell-check and a dictionary to check the spelling in your revision of Inez's paragraph. *All words are spelled correctly in the original paragraph.*

2. Correct any misspelled words.

 Now rewrite Inez's paragraph again with your editing corrections.

Reading Your Own Definition Paragraph

Reading
Strategy

Returning to the definition paragraph you wrote earlier in this chapter, you are now ready to revise and edit your own writing. You will first read your paragraph with the same reading strategy you have applied to other reading tasks in this chapter so you can look at it as your reader might.

READING CRITICALLY
Reacting Critically to Your Own Paragraph

As you begin to rework your paragraph, use the same technique you have practiced throughout the chapter. Just as you identified the author's ideas and recorded your reactions to them to help you understand what the paragraph was saying, record the ideas from your own writing on the left side of a piece of paper and your reactions to them on the right. Expand your paragraph with any new ideas that surface from this exercise.

Revising and Editing Your Own Paragraph

The checklists here will help you apply what you have learned in this chapter to your paragraph. Work first with the content, making sure your thoughts are fully developed and effectively organized. Then find and correct your grammar and usage errors.

Revising Your Own Paragraph

For Revising Peer Evaluation Forms, go to Appendix 4.

TOPIC SENTENCE

☐ Does the topic sentence convey the paragraph's controlling idea?

☐ Does the topic sentence appear as the first or last sentence of the paragraph?

1. What are you defining?

   _____

2. Put brackets around your topic sentence. Does it explain what you are defining?

   _____

3. Make sure it introduces all the ideas in your paragraph.

   _____

DEVELOPMENT

☐ Does the paragraph contain *specific* details that support the topic sentence?

☐ Does the paragraph include *enough* details to fully explain the topic sentence?

1. Do your details help you define your term or concept?

_____

2. Do you rely on synonyms, categories, or negation to develop your definition?

_____

3. Where do you need more information?

_____

4. Add at least one other detail to your paragraph.

UNITY

☐ Do all the sentences in the paragraph support the topic sentence?

1. Read each of your sentences with your topic sentence in mind.

2. Drop or rewrite any sentences that are not directly related to your topic sentence.

ORGANIZATION

☐ Is the paragraph organized logically?

1. Read your paragraph again to see if all the sentences are arranged logically.

2. What method of organization did you use?

_____

3. What word clues from your paragraph tell your readers how it is organized?

_____

COHERENCE

For a list of transitions, see pages 59–60.

☐ Do the sentences move smoothly and logically from one to the next?

1. Circle three transitions.

2. Add one transition to your paragraph, and explain how it makes your paragraph easier to read.

_____

_____

 Now rewrite your paragraph with your revisions.

Editing Your Own Paragraph

For Editing Peer Evaluation Forms, go to Appendix 6.

SENTENCES

Subjects and Verbs

☐ Does each sentence have a main subject and verb?

1. Underline the subjects once and verbs twice in your revised paragraph. Remember that sentences can have more than one subject-verb set.

For help with subjects and verbs, see Chapter 20.

2. Does each of your sentences have at least one subject and verb that can stand alone?

3. Correct any fragments you have written.
4. Correct any run-together sentences you have written.

For help with fragments, see Chapter 21.
For help with run-togethers, see Chapter 22.

Subject-Verb Agreement

☐ Do all subjects and verbs agree?

1. Read aloud the subjects and verbs you underlined in your revised paragraph.

For help with subject-verb agreement, see Chapter 25.

2. Correct any subjects and verbs that do not agree.

Pronoun Agreement

☐ Do all pronouns agree with their nouns?

1. Find any pronouns in your revised paragraph that do not agree with their nouns.

For help with pronoun agreement, see Chapter 29.

2. Correct any pronouns that do not agree with their nouns.

Modifier Errors

☐ Are modifiers as close as possible to the words they modify?

1. Find any modifiers in your revised paragraph that are not as close as possible to the words they modify.

For help with modifier errors, see Chapter 32.

2. Rewrite sentences if necessary so that your modifiers are as close as possible to the words they modify.

PUNCTUATION AND MECHANICS

Punctuation

☐ Are sentences punctuated correctly?

For help with punctuation, see Chapters 33–37.

1. Read your revised paragraph for any errors in punctuation.

2. Make sure any fragments and run-together sentences you revised are punctuated correctly.

Mechanics

☐ Are words capitalized properly?

For help with capitalization, see Chapter 38.

1. Read your revised paragraph for any errors in capitalization.

2. Be sure to check your capitalization in any fragments or run-together sentences you revised.

WORD CHOICE AND SPELLING

Word Choice

☐ Are words used correctly?

For help with confused words, see Chapter 44.

1. Find any words used incorrectly in your revised paragraph.

2. Correct any errors you find.

For help with spelling, see Chapter 45.

Spelling

☐ Are words spelled correctly?

To make a personal log of your grammar/usage errors, go to Appendix 7.

1. Use spell-check and a dictionary to check your spelling.

2. Correct any misspelled words.

To make a personal log of your spelling errors, go to Appendix 8.

⬛ Now rewrite your paragraph again with your editing corrections.

MyWritingLab | **More Helpful Hints**

- **Do you need some reminders about revising?** Definition paragraphs require a lot of detail and rely heavily on clarity, so you need to pay special attention to these features as you revise. Go to **Revising the Paragraph** in **The Craft of Writing** module in **MyWritingLab** for some helpful guidelines.

- **Do you have any lists or series in your paragraph?** Lists are often helpful when defining a subject, but they can be confusing if all of the items in the list aren't in parallel structure. To find out if your list is grammatically correct, go to **Parallelism** in the **Sentence Skills** module in **MyWritingLab.**

PRACTICING DEFINITION: FROM READING TO WRITING

This final section lets you practice the reading and writing skills you learned in this chapter. It includes two reading selections and several writing assignments on "your reading" and "your world." The section then offers guidance in peer evaluation and reflection, ending with suggestions about how to lead your instructor through your writing in ways that will benefit both of you.

Reading Workshop

Here are two essays that show how definition works in the context of a full essay. "The Fire Inside" by Gary Mack provides a clear definition of motivation as it works in human beings. The second essay, "What Is Poverty?" by Jo Goodwin Parker, defines poverty from the author's personal experience.

THE FIRE INSIDE
by Gary Mack

Focusing Your Attention

1. Do you think there are different types of motivation? What are they?

2. The essay you are about to read defines *motivation*. What is the clearest goal in your life right now? What moves you toward that goal?

Expanding Your Vocabulary

The following word is important to your understanding of this essay. Highlight it in the essay before you begin to read. Then refer to this definition when you get to this word in the essay.

elite: a group of people considered by some to be superior (paragraph 11)

READING CRITICALLY
Reacting Critically to Your Reading

As you have throughout this chapter, practice generating your reactions to your reading by recording the author's ideas on the left side of a piece of paper and your own reactions on the right. These notes will also help you understand the essay on an analytical level. Share your notes with someone in the class.

SUMMARY
In this essay, Gary Mack defines *motivation* through examples from the world of sports.

READABILITY
(Flesch-Kincaid grade level)
6.5

INSTRUCTOR'S
RESOURCE MANUAL
For additional teaching strategies, for journal entries, for vocabulary and reading quizzes, and for more writing assignments, see the *Instructor's Resource Manual*, Section II, Part II.

THE FIRE INSIDE[1]
by Gary Mack

Each of us has a fire in our hearts for something. It's our goal in life to find it and keep it lit.

—Mary Lou Retton

All I want out of life is that when I walk down the street folks will say, "There goes the greatest hitter who ever lived."

—Ted Williams

1   He remembers gazing into the night sky as a boy, long, long ago. Each time he saw a falling star, he made a wish. "Please," he said, "let me be the hitter I want to be." As he grew older, his love for hitting a baseball didn't fade as many childhood infatuations do. The art form became his focus, his passion, his singular goal. "A man has to have goals, for a day, for a lifetime," he said upon reflection. "Mine was to have people say, 'There goes Ted Williams, the greatest hitter who ever lived.'"

2   On July 13, 1999, major league baseball staged its annual midsummer classic at Fenway Park in Boston. It was a glorious evening, perfect for stargazing. As part of the pregame festivities, the National and American League All-Star teams were introduced to the sellout crowd. So were the legends of the game. One by one, the announcer presented the members of baseball's All-Century team.

3   Near the end of the roll call, a golf cart appeared in the old ballpark. Along with millions of other TV viewers, I watched as it slowly paraded around the field, its heroic passenger smiling, waving, greeted with warm cheers.

4   Cameras flashed like winking stars, and when the announcer welcomed him and honored him, his voice was close to reverence. "That's Ted Williams! The greatest hitter who ever lived."

5   Motivation is a popular word, especially in sports. It comes from a Latin word meaning "to move." Athletes can move in one of two ways, either toward seeking pleasure (rewards) or toward avoiding pain (punishment). Motivation can be the desire to succeed or the fear of failure. I believe the best and healthiest motivation is the one that pushed Ted Williams, the last major leaguer to hit over .400 in one season, to reach his goal and live his dream.

6   An athlete's success is said to depend upon four factors—physical ability, physical training, mental training, and desire or drive. The desire to succeed needs to be stronger than the fear of failure.

7   "You hear a lot of athletes who say they are motivated by a fear of failure," pitcher David Cone said. "I couldn't disagree more. To me, it's an opportunity. This

---

[1] Gary Mack, with David Casstevens, "The Fire Inside" from *Mind Gym: An Athlete's Guide to Inner Excellence*, pp. 87–91. Copyright © 2001 by Gary Mack. Reprinted by permission of The McGraw-Hill Companies, Inc.

is what we live and play for. There's no place I'd rather be than right here, right now, pitching big games down the stretch for the Yankees."

Muhammad Ali illustrates one of my favorite stories about motivation. When he was growing up in Louisville, he got a job sacking groceries. He didn't make much money, but he saved enough to buy a secondhand bicycle. He loved that blue bicycle. He was proud of it. He had worked hard for it and earned it. One day someone stole his bike. He was heartbroken. "I walked all over Louisville that summer, looking for that bicycle," Ali said, picking up the narrative. "I walked and looked, looked and walked. Never found it to this day. But every time I got into the ring, I looked across at the other fighter, and I told myself, 'Hey, that's the guy who stole my bicycle!'"

Athletes find motivation in different ways. Roger Clemens said he thrived on the doubts that others had of him. The pitcher went into the 1997 season intent on proving the Red Sox had made a mistake by letting him go.

The most successful athletes are self-motivated. "The most important thing is to love your sport," said Peggy Fleming, the former Olympic figure-skating champion. "Never do it to please someone else; it has to be yours. That is all that will justify the hard work needed to achieve success."

At a workshop with elite teenage athletes, I asked one young man to relate his most enjoyable sports experience. He recalled being 10 or 11 years old. He talked about how much fun he had shooting hoops. As the teen relived the memory, his father's eyes welled with tears. The young man who wanted to quit his high school team was still playing basketball for his father's sake. It was his dad's dream, not his own.

What we associate with pleasure we pursue. What we associate with pain we avoid. Playing sports as a kid should be an enjoyable, positive, and rewarding experience. But too often, impressionable youngsters are embarrassed by a coach, or they worry about pleasing their parents. Participating in sports then becomes a painful, even punishing experience. As a coach, I would want my kids to have fun. I would want them to be eager and excited. I would want them to feel they are improving and focusing on the process rather than the outcome.

Motivation gets you moving in a direction. Being on a mission provides the emotion. Clemens was on a mission after he left the Red Sox. Arnold Schwarzenegger also had a mission. His vision created what he calls "want power." Schwarzenegger said, "My wanting to be Mr. Universe came about because I saw myself so clearly, being up there on the stage and winning."

Carl Lewis had an ambitious mission and a powerful vision, too. "I want to be remembered as a person who felt there was no limitation to what the human body and mind can do, and be the inspiration to lead people, and do things they never hoped to do."

At spring training, Alex Rodriguez designed T-shirts for himself and his Seattle Mariners teammates. The printed message read, "We're On A Mission, Sir."

How about you? Does a fire burn inside you? Do you have a mission? What is it? What motivates you? If it is fear of failure, let that emotion go. The best motivation is "want" power, that prideful desire to achieve.

8 9 10 11 12 13 14 15 16

ANSWERS TO QUESTIONS

Thinking Critically About Content

1. Mack defines motivation as movement toward pleasurable rewards or avoidance of pain and punishment (para. 5).
2. Athletes are motivated in different ways, but they are all strongly moved to achieve in their sport.
3. Physical ability, physical training, mental training, and desire or drive (para. 6) regulate an athlete's success.

Thinking Critically About Purpose and Audience

4. Mack wrote this essay to explain that motivation is a component of achievement in athletics as well as in many other areas of life.
5. Mack's primary audience is aspiring athletes, yet this essay pertains to anyone with the desire to achieve.
6. Answers will vary.

Thinking Critically About Paragraphs

7. "Want power" is Schwarzenegger's term for the vision of success. The author probably repeats this term to bring attention to it.

Thinking Critically About Content

1. How does the author define motivation?

2. How are motivation and athletes related?

3. According to Mack, what four factors regulate an athlete's success?

Thinking Critically About Purpose and Audience

4. Why do you think Mack wrote this essay?

5. Who do you think is his primary audience?

6. How do you find motivation when you are in a competitive situation?

Thinking Critically About Paragraphs

7. The author repeats the phrase "want power" twice (paragraphs 13 and 16). What is this type of power? Why does the author repeat these words in the essay?

8. How is paragraph 5 organized? Why do you think Mack puts these details in this particular order?

9. Choose one paragraph, and explain its tone or mood.

10. Write a summary of this essay for your English class.

WHAT IS POVERTY?
by Jo Goodwin Parker

Focusing Your Attention

1. How do you generally feel about people who are less fortunate than you? Why do you feel this way?

2. In the essay you are about to read, the author defines poverty from her own experience. How would you define poverty? On what do you base your definition?

Expanding Your Vocabulary

The following words are important to your understanding of this essay. Highlight them throughout the essay before you begin to read. Then refer to this list as you get to these words in the essay.

stench: stink, foul odor (paragraph 1)

privy: toilet (paragraph 2)

grits: cornmeal mush (paragraph 4)

oleo: margarine (paragraph 4)

devour: eat (paragraph 5)

antihistamines: medications for colds and allergies (paragraph 5)

repossessed: taken away for failing to make installment payments (paragraph 8)

surplus commodities program: a government-run program that provides poor families with certain basic products free of charge (paragraph 11)

READING CRITICALLY
Reacting Critically as You Read

Once again, practice generating your reactions to your reading by recording the author's ideas on the left side of a piece of paper and your own reactions on the right. This activity will help you understand this essay at a deeper level than reading without annotating it. Share your notes with someone in the class.

WHAT IS POVERTY?[2]
by Jo Goodwin Parker

You ask me what is poverty? Listen to me. Here I am, dirty, smelly, and with no "proper" underwear on and with the stench of my rotting teeth near you. I will tell you. Listen to me. Listen without pity. I cannot use your pity. Listen with understanding. Put yourself in my dirty, worn out, ill-fitting shoes, and hear me.

1

Poverty is getting up every morning from a dirt-and-illness-stained mattress. The sheets have long since been used for diapers. Poverty is living in a smell that never leaves. This is a smell of urine, sour milk, and spoiling food sometimes joined with the strong smell of long-cooked onions. Onions are cheap. If you have smelled this smell, you did not know how it came. It is the smell of the outdoor privy. It is the smell of young children who cannot walk the long dark way in the night. It is the smell of the milk which has gone sour because the refrigerator long has not worked, and it costs money to get it fixed. It is the smell of rotting garbage. I could bury it, but where is the shovel? Shovels cost money.

2

---

[2] Jo Goodwin Parker, "What Is Poverty?" from *America's Other Children: Public Schools Outside Suburbia*, ed. George Henderson. Copyright © 1971 by University of Oklahoma Press. Reprinted by permission of the publisher.

3   Poverty is being tired. I have always been tired. They told me at the hospital when the last baby came that I had chronic anemia caused from poor diet, a bad case of worms, and that I needed a corrective operation. I listened politely—the poor are always polite. The poor always listen. They don't say that there is no money for iron pills or better food or worm medicine. The idea of an operation is frightening and costs so much that, if I had dared, I would have laughed. Who takes care of my children? Recovery from an operation takes a long time. I have three children. When I left them with "Granny" the last time I had a job, I came home to find the baby covered with fly specks and a diaper that had not been changed since I left. When the dried diaper came off, bits of my baby's flesh came with it. My other child was playing with a sharp bit of broken glass, and my oldest was playing alone at the edge of a lake. I made twenty-two dollars a week, and a good nursery school costs twenty dollars a week for three children. I quit my job.

4   Poverty is dirt. You can say in your clean clothes coming from your clean house, "Anybody can be clean." Let me explain about housekeeping with no money. For breakfast I give my children grits with no oleo or cornbread without eggs and oleo. This does not use up many dishes. What dishes there are, I wash in cold water and with no soap. Even the cheapest soap has to be saved for the baby's diapers. Look at my hands, so cracked and red. Once I saved for months to buy a jar of Vaseline for my hands and the baby's diaper rash. When I had saved enough, I went to buy it and the price had gone up two cents. The baby and I suffered on. I have to decide every day if I can bear to put my cracked sore hands into the cold water and strong soap. But you ask, why not hot water? Fuel costs money. If you have a wood fire it costs money. If you burn electricity, it costs money. Hot water is a luxury. I do not have luxuries. I know you will be surprised when I tell you how young I am. I look so much older. My back has been bent over the wash tubs every day for so long I cannot remember when I ever did anything else. Every night I wash every stitch my school age child has on and just hope her clothes will be dry by morning.

5   Poverty is staying up all night on cold nights to watch the fire, knowing one spark on the newspaper covering the walls means your sleeping child dies in flames. In summer, poverty is watching gnats and flies devour your baby's tears when he cries. The screens are torn, and you pay so little rent you know they will never be fixed. Poverty means insects in your food, in your nose, in your eyes, and crawling over you when you sleep. Poverty is hoping it never rains because diapers won't dry when it rains and soon you are using newspapers. Poverty is seeing your children forever with runny noses. Paper handkerchiefs cost money, and all your rags you need for other things. Even more costly are antihistamines. Poverty is cooking without food and cleaning without soap.

6   Poverty is asking for help. Have you ever had to ask for help, knowing your children will suffer unless you get it? Think about asking for a loan from a relative, if this is the only way you can imagine asking for help. I will tell you how it feels. You find out where the office is that you are supposed to visit. You circle that block four or five times. Thinking of your children, you go in. Everyone is busy. Finally, someone comes out, and you tell her that you need help. That never is the person you need to see. You go see another person, and after spilling the whole shame of your poverty all

over the desk between you, you find that this isn't the right office after all—you must repeat the whole process, and it never is any easier at the next place.

You have asked for help, and after all it has a cost. You are again told to wait. You are told why, but you don't really hear because of the red cloud of shame and the rising cloud of despair.

7

Poverty is remembering. It is remembering quitting school in junior high because "nice" children had been so cruel about my clothes and my smell. The attendance officer came. My mother told him I was pregnant. I wasn't, but she thought I could get a job and help out. I had jobs off and on, but never long enough to learn anything. Mostly, I remember being married. I was so young then. I am still young. For a time, we had all the things you have. There was a little house in another town, hot water and everything. Then my husband lost his job. There was unemployment insurance for a while and what few jobs I could get. Soon, all our nice things were repossessed and we moved back here. I was pregnant then. This house didn't look so bad when we first moved in. Every week it gets worse. Nothing is ever fixed. We now had no money. There were a few odd jobs for my husband, but everything went for food then, as it does now. I don't know how we lived through three years and three babies, but we did. I'll tell you something: After the last baby died, I destroyed my marriage. It had been a good one, but could you keep on bringing children in this dirt? Did you ever think how much it costs for any kind of birth control? I knew my husband was leaving the day he left, but there were no goodbyes between us. I hope he has been able to climb out of this mess somewhere. He never could hope with us to drag him down.

8

That's when I asked for help. When I got it, you know how much it was? It was, and is, seventy-eight dollars a month for the four of us; that is all I ever can get. Now you know why there is no soap, no needles and thread, no hot water, no aspirin, no worm medicine, no hand cream, no shampoo. None of these things forever and ever and ever. So that you can see clearly, I pay twenty dollars a month rent, and most of the rest goes for food. For grits and cornmeal, and rice and milk and beans. I try my best to use only the minimum electricity. If I use more, there is that much less for food.

9

Poverty is looking into a black future. Your children won't play with my boys. They will turn to other boys who steal to get what they want. I can already see them behind the bars of their prison instead of behind the bars of my poverty. Or will they turn to the freedom of alcohol or drugs and find themselves enslaved. And my daughter? At best, there is for her a life like mine.

But you say to me, there are schools. Yes, there are schools. My children have no extra books, no magazines, no extra pencils, or crayons, or paper and most important of all, they do not have health. They have worms, they have infections, they have pink-eye all summer. They do not sleep well on the floor or with me in my one bed. They do not suffer from hunger, my seventy-eight dollars keeps us alive, but they do suffer from malnutrition. Oh yes, I do remember what I was taught about health in school. It doesn't do much good. In some places there is a surplus commodities program. Not here. The county said it cost too much. There is a school lunch program. But I have two children who will already be damaged by the time they get to school.

11

of poverty in the hope that someone will respond to her pleas for help.

5. Parker is addressing all of us, but especially those who do not understand how anyone can live in Parker's position and who look down on her because she lives the way she does.

6. Answers will vary.

Thinking Critically About Paragraphs

7. Parker is stating that she knows she repulses many people, but she must expose herself fully and assertively to get people to listen. Parker is attempting to shock readers with her bluntness in order to capture their attention.

8. Here are some examples of Parker's lists from paragraph 11:

"no extra books, no magazines, no extra pencils, or crayons, or paper"

"They have worms, they have infections, they have pink-eye all summer"

"They do not sleep well....They do not suffer from hunger...they do suffer from malnutrition"

These lists create the feeling that

12   But, you say to me, there are health clinics. Yes, there are health clinics, and they are in the town. I live out here eight miles from town. I can walk that far (even if it is 16 miles both ways), but can my little children? My neighbor will take me when he goes; but he expects to get paid, one way or another. I bet you know my neighbor. He is that large man who spends his time at the gas station, the barbershop, and the corner store complaining about the government spending money on the immoral mothers of illegitimate children.

13   Poverty is an acid that drips on pride until all pride is worn away. Poverty is a chisel that chips on honor until honor is worn away. Some of you say that you would do something in my situation, and maybe you would, for the first week or the first month, but for year after year after year?

14   Even the poor can dream—a dream of a time when there is money. Money for the right kinds of foods, for worm medicine, for iron pills, for toothbrushes, for hand cream, for hammer and nails and a bit of screening, for a shovel, for a bit of paint, for some sheeting, for needles and thread. Money to pay for a trip to town. And, oh, money for hot water and money for soap. A dream of when asking for help does not eat away the last bit of pride. When the office you visit is as nice as the offices of other governmental agencies, when there are enough workers to help you quickly, when workers do not quit in defeat and despair. When you have to tell your story to only one person and that person can send you for other help and you don't have to prove your poverty over and over again.

15   I have come out of my despair to tell you this. Remember I did not come from another place or another time. Others like me are all around you. Look at us with an angry heart; anger will help you help me. Anger that will let you tell of me. The poor are always silent. Can you be silent too?

Thinking Critically About Content

1. Parker develops her definition of poverty with a series of examples from her own life. Which of these examples communicates most clearly to you what poverty is? Explain your answer.

2. Explain the meaning of Parker's final paragraph. What is the main message of this paragraph?

3. Do you think the level of poverty that Parker describes is still a major part of our society? Give evidence for your answer.

Thinking Critically About Purpose and Audience

4. Why do you think Parker wrote this essay?

5. Who do you think is Parker's audience in this essay? Explain your answer.

6. Does this essay make you feel more or less pity for those who live below the poverty line? Explain your answer.

Thinking Critically About Paragraphs

7. What do you think Parker is saying in her first paragraph? Why do you think she starts her essay this way?

8. Parker's style is very curt and to the point in this essay. Instead of transitions, she uses parallel lists and pronouns to give her paragraphs coherence. Look specifically at paragraph 11. Underline the words and phrases that are in list form. (Refer to Chapter 41 for information on parallel structure.) Then explain the feeling these lists create in the paragraph.

9. Many of Parker's paragraphs start with a definition of poverty, "Poverty is . . . ." What effect does this repetition have on the essay as a whole?

10. Paragraph 13 is a collection of metaphors that explain poverty. Metaphors are comparisons expressed without using *like* or *as* with words that cannot be taken literally. Make sure you understand the two metaphors Parker uses in the first two sentences. Then rewrite this paragraph in your own words.

Writing Workshop

This section gives you the opportunity to apply what you have learned in this chapter to another writing assignment. This time, we provide you with the guidelines only and let you go through your own writing process with occasional feedback from your peers. Refer to sections of the chapter as necessary until the process of producing a paragraph becomes automatic for you.

Guidelines for Writing a Definition Paragraph

1. State your purpose in your topic sentence.
2. Decide how you want to define your term or idea.
3. Use examples to expand on your definition.
4. Organize your examples to communicate your definition as clearly as possible.

Writing About Your Reading

1. In the first essay, Gary Mack defines *motivation*. Write your own definition of *motivation* or of another aspect of life, such as *pleasure*, *recreation*, or *athletics*.

2. Using Jo Goodwin Parker's method of development through examples, define *wealth*.

her problems are endless. They do not move from one to the next; they all seem to be present constantly.

9. The repetition of "poverty is" doesn't let readers forget the subject of her essay. Just when Parker finishes an intense description of one aspect of poverty, she reminds readers there is more to come.

10. Answers will vary.

To keep track of your critical thinking progress, go to Appendix 1.

ADDITIONAL WRITING TOPIC
Ask your students to expand the paragraphs they wrote on page 254 into well-developed essays.

TEACHING ON THE WEB
Discussion Topic: After a few clicks in a search engine, people can have definitions and information at their fingertips. Divide students into groups of three or four, and have them discuss the advantages and disadvantages of finding information so quickly. What is society losing by not using a library?

TEACHING ON THE WEB
Links: Provide students with a complex term, and have them link to Web sites that define the term. How does each site use definition? Which site defines the term most

clearly? Possible sites for the topic *homeopathy*:

Homeopathy World, homeopathyworld.com/ homeopathy.htm

Standard & Hyland's Homeopathic Products, homeopathy-soh.org/ about-homeopathy/ what-is-homeopathy/

Hahnemann Labs, hahnemannlabs.com/about_ homeopathy.html

TEACHING ON THE WEB *Research:* Provide students with an abstract concept like freedom or liberty, and have them search Web sites for a definition of these terms. Which Web site had the best definition? Why, in the context of the overall Web site, do the students think this is so?

3. Now that you have studied different approaches to the process of definition, what makes a definition effective or useful for you? Apply what you have studied about definition to your answer.

Writing About Your World

Lawrence Migdale/Science Source

1. Define *parenthood* from your point of view.

2. Define *relaxation* or *stress*, depending on your mood today.

3. Define one of the following abstract terms: *knowledge, fear, love, inferiority, wonder, pride, self-control, discipline, anger, freedom, violence, assertiveness, fellowship, friendship, courtesy, kindness.*

4. Create your own definition assignment (with the help of your instructor), and write a response to it.

Revising

Small Group Activity (5–10 minutes per writer) Working in groups of three or four, read your definition papers to each other.

Those listening should record their reactions on a copy of the Revising Peer Evaluation Forms in Appendix 4. After your group goes through this process, give your evaluation forms to the appropriate writers so that each writer has two or three peer comment sheets for revising.

Paired Activity (5 minutes per writer) Using the completed Peer Evaluation Forms, work in pairs to decide what you should revise. If time allows, rewrite some of your sentences, and have your partner check them.

Individual Activity Rewrite your paper using the revising feedback you received from other students.

Editing

Paired Activity (5–10 minutes per writer) Swap papers with a classmate, and use the Editing Peer Evaluation Form in Appendix 6 to identify as many grammar, punctuation, mechanics, and spelling errors as you can. If time allows, correct some of your errors, and have your partner check them. Record your grammar, punctuation, and mechanics errors in the Error Log (Appendix 7) and your spelling errors in the Spelling Log (Appendix 8).

Individual Activity Rewrite your paper again using the editing feedback you received from other students.

Reflecting on Your Writing   When you have completed your own paragraph, answer these six questions:

1. What was most difficult about this assignment?

2. What was easiest?

3. What did you learn about definition by completing this assignment?

4. What do you think are the strengths of your definition? Place a wavy line by the parts of your paragraph that you feel are very good.

5. What are the weaknesses, if any, of your paper? Place an X by the parts of your paragraph you would like help with. Write any questions you have in the margins.

6. What did you learn from this assignment about your own writing process—about preparing to write, about writing the first draft, about revising, and about editing?

Analyzing Causes and Effects

"You can't wait for inspiration. You have to go after it with a club."

—JACK LONDON

We all analyze causes and effects without even realizing it. Consider the following thoughts that might have crossed your mind:

- Why you find someone attractive;
- The reasons you thought a movie was good;
- The effects of cutting your English class;
- Your reaction to a political debate;
- The consequences of going out with your friends instead of studying for an exam.

Wanting to know why something happens is a natural interest that surfaces early in life—"Why can't I play outside today?" Not only do we want to know *why*, but we also want to know *what* will happen as a result of our actions. In like manner, your college courses often want you to analyze causes and effects. For example, an essay exam in a psychology course might ask "Why are some people superstitious?" Or a history question might be "What were the positive effects of the Spanish-American War?"

When we work with **causes and effects,** we are searching for connections and reasons. To understand a **cause,** we look to the past for reasons why something is the way it is. To discover an **effect,** we look to the future to figure out what the possible results of a particular action might be. In other words, we break an action or situation into parts and look at how these different parts relate to each other so that we can better understand the world around us.

In a book titled *Immigrant Kids*, Russell Freedman analyzes why the children of immigrants reject their parents' language and customs. He then discusses the results of this rejection. Can you see the difference between the causes and effects in this paragraph?

The children became Americanized much faster than their parents. Often this caused painful conflicts in immigrant families. A gap appeared between the children and their parents. The parents spoke English with heavy accents, if they spoke it at all. They clung to Old World customs and beliefs. The kids spoke English all day with their friends. They thought in American terms. More than anything else, they wanted to be accepted as equals in their adopted land. In their anxiety to become fully "American," some immigrant children rejected their Old World heritage and the traditional values of their parents. They felt embarrassed or even ashamed by their parents' immigrant ways.

You will refer to this passage again when you are learning the guidelines for writing a good cause/effect paragraph.

MyWritingLab

Understanding Cause and Effect

By now, you know the basics of analyzing causes and effects. To enhance your understanding, go to **MyWritingLab.com,** and click on **Cause and Effect** in the **Paragraph Development** module. For this topic, read the **Overview,** watch the **Animation** video, and complete the **Recall, Apply,** and **Write** activities. Then check your understanding of this material by taking the **Post-test.**

PREPARING TO WRITE A CAUSE/EFFECT PARAGRAPH

Learning how to read cause/effect paragraphs critically will improve your writing. Understanding how a reading selection actually works (in both form and content) will show you how to develop your own writing assignments. Like two parts of a whole, reading and writing work together to increase your ability to perform other tasks in all facets of life.

To begin with, you need to learn how to read cause/effect paragraphs critically. A sample paragraph will help you understand more clearly how good cause/effect reasoning works. First, you will apply a specific reading strategy to the paragraph. Next, you will answer some questions about the paragraph in an attempt to discover how it functions. With a detailed understanding of your reading, you will have more tools at your disposal for your writing.

After they complete the diagram, discuss with students the causes and effects for each article, paying particular attention to how a cause creates an effect that turns into a cause that becomes an effect, and so on. This exercise shows the importance of organization in cause/effect essays.

Student Comment: "**Cause and Effect** was the most helpful topic to me because I now feel more confident in writing cause and effect paragraphs and essays."

Coincidence vs. cause and effect is a difficult concept for students to grasp. Spend some time in class providing clear, specific examples of this concept before your students go to MyWritingLab.

For more detailed information on making connections, see pages 20–21 in Chapter 2.

READING CRITICALLY
Making Connections in a Professional Paragraph

Distinguishing causes from effects is an important part of understanding a cause/effect paragraph. After the first reading of a cause/effect paragraph, divide a sheet of paper into two parts with a vertical line. Then, as you read the paragraph for a second time, record the causes in the left column and the results in the right. Draw lines from each cause to its related effect (if applicable). Be prepared to explain the connections between your lists and the details in the paragraph.

Reading Strategy

Reading a Cause/Effect Paragraph

In this paragraph, Robert Hine writes about his life when surgery restored his eyesight after many years of blindness. The author focuses on points of contact among humans. Does the author deal with both causes and effects in this paragraph? Make two lists with arrows so you can see how Hine's paragraph works. Then answer the questions after the paragraph.

We assume that the face is the primary means of human contact. "Face-to-face" is a basic term in the language. It refers to one-on-one relationships, fundamental in the building of strong traditional communities. What then for the blind? Because they do not see faces, are they excluded from community? Obviously not. The blind do not need to "face" one another (though they often do so, turning toward the voice as a gesture of respect or an effort to conform). Theirs is the special bonding based either on their own internal images from voices or on some spiritual sense. Though faces are newly precious to me, for myself or for my community, I realize that the blind have their own form of face-to-face relationships.

Discovering How This Paragraph Works

To help you discover the elements that make this an effective cause/effect paragraph so you can use them in your own writing, answer the following questions in as much detail as possible.

1. What is Hine analyzing in this paragraph?

   Face-to-face relationships in both sighted and unsighted people's lives

2. Does Hine's topic sentence capture this focus? Explain your answer.

Yes, in general terms. Answers will vary beyond this.

3. What one cause and one effect does Hine cite? How does each relate to the topic sentence?

Cause	Relation to Topic Sentence
The blind do not see faces.	*only one aspect of face-to-face contact*

Effects	
The blind turn their faces toward the voice.	*another form of face-to-face contact*

4. Do you feel that Hine gets to the real causes and effects connected with face-to-face relationships among the blind? Explain your answer.

Answers will vary.

5. How does Hine organize the details in his paragraph: chronologically or from one extreme to another?

From one extreme to another—least to most important aspects of human contact

WRITING A CAUSE/EFFECT PARAGRAPH

Now that you have read and studied a cause/effect paragraph, you will be writing one of your own. This section will help you generate a rough draft that you will then revise and edit in the third section of this chapter. It will guide you through a careful reading of the writing assignment, give you several ways to generate ideas, and finally furnish you with concrete guidelines for writing an effective cause/effect paragraph. We encourage you to write notes and lists throughout this section so you can use them when you write a draft of your paragraph at the end of this section.

Reading the Prompt

Reading Strategy

The very first step in writing a good paragraph is making sure you understand the writing assignment or "prompt." An assignment attempts to "prompt" you to respond to a specific issue or question. The more clearly you understand the prompt, the better paragraph or essay you will create.

Applying the chapter reading strategy to your writing assignment is a good way to accomplish this goal.

READING CRITICALLY
Making Connections in the Prompt

What are the tasks you need to perform in the writing prompt that follows? Put a vertical line down the center of a blank sheet of paper, and list the assignment tasks on the left and what you need to do to complete those tasks on the right. Then write as many personal notes as you can in the margins of your lists. Finally, underline the key words for completing this assignment.

Writing Prompt

Complete this **Writing Prompt** at **mywritinglab.com**

Why did you choose the college you are attending today? Explain in a paragraph the events that led up to your decision and the results you expect from attending this college. Be as thorough as possible in your explanation. Use the guidelines below to get yourself started on your paragraph.

Thinking About the Prompt

Before you focus on a specific topic, you should generate as many ideas as you can so you have several to choose from. List all the factors you can think of that played a part in your college decision. Were any of these factors more important than others? Put a star by the two or three fundamental reasons behind your decision. In another column, list all the consequences of the choice you made. Put a star by the two or three main results. Use one or more of the prewriting techniques you learned in Chapter 3 to generate and record as many thoughts as possible about your college choice.

Guidelines for Writing a Cause/Effect Paragraph

Writing about causes and effects requires careful critical thinking. To do this well, you must discover connections between two or more events or ideas and explain the connection. Although this is a complex form of writing, good cause/effect paragraphs follow a few simple guidelines. We use Russell Freedman's paragraph at the beginning of this chapter to demonstrate each step.

1. **Write a topic sentence that makes a clear statement about what you are going to analyze.** This should always be the first step in a cause/effect paragraph. You need to decide what you are analyzing and whether you

PREWRITING EXERCISE
Have students use the prewriting method they prefer to start thinking about why they chose the college they're attending today. What separated this school from the other possibilities?

TEACHING TIPS
The following eight teaching tips are based on Howard Gardner's list of multiple intelligences:

Verbal/Linguistic
Have students find a short cause/effect article in a magazine and search for all the causes and effects. What words in the article help a reader know when either a cause or an effect

are going to focus on causes (activities leading up to the event), effects (the results of an event), or both. These decisions will give focus and coherence to the rest of your paragraph.

In the Reading: In Russell Freedman's paragraph, Freedman writes a very clear topic sentence: "The children became Americanized much faster than their parents." His topic sentence suggests that he will be discussing both the causes and effects of this observation.

In Your Writing: As you think about your college decision, what will you analyze in your paragraph? Write a rough draft of your topic sentence? Does this sentence say what you are going to analyze?

2. **Choose facts and details to support your topic sentence.** These facts and details are the causes and effects that fully explain your topic sentence. To generate this material, try to anticipate your readers' questions and then answer them in your paragraph.

In the Reading: In Freedman's paragraph, the author cites two *results* of Americanization at the beginning of the paragraph:

> often caused painful conflicts

> gaps appeared between children and parents

Then he discusses seven *causes* of this situation—two from the parents' side of the conflict:

> spoke English with heavy accents

> clung to Old World customs

and five from the children's side:

> spoke English all day long

> thought in American terms

> wanted to be accepted as equals

> rejected Old World customs

> were embarrassed by their parents' immigrant ways

In Your Writing: Expand your prewriting list of causes and effects so that you have as many details to work with as possible. Based on these additions, do your top five items change on either list?

3. **Make sure you include the *real* causes and effects of your topic.** Just as you wouldn't stop reading halfway through a good murder mystery, you shouldn't stop too early in your analysis of causes and effects. For example, a student might fail a biology exam because she was sick. However, if you dig a little deeper, you may find that she missed several lectures, didn't study very much, and is exhausted holding down two jobs. Similarly, failing the exam probably has many effects: She may quit one job, promise herself to attend class regularly, and study harder

is being described? What words, if removed from the article, weaken the cause/effect relationships?

Musical/Rhythmic

Listen to an old song that you had an emotional connection with years ago. What feeling does this song stimulate? What causes this song to have such an effect on you?

Logical/Mathematical

Have students diagram the causes and effects associated with a class.

For example,

Cause	Effect
Class is interesting and informative.	Grade of A
I didn't understand and didn't study hard.	Grade of D

Visual/Spatial

Bring in numerous pictures (without any words) that depict cause/effect relationships. For example, you might bring in pictures of a flood: people trying desperately to place sandbags around their homes, water breaking through the barrier, a home floating down a river, a family stranded at a Red Cross facility, and a family looking at where their home used to stand. Then ask students to put the pictures into a logical order. Finally, have them justify and explain the order.

Bodily/Kinesthetic

Have students play Jenga, a game that tests their ability to understand critical thinking skills. But before they remove a piece from the structure, have them state what the effects of removing the piece will be (for example, "This will not weaken the structure, but it will cause the next move to weaken it"). If they miscalculate, have them state the causes of the tower's destruction.

Intrapersonal

Have students think about times when they tried to study or work but were distracted. What were the causes of the distraction? What effects did these causes produce? How would students make sure these distractions don't occur again?

Interpersonal

Have a group of students go to a magic store and ask a magician to show them some tricks. Then have students try to figure out the causes that make the tricks work (effects).

Naturalist

Have students film a video or take pictures that show the influence of humans on nature. What are the causes and effects of the human influence on nature?

INSTRUCTOR'S RESOURCE MANUAL For additional material about teaching cause/effect, for journal entries, and for various tests, see the *Instructor's Resource Manual*, Section II, Part II.

for the next test. In other words, the actual causes and effects may not be the most obvious ones. This digging for the basic causes and effects will help you avoid confusing causes and effects with coincidences.

In the Reading: In the sample paragraph, Freedman keeps digging for the "real" reasons for the conflict and tension in immigrant families. He first lists ways children try to become more American and finally realizes that they are basically embarrassed by their heritage.

In Your Writing: Does your list include the *real* causes and effects? If you explore any of the items on your lists, would you discover deeper reasons for your choice of colleges? Dig even further into this topic by making another list of causes and results related to your choice of colleges.

4. **Organize your material so that it communicates your message as clearly as possible.** You should present your details in a logical order—perhaps chronologically or from one extreme to another. Chronological order follows a time sequence; from one extreme to another could involve any two extremes.

In the Reading: Freedman organizes his paragraph from least serious to most serious according to the two different groups he is discussing. He first takes up the parents' point of view (from accent to customs) and then deals with the children's side (from their speaking English all day to their feelings of embarrassment and shame).

In Your Writing: How will you organize the details in your paragraph: general to specific, specific to general, spatial, chronological, or from one extreme to another? (See Chapter 3 for explanations of these.) Is this method of organization the best choice for achieving your purpose? Reorganize your lists to fit this method of organization so you are ready to write your paragraph.

Writing a Draft of Your Paragraph

Now is the time to collect all your associations, your conclusions, your notes, your prewriting exercises, and your lists as you generate the first draft of your paragraph. You might want to review the professional essay, the writing assignment, and the chapter guidelines to help you write a draft of your paragraph. At this point, don't think about revising or editing; just get a rough draft of your ideas down on paper in response to the writing prompt.

MyWritingLab **Helpful Hints**

- **Need more ideas now that you are going to write?** Generate more ideas through prewriting; visit **Prewriting** in **The Craft of Writing** module in **MyWritingLab** to find out how.

- **Do you have enough details?** Including detailed definitions to support your cause/effect paragraph can help you convey a specific point. For more information about how to define your subject, see **Defining** in the **Paragraph Development** module in **MyWritingLab.**

REVISING AND EDITING

You are now ready to learn how to revise and edit. This section will guide you through the process of revising and editing cause/effect paragraphs in reference to two writing samples: another student's paragraph and your own paragraph. Finding strengths and weaknesses in another person's writing is often much easier than evaluating your own, so you will be reviewing the chapter guidelines by revising and editing another student's writing before applying the same guidelines to your own writing.

Reading a Student Paragraph

Here is a cause/effect paragraph written by a student named Matthew Machias. His paragraph analyzes the causes and effects of his experience with jury duty. Do you think Matthew gets to the real causes and effects of the jury's verdict in this paragraph?

Reading Strategy

READING CRITICALLY
Making Connections in the Student Paragraph

As you read Matthew's paragraph, see if you can find the points in his draft where he deals with causes. When does he focus on effects? After a first reading of the paragraph, divide a sheet of paper into two parts with a vertical line. As you read the paragraph a second time, record the causes in the left column and the results on the right. Draw lines from each cause to its related effect (if applicable). Try to find the deepest level of cause and effect that Matthew discusses. Be prepared to explain the connection between your lists and the details in the paragraph.

REVISING AND EDITING OPTIONS
Consider teaching revising and editing in a class discussion, in small groups, or in pairs.

CLASS ACTIVITY
Find a professionally written cause/effect paragraph that incorporates many of the other rhetorical modes. Have the students identify the instances of other modes, and then ask them how they think these other strategies help establish the cause/effect relationships in the paragraph as a whole.

[1]Serving on a jury and determining someone's future are the toughest tasks I've ever had to do. [2]We had finished listening to both sides present evidence, examine witnesses, and summarize their arguments. [3]We had looked at photographs of the terrible automobile accident, shots of the wreckage, close-ups of the defendant's best

friend, and even photos of him being taken away. ⁴We heard that Grant (the defendant) had been driving while intoxicated on Highway 281 at 2 a.m. after a party. ⁵His blood alcohol level was .11. ⁶Well over the legal limit. ⁷Grant had been convicted of drunk driving on previous occasions during 2012. ⁸Grant didn't know that his actions would lead to his best friend's death. ⁹Grant had completed a special program for drunk drivers in mid-May. ¹⁰I've heard those programs don't work well. ¹¹I don't know why those programs keep running. ¹²Grant was driving over 80 mph while drunk, even though his license had been suspended. ¹³When Grant's friend got in the car with him that night, was Grant's friend partly to blame for his own death. ¹⁴What a tough question this is? ¹⁵Even though the 22-year-old defendant looked like a nice person, he was guilty. ¹⁶Grant and his friend knew what they were doing when he drove to the party that night. ¹⁷He knew what he was doing when he took that first drink. ¹⁸Grant's friend trusted him. ¹⁹That was the last decision he was ever able to make. ²⁰After we filed back into the jury box. ²¹The foreman read our verdict of second-degree murder. ²²I knew that the group's judgment was the right one, even though I still felt sorry for the defendant.

Revising and Editing the Student Paragraph

This paragraph is Matthew's first draft, which now needs to be revised and edited. First, apply the following Revising Checklist to the content of Matthew's draft. When you are satisfied that his ideas are fully developed and well organized, use the Editing Checklist to correct his grammar and mechanics errors. Answer the questions, and complete the tasks in each category. Then write your suggested changes directly on Matthew's draft.

REVISING STRATEGIES
This chapter focuses on the following revising elements:
Unity
Organization
Coherence

Revising the Student Paragraph

TOPIC SENTENCE

✔ Does the topic sentence convey the paragraph's controlling idea?

✔ Does the topic sentence appear as the first or last sentence of the paragraph?

1. What is Matthew analyzing in his paragraph?

   A jury decision about a drunk driving case

2. Put brackets around Matthew's topic sentence. Does it capture the paragraph's focus?

   [Serving on a jury and determining someone's future are the toughest

   tasks I've ever had to do.] Yes

3. Make sure it introduces all the ideas in Matthew's paragraph.

DEVELOPMENT

✔ Does the paragraph contain *specific* details that support the topic sentence?

✔ Does the paragraph include *enough* details to fully explain the topic sentence?

1. Do the details in the paragraph refer to specific causes and effects?

   Yes

2. Where does Matthew deal with causes? Where does he deal with effects?
   Answers will vary.

Causes	Effects
Jury looked at evidence	*Jury convicted Grant*
Grant was driving drunk	*Grant wrecked car*
Grant wrecked his car	*Friend died*

UNITY

✔ Do all the sentences in the paragraph support the topic sentence?

1. Read each of Matthew's sentences with his topic sentence (revised, if necessary) in mind.

2. Cross out the two sentences that are not directly related to Matthew's topic sentence.   *Sentences 10 and 11*

ORGANIZATION

✔ Is the paragraph organized logically?

1. Read Matthew's paragraph again to see if all the sentences are arranged logically.

2. Identify Matthew's method of organization.

   Chronological

3. Move the one example that seems to be out of order.   *Move sentence 12 before sentence 5.*

COHERENCE

✔ Do the sentences move smoothly and logically from one to the next?

1. Circle three pronouns Matthew uses.

2. Change three references to Grant to pronouns, and explain how they affect Matthew's paragraph.

   For a list of pronouns, see page 365.

   Answers will vary.

  Now rewrite Matthew's paragraph with your revisions.

EDITING STRATEGIES

This chapter focuses on the following editing problems:

Fragments

Pronoun agreement

End punctuation

Editing the Student Paragraph

SENTENCES

Subject and Verbs

✔ Does each sentence have a main subject and verb?

For help with subjects and verbs, see Chapter 20.

1. Underline the subjects once and verbs twice in your revision of Matthew's paragraph. Remember that sentences can have more than one subject-verb set.

2. Does each of the sentences have at least one subject and verb that can stand alone?

   No, not in the original paragraph

For help with fragments, see Chapter 21.

3. Did you find and correct Matthew's two fragments? If not, find and correct them now.   *Sentences 6 and 20*

Subject-Verb Agreement

✔ Do all subjects and verbs agree?

For help with subject-verb agreement, see Chapter 25.

1. Read aloud the subjects and verbs you underlined in your revision of Matthew's paragraph.

2. Correct any subjects and verbs that do not agree.   *All subjects agree with their verbs in the original paragraph.*

Pronoun Agreement

✔ Do all pronouns agree with their nouns?

For help with pronoun agreement, see Chapter 29.

1. Find any pronouns in your revision of Matthew's paragraph that do not agree with their nouns.   *Grant and his friend/he (sentence 16), antecedent of he and he (sentence 17), antecedent of he (sentence 19)*

2. Did you find and correct the four pronoun agreement errors in Matthew's paragraph? If not, find and correct them now.   *they (sentence 16), Grant or his friend/he (sentence 17), Grant or his friend (sentence 19)*

Modifier Errors

✔ Are modifiers as close as possible to the words they modify?

For help with modifier errors, see Chapter 32.

1. Find any modifiers in your revision of Matthew's paragraph that are not as close as possible to the words they modify.   *There are no modifier errors in the original paragraph.*

2. Rewrite sentences if necessary so that the modifiers are as close as possible to the words they modify.

PUNCTUATION AND MECHANICS

Punctuation

✔ Are sentences punctuated correctly?

1. Read your revision of Matthew's paragraph for any errors in punctuation.

2. Find the two fragments you revised, and make sure they are punctuated correctly.

3. Did you find and correct two errors in end punctuation in Matthew's paragraph? If not, find and correct them now. *Sentence 13 needs a question mark, and sentence 14 needs an exclamation point.*

For help with punctuation, see Chapters 33–37.

Mechanics
✔ Are words capitalized properly?

1. Read your revision of Matthew's paragraph for any errors in capitalization. *All capitals are correct in the original paragraph.*
2. Be sure to check Matthew's capitalization in the fragments you revised.

For help with capitalization, see Chapter 38.

WORD CHOICE AND SPELLING

Word Choice
✔ Are words used correctly?

1. Find any words used incorrectly in your revision of Matthew's paragraph. *All words are used correctly in the original paragraph.*
2. Correct any errors you find.

For help with confused words, see Chapter 44.

Spelling
✔ Are words spelled correctly?

1. Use spell-check and a dictionary to check the spelling in your revision of Matthew's paragraph. *All words are spelled correctly in the original paragraph.*

2. Correct any misspelled words.

For help with spelling see Chapter 45.

 Now rewrite Matthew's paragraph again with your editing corrections.

Reading Your Own Cause/Effect Paragraph

Returning to the cause/effect paragraph you wrote earlier in this chapter, you are now ready to revise and edit your own writing. You will first read your paragraph with the same reading strategy you have applied to other reading tasks in this chapter so you can look at it as your reader might.

READING CRITICALLY
Making Connections in
Your Own Paragraph

As you begin to rework your paragraph, use the same technique on it that you have been practicing throughout this chapter. List the causes and effects that you discuss in your essay in two columns. Then draw lines from causes to related effects, making sure the relationship between these items is clear to your readers. Revise any connections that are unclear.

Revising and Editing Your Own Paragraph

The checklists here will help you apply what you have learned in this chapter to your own paragraph. Consider your content first, making sure your paragraph is well developed and effectively organized. Then find and correct your grammar and usage errors.

For Revising Peer Evaluation Forms, go to Appendix 4.

Revising Your Own Paragraph

TOPIC SENTENCE

☐ Does the topic sentence convey the paragraph's controlling idea?

☐ Does the topic sentence appear as the first or last sentence of the paragraph?

1. What are you analyzing in your paragraph?

_____

2. Underline your topic sentence. Does it capture the focus of your paragraph?

_____

3. Make sure it introduces all the ideas in your paragraph.

DEVELOPMENT

☐ Does the paragraph contain *specific* details that support the topic sentence?

☐ Does the paragraph include *enough* details to fully explain the topic sentence?

1. Do the details in your paragraph refer to specific causes and effects?

_____

2. Where do you deal with causes? Where do you deal with effects?

Causes	Effects
_____	_____
_____	_____
_____	_____
_____	_____

UNITY

☐ Do all the sentences in the paragraph support the topic sentence?

1. Read each of your sentences with your topic sentence in mind.

2. Drop or rewrite any sentences that are not directly related to your topic sentence.

ORGANIZATION

☐ Is the paragraph organized logically?

1. Read your paragraph again to see if all the sentences are arranged logically.

2. What method of organization did you use for your paragraph?

_____

3. What word clues from your paragraph tell your readers how it is organized?

_____

COHERENCE

☐ Do the sentences move smoothly and logically from one to the next?

1. Circle three pronouns you use.

2. Add at least one pronoun to your paragraph, and explain how it makes your paragraph easier to read.

For a list of pronouns, see page 365.

_____

_____

  Now rewrite your paragraph with your revisions.

Editing Your Own Paragraph

For Editing Peer Evaluation Forms, go to Appendix 6.

SENTENCES

Subject and Verbs

☐ Does each sentence have a main subject and verb?

1. Underline the subjects once and verbs twice in your revised paragraph. Remember that sentences can have more than one subject-verb set.

For help with subjects and verbs, see Chapter 20.

2. Does each of your sentences have at least one subject and verb that can stand alone?

For help with fragments, see Chapter 21.

For help with run-togethers, see Chapter 22.

3. Correct any fragments you have written.

4. Correct any run-together sentences you have written.

Subject-Verb Agreement
☐ Do all subjects and verbs agree?

For help with subject-verb agreement, see Chapter 25.

1. Read aloud the subjects and verbs you underlined in your revised paragraph.

2. Correct any subjects and verbs that do not agree.

Pronoun Agreement
☐ Do all pronouns agree with their nouns?

For help with pronoun agreement, see Chapter 29.

1. Find any pronouns in your revised paragraph that do not agree with their nouns.

2. Correct any pronouns that do not agree with their nouns.

Modifier Errors
☐ Are modifiers as close as possible to the words they modify?

For help with modifier errors, see Chapter 32.

1. Find any modifiers in your revised paragraph that are not as close as possible to the words they modify.

2. Rewrite sentences if necessary so that your modifiers are as close as possible to the words they modify.

PUNCTUATION AND MECHANICS

Punctuation
☐ Are sentences punctuated correctly?

For help with punctuation, see Chapters 33–37.

1. Read your revised paragraph for any errors in punctuation.

2. Make sure any fragments and run-together sentences you revised are punctuated correctly.

Mechanics
☐ Are words capitalized properly?

For help with capitalization, see Chapter 38.

1. Read your revised paragraph for any errors in capitalization.

2. Be sure to check your capitalization in any fragments and run-together sentences you revised.

WORD CHOICE AND SPELLING

Word Choice

☐ Are words used correctly?

1. Find any words used incorrectly in your revised paragraph.
2. Correct any errors you find.

For help with confused words, see Chapter 44.

Spelling

☐ Are words spelled correctly?

1. Use spell-check and a dictionary to check your spelling.
2. Correct any misspelled words.

For help with spelling, see Chapter 45.

To make a personal log of your grammar/usage errors, go to Appendix 7.

To make a personal log of your spelling errors, go to Appendix 8.

Now rewrite your paragraph again with your editing corrections.

MyWritingLab More Helpful Hints

- **Do you need some reminders about revising?** Cause-and-effect paragraphs require clear structure and detailed examples, so you need to pay special attention to these features as you revise. Go to **Revising the Paragraph** in **The Craft of Writing** module in **MyWritingLab** to get some help with these aspects of the revising process.
- **Do you know the difference between active and passive voice?** Using active voice can help you create a clear picture of a cause/effect relationship. To learn more about how to use the active voice, go to **Consistent Verb Tense and Active Voice** in the **Sentence Skills** module in **MyWritingLab.**

PRACTICING CAUSE/EFFECT: FROM READING TO WRITING

This final section lets you practice the reading and writing skills you learned in this chapter. It includes two reading selections and several writing assignments on "your reading" and "your world." The section then offers guidance in peer evaluation and reflection, ending with suggestions about how to lead your instructor through your writing in ways that will benefit both of you.

Reading
Strategy

Reading Workshop

Here are two essays that follow the guidelines you have studied in this chapter. In "Does Game Violence Make Teens Aggressive?," Kristin Kalning discusses the connection between violent video games and real violence, and in "Life Sentences," Corky Clifton analyzes the role of writing in his life as a prisoner. As you read, notice how the writers make their points through well-thought-out, detailed reasoning.

DOES GAME VIOLENCE MAKE TEENS AGGRESSIVE?
by Kristin Kalning

SUMMARY
In this essay, Kristin Kalning studies the connection between violent video games and violent behavior.

READABILITY
(Flesch-Kincaid grade level) 11.8

INSTRUCTOR'S RESOURCE MANUAL
For additional teaching strategies, for journal entries, for vocabulary and reading quizzes, and for more writing assignments, see the *Instructor's Resource Manual,* Section II, Part II.

Focusing Your Attention

1. Do you play violent video games and/or watch violent movies? If so, how do you feel after observing this type of violence?

2. The essay you are about to read openly discusses the relationship between game violence and real violence. What do you think this relationship is? How do you think we might control this relationship?

Expanding Your Vocabulary

The following words are important to your understanding of this essay. As you read, circle any words you don't know beyond this list. Then break into groups, and help each other figure out the meanings of these unknown words.

inhibition: self-consciousness (paragraph 1)

MRIs: Magnetic resonance imaging, a medical imaging technique used in radiology to visualize the functions of specific body parts (paragraph 4)

gravitate: move (paragraph 13)

epidemic: major outbreak (paragraph 14)

READING CRITICALLY
Making Connections in Your Reading

As you learned throughout this chapter, practice recognizing causes and effects by listing those that appear in the following essay. Put them in two columns on a separate sheet of paper. These lists will help you understand the essay on an analytical level. Compare your notes with those of a classmate.

DOES GAME VIOLENCE MAKE TEENS AGGRESSIVE?[1]
by Kristin Kalning

1. Can video games make kids more violent? A study employing state-of-the-art brain-scanning technology says that the answer may be yes. Researchers at the Indiana University School of Medicine say that brain scans of kids who played a violent video game showed an increase in emotional arousal—and a corresponding decrease of activity in brain areas involved in self-control, inhibition, and attention. Does this mean that your teenager will feel an uncontrollable urge to go on a shooting rampage after playing "Call of Duty?"

2. Vince Mathews, the principal investigator on the study, hesitates to make that leap. But he says he does think that the study should encourage parents to look more closely at the types of games their kids are playing: "Based on our results, I think parents should be aware of the relationship between violent video-game playing and brain function."

3. Mathews and his colleagues chose two action games to include in their research— one violent the other not. The first game was the high-octane but non-violent racing game "Need for Speed: Underground." The other was the ultra-violent, first-person shooter "Medal of Honor: Frontline."

4. The team divided a group of 44 adolescents into two groups and randomly assigned the kids to play one of the two games. Immediately after the play sessions, the children were given MRIs of their brains. The scans showed a negative effect on the brains of the teens who played "Medal of Honor" for 30 minutes. That same effect was not present in the kids who played "Need for Speed." The only difference? Violent content.

5. What's not clear is whether the activity picked up by the MRIs indicates a lingering—or worse, permanent—effect on the kids' brains. And it's also not known what effect longer play times might have. The scope of this study was 30 minutes of play and one brain scan per kid, although further research is in the works.

6. But what about violent TV shows? Or violent films? Has anyone ever done a brain scan of kids who have just watched a violent movie? John P. Murray, a psychology professor at Kansas State University, conducted a very similar experiment, employing the same technology used in Mathews' study. His findings are similar. Kids in his study experienced increased emotional arousal when watching short clips from the boxing movie "Rocky IV."

7. So, why is everyone picking on video games? Probably because there's a much smaller body of research on video games. They just haven't been around as long as TV and movies, so the potential effects on children are a bigger unknown. That's a scary thing for a parent.

---

[1] Kristin Kalning, "Does Game Violence Make Teens Aggressive?" MSNBC.com, December 8, 2006. Copyright 2006 by MSNBC Interactive News, LLC. Reproduced with permission of MSNBC Interactive News, LLC in the format Textbook via Copyright Clearance Center.

8   Larry Ley, the director and coordinator of research for the Center for Successful Parenting, which funded Mathews' study, says the purpose of the research was to help parents make informed decisions. "There's enough data that clearly indicates that [game violence] is a problem," he says. "And it's not just a problem for kids with behavior disorders."

9   But not everyone is convinced that this latest research adds much to the debate—particularly the game development community. One such naysayer is Doug Lowenstein, president of the Entertainment Software Association: "We've seen other studies in this field that have made dramatic claims but turn out to be less persuasive when objectively analyzed."

10   The ESA has a whole section of its Web site dedicated to the topic of video game violence, which would suggest that they get asked about it a lot. And they've got plenty of answers at the ready for the critics who want to lay school shootings or teen aggression at the feet of the game industry. Several studies cited by the ESA point to games' potential benefits for developing decision-making skills or bettering reaction times.

11   Ley, however, argues such studies aren't credible because they were produced by "hired guns" funded by the multi-billion-dollar game industry. "We're not trying to sell [parents] anything," he says. "We don't have a product. The video game industry does."

12   Increasingly parents are more accepting of video game violence, chalking it up to being a part of growing up. "I was dead-set against violent video games," says Kelley Windfield, a Sammamish, Wa.-based mother of two. "But my husband told me I had to start loosening up."

13   Laura Best, a mother of three from Clovis, California, says she looks for age-appropriate games for her 14 year-old son, Kyle. And although he doesn't play a lot of games, he does tend to gravitate towards shooters like "Medal of Honor." But she isn't concerned that Kyle will become aggressive as a result. "That's like saying a soccer game or a football game will make a kid more aggressive," she says. "It's about self-control, and you've got to learn it."

14   Ley says he believes further research, for which the Center for Successful Parenting is trying to arrange, will prove a cause-and-effect relationship between game violence and off-screen aggression. But for now, he says, this study gives his organization the ammunition it needs to prove that parents need to be more aware of how kids are using their free time. "Let's quit using various Xboxes as babysitters instead of doing healthful activities," says Ley, citing the growing epidemic of childhood obesity in the United States. And who, really, can argue with that?

Thinking Critically About Content

1. According to the study conducted by Vince Mathews and his colleagues, what is the relationship between violence and video games?

2. According to this essay, what do similar studies show about the effects of violent movies on viewers?

3. According to the Entertainment Software Association, what are two benefits of playing video games?

Thinking Critically About Purpose and Audience

4. What do you think is Kalning's purpose in this essay?

5. Who do you think is her primary audience?

6. Why do you think parents are becoming more accepting of video games?

Thinking Critically About Paragraphs

7. What questions about the relationship between violence and video games remain unanswered? Why do you think the author brings up these issues? Explain your answer.

8. What games did the researchers use in their study? How many participants did you study? How long did they study these games? What is the value of furnishing these details in this essay?

9. What other consequences, besides violence, does Larry Ley attribute to the video game industry? Is this an effective ending to this essay?

10. Write a paragraph about the role of video games or violent movies in your life. Do you want to change the part they play in your life?

8. The researchers used "Need for Speed: Underground" (a non-violent racing game) and "Medal of Honor: Frontline" (a very violent shooter game) in their study; they studied 44 participants who played one of these games for 30 minutes and then underwent an MRI. Furnishing these details makes the study transparent and clear to the readers.

9. Ley attributes obesity to the video game industry, which is a striking way to end the essay.

10. Answers will vary.

To keep track of your critical thinking progress, go to Appendix 1.

LIFE SENTENCES
by Corky Clifton

Focusing Your Attention

1. Think of a time when you acted without carefully analyzing the situation. What were the results?

2. In the essay you are about to read, the writer analyzes his reasons for risking his life to escape from prison. Think of the most difficult decision you have ever had to make. In what way did you analyze the situation and circumstances before you made the decision? Did you think about it for a long time? Discuss it with others? Write about it?

Expanding Your Vocabulary

The following words are important to your understanding of this essay. As you read, circle any words you don't know beyond this list. Then break into groups, and help each other figure out the meanings of these unknown words.

disciplinary reports: reports of misconduct (paragraph 4)

D.A.: district attorney, prosecutor for the government (paragraph 4)

inflict: commit (paragraph 5)

SUMMARY
In this essay, Clifton describes his decision to escape from the Louisiana State Penitentiary.

READABILITY
(Flesch-Kincaid grade level) 7.8

INSTRUCTOR'S RESOURCE MANUAL
For additional teaching strategies, for journal entries, for vocabulary and reading quizzes, and for more writing assignments, see the *Instructor's Resource Manual,* Section II, Part II.

READING CRITICALLY
Making Connections to Your Reading

As you did with the previous essay, list the causes and effects in the following essay on a separate sheet of paper. Then draw lines from specific causes to the related effects. This process will give you some good insights into the author's approach to his topic and his methods of developing his ideas. Compare your notes with those of one of your classmates.

LIFE SENTENCES[2]
by Corky Clifton

1   Why did I escape? I suppose it was for the same reason that men have fought wars and died for throughout history. I wanted to be free.

2   For 27 years, I have submitted to discipline, the rules, the harsh conditions, the torment of my children growing from babies into men—without ever seeing them. I've never had a visit from any of my family during these 27 years because, being from Ohio, no one could afford the trip here to Louisiana.

3   I once thought, as most people do, that all you had to do in order to get out of prison was just be good and they'll let you out someday. One does not have to be in the prison system very long to learn what a joke that is.

4   If Jesus Christ himself was in here with a life sentence, he couldn't get out unless he had money to put in the right places. I've always been a pretty stubborn person, so even though I was told how the political and Pardon Board system works, I freely submitted to all the prison rules and discipline. After 12 years with a perfect record—no disciplinary reports—I applied to the Pardon Board and was denied any consideration for relief. So I waited 10 more years and applied again, still with an excellent prison record. This time they wouldn't even hear my case. In 1983, I applied to the board for the third time and the Pardon Board cut my time to 50 years. However, the judge and D.A., retired, simply called the governor's legal staff and told them they don't want me to be free—so, end of case. When I applied for my pardon in 1983, the D.A. published an article in the newspaper saying I was a very dangerous man that would kill anyone who got into my way. He said a lot of things which were all designed to turn public opinion against me and justify his reason for protesting my release.

---

[2] Corky Clifton, in an article by Wilbert Rideau and Ron Wikberg from *The Angolite: The Prison News Magazine*, June 1989. Reprinted by permission of Louisiana State Penitentiary, Angola, Louisiana.

In spite of having to endure the torment of prison life all these years without hope, I was still determined to better myself, no longer with any hope that a nice record would get me my freedom but because the years of discipline and hardships had molded my personality to the extent that I no longer desired to do anything criminal. I could not even inflict revenge on my enemies within prison.

I taught myself how to repair watches, and for more than 20 years I repaired watches for other prisoners as well as guards. I also taught myself how to paint pictures. At the 1988 Angola Arts & Crafts Festival, I won a second place for one of my watercolors. Aside from all my other accomplishments within prison, I have only two disciplinary reports in 27 years. I proved my honesty and sincerity many times over. Every time I made a friend through correspondence, one of the first things they wanted to know is how come I'm still in prison. I'm always tempted to use up several legal pads trying to explain about the corrupt legal and political system here in Louisiana. But who's gonna believe a man can be kept in here all his life just because some big shot out there doesn't want him out? Well, I am one example of it, and there are hundreds more lifers in here, many of them I know personally, who are in here for no other reason than because some big shot out there doesn't want them to go free. The only way you can get around that is *money*—in the right places.

Since the sheriff, the D.A., and/or the judge can dictate who can get out and who can't, then what's the purpose of a pardon board? Why the waste of taxpayers' money? I spent many years in here struggling for freedom. There are many people here in prison, as well as outside, who believe I should be free, but the judge and D.A. say they intend to see that I never go free, as long as I live. How am I supposed to handle that?

I'm not Charles Manson or some other mass murderer. I didn't torture or mutilate some child. When I was 23 years old, I killed a man in a robbery. That's bad enough. But the point is, hundreds of prisoners in here for the same and even worse crimes have been pardoned throughout all the years I've been here. The majority of them served only half or less time than I have.

Of course, it's no mystery to me why I'm still in prison. The judge and D.A. are keeping me here. But I say that's unfair—should, in fact, be illegal. They prosecuted and sentenced me 27 years ago, and that should be the end of their involvement in my case. They justify keeping me in here by claiming I am still the same dangerous man I was 27 years ago. If this were true, then I would like for someone to explain why, when I escaped a few weeks ago, I did not steal a car, knock someone in the head, or break into one of the many houses I passed.

On the night of April 15, when I finally made up my mind to escape, I knew the odds were against me. I was 52 years old and had already suffered two heart attacks. In those final few days before April 15, I fought many emotional battles with myself. I had a lot to lose, and I'd be letting down a lot of good people who'd put their trust in me. But desperation is pretty hard to win a rational argument with. My time was running out. Had run out, really, because I was certainly in no condition to run through that jungle in the Tunica Hills. But even against all odds, I went for it anyway.

I struggled through those hills, mountains really, for five days and six nights, sleeping on the ground, with no food and very little water. I ended up in Mississippi. I saw a lot of people, and I even talked to a few.

5

6

ANSWERS TO QUESTIONS

Thinking Critically About Content

1. Clifton is analyzing what he thinks is the unfairness of the Louisiana prison system. The title helps focus this analysis because readers understand from the beginning that Clifton is referring to something that will last for the rest of his life.

7

8

2. Answers will vary. Here are some examples:

Cause: escaping from prison

Effect: on the run for five days

Cause: could no longer commit crimes

9

Effect: had to give himself up to the authorities because he couldn't make it another day

10

3. Clifton ends with a question because he wants readers to think of themselves in his position. It is effective because not only do readers

11

think about their
own lives in this sit-
uation but they also
wonder which route
Clifton chooses.

**Thinking Critically
About Purpose and
Audience**

4. Clifton wrote this
essay to try to ex-
plain his actions and
to reveal the injus-
tice of the Louisiana
prison system.

5. Clifton's primary
audience is the
general public, who
would benefit from
knowing about the
prison corruption
that he discusses.

6. Answers will vary.

**Thinking Critically
About Paragraphs**

7. Clifton wants read-
ers to feel sorry
for him before he
tells them about his
crime. He thinks
that if he can elicit
their sympathy, they
won't feel his crime
was as bad as it was.

8. *Causes:* paragraphs
1–9. *Effects:* para-
graphs 10–15. It
is a good balance
because readers can
fully understand
why Clifton would
both choose to leave
and wish to return.
This balance also
helps readers un-
derstand Clifton's
last paragraph.

9. Paragraph 12 is or-
ganized from general
to particular moving
from the general
idea of committing

12   After a couple days I knew it would be impossible for me to get away unless I stole a car or knocked someone in the head. Not far from Woodville, Mississippi, I came across a house trailer. I sat in the bushes watching the trailer from about 50 yards away. I watched a woman drive up and unlock the door and go in alone. A few minutes later, she came out and washed her car. I could have knocked her in the head, or even killed her, took her car, and been long gone. But I couldn't bring myself to do that.

13   I discovered that in reality I could no longer commit the crimes that I once did. So here I stood in those bushes, watching that house trailer, that car, and that lady—my ticket to freedom—and discover I can't pay the price. I can't think of any words that could truly describe the dejection and hopelessness I felt at that moment. There was no way I could continue on as I had those five days past. There was just no strength left in my legs to go on. Resigned to my fate, I walked several hundred yards to the highway and gave myself up.

14   So now I am left with only two ways left to escape my torment. Just sit here for God knows how many more years and wait on a natural death. Or I can avoid all those senseless years of misery and take my own life now.

15   Having to sit in this cell now for several weeks with nothing—even being denied my cigarettes—I have thought a lot about suicide, and it seems to be the most humane way out of a prison I no longer care to struggle in. Suicide or endless torment. Which would you choose?

Thinking Critically About Content

1. What is Clifton analyzing in this essay? How does his title help focus his analysis?

2. Explain two causes and two effects of Clifton's escape from prison.

3. Why do you think Clifton ends this essay with a question? Is this an effective conclusion?

Thinking Critically About Purpose and Audience

4. Why do you think Clifton wrote this essay?

5. Who do you think Clifton's audience is in this essay? Explain your answer.

6. Did the fact that this excerpt was written by a convicted criminal have any effect on you? Explain your answer.

Thinking Critically About Paragraphs

7. In paragraph 2 of his essay, the author mentions the "torment" of not being able to see his children growing up, yet he doesn't mention the crime he committed until paragraph 8. Why do you think he presents his material in this order?

8. Which of Clifton's paragraphs deal with the causes of his escape? Which deal with the effects? Do you think this is a good balance for Clifton's purpose? Explain your answer.

9. How does Clifton organize the details in paragraph 12? Why do you think he chose this method of organization?

10. If you were the district attorney who prosecuted Corky Clifton, how would you respond to Clifton's analysis? Write your response to him in the form of a letter.

Writing Workshop

Now you have the opportunity to apply what you have learned in this chapter to another writing assignment. This time, we provide you with the guidelines only and let you go through your own writing process with occasional feedback from your peers. Refer to sections of the chapter as necessary until the process of producing a paragraph becomes automatic for you.

Guidelines for Writing a Cause/Effect Paragraph

1. Write a topic sentence that makes a clear statement about what you are going to analyze.
2. Choose facts and details to support your topic sentence.
3. Make sure you include the real causes and effects of your topic.
4. Organize your material so that it communicates your message as clearly as possible.

Writing About Your Reading

1. Many significant studies have established the connection between TV watching and violent behavior. What other reasons might there be for an increase in aggression in our society? Explain your answer.

2. In "Life Sentences," Corky Clifton explains that he is desperate to escape from prison. He can no longer stand "the torment." Have you ever wanted to escape from certain people or a specific situation in your life? How do you escape when you want to?

3. How would looking closely at causes and effects help you live a better life? How would the process of discovering causes and effects help you think through your decisions and problems more logically? Explain your answer.

a crime to the notion of killing a specific person. This method of organization builds suspense in this paragraph.

10. Answers will vary.

To keep track of your critical thinking progress, go to Appendix 1.

ADDITIONAL WRITING TOPIC
Let your students expand the paragraphs they wrote on page 280 into well-developed essays.

TEACHING ON THE WEB
Discussion Topic: Divide students into groups of three or four, and have them discuss the effects of the Internet on society today. What are some of the effects of the Internet on businesses, homes, and social clubs? Are all the effects positive?

TEACHING ON THE WEB
Links: Think of a recent disaster in the United States, and have students link to news Web sites to see how the news agencies reported the story. How does each use cause and effect differently to recount what happened?
Possible sites:
MSNBC, msnbc.com
Time magazine, time.com
USA Today, usatoday.com

TEACHING ON THE WEB
Research: Have students find a Web site that explains a recent scientific discovery. What is the discovery, and how will it affect the world? What causes made this discovery possible?

Writing About Your World

Georg Gerster/Science Source

1. Write an explanation of how the area in the photo above became such a wasteland. Analyze what happened before this picture was taken. Why did it happen? Or focus on what might happen in this area in the future.

2. Write a paragraph about an important event that changed your attitude toward an authority figure in your life (a parent, a religious leader, a teacher, a club sponsor, a supervisor or boss). What brought about the change? What were the results of the change?

3. Choose a major problem you see in society today, and analyze its causes and effects. Can you propose a solution to this problem?

4. Create your own cause/effect assignment (with the help of your instructor), and write a response to it.

Revising

Small Group Activity (5–10 minutes per writer) Working in groups of three or four, read your cause/effect papers to each other. Those listening should record their reactions on a copy of the Revising Peer Evaluation Forms in Appendix 4. After your group goes through this process, give your evaluation forms to the appropriate writers so that each writer has two or three peer comment sheets for revising.

Paired Activity (5 minutes per writer) Using the completed Peer Evaluation Forms, work in pairs to decide what you should revise. If time allows, rewrite some of your sentences, and have your partner check them.

Individual Activity Rewrite your paper using the revising feedback you received from other students.

Editing

Paired Activity (5–10 minutes per writer) Swap papers with a classmate, and use the Editing Peer Evaluation Form in Appendix 6 to identify as many grammar, punctuation, mechanics, and spelling errors as you can. If time allows, correct some of your errors, and have your partner check them. Record your grammar, punctuation, and mechanics errors in the Error Log (Appendix 7) and your spelling errors in the Spelling Log (Appendix 8).

Individual Activity Rewrite your paper again using the editing feedback you received from other students.

Reflecting on Your Writing   When you have completed your own paragraph, answer these six questions:

1. What was most difficult about this assignment?

2. What was easiest?

3. What did you learn about cause/effect by completing this assignment?

4. What do you think are the strengths of your cause/effect? Place a wavy line by the parts of your paragraph that you feel are very good.

5. What are the weaknesses, if any, of your paper? Place an X by the parts of your paragraph you would like help with. Write any questions you have in the margins.

6. What did you learn from this assignment about your own writing process—about preparing to write, about writing the first draft, about revising, and about editing?

Arguing

"My task, which I am trying to achieve, is, by the power of the written word, to make you hear, to make you feel—it is, before all, to make you see."

—JOSEPH CONRAD

When was the last time you tried to talk someone into doing something? Was it when you wanted:

- your wife to go to a movie you were excited to see?
- your parents to let you use the car?
- your sister to lend you money?
- a professor to give you a little more time to submit a paper?
- the garage mechanic to fix your car without charging you more than the car was worth?

So much of what we say or do is an attempt to convince someone to do something. If you dress up for a job interview, you are trying to persuade the employer that you should be hired. If you argue with a friend about gun control, you are trying to persuade your friend to agree with you. And think of all the television, magazine, and billboard ads that try to persuade you into buying a certain product. Life is filled with opportunities to argue with others and to convince them of your point of view.

The purpose of **arguing** is to persuade your readers to take some action or to think or feel a certain way. So arguing and persuading work closely together. Because we live in a society that allows us to voice our opinions freely, learning how to express our thoughts in a polite and reasonable way is one goal we should all strive for. The ability to argue well is a powerful tool.

In the following paragraph, Karen Goldberg Goff claims that social networking has important benefits for our society. In it, she argues that social networking helps us communicate in ways that sustain and promote our culture. Does she persuade you?

Co-author Lisa Tripp, now an assistant professor at Florida State University, says technology, including YouTube, iPods, and podcasting, creates avenues for extending one's circle of friends, boosts self-directed learning, and fosters independence. "Certain technical skills in the coming years are not going to be just about consuming media," she says. "It is also going to be about producing media. It is not just about writing a blog, but also how to leave comments that say something. Learning to communicate like this is contributing to the general circulation of culture." That means anything from a video clip to a profile page is going to reflect the self-expression skills one has, so teens might as well practice what will say who they are.

You will refer to this passage again when you are learning the guidelines for writing a good cause/effect paragraph.

MyWritingLab

Understanding Argument

Now that you have been introduced to argument, test your knowledge by going to **MyWritingLab.com** and clicking on **Argument** in the **Paragraph Development** module. At this point, read the **Overview,** watch the **Animation** video, and complete the **Recall, Apply,** and **Write** activities. Then check your understanding of persuasive paragraphs by taking the **Post-test.**

Sidebar notes:

who did not change sides why the other side's most persuasive arguments did not convince them. Through this dialogue, which elicits useful information on how arguments work, students will become aware of how to argue their points more effectively.

Student Comment: "The fact that you can fail an assignment, learn from it, and try it again was the best part of **MyWritingLab** for me."

MyWritingLab uses the words *argumentative* and *persuasive* interchangeably. Make sure your students are prepared for this when they go to MyWritingLab.

PREPARING TO WRITE AN ARGUMENT PARAGRAPH

Reading arguments critically will help you write arguments critically, which are both necessary skills for success in college and in life beyond college. You need to be conscious of the process you use to understand your reading so you can use this strategy just as effectively in your writing. Like two halves of a whole, these processes work together to create a coherent approach to important tasks.

To begin with, you need to learn how to read critically. A sample paragraph will help you learn how good arguments work. First, you will apply a specific reading strategy to the paragraph. Next, you will answer some questions about the paragraph in an attempt to discover how it functions. With a detailed understanding of your reading, you will have more tools at your disposal when you write.

For more detailed information on recognizing facts and opinions and on responding to them, see pages 21–22 in Chapter 2.

READING CRITICALLY
Recognizing Facts and Opinions in a Professional Paragraph

Reading an argument critically calls for very high-level skills. You need to understand your reading on a literal level, know the difference between opinions and facts, and come up with your own thoughts on the topic by challenging the author's ideas. As you read the following paragraph for the first time, highlight facts in one color and the author's opinions in another color. Then, put an X by any facts or opinions that you do not agree with or that you want to question in some way. Be prepared to explain any marks you make.

Reading Strategy

Reading an Argument Paragraph

This paragraph, by Marie Winn, argues that TV watching is an addiction. As you read this passage, highlight the facts and opinions and then add Xs to the margins. Finally, respond to the questions after the paragraph.

Not unlike drugs or alcohol, the television experience allows the participant to blot out the real world and enter into a pleasurable and passive mental state. The worries and anxieties of reality are as effectively deferred by becoming absorbed in a television program as by going on a "trip" induced by drugs or alcohol. And just as alcoholics are only vaguely aware of their addiction, feeling that they control their drinking more than they really do ("I can cut it out any time I want—I just like to have three or four drinks before dinner"), people similarly overestimate their control over television watching. Even as they put off other activities to spend hour after hour watching television, they feel they could easily resume living in a different, less passive style. But somehow or other, while the television set is present in their homes, the click doesn't sound. With television pleasures available, those other experiences seem less attractive, more difficult somehow.

Discovering How This Paragraph Works

To help you discover the elements that make this an effective argument paragraph so you can use them in your own writing, answer the following questions in as much detail as possible.

1. What is Winn's topic sentence?

    Not unlike drugs or alcohol, the television experience allows the participant to

    blot out the real world and enter into a pleasurable and passive mental state.

Does it state her opinion about a certain issue? *Yes*

Is it debatable? (Does it have more than one side?) *Yes*

2. Whom do you think Winn is addressing in this paragraph? How did you come to this conclusion?

She is addressing the general population with televisions in their homes.

3. What evidence does the author use to support her topic sentence? How would you classify her major pieces of evidence (facts, statistics, statements from authorities, or examples/personal stories)?

Evidence	Type
Worries and anxieties deferred by TV	*statement from authority*
Overestimated control over TV watching	*fact*
Activities put off while TV is on	*fact*
TV not turned off when it is on	*fact*

4. How does Winn organize her paragraph: general to particular, particular to general, or from one extreme to another?

General to particular—from TV watching is an addiction to the details of that addiction

WRITING AN ARGUMENT PARAGRAPH

Now that you have read and studied a paragraph, you will be writing one of your own. This section will help you generate a rough draft that you will then revise and edit in the third section of this chapter. It will guide you through a careful reading of the writing assignment, give you several ways to generate ideas, and finally furnish you with concrete guidelines for writing an effective argument paragraph. We encourage you to write notes and lists throughout this section so you can use them when you write a draft of your paragraph.

Reading the Prompt

Reading
Strategy

The very first step in writing a good paragraph is making sure you understand the writing assignment or "prompt." An assignment attempts to "prompt" you to respond to a specific issue or question. The more clearly you understand the prompt, the better paragraph or essay you will create. Applying the chapter reading strategy to your writing assignment is a good way to accomplish this goal.

READING CRITICALLY
Recognizing Facts and Opinions in the Prompt

As you read the following prompt for the first time, highlight directions in one color and clues about the content in another color. Then put an X by any parts of the assignment you want to question in some way. Be prepared to explain any marks you make on the assignment. Next, as you read the assignment again, write on a separate piece of paper some possible topics on the left and your opinions about those topics on the right side of the page. Finally, highlight all the key directions in the assignment so you are sure to address all aspects of the prompt.

Writing Prompt

 Complete this **Writing Prompt** at **mywritinglab.com**

Choose a controversial issue on your campus, and write a paragraph that presents your opinion about it. When writing your paragraph, be sure to back up your opinion with reasons. Use the guidelines below to get you started on your paragraph.

Thinking About the Prompt

PREWRITING EXERCISE
Have students use the prewriting method they prefer to start thinking about a controversial issue on campus. What can be done to remedy the situation?

Before you focus on a specific topic, you should generate as many ideas as you can so you have several to choose from. On a separate piece of paper, record some possible topics on the left and your opinions about those topics on the right side of the page. Why are these issues controversial? Do you have strong opinions about all of them? Which do you feel most passionate about? Choose one of these topics, and use one or more of the prewriting techniques you learned in Chapter 3 to generate and record as many thoughts as possible about the issue.

Guidelines for Writing an Argument Paragraph

TEACHING TIPS
The following eight teaching tips are based on Howard Gardner's list of multiple intelligences:

Verbal/Linguistic
Have students prepare a list of words and phrases that can help their communication in an argument essay. How can choosing the right word strengthen or weaken an argument? What are some words and phrases that can weaken arguments?

When you are writing an argument, you must present evidence that convinces your readers to agree with you on a particular topic. This isn't always as easy as it sounds. All too often your reader will have a different opinion. Your evidence, therefore, must be accurate and logical. In fact, evidence is the most important ingredient in an argument. Without supporting evidence, your paragraph will be nothing more than a statement of your opinion. Convincing evidence, however, helps your readers understand and perhaps agree with your views. The following guidelines will help you organize and develop a good argument/persuasion paragraph. Each step points to Karen Goldberg Goff's paragraph at the beginning of this chapter as an example.

1. **State your opinion on the issue in your topic sentence.** This sentence should state your position on an issue that can be argued and does not

have a clear answer. Usually the first sentence, it sets up your point of view and prepares your readers for the evidence you plan to give them.

In the Reading: Goff starts her paragraph with a statement that readers might dispute: "technology, including YouTube, iPods, and podcasting, creates avenues for extending one's circle of friends, boosts self-directed learning, and fosters independence." Goff's first sentence sets up the rest of her paragraph, in which she supports her position.

In Your Writing: Consider the paragraph you will be writing on a controversial issue on your campus. What will you include in your topic sentence? Jot down your subject and your opinion about that subject.

2. **Find out as much as you can about your audience before you write.** Knowing your audience's background and feelings toward your topic will help you choose supporting details and examples. If you are trying to convince people in two different age groups not to smoke, you might tell teenagers that cigarettes make their breath rancid, their teeth yellow, and their clothes smell bad. On the other hand, you might persuade parents and other adults to stop smoking with some long-term statistics on lung and heart disease in smokers.

In the Reading: Goff's paragraph addresses the general public with references to a variety of age groups. Through quotations, she makes some general claims about the benefits of social networking that apply to all ages and ends her paragraph with a reference to teens. Goff's knowledge of her audience helps her develop the rest of her paragraph, making effective choices as she writes.

In Your Writing: What do you know about the people who will be reading your paragraph on a controversial campus issue? Can you find out any more about them? Are the details listed in your prewriting exercise geared toward this audience? Revise your list so it relates directly to the audience you have identified.

3. **Choose appropriate evidence that supports your topic sentence.** Evidence usually takes the form of (a) facts, (b) statistics, (c) statements from authorities, or (d) examples and personal stories. You can use one of these types of evidence or a combination of them in any argument paragraph. Opinions—your own or other people's—are not evidence.

In the Reading: Goff's paragraph cites three pieces of evidence that fall into two of these categories:

Evidence	Type
"Certain technical skills in the coming years are not going to be just about consuming media."	statement from authority
"It is also going to be about producing media."	statement from authority

Musical Rhythmic

Have students create a rap song that tries to persuade people that rap music either has value in our society or should be banned. At what audience should this song be aimed?

Logical/Mathematical

Provide students with a short argumentative article. Have students identify key arguments and explain why they are organized as they are. Have them change the order of the argumentative points and explain why the new order either strengthens or weakens the argument.

Visual/Spatial

Provide students with a short argumentative essay, and have them sketch an outline of the essay. Does knowing the blueprint of the argument make the essay more or less persuasive?

Bodily/Kinesthetic

Have students try to persuade a friend on campus to do something for them, such as sit on a bench or sign his or her name to a card, without using words. Then ask students to explain how difficult using only facial expressions and actions to persuade people was.

Intrapersonal

Have students find an article in the library or on the Internet that they believe is well argued. What makes the argument so persuasive? How can other students learn from this essay?

Interpersonal

Have students openly debate a current issue in your state. Have them try to persuade others to believe their opinions and

join the opposing side of
the issue. How heated does
the debate become? How
many people altered their
beliefs? What caused them
to do so?

Naturalist
Have students think of an
outdoor activity they like
to do but that others think
is dangerous or risky. Have
students try to persuade
someone who thinks the
activity is dangerous to try
it. Can the other person be
swayed?

**INSTRUCTOR'S
RESOURCE MANUAL**
For additional material
about teaching argument,
for journal entries, and
for various tests, see the
*Instructor's Resource
Manual,* Section II, Part II.

Evidence	Type
"It is not just about writing a blog, but also how to leave comments that say something."	example
anything from a video clip to a profile page is going to reflect the self-expression skills one has	example

In Your Writing: What types of evidence will you use in your paragraph? Chart your evidence, and decide if you need to add any more information. Should this new information be a different type of evidence? Expand your list of evidence with enough details to make your argument convincing to your audience.

4. **Organize your evidence so that it supports your argument as effectively as possible.** The organization of your material in an argument paragraph depends to a great extent on the opinions of your readers. Your paragraph should be arranged from general to particular, from particular to general, or from one extreme to another. When you know that your readers already agree with you, you should arrange your paragraph from a general statement to particular examples or from most to least important. This way, your audience will move through your argument with you from beginning to end, and you will be building on their loyalty and enthusiasm. When you are dealing with readers who probably disagree with you, you should work from details and examples to a single general statement or from least to most important. With this method of organization, you can lead your readers through your reasoning as you use your examples to pull them into your way of thinking.

In the Reading: In her paragraph, Goff starts with a general statement and then organizes her proof from general (technology encourages communication) to particular examples (video clip, profile page). She is trying to persuade her readers that social networking does have value for individuals and for society.

In Your Writing: How will you organize your paragraph—from general to particular, from particular to general, or from one extreme to another? Is this the most effective order for what you are trying to say to your particular audience? Would another method of organization be more effective? Rearrange the details on your list until you are sure they are in the best order for what you are trying to achieve.

Writing a Draft of Your Paragraph

Now is the time to collect all your conclusions, your notes, your prewriting exercises, and your lists as you generate the first draft of your paragraph. You might want to review the professional essay, the writing assignment, and the chapter guidelines to help you write a draft of your paragraph. At this point, don't think about revising or editing; just get a rough draft of your ideas down on paper in response to the writing prompt.

MyWritingLab **Helpful Hints**

- **Does your paragraph need to be more convincing?** Argumentative paragraphs often use comparison or contrast to help prove or clarify a point. To find out more about comparison/contrast, go to **Comparing and Contrasting** in the **Paragraph Development** module in **MyWritingLab.**

- **Does your paragraph seem chaotic?** Use what you know about other methods of thinking to help organize your ideas—for example, the way division and classification group and sort points. Review **Dividing and Classifying** in the **Paragraph Development** module in **MyWritingLab** for more ideas about how to bring order to your paragraph.

REVISING AND EDITING

You are now ready to learn how to revise and edit. This section will guide you through the process of revising and editing argument paragraphs in reference to two writing samples: another student's paragraph and your own paragraph. Finding strengths and weaknesses in another person's writing is often much easier than evaluating your own, so you will be reviewing the chapter guidelines by revising and editing another student's writing before applying the same guidelines to your own writing.

REVISING AND EDITING OPTIONS
Consider teaching revising and editing in a class discussion, in small groups, or in pairs.

Reading a Student Paragraph

Here is a paragraph written by Anthony Barone arguing against home schooling for children. Notice how this student writer organizes and presents his evidence on this subject.

Reading Strategy

READING CRITICALLY
Recognizing Facts and Opinions in the Student Paragraph

As you read Anthony's paragraph, highlight his facts in one color and his opinions in another. In the margins, put an X next to items you question or disagree with and a √ by items you agree with. Be prepared to explain the connection between your margin symbols and the material in the paragraph.

CLASS ACTIVITY
Write an argument paragraph on the board filled with "I believe," "I think," and "in my opinion" statements. Demonstrate to students how these types of personal statements weaken rather than strengthen arguments.

[1]Being educated at home is not in the best interest of children. [2]I do not think it should be allowed unless a child is sick or lives to far from school to go home every day. [3]Most parents say the world is too dangerous for their children who teach they're kids at home. [4]Parents also need to consider that children do not learn to work together by staying home, they need to be around other children to learn how to argue, how to solve problems, and how to develop a strong value system. [5]But if one child is unsafe. [6]All children are unsafe that I know. [7]The community should get together and make the area safe for these children. [8]Children can learn more then academic subjects in school they can also learn about life. [9]Parents should volunteer at there child's school. [10]And pass their knowledge on to other children too.

Revising and Editing the Student Paragraph

This paragraph is Anthony's first draft, which now needs to be revised and edited. First, apply the following Revising Checklist to the content of Anthony's draft. When you are satisfied that his ideas are fully developed and well organized, use the Editing Checklist to correct his grammar and mechanics errors. Answer the questions, and complete the tasks in each category. Then write your suggested changes directly on Anthony's draft.

REVISING STRATEGIES
This chapter focuses on the following revising element:

Organization

Revising the Student Paragraph

TOPIC SENTENCE

✔ Does the topic sentence convey the paragraph's controlling idea?

✔ Does the topic sentence appear as the first or last sentence of the paragraph?

1. What is the subject of Anthony's paragraph?

   Home schooling

2. What is his opinion on this subject?

   He believes home schooling is not in the best interest of children.

3. Put brackets around Anthony's topic sentence. Does it communicate the subject and his opinion on it?

   [Being educated at home is not in the best interest of children.] Yes

4. Make sure it introduces all the ideas in Anthony's paragraph.

DEVELOPMENT

✔ Does the paragraph contain *specific* details that support the topic sentence?

✔ Does the paragraph include *enough* details to fully explain the topic sentence?

1. What types of support does Anthony supply for his topic sentence?

Evidence	Type
parents' think children unsafe at school	*example*
children need other children	*fact*
children can learn more than academics	*fact*

2. Where do you need more information?

   Answers will vary.

UNITY

✔ Do all the sentences in the paragraph support the topic sentence?

1. Read each of Anthony's sentences with his topic sentence (revised, if necessary) in mind.

2. Drop or rewrite any of his sentences that are not directly related to his topic sentence. *All sentences are related to the topic sentence.*

ORGANIZATION

✔ Is the paragraph organized logically?

1. Read Anthony's paragraph again to see if all sentences are arranged logically.

2. Identify Anthony's method of organization.

   From one extreme to another—from least to most important

3. Move the one example that seems to be out of order. *Move sentences 5–7 after sentence 3.*

COHERENCE

✔ Do the sentences move smoothly and logically from one to the next?

1. Circle three transitions, repetitions, synonyms, or pronouns Anthony uses. *Answers will vary.*

   For a list of transitions, see pages 59–60.

2. Change at least one of these in Anthony's paragraph, and explain how your change makes the paragraph easier to read.

   Answers will vary.

   For a list of pronouns, see page 365.

 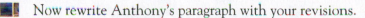

Now rewrite Anthony's paragraph with your revisions.

Editing the Student Paragraph

SENTENCES

Subjects and Verbs

✔ Does each sentence have a main subject and verb?

For help with subjects and verbs, see Chapter 20.

1. Underline the subjects once and verbs twice in your revision of Anthony's paragraph. Remember that sentences can have more than one subject-verb set.

2. Does each of Anthony's sentences have at least one subject and verb that can stand alone? *No*

For help with fragments, see Chapter 21.

3. Did you find and correct Anthony's two fragments? If not, find and correct them now. *Sentences 5 and 10*

For help with run-togethers, see Chapter 22.

4. Did you find and correct Anthony's two run-together sentences? If not, find and correct them now. *Sentences 4 and 8*

Subject-Verb Agreement

✔ Do all subjects and verbs agree?

For help with subject-verb agreement, see Chapter 25.

1. Read aloud the subjects and verbs you underlined in your revision of Anthony's paragraph.

2. Correct any subjects and verbs that do not agree. *All subjects agree with their verbs in the original paragraph.*

Pronoun Agreement

✔ Do all pronouns agree with their nouns?

For help with pronoun agreement, see Chapter 29.

1. Find any pronouns in your revision of Anthony's paragraph that do not agree with their nouns. *All pronouns agree with their nouns in the original paragraph.*

2. Correct any pronouns that do not agree with their nouns.

Modifier Errors

✔ Are modifiers as close as possible to the words they modify?

For help with modifier errors, see Chapter 32.

1. Find any modifiers in your revision of Anthony's paragraph that are not as close as possible to the words they modify. *Sentences 3 and 6*

2. Did you find and correct Anthony's two modifier errors? If not, find and correct them now. *Parents who teach they're kids at home, children that I know*

PUNCTUATION AND MECHANICS

Punctuation

✔ Are sentences punctuated correctly?

For help with punctuation, see Chapters 33–37.

1. Read your revision of Anthony's paragraph for any errors in punctuation.

2. Find the two run-together sentences and two fragments you revised, and make sure they are punctuated correctly.

Mechanics

✔ Are words capitalized properly?

1. Read your revision of Anthony's paragraph for any errors in capitalization. *All capitals are correct in the original paragraph.*
2. Be sure to check Anthony's capitalization in the fragments and run-together sentences you revised.

For help with capitalization, see Chapter 38.

WORD CHOICE AND SPELLING

Word Choice

✔ Are words used correctly?

1. Find any words used incorrectly in your revision of Anthony's paragraph. *to (sentence 2), they're (sentence 3), then (sentence 8), there (sentence 9)*
2. Did you find and correct the four words Anthony uses incorrectly? If not, find and correct them now. *to/too, they're/their, then/than, there/their*

For help with confused words, see Chapter 44.

Spelling

✔ Are words spelled correctly?

1. Use spell-check and a dictionary to check the spelling in your revision of Anthony's paragraph. *All words are spelled correctly in the original paragraph.*
2. Correct any misspelled words.

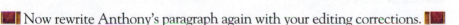

 Now rewrite Anthony's paragraph again with your editing corrections. ■▮

Reading Your Own Argument Paragraph

Reading Strategy

Returning to the argument paragraph you wrote earlier in this chapter, revise and edit your own writing. You will first read your paragraph with the same reading strategy you have applied to other reading tasks in this chapter so you can look at it as your reader might.

READING CRITICALLY
Recognizing Facts and Opinions
in Your Own Paragraph

As you begin to rework your paragraph, apply the same technique to your writing that you have been practicing throughout this chapter. Highlight your own opinions and facts in two different colors to demonstrate that you see the difference between the two. Then check to see that you support each of your main ideas with enough details to make your point.

Revising and Editing Your Own Paragraph

The checklists here will help you apply what you have learned in this chapter to your own paragraph. Work first with the content, making sure your thoughts are fully developed and effectively organized before you consider your grammar and usage errors.

For Revising Peer Evaluation Forms, go to Appendix 4.

Revising Your Own Paragraph

TOPIC SENTENCE

☐ Does the topic sentence convey the paragraph's controlling idea?

☐ Does the topic sentence appear as the first or last sentence of the paragraph?

1. What is the subject of your paragraph?

   _____

2. What is your opinion on this subject?

   _____

3. Put brackets around your topic sentence. Does it communicate your subject and opinion? _____

4. Make sure it introduces all the ideas in your paragraph.

DEVELOPMENT

☐ Does the paragraph contain *specific* details that support the topic sentence?

☐ Does the paragraph include *enough* details to fully explain the topic sentence?

1. What type of support do you supply for your topic sentence?

Evidence	Type
_____	_____
_____	_____
_____	_____
_____	_____

2. Where do you think you need to give more information?

   _____

UNITY

☐ Do all the sentences in the paragraph support the topic sentence?

1. Read each of your sentences with your topic sentence in mind.

2. Drop or rewrite any sentences that are not directly related to your topic sentence.

ORGANIZATION

☐ Is the paragraph organized logically?

1. Read your paragraph again to see if all the sentences are arranged logically.

2. How did you organize the evidence in your paragraph?

_____

3. What word clues from your paragraph tell your readers how it is organized?

_____

COHERENCE

☐ Do the sentences move smoothly and logically from one to the next?

1. Circle three transitions, repetitions, synonyms, or pronouns you use.

2. Change at least one of these in your paragraph, and explain how your change makes your paragraph easier to read.

_____

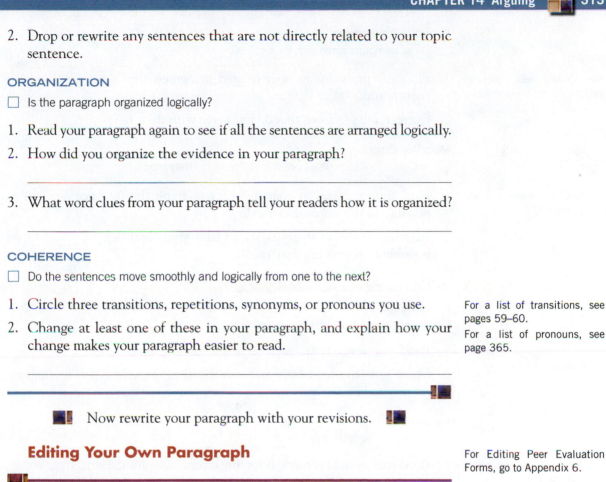

Now rewrite your paragraph with your revisions.

For a list of transitions, see pages 59–60.
For a list of pronouns, see page 365.

Editing Your Own Paragraph

For Editing Peer Evaluation Forms, go to Appendix 6.

SENTENCES

Subjects and Verbs

✔ Does each sentence have a main subject and verb?

1. Underline the subjects once and verbs twice in your revised paragraph. Remember that sentences can have more than one subject-verb set.

For help with subjects and verbs, see Chapter 20.

2. Does each of your sentences have at least one subject and verb that can stand alone? _____

3. Correct any fragments you have written.

For help with fragments, see Chapter 21.

4. Correct any run-together sentences you have written.

For help with run-togethers, see Chapter 22.

Subject-Verb Agreement

☐ Do all subjects and verbs agree?

1. Read aloud the subjects and verbs you underlined in your revised paragraph.

For help with subject-verb agreement, see Chapter 25.

2. Correct any subjects and verbs that do not agree.

Pronoun Agreement

☐ Do all pronouns agree with their nouns?

For help with pronoun agreement, see Chapter 29.

1. Find any pronouns in your revised paragraph that do not agree with their nouns.

2. Correct any pronouns that do not agree with their nouns.

Modifier Errors

☐ Are modifiers as close as possible to the words they modify?

For help with modifier errors, see Chapter 32.

1. Find any modifiers in your revised paragraph that are not as close as possible to the words they modify.

2. Rewrite sentences if necessary so that your modifiers are as close as possible to the words they modify.

PUNCTUATION AND MECHANICS

Punctuation

☐ Are sentences punctuated correctly?

For help with punctuation, see Chapters 33–37.

1. Read your revised paragraph for any errors in punctuation.

2. Make sure any fragments and run-together sentences you revised are punctuated correctly.

Mechanics

☐ Are words capitalized properly?

For help with capitalization, see Chapter 38.

1. Read your revised paragraph for any errors in capitalization.

2. Be sure to check your capitalization in any fragments or run-together sentences you revised.

WORD CHOICE AND SPELLING

Word Choice

☐ Are words used correctly?

For help with confused words, see Chapter 44.

1. Find any words used incorrectly in your revised paragraph.

2. Correct any errors you find.

Spelling

For help with spelling, see Chapter 45.

☐ Are words spelled correctly?

To make a personal log of your grammar/usage errors, go to Appendix 7.

1. Use spell-check and a dictionary to check your spelling.

2. Correct any misspelled words.

To make a personal log of your spelling errors, go to Appendix 8.

Now rewrite your paragraph again with your editing corrections.

MyWritingLab
More Helpful Hints

- **Do you need some reminders about revising?** Argument paragraphs require strong supporting details and an appropriate tone, so you need to pay special attention to these features as you revise. Go to **Revising Your Paragraph** in **The Craft of Writing** module in **MyWritingLab** to get some help with these aspects of the revising process.

- **Have you been told you need help with Fused Sentences and Comma Splices?** Run-Ons interfere with how well readers understand your message. To learn how to avoid these errors and increase the persuasive power of your paragraph, go to **Run-Ons** in the **Sentence Skills** module in **MyWritingLab**.

PRACTICING ARGUMENT: FROM READING TO WRITING

This final section lets you practice the reading and writing skills you learned in this chapter. It includes three reading selections and several writing assignments on "your reading" and "your world." The section then offers guidance in peer evaluation and reflection, ending with suggestions about how to lead your instructor through your writing in ways that will benefit both of you.

Reading Workshop

Here are three essays that follow the guidelines you have studied in this chapter. The first is an essay by Juan Guzmán and Raul Jara called "The Economic Benefits of Passing the DREAM Act," which discusses the financial effects of the Dream Act. The other two essays are about social networking: "The Flight from Conversation" by Sherry Turkle and "Social Media's Small, Positive Role in Human Relationships" by Zeynep Tufekci. As you read, notice how the writers make their points through clear, well-chosen evidence.

THE ECONOMIC BENEFITS OF PASSING THE DREAM ACT
by Juan Guzmán and Raúl Jara

Focusing Your Attention

1. In your opinion, who should be allowed to immigrate to the United States? How should we handle illegal immigrants? What about children who were brought to the United States illegally?

SUMMARY
This essay outlines some of the economic benefits of the DREAM (Development, Relief, and Education of Alien Minors) Act, a bipartisan bill introduced to Congress in 2001 and reintroduced in 2009 by Utah Republican

Senator Orrin Hatch and Illinois Democrat Senator Dick Durbin.

READABILITY
(Flesch-Kincaid grade level) 12

INSTRUCTOR'S RESOURCE MANUAL
For additional teaching strategies, for journal entries, for vocabulary and reading quizzes, and for more writing assignments, see the *Instructor's Resource Manual,* Section II, Part II.

ANSWERS TO QUESTIONS

Thinking Critically About Content

1. Guzmán and Jara argue that the DREAM Act will benefit America's economy by granting young undocumented persons access to higher education and better jobs, which would then translate into more money in our economy and new jobs.

2. The Development, Relief, and Education for Alien Minors (DREAM) Act would grant undocumented persons who were brought to the United States at a young age a path to legal status upon attending college or serving in the military.

3. Answers will vary.

2. You are about to read an essay that represents some of the economic benefits of the DREAM (Development, Relief, and Education of Alien Minors) Act. What do you think are the relevant issues? Why would American citizens care about these issues?

Expanding Your Vocabulary

The following words are important to your understanding of this essay. To help you add them to your vocabulary, write out a synonym and an example from your own experience for each new word.

fiscal: financial (paragraph 2)

incentive: motivation (paragraph 4)

consumption: spending (paragraph 5)

trajectory: path (paragraph 6)

naturalization: citizenship (paragraph 8)

READING CRITICALLY
Recognizing Facts and Opinions in Your Reading

As you have practiced throughout this chapter, separate the facts and opinions in the following essay by highlighting them in two different colors. Then write in the margins your reactions to each paragraph's main idea. These notes will give you insights into the topic and guide you to a deeper level of understanding. Compare your notes with someone else's in the class.

THE ECONOMIC BENEFITS OF PASSING THE DREAM ACT[1]
by Juan Guzmán and Raúl Jara

1   Until now, much of the debate surrounding the Development, Relief, and Education for Alien Minors Act, or DREAM Act—a bill to provide a pathway to legal status for eligible young people who were brought here as children and who complete high school and some college or military service—focused on legal, ethical, and

[1] Center for American Progress, 2013; www.americanprogress.org/issues/immigration/report/2012/09/30/39567/the-economic-benefits-of-passing-the-dream-act/.

logistical concerns. But there are other important benefits of enacting the DREAM Act, most importantly the boost to the economy.

This report takes a close look at this economic perspective. We present an analysis to understand what would happen if the United States were to grant a pathway to legal status to an estimated 2.1 million eligible youth in our country by passing the DREAM Act. Overall, we find that the passage of the DREAM Act would add $329 billion to the U.S. economy and create 1.4 million new jobs by 2030, demonstrating the potential of the proposed law to boost economic growth and improve our nation's fiscal health.

In making these projections we used American Community Survey data from 2006 to 2010 to calculate the number of eligible unauthorized youth that would qualify for the DREAM Act—creating the largest dataset of unauthorized immigrants to date—and then put the data into a robust model of the likely educational and job attainment potential of eligible DREAMers to estimate their likely future earnings. This model takes into account factors such as educational level, age, sex, race, and ethnicity and constitutes our estimate of the direct economic consequences of the DREAM Act. This is similar to the methodology used by education economist Luis Crouch and many of his colleagues in the field.

We find in this report that enabling these 2.1 million eager-to-be-Americans to contribute to building the American Dream would deliver a double boost to our economy. First, enacting the law would provide an incentive for their further education because for most of those who would be eligible the legalization provisions can only be attained through completion of high school and some college. Receiving more education opens access to higher-paying jobs, enabling these undocumented youth to become much more productive members of our society. Second, gaining legal status itself translates into higher earnings for these youth since legal status allows DREAMers to apply to a broader range of high-paying jobs rather than having to resort to low-wage jobs from employers who are willing to pay them under the table.

Thus our projections track both the gap in current earnings between unauthorized individuals at various levels of education and their U.S.-born counterparts, as well as the gains in earnings from attaining more education. Overall, our research finds that by 2030 the eligible DREAMer population will earn 19 percent more in earnings than without passage of the DREAM Act, in turn increasing their consumption and contributing more in the way of tax revenue to the federal government.

In detailing the ways in which passage of the DREAM Act will add significant value, jobs, and tax revenue to the American economy, it is important to note that the benefits would not simply be a one-time addition but instead unfold over time, with the economic benefits growing larger as time goes on. This upward trajectory comes because eligible DREAMers will have a staggered entrance into the workforce, with many eligible youth still in elementary or secondary school at the time of passage.

While studies by groups in favor of restricting immigration tend to take a snapshot view of the costs and benefits of immigrants at one specific point in time—usually finding high education costs from the children of immigrants—our study finds that investments in these students will pay off greatly in the future. The passage of the DREAM Act will ensure that a steady stream of people is able to attend college and achieve better jobs.

Thinking Critically About Purpose and Audience

4. Guzmán and Jara's purpose is to persuade readers that the DREAM Act provides practical economic benefits to the country by citing the American Community Survey data and presenting the potential outcomes from the data.

5. Most American citizens would be interested in this essay.

6. Guzmán and Jara immediately show the reader from the beginning of the essay how the DREAM Act would potentially boost the nation's economy. They then mention opposing points of view while reinforcing the idea that the DREAM Act is both practical and fair. Overall, Guzmán and Jara capture the reader's attention by emphasizing how the bill affects all Americans.

Thinking Critically About Paragraphs

7. Since the definition that begins the essay and the position statement that ends the essay both emphasize the idea that the DREAM Act will benefit the entire country, the authors hold the

readers' attention for the entire essay. Beyond this, answers to this question will vary.

8. Guzmán and Jara begin with a definition of the act and then cite statistics that suggest that the DREAM Act will boost the U.S. economy. They then trace the process that would occur to accomplish the economic results they discuss. They note some objections of the opposition and finally explain that DREAMers will not displace native-born workers. Guzmán and Jara end their essay by restating their position on the DREAM Act.

9. Gomez presents the following points in his essay. Beyond this, answers to this question will vary.

Pros of the DREAM Act

provides undocumented immigrants with access to college/ military

provides undocumented immigrants with access to better jobs

grants undocumented immigrants legal status

will encourage immigrant workers to complement native workers

8 One important caveat is necessary: This study looks solely at the economic benefits from passing the DREAM Act and not any costs that may be incurred. But we believe future costs from the DREAM Act will be limited. Eligible DREAMers will still be subject to the same ineligibility for most public benefits as other legal immigrants and would only be allowed to receive most non-emergency federal benefits after five years of lawful permanent residence—holding a green card or becoming a citizen through naturalization. The DREAM Act itself contains a safety valve to contain costs, since recipients must wait a 10-year conditional period, by which time we assume the DREAM Act population as a whole will be contributing significantly to the economy.

9 The U.S. economy is not a zero-sum game, and increased earnings from DREAMers create greater demand for services among the most important drivers of job growth in the country, expanding opportunities for all Americans. There are also very good reasons to think that the DREAMers will not be displacing American workers.

10 First, many economists find that immigrants tend to complement the skills of native workers rather than compete with them, especially as immigrants move up the education and skills chain. Increasing the education of immigrant workers would therefore decrease the competition between DREAMers and the native-born.

11 Second, research shows that an increase in college-educated immigrants directly increases U.S. gross domestic product—the largest measure of economic growth— which correlates to more jobs for American workers. In the 1990s, for example, the increase in college-educated immigrants was found to be responsible for a 1.4 percent to 2.4 percent increase in U.S. GDP. Finally, by giving legal status to DREAMers, fewer employers would be able to pay workers under the table and more would have to abide by a system that is fair to all workers.

12 This study's findings are clear: Passage of the DREAM Act would improve the American economy and contribute to the economic recovery and our future economic stability.

Thinking Critically About Content

1. What is Guzmán and Jara's main claim in this essay?

2. Explain the DREAM Act in your own words.

3. At the end of the essay, are you convinced that the DREAM Act "would improve the American economy and contribute to the economic recovery and our future economic stability" (paragraph 12)? Explain your answer.

Thinking Critically About Purpose and Audience

4. What do you think is the authors' purpose in writing this essay?

5. Who do you think would be most interested in this essay?

6. An essential ingredient in writing an effective argument is to pull the readers into the situation. How do Guzmán and Jara accomplish this? Explain your answer.

Thinking Critically About Paragraphs

7. The authors begin this essay with a definition of the DREAM Act and end it with a clear statement of their position on the issues surrounding the act. Is this an effective beginning and ending for their argument? Explain your answer.

8. How do the authors organize their evidence to prove that the DREAM Act will improve our country's economy? Is this an effective approach to their thesis?

9. Do Guzmán and Jara represent any opposing sides of the argument on this topic? List the pro and con points from the essay in two columns. Which side is most convincing to you? Explain your answer.

10. From your perspective, write a personal response to Guzmán and Jara.

will contribute to the nation's economy over decades

Cons of the DREAM Act

generates high education costs for immigrant children

provides undocumented immigrants legal status

encourages undocumented immigrants to compete for jobs with native-born workers

10. Answers will vary.

To keep track of your critical thinking progress, go to Appendix 1.

ARGUING A POSITION

Focusing Your Attention

1. What role does social networking play in your life? Is it important to you? What percentage of your day do you spend on social network sites?

2. In the two essays that you will be reading, one writer tries to persuade the readers that social networking has important advantages for its users while the other essay tells readers that social networking is dangerous in many ways. Although you have not yet read the essays, which one do you think you will agree with?

READING CRITICALLY
Recognizing Facts and Opinions in Your Reading

Once again, highlight the facts and opinions in both of the following essays. Then, to help you form your own opinions about the issues surrounding social networking, write in the margins your reactions to each paragraph's main idea. Be prepared to defend your thoughts with details from the essays and examples from your own experience.

THE FLIGHT FROM CONVERSATION
by Sherry Turkle

SUMMARY
This first essay argues that social networking has an adverse effect on our ability to converse and respond to one another.

READABILITY
(Flesch-Kincaid grade level) 10.8

INSTRUCTOR'S RESOURCE MANUAL
For additional teaching strategies, for journal entries, for vocabulary and reading quizzes, and for more writing assignments, see the *Instructor's Resource Manual,* Section II, Part II.

Expanding Your Vocabulary

The following words are important to your understanding of this essay. To help you add them to your vocabulary, write out a synonym and an example from your own experience for each new word.

customize (paragraph 3): modify

wistfully (paragraph 6): sadly

suite (paragraph 6): collection

shortchange (paragraph 9): treat unfairly

commerce (paragraph 10): trade

nuance (paragraph 11): subtle difference

delusion (paragraph 17): false belief

partisan (paragraph 22): supporter

THE FLIGHT FROM CONVERSATION[2]
by Sherry Turkle

1 We live in a technological universe in which we are always communicating. And yet we have sacrificed conversation for mere connection. At home, families sit together, texting and reading e-mail. At work executives text during board meetings. We text (and shop and go on Facebook) during classes and when we're on dates. My students tell me about an important new skill: it involves maintaining eye contact with someone while you text someone else; it's hard, but it can be done.

2 Over the past 15 years, I've studied technologies of mobile connection and talked to hundreds of people of all ages and circumstances about their plugged-in lives. I've learned that the little devices most of us carry around are so powerful that they change not only what we do, but also who we are.

3 We've become accustomed to a new way of being "alone together." Technology-enabled, we are able to be with one another and also elsewhere, connected to wherever we want to be. We want to customize our lives. We want to move in and out of

---

[2] http://www.nytimes.com/2012/04/22/opinion/sunday/the-flight-from-conversation.html?pagewanted=all&_r=0. April 21, 2012.

where we are because the thing we value most is control over where we focus our attention. We have gotten used to the idea of being in a tribe of one, loyal to our own party.

Our colleagues want to go to that board meeting but pay attention only to what interests them. To some this seems like a good idea, but we can end up hiding from one another, even as we are constantly connected to one another.

A businessman laments that he no longer has colleagues at work. He doesn't stop by to talk; he doesn't call. He says that he doesn't want to interrupt them. He says they're "too busy on their e-mail." But then he pauses and corrects himself. "I'm not telling the truth. I'm the one who doesn't want to be interrupted. I think I should. But I'd rather just do things on my BlackBerry."

A 16-year-old boy who relies on texting for almost everything says almost wistfully, "Someday, someday, but certainly not now, I'd like to learn how to have a conversation." In today's workplace, young people who have grown up fearing conversation show up on the job wearing earphones. Walking through a college library or the campus of a high-tech start-up, one sees the same thing: we are together, but each of us is in our own bubble, furiously connected to keyboards and tiny touch screens. A senior partner at a Boston law firm describes a scene in his office. Young associates lay out their suite of technologies: laptops, iPods, and multiple phones. And then they put their earphones on. "Big ones. Like pilots. They turn their desks into cockpits." With the young lawyers in their cockpits, the office is quiet, a quiet that does not ask to be broken.

In the silence of connection, people are comforted by being in touch with a lot of people—carefully kept at bay. We can't get enough of one another if we can use technology to keep one another at distances we can control: not too close, not too far, just right. I think of it as a Goldilocks effect.

Texting and e-mail and posting let us present the self we want to be. This means we can edit. And if we wish to, we can delete—or retouch: the voice, the flesh, the face, the body. Not too much, not too little—just right.

Human relationships are rich; they're messy and demanding. We have learned the habit of cleaning them up with technology. And the move from conversation to connection is part of this. But it's a process in which we shortchange ourselves. Worse, it seems that over time we stop caring; we forget that there is a difference.

We are tempted to think that our little "sips" of online connection add up to a big gulp of real conversation. But they don't. E-mail, Twitter, Facebook, all of these have their places—in politics, commerce, romance, and friendship. But no matter how valuable, they do not substitute for conversation.

Connecting in sips may work for gathering discrete bits of information or for saying, "I am thinking about you." Or even for saying, "I love you." But connecting in sips doesn't work as well when it comes to understanding and knowing one another. In conversation we tend to one another. (The word itself is kinetic; it's derived from words that mean to move, together.) We can attend to tone and nuance. In conversation, we are called upon to see things from another's point of view.

Face-to-face conversation unfolds slowly. It teaches patience. When we communicate on our digital devices, we learn different habits. As we ramp up the volume and velocity of online connections, we start to expect faster answers. To get these, we ask one another simpler questions; we dumb down our communications, even on the most important matters. It is as though we have all put ourselves on cable news. Shakespeare might have said, "We are consum'd with that which we were nourish'd by."

13 And we use conversation with others to learn to converse with ourselves. So our flight from conversation can mean diminished chances to learn skills of self-reflection. These days, social media continually ask us what's "on our mind," but we have little motivation to say something truly self-reflective. Self-reflection in conversation requires trust. It's hard to do anything with 3,000 Facebook friends except connect.

14 As we get used to being shortchanged on conversation and to getting by with less, we seem almost willing to dispense with people altogether. Serious people muse about the future of computer programs as psychiatrists. A high school sophomore confides to me that he wishes he could talk to an artificial intelligence program instead of his dad about dating; he says the A.I. would have so much more in its database. Indeed, many people tell me they hope that as Siri, the digital assistant on Apple's iPhone, becomes more advanced, "she" will be more and more like a best friend—one who will listen when others won't.

15 During the years I have spent researching people and their relationships with technology, I have often heard the sentiment "No one is listening to me." I believe this feeling helps explain why it is so appealing to have a Facebook page or a Twitter feed—each provides so many automatic listeners. And it helps explain why—against all reason—so many of us are willing to talk to machines that seem to care about us. Researchers around the world are busy inventing sociable robots, designed to be companions to the elderly, to children, to all of us.

16 One of the most haunting experiences during my research came when I brought one of these robots, designed in the shape of a baby seal, to an elder-care facility, and an older woman began to talk to it about the loss of her child. The robot seemed to be looking into her eyes. It seemed to be following the conversation. The woman was comforted.

17 And so many people found this amazing. Like the sophomore who wants advice about dating from artificial intelligence and those who look forward to computer psychiatry, this enthusiasm speaks to how much we have confused conversation with connection and collectively seem to have embraced a new kind of delusion that accepts the simulation of compassion as sufficient unto the day. And why would we want to talk about love and loss with a machine that has no experience of the arc of human life? Have we so lost confidence that we will be there for one another?

18 We expect more from technology and less from one another and seem increasingly drawn to technologies that provide the illusion of companionship without the demands of relationship. Always-on/always-on-you devices provide three powerful fantasies: that we will always be heard; that we can put our attention wherever we want it to be; and that we never have to be alone. Indeed our new devices have turned being alone into a problem that can be solved.

When people are alone, even for a few moments, they fidget and reach for a device. Here connection works like a symptom, not a cure, and our constant, reflexive impulse to connect shapes a new way of being. Think of it as "I share; therefore I am." We use technology to define ourselves by sharing our thoughts and feelings as we're having them. We used to think, "I have a feeling; I want to make a call." Now our impulse is, "I want to have a feeling; I need to send a text." 19

So, in order to feel more and to feel more like ourselves, we connect. But in our rush to connect, we flee from solitude, our ability to be separate and gather ourselves. Lacking the capacity for solitude, we turn to other people but don't experience them as they are. It is as though we use them, need them as spare parts to support our increasingly fragile selves. 20

We think constant connection will make us feel less lonely. The opposite is true. If we are unable to be alone, we are far more likely to be lonely. If we don't teach our children to be alone, they will know only how to be lonely. 21

I am a partisan for conversation. To make room for it, I see some first, deliberate steps. At home, we can create sacred spaces: the kitchen, the dining room. We can make our cars "device-free zones." We can demonstrate the value of conversation to our children. And we can do the same thing at work. There we are so busy communicating that we often don't have time to talk to one another about what really matters. Employees asked for casual Fridays; perhaps managers should introduce conversational Thursdays. Most of all, we need to remember—in between texts and e-mails and Facebook posts—to listen to one another, even to the boring bits, because it is often in unedited moments, moments in which we hesitate and stutter and go silent, that we reveal ourselves to one another. 22

I spend the summers at a cottage on Cape Cod, and for decades I walked the same dunes that Thoreau once walked. Not too long ago, people walked with their heads up, looking at the water, the sky, the sand, and at one another, talking. Now they often walk with their heads down, typing. Even when they are with friends, partners, children, everyone is on their own devices. 23

So I say, look up, look at one another, and let's start the conversation. 24

SOCIAL MEDIA'S SMALL, POSITIVE ROLE IN HUMAN RELATIONSHIPS
by Zeynep Tufekci

Expanding Your Vocabulary

The following words are important to your understanding of this essay. To help you add them to your vocabulary, write out a synonym and an example from your own experience for each new word.

automating (paragraph 2): making automatic

autism (paragraph 2): a psychological condition that affects a person's ability to form relationships and understand the world

SUMMARY
This opposing essay argues that social networking has important benefits for all who use these sites.

READABILITY
(Flesch-Kincaid grade level) 13.2

INSTRUCTOR'S
RESOURCE MANUAL
For additional teaching
strategies, for journal
entries, for vocabulary and
reading quizzes, and for
more writing assignments,
see the *Instructor's
Resource Manual,*
Section II, Part II.

endeavor (paragraph 2): plan

devaluation (paragraph 4): lack of respect for

displacement (paragraph 6): shift

verbatim (paragraph 7): exactly

SOCIAL MEDIA'S SMALL, POSITIVE ROLE IN HUMAN RELATIONSHIPS[3]
by Zeynep Tufekci

1   A few years ago I had an interview for a job at one of the leading academic departments in my field. Maybe because I knew that I wasn't likely to be offered the job, I saw the day as a relaxed opportunity to meet people carrying out interesting research. My comfort with the day was shaken, however, when a faculty member showed me ongoing research on avatars—bots—designed to interact with (and provide therapy for) human children with autism. I squirmed. I squinted. I tried to voice my discomfort. I lost my voice. I turned away. I was shaken for the rest of the day and on my way back. That flickering image of the bot we'd one day turn our children over to still haunts me.

2   I don't discount the appeal of automating such therapy. Working with children with autism is difficult, tiring work, especially since the social rewards—the smile, the eye-contact, the hug, the thank you—that make most of us tick are few and far between. I've never tried such an endeavor; I'm in no position to judge anyone.

3   Still the barely pixelated, realistic face of the "therapist" talking on the screen scares me because it is indeed an indicator of one possible future. Much of what ails our modern life is exactly because we reduce the value of a human being to a number, say salary or consumer power. And the first to be thrown overboard tend to be the elderly, the disabled, and anyone not integrated tightly into the global supply-chain. This phenomenon, coupled with the growing powers of automation and artificial intelligence, which promises to make replacing human beings even cheaper, means there is a very important conversation we need to be having—but that conversation is not about the effects of social media.

4   That might not have been apparent to those who picked up their Sunday *New York Times* to find Sherry Turkle's latest essay arguing that social media are driving us apart. If anything, social media is a counterweight to the ongoing devaluation of human lives. Social media's rapid rise is a loud, desperate, emerging attempt by

[3] http://www.theatlantic.com/technology/archive/2012/04/social-medias-small-positive-role-in-human-relationships/256346/. April 21, 2012.

people everywhere to connect with *each other* in the face of all the obstacles that modernity imposes on our lives: suburbanization that isolates us from each other, long working-hours and commutes that are required to make ends meet, the global migration that scatters families across the globe, the military-industrial-consumption machine that drives so many key decisions, and, last but not least, the television—the ultimate alienation machine—which remains the dominant form of media. (For most people, the choice is not leisurely walks on Cape Cod versus social media. It's television versus social media.)

As a social media researcher and a user, every time I read one of these "let's panic" articles about social media (and there are many), I want to shout: Look at TV! Look at commutes! Look at suburbs! Look at long work hours! That is, essentially, my response to Stephen Marche's "Facebook Is Making Us Lonely," which ran in *The Atlantic* magazine. And then, please, look at the extensive amount of data that show that social-media users are having more conversations with people—online and off!

What evidence we do have does not suggest a displacement of one type of conversation (offline) with another (online). All data I've seen say that people who use social media are either also more social offline; that they have benefited from social media to keep in touch with people they otherwise could not; or that many people find fellows, peers, and like-minded individuals they otherwise could not find. In other words, texting, Facebook-status updates, and Twitter conversations are not displacing face-to-face socializing—on average, they are making them stronger. Social media is enhancing human connectivity as people can converse in ways that were once not possible. Surveys also show that most families think social media enhances their family life—they can stay in touch better, more frequently. (Obviously, there are many complex impacts and not every person is going to "average" impacts.)

In other words, the people Turkle sees with their heads down on their devices while on a train somewhere are connecting to people they deem important in their lives. They are not talking to bots. Why would they be talking to bots? People tend to hate talking to bots. Anyone who's active on social media would see that. And social media are certainly easy to dismiss from afar. But close up, it's alive and brimming with humanity (and all the good and bad that comes along with that). And, as with all conversational settings, social media do not make much sense taken out of the context. (Ever seen verbatim transcripts of face-to-face conversations? They are almost incomprehensible even though they make perfect sense in the moment.)

One other category that is often overlooked is people who are either not that comfortable at some aspects of face-to-face conversation but find online interaction to be liberating. It's not that these people are not seeking human contact. It's just that they find it hard to make that initial connection. They are the people who don't dominate conversations, the people who appear shy, are less outgoing, who feel nervous talking to new people. Sometimes it's because they are different from the people around them.

From Arab Spring dissidents who were minorities in their communities to my students from a variety of backgrounds, from gay teens in rural areas to just people who feel awkward when in company of new people, I've heard the sentiment again and again that new communication tools are what saved their (offline) social lives.

10   So far, I've talked about two categories of people—those who were already social and who are becoming even more social offline as a result of offline connectivity, and those who have felt awkward offline and who are benefiting from online socializing. What I've not seen in the data I look at extensively (national surveys, qualitative research, and other accounts) are significant numbers of people who were otherwise able and willing to be social face-to-face and are now lost to their devices. It is true that the rise of the Internet may result in some people feeling more isolated than before, but those will likely be the people who do not or cannot use these new tools to engage their social ties. Such people, who reluctantly socialize via online methods due to skill or cost or personal disposition, may well find themselves *left out* of conversation.

11   One twist is that as people are increasingly able to find people based on interests—rather than interacting in the old manner with people with whom they happen to be in the same geographic proximity—people who depended on geographic proximity or family ties to provide social connectivity may indeed find themselves at a disadvantage if they are not able to develop their own networks. This is certainly a disruption and involves a certain kind of loss; however, it is hard to argue that it is all negative.

12   Finally, I've previously argued that some people may be "cyberasocial"; that is, they are unable or unwilling to invoke a sense of social presence through mediated communication, somewhat similar to the way we invoke language—a fundamentally oral form—through reading, which is a hack in our brain. I suspect such people may well be at a major disadvantage similar to the way people who could not or would not talk on the telephone would be in late 20th century.

13   In sum, social media is propelling transitions and disruptions in the composition of social networks. Increasingly, what used to be a given (social ties you inherited by the virtue of where you lived or your familial ties) is now a task (social ties based on shared interests and mutual interest). Surely, there will be new winners and losers. None of this, however, indicates a flight from human contact.

14   Is there a qualitative loss, then? Maybe. Such a subjective argument cannot be refuted with all the data showing people are just as much, if not more, connected now compared with most of 20th century. My sense is that what qualitative loss there is happens to be less so than many other forms of conversation avoidance. In fact, I can't count the number of times I was disturbed upon entering a house—especially in Turkey where this is common—because the television was glaring. Most people use the TV exactly like that—a conversation killer. At least, if people are texting, they are texting a human being. Similarly, I doubt that anyone has not seen how a person can open the newspaper at the kitchen table to block out conversation.

15   Take the much-maligned teenagers. What have we done to them? First, we move to the suburbs. So, they can't get around unless they drive (which is pretty dangerous). Parents often only take them to organized activities where the activity—hockey, violin, debate club—dominates, not the leisurely social conversation with each other adolescents naturally crave. Or they can hang out at . . . shopping malls. I need not say more about soul-killing.

16   And then when teenagers attempt to break out of this asocial, unnatural, and bizarre prison constructed of highways, no-recess time, and isolated single-family homes by connecting to *each other* through social media, we "tsk-tsk" them on how

they don't know how to actually talk or that they are narcissists because now we can see their status updates. Hint: Not much new going on here except teenage behavior is now visible thanks to technology, and everyone else seems to have forgotten what it was like to be that age. And, yeah, mom and dad, sometimes they want to talk to their peers and not to you. That is not new. It's not even your fault. It's called being a teenager. A bit of a pain, perhaps, but the kids are neither the smartest, nor the dumbest, nor the most narcissistic, nor the most non-conversationalist generation ever.

Or consider the elderly—the most poignant example Turkle raises. Data say they are now online in growing numbers. Why? So they can talk to people. Old classmates. Grandchildren. Each other. I've heard of many similar stories from people with disabilities: Social media allow them to connect in a world which does not otherwise allow them easy access. The fact that, rather than being separate "real" and "virtual" worlds, online and offline spheres are integrated is exactly why people can attempt to break away from the constraints in their offline lives by hacking their connectivity through online interaction. Can't be close to your family because your job took you to the other end of the planet? You can still share updates on Facebook. Your government is censoring news of your protest? You can tweet photos of it. You cannot find people interested in a particular kind of music that moves you? Surely, there is a community.

I concur with Sherry Turkle and others that there needs to be a deep and serious conversation about valuing each other—as humans, nothing more or less. And perhaps the impact of these rapidly evolving technologies on the "least among us" (as modern economic structures define them) is the correct place to start this conversation. However, to the degree this discussion can take place, it will mostly be because social media allow for such broad and deep conversations *among* the masses, who are reading and sharing rather than being lectured at and advertised to from their television screens.

Thinking Critically About Content

1. What is the main argument of each essay?

2. Do you agree with Turkle when she says that what we value most is "control over where we focus our attention" (paragraph 3)? Explain your answer.

3. How does Tufekci introduce her main point about social networking? Is this an effective approach to her argument? Explain your answer.

Thinking Critically About Purpose and Audience

4. What type of audience do you think would be most interested in the topic of these two essays? Explain your answer.

5. What tone do the authors use in these essays?

Thinking Critically About Purpose and Audience

4. Although these essays appeal to a general audience, social media users would benefit from its discussion because digital technology constantly shapes their lives.

5. Turkle uses an urgent and occasionally frustrated tone while Tufekci uses a relaxed and good-humored tone.

6. Answers will vary.

Thinking Critically About Paragraphs

7. Turkle provides examples of the ways people use digital technology in extreme ways before she makes her points about the effects of constant connectivity. On the other hand, Tufekci makes her points about social media before she illustrates those points with specific examples. However, both writers use personal examples throughout their respective essays, and both end their essays with calls to action.

8. Turkle and Tufekci conclude their essays with calls to action. Turkle provides an emotional appeal about how digital technology has invaded her

17

18

cottage on Cape Cod before she pleads with the readers to look up from their devices and have conversations with others. Tufekci also encourages readers to have serious conversations with each other, but she wants them to embrace social media and steer away from isolating devices like televisions.

9. Answers will vary.
10. Answers will vary.

To keep track of your critical thinking progress, go to Appendix 1.

ADDITIONAL WRITING TOPIC
Ask students to expand the paragraphs they wrote on page 306 into well-developed essays.

TEACHING ON THE WEB
Discussion Topic: Divide students into groups of three or four, and ask them to discuss the unlimited amount of information available on the Web. How can they determine which Web sites are trustworthy and which aren't? What role does persuasion play in the Web sites that aren't credible?

TEACHING ON THE WEB
Links: Have students link to Web sites that argue a controversial issue. How do the Web sites try to persuade people to think a certain way? Are the sites biased in any way?
Possible sites for the issue "Should marijuana be legalized?":
Mary Jane's Garden, maryjanesgarden.com/

6. Which essay do you agree with more? Did you agree with that position before you read the essays? If you changed your mind as a result of reading one of these essays, which part of the essay made you change your mind? Explain your answer in detail.

Thinking Critically About Paragraphs

7. Discuss the authors' methods of organizing their ideas. How are their methods of organization different in these essays? How are they the same?

8. Compare the conclusions in these two essays. Do these conclusions each reflect the main points of their essays?

9. Which paragraph is most convincing to you in each essay? What makes each one so convincing?

10. Write a paragraph explaining one of the ideas or facts that both essays agree on.

Writing Workshop

This section gives you the opportunity to apply what you have learned in this chapter to another writing assignment. This time, we provide you with the guidelines only and let you go through your own writing process with occasional feedback from your peers. Refer to sections of the chapter as necessary until the process of producing a paragraph becomes automatic for you.

Guidelines for Writing an Argument Paragraph

1. State your opinion on the issue in the topic sentence.
2. Find out as much as you can about your audience before you write.
3. Choose appropriate evidence that supports your topic sentence.
4. Organize your evidence so that it supports your argument as effectively as possible.

Writing About Your Reading

1. "The Economic Benefits of Passing the DREAM Act" discusses the complex issues surrounding illegal immigrants in our country. Choose another controversial subject related to immigration, and discuss its complexities in a way similar to Guzmán and Jara.

2. The two essays on social networking are both concerned with our ability to be connected with others in meaningful ways and our ability

to be alone. What suggestions do you have for this ongoing problem associated with social networking? Think of a strategy that will help young people strike a healthy balance between these two important goals, and attempt to convince a group of your peers that your solution will work. Gather as much evidence as you can before you begin to write.

3. How can being able to develop good arguments and persuade people of your point of view help you in real life? How might this ability give you the edge over other people in the job market?

Writing About Your World

Robert Landau/CORBIS

1. Explain how the billboard ad above is trying to persuade people to buy cigarettes. How does it appeal to its viewers? What line of reasoning does it follow? Write a paragraph about what the ad would say if it could talk directly to you.

2. We all have strong opinions on controversial issues. A newspaper or newscast might remind you of some of these subjects. Choose a current controversial issue, and, presenting your evidence in an essay, try to convince your classmates that your opinion is right.

3. Persuade the leader of an organization that your position on an important topic affecting the organization is the best choice. To find a topic, think of your own work experience, or talk to someone who has work experience. Organize your evidence as effectively as possible.

4. Create your own argument/persuasion assignment (with the help of your instructor), and write a response to it.

legalization-marijuana-california.php
    Working to Reform Marijuana Laws, norml.org/
    The DEA [Drug Enforcement Administration] Position on Marijuana,justice.gov/dea/docs/marijuana_position_2011.pdf

Revising

Small Group Activity (5–10 minutes per writer) Working in groups of three or four, read your arguments to each other. Those listening should record their reactions on a copy of the Revising Peer Evaluation Forms in Appendix 4. After your group goes through this process, give your evaluation forms to the appropriate writers so that each writer has two or three peer comment sheets for revising.

Paired Activity (5 minutes per writer) Using the completed Peer Evaluation Forms, work in pairs to decide what you should revise. If time allows, rewrite some of your sentences, and have your partner check them.

Individual Activity Rewrite your paper using the revising feedback you received from other students.

Editing

Paired Activity (5–10 minutes per writer) Swap papers with a classmate, and use the Editing Peer Evaluation Form in Appendix 6 to identify as many grammar, punctuation, mechanics, and spelling errors as you can. If time allows, correct some of your errors, and have your partner check them. Record your grammar, punctuation, and mechanics errors in the Error Log (Appendix 7) and your spelling errors in the Spelling Log (Appendix 8).

Individual Activity Rewrite your paper again using the editing feedback you received from other students.

Reflecting on Your Writing When you have completed your own paragraph, answer these six questions:

1. What was most difficult about this assignment?

2. What was easiest?

3. What did you learn about argument by completing this assignment?

4. What do you think are the strengths of your argument? Place a wavy line by the parts of your paragraph that you feel are very good.

5. What are the weaknesses, if any, of your paper? Place an X by the parts of your paragraph you would like help with. Write any questions you have in the margins.

6. What did you learn from this assignment about your own writing process—about preparing to write, about writing the first draft, about revising, and about editing?

Essays: Paragraphs in Context

❝Easy reading is damn hard writing.**❞**

—NATHANIEL HAWTHORNE

Part III explains what an essay is. It tells you not only how to identify an essay but also how to read and write one—step by step. It provides both a professional model and a student model for you to work with. Then it demonstrates how to apply specific revising and editing guidelines to an essay.

15

How to Read an Essay

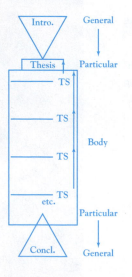

In content, essays are "nonfiction." That is, they are about real-life subjects rather than made-up ones. Most essays focus on one specific subject, a single purpose, and a particular audience (for example, telling college students how to get a good job). A successful essay gets the reaction from the readers that its author hopes for, whether this response is to appreciate a special scene, identify with someone's grief, or leap to action on a controversial issue.

Although essays may differ a great deal in approach and content, they share certain features that distinguish them from other types of writing. First, an essay usually has a title that names its general subject. When writers move from one topic to another, they start a new paragraph by indenting the first line a few spaces. In addition, most essays contain a thesis statement (a controlling idea for the entire essay) in the introduction. Several body paragraphs explain and support that thesis, and a conclusion draws the essay to a close.

To learn how essays actually function, you should look at them from two different perspectives—from both reading and writing. As you progress through these next two chapters, you will learn reading and writing are companion activities that help people create meaning. When you read an essay, you work with the writer to understand his or her message; in other words, you convert words and sentences into ideas and thoughts. When you write an essay, your job is to put your own thoughts into language that communicates your message to your reader(s). In either case, you are in a partnership with the text to create meaning from the words on the page.

Ideally, you should read an essay three times to understand it as thoroughly as possible. But first, you should prepare to read; this involves looking closely at the title, finding out some information about the author, and focusing your attention. Then, the first reading includes scanning the essay for difficult words, applying a reading strategy to the essay as you read it, and understanding the author's purpose and audience. The next stage is your first rereading, during which you should consider the essay's assumptions and look for important relationships between ideas. And the final reading requires you to ask some of your own questions about the reading in a conscious attempt to reach an analytical understanding of the essay.

A good way to approach your reading is to discover for yourself exactly how an essay works. You will then understand more clearly the choices you can make as a writer. To accomplish this goal, follow the guidelines in this chapter as you read an essay by Scott Russell Sanders. Once you understand these guidelines, you will learn for yourself the various features at work in a good essay and be able to apply this new knowledge to your own reading and writing.

MyWritingLab | ### Recognizing an Essay

To make sure that you fully understand what an essay entails, go to **MyWritingLab.com,** and click on **Recognizing an Essay** in the **Essay Development** module. Watch the **Animation** video called **Essays: Recognizing an Essay,** and learn about the main features of this type of writing.

The following essay, by Scott Russell Sanders, is from a book entitled *Hunting for Hope*.

FIDELITY[1]
by Scott Russell Sanders

A cause needn't be grand, it needn't impress a crowd, to be worthy of our com-   1
mitment. I knew a man, a lifelong Quaker, who visited prisoners in our county jail, week in and week out, for decades. He would write letters for them, carry messages for them, fetch them clothing or books. But mainly he just offered himself, a very tall and spare and gentle man, with a full shock of white hair in his later years and a rumbling voice that never wasted a word. He didn't ask whether the prisoners were innocent or guilty of the charges that had landed them in jail. All that mattered was that they were

[1] From *Hunting for Hope* by Scott Russell Sanders. Copyright © 1998 by Scott Russell Sanders. Reprinted by permission of Beacon Press, Boston.

Since students have been working intensively with topic sentences in Part II, you might start the discussion of essays by showing them how the topic sentence of a paragraph relates to the thesis statement of an essay. Explain how the thesis statement controls the entire essay and its topic sentences become supporting ideas to the thesis. Then show students how the same principles they've been studying in previous chapters apply to essays; students just have to adjust their thinking to a larger scale.

How to Read an Essay To help students find the answers to the questions in this chapter, have them work in one of the following ways.

Learning how to read analytically from others is always a good strategy.

- In pairs
- In groups of three or four
- With a tutor

INSTRUCTOR'S RESOURCE MANUAL For additional material about teaching essays, for journal entries, and for various tests, see the *Instructor's Resource Manual,* Section II, Part III.

in trouble. He didn't preach to them, didn't pick and choose between the likable and the nasty, didn't look for any return on his time. Nor did he call attention to his kindness; I had known him for several years before I found out about his visits to the jail. Why did he go spend time with outcasts, every week without fail, when he could have been golfing or shopping or watching TV? "I go," he told me once, "in case everyone else has given up on them. I never give up."

2   Never giving up is a trait we honor in athletes, in soldiers, in climbers marooned by avalanches, in survivors of shipwreck, in patients recovering from severe injuries. If you struggle bravely against overwhelming odds, you're liable to wind up on the evening news. A fireman rescues three children from a burning house, then goes back inside a fourth time to rescue the dog. A childless washerwoman in the deep South, who never dreamed of going to college herself, lives modestly and saves her pennies and in old age donates everything she's saved, over a hundred thousand dollars, for university scholarships. A pilot flies his flimsy plane through a blizzard, searching for a pickup truck in which a woman is trapped; gliding and banking through a whirl of white, he catches signals from her cellular phone, ever so faint; the snow blinds him, the wind tosses him around, his fuel runs low, but he circles and circles, homing in on that faint signal; then just before dark he spies the truck, radios the position to a helicopter crew, and the woman is saved. What kept him searching? "I hadn't found her yet," he tells the camera. "I don't quit so long as I have gas."

3   Striking examples of perseverance catch our eye, and rightly so. But in less flashy, less newsworthy forms, fidelity to a mission or a person or an occupation shows up in countless lives all around us, all the time. It shows up in parents who will not quit loving their son no matter how much trouble he causes, in parents who will not quit loving their daughter even after she dyes her hair purple and tattoos her belly and runs off with a rock band. It shows up in couples who choose to mend their marriages instead of filing for divorce. It shows up in farmers who stick to their land through droughts and hailstorms and floods. It shows up in community organizers who struggle year after year for justice, in advocates for the homeless and the elderly, in volunteers at the hospital or library or women's shelter or soup kitchen. It shows up in the unsung people everywhere who do their jobs well, not because a supervisor is watching or because they are paid gobs of money but because they know their work matters.

4   When Jesse was in sixth grade, early in the school year, his teacher was diagnosed as having breast cancer. She gathered the children and told them frankly about the disease, about the surgery and therapy she would be undergoing, and about her hopes for recovery. Jesse came home deeply impressed that she had trusted them with her news. Before going to the hospital, she laid out lesson plans for the teacher who would be replacing her. Although she could have stayed home for the rest of the year on medical leave while the substitute handled her class, as soon as she healed from the mastectomy, she began going in to school one afternoon a week, then two, then a full day, then two days and three, to read with the children and talk with them and see how they were getting on. When a parent worried aloud that she might be risking her health for the sake of the children, the teacher scoffed, "Oh, heavens no! They're my best medicine." Besides, these children would only be in sixth grade once, and she meant to help them all she could while she had the chance.

The therapy must have worked, because seven years later she's going strong. When Ruth and I see her around town, she always asks about Jesse. Is he still so funny, so bright, so excited about learning? Yes he is, we tell her, and she beams.

I have a friend who builds houses Monday through Friday for people who can pay him and then builds other houses on Saturday, with Habitat for Humanity, for people who can't pay him. I have another friend who bought land that had been stripped of topsoil by bad farming, and who is slowly turning those battered acres into a wildlife sanctuary by halting erosion and spreading manure and planting trees. A neighbor of ours who comes from an immigrant family makes herself available night and day to international students and their families, unriddling for them the puzzles of living in this new place. Other neighbors coach soccer teams, visit the sick, give rides to the housebound, go door to door raising funds for charity, tutor dropouts, teach adults to read; and they do these things not just for a month or a season but for years.   5

There's a man in our town who has been fighting the U.S. Forest Service for two decades, trying to persuade them to quit clear-cutting, quit selling timber at a loss, quit breaking their own rules in the Hoosier National Forest. All the while, those who make money from tearing up the woods call for more cutting, more road-building, more board feet. This man makes no money from carrying on his crusade, but he makes plenty of enemies, many of whom own chain saws and guns. He won't back down, though, because he loves the forest and loves the creatures that depend on the forest. Hearing him talk, you realize that he sees himself as one of those creatures, like any warbler or fox.   6

I could multiply these examples a hundredfold without ever leaving my county. Most likely you could do the same in yours. Any community worth living in must have a web of people faithful to good work and to one another, or that community would fall apart.   7

PREPARING TO READ

The questions here are designed to focus your attention on the subject of the essay before you read it for the first time. In this book, prereading questions are furnished for you. But in most cases, you must supply these questions yourself. Answer the following questions in your journal or on a separate piece of paper—in preparation for a close reading of Sanders's essay "Fidelity."

Focuing Your Attention

1. Think of a person you admire: your mom, a Hollywood star, your dad, your sister, a president, an athlete. Then make a list of the qualities you appreciate in this person.

2. In the essay "Fidelity," Sanders recounts the stories of several people who consistently give of themselves to help others. Think of something special someone has done. What details of the activity made the strongest impressions on you?

Expanding Your Vocabulary

The next natural step is identifying difficult words. In this text, these words are furnished for you. In other reading situations, you need to find these words yourself, including names of people and places.

perseverance: determination (paragraph 3)

Hoosier National Forest: a 644,163-acre area of rolling hills in southern Indiana (paragraph 6)

FIRST READING

The guidelines in this section teach you a specific way of approaching your reading that can help you not only understand what you read but also discover the relationship of the writer's ideas to one another and to your own thoughts. These reading techniques can also help clarify for you the connection between the writer's topic, his or her means of expression, and your own composing process. In other words, the strategies and questions are designed to help you understand and generate ideas, discover various choices writers make in composing their essays, and then realize the freedom you have to make related choices in your own writing. Such an approach to the process of reading takes some of the mystery out of reading and writing and makes them manageable tasks at which anyone can succeed.

Choosing a Reading Strategy

Choose one of the strategies explained in Chapter 2, and apply it to the Sanders essay. This process will help you begin to move toward a deep understanding of your reading assignment.

Discovering How the Essay Works

You are now ready to discover how the essay works. As you become an analytical reader, you will be able to generate these questions on your own as you read. But here is a sample of the type of questions that will help you learn how the essay functions and makes its points. Once you realize the choices the writer made to create the essay, you will understand the types of choices you have to make when you write. Once again, answer the questions in your journal or on a separate piece of paper.

1. What is the subject of this essay?

   The benefits of performing selfless acts to help others

2. What is its thesis statement?

   The first sentence in the first paragraph.

3. Does the thesis state the author's position on the subject?

Yes. It carefully sets up all the supporting body paragraphs.

4. How does the writer capture the readers' attention in the introduction?

The introduction uses a brief story, a question, and an answer.

Is this strategy effective for this subject? Why or why not?

Answers will vary.

5. How many body paragraphs does the author include in this essay?

Sanders's essay contains five body paragraphs.

List the topic sentence of each body paragraph:

Paragraph   Topic Sentence

2

3

4

5

6

6. Does the author use enough specific details to communicate his message?

Answers will vary.

7. Do the sentences in each paragraph support the topic sentence?

Yes.

8. Is the essay organized logically? Give an example to support your answer.

Yes. Examples will vary.

9. Do the sentences and paragraphs move smoothly and logically from one to the next? Give an example to support your answer.

Yes. Examples will vary.

10. What strategy does the author use to conclude the essay?

He summarizes, extends his observations, and calls his readers to action.

Is this strategy effective? Explain your answer.

Answers will vary.

11. How does the title relate to the author's thesis statement?

Fidelity means loyalty or faithfulness, which is what this essay is about.

Is this an effective title? Explain your answer.

Answers will vary.

12. Did you find the essay interesting?

Answers will vary.

FIRST REREADING

The first rereading will naturally move you more deeply into the subject. You will see relationships in the essay that you did not notice the first time, and you will probably start thinking, if you haven't already, of your reactions to various ideas in the essay. The following types of questions, which appear after each essay in this text, will guide you through this process. Answer them in your journal or on a separate piece of paper.

Thinking Critically About Content

1. Name three "causes" that Sanders discusses in this essay.

   Sanders talks about helping prisoners, rescuing people, persevering in everyday life,

   recovering from breast cancer, doing generous acts for neighbors, and saving a forest.

2. Have you or someone you know ever done any selfless acts like the people in this essay? If so, what were they?

   Answers will vary.

3. What does the author mean when he says, "Any community worth living in must have a web of people faithful to good work and to one another, or that community would fall apart"?

   Communities that survive have selfless people who help one another.

Thinking Critically About Purpose and Audience

4. What do you think Sanders's purpose is in this essay?

   To explain the advantages of selfless acts

5. What type of audience do you think would most appreciate this essay? Why do you admire this person?

   Answers will vary.

6. Whom do you admire most from this essay for his or her selfless acts? Why do you admire this person?

   Answers will vary.

Thinking Critically About Essays

7. Does Sanders give enough examples to convince you of his main point?

   Answers will vary.

8. What is Sanders's thesis in this essay?

   The first sentence of the first paragraph.

9. Does each topic sentence in this essay support the thesis statement? Explain your answer.

   The topic sentences support the thesis statement by expanding it in each case.

10. Write a paragraph about someone you know who performed a selfless act to help someone else. What was the value of this act?

SECOND REREADING

The second rereading requires the most energy on your part because you have to produce questions about the essay as it moves from point to point. Even though this third reading takes the most energy, it is also the most satisfying because your mind gets to exercise and grapple with ideas on a level that will help you understand both your reading and writing assignments more completely.

To accomplish this level, you should ask questions that go beyond the words on the page and then answer them in writing.

- Ask yourself "how" and "why" questions;
- Answer those questions;
- Record your opinions; and
- Analyze your thoughts as they occur.

To check your understanding and interpretations, talk to others in your class as you go through this process.

The remainder of Part III in this text will guide you step by step through the process of writing your own essay in response to a specific topic related to this reading. As you move through this section, the information on the reading and writing processes provided in Part I will help you answer the questions in each chapter.

16

How to Write an Essay

As you learned in Chapter 15, writing is a companion activity to reading. In fact, you can learn a great deal about how to write by reading. When you read an essay, you can see how the writer thinks and puts words together to create meaning. Then, when you write, you are putting your own thoughts into words so you can communicate a specific message to your reader(s). In both cases, you must work together with the words to create meaning.

Writing an essay is very similar to writing a paragraph, although we call some elements of an essay by different names than we use for similar elements in a paragraph. The following chart demonstrates the correspondences:

Paragraph	Essay
Topic sentence	Introduction with thesis statement
Examples, details, support	Body paragraphs
Concluding sentence	Concluding paragraph

Keeping these similarities in mind will help you learn in this chapter how to construct a good essay. Here is the writing prompt for this chapter.

Writing Prompt   **Complete** this **Writing Prompt** at **mywritinglab.com**

Write an essay explaining your feelings, observations, and thoughts about a significant event in your life with someone you admire. Why do you admire this person? What has this person done that separates him or her from others? Focus on a single activity, and explain its significance in a well-developed essay.

As we address this writing assignment, we will demonstrate each stage of the writing process by observing how a writer named Jolene Christie developed an essay in response to this topic.

MyWritingLab

How to Write an Essay

To make sure that you fully understand what an essay entails, go to MyWritingLab.com, and click on **Recognizing an Essay** in the **Essay Development** module. Watch the **Animation** video called **Essays: Essay Writing,** and learn about the main features of this type of writing. When you feel comfortable with these ideas, complete the **Recall, Apply,** and **Write** activities in **MyWritingLab.** Then check your understanding by doing the **Posttest.**

PREPARING TO WRITE

Prewriting refers to activities that help you explore a general subject, generate ideas about it, select a specific topic, establish a purpose, and learn as much as possible about your readers or audience. Your mission at this stage is to stimulate your thinking before and during the act of writing.

Whenever you generate new material throughout the writing process, you are prewriting. The most common prewriting activities are freewriting, brainstorming, clustering, questioning, and discussing. (See Chapter 3 for an explanation of each of these techniques.) The more ideas you generate now and throughout the entire writing process, the more you have to work with as you draft your essay.

Once you generate ideas, you need to map out your essay and write a thesis statement that you can use as an anchor throughout the writing process. Your "plan" and your thesis might change as your essay develops, but they both give you something to start with as you approach a writing assignment.

Choosing a Topic

You might be choosing a subject from infinite possibilities or selecting a topic based on a writing assignment, as in this situation. Whatever the case, make sure you decide on a topic you can handle comfortably within the required length. That means you might choose a subject, like pets, and then narrow the subject further to fulfill the assignment:

General subject: pets
  More specific: dogs
    More specific: golden retrievers
      More specific: training your golden retriever

Jolene's Brainstorming Our student writer decided immediately that she wanted to write about her dad, but she didn't know how to limit her

TEACHING HOW TO WRITE AN ESSAY
Have the students as a class come up with a topic that they would like to write an essay on. Make sure the topic is neither too narrow nor too broad.

After the students settle on a topic, have the class as a whole write a thesis statement for the topic. Once you decide that the thesis statement is a good controlling idea, have students come up with three (or any number that you set) topic sentences that would support the thesis statement. Then decide on the order of the topic sentences.

After the class has developed a good thesis statement and the topic sentences, divide the class into five or more groups, and have each group work on one part of the essay (introduction, three or more body paragraphs, or conclusion). For instance, group 1 will write the introduction, groups 2 through 4 will each get a topic sentence to write on, and group 5 will write the conclusion. Do not let the groups know what the

topic. So she decided to brainstorm to see where that activity would take her. Here is a list of Jolene's ideas in response to this essay prompt:

my dad

the city

train ride

excitement

feeling lost

looking successful

my friends don't care

my dad was special

meeting him

just the beginning

Your Brainstorming   Make a list of some of the ideas that are on your mind in reference to this assignment.

Planning

Writing an essay takes planning, and the more thought you put into your essay before you start writing, the more direction you will have as you write. If you make some decisions about your topic, purpose, and audience before you actually write, the job of writing will be much smoother and less stressful than it would be otherwise.

Jolene's Plans   Jolene decides that the single activity she would like to focus on is the day she met her father for the first time. But she wants to build up to this event by keeping the reader guessing what is happening. She wants the readers to feel some of the excitement and surprise she felt as she approached and carried out this event. She will concentrate on narration, showing rather than telling her readers about the significance of this day in her life. She will be writing for her English class.

Subject:	Meeting her father for the first time
Purpose:	To share the excitement and surprise of this experience
Audience:	Her classmates

Your Plans   What activity will you focus on in response to this writing assignment? Also, what are your purpose and audience for this essay?

Writing a Thesis Statement

Just as a topic sentence is the controlling idea of a paragraph, a thesis statement provides the controlling idea for an essay. It guides the writing of your entire essay. Like a high-powered telescope pointed at a distant star, your thesis statement focuses on a single aspect of your subject.

Your essay's thesis statement is also a contract between you and your readers. The thesis statement tells your readers what the main idea of your essay will be and what the body paragraphs will be about. If you don't deliver what your thesis statement promises, your readers will be confused and disappointed.

To write a thesis statement, begin by stating your position on your topic. This sentence moves you from the broad subject of your essay to your own perspective or feeling about the topic.

> **Thesis statement:**   Training your golden retriever is important for your dog's safety and for your enjoyment of each other.

In this case, the writer states a position (training is important) and gives reasons for this position (safety and enjoyment).

When you feel you have a good working thesis statement, turn it into a question as an exercise to guide you through your draft. Then the rest of your essay should answer this question.

> **Thesis question:**   In what ways is training your golden retriever important for your dog's safety and for your enjoyment of each other?

Usually, the thesis statement is the final sentence in the introduction. This placement gives the reader a road map for reading the rest of your essay.

Jolene's Thesis Statement   Jolene wanted to end her introduction with a reference to meeting her father as an event she would never forget. So she writes the following thesis statement:

> **Topic:**   Meeting my dad.
> **Thesis/Position:** I'll never forget that day.
> **Thesis question:** How did meeting my father affect me?

Your Thesis Statement   Write out a tentative thesis statement for your essay based on the decisions you have already made.

WRITING

Four more general guidelines will help you develop the first draft of your essay. They range from writing a complete introduction to bringing your essay to a close with a conclusion that reflects the introduction. Between the introduction and conclusion must be the paragraphs that support your thesis statement.

1. **Construct an introduction that leads up to your thesis statement.** The introduction to an essay is your chance to make a great first impression. Just like a firm handshake and a warm smile in a job interview, an essay's introduction should capture your readers' interest, set the tone for your essay, and state your specific purpose. Introductions often take on a funnel shape: they typically begin with general information and then narrow their focus to your position on a particular issue. Regardless of your approach, your introduction should "hook" your readers by grabbing their attention.

   Some effective ways of catching your audience's attention and giving necessary background information are (1) to furnish a quotation; (2) to tell a story that relates to your topic; (3) to provide a revealing fact, statistic, or definition; (4) to offer an interesting comparison; or (5) to ask an intriguing question.

   Jolene's Introduction   Jolene wants to set the scene for her essay and keep the element of surprise as long as she can. In her first paragraph, she has to set up some background for her essay and introduce the scene she is going to focus on.

   > My mother is a single mother, and she lived in a small town her whole life. She had me at a very young age. I never knew my father, and she never mentioned anything about him. On numerous occasions I would ask about him, and around the age of 15, my mother decided that it might be best if I knew who my father was. I'll never forget that day.

   Your Introduction   Drawing on all this important advice, draft an introduction for your essay.

2. **Develop as many supporting paragraphs or body paragraphs as necessary to explain your thesis statement.** Following the introductory paragraph, an essay includes several body paragraphs that support and explain the essay's thesis. Each body paragraph deals with a topic that is directly related to your thesis statement.

   At least one supporting paragraph should cover each topic in your essay. Supporting paragraphs usually include a topic sentence (a general statement about the paragraph's content) and examples or details that support the topic sentence. See Chapter 3 for methods of developing and organizing these paragraphs.

Jolene's Body Paragraphs   Jolene has four ideas she thinks should be developed into body paragraphs. Each one supports her thesis statement.

Topic	Point
1	research on my father
2	traveling to see my dad
3	trying to locate my dad
4	connecting with my dad

Your Body Paragraph   List the topics of your possible body paragraphs. Like the foundation of a solid building, these paragraphs must provide support for the point you express in your thesis statement. The stronger the supporting paragraphs are, the stronger the essay.

3. **Write a concluding paragraph.** The concluding paragraph is the final paragraph of an essay. In its most basic form, it should summarize the main points of your essay and remind readers of your thesis statement.

   The best conclusions expand on these basic requirements and conclude the essay with one of these creative strategies: (1) ask a question that provokes new ideas, (2) predict the future, (3) offer a solution to a problem, or (4) call the reader to action. Each of these options sends a specific message and creates a slightly different effect at the end of an essay. The most important responsibility of the last paragraph, however, is to bring the essay to a close.

Jolene's Conclusion   Jolene wanted to stress the excitement she felt on the day she met her dad and explain the significance of this day in her life. Her conclusion needs to close her essay as it also explains indirectly why she wrote it.

   I will never forget my first encounter with this city. I glance once more at my father as we walk out of the station. I suddenly feel as if this city, this place where my father lives, has always been a part of me. I am ready to venture out toward a new life.

Your Conclusion   How will you bring your essay to a close? Choose a strategy you will use, and think of a way to remind your readers of your controlling idea. Then write a rough draft of your conclusion.

4. **Give your essay a catchy title.** Now you should think of a title for your essay. Much like well-chosen clothes for a job interview, your title is what your reader sees first. Titles are phrases, usually no more

than a few words, placed at the beginning of your essay that suggest or sum up the subject, purpose, or focus of your essay. Besides forecasting an essay's purpose, a good title catches an audience's attention. The title chosen for this book, *Mosaics*, reflects a specific view of the writing process—a collection of brightly colored individual pieces that fit together to form a complete whole. Whereas this title vividly conveys the textbook's purpose, the title for this chapter is a more straightforward label: "How to Write an Essay." These are just two of many approaches to creating a title.

Jolene's Title   Jolene wants to get her readers' attention in some unique way. But she doesn't want her title to say too much. She wants to whet her readers' curiosity without revealing any of her surprises. That's exactly what a title should do—make your readers want to read your essay.

My First Encounter with the City

Your Title   What do you want to reveal in your title? Record several possible titles for your essay that suggest its purpose and attract the readers' attention at the same time.

5. **Write a first draft from the work you have done in this section.** Follow your notes and continue to generate ideas as you write your first draft. You will then revise and edit this draft until it says exactly what you want it to say and is free from all grammar and usage errors.

Jolene's First Draft   After working through these guidelines, Jolene was ready to write out her first draft. She knew she would be revisiting this draft several times to revise and edit it carefully.

My First Encounter with the City

1   My mother is a single mother, and she lived in a small town her whole life. She had me at a very young age. I never knew my father, she never mentioned anything about him. On numerous occasions I would ask about him, and around the age of 15, my mother decided that it might be best if I knew who my father was. I'll never forget that day.

2   I went out to do some research on my newfound father. I asked about him and tried to find out what kind of person he was. I didn't find a lot of information, but at the time it was enough for a 15-year-old. Just after my 18th birthday, I thought that I was mentally ready to take another step forward. I managed to find

his phone number. It took me about six months to work up the courage to call him. I was afraid that he wouldn't believe that I be his daughter and would reject me, but I was pleasantly surprised. Now, two months later, I am excited about our first encounter. Especially in the city!

My thoughts are interrupted as I notice that the bus is pulling   3
into the station. People are everywhere! Some are strolling down the sidewalks gazing through store windows; others are speed-walking with there cell phones glued to their ears. I look out the window and take a deep breath. There is wall-to-wall traffic, with people honking their horns and slamming on their brakes. I can feel the terror filling up inside of me. I grab my backpack and suitcase, adjust my load, and step off the bus. Just as I step down, someone bowls me over to catch another bus. I pick up my bags from the filthy ground, readjust, and sigh. I feel as if my legs are rooted to the cement and, if I try to move them, they will turn to Jell-O.

I see a man walking toward me. He have a mound of long, greasy   4
gray hair that resembles a used bird's nest. He also has a long, scraggly beard and mustache. He has beady little eyes that I can feel penetrating and paralyzing me. His clothes are ragged, ripped, and falling off of him. My heart sinks as I realize this man could be my father, Samuel Bride. I cannot align my emotions and expectations with the man who is staring directly into my eyes.

As I scan the station trying to find the courage to approach him,   5
my eyes spot a man wearing a suit and tie. He is holding a sign with my name written in black and a bouquet of white and yellow roses. I hesitantly walk over to him with an uncomfortable smile. I give him an awkward hug, and he returns the gesture. After a moment of silence, he asks me how my trip was, and I can't help but look back at the bedraggled man. I suddenly feel sorry for him, ashamed that I had desperately wanted someone else as my father. I look up at my successful, charming father and, in my anxious emotional state, can only respond with a smile.

I will never forget my first encounter with this city. I glance   6
once more at my father as we walk out of the station. I suddenly feel as if this city, this place where my father lives, has always been a part of me. I am ready to venture out toward a new life.

First Draft   Write a draft of your own essay that represents all the ideas you want to communicate on the assigned topic. Review the guidelines in this chapter one by one to help you draft your essay.

REVISING AND EDITING

The drafts now need to go through the final stages of revising and editing.

Revising and Editing the Student Essay

Jolene's first draft now needs to be revised and edited. First, apply the following Revising Checklist to the content of Jolene's draft. When you are satisfied that her ideas are fully developed and well organized, use the Editing Checklist to correct her grammar and mechanics errors. Answer the questions, and complete the tasks in each category. Then write your suggested changes directly on Jolene's draft.

 ## Understanding Revising

To revise an essay, you are reconsidering its content or substance. For a review of the revising process, go to **Revising the Essay** in the **Essay Development** module in **MyWritingLab.** First, read the **Overview** and watch the **Animation** videos to learn to revise specific parts of essays. Next, complete the **Recall, Apply,** and **Write** activities to make sure you have learned all the elements of this process. Then check your understanding of this topic by taking the **Post-test.**

Revising the Student Essay

THESIS STATEMENT

✔ Does the thesis statement contain the essay's controlling idea and an opinion about that idea?

✔ Does the thesis appear as the last sentence of the introduction?

1. What is Jolene's main idea in this essay?

   She is meeting her dad for the first time.

2. Put brackets around the last sentence in Jolene's introduction. Does it introduce her main idea?

   [I'll never forget that day.] No

3. Rewrite Jolene's thesis statement if necessary so it states her main point and introduces her topics.

   One possibility: I will never forget a very special meeting that changed my life.

BASIC ELEMENTS

✔ Does the title draw in the readers?

✔ Does the introduction capture the readers' attention and build up effectively to the thesis statement?

✔ Does each body paragraph deal with a single topic?

✔ Does the conclusion bring the essay to a close in an interesting way?

1. Give Jolene's essay an alternate title.

   Answers will vary.

2. Rewrite Jolene's introduction so it captures the readers' attention and builds up to the thesis statement at the end of the paragraph.

   Answers will vary.

3. Does each of Jolene's body paragraphs deal with only one topic?

   Yes

4. Rewrite Jolene's conclusion using at least one suggestion from item 3 under "Writing" in this chapter.

   Answers may vary.

DEVELOPMENT

✔ Do the body paragraphs adequately support the thesis statement?

✔ Does each body paragraph have a focused topic sentence?

✔ Does each body paragraph contain *specific* details that support the topic sentence?

✔ Does each body paragraph include *enough* details to fully explain the topic sentence?

1. Write out Jolene's thesis statement (revised, if necessary), and list her four topic sentences below it.

   Thesis statement: *Answers will vary.*

   Topic 1: *I went out to do some research on my newfound father.*

   Topic 2: *My thoughts are interrupted as I notice that the bus is pulling into the station.*

   Topic 3: *I see a man walking toward me.*

   Topic 4: *As I scan the station trying to find the courage to approach him . . .*

2. Do Jolene's topics adequately support her thesis statement? *Yes*

3. Does each body paragraph have a focused topic sentence? *Yes*

4. Are Jolene's examples specific? *Yes*

   Add another more specific detail to one of the examples in her essay.

5. Does she offer enough examples to make her point? *Answers will vary.*

   Add at least one new example to strengthen Jolene's essay.

UNITY

✔ Do the essay's topic sentences relate directly to the thesis statement?

✔ Do the details in each body paragraph support the paragraph's topic sentence?

1. Read each of Jolene's topic sentences with her thesis statement (revised, if necessary) in mind. Do they go together? *Answers will vary.*

2. Revise her topic sentences if necessary so they are directly related.
   Answers will vary.

3. Read each of Jolene's sentences with its topic sentence in mind.

4. Drop or rewrite any sentences that are not directly related to their topic sentence. *All sentences are related.*

ORGANIZATION

✔ Is the essay organized logically?

✔ Is each body paragraph organized logically?

1. Review your list of Jolene's topics in item 2 under "Writing" in this chapter, and decide if her body paragraphs are organized logically.

2. What is her method of organization? *Chronological*

3. Look closely at Jolene's body paragraphs to see if all her sentences are arranged logically within paragraphs.

4. Move any sentences that are out of order. *All sentences are arranged logically.*

COHERENCE

✔ Are transitions used effectively so that paragraphs move smoothly and logically from one to the next?

✔ Do the sentences move smoothly and logically from one to the next?

1. Circle five transitions Jolene uses.   *Answers will vary.*

2. Explain how two of these transitions make Jolene's essay easier to read.
   Answers will vary.

 Now rewrite Jolene's essay with your revisions.

For a list of transitions, see pages 59–60.

 MyWritingLab | ## Understanding Editing

Editing deals with the grammar and mechanics of an essay. If you need a review before you edit this student paper, go to **MyWritingLab.com,** and choose **Editing the Essay** in the **Essay Development** module. To understand the basics of editing and proofreading, read the **Overview,** and watch the four **Animation** videos. Then complete the **Recall, Apply,** and **Write** activities. Finally, check your understanding of the editing process in the **Post-test.**

Editing the Student Essay

SENTENCES

Subjects and Verbs
✔ Does each sentence have a main subject and verb?

1. In paragraphs 1 and 2 of your revision, underline Jolene's subjects once and verbs twice. Remember that sentences can have more than one subject-verb set.   *See Jolene's first draft.*

2. Does each sentence in these paragraphs have at least one subject and verb that can stand alone? *No*

3. Correct any fragments you find.   *Paragraph 2, last sentence*

4. Correct any run-together sentences you find.   *Paragraph 1, sentence 3*

Subject-Verb Agreement
✔ Do all subjects and verbs agree?

1. Read aloud the subjects and verbs you underlined in Jolene's first two paragraphs.

For help with subjects and verbs, see Chapter 20.

For help with fragments, see Chapter 21.

For help with run-togethers, see Chapter 22.

For help with subject-verb agreement, see Chapter 25.

2. Correct any subjects and verbs that do not agree.   *I be, paragraph 2*

3. Now read aloud all the subjects and verbs in the rest of her revised paragraphs.

4. Correct any subjects and verbs that do not agree.   *He have, paragraph 4, sentence 2*

Pronoun Agreement
✔ Do all pronouns agree with their nouns?

For help with pronoun agreement, see Chapter 29.

1. Find any pronouns in your revision of Jolene's essay that do not agree with their nouns.   *All pronouns agree with their nouns.*

2. Correct any pronouns that do not agree with their nouns.

Modifier Errors
✔ Are modifiers as close as possible to the words they modify?

For help with modifier errors, see Chapter 32.

1. Find any modifiers in your revision of Jolene's essay that are not as close as possible to the words they modify.   *There are no modifier errors.*

2. Rewrite sentences if necessary so that modifiers are as close as possible to the words they modify.

PUNCTUATION AND MECHANICS

Punctuation
✔ Are sentences punctuated correctly?

For help with punctuation, see Chapters 33–37.

1. Read your revision of Jolene's essay for any errors in punctuation.   *There are no punctuation errors.*

2. Make sure any fragments and run-together sentences you revised are punctuated correctly.

Mechanics
✔ Are words capitalized properly?

For help with capitalization, see Chapter 38.

1. Read your revision of Jolene's essay for any errors in capitalization.   *All capitals are correct.*

2. Be sure to check her capitalization in any fragments or run-together sentences you revised.

WORD CHOICE AND SPELLING

Word Choice
✔ Are words used correctly?

For help with confused words, see Chapter 44.

1. Find any words used incorrectly in your revision of Jolene's essay.   *there (paragraph 3, sentence 4)*

2. Correct any errors you find.   *there/their*

Spelling

✔ Are words spelled correctly?

1. Use spell-check and a dictionary to check the spelling in your revision of Jolene's essay. *All words are spelled correctly.*

For help with spelling, see Chapter 45.

2. Correct any misspelled words.

  Now rewrite Jolene's paragraph again with your editing corrections.

Revising and Editing Your Own Essay

Returning to the essay you wrote earlier in this chapter, revise and edit your own writing following the guidelines you just used on the student essay.

Writing Workshop

Guidelines for Writing an Essay

1. Choose a subject.
2. Plan your essay.
3. Write a thesis statement about your subject.
4. Construct an introduction that leads up to your thesis statement.
5. Develop as many supporting paragraphs or body paragraphs as necessary to explain your thesis statement.
6. Write a concluding paragraph.
7. Give your essay a catchy title.
8. Revise and edit your essay.

WRITING AN ESSAY

Steve Mack/Getty Images

1. Find someone who does community service or volunteer work as in the photo on the previous page. What type of service does this person do? Why is the person attracted to this type of work? Whom does he or she help? What does this activity do for the community? What does it do for you? Write an essay about this person's contributions to society.

2. You have been asked by the editor of your campus newspaper to relate your weirdest experience. Write an essay about this experience, including what you learned from it.

3. In an essay, analyze a relationship you have with another person by explaining its causes and effects.

4. Come up with your own essay assignment (with the help of your instructor), and write a response to it.

REVISING WORKSHOP

Small Group Activity (5–10 minutes per writer) Working in groups of three or four, read your essays to each other. Those listening should record their reactions on a copy of the Revising Peer Evaluation Form in Appendix 5. After your group goes through this process, give your evaluation forms to the appropriate writers so that each writer has two or three peer comment sheets for revising.

Paired Activity (5 minutes per writer) Using the completed Peer Evaluation Forms, work in pairs to decide what you should revise in your essay. If time allows, rewrite some of your sentences, and have your partner look at them.

Individual Activity Rewrite your paper, using the revising feedback you received from other students.

EDITING WORKSHOP

Paired Activity (5–10 minutes per writer) Swap papers with a classmate, and use the Editing Peer Evaluation Form in Appendix 6 to identify as many grammar, punctuation, mechanics, and spelling errors as you can. If time allows, correct some of your errors, and have your partner look at them. Record your grammar, punctuation, and mechanics errors in the Error Log (Appendix 7) and your spelling errors in the Spelling Log (Appendix 8).

Individual Activity Rewrite your paper again, using the editing feedback you received from other students.

view about having the job of carrying something so important and so large for the benefit of the other ants.

Bodily/Kinesthetic

Working in pairs, blindfold a fellow student, and put an unusual object in his or her hands (for example, a dog biscuit or jello). Have the blindfolded student describe the item while you write down the description. After the student finishes describing the item, remove the item and then the blindfold, and let your partner write a brief essay about what the item might be and how he or she came to this conclusion. Then reverse roles.

Intrapersonal

Listen to a series of nature CDs (ocean sounds, thunderstorms, and tropical rain forests), and reflect on how each sound makes you feel. Write an essay about how the sounds evoke different emotions in you.

Interpersonal

Go to a local park, and watch some children discover different aspects of nature. Write an essay describing your observations. Be sure to include the reactions of the children who notice something in nature for the first time.

Naturalist

Go to the nearest botanical garden (or the equivalent) in your city, and look at the different varieties of trees, flowers, and plants. Pay particular attention to where the varieties grow naturally. Write an essay about where you might want to live based on the trees, flowers, and plants you prefer. Why did you choose this particular place?

Student Comment:
"Pearson Tutor Services was incredibly helpful because someone took the time to go over my essay and tell me how and why I should revise it. This was particularly helpful because I didn't have time to go to the tutoring center."

Pearson Tutor Services takes approximately 24–48 hours, so be sure students submit their papers with enough time to revise. Also, because students will be asked to provide the paper's instructions, give them this information with their assignment so they know how to submit their papers for review.

INSTRUCTOR'S RESOURCE MANUAL For additional material about teaching writing and for journal entries, see the *Instructor's Resource Manual,* Section II, Part III.

MyWritingLab **Helpful Hints**

Want another set of eyes on your essay? Pearson Tutor Services allows you to submit your papers (up to 15 pages long) on any subject and have personalized feedback within 24 to 48 hours from someone with a Master's degree or Ph.D. in that subject. On your course page in **MyWritingLab,** click **Pearson Tutor Services** for more information on this extremely beneficial service.

REFLECTING ON YOUR WRITING

When you have completed your own essay, answer these six questions:

1. What was most difficult about this assignment?

2. What was easiest?

3. What did you learn about writing essays by completing this assignment?

4. What do you think are the strengths of your essay? Put a wavy line by the parts of your essay that you feel are very good.

5. What are the weaknesses, if any, of your paper? Put an X by the parts of your essay you would like help with. Write in the margins any questions you have.

6. What did you learn from this assignment about your own writing process—about preparing to write, about writing the first draft, about revising, and about editing?

The Handbook

This part of *Mosaics* provides you with a complete handbook for editing your writing. You can use it as a reference tool as you write or as a source of instruction and practice in areas where you need work. This handbook consists of nine units:

INSTRUCTOR'S
RESOURCE MANUAL
In the *Instructor's Resource Manual* are Unit Quizzes you can give students to check their mastery of the combined skills in each unit. First, two pre-tests are provided that ask students to apply what they have learned in each unit. The first test is made up of separate, numbered sentences so students can concentrate on individual skills; the second asks them to apply their knowledge to an entire paragraph as they would in their own writing and in peer evaluation exercises. Two similar post-tests are furnished for each unit, followed by Unit Quizzes.

The chapters in each unit start with a **self-test** to help you identify your strengths and weaknesses in that area. Then the chapters teach specific grammar skills and provide exercises so you can practice what you have learned. You will really know this material when you can use it in your own writing. As a result, each chapter ends with an exercise that asks you to **write your own sentences** and then work with another student to **edit each other's writing.**

The **Editing Symbols** on the inside back cover are marks you can use to highlight errors in your papers. In addition, the **Error Log (Appendix 7)** and **Spelling Log (Appendix 8)** will help you tailor the instruction to your own needs and keep track of your progress.

The Basics

This handbook uses very little terminology. But sometimes talking about language and the way it works is difficult without a shared understanding of certain basic grammar terms. For this reason, your instructor may ask you to study parts of this unit to review basic grammar—parts of speech, phrases, and clauses. You might also use this unit for reference.

This section has two chapters:

Chapter 18: Parts of Speech
Chapter 19: Phrases and Clauses

18

Parts of Speech

UNIT PRETESTS
To check your students' abilities with the collective skills in this unit, two Unit Pretests are available in the *Instructor's Resource Manual.*

TEACHING PARTS OF SPEECH
Play a game of Memory (Concentration) by creating two identical batches of words on index cards. For instance, have two cards for each of the following words: *walk, house, you, red, never, during, can't,* and *Hey!* Make sure you have many sets of words representing each part of speech. Shuffle the cards, and number the back of each card, starting with 1.

Line your wall with butcher paper, and attach a piece of removable tape to the front of each index card (so that each card can be removed and placed back into position many times). Place the index cards, word side down, on the paper in the order of their numbers. For instance, put 1–10 in the first row, 11–20 in the second row, and so on.

TEST YOURSELF

In the following paragraph, label the parts of speech listed here:

3 verbs (v)	2 adverbs (adv)
3 nouns (n)	2 prepositions (prep)
2 pronouns (pro)	2 conjunctions (conj)
2 adjectives (adj)	2 interjections (int)

The personality trait that I like best about myself is my healthy sense of humor. No matter how bad a situation is, I can usually say something funny to everyone. When Toby's ancient car was stolen, I told him it was a piece of junk anyway, and I felt sorry for the foolish person who stole it. Man, we laughed so hard, imagining the car thief stalled on the side of the road somewhere in town. Oh, there are some things that I don't ever joke about, like death and diseases. A person would be extremely insensitive to joke about those situations.

(Answers are in Appendix 3.)

Every sentence is made up of a variety of words that play different roles. Each word, like each part of a coordinated outfit, serves a distinct function. These functions fall into eight categories:

1. Verbs
2. Nouns
3. Pronouns
4. Adjectives

5. Adverbs

6. Prepositions

7. Conjunctions

8. Interjections

Some words, such as *is*, can function in only one way—in this case, as a verb. Other words, however, can serve as different parts of speech depending on how they are used in a sentence. For example, look at the different ways the word *burn* can be used:

Verb: The farmers **burn** the fields after every harvest.
              (*Burn* is a verb here, telling what the farmers do.)

Noun: Yolanda's **burn** healed well.
              (*Burn* functions as a noun here, telling what healed.)

Adjective: My mom found two **burn** marks on the sofa.
              (*Burn* is an adjective here, modifying, or explaining, the noun *marks*.)

MyWritingLab **Understanding Parts of Speech**

To learn more about parts of speech, go to **MyWritingLab.com,** and choose **Parts of Speech, Phrases, and Clauses** in the **Basic Grammar** module. From there, watch the video called **Animation: Parts of Speech, Phrases, and Clauses.** Then return to this chapter, which will go into more detail about parts of speech and give you opportunities to practice using them. Finally, you will apply your understanding of parts of speech to your own writing.

VERBS

The **verb** is the most important word in a sentence because every other word depends on it in some way. Verbs tell what's going on in a sentence.

There are three types of verbs: action, linking, and helping. An **action verb** tells what someone or something is doing. A **linking verb** tells what someone or something is, feels, or looks like. Sometimes an action or linking verb has **helping verbs**—words that add information, such as when an action is taking place. A **complete verb** consists of an action or linking verb and any helping verbs.

Action: We **started** the fire too close to the tent.

Action: Mark **voted** in the election.

Have students form teams of three or four and try to find the matching words. When a team uncovers two words that match, it must identify the part of speech before getting credit for the match. Otherwise, the pair goes back onto the board for another team to uncover and label.

The team that accumulates the most cards wins.

INSTRUCTOR'S RESOURCE MANUAL
For more sample words, for more exercises, and for quizzes, see the *Instructor's Resource Manual,* Section II, Part IV.

Student Comment:
"After being out of school for over 20 years, I forgot a lot about writing—especially grammar. The **Parts of Speech** topic helped me brush up on what I had forgotten."

UNIT POSTTESTS
To check your students' mastery of the collective skills in this unit, two Unit Posttests are available in the *Instructor's Resource Manual.*

Linking:	We **felt** really smart.
Linking:	It **was** the most embarrassing moment in my life.
Helping:	She **will be** arriving tomorrow.
Helping:	I **have** been so tired lately.
Complete Verb:	She **will be arriving** tomorrow.
Complete Verb:	I **have been** so tired lately.

Reviewing Verbs

Define each of the following types of verbs, and give an example of each.

Action: *Tells what someone or something is doing*

Examples will vary.

Linking: *Tells what someone or something is, feels, or looks like*

Examples will vary.

Helping: *Adds information such as when action is taking place*

Examples will vary.

What is a complete verb? Give an example with your definition.

A complete verb consists of an action or linking verb and all the helping

verbs. Examples will vary.

PRACTICE 1: Recall/Identify In each of the following sentences, underline the complete verbs. Some sentences have more than one verb.

1. We <u>left</u> on our fishing expedition when we <u>got</u> off work.

2. My brother <u>has felt</u> guilty since he <u>took</u> my money.

3. People sometimes <u>think</u> more than they <u>act</u>.

4. The first sign of trouble <u>came</u> almost immediately.

5. Next weekend, we <u>will be going</u> Christmas shopping at the mall.

PRACTICE 2: Apply Fill in each blank in the following paragraph with a verb. *Answers will vary.*

Last weekend, we (1) _____ to go shopping at a nearby outlet mall. Before we got out of the city limits, Maryl (2) _____ that she was really thirsty and Kurt

(3) _____ hungry. So we stopped at the first conve-
nience store we saw. While Kurt and Maryl were inside the store, I
(4) _____ steam coming from under the hood of my car.
After checking it out, I (5) _____ water leaking from the
radiator, so we canceled the trip and went home.

PRACTICE 3: Write Your Own Write a sentence of your own for each of the
following verbs.   *Answers will vary.*

1. had been going _____

2. chuckled _____

3. appeared _____

4. did become _____

5. whispers _____

NOUNS

People often think of **nouns** as "naming words" because they identify—
or name—people (*friend, Brian, dad, officer*), places (*town, lake, Greenville*),
or things (*tree, boat, table, belt*). Nouns also name ideas (*freedom, democracy*), qualities (*honesty, courage*), emotions (*fear, anxiety*), and actions
(*competition, negotiations*). A **common noun** names something general
(*actor, mountain, soda, restaurant*). A **proper noun** names something specific (*Julia Roberts, Mt. McKinley, Pepsi, Burger King*).

Hint: To test whether a word is a noun, try putting *a, an,* or *the* in front
of it:

Nouns:	a friend, an apple, the love
NOT Nouns:	a silly, an around, the sing

This test does not work with proper nouns:

NOT:	a Ken, the Seattle

Reviewing Nouns

What is a noun?

A noun names people, places, things, ideas, qualities, emotions, and

actions.

What is the difference between a common noun and a proper noun? Give an example of each.

Common noun: *A common noun names something general.*

Examples will vary.

Proper noun: *A proper noun names something specific.*

Examples will vary.

PRACTICE 4: Recall/Identify Underline all the nouns in the following sentences.

1. <u>Students</u> in <u>college</u> have many <u>responsibilities</u>.

2. Before my <u>friend</u> ran in the <u>marathon</u>, she trained for <u>months</u>.

3. Last <u>fall</u>, my <u>husband</u> and I bought our first <u>house</u>.

4. <u>David</u> nodded his <u>head</u> while I presented my <u>ideas</u>.

5. <u>Minnesota</u> is known for its many <u>lakes</u> and excellent <u>universities</u>.

PRACTICE 5: Apply Fill in each blank in the following paragraph with a noun that will make each sentence complete. *Answers will vary.*

     My best (1) _____ is my brother Ben. He is 18, about six feet tall with curly brown hair. He is really a neat (2) _____ I have to say that he is unusual and does his own thing. For example, he likes to wear (3) _____ during the wintertime. When he goes out, people usually point and stare. Ben just shakes his (4) _____ and keeps on walking. But Ben's best qualities are his (5) _____ and his (6) _____ to help people.

PRACTICE 6: Write Your Own Write a sentence of your own for each of the following nouns. *Answers will vary.*

1. jury _____

2. point _____

3. lateness _____

4. determination _____

5. Michael Jordan _____

PRONOUNS

Pronouns can do anything nouns can do. In fact, **pronouns** can take the place of nouns. Without pronouns, you would find yourself repeating nouns and producing boring sentences. Compare the following sentences, for example:

Maxine picked up **Maxine's** cell phone and called **Maxine's** friend Sam to say **Maxine** was on **Maxine's** way.

Maxine picked up **her** cell phone and called **her** friend Sam to say **she** was on **her** way.

There are many different types of pronouns, but you only need to focus on the following four types for now:

Most Common Pronouns

Personal (refer to people or things)

Singular:	*First Person:*	*I, me, my, mine*
	Second Person:	*you, your, yours*
	Third Person:	*he, she, it, him, her, hers, his, its*
Plural:	*First Person:*	*we, us, our, ours*
	Second Person:	*you, your, yours*
	Third Person:	*they, them, their, theirs*

Demonstrative (point out someone or something)

Singular:	*this, that*
Plural:	*these, those*

Relative (introduce a dependent clause)

who, whom, whose, which, that

Indefinite (refer to someone or something general, not specific)

Singular:	*another, anybody, anyone, anything, each, either, everybody, everyone, everything, little, much, neither, nobody, none, no one, nothing, one, other, somebody, someone, something*
Plural:	*both, few, many, others, several*

Either Singular or Plural: *all, any, more, most, some*

Hint: When any of these words are used with nouns, they are pronouns used as adjectives.

Adjective: She can have **some cookies.**

Pronoun: She can have **some.**

Adjective: I want **that car.**

Pronoun: I want **that.**

Reviewing Pronouns

What is a pronoun?

A pronoun is a word that can take the place of a noun.

Define the four most common types of pronouns, and give two examples of each.

Personal: Refer to people or things. Examples will vary.

Demonstrative: Point out someone or something. Examples will vary.

Relative: Introduce a dependent clause. Examples will vary.

Indefinite: Refer to someone or something in general. Examples will vary.

PRACTICE 7: Recall/Identify Underline all the pronouns in the following sentences. Don't underline pronouns that are really adjectives.

1. <u>Some</u> of the fruit was shipped from Florida.

2. I don't believe <u>he</u> could have committed such crimes.

3. <u>Whoever</u> took the last piece of pie should confess!

4. If <u>we</u> help each other, <u>we</u> can finish by Sunday.

5. <u>This</u> is the last time <u>I</u> spend <u>any</u> of my money calling a psychic hotline.

PRACTICE 8: Apply In the following paragraph, replace the nouns in parentheses with pronouns.

Have you ever received an anonymous card or letter? I did. In fact, I received several cards. To this day, I still don't know who sent (1) _____them_____ (the cards). I remember when I got the first card. (2) _____It_____ (the card) was written in a scratchy handwriting and signed "Your Secret Admirer." Of course, I asked my friends Amy and Beth whether (3) _____ *they* _____ (Amy and Beth) knew who had sent it. Though (4) _____ *they* _____ (Amy and Beth) denied it, I think Amy was more involved than (5) _____ *she* _____ (Amy) admits.

PRACTICE 9: Write Your Own Write a sentence of your own for each of the following pronouns. *Answers will vary.*

1. they _____

2. anybody _____

3. those _____

4. who _____

5. few _____

ADJECTIVES

Adjectives modify, or describe, nouns or pronouns. Adjectives generally make sentences clear and vivid.

Without Adjectives:	We had our rods, a cooler, and some sandwiches for the trip.
With Adjectives:	We had our **trusty fly** rods, a **white plastic** cooler, and **several tuna** sandwiches for the trip.

Reviewing Adjectives

What is an adjective?

An adjective modifies or describes a noun or pronoun.

Give three examples of adjectives.

Examples will vary.

PRACTICE 10: Recall/Identify Underline all the adjectives in the following sentences.

1. Her long red hair bounced as she walked down the sunlit street.

2. Carl's successful career results from his hard work and pure determination.

3. Ali's poor old car needs two new tires and a complete under-the-hood check.

4. If you want to go on the camping trip, turn in the registration slip.

5. My little brother lost the remote control for our big-screen TV.

PRACTICE 11: Apply Fill in each blank in the following paragraph with an adjective.   *Answers will vary.*

We went to a (1) _____ play at the Little Theater on campus. It was a (2) _____ comedy written by a (3) _____ student at our school. The lead actor was a (4) _____ guy who kept everyone laughing with his (5) _____ faces and clever lines.

PRACTICE 12: Write Your Own Write a sentence of your own for each of the following adjectives.   *Answers will vary.*

1. sparkling _____

2. tasty _____

3. upset _____

4. fourth _____

5. thrilling _____

ADVERBS

Adverbs modify, or describe, adjectives, verbs, and other adverbs. They do *not* modify nouns. Adverbs also answer the following questions:

How?	*carefully, fast, quickly, slowly*
When?	*yesterday, lately, early, now*
Where?	*outside, here, there, deeply*
How often?	*usually, seldom, regularly, promptly*
To what extent?	*very, almost, too, hardly*

Hint: Notice that adverbs often end in *-ly*. That might help you recognize them.

Reviewing Adverbs

What is an adverb?

An adverb modifies or describes an adjective, a verb, or another adverb.

What are the five questions that adverbs answer?

How?   *When?*   *Where?*

How often?   *To what extent?*

Give one example of an adverb that answers each question.

Examples will vary.

PRACTICE 13: Recall/Identify Underline all the adverbs in the following sentences.

1. My curious cat sat <u>very</u> quietly for a few seconds before she <u>quickly</u> pounced on the fly.

2. Steve was <u>quite</u> upset after <u>badly</u> missing the shot.

3. We will <u>never</u> do business with the Simpsons <u>again</u>.

4. <u>Often</u> Mr. Ringold asks, "Are you working hard or <u>hardly</u> working?"

5. I don't <u>necessarily</u> think we need to go <u>there</u> tomorrow.

PRACTICE 14: Apply Fill in each blank in the following paragraph with an adverb. *Answers will vary.*

(1) _____ I decided to find a new job, a (2) _____ easy task, or so I thought. I began by (3) _____ going through the phone book and listing each business that I thought would be hiring (4) _____ After calling ten businesses that said they weren't hiring, I (5) _____ realized this job hunt would be more difficult than I first thought.

PRACTICE 15: Write Your Own Write a sentence of your own for each of the following adverbs. *Answers will vary.*

1. quickly _____

2. fast _____

3. sometimes _____

4. down _____

5. always _____

PREPOSITIONS

Prepositions indicate relationships among the ideas in a sentence. Something is *up, down, next to, behind, around, near,* or *under* something else. A preposition is always followed by a noun or a pronoun called the **object of the preposition.** Together, they form a **prepositional phrase.**

Preposition	+	Object	=	Prepositional Phrase
of	+	the supplies	=	of the supplies
for	+	the lake	=	for the lake

Here is a list of some common prepositions:

Common Prepositions

about	beside	into	since
above	between	like	through
across	beyond	near	throughout
after	by	next to	to
against	despite	of	toward
among	down	off	under
around	during	on	until
as	except	on top of	up
at	for	out	upon
before	from	out of	up to
behind	in	outside	with
below	in front of	over	within
beneath	inside	past	without

Hint: *To* + a verb (as in *to go, to come, to feel*) is not a prepositional phrase. It is a verb phrase, which we will deal with later in this chapter.

Reviewing Prepositions

What is a preposition?

A preposition indicates relationships among the ideas in a sentence.

Give two examples of prepositions:

Examples will vary.

What is a prepositional phrase?

A prepositional phrase consists of a preposition and its object.

Give two examples of prepositional phrases:

Examples will vary.

PRACTICE 16: Recall/Identify Underline all the prepositions in the following sentences.

1. James said the concert by the college jazz band would take place during the last week of May.

2. Carlos was with us when we talked after the party.

3. Before the movie, we talked among ourselves in a downtown park.

4. Sharon was lying on the couch watching *Jeopardy* on TV when I walked into the room.

5. Colin looked under his bed and inside his closet, but he never found his math book.

PRACTICE 17: Apply Fill in each blank in the following paragraph with a preposition.   *Answers will vary.*

One day as I waited (1) _____ the bus, a tall man sat down (2) _____ me on the bench and began talking (3) _____ the weather. I agreed that it certainly had been hot (4) _____ the city. As we were talking, a police officer came around the corner and began walking (5) _____ the sidewalk toward us. For some strange reason, the man quickly stood up and walked away.

PRACTICE 18: Write Your Own Write a sentence of your own for each of the following prepositions.   *Answers will vary.*

1. of _____

2. without _____

3. along _____

4. like _____

5. despite _____

CONJUNCTIONS

Conjunctions connect groups of words. Without conjunctions, most of our writing would be choppy and boring. The two types of conjunctions are easy to remember because their names state their purpose: *Coordinating conjunctions* link equal ideas, and *subordinating conjunctions* make one idea subordinate to—or dependent on—another.

Coordinating conjunctions connect parts of a sentence of equal importance or weight. These parts can be **independent clauses**—a group of words with a subject and verb that can stand alone as a sentence. (See page 381.)

There are only seven coordinating conjunctions:

Coordinating Conjunctions

and, but, or, nor, for, so, yet

Coordinating:	I wanted to explore the caves, **and** Greg wanted to go up in a hot air balloon.
Coordinating:	Our adventure turned into a nightmare, **but** we learned an important lesson.

Subordinating conjunctions join two ideas by making one dependent on the other. The idea introduced by the subordinating conjunction becomes a **dependent clause,** a group of words with a subject and a verb that cannot stand alone as a sentence. (See page 381.) The other part of the sentence is an independent clause.

Here are some common subordinating conjunctions:

Common Subordinating Conjunctions

after	because	since	until
although	before	so	when
as	even if	so that	whenever

as if	even though	than	where
as long as	how	that	wherever
as soon as	if	though	whether
as though	in order that	unless	while

Subordinating: Dependent Clause
I don't know **when** I will return.

Subordinating: Dependent Clause
If we save enough money, we can go to Disneyland.

Reviewing Conjunctions

What is a coordinating conjunction?

A coordinating conjunction connects parts of a sentence of equal importance or weight.

Name the seven coordinating conjunctions.

and   but   for

nor   or   so

yet

What is a subordinating conjunction?

A subordinating conjunction joins two ideas by making one dependent on the other.

Write a sentence using a subordinating conjunction.

Answers will vary.

PRACTICE 19: Recall/Identify Underline all the conjunctions in the following sentences.

1. I hate going grocery shopping, though I love to cook.

2. Whether or not you're ready for it, becoming a parent will change your life.

3. You can't rent a car <u>unless</u> you have a credit card.

4. Pedro would make a great attorney, <u>and</u> he would get paid to argue.

5. I thought this class was easy <u>until</u> we took the midterm.

PRACTICE 20: Apply Fill in each blank in the following paragraph with a conjunction.   *Answers will vary.*

(1) _____ I work two jobs and go to school, I have little spare time. Whenever possible, I try very hard to find time for myself. (2) _____ I have so many things to do, I sit down and write out everything in the order it has to be done. I try to make a schedule, (3) _____ I have a tendency to get side-tracked. For example, (4) _____ I have homework, it has to be my first priority. But (5) _____ work and school are finished, I make sure I save time for my friends.

PRACTICE 21: Write Your Own Write a sentence of your own for each of the following conjunctions.

Answers will vary.

1. after _____
2. because _____
3. but _____
4. so _____
5. although _____

INTERJECTIONS

Interjections are words that express strong emotion, surprise, or disappointment. An interjection is usually followed by an exclamation point or a comma.

Interjection: **Help!** The boat is drifting away.
Interjection: **Wow,** what an unbelievable game!

Other common interjections include *aha, awesome, great, hallelujah, neat, oh, oops, ouch, well, whoa, yeah,* and *yippee.*

Reviewing Interjections

What is an interjection?

An interjection is a word that expresses strong emotion, surprise, or

disappointment.

Write a sentence using an interjection.

Answers will vary.

PRACTICE 22: Recall/Identify Underline all the interjections in the following sentences.

1. Yeah! We got the best seats in the house!

2. Man, my legs are tired after running ten miles.

3. Oh, I almost forgot that I have a dentist appointment.

4. That was the best grade I've ever received in math. Hallelujah!

5. Ouch! I stubbed my toe.

PRACTICE 23: Apply Fill in each blank in the following paragraph with an interjection. *Answers will vary.*

(1) _____, was I tired last night! I woke up yesterday morning at the crack of dawn, climbed into the shower, and slipped on the bar of soap before I could even get my eyes completely open. (2) _____! Then I got into my car and, (3) _____, it wouldn't start. After calling a friend to give me a ride to work, I got to my desk to find an emergency project that needed to be completed before the end of my shift. (4) _____, I worked on it all day, though I had to stay late to finish it. (5) _____! I am so glad that day is over!

PRACTICE 24: Write Your Own Write a sentence of your own for each of the following interjections. *Answers will vary.*

1. cool _____

2. help _____

3. good gracious _____

4. oh _____

5. oops _____

CHAPTER REVIEW

This topic goes over
many different parts of
speech in great detail,
which is particularly
helpful for ESL
students and for other
students who might
need a grammar review.

MyWritingLab   **Reviewing Parts of Speech**

To review this material before you complete the Review Practices, watch
Animation: Parts of Speech, Phrases, and Clauses at **MyWritingLab.
com** one more time. This time, keep the video open as you complete the rest of the practices in this chapter. For best results, do the
MyWritingLab exercises online as well as the Chapter Review practices
in the book.

REVIEW PRACTICE 1: Recall/Identify Use the following abbreviations to label
the underlined words in these sentences.

v	verb	adv	adverb
n	noun	prep	preposition
pro	pronoun	conj	conjunction
adj	adjective	int	interjection
ph	phrase	cl	clause

        int   *prep adj*   *n*   *prep*   *n*

1. Hey, remember to meet with your counselor before choosing your classes.

          v   *adj*   *v*   *adj*

2. Stacy works as a telephone salesperson and has to meet a daily quota.

        n   *n*   *conj*

3. An education enables people to obtain knowledge, confidence, and

    marketable skills.

     conj   *ph*   *ph*   *pro*

4. While we were eating dinner at Jake's Tex Mex, my parents and I were

                  adj

    discussing my college bills.

5. The best _{adj} movie made in 2002 _{ph} was Chicago _n.

   5. The *best* movie made *in 2002* was *Chicago*.

           adj   *ph*   *n*

   6. Men *who hunt wild game* are not *necessarily* trying *to destroy nature*.

           cl   *adv*   *ph*

   7. My brother *lives in* Virginia because *he* is *in the Navy*.

          v prep   *prob*   *ph*

   8. There is *nothing* better than a *warm* fire on a *cold* day.

          pro   *adj*   *adj*

   9. Tom *wanted* to date *Susan*, but *she* *is* dating Damian.

        v   *n*   *pro v*

  10. If you *maintain* a B+ average, you will *likely* qualify *for* grants *or* scholarships.

        v   *adv*   *prep*   *conj*

MyWritingLab

Practicing Parts of Speech

Now complete the **Recall** activities for **Parts of Speech, Phrases, and Clauses** in the **Basic Grammar** module of **MyWritingLab.** If you're having a difficult time with a question, open up the video in the lower right-hand corner for some help.

REVIEW PRACTICE 2: Apply Fill in each blank in the following paragraph with an appropriate word as indicated. *Answers will vary.*

I saved money for six months to buy a new (1) _____ (noun) for my (2) _____ (adjective) car. I found a store where I could (3) _____ (verb) this product, (4) _____ (conjunction) I waited an extra week for it to go on sale. The store was located (5) _____ (preposition) town, but it was worth the drive. (6) _____ (interjection)! I had wanted this thing for a long time! On my next day off work, I (7) _____ (adverb) drove to the store and made the purchase. I talked to the salesperson for about an hour, and (8) _____ (pronoun) assured me I was making a wise purchase. But when I finally had time to enjoy my (9) _____ (noun), the item I had saved so long for did not work properly, and I completely lost my temper. I picked the thing up and (10) _____ (adverb) threw it away.

Practicing Parts of Speech

Next, complete the **Apply** activity for **Parts of Speech, Phrases, and Clauses** in the **Basic Grammar** module of **MyWritingLab.** Pay close attention to the directions, and click only on what you're asked to.

⚙️•⌐**Complete** this **Writing Prompt** at **mywritinglab.com**

REVIEW PRACTICE 3: Write Your Own Write your own paragraph about your favorite pastime. What does it entail? Why do you like it? *Answers will vary.*

MyWritingLab **Practicing Parts of Speech**

For more practice, complete the **Write** activity for **Parts of Speech, Phrases, and Clauses** in the **Basic Grammar** module of **MyWritingLab. com.** Make sure to pay close attention to the use of phrases and clauses.

REVIEW PRACTICE 4: Editing Your Writing Exchange paragraphs from Review Practice 3 with a classmate, and do the following: *Answers will vary.*

1. Circle any words that are used incorrectly.

2. Underline any phrases that do not read smoothly.

3. Put an X in the margin where you find a dependent clause that is not connected to an independent clause.

Then return the paragraph to its writer, and use the information in the Introduction to edit your own paragraph. Record your errors on the Error Log in Appendix 7.

Phrases and Clauses

Underline the phrases and put the clauses in brackets in the following sentences.

- After the concert, we decided to get some food.
- To get a good grade on the test, I know I have to study harder.
- Mallory will get what she wants out of life because she is assertive.
- Benito lives in the brick house at the end of the block behind the park.
- Do you want to see a movie with us?

(Answers are in Appendix 3.)

UNIT PRE-TESTS
To check your students' abilities with the collective skills in this unit, two Unit Pre-tests are available in the *Instructor's Resource Manual*.

Understanding the difference between phrases and clauses is the first step toward writing correct, effective sentences. This chapter will give you that information that you can then use in your own writing.

MyWritingLab

Understanding Phrases and Clauses

To learn more about phrases and clauses, go to **MyWritingLab.com**, and choose **Parts of Speech, Phrases, and Clauses** in the **Basic Grammar** module. For this topic, watch the video called **Animation: Parts of Speech, Phrases, and Clauses.** Then, return to this chapter, which will go into more detail about phrases and clauses and give you opportunities to practice using them. Finally, you will apply your understanding of phrases and clauses to your own writing.

Student Comment:
"From a combination of **MyWritingLab** and *Mosaics*, I now understand that seeing the difference between phrases and clauses is essential for writing correct sentences."

TEACHING PHRASES
Divide students into two
groups, and provide them
with a series of cards
containing phrases that can
be made into five different
sentences. Here are some
examples:

baking early in the morning/
is creating/long days

my best friend/has enjoyed/
her new job/in my father's
bakery

my father/has owned/
a bakery/for many years

running a bakery/has been/
a challenge/for my father

my mother/has been trying/
to get me/to become a
baker too

The sentences should all
focus on the same theme.
   Give students the cards
in random order, and have
them try to create five
sentences that all make
sense. For instance, if they
create the sentence *My best
friend has enjoyed her new
job baking in the morning,*
and if they get the last three
sentences correct, they will
be left with *in my father's
bakery is causing long days.*
Obviously, this does not
make sense, so they will
have to figure out how
to make all the sentences
work. The first group to get
all five sentences in a logical
order wins. Remember
that the sentences can
be rearranged and still be
logical.
   The major objective
of this exercise is to show
students how phrases
work as a part of a larger
whole—a sentence.

PHRASES

A **phrase** is a group of words that function together as a unit. Phrases cannot stand alone, however, because they are missing a subject, a verb, or both.

Phrases:	the black mountain bike, a happy person
Phrases:	turned up the music, cruised the mall, opened my present
Phrases:	after school, in the back room, by myself, on the green grass
Phrases:	telling us the answer, to be fooled

Notice that all these groups of words are missing a subject, a verb, or both.

Reviewing Phrases

What is a phrase?

A phrase is a group of words that function together as a unit but cannot

stand alone.

Give two examples of phrases.

Examples will vary.

PRACTICE 1: Recall/Identify Underline eight phrases in the following sentences.

1. Looking out the window, I watched the countryside from the train.

2. I like to do adventurous things like skydiving and rock climbing.

3. My favorite vacation was our trip to the Bahamas three years ago.

4. Customers should have completed their deposit slips.

5. Save energy by turning off the lights after everyone has left the room.

PRACTICE 2: Apply Fill in each blank in the following paragraph with a phrase. *Answers will vary.*

   Sang went (1) _____ early because he had worked overtime yesterday afternoon. But since his roommate was cleaning the apartment, (2) _____, and (3) _____, Sang knew he would not be able to sleep. Tony, Sang's roommate, wanted everything clean because his parents (4) _____. His last chore was to get a can of air freshener (5) _____ and spray it around the apartment.

PRACTICE 3: Write Your Own Write a sentence of your own for each of the following phrases.   *Answers will vary.*

1. the timid first-grader _____

2. is sending out invitations _____

3. in the river _____

4. to attend college _____

5. energized by food and sleep _____

CLAUSES

Like phrases, **clauses** are groups of words. But unlike phrases, a clause always contains a subject and a verb. There are two types of clauses: *independent* and *dependent*.

An **independent clause** contains a subject and a verb and can stand alone and make sense by itself. Every complete sentence must have at least one independent clause.

Independent Clause: We planned our vacation very carefully.

Now look at the following group of words. It is a clause because it contains a subject and a verb. But it is a **dependent clause** because it is introduced by a word that makes it dependent, *since*.

Dependent Clause: **Since** we planned our vacation very carefully.

This clause cannot stand alone. It must be connected to an independent clause to make sense. Here is one way to complete the dependent clause and form a complete sentence.

        Dependent   Independent

Since we planned our vacation very carefully, we had a great time.

Hint: Subordinating conjunctions (such as *since, although, because, while*) and relative pronouns (*who, whom, whose, which, that*) make clauses dependent. (For more information on subordinating conjunctions, see pages 372–373, and on relative pronouns, see page 365.)

INSTRUCTOR'S RESOURCE MANUAL
For more sample phrases, and sentences, for more exercises, and for quizzes, see the *Instructor's Resource Manual*, Section II, Part IV.

TEACHING CLAUSES
For about five minutes, have students write down as many song titles as they can think of—no made-up titles allowed. Be sure they write down the full titles. After they have completed their lists, have them cross out all song titles that are only phrases, leaving only titles that are clauses. The student with the most titles that are clauses wins.

INSTRUCTOR'S RESOURCE MANUAL
For more exercises and for quizzes, see the *Instructor's Resource Manual*, Section II, Part IV.

UNIT POST-TESTS
To check your students' mastery of the collective skills in this unit, two Unit Post-tests are available in the *Instructor's Resource Manual*.

Reviewing Clauses

For a group of words to be a clause, it must have a __subject__ *and a* __verb__ .

What is an independent clause?

An independent clause contains a subject and a verb and can stand alone

and make sense by itself.

What is a dependent clause?

A dependent clause contains a subject and a verb but cannot stand alone.

Name the two kinds of words that can begin a dependent clause.

subordinating conjunctions   relative pronouns

Name five subordinating conjunctions.

Answers will vary.

Name the five relative pronouns.

who   whom   whose

which   that

PRACTICE 4: Recall/Identify Each of the following sentences is made up of two clauses. Circle the coordinating or subordinating conjunctions and relative pronouns. Then label each clause either independent (Ind) or dependent (Dep).

1. *Dep* (When) Veronica got up, she made her bed *Ind* (and) brushed her teeth.

2. *Ind* The truck swerved toward his car, (and) *Ind* Jason veered to the side of the road.

3. *Dep* (Unless) you are planning to major in science, *Ind* you don't need to take chemistry.

4. *Ind* I am familiar with the person (who) *Dep* won the contest.

5. *Dep* (Until) he makes the team, *Ind* Chan will continue to practice his swing.

PRACTICE 5: Apply Add an independent or dependent clause that will complete each sentence and make sense.   *Answers will vary.*

Matt is an artist (1) who _____. (2) He _____.
He buys supplies with half of his earnings, (3) and _____.
His most recent drawing won a prize, (4) which _____. He
says he will never sell it (5) because _____.

PRACTICE 6: Write Your Own Write five independent clauses. Then add at least one dependent clause to each independent clause.   *Answers will vary.*

_____

_____

_____

_____

_____

CHAPTER REVIEW

MyWritingLab **Reviewing Phrases and Clauses**

To review this material before you complete the Review Practices, watch **Animation: Parts of Speech, Phrases, and Clauses** at **MyWritingLab.com** one more time. This time, keep the video open as you complete the rest of the practices in this chapter. For best results, do the **MyWritingLab** exercises online as well as the Chapter Review practices in the book.

Students might have seen this video in the previous chapter, but in this case, they should be focused on phrases and clauses rather than parts of speech. To prepare your students for this material, you might want to review the parts of speech with them.

REVIEW PRACTICE 1: Recall/Identify Underline the phrases and put the clauses in brackets in each of the following sentences.

1. [She wants to study][before she takes the exam tomorrow].

2. [When you leave], [I'll give you a map].

3. [Why do you think][she got mad]?

4. [While they laughed], [Mel and I walked away].

5. [Jorge wanted to meet Beth][but she works tonight].

6. [When you return to the house], [I have a question for you].

7. After the practice, [the team felt very good about their chances to win the next day].

8. [I was surprised to learn][that snow boarding is really fun].

9. [I can't borrow the car again][because I got a ticket last time].

10. [When you go to the party], [I will stay at home].

MyWritingLab **Practicing Phrases and Clauses**

Now complete the **Recall** activities for **Parts of Speech, Phrases, and Clauses** in the **Basic Grammar** module of **MyWritingLab.com.** If you're having a difficult time with a question, open up the video in the lower right-hand corner for some help.

REVIEW PRACTICE 2: Apply Fill in each blank in the following paragraph with an appropriate phrase or clause, as indicated. *Answers will vary.*

I can't remember when I laughed so much. The group got along well; the _____ (phrase) were exciting; and I spent all day with my _____ (phrase). _____ (clause), I will definitely want to do this again. But next time, I'll have to bring more money. I had no idea the day's activities _____ (phrase). After we paid our fees and bought some food, (clause). When we return, we should _____ (phrase)

MyWritingLab **Practicing Phrases and Clauses**

Next, complete the **Apply** activity for **Parts of Speech, Phrases, and Clauses** in the **Basic Grammar** module of **MyWritingLab.com.** Pay close attention to the directions, and click only on what you're asked to.

⚙️ Complete this **Writing Prompt** at **mywritinglab.com**

REVIEW PRACTICE 3: Write Your Own Write your own paragraph about your favorite food. Why do you like this food? When were you first introduced to it? *Answers will vary.*

MyWritingLab **Practicing Phrases and Clauses**

For more practice, complete the **Write** activity for **Parts of Speech, Phrases, and Clauses** in the **Basic Grammar** module of **MyWritingLab. com.** Make sure to pay close attention to the use of phrases and clauses.

REVIEW PRACTICE 4: Editing Your Writing Exchange paragraphs from Review Practice 3 with a classmate, and do the following: *Answers will vary.*

1. Circle any words that are used incorrectly.

2. Underline any phrases that do not read smoothly.

3. Put an X in the margin where you find a dependent clause that is not connected to an independent clause.

Then return the paragraph to its writer, and use the information in the Introduction to edit your own paragraph. Record your errors on the Error Log in Appendix 7.

Sentences

Writing complete, correct sentences is one of the most difficult tasks for college writers. It involves understanding the transition from oral to written English. As a student, you must make decisions about sentences that you don't have to deal with when you speak, such as what makes up a sentence and how to punctuate it. What is important, however, is that you address these issues. This unit will help you start making the transfer from oral to written English.

To help you start editing your writing, we will focus on the following sentence elements:

Subjects and Verbs

UNIT PRE-TESTS
To check your students'
abilities with the collective
skills in this unit, two Unit
Pre-tests are available in
the *Instructor's Resource
Manual.*

TEST YOURSELF

Circle the subjects and underline the verbs in each sentence.

- We really liked the movie.
- Melissa and Giselle left early.
- She is in class.
- Clean your room.
- The Masons have never remodeled their kitchen.
- She checked the oil and put air in the tires.

(Answers are in Appendix 3.)

A sentence has a message to communicate, but for communication to take place, it must have a subject and a verb. The subject is the topic of the sentence or what the sentence is about. The verb is the sentence's motor. It moves the message forward to its destination. Without these two parts, the sentence is not complete.

MyWritingLab

Understanding Subjects and Verbs

To find out more about this topic, go to **MyWritingLab.com,** and choose **Subjects and Verbs** in the **Basic Grammar** module. Then, watch the video called **Animation: Subjects and Verbs.** Next, return to this chapter, which will go into more detail about these elements and give you opportunities to practice them. Finally, you will apply your understanding of subjects and verbs to your own writing.

Student Comment
"The program lets me go back and look at a topic again if I feel like I didn't get it. With lectures, there's no rewind button."

SUBJECTS

To be complete, every sentence must have a subject. The **subject** tells whom or what the sentence is about.

Subject
↓

She   never liked movies at all.

Mystery **novels**   appeal to everyone.

Compound Subjects

When two or more separate words tell what the sentence is about, the sentence has a **compound subject.**

Compound Subject: **Hamburgers** and **hotdogs** are my favorite foods.

Compound Subject: **Margaret** and **I** watch movies every night.

Hint: Note that *and* is not part of the compound subject.

Unstated Subjects

Sometimes a subject does not actually appear in a sentence but is understood. This occurs in commands and requests. The understood subject is always *you*, meaning either someone specific or anyone in general.

Command: Call your boss in the morning.
                                s
Unstated Subject: **(You)** call your boss in the morning.

Request: Pass me the salt, please.
                                s
Unstated Subject: **(You)** pass me the salt, please.

Subjects and Prepositional Phrases

The subject of a sentence cannot be part of a prepositional phrase. A **prepositional phrase** is a group of words that begins with a **preposition,** a word like *in, on, under, after,* or *from.* Here are some examples of prepositional phrases:

in the hall	**next to** me	**on** the stairs
under your pillow	**with** Brad	**behind** the car
after lunch	**into** the cave	**around** the block
from the mayor's office	**during** the day	**at** home
before dinner	**instead of** you	**across** the street

(See page 370 for a more complete list of prepositions.)

If you are looking for the subject of a sentence, first cross out all the prepositional phrases. Then figure out what the sentence is about.

~~After dinner~~, my friend and I went home.
(s above dinner, s above friend, s above I)

The classified ads ~~in the local newspaper~~ were misleading.
(s above ads)

One ~~of our cows~~ got ~~into a neighboring pasture~~ last night.
(s above One)

Reviewing Subjects

What is a subject?

The subject tells whom or what the sentence is about.

What is a compound subject?

A compound subject is two or more separate words that tell what the sentence is about.

What is an unstated subject?

An unstated subject does not appear in the sentence but is understood.

How can you find the subject of a sentence?

First, cross out all the prepositional phrases, and then figure out what the sentence is about.

PRACTICE 1: Recall/Identify Cross out the prepositional phrases in each of the following sentences, and then underline the subjects.

1. The <u>boxers</u> stood ~~in their corners~~.

2. <u>One</u> ~~of the artists~~ is showing his paintings ~~at a gallery in New York City~~.

3. <u>Manuel</u> and <u>Jack</u> are both good guitar players.

4. ~~After the first of the year~~, <u>I</u> will begin preparing my taxes.

5. Start working ~~on your term paper~~ immediately.   *You understood*

PRACTICE 2: Apply Fill in each blank in the following sentences with a subject without using a person's name. *Answers will vary.*

1. _____ slept fitfully last night.

2. _____ strutted across the stage to a cheering crowd.

3. Sitting high above the pool, _____thought about life.

4. Sometimes _____ comes out all wrong.

5. _____ are always backing out at the last moment.

PRACTICE 3: Write Your Own Write five sentences of your own, and circle the subjects. *Answers will vary.*

_____

_____

_____

_____

_____

VERBS

To be complete, a sentence must have a verb as well as a subject. A **verb** tells what the subject is doing or what is happening.

Verb
↓

She   never **liked** movies at all.

Mystery novels   **appeal** to everyone.

Action Verbs

An **action verb** tells what a subject is doing. Some examples of action verbs are *run*, *skate*, *discuss*, *hurt*, *allow*, *forget*, *pretend*, *hope*, *laugh*, *increase*, *listen*, and *hurry*.

Action: The players **raced** down the court.

Action: The bus **stopped** at the bus stop.

Linking Verbs

A **linking verb** connects the subject to other words in the sentence that say something about it. Linking verbs are also called **state-of-being verbs**

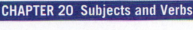
because they do not show action. Rather, they say that something "is" a particular way. The most common linking verb is *be* (*am, are, is, was, were*).

Linking: The cats **are** in the other room.

Linking: He **was** very happy to see her.

Other common linking verbs are *become, feel, look, appear,* and *seem*.

Linking: She **became** a lawyer.

Linking: Mom **feels** sick.

Linking: His beard **looks** rough and scratchy.

Linking: Ashley and Jack **appear** very worried.

Linking: My brother **seems** happy with his choice of career.

Some words, like *smell* and *taste*, can be either action verbs or linking verbs.

Action: I **smell** a skunk.
Linking: This rose **smells** so fragrant.

Action: I **tasted** the stew.
Linking: It **tasted** very good.

Compound Verbs

Just as a verb can have more than one subject, some subjects can have more than one verb. These are called **compound verbs.**

Compound: She **watches** and **feeds** his dog on the weekends.

Compound: I **visit** my grandparents and **play** cards with them.

Hint: A sentence can have both a compound subject and a compound verb.

     s   s   v   v
Gus and **Burt ran** from the car and **dove** into the water.

Helping Verbs

Often, the **main verb** (the action verb or linking verb) in a sentence needs help to convey its meaning. **Helping verbs** add information, such as when an action took place. The **complete verb** consists of a main verb and all its helping verbs.

Complete Verb: The horses <u>**are**</u> **galloping** to the finish line.

Complete Verb: Angelica <u>**did**</u> **feel** angry.

Complete Verb: They <u>**might**</u> come with us.

Complete Verb: Maybe we <u>**should have**</u> gone to the library.

Complete Verb: My favorite teacher <u>**used to**</u> give a quiz every week.

Complete Verb: Duane <u>**will**</u> not <u>**be**</u> graduating this year.

Hint: Note that *not* isn't part of the helping verb. Similarly, *never, always, only, just,* and *still* are never part of the verb.

Complete Verb: I <u>**have**</u> never <u>**been**</u> so insulted in my life.

The most common helping verbs are

> *be, am, is, are, was, were*
> *have, has, had*
> *do, did*

Other common helping verbs are

> *may, might*
> *can, could*
> *will, would*
> *should, used to, ought to*

Reviewing Verbs

What is a verb?

A verb tells what the subject is doing or what is happening

_____

What is the difference between action and linking verbs?

An action verb tells what the subject is doing. A linking verb connects the subject

to other words in the sentence.

Give an example of a compound verb.   *Examples will vary.*

Give an example of a helping verb.   *Examples will vary.*

What is the difference between a subject and a verb?

The subject tells whom or what the sentence is about, and the verb tells

what the subject is doing or what is happening.

PRACTICE 4: Recall/Identify   Underline the complete verbs in each of the following sentences.

1. The workers <u>became</u> tired early.

2. *O, The Oprah Magazine*, <u>has been recognized</u> as a very popular magazine.

3. One young woman with too many problems <u>left</u> school early.

4. If she <u>succeeds</u>, she <u>feels</u> happy and fulfilled.

5. <u>Don't</u> <u>encourage</u> her.

PRACTICE 5: Apply Fill in each blank in the following sentences with a verb. Avoid using *is*, *are*, *was*, and *were* except as helping verbs. *Answers will vary.*

1. Orlando _____ extremely lucky.

2. The field workers _____ tired.

3. My manager _____ crossword puzzles every day.

4. Both the instructors and the deans _____ patiently for the meeting to begin.

5. Computers _____ our daily lives.

PRACTICE 6: Write Your Own Write five sentences of your own, and underline all the verbs in each. *Answers will vary.*

_____

_____

_____

_____

_____

CHAPTER REVIEW

MyWritingLab **Reviewing Subjects and Verbs**

To review this material before you complete the Review Practices, watch **Animation: Subjects and Verbs** at **MyWritingLab.com** one more time. This time, keep the video open as you complete the rest of the practices in this chapter. For best results, do the **MyWritingLab** exercises online as well as the Chapter Review practices in the book.

Remind students that they can save their work in the Write activity and come back to it later.

REVIEW PRACTICE 1: Recall/Identify Underline the subjects once and the verbs twice in each of the following sentences. Cross out the prepositional phrases first.

1. The competitors eyed one another warily and looked ready ~~for the game~~.

2. Sculptors work ~~from a variety of raw material~~.

3. David was quite a good piano player.

4. ~~After April 15th~~, she will begin my campaign ~~for office~~.

5. Every year, her parents put money ~~into her college fund~~.

6. The first three scenes ~~in the horror film~~ were frightening.

7. The earth and the buildings shook and cracked.

8. The singer couldn't remember the right words ~~to the song~~.

9. Professional athletes and movie stars have the highest paying jobs ~~in America~~.

10. My brother doesn't like his current job.

MyWritingLab **Practicing Subjects and Verbs**

Now complete the **Recall** activities for **Subjects and Verbs** in the **Basic Grammar** module of **MyWritingLab.com**. Remember to read the answers carefully because many of them look similar.

REVIEW PRACTICE 2: Apply Fill in the missing subjects or verbs in each of the following sentences. *Answers will vary.*

1. _____ got the best seats in the house.

2. Usually _____ just waited and hoped for someone else to volunteer.

3. Mark and Mabel to _____ stay at the fancy hotel.

4. Every day _____ leaves the house to go to work in the grocery store.

5. Carrying the grand piano _____ a difficult task.

6. Certainly, _____ returned a little later and a midnight movie.

7. In the spring, we usually _____ our house really well and _____ a huge garage sale.

8. Most of the time, my uncle _____ does the cooking, and my aunt _____ takes care of the lawn.

9. I _____ not _____ to scream.

10. _____ often is caught reading newspapers and magazines.

MyWritingLab   **Practicing Subjects and Verbs**

Next, complete the **Apply** activity for **Subjects and Verbs** in the **Basic Grammar** module of **MyWritingLab.com.** If you're stuck, you can go to the lower right-hand corner and open up the video again, or you can click on the hint button.

⚙️─[**Complete** this **Writing Prompt** at **mywritinglab.com**

REVIEW PRACTICE 3: Write Your Own Write a paragraph explaining what you would do if you won the lottery.   *Answers will vary.*

MyWritingLab   **Practicing Subjects and Verbs**

For more practice, complete the **Write** activity for **Subjects and Verbs** in the **Basic Grammar** module of **MyWritingLab.com.** Make sure to pay close attention to subjects and verbs in your paragraph.

REVIEW PRACTICE 4: Editing Through Collaboration Exchange paragraphs from Review Practice 3 with another student, and do the following: *Answers will vary.*

1. Circle the subjects.

2. Underline the verbs.

Then return the paragraph to its writer, and edit any sentences in your own paragraph that do not have both a subject and a verb. Record your errors on the Error Log in Appendix 7.

Fragments

UNIT PRE-TESTS
To check your students'
abilities with the collective
skills in this unit, two Unit
Pre-tests are available in
the *Instructor's Resource
Manual.*

TEST YOURSELF

Put an X by the sentences that are fragments.

- _____ We were hoping that the test would be easy.
- _____ Which he did not see at first.
- _____ She wanted to become a musician.
- _____ Running to catch the plane, with her suitcase flying.
- _____ Since the newspaper had reported it.

(Answers are in Appendix 3.)

One of the most common errors in college writing is the fragment. A fragment is a piece of a sentence that is punctuated as a complete sentence. But it does not express a complete thought. Once you learn how to identify fragments, you can avoid them in your writing.

ABOUT FRAGMENTS

A complete sentence must have both a subject and a verb. If one or both are missing or if the subject and verb are introduced by a dependent word, you have only part of a sentence, a **fragment.** Even if it begins with a capital letter and ends with a period, it cannot stand alone and must be corrected in your writing. The five most common types of fragments are explained in this chapter.

Type 1: Afterthought Fragments
He works out at the gym. **And runs several miles a week.**

Type 2: *-ing* Fragments
Finding no food in the refrigerator. LaKesha went to the store.

Type 3: *to* Fragments
The company sponsored a national training program. **To increase its sales by 20 percent.**

Type 4: Dependent-Clause Fragments
Since he bought a Chevy Blazer. His insurance has gone up.

Type 5: Relative-Clause Fragments
I climbed Mt. Everest. **Which is the tallest mountain in the world.**

Reviewing Fragments

What is a sentence fragment?

A sentence fragment is punctuated like a sentence but is missing

a subject and/or verb or is introduced by a dependent word.

What are the five types of fragments?

afterthought fragment   dependent-clause fragment

-ing fragment   relative-clause fragment

to fragment

MyWritingLab   ## Understanding Fragments

To help you understand this sentence error, go to **MyWritingLab.com**, and choose **Fragments** in the **Sentence Skills** module. From there, watch the video called **Animation: Fragments.** Then return to this chapter, which will go into more detail about these errors and give you opportunities to practice correcting them. Finally, you will apply your understanding of fragments to your own writing.

IDENTIFYING AND CORRECTING FRAGMENTS

Once you have identified a fragment, you have two options for correcting it. The rest of this chapter discusses the five types of fragments and the corrections for each type.

Correction 1:   *Connect the fragment to the sentence before or after it.*

Correction 2:   *Make the fragment into an independent clause:*

(a) either add the missing subject and/or verb, or

(b) drop the subordinating word before the fragment.

TEACHING FRAGMENTS
Buy blank flash cards in an educational supply store, and on each card, put words and phrases that can be combined to form sentences: subordinating conjunctions, relative pronouns, phrases, subjects, verbs, and so on.

Give each student a certain number of flash

cards with words on them. Then have students create sentences out of their words and stand in front of the class in the order of their sentence. For instance, three students might hold up the sentence *the car/was swerving/on the street.* Have another student add *because* to the beginning of the sentence to show how one word can create a fragment.

Have students make other sentences in the same way. Then add and subtract words from these sentences so that students can see the way fragments are both formed and fixed.

INSTRUCTOR'S RESOURCE MANUAL For suggested words, phrases, and clauses, for more exercises, and for quizzes, see the *Instructor's Resource Manual,* Section II, Part IV.

UNIT POST-TESTS To check your students' mastery of the collective skills in this unit, two Unit Post-tests are available in the *Instructor's Resource Manual.*

Type 1: Afterthought Fragments

Afterthought fragments occur when you add an idea to a sentence but don't punctuate it correctly.

> **Fragment:**   He works out at the gym. **And runs several miles a week.**

The phrase *And runs several miles a week* is punctuated and capitalized as a complete sentence. Because this group of words lacks a subject, however, it is a fragment.

> **Correction 1:**   *Connect the fragment to the sentence before or after it.*
> **Example:**   He works out at the gym **and** runs several miles a week.
> **Correction 2:**   *Make the fragment into an independent clause.*
> **Example:**   He works out at the gym. **He** runs several miles a week.

The first correction connects the fragment to the sentence before it or after it. The second correction makes the fragment an independent clause with its own subject and verb.

Reviewing Afterthought Fragments

What is an afterthought fragment?

An idea added to a sentence but not punctuated correctly

_____

Give an example of an afterthought fragment.

Examples will vary.

_____

What are the two ways to correct an afterthought fragment?

1. *Connect it to the sentence before or after it.*

_____

2. *Make it into an independent clause by adding the missing subject and/or verb to it.*

PRACTICE 1A: Recall/Identify Underline the afterthought fragments in each of the following sentences.

1. The competition was tough. We were all afraid to play them. <u>Including me.</u>

2. <u>With his face against the window.</u> He could see his keys lying on the end table.

3. She stayed up late last night. Now she's sleeping. <u>In class.</u>

4. Spring is my favorite time of year. <u>With all the flowers in bloom. And lovers holding hands.</u>

5. Aikio was very nervous. <u>Before her job interview.</u> I hope she calms down.

PRACTICE 1B: Correct Correct the fragments in Practice 1A by rewriting each sentence.   *Answers will vary.*

PRACTICE 2: Apply Correct the following afterthought fragments using both correction 1 and correction 2. Rewrite any corrected sentences that could be smoother.   *Answers will vary.*

1. She found a beautiful vase at the yard sale. Also some antique chairs.

   _____

2. Benny studied really hard. Lisa too.

   _____

3. My mom makes the best brownies. Sometimes with walnuts and frosting.

   _____

4. They married December 6. In Las Vegas.

   _____

5. The mysterious woman stood in the doorway. And stared at him.

   _____

PRACTICE 3: Write Your Own Write five afterthought fragments of your own, and correct them.   *Answers will vary.*

_____

_____

_____

_____

_____

Type 2: -ing Fragments

Words that end in *-ing* are forms of verbs but cannot be the main verbs in their sentences. For an *-ing* word to function as a verb, it must have a helping verb with it. (See pages 391–392.)

Fragment: **Finding no food in the refrigerator.** LaKesha went to the store.

Finding is not a verb in this sentence because it has no helping verb. Also, this group of words is a fragment because it has no subject.

Correction 1: *Connect the fragment to the sentence before or after it.*
Example: **Finding no food in the refrigerator,** LaKesha went to the store.

Correction 2: *Make the fragment into an independent clause.*
Example: **She found no food in the refrigerator.** LaKesha went to the store.

Hint: When you connect an *-ing* fragment to a sentence, insert a comma between the two sentence parts. You should insert the comma whether the *-ing* part comes at the beginning or the end of the sentence.

LaKesha went to the store, **finding no food in the refrigerator.**

Finding no food in the refrigerator, LaKesha went to the store.

Reviewing *-ing* Fragments

How can you tell if an -ing word is part of a fragment or is a main verb?

If the -ing word has a helping verb, it is part of the main verb.

Otherwise, it could be part of a fragment.

Give an example of an -ing fragment.

Examples will vary.

What are the two ways to correct an -ing fragment?

1. Connect it to the sentence before or after it.

2. Make it into an independent clause by adding the missing subject and/or verb to it.

What kind of punctuation should you use when you join an -ing fragment to another sentence?

Use a comma when joining an -ing fragment to another sentence.

PRACTICE 4A: Recall/Identify Underline the *-ing* fragments in each of the following sentences.

1. <u>Driving like a maniac.</u> She made the trip in 10 hours.

2. Yvonne joined a health club. <u>Thinking that would motivate her to exercise.</u>

3. <u>Threatening the Florida coast.</u> The hurricane grew in force.

4. Drew cleaned his house thoroughly. <u>Vacuuming, dusting, and washing windows.</u>

5. He's at the student union. <u>Hanging out.</u>

PRACTICE 4B: Correct Correct the fragments in Practice 4A by rewriting each sentence. *Answers will vary.*

PRACTICE 5: Apply Correct each of the following *-ing* fragments using both methods. Remember to insert a comma when using correction. *Answers will vary.*

1. We'll either walk or drive. Depending on the weather.

   _____

2. You can find him at home every night. Playing his electric guitar.

   _____

3. The car lurched and stopped suddenly. Spilling the soda on the seat.

   _____

4. Loving every minute on stage. She is a talented performer.

   _____

5. Mrs. Weeks volunteers at the hospital. Delivering flowers and cards to patients.

   _____

PRACTICE 6: Write Your Own Write five *-ing* fragments of your own, and correct them. *Answers will vary.*

   _____

   _____

   _____

   _____

   _____

Type 3: *to* Fragments

When *to* is added to a verb (*to see, to hop, to skip, to jump*), the combination cannot be a main verb in its sentence. As a result, this group of words is often involved in a fragment.

> **Fragment:**   The company sponsored a national training program.
> **To increase its sales by 20 percent.**

Because *to* + a verb cannot function as the main verb of its sentence, *to increase its sales by 20 percent* is a fragment as it is punctuated here.

> **Correction 1:**   *Connect the fragment to the sentence before or after it.*
> **Example:**   The company sponsored a national training program **to increase its sales by 20 percent.**

> **Correction 2:**   *Make the fragment into an independent clause.*
> **Example:**   The company sponsored a national training program.
> **It decided to increase its sales by 20 percent.**

Hint: A *to* fragment can also occur at the beginning of a sentence. In this case, insert a comma between the two sentence parts when correcting the fragment.

> **To increase its sales by 20 percent,** the company sponsored a national training program.

Reviewing *to* Fragments

What does a *to* fragment consist of?

A to fragment consists of to plus a verb.

Give an example of a *to* fragment.

Examples will vary.

What are the two ways to correct a *to* fragment?

1. *Connect it to the sentence before or after it.*

2. *Make it into an independent clause by adding the missing subject and/or verb to it.*

PRACTICE 7A: Recall/Identify Underline the *to* fragments in each of the following sentences.

1. We want to stay home tonight. To see the MTV awards.

2. To get an A in English. That's Shonda's goal.

3. Would you please call Jerry? <u>To remind him to bring his cooler.</u>

4. The environmental group Greenpeace will be there. <u>To protest whaling.</u>

5. I have only one New Year's resolution. <u>To stop smoking.</u>

PRACTICE 7B: Correct Correct the fragments in Practice 7A by rewriting each sentence.   *Answers will vary.*

PRACTICE 8: Apply Correct the following *to* fragments using both correction 1 and correction 2. Try putting the fragment at the beginning of the sentence instead of always at the end. Remember to insert a comma when you add the *to* fragment to the beginning of a sentence.   *Answers will vary.*

1. To improve her strength and flexibility. She has started a new exercise program.

   _____

2. He works full time and takes classes at night. To get his degree in accounting.

   _____

3. Megan and Bethany are saving their money. To go to Florida for spring vacation.

   _____

4. To warn approaching ships. The captain sounded the foghorn.

   _____

5. He bought two pounds of coffee. To be sure he didn't run out.

   _____

PRACTICE 9: Write Your Own Write five *to* fragments of your own, and correct them.   *Answers will vary.*

_____

_____

_____

_____

_____

Type 4: Dependent-Clause Fragments

A group of words that begins with a **subordinating conjunction** (see the following list) is called a **dependent clause** and cannot stand alone. Even though it has a subject and a verb, it is a fragment because it depends on an independent clause to complete its meaning. An **independent clause** is a group of words with a subject and a verb that can stand alone. (See pages 381–383 for help with clauses.)

Here is a list of some commonly used subordinating conjunctions that create dependent clauses:

Subordinating Conjunctions

after	because	since	until
although	before	so	when
as	even if	so that	whenever
as if	even though	than	where
as long as	how	that	wherever
as soon as	if	though	whether
as though	in order that	unless	while

Fragment: <u>Since he bought a Chevy Blazer.</u> His insurance has gone up.

This sentence has a subject and a verb, but it is introduced by a subordinating conjunction, *since*. As a result, this sentence is a dependent clause and cannot stand alone.

Correction 1:   *Connect the fragment to the sentence before or after it.*
Example: **Since he bought a Chevy Blazer,** his insurance has gone up.

Correction 2:   *Make the fragment into an independent clause.*
Example: ~~Since~~ **He** bought a Chevy Blazer. His insurance has gone up.

Hint: If the dependent clause comes first, put a comma between the two parts of the sentence. If the dependent clause comes second, the comma is not necessary.

Since he bought a Chevy Blazer, his insurance has gone up.
His insurance has gone up **since he bought a Chevy Blazer.**

Reviewing Dependent-Clause Fragments

What is a dependent-clause fragment?

A group of words with a subject and verb that cannot stand alone.

What types of words make a clause dependent?

subordinating conjunction   relative pronoun

What is an independent clause?

A group of words with a subject and verb that can stand alone.

Give an example of a dependent-clause fragment.

Examples will vary.

What are the two ways to correct a dependent-clause fragment?

1. *Connect it to the sentence before or after it.*

2. *Make it into an independent clause by dropping the subordinating word before it.*

PRACTICE 10A: Recall/Identify Underline the dependent-clause fragments in each of the following sentences.

1. Let's wait under this awning. <u>Until it stops raining.</u>

2. We rented the apartment on Lee Street. <u>So that I can walk to campus.</u>

3. Ana took two aspirin. <u>Because she has a headache.</u>

4. <u>If you are interested.</u> I can show you how to install the new software.

5. Wait one minute, please. <u>While I get my coat.</u>

PRACTICE 10B: Correct Correct the fragments in Practice 10A by rewriting each sentence.   *Answers will vary.*

PRACTICE 11: Apply Correct the following dependent-clause fragments using both correction 1 and correction 2. When you use correction 1, remember to add a comma if the dependent clause comes first.   *Answers will vary.*

1. Although Jeff doesn't have any money. He manages to go to every Lakers game.

2. As long as you're up. Would you please get me a Coke?

_____

3. I don't watch much TV. Unless *Ellen* is on.

_____

4. You can save a lot of money. If you clip coupons.

_____

5. The checkbook is on the kitchen counter. Where I left it.

_____

PRACTICE 12: Write Your Own Write five dependent-clause fragments of your own, and correct them.   *Answers will vary.*

_____

_____

_____

_____

Type 5: Relative-Clause Fragments

A **relative clause** is a dependent clause that begins with a relative pro-noun: *who, whom, whose, which,* or *that.* When a relative clause is punctuated as a sentence, the result is a fragment.

Fragment: I climbed Mt. Everest. **Which is the tallest mountain in the world.**

Which is the tallest mountain in the world is a clause fragment that begins with the relative pronoun *which.* This word automatically makes the words that follow it a dependent clause, so they cannot stand alone as a sentence.

Correction 1: *Connect the fragment to the sentence before or after it.*
Example: I climbed Mt. Everest, **which** is the tallest mountain in the world.

Correction 2: *Make the fragment into an independent clause.*
Example: I climbed Mt. Everest. **It** is the tallest mountain in the world.

Reviewing Relative-Clause Fragments

How is a relative-clause fragment different from a dependent-clause fragment?

A relative-clause fragment begins with a relative pronoun rather than a subordinating conjunction.

Give an example of a relative-clause fragment.

Examples will vary.

What are the two ways to correct a relative-clause fragment?

1. Connect it to the sentence before or after it.

2. Make it into an independent clause that can stand alone.

PRACTICE 13A: Recall/Identify Underline the relative-clause fragments in the following sentences.

1. I have Professor Shannon. Whose wife also teaches here.

2. She takes courses online. Which allows her to also work full time.

3. Ronya is going to stay with her sister. Who lives in Brooklyn.

4. He's thinking of getting a laptop computer. That he can take on trips.

5. Traffic was bumper to bumper. Which always makes me impatient.

PRACTICE 13B: Correct Correct the fragments in Practice 13A by rewriting each sentence. Answers will vary.

PRACTICE 14: Apply Correct the following relative-clause fragments using both correction 1 and correction 2. Answers will vary.

1. The shark circled the boat. Which made me very nervous.

2. She's dating Kevin. Whom I dated last year.

3. The movie stars Tom Hanks. Who has already won two Oscars.

4. He read every short story. That was published in 2004.

_____

5. She watched the professor. Whose glasses kept slipping down his nose.

_____

PRACTICE 15: Write Your Own Write five relative-clause fragments of your own, and correct them. *Answers will vary.*

_____

_____

_____

_____

CHAPTER REVIEW

If students are stuck on the Grammar Apply, have them click "Hint" to receive helpful information about the exercise.

MyWritingLab   **Reviewing Fragments**

To review this material before you complete the Review Practices, watch **Animation: Fragments** at **MyWritingLab.com** one more time. This time, keep the video open as you complete the rest of the practices in this chapter. For best results, do the **MyWritingLab** exercises online as well as the Chapter Review practices in the book.

REVIEW PRACTICE 1: Recall/Identify Underline the fragments in the following paragraph.

The worst day of my life was last week. My sister promised to help me move into my new apartment. And didn't show up. Which I couldn't believe at first. When I called her to make arrangements, I should have known I was in trouble. Because she didn't sound like she was listening to me on the phone. This was my first clue. Anyway, I was counting on her. A big mistake. I kept expecting her to arrive all night. But she never came. I found out afterwards. That she forgot. This was what it was like growing up with her too. She remembered what she wanted to remember. And not any more. <u>Which got her this far in life.</u> But how much more can her family and friends forgive and forget?

MyWritingLab — Practicing Fragments

Now complete the **Recall** activities for **Fragments** in the **Sentence Skills** module of **MyWritingLab.com.** Remember to read the answers carefully because many of them look similar.

REVIEW PRACTICE 2: Apply Correct all the fragments you underlined in Review Practice 1 by rewriting the paragraph. *Answers will vary.*

MyWritingLab — Practicing Fragments

Next, complete the **Apply** activity for **Fragments** in the **Sentence Skills** module of **MyWritingLab.com.** Pay close attention to the directions, and click only on what you're asked to.

Complete this **Writing Prompt** at **mywritinglab.com**

REVIEW PRACTICE 3: Write Your Own Write a paragraph about your favorite restaurant. Where is this restaurant? What does it specialize in? Why do you like it? What is your favorite meal? *Answers will vary.*

MyWritingLab — Practicing Fragments

For more practice, complete the **Write** activity for **Fragments** in the **Sentence Skills** module of **MyWritingLab.com.** Make sure to pay close attention to which sentences might be potential sentence fragments.

REVIEW PRACTICE 4: Editing through Collaboration Exchange paragraphs from Review Practice 3 with another student, and do the following: *Answers will vary.*

1. Put brackets around any fragments you find.

2. Identify the types of fragments you find.

Then return the paper to its writer, and use the information in this chapter to correct any fragments in your own paragraph. Record your errors on the Error Log in Appendix 7.

Fused Sentences
and Comma Splices

UNIT PRE-TESTS
To check your students'
abilities with the collective
skills in this unit, two Unit
Pre-tests are available in
the *Instructor's Resource
Manual.*

TEST YOURSELF

Mark any incorrect sentences here with a slash between the independent clauses that are not joined properly.

- Jennifer was elected Academic President, I voted for her.
- The beach is a great getaway we're fortunate it's only 45 minutes away.
- He wanted to participate, but he wasn't sure of the rules.
- Casey is hard to get to know she hides her thoughts and feelings well.
- I hope I get into Dr. Jones's class, I hear he's the best teacher to get.

(Answers are in Appendix 3.)

When we cram two separate statements into a single sentence without correct punctuation, we create *fused sentences* and *comma splices*. These run-together sentences generally distort our message and cause problems for our readers. In this chapter, you will learn how to identify and avoid these errors in your writing.

IDENTIFYING FUSED SENTENCES AND COMMA SPLICES

Whereas a fragment is a piece of a sentence, **fused sentences** and **comma splices** are made up of two sentences written as one. In both cases, the first sentence runs into the next without the proper punctuation between the two.

Fused Sentence: The car slowly rolled to a stop we hopped out.

Comma Splice: The car slowly rolled to a stop, we hopped out.

Both of these sentences incorrectly join two independent clauses. The difference between them is a single comma.

MyWritingLab

Understanding Fused Sentences and Comma Splices

To learn more about these sentence errors, go to **MyWritingLab.com,** and choose **Run-Ons** in the **Sentence Skills** module. From there, watch the video called **Animation: Run-Ons.** For this topic, return to this chapter, which will go into more detail about these errors and give you opportunities to practice correcting them. Finally, you will apply your understanding of fused sentences and comma splices to your own writing.

A **fused sentence** is two sentences "fused" or jammed together without any punctuation. Look at these examples:

Fused Sentence: Kinya's favorite event is the pole vault he always scores very high in it.

This example consists of two independent clauses with no punctuation between them:

1. Kinya's favorite event is the pole vault.
2. He always scores very high in it.

Fused Sentence: My brother loves to cook he doesn't like others to cook for him.

This example also consists of two independent clauses with no punctuation between them:

1. My brother loves to cook.
2. He doesn't like others to cook for him.

Like a fused sentence, a **comma splice** incorrectly joins two independent clauses. However, a comma splice puts a comma between the two independent clauses. The only difference between a fused sentence and a comma splice is the comma. Look at the following examples:

Comma Splice: Kinya's favorite event is the pole vault, he always scores very high in it.

Comma Splice: My brother loves to cook, he doesn't like others to cook for him.

Student Comment:
"The videos are great! I finally get comma splices!"

TEACHING FUSED SENTENCES AND COMMA SPLICES
One of the major misconceptions about run-together sentences is that long sentences are usually fused sentences and comma splices. After all, they run on and on and on. One way to dispel this myth is to write two sentences on the board (one very short and one very long) and ask students to identify the run-together sentence. For this to work, make sure the run-together is the very short sentence. Here is an example:
    Which of the following is the run-together sentence?
    I love chocolate it tastes good.
    I love chocolate, not only because it tastes good but also because it reminds me of all the fun times that my sister and I had when we were little kids and would buy all different types of candy that we would eat until we got sick.
    Students will invariably choose the longer sentence

Both of these sentences consist of two independent clauses. But a comma is not the proper punctuation to separate these two clauses.

Reviewing Fused Sentences and Comma Splices

What are the two types of run-together sentences?

fused sentence   comma splice

What is the difference between them?

A fused sentence has no punctuation between the run-together sentences, and

a comma splice has a comma between them.

PRACTICE 1: Recall/Identify Put a slash between the independent clauses that are not joined correctly.

1. Cedric goes out on a date every Saturday night/he usually spends less than $20.

2. Toni Morrison wrote the novels *Beloved* and *The Bluest Eye*/she won a Nobel Prize for literature.

3. The party begins at six, but the food isn't served until seven,/there's a choice between chicken and beef.

4. The carnation is my favorite flower, but I still like the rose/it is also beautiful.

5. Peanut butter and chocolate is my favorite ice cream flavor, but macadamia nuts in vanilla ice cream is a close second,/the peanut butter makes my taste buds tingle.

PRACTICE 2: Recall/Identify For each incorrect sentence in the following paragraph, put a slash between the independent clauses that are not joined properly.

The day I started my first job was the most frustrating day of my life. I arrived at the restaurant early/no one showed me which door to enter, so I stood outside banging on the wrong door for several minutes. One of the cooks heard me,/he laughed and told the other employees. This embarrassed me from the start. I didn't know that my white shirt was wrong either,/it had two pockets instead of one. Sherri, my manager, pointed this out. She said the personnel director should have told me about the dress code/I said he had told me nothing but wear a white shirt. Anyway, the most frustrating part of the day was watching videos about setting a table, serving, and performing other duties. It was boring/I had worked two years at the country club and knew what to do. I wanted to get out on the floor. The day was too long,/I knew things had to get better!

PRACTICE 3: Write Your Own Write five fused sentences. Then write the same sentences as comma splices.

Answers will vary.

_____

_____

_____

_____

CORRECTING FUSED SENTENCES AND COMMA SPLICES

You have four different options for correcting your run-together sentences.

1. *Separate the two sentences with a period, and capitalize the next word.*

2. *Separate the two sentences with a comma, and add a coordinating conjunction* (and, but, for, nor, or, so, *or* yet).

3. *Change one of the sentences into a dependent clause with a subordinating conjunction (such as* if, because, since, after, *or* when) *or a relative pronoun* (who, whom, whose, which, *or* that).

4. *Separate the two sentences with a semicolon.*

Correction 1: Use a Period

Separate the two sentences with a period, and capitalize the next word.

Kinya's favorite event is the pole vault. **He** always scores very high in it.
My brother loves to cook. **He** doesn't like others to cook for him.

PRACTICE 4: Correct Correct all of the sentences in Practice 1 using correction 1. *Students should insert a period where the slashes are and capitalize the next word.*

PRACTICE 5: Correct Correct the paragraph in Practice 2 using correction 1. *Students should insert a period where the slashes are and capitalize the next word.*

PRACTICE 6: Write Your Own Correct the sentences you wrote in Practice 3 using correction 1.

Answers will vary.

_____

_____

_____

_____

Correction 2: Use a Coordinating Conjunction

Separate the two sentences with a comma, and add a coordinating conjunction (and, but, for, nor, or, so, *or* yet).

Kinya's favorite event is the pole vault, **so** he always scores very high in it.

My brother loves to cook, **but** he doesn't like others to cook for him.

PRACTICE 7: Correct Correct all the sentences in Practice 1 using correction 2. *Students should insert a comma and a coordinating conjunction where the slashes are.*

PRACTICE 8: Correct Correct the paragraph in Practice 2 using correction 2. *Students should insert a comma and a coordinating conjunction where the slashes are.*

PRACTICE 9: Write Your Own Correct the sentences you wrote in Practice 3 using correction 2.

Answers will vary.

_____

_____

_____

_____

Correction 3: Create a Dependent Clause

Change one of the sentences into a dependent clause with a subordinating conjunction (such as if, because, since, after, *or* when) *or a relative pronoun* (who, whom, whose, which, *or* that).

Kinya's favorite event is the pole vault **because** he always scores very high in it.

Even though my brother loves to cook, he doesn't like others to cook for him.

For a list of subordinating conjunctions, see pages 372–373.

Hint: If you put the dependent clause at the beginning of the sentence, add a comma between the two sentence parts.

Because he always scores very high in it, Kinya's favorite event is the pole vault.

PRACTICE 10: Correct Correct all the sentences in Practice 1 using correction 3. *Students should change one of the sentences in each run-together into a dependent clause with a subordinating conjunction.*

PRACTICE 11: Correct Correct the paragraph in Practice 2 using correction 3. *Students should change one of the sentences in each run-together into a dependent clause with a subordinating conjunction.*

PRACTICE 12: Write Your Own Correct the sentences you wrote in Practice 3 using correction 3.

Answers will vary. _____

_____

_____

_____

_____

Correction 4: Use a Semicolon

Separate the two sentences with a semicolon.

Kinya's favorite event is the pole vault; he always scores very high in it.

My brother loves to cook; he doesn't like others to cook for him.

You can also use a **transition,** a word or expression that indicates how the two parts of the sentence are related, with a semicolon. A transition often makes the sentence smoother. It is preceded by a semicolon and followed by a comma.

Kinya's favorite event is the pole vault; **as a result,** he always scores very high in it.

My brother loves to cook; **however,** he doesn't like others to cook for him.

Here are some transitions commonly used with semicolons:

Transitions Used with a Semicolon
Before and a Comma After

also	however	furthermore	instead
meanwhile	consequently	for example	similarly
in contrast	therefore	for instance	otherwise
of course	finally	in fact	nevertheless

PRACTICE 13: Correct Correct all the sentences in Practice 1 using correction 4.   *Students should put semicolons where the slashes are.*

PRACTICE 14: Correct Correct the paragraph in Practice 2 using correction 4.   *Students should put semicolons where the slashes are.*

PRACTICE 15: Write Your Own Correct the sentences you wrote in Practice 3 using correction 4.

Answers will vary

_____

_____

_____

_____

Reviewing Methods of Correcting Fused Sentences and Comma Splices

What are the four ways to correct a fused sentence or comma splice?

1. *Separate the two sentences with a period, and capitalize the next word.*

2. *Separate the two sentences with a comma, and add a coordinating conjunction.*

3. *Change one of the sentences into a dependent clause with a subordinating conjunction.*

4. *Use a semicolon between the two sentences with or without a transition.*

Why is correcting fused sentences and comma splices important?

They distort a writer's message and cause readers problems.

CHAPTER REVIEW

| **MyWritingLab** | ### Reviewing Fused Sentences and Comma Splices |

To review this material before you complete the Review Practices, watch **Animation: Run-Ons** at **MyWritingLab.com** one more time. This time, keep the video open as you complete the rest of the practices in this chapter. For best results, do the **MyWritingLab** exercises online as well as the Chapter Review practices in the book.

Since many students struggle with fused sentences and comma splices, they may be anxious about completing the Run-Ons topic in MyWritingLab. As a result, they might need a little extra encouragement when completing this topic.

REVIEW PRACTICE 1: Recall/Identify Label each of the following sentences as fused (F), comma splice (CS), or correct (C).

1. __F__ The small girls fidgeted in their colorful outfits they waited for their cue to go on stage.

2. __C__ A hubcap came off the car as the car continued down the street.

3. __F__ Alanna grabbed for the pen that worked she didn't want to forget his phone number.

4. __CS__ Stanley waited, but Tia never showed up, her car must have gotten stuck.

5. __C__ Now that winter is approaching, the ski slopes will get very crowded.

6. __CS__ Both women would graduate at the end of the fall quarter, it was three weeks away.

7. __F__ Sitting on top of flagpoles was an activity in the 1920s it was a great pastime.

8. __CS__ The library has over 1,000 journals, they can be found online.

9. __CS__ Some people get nervous when they meet movie stars, they're no different than regular people.

10. __F__ Larissa is graduating with a degree in geology this year she's throwing a big party to celebrate.

MyWritingLab

Practicing Fused Sentences and Comma Splices

Now complete the **Recall** activities for **Run-Ons** in the **Sentence Skills** module of **MyWritingLab.com.** If you're having a difficult time with a question, open up the video in the lower right-hand corner for some help.

REVIEW PRACTICE 2: Correct Correct the fused sentences and comma splices in Review Practice 1.   *Answers will vary.*

MyWritingLab

Practicing Fused Sentences and Comma Splices

Next, complete the **Apply** activity for **Run-Ons** in the **Sentence Skills** module of **MyWritingLab.com.** If you're stuck, you can click on the hint button.

⚙️┌**Complete** this **Writing Prompt** at **mywritinglab.com**

REVIEW PRACTICE 3: Write Your Own Write a paragraph about a "first" in your life (for example, your first date, your first pizza, your first job).   *Answers will vary.*

MyWritingLab

Practicing Fused Sentences and Comma Splices

For more practice, complete the **Write** activity for **Run-Ons** in the **Sentence Skills** module of **MyWritingLab.com.** Make sure to pay close attention to which sentences are fused sentences and which are comma splices.

REVIEW PRACTICE 4: Editing Through Collaboration Exchange paragraphs from Review Practice 3 with another student, and do the following: *Answers will vary.*

1. Put brackets around any sentences that have more than one independent clause.

2. Circle the words that connect these clauses.

Then return the paper to its writer, and use the information in this chapter to correct any run-together sentences in your own paragraph. Record your errors on the Error Log in Appendix 7.

Verbs

Verbs can do just about anything we ask them to do. Because they have so many forms, they can play lots of different roles in a sentence: The bells *ring* on the hour; voices *rang* through the air; we could hear the clock *ringing* miles away. As you can see from these examples, even small changes, like a single letter, mean something; as a result, verbs make communication more interesting and accurate. But using verbs correctly takes concentration and effort.

In this unit, we will discuss the following aspects of verbs and their use:

Regular and Irregular Verbs

UNIT PRE-TESTS
To check your students'
abilities with the collective
skills in this unit, two Unit
Pre-tests are available in
the *Instructor's Resource
Manual.*

TEST YOURSELF

Underline the complete verbs in each of the following sentences. Then mark an X if the form of any of the verbs is incorrect.

- _____ We brang our new neighbor a pizza for dinner.
- _____ My brother married on February 14—Valentine's Day.
- _____ He drug the heavy suitcase down the street.
- _____ This CD costed $15.
- _____ My roommate's water bed has sprang a leak.

(Answers are in Appendix 3.)

All verbs are either regular or irregular. *Regular verbs* form the past tense and past participle by adding *-d* or *-ed* to the present tense. If a verb does not form its past tense and past participle this way, it is called an *irregular verb*.

Student Comment:
"As a non-English speaker,
MyWritingLab helps me
remember grammar rules."

MyWritingLab

Understanding Regular and Irregular Verbs

To improve your understanding of verbs, go to **MyWritingLab.com**, and choose **Regular and Irregular Verbs** in the **Basic Grammar** module. From there, watch the video called **Animation: Regular and Irregular Verbs.** Then, return to this chapter, which will go into more detail about verbs and give you opportunities to practice them. Finally, you will apply your understanding of regular and irregular verbs to your own writing.

REGULAR VERBS

Here are the principal parts (present, past, and past participle forms) of some regular verbs. They are **regular verbs** because their past tense and past participle end in *-d* or *-ed*. The past participle is the verb form often used with helping verbs like *have*, *has*, or *had*.

Some Regular Verbs

PRESENT TENSE	PAST TENSE	PAST PARTICIPLE (USED WITH HELPING WORDS LIKE *HAVE, HAS, HAD*)
talk	talk**ed**	talk**ed**
sigh	sigh**ed**	sigh**ed**
drag	drag**ged**	drag**ged**
enter	enter**ed**	enter**ed**
consider	consider**ed**	consider**ed**

The different forms of a verb tell when something happened—in the *present* (I *walk*) or in the *past* (I *walked*, I *have walked*, I *had walked*).

Reviewing Regular Verbs

What is a regular verb?

A regular verb forms its past tense and past participle by adding -d or -ed.

Identify three forms of a regular verb.

present tense _____   past tense _____

past participle _____

PRACTICE 1: Recall/Identify Put an X to the left of the incorrect verb forms in the following chart.

Present Tense	Past Tense	Past Participle
1. _____ skip	_X_ skipt	_____ skipped
2. _____ paint	_____ painted	_____ painted
3. _X_ danced	_X_ dance	_____ danced

| 4. _____ play | _____ played | _X_ playen |
| 5. _____ cook | _____ cooked | _X_ cooken |

PRACTICE 2: Apply Write the correct forms of the following regular verbs.

	Present Tense	Past Tense	Past Participle
1. act	act	acted	acted
2. invent	invent	invented	invented
3. follow	follow	followed	followed
4. drag	drag	dragged	dragged
5. create	create	created	created

PRACTICE 3: Write Your Own Write five sentences using at least five of the verb forms from Practice 2.   *Answers will vary.*

_____

_____

_____

_____

_____

IRREGULAR VERBS

Irregular verbs do not form their past tense and past participle with *-d* or *-ed*. That is why they are irregular. Some follow certain patterns (*sing, sang, sung; ring, rang, rung; drink, drank, drunk; shrink, shrank, shrunk*). But the only sure way to know the forms of an irregular verb is to spend time learning them. As you write, you can check a dictionary or the following list.

Irregular Verbs

PRESENT	PAST	PAST PARTICIPLE (USED WITH HELPING WORDS LIKE *HAVE, HAS, HAD*)
am	was	been
are	were	been
be	was	been

bear	bore	borne, born
beat	beat	beaten
begin	began	begun
bend	bent	bent
bid	bid	bid
bind	bound	bound
bite	bit	bitten
blow	blew	blown
break	broke	broken
bring	brought (not brang)	brought (not brung)
build	built	built
burst	burst (not bursted)	burst
buy	bought	bought
choose	chose	chosen
come	came	come
cost	cost (not costed)	cost
cut	cut	cut
deal	dealt	dealt
do	did (not done)	done
draw	drew	drawn
drink	drank	drunk
drive	drove	driven
eat	ate	eaten
fall	fell	fallen
feed	fed	fed
feel	felt	felt
fight	fought	fought
find	found	found
flee	fled	fled
fly	flew	flown
forget	forgot	forgotten
forgive	forgave	forgiven
freeze	froze	frozen
get	got	got, gotten

(*continued*)

Irregular Verbs

PRESENT	PAST	PAST PARTICIPLE (USED WITH HELPING WORDS LIKE *HAVE, HAS, HAD*)
go	went	gone
grow	grew	grown
hang[1] *(a picture)*	hung	hung
has	had	had
have	had	had
hide	hid	hidden
hear	heard	heard
hurt	hurt (not hurted)	hurt
is	was	been
know	knew	known
lay	laid	laid
lead	led	led
leave	left	left
lend	lent	lent
lie[2]	lay	lain
lose	lost	lost
meet	met	met
pay	paid	paid
prove	proved	proved, proven
put	put	put
read [rēēd]	read [rĕd]	read [rĕd]
ride	rode	ridden
ring	rang	rung
rise	rose	risen
run	ran	run
say	said	said
see	saw (not seen)	seen
set	set	set
shake	shook	shaken
shine[3] *(a light)*	shone	shone
shrink	shrank	shrunk

sing	sang	sung
sink	sank	sunk
sit	sat	sat
sleep	slept	slept
speak	spoke	spoken
spend	spent	spent
spread	spread	spread
spring	sprang (not sprung)	sprung
stand	stood	stood
steal	stole	stolen
stick	stuck	stuck
stink	stank (not stunk)	stunk
strike	struck	struck, stricken
strive	strove	striven
swear	swore	sworn
sweep	swept	swept
swell	swelled	swelled, swollen
swim	swam	swum
swing	swung	swung
take	took	taken
teach	taught	taught
tear	tore	torn
tell	told	told
think	thought	thought
throw	threw	thrown
understand	understood	understood
wake	woke	woken
wear	wore	worn
weave	wove	woven
win	won	won
wring	wrung	wrung
write	wrote	written

1. *Hang* meaning "execute by hanging" is regular: *hang, hanged, hanged*.
2. *Lie* meaning "tell a lie" is regular: *lie, lied, lied*.
3. *Shine* meaning "brighten by polishing" is regular: *shine, shined, shined*.

Reviewing Irregular Verbs

What is the difference between regular and irregular verbs?

Irregular verbs do not form their past tense and past participle with -d or -ed.

What is the best way to learn the past tense and past participle forms of irregular verbs?

The best way to learn these forms is to spend time becoming familiar with them.

PRACTICE 4: Recall/Identify Put an X to the left of the incorrect verb forms in the following chart.

Present Tense	Past Tense	Past Participle
1. _X_ bust	_X_ bursted	_____ burst
2. _____ ring	_X_ rung	_____ rung
3. _X_ took	_X_ taken	_____ taken
4. _____ sleep	_____ slept	_X_ slepted
5. _____ drink	_____ drank	_____ drunk

PRACTICE 5: Apply Write the correct forms of the following irregular verbs.

	Present Tense	Past Tense	Past Participle
1. hide	*hide*	*hid*	*hidden*
2. sing	*sing*	*sang*	*sung*
3. bring	*bring*	*brought*	*brought*
4. write	*write*	*wrote*	*written*
5. cost	*cost*	*cost*	*cost*

PRACTICE 6: Write Your Own Write five sentences using at least five of the verb forms from the chart in Practice 5.   *Answers will vary.*

_____

_____

_____

_____

_____

USING *LIE/LAY* AND *SIT/SET* CORRECTLY

Two pairs of verbs are often used incorrectly—*lie/lay* and *sit/set*.

Lie/Lay

	Present Tense	Past Tense	Past Participle
lie *(recline or lie down)*	lie	lay	(have, has, had) lain
lay *(put or place down)*	lay	laid	(have, has, had) laid

The verb *lay* always takes an object. You must lay something down:

Lay down *what?*
Lay down *your books*.

Sit/Set

	Present tense	Past tense	Past Participle
sit *(get into a seated position)*	sit	sat	(have, has, had) sat
set *(put or place down)*	set	set	(have, has, had) set

Like the verb *lay*, the verb *set* must always have an object. You must set something down:

Set *what?*
Set *the presents* over here.

Reviewing *Lie/Lay* **and** *Sit/Set*

What do lie *and* lay *mean?*

Lie means recline or lie down; lay means put or place down.

What are the principal parts of lie *and* lay*?*

Lie, lay, lain *and* lay, laid, laid

What do sit *and* set *mean?*

Sit means get into a seated position; set means put or place down.

What are the principal parts of sit *and* set*?*

Sit, sat, sat *and* set, set, set

Which of these verbs always take an object?

Lay *and* set

MyWritingLab **Understanding Frequently Confused Verbs**

To learn more about verbs that are often confused, go to **MyWritingLab.com**, and choose **Regular and Irregular Verbs** in the **Basic Grammar** module. From there, watch the video called **Animation: Frequently Confused Verbs.** Keep the video open as you complete the practice exercises in this section of the book.

PRACTICE 7: Recall/Identify Underline the correct verb in the following sentences.

1. She has always (set, sat) in the front row.

2. Please (set, sit) the box of tissues on the nightstand.

3. You have (laid, lain) on the couch all morning.

4. At the concert, we (set, <u>sat</u>) with Howie and Carol.

5. The installers are coming to (lay, lie) the new carpeting.

PRACTICE 8: Apply Fill in each blank in the following sentences with the correct form of *lie/lay* or *sit/set*.

1. I like to _____*sit*_____ next to the window on an airplane.

2. She has _____*laid*_____ out the clothes she will take on her trip.

3. _____*Set*_____ the box on the table.

4. I'm exhausted. I have to _____*lie*_____ down.

5. _____*Set*_____ the tray over here.

PRACTICE 9: Write Your Own Write five sentences using variations of *lie/lay* or *sit/set*. *Answers will vary.*

_____

_____

_____

_____

_____

CHAPTER REVIEW

MyWritingLab **Reviewing Regular and Irregular Verbs**

Remind your students that spelling counts in the Apply section.

To review this material before you complete the Review Practices, watch **Animation: Regular and Irregular Verbs** at **MyWritingLab. com** one more time. This time, keep the video open as you complete the rest of the practices in this chapter. For best results, do the **MyWritingLab** exercises online as well as the Chapter Review practices in the book.

REVIEW PRACTICE 1: Recall/Identify Write out the past tense and past participle of each verb listed here, and then identify the verb as either regular or irregular.

Present Tense	Past Tense	Past Participle	Type of Verb
1. react	reacted	reacted	regular
2. hesitate	hesitated	hesitated	regular
3. sing	sang	sung	irregular
4. treat	treated	treated	regular
5. bring	brought	brought	irregular
6. suffer	suffered	suffered	regular
7. read	read	read	irregular
8. stink	stunk	stank	irregular
9. take	took	taken	irregular
10. speak	spoke	spoken	irregular

MyWritingLab   **Practicing Regular and Irregular Verbs**

Now complete the **Recall** activities for **Regular and Irregular Verbs** in the **Basic Grammar** module of **MyWritingLab.com**. Remember to read the answers carefully because many of them look similar.

REVIEW PRACTICE 2: Apply Fill in each blank in the following sentences with a regular or irregular verb that makes sense.   *Answers may vary.*

1. No one believed that he had _____won_____ the lottery.

2. I was so tired, I _____went_____ home.

3. We _____listened_____ to the music until after midnight.

4. Because I have a cold, I have _____lain_____ in bed all day.

5. In the sixties, he ____had or grew____ a beard and an outrageous afro.

6. Brian has always _____*been*_____ a wonderful father to his daughter.

7. Every time the choir performs, my grandfather _____*goes*_____ to the concert.

8. Please _____*set*_____ the groceries on the kitchen table.

9. She has _____*gone*_____ to the store to buy cheesecake.

10. At the football game, we _____*sit or sat*_____ in the stands closest to the 50-yard line.

MyWritingLab   **Practicing Regular and Irregular Verbs**

Next, complete the **Apply** activity for **Regular and Irregular Verbs** in the **Basic Grammar** module of **MyWritingLab.com**. Remember that spelling counts.

⚙️◖**Complete** this **Writing Prompt** at **mywritinglab.com**

REVIEW PRACTICE 3: Write Your Own Write a paragraph explaining how active or inactive you are in life. What are the reasons for the choices you have made regarding your level of daily activity?   *Answers will vary.*

MyWritingLab   **Practicing Regular and Irregular Verbs**

For more practice, complete the **Write** activity for **Regular and Irregular Verbs** in the **Basic Grammar** module of **MyWritingLab.com**. Make sure to pay close attention to which verbs need to be changed because they are irregular.

REVIEW PRACTICE 4: Editing Through Collaboration Exchange paragraphs from Review Practice 3 with another student, and do the following. *Answers will vary.*

1. Circle any verb forms that are not correct.

2. Suggest a correction for these incorrect forms.

Then return the paper to its writer, and use the information in this chapter to correct the verb forms in your own paragraph. Record your errors on the Error Log in Appendix 7.

Verb Tense

UNIT PRE-TESTS
To check your students'
abilities with the collective
skills in this unit, two Unit
Pre-tests are available in
the *Instructor's Resource
Manual.*

TEST YOURSELF

Underline the complete verbs in each sentence. Then mark an X if the
form of any of the verbs is incorrect.

- _____ We be planning on leaving in the morning.
- _____ The team chose an alligator as its mascot.
- _____ My sister practice the flute every day.
- _____ He don't look old enough to drive.
- _____ Over 1,000 students apply to my college this year.

(Answers are in Appendix 3.)

When we hear the word *verb*, we often think of action. We also know
that action occurs in time. We are naturally interested in whether something happened today or yesterday or if it will happen at some time in the
future. The time of an action is indicated by the **tense** of a verb, specifically
in the ending of a verb or in a helping word. This chapter discusses the
most common errors in using verb tense.

Student Comment:
"I got to watch the **Verb
Tense** video three times.
In a lecture, I'd only get
to hear it once."

MyWritingLab

Understanding Verb Tense

To find out more about this subject, go to **MyWritingLab.com,** and choose
Tense in the **Basic Grammar** module. From there, watch the video called
Animation: Tense. Then, return to this chapter, which will go into more
detail about tense and give you opportunities to practice it. Finally, you
will apply your understanding of verb tense to your own writing.

PRESENT TENSE

One of the most common errors in college writing is reversing the present-tense endings—adding an *-s* where none is needed and omitting the *-s* where it is required. This error causes problems in subject-verb agreement. Make sure you understand this mistake, and then proofread carefully to avoid it in your writing.

Present Tense

Singular		Plural	
INCORRECT	CORRECT	INCORRECT	CORRECT
NOT *I talks*	*I talk*	**NOT** *we talks*	*we talk*
NOT *you talks*	*you talk*	**NOT** *you talks*	*you talk*
NOT *he, she, it talk*	*he, she, it talks*	**NOT** *they talks*	*they talk*

You also need to be able to spot these same errors in sentences.

Incorrect

Brad run to the store.

She like my tie.

You goes next.

They plants a garden every year.

Correct

Brad runs to the store.

She likes my tie.

You go next.

They plant a garden every year.

Reviewing Present-Tense Errors

What is the most common error in using the present tense?

Reversing the present-tense endings—adding an -s when not needed or omitting

it when it is required

How can you prevent this error?

By learning the correct forms and proofreading carefully

PRACTICE 1A: Recall/Identify Underline the present-tense errors in each of the following sentences.

1. Larry and Sara <u>wants</u> to join our study group.   *(want)*

2. Rhoda <u>make</u> herself breakfast every morning.   *(makes)*

3. At night, we <u>hears</u> coyotes and owls.   *(hear)*

4. That jacket <u>look</u> good on you.   *(looks)*

5. Our mail always <u>come</u> by noon.   *(comes)*

UNIT POST-TESTS
To check your students'
mastery of the collective
skills in this unit, two Unit
Post-tests are available in
the *Instructor's Resource
Manual.*

PRACTICE 1B: Correct Correct the present-tense errors in Practice 1A by rewriting each sentence. *See Practice 1A.*

PRACTICE 2: Apply Fill in each blank in the following paragraph with the correct present-tense verbs. *Answers will vary.*

My mom always (1) _____ me to watch my little sister every time she goes out. Whether she goes to the store or on an errand, she always (2) _____ me in charge. I don't really mind, except sometimes my sister (3) _____ me into trouble because she doesn't like to listen to me. But I tend to let her do whatever she (4) _____. This is probably why she doesn't listen to me all the time. We do have a lot of fun together, so in the end, I guess I (5) _____ the time we have together.

PRACTICE 3: Write Your Own Write a sentence of your own for each of the following present-tense verbs. *Answers will vary.*

1. runs _____
2. feel _____
3. bring _____
4. believes _____
5. wants _____

PAST TENSE

Just as we know by its ending that a verb is in the present tense, we can tell that a verb is in the past tense by its ending. Regular verbs form the past tense by adding *-d* or *-ed*. But some writers forget the ending when they are writing the past tense. Understanding this problem and then proofreading carefully will help you catch this error.

Past Tense

Singular		Plural	
INCORRECT	CORRECT	INCORRECT	CORRECT
NOT I talk	I talked	**NOT** we talk	we talked
NOT you talk	you talked	**NOT** you talk	you talked
NOT he, she, it talk	he, she, it talked	**NOT** they talk	they talked

You also need to be able to spot these same errors in sentences.

Incorrect	**Correct**
He love the game.	**He loved** the game.
She try not to laugh.	**She tried** not to laugh.
The kids watch old movies for hours.	**The kids watched** old movies for hours.
Yes, **we study** for the test.	Yes, **we studied** for the test.

Reviewing Past-Tense Errors

What is the most common error made with the past tense?

Forgetting the past tense ending (-d or -ed)

How can you prevent this error?

By learning the correct forms and proofreading carefully

PRACTICE 4A: Recall/Identify Underline the past-tense errors in the following sentences.

1. We <u>share</u> a hot dog and a Coke at the game. *(shared)*

2. When she left, she <u>lock</u> the door. *(locked)*

3. He <u>ignore</u> the stop sign and almost <u>kill</u> himself. *(ignored; killed)*

4. Tina <u>wrap</u> the gift herself. *(wrapped)*

5. Anya and Sandra <u>watch</u> the little sailboat get smaller and smaller. *(watched)*

PRACTICE 4B: Correct Correct the past-tense errors in Practice 4A by rewriting each sentence. *See Practice 4A.*

PRACTICE 5: Apply Fill in each blank in the following paragraph with the correct past-tense verb.

Last year, our club held a fund-raiser to raise money for a local boys' club. We (1) _____ more than $5,000 by selling chocolate in tin tubs. We had all different kinds of chocolate, but the kind that (2) _____ the most was the chocolate turtles, which (3) _____ chocolate, caramel, and pecans.

I actually (4) _____ five of these tins for my mom. We
(5) _____ quite a lot of money for the boys' club. We are
ready to beat last year's record this year.

PRACTICE 6: Write Your Own Write a sentence of your own for each of the
following past-tense verbs.   *Answers will vary.*

1. ran _____

2. was _____

3. brought _____

4. thought _____

5. saw _____

USING HELPING WORDS WITH PAST PARTICIPLES

Helping words are used only with the past participle form, *not* with the
past-tense form. It is therefore incorrect to use a helping verb (such as *is*,
was, *were*, *have*, *has*, or *had*) with the past tense. Make sure you understand
how to use helping words with past participles, and then proofread your
written work to avoid making these errors.

Incorrect	**Correct**
He **has went.**	He **has gone.**
She **has chose** to stay home.	She **has chosen** to stay home.
I **have ate** at Jimmy's restaurant.	I **have eaten** at Jimmy's restaurant.
We **had flew** into Memphis.	We **had flown** into Memphis.

Reviewing Errors with Helping Words and Past Participles

*What is the most common sentence error made with past
participles?*

Using a helping word with the past tense instead of the past participle

How can you prevent this error?

By learning the correct forms and proofreading carefully

PRACTICE 7A: Recall/Identify Underline the incorrect helping words and past participles in each of the following sentences.

1. Dawn <u>had forgot</u> that she promised to go with me. *(had forgotten)*

2. The Wildcats <u>have beat</u> the Spartans every year since 2000. *(have beaten)*

3. He <u>has broke</u> the world record! *(has broken)*

4. The lawyer <u>has went</u> to court. *(has gone)*

5. You <u>have drank</u> all the orange juice. *(have drunk)*

PRACTICE 7B: Correct Correct the helping verb and past participle errors in Practice 7A by rewriting each sentence. *See Practice 7A.*

PRACTICE 8: Apply Fill in each blank in the following paragraph with helping verbs and past participles that make sense. *Answers will vary.*

I thought you (1) _____ the money we talked about for spring break. But I guess you (2) _____ your mind. The last time we (3) _____ I thought our trip (4) _____. But I am glad to see it is on again. This time I (5) _____ to enjoy myself—whatever adjustments I have to make.

PRACTICE 9: Write Your Own Write a sentence of your own for each of the following helping words and past participles. *Answers will vary.*

1. has run _____

2. have gone _____

3. had brought _____

4. is broken _____

5. have written _____

USING *-ING* VERBS CORRECTLY

Verbs ending in *-ing* describe action that is going on or that was going on for a while. To be a complete verb, an *-ing* verb is always used with a helping verb. Two common errors occur with *-ing* verbs:

1. Using *be* or *been* instead of the correct helping verb

2. Using no helping verb at all

Learn the correct forms, and proofread carefully to catch these errors.

Incorrect	Correct
The dog **be chasing** the cat.	The dog **is chasing** the cat.
	The dog **was chasing** the cat.
The dog **been chasing** the cat.	The dog **has been chasing** the cat.
	The dog **had been chasing** the cat.
We **drinking** Dr. Pepper.	We **are drinking** Dr. Pepper.
	We **have been drinking** Dr. Pepper.
	We **were drinking** Dr. Pepper.
	We **had been drinking** Dr. Pepper.

Reviewing -*ing* Verb Errors

What two kinds of errors occur with -ing verbs?

Using be or been instead of the correct helping verb

Not using any helping verb at all

How can you prevent these errors?

By learning the correct forms and proofreading carefully

PRACTICE 10A: Recall/Identify Underline the incorrect helping verbs and -*ing* forms in each of the following sentences.

1. Mrs. Trent <u>been collecting</u> teapots her whole life. *(has been collecting)*

2. The ambulance <u>be taking</u> the victim to the hospital. *(is taking)*

3. I <u>been thinking</u> that I should invite his family to dinner. *(was or have been thinking)*

4. If you <u>be following</u> your dreams, you will be happy. *(are following)*

5. Stan's not here; he <u>renewing</u> his driver's license downtown. *(is renewing)*

PRACTICE 10B: Correct Correct the verb form errors in Practice 10A by rewriting each sentence. *See Practice 10A.*

PRACTICE 11: Apply Fill in each blank in the following paragraph with the correct helping verb and -*ing* form. *Answers will vary.*

Today I can already tell I (1) _____ one of those days you wish you could start over. It began while I (2) _____ through my alarm. I then had only 10 minutes to get to school before a test. All through the test, I felt like I (3) _____ to catch my breath because I still felt rushed. After I finished, I went to my car and actually found that a police officer (4) _____ me a ticket for parking illegally. I tried to persuade her to look the other way, but she wouldn't. At 10:45 in the morning, I (5) _____ to just lock myself in my house until tomorrow.

PRACTICE 12: Write Your Own Write a sentence of your own for each of the following verbs. *Answers will vary.*

1. is thinking _____

2. has been feeling _____

3. were going _____

4. was reading _____

5. had been jogging _____

PROBLEMS WITH *BE*

The verb *be* can cause problems in both the present tense and the past tense. The following chart demonstrates these problems. Learn how to use these forms correctly, and then always proofread your written work carefully to avoid these errors.

The Verb *be*

Present Tense

Singular		Plural	
INCORRECT	CORRECT	INCORRECT	CORRECT
NOT *I* **be/ain't**	*I* **am/am not**	**NOT** *we* **be/ain't**	*we* **are/are not**
NOT *you* **be/ain't**	*you* **are/are not**	**NOT** *you* **be/ain't**	*you* **are/are not**
NOT *he, she, it* **be/ain't**	*he, she, it* **is/is not**	**NOT** *they* **be/ain't**	*they* **are/are not**

Past Tense

Singular		Plural	
INCORRECT	CORRECT	INCORRECT	CORRECT
NOT I **were**	I **was**	**NOT** we **was**	we **were**
NOT you **was**	you **were**	**NOT** you **was**	you **were**
NOT he, she, it **were**	he, she, it **was**	**NOT** they **was**	they **were**

Reviewing Problems with *be*

What are two common errors made with be?

In the present tense, using be and ain't instead of the correct verb forms

In the past tense, confusing was and were

How can you prevent these errors?

By learning the correct forms and proofreading carefully

PRACTICE 13A: Recall/Identify Underline the incorrect forms of *be* in each of the following sentences.

1. She be in my dormitory, but we ain't friends.   *(is; aren't)*

2. We was hungry and freezing cold.   *(were)*

3. It ain't too late to change your mind.   *(isn't)*

4. You wasn't supposed to know about the party.   *(weren't)*

5. All in all, they was a good-natured group.   *(were)*

PRACTICE 13B: Correct Correct the incorrect forms of *be* in Practice 13A by rewriting each sentence.   *See Practice 13A.*

PRACTICE 14: Apply Fill in each blank in the following paragraph with the correct form of *be*.

Fishing (1) _____*is*_____ the center of my dad's universe. He (2) _____*has been*_____ a good fisherman from the time he was a young boy. Fishing (3) _____*is*_____ a sport that has been in my dad's family for years—his dad taught him, his dad's dad taught his dad,

and so on. My dad taught me to fish when I (4) _____ *was* _____
three years old. We love to go out on long weekends. It is really more
about being together than anything else. It is really more
about being together than anything else. My dad (5) _____ *is* _____
always happiest when we are together on a fishing trip.

PRACTICE 15: Write Your Own Write a sentence of your own for each of the
following verbs.   *Answers will vary.*

1. was _____

2. is _____

3. am _____

4. were _____

5. are _____

PROBLEMS WITH *DO*

Another verb that causes sentence problems in the present and past
tenses is *do*. The following chart shows these problems. Learn the correct
forms, and proofread to avoid errors.

The Verb *do*

Present Tense

Singular		Plural	
INCORRECT	CORRECT	INCORRECT	CORRECT
NOT *I* **does**	*I* **do**	**NOT** *we* **does**	*we* **do**
NOT *you* **does**	*you* **do**	**NOT** *you* **does**	*you* **do**
NOT *he, she, it* **do**	*he, she, it* **does**	**NOT** *they* **does**	*they* **do**

Past Tense

Singular		Plural	
INCORRECT	CORRECT	INCORRECT	CORRECT
NOT *I* **done**	*I* **did**	**NOT** *we* **done**	*we* **did**
NOT *you* **done**	*you* **did**	**NOT** *you* **done**	*you* **did**
NOT *he, she, it* **done**	*he, she, it* **did**	**NOT** *they* **done**	*they* **did**

Reviewing Problems with *do*

What are two common errors made with do?

In the present tense, confusing does and do

In the past tense, confusing done and did

How can you prevent these errors?

By learning the correct forms and proofreading carefully

PRACTICE 16A: Recall/Identify Underline the incorrect forms of *do* in each of the following sentences.

1. She done the dishes today and yesterday. *(did)*

2. She thinks she knows me, but she don't. *(doesn't)*

3. I done most of my research on the Internet. *(did)*

4. Don't worry; it don't matter if you're late. *(doesn't)*

5. If he don't have the remote control, and you don't have it, where is it? *(doesn't)*

PRACTICE 16B: Correct Correct the incorrect forms of *do* in Practice 16A by rewriting each sentence. *See Practice 16A.*

PRACTICE 17: Apply Fill in each blank in the following paragraph with the correct form of *do*.

I (1) _____did_____ my final presentation for sociology in less than 5 minutes. My teacher told us we could (2) _____do_____ the reports in 10–15 minutes, but I talked so fast that I (3) _____did_____ mine in only half the time. I always (4) _____do_____ this to myself. I talk so fast that I speed up my oral reports. Usually the teachers are nice about my fast-talking performances and tell me I (5) _____did_____ a good job.

PRACTICE 18: Write Your Own Write a sentence of your own for each of the following verbs. *Answers will vary.*

1. do _____

2. did _____

3. does _____

4. did _____

5. do _____

PROBLEMS WITH *HAVE*

Along with *be* and *do*, the verb *have* causes sentence problems in the present and past tenses. The following chart demonstrates these problems. Learn the correct forms, and proofread to avoid errors with *have*.

The Verb *have*

Present Tense

Singular		Plural	
INCORRECT	CORRECT	INCORRECT	CORRECT
NOT I *has*	I *have*	**NOT** we *has*	we *have*
NOT you *has*	you *have*	**NOT** you *has*	you *have*
NOT he, she, it *have*	he, she, it *has*	**NOT** they *has*	they *have*

Past Tense

Singular		Plural	
INCORRECT	CORRECT	INCORRECT	CORRECT
NOT I *has*	I *had*	**NOT** we *has*	we *had*
NOT you *have*	you *had*	**NOT** you *has*	you *had*
NOT he, she, it *have*	he, she, it *had*	**NOT** they *has*	they *had*

Reviewing Problems with *have*

What are two common errors made with have?

In the present tense, confusing has and have

In the past tense, confusing has or have and had

How can you prevent these errors?

By learning the correct forms and proofreading carefully

PRACTICE 19A: Recall/Identify Underline the incorrect forms of *have* in each of the following sentences.

1. She <u>have</u> a wonderful sense of humor.   *(has)*

2. They <u>has</u> a great time at the movies.   *(have)*

3. You <u>has</u> some mail on the kitchen counter.   *(have)*

4. Lisa and Kayla <u>has</u> adopted a kitten from the shelter.   *(have)*

5. She <u>have</u> come to class late for a week.   *(has)*

PRACTICE 19B: Correct Correct the incorrect forms of *have* in Practice 19A by rewriting each sentence.   *See Practice 19A.*

PRACTICE 20: Apply Fill in each blank in the following paragraph with the correct form of *have*.

I (1) _____*had*_____ a fabulous spring break! My friends and I went to Padre Island and (2) _____*had*_____ the best times of our lives. Since we got home, we (3) _____*have*_____ not stopped talking about all the people we met and parties we (4) _____*had*_____ We know for sure we are going back next year! Now all we (5) _____*have*_____ to do is start saving our money for next year.

PRACTICE 21: Write Your Own Write a sentence of your own for each of the following verbs.   *Answers will vary.*

1. has _____

2. have _____

3. had _____

4. have _____

5. had _____

CHAPTER REVIEW

MyWritingLab   **Reviewing Verb Tense**

To review this material before you complete the Review Practices, watch **Animation: Tense** at **MyWritingLab.com** one more time. This

Remind students that they lose points in MyWritingLab for every incorrect answer (as well as when they take hints) in the Grammar Apply.

time, keep the video open as you complete the rest of the practices in this chapter. For best results, do the **MyWritingLab** exercises online as well as the Chapter Review practices in the book.

REVIEW PRACTICE 1: Recall/Identify Underline the incorrect verb forms in the following sentences. Check problem areas carefully: Is an -s needed, or is there an unnecessary -s ending? Do all past-tense regular verbs end in -d or -ed? Is the past participle used with helping words? Is the correct helping verb used with -ing verbs? Are the forms of be, do, and have correct?

1. She be training for a new job at the bank. *(is training)*

2. Harper study very hard for the final exam. *(studies/studied)*

3. She walk along the beach and pick up seashells. *(walks/walked, picks/picked)*

4. We has a family reunion every Memorial Day. *(have)*

5. That little frog been jumping from lily pad to lily pad all afternoon. *(has been jumping)*

6. This is the second time she be reading that book. *(is reading)*

7. My dog, Otto, goes everywhere I does. *(do)*

8. He be bicycling to work every day. *(is/has been bicycling)*

9. We been standing at the bus stop when the storm struck. *(were standing)*

10. She always have a backup file when she be working on the computer. *(has, is working)*

MyWritingLab **Practicing Verb Tense**

Now complete the **Recall** activities for **Tense** in the **Basic Grammar** module of **MyWritingLab.com**. Remember to read the answers carefully. If you're having a difficult time with a question, open up the video in the lower right-hand corner for some help.

REVIEW PRACTICE 2: Apply Correct the errors in Review Practice 1 by rewriting each sentence. *See Review Practice 1.*

MyWritingLab   **Practicing Verb Tense**

Next, complete the **Apply** activity for **Tense** in the **Basic Grammar** module of **MyWritingLab.com.** If you're stuck, you can click on the hint button.

Complete this **Writing Prompt** at **mywritinglab.com**

REVIEW PRACTICE 3: Write Your Own Write a paragraph describing your best friend. Be careful to use all verbs in the correct tense. Check in particular for errors with *be, do,* and *have*.   *Answers will vary.*

MyWritingLab   **Practicing Verb Tense**

For more practice, complete the **Write** activity for **Tense** in the **Basic Grammar** module of **MyWritingLab.com.** Make sure to pay close attention to which verbs have tense errors.

REVIEW PRACTICE 4: Editing Through Collaboration Exchange paragraphs from Review Practice 3 with another student, and do the following: *Answers will vary.*

1. Underline any incorrect tenses.

2. Circle any incorrect verb forms.

Then return the paper to its writer, and use the information in this chapter to correct any verb errors in your own paragraph. Record your errors on the Error Log in Appendix 7.

Subject-Verb Agreement

Underline the subjects once and the complete verbs twice in the following sentences. Put an X by the sentence if its subject and verb do not agree.

- _____ Ben and Tess has become great friends.
- _____ Each of the nurses are with a patient.
- _____ Macaroni and cheese are my favorite food.
- _____ There are two trains to Baltimore in the morning.
- _____ Everyone are ready to leave.

(Answers are in Appendix 3.)

UNIT PRE-TESTS
To check your students' abilities with the collective skills in this unit, two Unit Pre-tests are available in the *Instructor's Resource Manual.*

Almost every day, we come across situations that require us to reach an agreement with someone. For example, you and a friend might have to agree on which movie to see, or you and your manager might have to agree on how many hours you'll work in the coming week. Whatever the issue, agreement is essential in most aspects of life—including writing. In this chapter, you will learn how to resolve conflicts in your sentences by making sure your subjects and verbs agree.

SUBJECT-VERB AGREEMENT

Subject-verb agreement simply means that singular subjects must be paired with singular verbs and plural subjects with plural verbs. Look at this example:

Singular: He lives in Cleveland.

The subject *he* is singular because it refers to only one person. The verb *lives* is singular and matches the singular subject. Here is the same sentence in plural form:

Plural: **They live** in Cleveland.

The subject *they* is plural, more than one person, and the verb *live* is also plural.

Reviewing Subject-Verb Agreement

What is the difference between singular and plural?

Singular refers to only one subject. Plural refers to more than one subject.

_____

What kind of verb goes with a singular subject?

A singular verb goes with a singular subject.

_____

What kind of verb goes with a plural subject?

A plural verb goes with a plural subject.

_____

MyWritingLab   ## Understanding Subject-Verb Agreement

To expand your understanding of this topic, go to **MyWritingLab. com,** and choose **Subject-Verb Agreement** in the **Sentence Skills** module. From there, watch the video called **Animation: Subject-Verb Agreement.** Then return to this chapter, which will go into more detail about this topic and give you opportunities to practice it. Finally, you will apply your understanding of subject-verb agreement to your own writing.

PRACTICE 1: Recall/Identfy Underline the verb that agrees with its subject in each of the following sentences.

1. On her vacations, Sylvia (enjoys, enjoy) reading romance novels.

2. Jerry (has, have) a large coin collection.

3. During the day, the farm hands (works, work) in the fields.

4. Unfortunately, the paychecks (was, were) lost in the mail.

5. The twins (does, do) not look alike.

PRACTICE 2: Apply Fill in each blank in the following sentences with a present-tense verb that agrees with its subject. *Answers will vary.*

1. The new clothing styles _____ bad on me.

2. Bob _____ his mom to visit.

3. Every night, the news _____ the latest disasters.

4. During the evening, Jake _____ for many hours.

5. The football team usually _____ its games.

PRACTICE 3: Write Your Own Write five sentences of your own, and underline the subjects and verbs. Make sure your subjects and verbs agree. *Answers will vary.*

_____

_____

_____

_____

WORDS SEPARATING SUBJECTS AND VERBS

With sentences as simple and direct as *He lives in Cleveland*, checking that the subject and verb agree is easy. But problems can arise when words come between the subject and the verb. Often, the words between the subject and verb are prepositional phrases. If you follow the advice given in Chapter 23, you will be able to find the subject and verb: *Cross out all the prepositional phrases in a sentence. The subject and verb will be among the words that are left.* Here are some examples:

                                         s   v
Prepositional Phrases: The **map** ~~of the Ozarks~~ **is** ~~in a small suitcase~~.

When you cross out the prepositional phrases, you can tell that the singular subject, *map*, and the singular verb, *is*, agree.

                                    s   v
Prepositional Phrases: **Classes** ~~at my college~~ **begin** ~~in August~~.

When you cross out the prepositional phrases, you can tell that the plural subject, *classes*, and the plural verb, *begin*, agree.

of poster board, and place squares of the other side of the Velcro on the backs of the index cards.

Now attach index cards to the poster board so that you create a few simple sentences with no words separating the subjects and their verbs. Next, add phrase cards to the sentences, separating the subjects and verbs to show students that verbs do not change even though information may come between a subject and its verb. Demonstrate some common agreement errors by placing incorrect verbs with subjects.

Once your students understand how subjects and verbs agree, test them by putting sentences with subject-verb agreement errors on the board and asking them to come to the board to find and correct the errors.

INSTRUCTOR'S RESOURCE MANUAL
For more sample sentences, for more exercises, and for quizzes, see the *Instructor's Resource Manual*, Section II, Part IV.

UNIT POST-TESTS
To check your students' mastery of the collective skills in this unit, two Unit Post-tests are available in the *Instructor's Resource Manual*.

Reviewing Words Separating Subjects and Verbs

What words often come between subjects and verbs?

Prepositional phrases often come between subjects and verbs.

What is an easy way to identify the subject and verb in a sentence?

Cross out the prepositional phrases first.

PRACTICE 4: Recall/Identify Underline the subject once and the verb twice in each of the following sentences. Cross out the prepositional phrases first. Put an X to the left of any sentence in which the subject and verb do not agree.

1. __X__ Her behavior ~~in front of adults~~ make us all sick.

2. _____ The blooming trees ~~in the orchard~~ are making me sneeze.

3. _____ ~~Unlike John~~, Katie gives ~~to the poor~~.

4. __X__ The house ~~in the mountains~~ were ~~for sale for one year~~.

5. __X__ Oscar, ~~along with his two sisters~~, are studying law.

PRACTICE 5: Apply Fill in each blank in the following sentences with a present-tense verb that agrees with its subject. Cross out the prepositional phrases first. *Answers will vary.*

1. Many students ~~at my college~~ _____ business administration.

2. Angie, ~~along with the entire math class~~, _____ the day could start over.

3. The police, ~~despite many obstacles~~, _____ many criminals every day.

4. Most teachers ~~at all grade levels~~ _____ the work they do.

5. The buses ~~in town~~ _____ many students ~~to school~~.

PRACTICE 6: Write Your Own Write five sentences of your own with at least one prepositional phrase in each, and underline the subjects and verbs. Make sure your subjects and verbs agree. *Answers will vary.*

_____

_____

_____

MORE THAN ONE SUBJECT

Sometimes a subject consists of more than one person, place, thing, or idea. These subjects are called **compound** (as discussed in Chapter 22). Follow these three rules when matching a verb to a compound subject:

1. When compound subjects are joined by *and*, use a plural verb.

   Plural: The **heat** and **humidity were** hard on Simone.

   The singular words *heat* and *humidity* together make a plural subject. Therefore, the plural verb *were* is needed.

2. When the subject appears to have more than one part but the parts refer to a single unit, use a singular verb.

   Singular: **Peanut butter and jelly is** Mindy's favorite sandwich.

   Peanut butter is one item and *jelly* is one item, but Mindy does not eat one without the other, so they form a single unit. Because they are a single unit, they require a singular verb—*is*.

3. When compound subjects are joined by *or* or *nor*, make the verb agree with the subject closest to it.

   Singular: Neither **leeches** nor miserable **weather was** enough to keep her from her goal.

   The part of the compound subject closest to the verb is *weather*, which is singular. Therefore, the verb must be singular—*was*.

   Plural: Neither miserable **weather** nor **leeches were** enough to keep her from her goal.

   This time, the part of the compound subject closest to the verb is *leeches*, which is plural. Therefore, the verb must be plural—*were*.

Reviewing Subject-Verb Agreement with More than One Subject

Do you use a singular or plural verb with compound subjects joined by and?

A plural verb

Why should you use a singular verb with a subject like macaroni and cheese?

Because it forms a single unit

> *If one part of a compound subject joined by* or *or* nor *is singular and the other is plural, how do you decide whether to use a singular or plural verb?*
>
> *Make the verb agree with the subject closest to it.*

PRACTICE 7: Recall/Identify Underline the verb that agrees with its subject in each of the following sentences. Cross out the prepositional phrases first.

1. The golfers and their caddies (looks, <u>look</u>) ready ~~for a day of golf~~.

2. Ham and cheese (are, <u>is</u>) my favorite kind ~~of sandwich~~.

3. Either the professor or his teaching assistants (grades, <u>grade</u>) exams.

4. The White Sox and the Cubs (is, <u>are</u>) both Chicago teams.

5. Checkers and chess (<u>take</u>, takes) a lot ~~of concentration~~.

PRACTICE 8: Apply Fill in each blank in the following sentences with a present-tense verb that agrees with its subject. Avoid *is* and *are*. Cross out the prepositional phrases first.   *Answers will vary.*

1. Music and film _____ the senses ~~with pleasure~~.

2. Either Omaha or Milwaukee _____ our choice ~~for a weekend trip~~.

3. Ice cream and cake _____ me happy ~~after a stressful day~~.

4. Neither my checkbook nor my credit cards _____ me out of debt when I have no money.

5. Teachers and counselors _____ the influence they have ~~over their students~~.

PRACTICE 9: Write Your Own Write a sentence of your own for each of the following compound subjects. Make sure your subjects and verbs agree.   *Answers will vary.*

1. either the memo or the reports

_____

2. jeans and coats

_____

3. neither Jim nor Belinda

_____

4. the mother and her baby girl

_____

5. mashed potatoes and gravy

_____

VERBS BEFORE SUBJECTS

When the subject follows its verb, the subject may be hard to find, which makes the process of agreeing subjects and verbs difficult. Subjects come after verbs in two particular situations—when the sentence begins with *Here* or *There* and when a question begins with *Who, What, Where, When, Why,* or *How.* Here are some examples:

Verb Before Subject: Here **are** the **decorations** ~~for the party~~.

Verb Before Subject: There **is iced tea** ~~in the refrigerator~~.

In sentences that begin with *here* or *there,* the verb always comes before the subject. Don't forget to cross out prepositional phrases to help you identify the subject. One of the words that's left will be the subject, and then you can check that the verb agrees with it.

                                      v   s

Verb Before Subject: Who **is** that **woman** ~~in red~~?

                                   v   s

Verb Before Subject: Where **are** the application **forms?**

                        v   s   v

Split Verb: What time **are you leaving** ~~for school~~?

In questions that begin with *Who, What, When, Where, Why,* and *How,* the verb comes before the subject, as in the first two examples, or is split by the subject, as in the last example.

Reviewing Verbs Before Subjects
Where will you find the verb in sentences that begin with **Here** *or* **There?**
Before the subject

> *Where will you find the verb in questions that begin with Who,*
> *What, Where, When, Why, and How?*
>
> *Before the subject* _____

PRACTICE 10: Recall/Identify Underline the subject once and the verb twice
in each of the following sentences. Cross out the prepositional phrases first.

1. Where is the speaker ~~for tonight's program~~?

2. There are scholarships available ~~for next year~~.

3. Who was the winner ~~of the Penn State–Purdue game~~?

4. Here comes the judge ~~with his briefcase~~.

5. Where is the best place ~~for our volleyball game~~?

PRACTICE 11: Apply Fill in each blank in the following sentences with a
verb that agrees with its subject. Cross out the prepositional phrases first.
Answers will vary.

1. What _____ that strange noise ~~in the basement~~?

2. There _____ several reasons ~~for staying in school~~.

3. Why _____ Michelle so quiet?

4. Here _____ the tree I planted ~~on Mother's Day~~.

5. When _____ he _____ smoking?

PRACTICE 12: Write Your Own Write a sentence of your own for each of the
following words and phrases. Make sure your subjects and verbs agree.
Answers will vary.

1. Here is _____

2. There are _____

3. Who made _____

4. How did you _____

5. When were _____

COLLECTIVE NOUNS

Collective nouns name a group of people or things. Examples include
such nouns as *army, audience, band, class, committee, crew, crowd, fam-*
ily, flock, gang, jury, majority, minority, orchestra, senate, team, and *troop.*

Collective nouns can be singular or plural. They are singular when they refer to a group as a single unit. They are plural when they refer to the individual actions or feelings of the group members.

                                  s   v

Singular: The marching **band plays** ~~at all home games~~.

Band refers to the entire unit or group. Therefore, it requires the singular verb *plays*.

                                  s   v

Plural: The marching **band get** their new uniforms today.

Here *band* refers to the individual members, who will each get a new uniform, so the plural verb *get* is used.

> ### Reviewing Collective Nouns
>
> **When is a collective noun singular?**
>
> *When it refers to a group as a single unit*
>
> _____
>
> **When is a collective noun plural?**
>
> *When it refers to the individual actions or feelings of the group members*
>
> _____

PRACTICE 13: Recall/Identify Underline the correct verb in each of the following sentences. Cross out the prepositional phrases first.

1. The crew (is, <u>are</u>) talking ~~to their loved ones on the phone~~.

2. The minority (<u>is</u>, are) still a vocal group.

3. The family (was, <u>were</u>) watching TV, eating, and sleeping when the fire alarm began screaming.

4. The class (feels, <u>feel</u>) proud ~~of raising enough money for a field~~ trip.

5. The carnival troupe (<u>performs</u>, perform) ~~in the spring~~.

PRACTICE 14: Apply Fill in each blank in the following sentences with a present-tense verb that agrees with its subject. Cross out the prepositional phrases first.
Answers will vary.

1. The audience always _____ their seats when the show starts.

2. The school band _____ old favorites when they perform on ~~Saturday~~.

3. Our team _____ wearing their letter sweaters.

4. Our committee _____ people who take action immediately.

5. A group ~~of tourists~~ _____ arriving ~~at noon~~.

PRACTICE 15: Write Your Own   Write a sentence of your own using each of the following words as a plural subject. Make sure that your subjects and verbs agree.   *Answers will vary.*

1. committee _____

2. team _____

3. family _____

4. jury _____

5. audience _____

INDEFINITE PRONOUNS

Indefinite pronouns do not refer to anyone or anything specific. Some indefinite pronouns are always singular, and some are always plural. A few can be either singular or plural, depending on the other words in the sentence. When an indefinite pronoun is the subject of a sentence, the verb must agree with the pronoun. Here is a list of indefinite pronouns:

Indefinite Pronouns

ALWAYS SINGULAR		ALWAYS PLURAL	EITHER SINGULAR OR PLURAL
another	*neither*	*both*	*all*
anybody	*nobody*	*few*	*any*
anyone	*none*	*many*	*more*
anything	*no one*	*others*	*most*
each	*nothing*	*several*	*some*
either	*one*		
everybody	*other*		
everyone	*somebody*		
everything	*someone*		
little	*something*		
much			

Singular: **No one answers** the phone when a customer calls.

    Everybody simply **listens** to the ringing phone.

Plural: **Many get** up and **walk** away.

    Others remain seated, tired, and unmotivated.

The pronouns that can be either singular or plural are singular when they refer to singular words and plural when they refer to plural words.

Singular: **Some** of Lamar's time **was** spent daydreaming.

Some is singular because it refers to *time*, which is singular. The singular verb *was* agrees with the singular subject *some*.

Plural: **Some** of Lamar's friends **were** late.

Some is plural because it refers to *friends*, which is plural. The plural verb *were* agrees with the plural subject *some*.

Reviewing Indefinite Pronouns

What is an indefinite pronoun?

A pronoun that doesn't refer to anyone or anything specific

When are all, any, more, most, and some singular or plural?

They are singular when they refer to singular words and plural when they refer to plural words.

PRACTICE 16: Recall/Identify Underline the verb that agrees with its subject in each of the following sentences. Cross out the prepositional phrases first.

1. ~~Of all the guests,~~ none (<u>was</u>, were) dressed appropriately.

2. Someone (sneak, <u>sneaks</u>) ~~into my room~~ while I am gone.

3. Some never (<u>seem</u>, seems) to learn ~~from their own mistakes.~~

4. In reference to the candidates, any who wish to apply for the job (need, needs) to fill out an application.

5. Somebody always (take, takes) Tabitha to lunch on Wednesdays.

PRACTICE 17: Apply Fill in each blank in the following sentences with a present-tense verb that agrees with its subject. Cross out the prepositional phrases first.   *Answers will vary.*

1. No one _____ he's innocent of the crime.

2. Each of the oranges _____ spoiled.

3. None of the cars _____ power windows or a rear window defroster.

4. Only a few of the senior employees _____ three weeks of vacation a year.

5. Most of my supply _____ gone.

PRACTICE 18: Write Your Own Write sentences of your own using each of the following words as a subject, combined with one of the following verbs: *is, are, was, were.* Make sure your subjects and verbs agree.   *Answers will vary.*

1. another _____

2. both _____

3. others _____

4. each _____

5. none _____

CHAPTER REVIEW

Students often have a hard time with **Subject-Verb Agreement** when it comes to compound, indefinite, and collective nouns. Going over this in class before the students complete the topic is helpful.

MyWritingLab   **Reviewing Subject-Verb Agreement**

To review this material before you complete the Review Practices, watch **Animation: Subject-Verb Agreement** at **MyWritingLab.com** one more time. This time, keep the video open as you complete the rest of the practices in this chapter. For best results, do the **MyWritingLab** exercises online as well as the Chapter Review practices in the book.

REVIEW PRACTICE 1A: Recall/Identify Underline the subject once and the verb twice in each of the following sentences. Cross out the prepositional phrases first. Then put an X to the left of each sentence in which the subject and verb do not agree.

1. _____ The orchestra ~~with new instruments~~ gets paid every Tuesday.

2. _____ Here are all the pieces ~~to the puzzle~~.

3. __X__ Neither the cheese nor the vegetables was fresh. *(were)*

4. _____ The class ~~down the hall~~ is studying math.

5. _____ Anyone ~~with questions~~ can speak ~~to the manager~~.

6. __X__ Why have that team ~~of dancers~~ left the show early? *(has left)*

7. __X__ Peanut butter and honey, when mixed together, are wonderful on ~~crackers~~. *(is)*

8. __X__ The cat and the duck ~~on my uncle's farm~~ makes an unlikely pair. *(make)*

9. _____ What is that flock ~~of birds~~ doing ~~on our tree~~?

10. __X__ There are most ~~of the water from the flood~~. *(is)*

REVIEW PRACTICE 1B: Correct Correct the subjects and verbs that don't agree in Review Practice 1A by rewriting the incorrect sentences. *See Review Practice 1A.*

MyWritingLab | **Practicing Subject-Verb Agreement**

Now complete the **Recall** activities for **Subject-Verb Agreement** in the **Sentence Skills** module of **MyWritingLab.com.** Remember to read the answers carefully because many of them look similar.

REVIEW PRACTICE 2: Apply Fill in each blank in the following sentences with a present-tense verb that agrees with its subject. *Answers will vary.*

1. Despite their ages, Angelica and Cindy _____ playing with each other at school.

2. The family with the most children _____ always seated first.

3. How _____ the levers and pulleys work?

4. Some of your apples _____ ripe.

5. Neither the curtains nor the comforter _____ the paint in the room.

MyWritingLab   **Practicing Subject-Verb Agreement**

Next, complete the **Apply** activity for **Subject-Verb Agreement** in the **Sentence Skills** module of **MyWritingLab.com.** Pay close attention to the directions and only click on what you're asked to.

⚙️—**Complete** this **Writing Prompt** at **mywritinglab.com**

REVIEW PRACTICE 3: Write Your Own Write a paragraph about an experience you have had participating on a team or observing a team. This could be in athletics, at work, in a club, at home, or at church.   *Answers will vary.*

MyWritingLab   **Practicing Subject-Verb Agreement**

For more practice, complete the **Write** activity for **Subject-Verb Agreement** in the **Sentence Skills** module of **MyWritingLab.com.** Make sure to pay close attention to which subjects and verbs do not agree.

REVIEW PRACTICE 4: Editing Through Collaboration Exchange paragraphs from Review Practice 3 with another student, and do the following: *Answers will vary.*

1. Underline the subject once in each sentence.

2. Underline the verbs twice.

3. Put an X by any verbs that do not agree with their subjects.

Then return the paper to its writer, and use the information in this chapter to correct any subject-verb agreement errors in your own paragraph. Record your errors on the Error Log in Appendix 7.

More on Verbs

Label each sentence I if the verb tenses are inconsistent or P if the sentence uses the passive voice.

- _____ When my brother won the gold medal, my father looks very proud.
- _____ All new employees are trained by a professional.
- _____ The child was saved by the firefighters.
- _____ My friend got home early, so we go to the movies.
- _____ The student was given the answers in advance.

(Answers are in Appendix 3.)

UNIT PRE-TESTS
To check your students' abilities with the collective skills in this unit, two Unit Pre-tests are available in the *Instructor's Resource Manual.*

Verbs communicate the action and time of each sentence. So it is important that you use verb tense consistently. Also, you should strive to write in the active, not the passive, voice. This chapter provides help with both of these sentence skills.

MyWritingLab Understanding More on Verbs

To learn more about verbs, go to **MyWritingLab.com,** and choose **Consistent Verb Tense and Active Voice** in the **Sentence Skills** module. From there, watch the video called **Animation: Active and Passive Voice.** Then, return to this chapter, which will go into more detail on verbs and give you opportunities to practice them. Finally, you will apply your understanding of verbs to your own writing.

Student Comment:
"This video on **Active and Passive Voice** helped me understand verbs better because they were fresh in my mind when I went back to write my papers. No more verb errors for me!"

TEACHING MORE ON VERBS
Create a short paragraph with inconsistent tenses. You might use words like *today* and *yesterday* to help create confusion. For example, "I am studying today for the hardest final I have ever taken. I had been studying for over two weeks, and I still will not feel like I'm prepared. The test was given tomorrow."

Have students rewrite the paragraph three times, once for each tense—past, present, and future. Make sure they adjust all words to indicate the correct time (for example, use *today* with the present and *yesterday* with the past).

INSTRUCTOR'S RESOURCE MANUAL
For more sample paragraphs, for more exercises, and for quizzes, see the *Instructor's Resource Manual*, Section II, Part IV.

UNIT POST-TESTS
To check your students' mastery of the collective skills in this unit, two Unit Post-tests are available in the *Instructor's Resource Manual*.

CONSISTENT VERB TENSE

Verb tense refers to the time an action takes place—in the present, the past, or the future. The verb tenses in a sentence should be consistent. That is, if you start out using one tense, you should not switch tenses unless absolutely necessary. Switching tenses can be confusing. Here are some examples:

                                Present
NOT   When the sun **sits** high in the sky, and the cloud
            Present   Past
            cover **is** just right, we **saw** the water glistening.

                                Present
Correct: When the sun **sits** high in the sky and the cloud
            Present   Present
            cover **is** just right, we **see** the water glistening.

                      Past
NOT   They **climbed** Mt. Shasta last week when the
            Present
            snowfall **is** heavy.

                      Past
Correct: They **climbed** Mt. Shasta last week when the
            Past
            snowfall **was** heavy.

                                Future
NOT   The astronauts **will finish** training this week, and then
            Present
            they **lead** the first mission to Saturn.

                                Future
Correct: The astronauts **will finish** training this week, and then
            Future
            they **will lead** the first mission to Saturn.

Reviewing Consistent Verb Tenses

Why should verb tenses be consistent?

Because time should be consistent within a sentence

What problem do inconsistent verb tenses create?

Inconsistent verb tenses can be confusing for the reader.

PRACTICE 1A: Recall/Identify In the following sentences, write C if the verb tense is consistent or I if it is inconsistent.

1. ___I___ The explorers will be leaving early in the morning and returned late at night.

2. ___I___ My dogs, Zak and Apollo, enjoy a day at the park and will love to play on the beach.

3. ___C___ Explaining the assignments to my sick roommate was hard, and it tried my patience.

4. ___I___ The summer movies looked interesting but will be big disappointments.

5. ___I___ The game was won with brute strength and is fun to watch.

PRACTICE 1B: Correct Correct the verb-tense errors in Practice 1A by re-writing the inconsistent sentences. *Answers will vary.*

PRACTICE 2: Apply Fill in each blank in the following sentences with consistent verbs. *Answers will vary.*

1. The stores _____ many sales and _____ a lot of money.

2. Most people _____ comedies and _____ tragedies.

3. Most people _____ forward to vacations because they _____ to rest.

4. Students _____ hard before they _____ final exams.

5. Samantha _____ her bike and _____ a scooter.

PRACTICE 3: Write Your Own Write five sentences of your own with at least two verbs in each. Make sure your tenses are consistent. *Answers will vary.*

_____

_____

_____

_____

_____

USING THE ACTIVE VOICE

In the **active voice,** the subject performs the action. In the **passive voice,** the subject receives the action. Compare the following two examples:

Passive Voice: The employees **were charged** with disturbing the peace **by the police.**

Active Voice: The **police charged** the employees with disturbing the peace.

The active voice adds energy to your writing. Here is another example. Notice the difference between active and passive.

Passive Voice: The water **was boiled** for the pasta **by Carmen.**

Active Voice: **Carmen boiled** the water for the pasta.

Reviewing Active and Passive Voice

What is the difference between the active and passive voice?

In the active voice, the subject performs the action. In the passive voice, the subject receives the action.

Why is the active voice usually better than the passive?

Because it adds energy to your writing

PRACTICE 4A: Recall/Identify Write A if the sentence is in the active voice and P if it is in the passive voice.

1. __P__ The mail was opened by Sarah.

2. __A__ Albert and Walter are sending flowers to their girlfriends.

3. __P__ My purse was stolen by someone!

4. __A__ The judge sentenced the criminals to serve five years.

5. __A__ I would like to walk on the beach with you.

PRACTICE 4B: Correct Rewrite the passive sentences in Practice 4A in the active voice.   *Answers will vary.*

PRACTICE 5: Apply Complete the following sentences in the active voice. *Answers will vary.*

1. Many styles of jeans _____.

2. A can of Coke _____.

3. A bowl of beans _____.

4. A vacation _____.

5. The baseball _____.

PRACTICE 6: Write Your Own Write five sentences in the passive voice. Then rewrite them in the active voice. *Answers will vary.*

_____

_____

_____

_____

_____

CHAPTER REVIEW

MyWritingLab **Reviewing More on Verbs**

To review this material before you complete the Review Practices, watch **Animation: Active and Passive Voice** at **MyWritingLab.com** one more time. This time, keep the video open as you complete the rest of the practices in this chapter. For best results, do the **MyWritingLab** exercises online as well as the Chapter Review practices in the book.

Remind students that clicking "Hint" will give them helpful information about an exercise.

REVIEW PRACTICE 1: Recall/Identify Label each sentence I if the verb tenses are inconsistent, P if the sentence is in the passive voice, or C if the sentence is correct. Then revise the inconsistent and passive sentences by rewriting them. *Corrections will vary.*

1. __P__ All of the chocolate doughnuts have been eaten by José.

2. __I__ Mr. Johnson walks five miles every day but has eaten whatever he likes.

3. __P__ The children were read to by Grandma Ginny.

4. ___P___ The lawns and gardens have always been groomed by Mr. Shultz, our gardener.

5. ___I___ The blue team raced down the hill, jumped the hurdles in their path, and then will cross the finish line.

6. ___I___ I love anything made with chocolate, but I will dislike the taste of mocha.

7. ___C___ Paul listens to classical music, particularly Beethoven.

8. ___I___ We quickly called home to see if we had any messages, and then were rushing back to the meeting.

9. ___C___ My dad bought a new car with the money he won on a TV game show.

10. ___I___ In her spare time, my Aunt Juaquita volunteers at the local animal shelter and also helped cook meals for the homeless shelter.

MyWritingLab **Practicing More on Verbs**

Now complete the **Recall** activities for **Consistent Verb Tense and Active Voice** in the **Sentence Skills** module of **MyWritingLab.com.** If you're having a difficult time with a question, open up the video in the lower right-hand corner for some help.

REVIEW PRACTICE 2: Apply Fill in each blank with consistent, active verbs.
Answers will vary.

1. Cheyenne always _____ the heat in summer and _____ the cold in winter.

2. The Key Club at our school _____ a bake sale and _____ all the money to charity.

3. The award-winning racehorse _____ through its routine.

4. Evan _____ to visit Tony in Las Vegas, but he _____ after only two days.

5. The soup for our dinner _____ on the stove.

 **Practicing More on Verbs**

Next, complete the **Apply** activity for **Consistent Verb Tense and Active Voice** in the **Sentence Skills** module of **MyWritingLab.com**. If you're stuck, you can click on the hint button.

⚙️—Complete this **Writing Prompt** at **mywritinglab.com**

REVIEW PRACTICE 3: Write Your Own Write a paragraph about your favorite college course. What do you like most about it? Why is it your favorite? Stay in the present tense, and use the active voice. *Answers will vary.*

MyWritingLab **Practicing More on Verbs**

For more practice, complete the **Write** activity for **Consistent Verb Tense and Active Voice** in the **Sentence Skills** module of **MyWritingLab.com**. Make sure to pay close attention to the use of active voice and verb tense consistency.

REVIEW PRACTICE 4: Editing Through Collaboration Exchange paragraphs from Review Practice 3 with another student, and do the following: *Answers will vary.*

1. Circle all verbs that are not consistent in tense.

2. Underline any verbs in the passive voice.

Then return the paper to its writer, and use the information in this chapter to correct any verb consistency or voice errors in your own paragraph. Record your errors on the Error Log in Appendix 7.

Pronouns

Pronouns generally go almost unnoticed in writing and speaking, even though these words can do anything nouns can do. In fact, much like your inborn sense of balance, pronouns work in sentences to make your writing precise and coherent. Without pronouns, writers and speakers would find themselves repeating nouns over and over, producing sentences that are unnatural and boring. For example, notice how awkward the following paragraph is without pronouns:

Robert wrote a rough draft of Robert's essay last night. Then Robert asked Robert's girlfriend to read over Robert's essay with Robert. After Robert's girlfriend helped Robert find errors, Robert made corrections. Then Robert set aside the essay for a day before Robert took the essay out and began revising again.

When we let pronouns take over and do their jobs, we produce a much more fluent paragraph:

Robert wrote a rough draft of his essay last night. Then he asked his girlfriend to read over his essay with him. After she helped Robert find errors, he made corrections. Then he set aside the essay for a day before he took it out and began revising again.

Problems with pronouns occur when the words pronouns refer to aren't clear or when pronouns and their antecedents—the words they refer to too far apart. In this unit, we will deal with the following aspects of pronouns:

Chapter 27: Pronoun Problems
Chapter 28: Pronoun Reference and Point of View
Chapter 29: Pronoun Agreement

Pronoun Problems

TEST YOURSELF

Correct the pronoun errors in the following sentences.

- The toy was hers' to begin with.
- Diego told Megan and I the funniest story.
- He can run a lot faster than me.
- Those there ballet shoes are Laura's.
- Ted and me are going to the game tonight.

(Answers are in Appendix 3.)

UNIT PRE-TESTS
To check your students' abilities with the collective skills in this unit, two Unit Pre-tests are available in the *Instructor's Resource Manual.*

Pronouns are words that take the place of nouns. They help us avoid repeating nouns. In this chapter, we'll discuss five types of pronoun problems: (1) using the wrong pronoun as a subject, (2) using the wrong pronoun as an object, (3) using an apostrophe with a possessive pronoun, (4) misusing pronouns in comparisons, and (5) misusing demonstrative pronouns.

MyWritingLab **Understanding Pronoun Problems**

To help you understand this topic, go to **MyWritingLab.com,** and choose **Pronoun Case** in the **Sentence Skills** module. For this topic, watch the video called **Animation: Pronoun Case.** Then, return to this chapter, which will go into more detail about pronouns and give you opportunities to practice them. Finally, you will apply your understanding of pronoun case to your own writing.

Student Comment:
"With **MyWritingLab,** I can try the exercises as many times as possible and not feel stupid."

TEACHING PRONOUN
PROBLEMS
Divide students into
groups of three or four,
and provide them with a
paragraph that has several
pronoun errors. Here is an
example:
   Mine brother can be so
selfish. He has difficulty
sharing. He believes that
these here books are only
to be read by he or that
them there clothes are only
for he to wear. He was
always more selfish than
me. I always loved to share
my stuff with others. You
would not even believe he
had the same parents as me
because him is so selfish.
I hope someday someone
teaches him about the art
of sharing.
   Ask students to correct
all the pronoun errors in
the paragraph.
   The first group to
correct all the pronoun
errors wins.

INSTRUCTOR'S
RESOURCE MANUAL
For more sample
paragraphs, for more
exercises, and for quizzes,
see the *Instructor's*
Resource Manual,
Section II, Part IV.

UNIT POST-TESTS
To check your students'
mastery of the collective
skills in this unit, two Unit
Post-tests are available in
the *Instructor's Resource*
Manual.

PRONOUNS AS SUBJECTS

Single pronouns as subjects usually don't cause problems.

Subject Pronoun:	**I** went to the movies with Jamie.
Subject Pronoun:	**They** moved to San Francisco.

You wouldn't say "*Me* went to the movies" or "*Them* moved to San Francisco." But an error often occurs when a sentence has a compound subject and one or more of the subjects is a pronoun.

NOT	**The Cardinals** and **us** tied for first place.
Correct:	**The Cardinals** and **we** tied for first place.

NOT	**Him** and **me** will wait on the porch.
Correct:	**He** and **I** will wait on the porch.

To test whether you have used the correct form of the pronoun in a compound subject, try each subject alone:

Subject Pronoun?	**The Cardinals** and **us** tied for first place.
Test:	**The Cardinals** tied for first place. **YES**
Test:	**Us** tied for first place. **NO**
Test:	**We** tied for first place. **YES**
Correction:	**The Cardinals** and **we** tied for first place.

Here is a list of subject pronouns:

Subject Pronouns

SINGULAR	PLURAL
I	*we*
you	*you*
he, she, it	*they*

Reviewing Pronouns as Subjects

Name two subject pronouns.

Answers will include two of the following: I, you, he, she, it, we, or they.

How can you test whether you are using the correct pronoun as the subject of a sentence?

Try each subject separately in its own sentence.

PRACTICE 1: Recall/Identify Underline the pronouns used as subjects in each of the following sentences.

1. Her favorite china pattern was no longer made because <u>it</u> was over 50 years old.

2. Paul got his feet massaged since <u>he</u> had worked hard all week.

3. <u>We</u> figured that the machinery had a crack in it.

4. <u>They</u> played a game of baseball just for a charitable organization.

5. "Some days are better than others for them," <u>he</u> said.

PRACTICE 2: Apply Fill in each blank in the following paragraph with a subject pronoun.

    Ron and Selma love to ride their bikes early in the morning. Selma bikes for pleasure, so _____*she*_____ rides in the countryside. On the other hand, Ron plans to race in competitions, so _____*he*_____ often bikes at the local university's track. Sometimes, however, _____*they*_____ bike together in the city. _____*It*_____ gives them a chance to visit each other. Personally, _____*I*_____ think it's wonderful that they have an interest in common.

PRACTICE 3: Write Your Own Write a sentence of your own for each of the following subject pronouns.   *Answers will vary.*

1. I _____

2. you _____

3. we _____

4. it _____

5. he _____

PRONOUNS AS OBJECTS

    One of the most frequent pronoun errors is using a subject pronoun when the sentence calls for an object pronoun. The sentence may require an object after a verb, showing that someone or something receives the action of the verb. Or it may be an object of a preposition that is required (see page 370 for a list of prepositions).

NOT	She invited Bob and **I** to dinner.
Correct:	She invited Bob and **me** to dinner.

NOT	This is between you and **I.**
Correct:	This is between you and **me.**

Like the subject pronoun error, the object pronoun error usually occurs with compound objects. Also like the subject pronoun error, you can test whether you are using the correct pronoun by using each object separately.

Object Pronoun?	She invited **Bob and I** to dinner.
Test:	She invited **Bob** to dinner. **YES**
Test:	She invited **I** to dinner. **NO**
Test:	She invited **me** to dinner. **YES**
Correction:	She invited **Bob and me** to dinner.

Here is a list of object pronouns:

Object Pronouns

SINGULAR	PLURAL
me	*us*
you	*you*
him, her, it	*them*

Reviewing Pronouns as Objects

In what two places are pronouns used as objects?
After a verb or after a preposition

How can you test whether you have used the correct pronoun as the object in a sentence?
Try each object separately in its own sentence.

PRACTICE 4: Recall/Identify Underline the correct object pronoun in each of the following sentences.

1. Crystal accidentally hit (he, <u>him</u>) with the ping-pong ball.

2. She played the violin for (<u>us</u>, we).

3. The mischievous child spilled milk all over Dana and (I, <u>me</u>).

4. Her grandmother took (she, <u>her</u>) shopping for a prom dress.

5. Mary picked a bouquet of flowers for (<u>them</u>, they).

PRACTICE 5: Apply Fill in each blank in the following sentences with an object pronoun. *Answers will vary.*

1. Alyssa gave _____ a Valentine's Day card.

2. Beau, my dog, bit Tina on the leg, but he didn't hurt _____.

3. I bought something for _____.

4. Mickey Mouse gave _____ a tour of Disneyland.

5. My grandmother lent the family pearls for the wedding.

PRACTICE 6: Write Your Own Write a sentence of your own for each of the following object pronouns. *Answers will vary.*

1. me _____

2. him _____

3. us _____

4. them _____

5. her _____

POSSESSIVE PRONOUNS

   Possessive pronouns show ownership (*my* wallet, *his* suitcase, *our* trip). (See page 365 for a list of pronouns.) An apostrophe is used with nouns to show ownership (*Tara's* car, the *clock's* hands, the *children's* toys). But an apostrophe is never used with possessive pronouns.

Possessive Pronouns

SINGULAR	PLURAL
my, mine	*our, ours*
your, yours	*you, yours*
his, her, hers	*their, theirs*

| NOT | That hairbrush is **hers'**. |
| Correct: | That hairbrush is **hers**. |

| NOT | The umbrella by the door is **your's**. |
| Correct: | The umbrella by the door is **yours**. |

| NOT | The puppy wanted **its'** tummy scratched. |
| Correct: | The puppy wanted **its** tummy scratched. |

Reviewing Possessive Pronouns

When do you use an apostrophe with a noun?

An apostrophe is used to show ownership with a noun.

Do possessive pronouns take apostrophes?

No, possessive pronouns never take apostrophes.

PRACTICE 7: Recall/Identify Underline the correct possessive pronoun in each of the following sentences.

1. Krista gave <u>her</u> hair and clothes a quick pat.

2. The Corvette needs <u>its</u> windshield fixed.

3. I believe that book on the dresser is <u>yours</u>.

4. <u>Their</u> bikes were left unattended, so they were stolen.

5. That dog should have <u>its</u> nails trimmed.

PRACTICE 8: Apply Fill in each blank in the following sentences with a possessive pronoun. *Answers will vary.*

1. _____ vacation to Mexico was fun and exciting, but not so relaxing.

2. The games are _____.

3. The grandfather clock is broken, but _____ face is still in good condition.

4. _____ sister makes the best chocolate fudge cake.

5. The dogs performing in the circus are _____.

PRACTICE 9: Write Your Own Write a sentence of your own for each of the following **possessive pronouns.** *Answers will vary.*

1. mine _____

2. her _____

3. its _____

4. our _____

5. theirs _____

PRONOUNS IN COMPARISONS

Sometimes pronoun problems occur in comparisons with *than* or *as.* An object pronoun may be mistakenly used instead of a subject pronoun. To find out if you are using the right pronoun, you should finish the sentence as shown here.

NOT	She can run a mile much faster than **me.**
Correct:	She can run a mile much faster than **I** [can run a mile].

NOT	Paula is not as good a cook as **him.**
Correct:	Paula is not as good a cook as **he** [is].

Hint: Sometimes an object pronoun is required in a *than* or *as* comparison. But errors rarely occur in this case because the subject pronoun sounds so unnatural.

NOT	Susan likes him more than she likes **I.**
Correct:	Susan likes him more than she likes **me.**

Reviewing Pronouns in Comparisons

What causes pronoun problems in comparisons?

Problems can occur when an object pronoun is mistakenly used instead of a subject pronoun.

How can you test whether to use a subject pronoun or an object pronoun in a than *or* as *comparison?*

Finish the sentence to test whether to use a subject pronoun or an object pronoun.

PRACTICE 10: Recall/Identify Underline the correct pronoun in each of the following comparisons.

1. Brenda can sew better than (<u>she</u>, her).

2. The kittens are much friskier than (<u>they</u>, them).

3. Martha isn't as outspoken as (<u>she</u>, her).

4. She is nicer to her friends than to (I, <u>me</u>).

5. My husband can fix a car as well as (him, <u>he</u>).

PRACTICE 11: Apply Fill in each blank in the following sentences with an appropriate pronoun for comparison.   *Answers will vary.*

1. Because Lupe grew up on a ranch, she is more relaxed around horses than _____.

2. She is a more accurate proofreader than _____.

3. Robert is just as smart as _____.

4. He makes you just as crazy as he makes _____.

5. Those girls ate more food than _____ did.

PRACTICE 12: Write Your Own Write a sentence of your own using each of the following pronouns in *than* or *as* comparisons.   *Answers will vary.*

1. I _____

2. we _____

3. he _____

4. she _____

5. they _____

DEMONSTRATIVE PRONOUNS

There are four demonstrative pronouns: *this*, *that*, *these*, and *those*. **Demonstrative pronouns** point to specific people or objects. Use *this* and *these* to refer to items that are near and *that* and *those* to refer to items farther away. Look at the following examples.

Demonstrative (near):   **This** tastes great.

Demonstrative (near):   **These** are delicious peaches.

Demonstrative (farther):   **That** will be decided later.

Demonstrative (farther):   **Those** are the clothes she brought with her.

Sometimes demonstrative pronouns are not used correctly.

NOT	Correct
this here, that there	this, that
these here, these ones	these
them, those there, those ones	those

NOT	**Them** are the boots she wants.
Correct:	**Those** are the boots she wants.

NOT	I'd like to order **these here** pictures.
Correct:	I'd like to order **these** pictures.

NOT	I made **those ones** by hand.
Correct:	I made **those** by hand.

NOT	**Those there** are the ones I ordered.
Correct:	**Those** are the ones I ordered.

When demonstrative pronouns are used with nouns, they become adjectives.

Pronoun:	**This** is his.
Adjective:	**This notebook** is his.

Pronoun:	**Those** are words you may regret.
Adjective:	You may regret **those words.**

The problems that occur with demonstrative pronouns can also occur when these pronouns act as adjectives.

NOT	Please hand me **that there** hammer.
Correct:	Please hand me **that** hammer.

Reviewing Demonstrative Pronouns

Name the four demonstrative pronouns.

this   that

these   those

Give two examples of errors with demonstrative pronouns.

Students should choose two from this here, that there, them, these here,

these ones, those there, and those ones.

PRACTICE 13A: Recall/Identify Underline the demonstrative pronoun errors in each of the following sentences.

1. <u>These here</u> dishes are dirty and those need to be put away. *(These)*

2. Yes, <u>these ones</u> can be taken back to the warehouse. *(these)*

3. <u>Them</u> classes are the hardest I have ever taken. *(These)*

4. I decided <u>those ones</u> will do nicely for the game. *(those)*

5. <u>That there</u> belongs to the girl waiting in line. *(That)*

PRACTICE 13B: Correct Correct the demonstrative pronoun errors in Practice 13A by rewriting the incorrect sentences. *See Practice 13A.*

PRACTICE 14: Apply Fill in each blank in the following sentences with a logical demonstrative pronoun.

1. Later on today, _____*this/that*_____ will be answered.

2. When seen from up close, _____*this/that*_____ looks quite large.

3. _____*These/those*_____ are the best seats in the house.

4. _____*These/those*_____ should be displayed in the window.

5. Mary had never seen any of _____*these/those*_____ before.

PRACTICE 15: Write Your Own Write four sentences of your own, one using each demonstrative pronoun. Be sure you don't use these pronouns as adjectives in your sentences. *Answers will vary.*

CHAPTER REVIEW

Remind students that they can save their work in the Apply exercise and come back to it later.

MyWritingLab   **Reviewing Pronoun Problems**

To review this material before you complete the Review Practices, watch **Animation: Pronoun Case** at **MyWritingLab.com** one more time. This time, keep the video open as you complete the rest of the practices in this chapter. For best results, do the **MyWritingLab** exercises online as well as the Chapter Review practices in the book.

REVIEW PRACTICE 1: Recall/Identify Underline the pronoun errors in each of the following sentences.

1. The ring is hers'.   *(hers)*

2. Ours' is the best short story out of those.   *(Ours)*

3. He is a better singer than me.   *(I)*

4. These here are our cars, which are expected to sell.   *(These)*

5. The children and us went for a Sunday drive in his new convertible.   *(we)*

6. Those ones may be out of fashion, but she still wears them.   *(Those)*

7. Her brother can play ball better than him.   *(he)*

8. Geoffrey used all of your art supplies when he drew a picture for she.   *(her)*

9. My little brother begged to go to the mall with Sarah and I.   *(me)*

10. This here is the car Mary thinks he should buy.   *(This)*

MyWritingLab **Practicing Pronoun Problems**

Now complete the **Recall** activities for **Pronoun Case** in the **Sentence Skills** module of **MyWritingLab.com.** Remember to read the answers carefully because many of them look similar.

REVIEW PRACTICE 2: Apply Correct the pronoun errors in Review Practice 1 by rewriting the incorrect sentences.   *See Review Practice 1.*

MyWritingLab **Practicing Pronoun Problems**

Next, complete the **Apply** activity for **Pronoun Case** in the **Sentence Skills** module of **MyWritingLab.com.** Remember that spelling counts.

⚙•[**Complete** this **Writing Prompt** at **mywritinglab.com**

REVIEW PRACTICE 3: Write Your Own Write a paragraph about the town you grew up in. What is one vivid memory you have of this place?   *Answers will vary.*

 **Practicing Pronoun Problems**

For more practice, complete the **Write** activity for **Pronoun Case** in the **Sentence Skills** module of **MyWritingLab.com.** Make sure to pay close attention to the case of all the pronouns.

REVIEW PRACTICE 4: Editing Through Collaboration Exchange paragraphs from Review Practice 3 with another student, and do the following: *Answers will vary.*

1. Circle all pronouns.

2. Put an X through any that are not in the correct form. Check that all the subject and object pronouns are used correctly. Also check that possessive pronouns, pronouns used in comparisons, and demonstrative pronouns are used correctly.

Then return the paper to its writer, and use the information in this chapter to correct the pronoun errors in your own paragraph. Record your errors on the Error Log in Appendix 7.

Pronoun Reference and Point of View

UNIT PRE-TESTS
To check your students' abilities with the collective skills in this unit, two Unit Pre-tests are available in the *Instructor's Resource Manual.*

TEST YOURSELF

Underline the pronouns in these sentences. Then put an X over any pronouns that are confusing or unclear.

- Emily and Grace decided that she would try out for the team.
- They say you should drink eight glasses of water a day.
- I take the bus because you can save a lot of money that way.
- The reporter did not check her facts or talk to the main witness, which she regretted.
- It says to notify the dean if you are dropping a class.

(Answers are in Appendix 3.)

Anytime you use a pronoun, it must clearly refer to a specific word. The word it refers to is called its **antecedent.** Two kinds of problems occur with pronoun references: The antecedent may be unclear, or the antecedent may be missing. You should also be careful to stick to the same point of view in your writing. If, for example, you start out talking about "I," you should not shift to "you" in the middle of the sentence.

MyWritingLab

Understanding Pronoun Reference and Point of View

To learn more about these pronoun features, go to **MyWritingLab.com**, and choose **Pronoun Reference and Point of View** in the **Sentence Skills** module. Next, watch the video called **Animation: Pronoun**

Student Comment:
"**MyWritingLab** along with **Mosaics** and help from my instructor really provided me with the ability to be a better writer."

Reference and Point of View. Then, return to this chapter, which will go into more detail about these topics and give you opportunities to practice them. Finally, you will apply your understanding of pronoun reference and point of view to your own writing.

PRONOUN REFERENCE

Sometimes a sentence is confusing because the reader can't tell what a pronoun is referring to. The confusion may occur because the pronoun's antecedent is unclear or is completely missing.

Unclear Antecedents

In the following examples, the word each pronoun is referring to is unclear.

Unclear: On the shelf, a camera sat next to a small tape recorder. As Mr. Crutcher reached for **it,** the shelf began to tip. (Was Mr. Crutcher reaching for the camera or the tape recorder? Only Mr. Crutcher knows for sure.)

Clear: On the shelf, a camera sat next to a small tape recorder. As Mr. Crutcher reached for **the camera,** the shelf began to tip.

Clear: On the shelf, a camera sat next to a small tape recorder. As Mr. Crutcher reached for **the tape recorder,** the shelf began to tip.

Unclear: Sarah agreed with April that **she** shouldn't get involved. (Does *she* refer to Sarah or April? Only the writer knows.)

Clear: Sarah agreed with April that **Sarah** shouldn't get involved.

Clear: Agreeing with April, **Sarah** vowed that **she** wouldn't get involved.

How can you be sure that every pronoun you use has a clear antecedent? First, you can proofread carefully. Probably an even better test, though, is to ask a friend to read what you have written and tell you if your meaning is clear or not.

Missing Antecedents

Every pronoun should have a clear antecedent, the word it refers to. But what happens when there is no antecedent at all? The writer's message is not communicated. Two words in particular should alert you to the possibility of missing antecedents: *it* and *they.*

The following sentences have missing antecedents:

skills in this unit, two Unit Post-tests are available in the *Instructor's Resource Manual.*

Missing Antecedent: In a recent study on teenage pregnancy, **it** says that counseling has a dramatically positive effect.
(What does *it* refer to? It has no antecedent.)

Clear: **A recent study on teenage pregnancy** says that counseling has a dramatically positive effect.

Missing Antecedent: **They** say that the early bird catches the worm.
(Who is *they?*)

Clear: **An old saying** claims that the early bird catches the worm.

Reviewing Pronoun Reference

What is an antecedent?

The word a pronoun refers to

How can you be sure every pronoun you use has a clear antecedent?

Proofread carefully, and ask a friend to read your writing and tell you if your

meaning is unclear.

What two words warn you that an antecedent may be missing?

it   they

PRACTICE 1A: Recall/Identify Underline the pronouns in each of the following sentences. Then put an X next to any sentences with missing or unclear antecedents.

1. _____ Five hot dog vendors were on the same street, and they were each trying to outsell the others.

2. __X__ The safety technician and the firefighter gave her speech in the park. *(their)*

3. __X__ Barbara's birthday and Sam's anniversary are coming soon; it is the same day as Valentine's Day. *(they are)*

4. __X__ In a recent study, it said, "Four times out of five, shoppers prefer Hallmark cards." *(A recent study said...)*

5. __X__ They say that most students have some debts. *(People)*

PRACTICE 1B: Correct Correct the sentences with pronoun errors in Practice 1A by rewriting them. *See Practice 1A.*

PRACTICE 2: Apply Correct the unclear or missing pronoun references in the following sentences by rewriting them. Pronouns that should be corrected are underlined. *Answers will vary.*

1. <u>It</u> says in the paper that tickets go on sale tomorrow.

2. I put the letters in my bag. Then I peeled an apple and an orange for a snack before I realized I hadn't addressed <u>them</u>.

3. Trish told Diana that <u>she</u> was going to have to move.

4. Mario told Lendel that <u>he</u> should go on a diet.

5. Both Pat and Danielle went to Mills College together. Then <u>she</u> finished her degree at the University of Maryland.

PRACTICE 3: Write Your Own Write five sentences of your own using pronouns with clear antecedents. *Answers will vary.*

_____

_____

_____

_____

_____

SHIFTING POINT OF VIEW

Point of view refers to whether a statement is made in the first person, the second person, or the third person. Each person—or point of view—requires different pronouns. The following chart lists the pronouns for each point of view.

Point of View

First Person:	*I, we*
Second Person:	*you, you*
Third Person:	*he, she, it, they*

If you begin writing from one point of view, you should stay in that point of view. Do not shift to another point of view. For example, if you start out writing "I," you should continue with "I" and not shift to "you." Shifting point of view is a very common error in college writing.

Shift:	If **a person** doesn't exercise regularly, **you** can lose flexibility and strength.
Correct:	If **a person** doesn't exercise regularly, **he or she** can lose flexibility and strength.

Shift:	**I** consulted a financial advisor because **you** can save money on interest payments.
Correct:	**I** consulted a financial advisor because **I** can save money on interest payments.

Reviewing Point of View

What is point of view?

Point of view refers to whether a statement is made in first, second, or third person.

What does it mean to shift point of view?

A shift occurs when a writer begins in one person and changes to another.

PRACTICE 4A: Recall/Identify Underline the pronouns that shift in point of view in the following sentences.

1. A person should avoid eating too much fat if you don't want to become overweight.   *(he or she doesn't)*

2. I think that the new tax laws should be revised because they are so complicated that you can't understand them.   *(people)*

3. Doctors must go to school for many years before they can practice medicine.

4. Since students have so little free time, you should always try to manage your time efficiently.   *(they, their)*

5. You should try to save money whenever you can because we never know when we might need it.   *(you, you)*

PRACTICE 4B: Correct Correct the point-of-view errors in Practice 4A by rewriting the incorrect sentences.   *See Practice 4A.*

PRACTICE 5: Apply Complete the following sentences with pronouns that stay in the same point of view.

1. I went shopping at the mall because I heard that _____*I*_____ could get some good bargains there.

2. A driver should always pay attention to others on the road if _____*he or she*_____ wants to avoid being in an accident.

3. The show was sold out so they checked the Internet since _____*they*_____ can usually find tickets for sale there.

4. If a person wants to make friends, _____*he or she*_____ should try to smile at others.

5. I always cook more than enough food for the picnic, for _____*I*_____ never know how many people will attend.

PRACTICE 6: Write Your Own Write a sentence of your own for each of the following pronouns. Be sure the pronouns have clear antecedents and do not shift point of view. *Answers will vary.*

1. you _____

2. they _____

3. we _____

4. it _____

5. them _____

CHAPTER REVIEW

If students are confused while completing the Recall/Apply activities, tell them they can watch the video while answering questions.

MyWritingLab

Reviewing Pronoun Reference and Point of View

To review this material before you complete the Review Practices, watch **Animation: Pronoun Reference and Point of View** at **MyWritingLab. com** one more time. This time, keep the video open as you complete the rest of the practices in this chapter. For best results, do the **MyWritingLab** exercises online as well as the Chapter Review practices in the book.

REVIEW PRACTICE 1: Recall/Identify Label the following sentences U if the antecedent is unclear, M if the antecedent is missing, or S if the sentence shifts point of view. Then correct the pronoun errors by rewriting the incorrect sentences.

1. ___S___ Alvin bought bananas, oranges, and apples at the store because you know fruit is healthy.

2. ___M___ They say a chef should train at home and abroad to be successful.

3. ___S___ You should hurry because we always need extra time.

4. ___U___ After my dog bit my neighbor's dog, he got sick.

5. ___M___ It is said that "every good dog deserves a bone."

6. ___U___ My mom often told my sister that she was a good dancer.

7. ___U___ Before Jan paints the garage and the house, she must clean it out.

8. ___S___ I drove to Cambria because you can really relax there.

9. ___M___ They tell me I should never walk down dark alleys alone.

10. ___U___ I watched a video on France since I have to write a report on it.

MyWritingLab

Practicing Pronoun Reference and Point of View

Now complete the **Recall** activities for **Pronoun Reference and Point of View** in the **Sentence Skills** module of **MyWritingLab.com.** Remember to read the answers carefully because many of them look similar.

REVIEW PRACTICE 2: Apply Correct the pronoun errors in the following sentences by rewriting each incorrect sentence. *Errors are underlined; answers will vary.*

1. Mary and Samantha are best friends, and she is my best friend too.

2. It is said that all people are created equal.

3. I am going to buy the most expensive dishwasher because you know that's the only way to get the best.

4. We have both chocolate and vanilla bon-bons, but it tastes better.

5. They believe that secondhand cigarette smoke can cause cancer.

6. I visited the animal shelter today since I believe you should always try to adopt a pet in need rather than one from a pet store.

7. Josephine and Yuki both went out tonight, but <u>she</u> didn't come home on time.

8. Shawn bought himself a hamburger, french fries, and a soda, but then left <u>it</u> sitting on the counter when he went to watch TV.

9. A person can always ask questions in this class, for how else are <u>you</u> going to learn the answers?

10. According to the statistics, <u>it</u> implies that a recession will soon hit our economy.

MyWritingLab

Practicing Pronoun Reference and Point of View

Next, complete the **Apply** activity for **Pronoun Reference and Point of View** in the **Sentence Skills** module of **MyWritingLab.com.** Pay close attention to the directions, and click only on what you're asked to.

Complete this **Writing Prompt** at **mywritinglab.com**

REVIEW PRACTICE 3: Write Your Own Using a variety of pronouns, write a paragraph about something you have learned from your friends this week. *Answers will vary.*

MyWritingLab

Practicing Pronoun Reference and Point of View

For more practice, complete the **Write** activity for **Pronoun Reference and Point of View** in the **Sentence Skills** module of **MyWritingLab.com.** Make sure to pay close attention to whether or not your pronouns have a clear reference.

REVIEW PRACTICE 4: Editing Through Collaboration Exchange paragraphs from Review Practice 3 with another student, and do the following: *Answers will vary.*

1. Underline all pronouns.

2. Draw arrows to the words they modify.

3. Put an X through any pronouns that do not refer to a clear antecedent or that shift point of view.

Then return the paper to its writer, and use the information in this chapter to correct any pronoun-reference and point-of-view errors in your own paragraph. Record your errors on the Error Log in Appendix 7.

Pronoun Agreement

UNIT PRE-TESTS
To check your students' abilities with the collective skills in this unit, two Unit Pre-tests are available in the *Instructor's Resource Manual.*

TEST YOURSELF

Underline the pronouns in each sentence, and draw an arrow to their antecedents. Put an X over any pronouns that do not agree with their antecedents.

- Harriett and Maureen walked their dogs in the park.
- Each person is responsible for their own transportation.
- Although the pieces of furniture were used, it looked new.
- Someone left their dirty dishes in the sink.
- Everyone contributed his work to the assignment.

(Answers are in Appendix 3.)

As you learned in Chapter 23, subjects and verbs must agree for clear communication. If the subject is singular, the verb must be singular; if the subject is plural, the verb must be plural. The same holds true for pronouns and the words they refer to—their *antecedents*. They must agree in number—both singular or both plural. Usually, pronoun agreement is not a problem, as these sentences show:

Singular: Jacob told **his** client to buy more stock.
Plural: Rosalinda and Hugo did **their** laundry yesterday.

MyWritingLab

Understanding Pronoun Agreement

For more information about this topic, go to **MyWritingLab.com,** and choose **Pronoun-Antecedent Agreement** in the **Sentence Skills** module. From there, watch the video called **Animation: Pronoun Agreement.** Then, return to this chapter, which will go into more detail about

Student Comment:
"Instructors always talked about pronouns agreeing with one another, and I always thought they just meant pronouns are friendly with one another. Now, I know that it's about the relationship between the pronouns and what they refer to."

pronoun agreement and give you opportunities to practice it. Finally, you will apply your understanding of pronoun agreement to your own writing.

INDEFINITE PRONOUNS

Pronoun agreement may become a problem with indefinite pronouns. Indefinite pronouns that are always singular give writers the most trouble.

NOT	**One** of the students turned in **their** paper late. (How many students were late? Only *one*, so use a singular pronoun.)
Correct:	**One** of the students turned in **her** paper late.
Correct:	**One** of the students turned in **his** paper late.
NOT	**Somebody** left **their** keys on the table. (How many people left keys? One person, so use a singular pronoun.)
Correct:	**Somebody** left **her** keys on the table.
Correct:	**Somebody** left **his** keys on the table.

Here is a list of indefinite pronouns that are always singular:

Singular Indefinite Pronouns

another	*everybody*	*neither*	*one*
anybody	*everyone*	*nobody*	*other*
anyone	*everything*	*none*	*somebody*
anything	*little*	*no one*	*someone*
each	*much*	*nothing*	*something*
either			

Hint: A few indefinite pronouns can be either singular or plural, depending on their meaning in the sentence. These pronouns are *any*, *all*, *more*, *most*, and *some*.

Singular:	**All** of the senior class had **its** picture taken.
Plural:	**All** of the seniors had **their** pictures taken.

In the first sentence, *class* is considered a single body, so the singular pronoun *its* is used. In the second sentence, the *seniors* are individuals, so the plural pronoun *their* is used.

TEACHING PRONOUN AGREEMENT
Create two sets of index cards: one of musical performers (made from pictures cut out of magazines) and another of personal pronouns. The performer cards should have pictures of both single performers and groups. Divide the students into small groups, and divide the performer cards evenly among the groups.

Provide sentences on the board, and ask teams to identify pronoun antecedent errors in the sentences. When a team gets an answer correct, give it a random pronoun card. The team should then match the pronoun card with a performer card (for example, a "her" card could go with Faith Hill or Madonna, a "their" card with Aerosmith or *NSync).

The first team to correctly match all their performer cards with pronoun cards wins.

INSTRUCTOR'S RESOURCE MANUAL
For sample sentences, for more exercises, and for quizzes, see the Instructor's Resource Manual, Section II, Part IV.

UNIT POST-TESTS
To check your students' mastery of the collective skills in this unit, two Unit Post-tests are available in the *Instructor's Resource Manual*.

Reviewing Indefinite Pronouns

Why should a pronoun agree with the word it refers to?

To communicate clearly

Name five indefinite pronouns that are always singular.

Answers will vary.

PRACTICE 1: Recall/Identify Underline the correct pronoun from the choices in parentheses, and be prepared to explain your choices.

1. Neither of the boys could give (<u>his</u>, their) opinion on the subject.

2. Before someone can appear on the program, (<u>he or she</u>, they) must audition.

3. Some of the bookstores put (its, <u>their</u>) books on sale for Father's Day.

4. Tom and Jack decided to hold (his, <u>their</u>) meetings on the first Thursday of each month.

5. Each of the dancers showed (<u>his or her</u>, their) dedication by practicing four hours a day.

PRACTICE 2: Apply Fill in each blank in the following sentences with a pronoun that agrees with its antecedent.

1. Joshua and Timothy explained _____*their*_____ method for cleaning chimneys.

2. Everyone should take the time to wash _____*his or her*_____ clothes.

3. Each of the trees has lost _____*its*_____ leaves.

4. Matthew asked _____*his*_____ brother to fix the car.

5. Because of the cold weather, someone will have to share _____*his or her*_____ warm clothes.

PRACTICE 3: Write Your Own Write a sentence of your own for each of the following pronouns. *Answers will vary.*

1. nobody _____

2. one _____

3. everyone _____

4. each _____

5. nothing _____

AVOIDING SEXISM

In the first section of this chapter, you learned to use singular pronouns to refer to singular indefinite pronouns. For example, the indefinite pronoun *someone* requires a singular pronoun—*his* or *her*, not the plural *their*. But what if you don't know whether the person referred to is male or female? Then you have a choice: (1) You can say "he or she" or "his or her"; (2) you can make the sentence plural; or (3) you can rewrite the sentence to avoid the problem altogether. What you should not do is ignore half the population by referring to all humans as a single gender.

NOT	If **anyone** wants to join us, then **he** can.
Correct:	If **anyone** wants to join us, then **he or she** can.
Correct:	**People** who want to can join us.

NOT	**Everyone** paid **his** dues this month.
Correct:	**Everyone** paid **his or her** dues this month.
Correct:	**All students** paid **their** dues this month.

Sexism in writing can also occur in ways other than with indefinite pronouns. We often assume that doctors, lawyers, and bank presidents are men and that nurses, schoolteachers, and secretaries are women. But that is not very accurate.

NOT	You should ask your **doctor** what **he** recommends. (Why automatically assume the doctor is a male instead of a female?)
Correct:	You should ask your **doctor** what **he or she** recommends.

NOT	The **policeman** gave me a warning but no ticket. (Since both men and women serve on police forces, the more correct term is *police officer* or *officer*.)
Correct:	The **police officer** gave me a warning but no ticket.

NOT	**A nurse** cannot let **herself** become too emotionally involved in **her** work. (Why leave the men who are nurses out of this sentence?)
Correct:	**A nurse** cannot let **him- or herself** become too emotionally involved in **his or her** work.
Correct:	**Nurses** cannot let **themselves** become too emotionally involved in **their** work.

Reviewing Sexism in Writing

What is sexism in writing?

Referring to unspecified people as either all male or all female

What are two ways to get around the problem of using male pronouns to refer to both women and men?

Use he or she.   *Make the sentence plural.*

Give two other examples of sexism in writing.

Examples will vary.

PRACTICE 4A: Recall/Identify Underline the sexist references in the following sentences.

1. At least one student did not memorize his test material.   *(his or her/plural)*

2. A judge will always give her verdict at the end of the trial.   *(his or her/ plural)*

3. A navy officer can wear his white uniform to weddings.   *(his or her/plural)*

4. A mailman knows he must deliver the mail rain or shine.   *(mail carrier, he or she/plural)*

5. A passenger usually can't fit all her luggage in the overhead bin.   *(his or her/plural)*

PRACTICE 4B: Correct Correct the sexist pronouns in Practice 4A by rewriting the incorrect sentences.   *See Practice 4A.*

PRACTICE 5: Apply Fill in each blank in the following sentences with an appropriate pronoun.

1. An athlete is always determined to overcome _____*his or her*_____ injury.

2. The contestant who sells the most candy can choose _____*his or her*_____ own prize.

3. An airplane pilot always has to make sure _____*he or she*_____ remains alert and awake.

4. A teacher should always explain _____*his or her*_____ assignments.

5. A truck driver can pull _____*his or her*_____ truck over to sleep for a few hours.

PRACTICE 6: Write Your Own Write a sentence of your own for each of the following antecedents. Include at least one pronoun in each sentence. *Answers will vary.*

1. doctor _____

2. professor _____

3. hair dresser _____

4. army recruit _____

5. senator _____

CHAPTER REVIEW

Be sure that students read the instructions for the Apply exercise carefully. They will be asked to click only on the pronoun, never on the antecedent. They will often have to change the verb of the sentence as well.

MyWritingLab | **Reviewing Pronoun Agreement**

To review this before material you complete the Review Practices, watch **Animation: Pronoun Agreement** at **MyWritingLab.com** one more time. This time, keep the video open as you complete the rest of the practices in this chapter. For best results, do the **MyWritingLab** exercises online as well as the Chapter Review practices in the book.

REVIEW PRACTICE 1: Recall/Identify Underline and correct the pronoun errors in the following sentences.

1. Neither of the women went to their parents' house for Thanksgiving. *(her)*

2. Each of the students picked up their test from the Psychology Department office. *(his or her)*

3. A newspaper writer can work on his assignment for months. *(his or her)*

4. Anyone can learn how to sew if they are patient. *(he or she is)*

5. A neat gardener always sweeps up after he mows the lawn. *(he or she)*

6. Something in the files seemed like they were confidential. *(it was)*

7. A coach constantly yells for his team to play harder. *(his or her)*

8. Someone in the crowd should stick up for their rights. *(his or her)*

9. Nobody ever believes their driving is bad. *(his or her)*

10. Everything in the sales bin has their price marked down. *(its)*

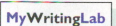

Practicing Pronoun Agreement

Now complete the **Recall** activities for **Pronoun-Antecedent Agreement** in the **Sentence Skills** module of **MyWritingLab.com.** If you're having a difficult time with a question, open up the video in the lower right-hand corner for some help.

REVIEW PRACTICE 2: Apply Correct the following pronoun errors by rewriting the following sentences.   *Answers will vary.*

1. None of the fraternity brothers were open about their rituals.

   _____

2. A doctor can choose his specialty from many different options.

   _____

3. Every one of the nurses has had their uniform cleaned for inspection.

   _____

4. Each of the people thought of their family as the story was being told.

   _____

5. A sales clerk is never allowed to take her vacation in December.

   _____

6. Everyone should have to watch her own performance on videotape.

   _____

7. A janitor is not responsible for purchasing all of his cleaning supplies.

   _____

8. Nobody wants their house robbed.

   _____

9. A firefighter must cover his face with protective gear.

   _____

10. Only one of the workers turned in their time sheet today.

   _____

MyWritingLab　　**Practicing Pronoun Agreement**

Next, complete the **Apply** activity for **Pronoun-Antecedent Agreement** in the **Sentence Skills** module of **MyWritingLab.com.** If you're stuck, you can click on the hint button.

🔧⚙─ **Complete** this **Writing Prompt** at **mywritinglab.com**

REVIEW PRACTICE 3:　Writing Your Own　Write a paragraph explaining what you think the qualities of a good teacher are.　*Answers will vary.*

MyWritingLab　　**Practicing Pronoun Agreement**

For more practice, complete the **Write** activity for **Pronoun-Antecedent Agreement** in the **Sentence Skills** module of **MyWritingLab.com.** Make sure to pay close attention to whether or not your pronouns and antecedents agree.

REVIEW PRACTICE 4:　Editing Through Collaboration　Exchange paragraphs from Review Practice 3 with another student, and do the following:　*Answers will vary.*

1.　Underline any pronouns.

2.　Circle any pronouns that do not agree with the words they refer to.

Then return the paper to its writer, and use the information in this chapter to correct any pronoun agreement errors in your own paragraph. Record your errors on the Error Log in Appendix 7.

Modifiers

Words that modify—usually called adjectives and adverbs—add details to sentences, either describing, limiting, or identifying so that sentences become more vivid and interesting. They work like accessories in our everyday lives. Without jewelry, scarves, ties, and cuff links, we are still dressed. But accessories give a little extra flair to our wardrobe. Without modifiers, our writing would be bland, boring, and lifeless. However, to use adjectives and adverbs correctly, you must learn about their different forms and functions.

In the chapters in this unit, you will learn about adjectives, adverbs, and various problems with the placement of these words in their sentences:

CHAPTER

30

Adjectives

UNIT PRE-TESTS
To check your students'
abilities with the collective
skills in this unit, two Unit
Pre-tests are available in
the *Instructor's Resource
Manual.*

TEST YOURSELF

Underline the adjectives in the following sentences. Then put an X over
the adjectives that are used incorrectly.

- The gray stingrays were very beautiful.
- We were more happier when the rain cooled the hot day.
- This is the worstest cold I've ever had.
- This textbook is more better than that one.
- She is the oldest of the two sisters.

(Answers are in Appendix 3.)

Adjectives are modifiers. They help us communicate more clearly (I have
a *red* sweater; I want a *blue* one) and vividly (her voice was *soft* and *gentle*).
Without adjectives, our language would be drab and boring.

MyWritingLab **Understanding Adjectives**

To understand more about this part of speech, go to **MyWritingLab.com,**
and choose **Adjectives and Adverbs** in the **Basic Grammar** module.
From there, watch the video called **Animation: Adjectives.** Then, return to this chapter, which will go into more detail about adjectives and
give you opportunities to practice using them. Finally, you will apply your
understanding of these modifiers to your own writing.

USING ADJECTIVES

TEACHING ADJECTIVES
Provide students with a
sentence that contains
no adjectives, and have
students draw a picture that

Adjectives are words that modify—or describe—nouns or pronouns.
Adjectives often tell how something or someone looks: *dark, light, tall,
short, large, small.* Most adjectives come before the words they modify, but

with linking verbs (such as *is, are, look, become,* and *feel*), adjectives follow the words they modify.

Adjectives Before a Noun:	We ate the **moist, sweet** cake.
Adjectives After a Linking Verb:	The cake was **moist** and **sweet**.

Reviewing Adjectives

What are adjectives?

Words that modify or describe nouns or pronouns

Where can you find adjectives in a sentence?

Before a noun or pronoun or after a linking verb

PRACTICE 1: Recall/Identify In the following sentences, underline the adjectives, and circle the words they modify.

1. I could eat a large (elephant) for lunch.

2. My biology (class) is difficult but interesting.

3. The good (news) is that her older (brother) volunteers for the Boy Scouts.

4. She owns an antique (store).

5. Our (yard) has both flowering (trees) and evergreen (trees).

PRACTICE 2: Apply Fill in each blank in the following sentences with logical adjectives. *Answers will vary.*

When my (1) _____ brother Nathan was in high school, he became (2) _____ at math. The teacher wanted to teach concepts according to the textbook, but Nathan always seemed to find a (3) _____ way to solve the math problems. Though he would have the right answers, the teacher would often take off points because of the process he used. After having (4) _____ conversations with the teacher, Nathan convinced her that he was (5) _____. He got an A in the course and became a good friend of the teacher's.

PRACTICE 3: Write Your Own Write a sentence of your own for each of the following adjectives. *Answers will vary.*

1. funny _____

2. seventeen _____

represents the sentence (for example, "the house on the street").

Restate the sentence, but this time add a few adjectives ("the two-story house on the narrow street"), and have students redraw the sentence on a new sheet of paper.

Continue this procedure a few more times until students are drawing an elaborate picture ("the two-story, red-brick house with a white, three-foot-tall picket fence on the narrow, shaded, deserted street").

Have students compare their first and last drawings to see the detail they added when a few adjectives were inserted into the description.

INSTRUCTOR'S RESOURCE MANUAL
For more sample sentences, for more exercises, and for quizzes, see the *Instructor's Resource Manual,* Section II, Part IV.

UNIT POST-TESTS
To check your students' mastery of the collective skills in this unit, two Unit Post-tests are available in the *Instructor's Resource Manual.*

3. long-lasting _____

4. reliable _____

5. stressful _____

COMPARING WITH ADJECTIVES

Most adjectives have three forms: a **basic** form, a **comparative** form (used to compare two items or indicate a greater degree), and a **superlative** form (used to compare three or more items or indicate the greatest degree).

For positive comparisons, adjectives form the comparative and superlative in two different ways.

1. For one-syllable adjectives and some two-syllable adjectives, use *-er* to compare two items and *-est* to compare three or more items.

Basic	Comparative (used to compare two items)	Superlative (used to compare three or more items)
tall	taller	tallest
old	older	oldest
hot	hotter	hottest

2. For some two-syllable adjectives and all longer adjectives, use *more* to compare two items and *most* to compare three or more items.

Basic	Comparative (used to compare two items)	Superlative (used to compare three or more items)
careful	more careful	most careful
relaxed	more relaxed	most relaxed
content	more content	most content

For negative comparisons, use *less* to compare two items and *least* to compare three or more items.

Basic	Comparative (used to compare two items)	Superlative (used to compare three or more items)
beautiful	less beautiful	least beautiful
familiar	less familiar	least familiar

Hint: Some adjectives are not usually compared. For example, one task cannot be "more complete" or "more impossible" than another. Here are some more examples.

complete	favorite	square
dead	horizontal	supreme
empty	impossible	unanimous
equal	pregnant	unique

Reviewing Adjective Forms

When do you use the comparative form of an adjective?

To compare two items

When do you use the superlative form of an adjective?

To compare three or more items

How do one-syllable and some two-syllable adjectives form the comparative and superlative in positive comparisons?

Add -er for the comparative and -est for the superlative.

How do some two-syllable adjectives and all longer adjectives form the comparative and superlative in positive comparisons?

With more and most

How do you form negative comparisons?

With less and least

PRACTICE 4: Recall/Identify Underline the adjectives, and note whether they are basic (B), comparative (C), or superlative (S).

1. __C, B__ The grass is always greener on the other side.
2. __B__ Your car will look good if you wash it.
3. __C__ Voters today are more educated.
4. __S, B__ The longest mile of the marathon is the last one.
5. __C__ My mother often asked my older brother to help her with the cooking.

PRACTICE 5: Apply Fill in each blank in the following paragraph with the correct comparative or superlative form of the adjective in parentheses.

Yesterday was the (1) _____*rainiest*_____ (rainy) day of the entire year. Consequently, my garden is looking (2) ___*more beautiful*___ (beautiful) today than it did two days ago. I have also seen the (3) _____*slimiest*_____ (slimy) earthworms on the sidewalk, wiggling faster than ever to get back into the dirt. Though I was pleased to see my flowers starting to bloom, I became even (4) ___*more excited*___ (excited) when I saw the tulip bulbs breaking through the ground. That means in a few weeks, my garden will be the (5) ___*most spectacular*___ (spectacular) one on the block.

PRACTICE 6: Write Your Own Write a sentence of your own for each of the following adjectives.   *Answers will vary.*

1. a superlative form of *happy* _____
2. the basic form of *practical* _____
3. a comparative form of *tight* _____
4. a superlative form of *disgusting* _____
5. a comparative form of *responsible* _____

COMMON ADJECTIVE ERRORS

Two types of problems occur with adjectives used in comparisons.

1. Instead of using one method for forming the comparative or superlative, both are used. That is, both *-er* and *more* or *less* are used to compare two items, or both *-est* and *most* or *least* are used to compare three or more items.

    NOT The top shelf is **more longer** than the bottom shelf.
    Correct: The top shelf is **longer** than the bottom shelf.

    NOT That is the **most silliest** hat I've ever seen.
    Correct: That is the **silliest** hat I've ever seen.

2. The second type of error occurs when the comparative or superlative is used with the wrong number of items. The comparative form should be used for two items and the superlative for three or more items.

    NOT Barb's chili recipe is the hott**est** of the **two.**
    Correct: Barb's chili recipe is the hott**er** of the **two.**

    NOT Ross is the young**er** of the **three** brothers.
    Correct: Ross is the young**est** of the **three** brothers.

Reviewing Common Adjective Errors

Can you ever use -er + more or -est + most?

No—you can't use both methods of comparison at the same time.

When do you use the comparative form of an adjective?

When comparing two items

When do you use the superlative form of an adjective?

When comparing three or more items

PRACTICE 7A: Recall/Identify In the following sentences, underline the adjectives that are used incorrectly in comparisons. Mark sentences that are correct with C.

1. _____ I always thought Lamar was more better at math than I was.
   (better)

2. _C_ Terry is the wildest of all her friends.

3. _____ Sean is the stronger of his five cousins.   *(strongest)*

4. _____ I've owned both a cat and a dog, and the cat was the cleanest of the two.   *(cleaner)*

5. _____ The most happiest day of my life was the day I got married.
   (happiest)

PRACTICE 7B: Correct Correct the adjective errors in Practice 7A by rewriting the incorrect sentences.   *See Practice 7A.*

PRACTICE 8: Apply Choose the correct adjective forms in the following paragraph to complete the sentences.

The (1) ____latest____ (latest/most latest) fads in cars are hard to keep up with. The (2) ___most common___ (more common/most common) of the many options now available is a car that uses both solar energy and natural gas for power. That way, if the solar cells are empty, the natural gas keeps the car running. What would be (3) ___sadder___ (sadder/more sadder) than running out of fuel while trying to meet a deadline or get to the hospital? Natural gas is

(4) _____cleaner_____ (more cleaner/cleaner) than the gasoline used by most cars today. Between these two sources, natural gas is the (5) _____easier_____ (easier/easiest) on the environment.

PRACTICE 9: Write Your Own Write a sentence of your own for each of the following adjectives.   *Answers will vary.*

1. most logical _____

2. happier _____

3. longest _____

4. more serious _____

5. scariest _____

USING *GOOD* AND *BAD* CORRECTLY

The adjectives *good* and *bad* are irregular. They do not form the comparative and superlative like most other adjectives. Here are the correct forms for these two irregular adjectives:

Basic	Comparative (used to compare two items)	Superlative (used to compare three or more items)
good	better	best
bad	worse	worst

Problems occur with *good* and *bad* when writers don't know how to form their comparative and superlative forms.

NOT   more better, more worse, worser, most best, most worst, bestest, worstest

Correct: better, worse, best, worst

These errors appear in sentences in the following ways:

NOT   That is the **bestest** play I have ever seen.

Correct: That is the **best** play I have ever seen.

NOT   His health is getting **more worse** as time goes by.

Correct: His health is getting **worse** as time goes by.

Reviewing *Good* and *Bad*

What are the three forms of good?

good   better

best

What are the three forms of bad?

bad   worse

worst

PRACTICE 10A: Recall/Identify In the following sentences, underline the forms of *good* and *bad* used correctly, and circle the forms of *good* and *bad* used incorrectly.

1. I got a C in chemistry, but did more better in Spanish.   *(better)*

2. The most best drawing is a bowl of fruit.   *(best)*

3. Even though he practiced, his soccer skills got more and more bad.
   (worse)

4. Going to work is better now that I am a manager.

5. I like my hair bestest when it is curly.   *(best)*

PRACTICE 10B: Correct Correct the errors with *good* and *bad* in Practice 10A by rewriting the incorrect sentences.   *See Practice 10A.*

PRACTICE 11: Apply Using the correct forms of *good* and *bad*, complete the following paragraph.

Dusting is definitely the (1) _____worst_____ household chore. I can't think of anything (2) _____worse_____ than having to take everything off a shelf just to wipe a rag across it. It would be (3) _____better_____ to buy those cans of compressed air and just spray the dust away instead of wiping the dust away. I can think of so many (4) _____better_____ things to do with my time than dusting. But according to Dear Abby, the (5) _____best_____ housekeepers have dust-free furniture.

PRACTICE 12: Write Your Own Write a sentence of your own for each of the following forms of *good* and *bad*.   *Answers will vary.*

1. bad _____

2. better _____

3. worst _____

4. good _____

5. best _____

CHAPTER REVIEW

While students are working on the exercises, have them make a chart on a sheet of paper, labeling the three forms of the word: basic, comparative, and superlative. This way, not only do they find out the answers for the questions, but they are also compiling a list of word forms and practicing as they go along.

MyWritingLab   **Reviewing Adjectives**

To review this material before you complete the Review Practices, watch **Animation: Adjectives** at **MyWritingLab.com** one more time. This time, keep the video open as you complete the rest of the practices in this chapter. For best results, do the **MyWritingLab** exercises online as well as the Chapter Review Practices in the book.

REVIEW PRACTICE 1: Recall/Identify Label the following adjectives basic (B), comparative (C), superlative (S), or not able to be compared (X).

1. ___S___ most lovable

2. ___C___ stickier

3. ___X___ final

4. ___C___ heavier

5. ___C___ more genuine

6. ___B___ new

7. ___X___ impossible

8. ___B___ delicious

9. ___B___ windy

10. ___S___ funniest

MyWritingLab **Practicing Adjectives**

Now complete the **Recall** activities for **Adjectives and Adverbs** in the **Basic Grammar** module of **MyWritingLab.com.** Remember to read the answers carefully because many of them look similar.

REVIEW PRACTICE 2: Apply Supply the comparative and superlative forms (both positive and negative) for each of the following adjectives.

Basic	Comparative	Superlative
1. tight	*tighter, less tight*	*tightest, least tight*
2. crooked	*more/less crooked*	*most/least crooked*
3. long	*longer, less long*	*longest, least long*
4. smart	*smarter, less smart*	*smartest, least smart*
5. greasy	*greasier, less greasy*	*greasiest, least greasy*
6. ignorant	*more/less ignorant*	*most/least ignorant*
7. great	*greater, less great*	*greatest, least great*
8. friendly	*friendlier, less friendly*	*friendliest, least friendly*
9. cheap	*cheaper, less cheap*	*cheapest, least cheap*
10. happy	*happier, less happy*	*happiest, least happy*

MyWritingLab **Practicing Adjectives**

Next, complete the **Apply** activity for **Adjectives and Adverbs** in the **Basic Grammar** module of **MyWritingLab.com.** Remember that spelling and spacing count.

⚙ Complete this **Writing Prompt** at **mywritinglab.com**

REVIEW PRACTICE 3: Write Your Own Write a paragraph describing one of the most memorable people you have ever met. What did the person look like? How did he or she talk? What did he or she wear? Where did you meet this person? Why is this person so memorable? *Answers will vary.*

| **MyWritingLab** | **Practicing Adjectives** |

For more practice, complete the **Write** activity for **Adjectives and Adverbs** in the **Basic Grammar** module of **MyWritingLab.com.** Make sure to pay close attention to which adjectives are used incorrectly.

REVIEW PRACTICE 4: Editing Through Collaboration Exchange paragraphs from Review Practice 3 with another student, and do the following: *Answers will vary.*

1. Underline all the adjectives.

2. Circle those that are not in the correct form.

Then return the paper to its writer, and use the information in this chapter to correct any adjective errors in your own paragraph. Record your errors on the Error Log in Appendix 7.

Adverbs

UNIT PRE-TESTS
To check your students' abilities with the collective skills in this unit, two Unit Pre-tests are available in the *Instructor's Resource Manual.*

TEST YOURSELF

Underline the adverbs in the following sentences. Then put an X over the adverbs that are used incorrectly.

- We were led quickly out the back door.
- He hugged her tight when he saw her.
- Tina left early because she wasn't feeling good.
- She feels badly that she couldn't stay.
- I can't never meet on Tuesdays because I work that night.

(Answers are in Appendix 3.)

Like adjectives, adverbs help us communicate more clearly (she walked *quickly*) and more vividly (she stopped *suddenly*). Adverbs make our sentences more interesting.

MyWritingLab **Understanding Adverbs**

To learn more about these modifiers, go to **MyWritingLab.com**, and choose **Adjectives and Adverbs** in the **Basic Grammar** module. From there, watch the video called **Animation: Adverbs.** Then, return to this chapter, which will go into more detail about adverbs and give you opportunities to practice using them. Finally, you will apply your understanding of this part of speech to your own writing.

Student Comment:
"Anytime you're having difficulty with your writing, refer back to **MyWritingLab** and review whatever it is you're having trouble with because it really does help."

USING ADVERBS

Adverbs modify verbs, adjectives, and other adverbs. They answer the questions *How? When? Where? How often?* and *To what extent?* Look at the following examples.

TEACHING ADVERBS
Choose a student, and give him or her oral directions, like "walk to the other side of the room."

The student should follow the directions.

Next, add an adverb to the sentence, and have the student again follow directions ("walk *slowly* to the other side of the room").

Continue changing or adding more adverbs to the directions so that students can see how adverbs affect the meaning of a sentence. Don't forget to add negative as well as positive words to remind students of the full range of adverbs ("do *not* walk to the other side of the room").

INSTRUCTOR'S RESOURCE MANUAL
For more sample sentences, for more exercises, and for quizzes, see the *Instructor's Resource Manual*, Section II, Part IV.

UNIT POST-TESTS
To check your students' mastery of the collective skills in this unit, two Unit Post-tests are available in the *Instructor's Resource Manual*.

How:	Zachary dusted the antiques **carefully.**
When:	The antique shop **always** opens on time.
Where:	The antique shop is **here.**
How often:	I shop there **regularly.**
To what extent:	The shop is **extremely** busy on Saturdays.

Some words are always adverbs, including *here, there, not, never, now, again, almost, often,* and *well.*

Other adverbs are formed by adding *-ly* to an adjective:

Adjective	Adverb
quiet	quietly
perfect	perfectly
strange	strangely

Hint: Not all words that end in *-ly* are adverbs. Some, such as *friendly, early, lonely, chilly,* and *lively,* are adjectives.

Reviewing Adverbs

What are adverbs?

Adverbs modify verbs, adjectives, and other adverbs.

What five questions do adverbs answer?

How?   *When?*

Where?   *How often?*

To what extent?

List four words that are always adverbs.

Answers will vary.

How do many adverbs end?

In -ly

PRACTICE 1: Recall/Identify In the following sentences, underline the adverbs, and circle the words they modify.

1. The little boy (cried) loudly.

2. That was a very (good) movie.

3. (Walk) quickly to the car because it's raining.

4. We never (miss) our favorite TV show.

5. The dimly (lit) restaurant served horrible food.

PRACTICE 2: Apply Fill in each blank in the following sentences with an adverb that makes sense.   *Answers will vary.*

Tom was (1) _____ tired after spending the day at Disneyland. He (2) _____ changed his clothes and (3) _____ crawled into bed. But before he closed his eyes, he heard a little fly (4) _____ buzzing around his head. Fortunately, his fatigue overpowered the buzzing, and he (5) _____ fell asleep.

PRACTICE 3: Write Your Own Write a sentence of your own for each of the following adverbs.   *Answers will vary.*

1. seemingly _____

2. almost _____

3. brightly _____

4. angrily _____

5. repeatedly _____

COMPARING WITH ADVERBS

Like adjectives, most adverbs have three forms: a **basic** form, a **comparative** form (used to compare two items), and a **superlative** form (used to compare three or more items).

For positive comparisons, adverbs form the comparative and superlative forms in two different ways:

1. For one-syllable adverbs, use *-er* and *-est* to form the comparative and superlative.

Basic	Comparative (used to compare two items)	Superlative (used to compare three or more items)
fast	faster	fastest
near	nearer	nearest
far	farther	farthest

2. For adverbs of two or more syllables, use *more* to compare two items and *most* to compare three or more items.

Basic	Comparative (used to compare two items)	Superlative (used to compare three or more items)
beautifully	more beautifully	most beautifully
awkwardly	more awkwardly	most awkwardly
loudly	more loudly	most loudly

For negative comparisons, adverbs, like adjectives, use *less* to compare two items and *least* to compare three or more items.

Basic	Comparative (used to compare two items)	Superlative (used to compare three or more items)
often	less often	least often
frequently	less frequently	least frequently
vividly	less vividly	least vividly

Hint: Like adjectives, certain adverbs are not usually compared. Something cannot last "more eternally" or work "more uniquely." The following adverbs cannot logically be compared.

endlessly	eternally	infinitely
equally	impossibly	invisibly

Reviewing Adverb Forms

When do you use the comparative form of an adverb?

To compare two items

When do you use the superlative form of an adverb?

To compare three or more items

How do one-syllable adverbs form the comparative and superlative in positive comparisons?

Add -er for the comparative and -est for the superlative

How do adverbs of two or more syllables form the comparative and superlative in positive comparisons?

With more and most

How do you form negative comparisons with adverbs?

With less and least

PRACTICE 4: Recall/Identify Underline the adverbs, and note whether they are basic (B), comparative (C), or superlative (S).

1. __C__ Can you drive <u>faster</u>?

2. __S__ This house is the <u>most beautifully</u> painted one in the neighborhood.

3. __C__ My sister speaks <u>more kindly</u> to me when Mom is in the room.

4. __B__ The crowd yelled <u>loudly</u> when the referee made a bad call.

5. __S__ They completed the project <u>most efficiently</u>.

PRACTICE 5: Apply Fill in each blank in the following paragraph with the correct comparative or superlative form of the adverb in parentheses.

Sasha gave the (1) __most creatively__ (creatively) presented oral report in the science class. Her visual aids were (2) __more colorfully__ (colorfully) decorated than Paul's, and Paul is an art major. Sasha even spoke (3) __more clearly__ (clearly) than Odella, who is a speech major. But best of all, she approached the assignment (4) __more cleverly__ (cleverly) than the best student in the class. She based her presentation on a popular TV game show. Everyone could identify with the information she presented, and (5) __most importantly__ (importantly), she kept our attention.

PRACTICE 6: Write Your Own Write a sentence of your own for each of the following adverbs.   *Answers will vary.*

1. the superlative form of *often* _____

2. the comparative form of *quickly* _____

3. the basic form of *selfishly* _____

4. the superlative form of *clearly* _____

5. the comparative form of *regularly* _____

ADJECTIVE OR ADVERB?

One of the most common errors with modifiers is using an adjective when an adverb is called for. Keep in mind that adjectives modify nouns and pronouns, whereas adverbs modify verbs, adjectives, and other adverbs. Adverbs *do not* modify nouns or pronouns. Here are some examples.

NOT   She spoke too **slow.** [adjective]
Correct: She spoke too **slowly.** [adverb]

NOT   He was **real** happy with the decision. [adjective]

Correct: He was **really** happy with the decision. [adverb]

Reviewing the Difference Between Adjectives and Adverbs

How do you know whether to use an adjective or an adverb in a sentence?

Adjectives modify nouns and pronouns. Adverbs modify verbs, adjectives, and other adverbs.

Give an example of an adverb in a sentence.

Examples will vary.

Give an example of an adjective in a sentence.

Examples will vary.

PRACTICE 7A: Recall/Identify Underline the adverbs in the following sentences. Write C next to the sentences that are correct.

1. _____ She talked <u>too quick</u> for me to understand.   *(quickly)*

2. _____ Your car engine runs <u>so quiet</u>.   *(quietly)*

3. __*C*__ I <u>patiently</u> read the same picture book five times.

4. _____ This is a <u>nice</u> decorated dorm room.   *(nicely)*

5. _____ The ducks began to quack <u>loud</u> when they saw us.   *(loudly)*

PRACTICE 7B: Correct Correct the adverb errors in Practice 7A by rewriting the incorrect sentences.   *See Practice 7A.*

PRACTICE 8: Apply Choose the correct adverb to complete the sentences in the following paragraph.

Last August, we drove to San Diego to visit a couple of friends that we hadn't seen in a (1) _____*really*_____ (real/really) long time. She is a doctor at a San Diego area hospital, and he stays (2) _____*incredibly*_____ (incredible/incredibly) busy doing his artwork and taking care of their two kids. After we arrived, they took us to the beach, and we laughed (3) _____*loudly*_____ (loudly/ loud) at the kids playing in the water. When it was time for us to go, we (4) _____*repeatedly*_____ (repeated/repeatedly) promised not to wait so long before the next visit. We hugged each other (5) _____*tightly*_____ (tightly/tight) and said goodbye.

PRACTICE 9: Write Your Own Write a sentence of your own for each of the following adverbs. *Answers will vary.*

1. loosely _____

2. especially _____

3. cheaply _____

4. honestly _____

5. thankfully _____

DOUBLE NEGATIVES

Another problem involving adverbs is the **double negative**—the use of two negative words in one clause. Examples of negative words include *no*, *not*, *never*, *none*, *nothing*, *neither*, *nowhere*, *nobody*, *barely*, and *hardly*. A double negative creates the opposite meaning of what is intended.

NOT   We **never** had **no** break today.

The actual meaning of these double negatives is "we did have a break today."

Correct: We had **no** break today.

NOT   Jim does **not** owe me **nothing.**

The actual meaning of these double negatives is "Jim does owe me something."

Correct: Jim does **not** owe me **anything.**

Double negatives often occur with contractions.

NOT   My mom does**n't hardly** get any time to herself.

The actual meaning of these double negatives is "My mom gets a lot of time to herself."

Correct: My mom **doesn't** get much time to herself.

Using two negatives is confusing and grammatically wrong. Be on the lookout for negative words, and use only one per clause.

Reviewing Double Negatives

What is a double negative?

The use of two negative words in one sentence

List five negative words.

Answers will vary.

Why should you avoid double negatives?

Because they create the opposite meaning of what is intended

PRACTICE 10A: Recall/Identify Mark each of the following sentences either correct (C) or incorrect (X).

1. __X__ I don't think you owe me nothing.   *(~~nothing~~ anything)*

2. __X__ Michelle couldn't hardly wait to go to the Bahamas.   *(couldn't hardly)*

3. __X__ Miguel can't barely fit in Tony's tennis shoes.   *(can't barely)*

4. __C__ The last one in the car is not really a rotten egg.

5. __X__ Having a driver's license doesn't say nothing about your driving skills.   *(~~nothing~~ anything)*

PRACTICE 10B: Correct Correct the double negatives in Practice 10A by rewriting the incorrect sentences.   *See Practice 10A.*

PRACTICE 11: Apply Choose the correct negative modifiers to complete the following paragraph.

The first time I went furniture shopping, I was (1) _____*hardly*_____ (hardly/not hardly) concerned with the quality of the furniture. I just wanted things that looked good, and I (2) _____*didn't*_____ (didn't/didn't never) think about how long they would last. I bought a plaid couch and was excited about decorating my living room around it, so I spent even more money on curtains, pillows, and wall hangings. Soon, I had a party at my house, and that couch was (3) _____*never*_____ (not never/never) so abused. One of my friends, who must weigh (4) _____*scarcely*_____ (scarcely/not scarcely) less than 300 pounds, plopped down on the couch, and it immediately broke. He apologized repeatedly, but no matter how he tried to fix it, there (5) _____*was nothing*_____ (wasn't nothing/was nothing) he could do. That's when I learned to buy things that last.

PRACTICE 12: Write Your Own Write a sentence of your own for each of the following negative words. *Answers will vary.*

1. nowhere _____

2. barely _____

3. not _____

4. never _____

5. nobody _____

USING *GOOD/WELL* AND *BAD/BADLY* CORRECTLY

The pairs *good/well* and *bad/badly* are so frequently misused that they deserve special attention. Good is an adjective; well is an adverb or an adjective.

Use *good* with a noun (n) or after a linking verb (lv).

                               n

Adjective: What a **good** dog.

                               lv

Adjective: The soup tastes **good.**

Use *well* for someone's health or after an action verb (av).

                            lv

Adverb: I am **well,** thank you. [health]

                            av

Adverb: She plays **well** with others.

Bad is an adjective; *badly* is an adverb.

Use *bad* with a noun (n) or after a linking verb (lv). Always use *bad* after *feel* if you're talking about emotions.

                               n

Adjective: That looks like a **bad** cut.

                            lv

Adjective: I feel **bad** that I lost the tickets.

Use *badly* with an adjective (adj) or after an action verb (av).

                               adj

Adverb: The steak is **badly** burned.

                           av

Adverb: She drives **badly.**

Reviewing *Good/Well* and *Bad/Badly*

When should you use the adjective good?

With a noun or after a linking verb

When should you use the adjective or adverb well?

Adjective—for someone's health; adverb—after an action verb

When should you use the adjective bad?

With a noun, after a linking verb, or after feel for emotions

When should you use the adverb badly?

With an adjective or after an action verb

PRACTICE 13A: Recall/Identify Label each of the following sentences either correct (C) or incorrect (X).

1. __X__ Gwyneth said she felt good enough to travel. *(good, well)*

2. __X__ Don't talk so bad about Mike. *(bad, badly)*

3. __C__ That one bad play cost us the game.

4. __X__ I want to do good in this class so my GPA improves. *(good, well)*

5. __C__ Tamika writes well.

PRACTICE 13B: Correct Correct the adverb errors in Practice 13A by rewriting the incorrect sentences. *See Practice 13A.*

PRACTICE 14: Apply Choose the correct modifiers to complete the following paragraph.

Remember when you were in third grade and wanted so (1) _____badly_____ (bad/badly) to have lots of friends? The worst feeling in the world is to be teased and shunned by peers. And third graders are very (2) _____good_____ (good/well) at creating nicknames that stay with a person for life. Nicknames often point out something unusual about your physical features or explain activities you don't play very (3) _____well_____ (good/well). Whatever kids find to tease you about, they repeat it and repeat it until you feel (4) _____bad_____ (bad/badly) about yourself—until you never want to return to school again. That is why parents should discourage name-calling and teasing. A child's self-image will affect how (5) _____well_____ (good/well) he or she handles all aspects of life.

PRACTICE 15: Write Your Own Write a sentence of your own for each of the following modifiers.   *Answers will vary.*

1. bad _____

2. well _____

3. badly _____

4. good _____

5. well _____

CHAPTER REVIEW

MyWritingLab   **Reviewing Adverbs**

To review this material before you complete the Review Practices, watch **Animation: Adverbs** at **MyWritingLab.com** one more time. This time, keep the video open as you complete the rest of the practices in this chapter. For best results, do the **MyWritingLab** exercises online as well as the Chapter Review practices in the book.

Students who have trouble with standard English are going to have more trouble with this topic. Remind them to look at the grammar of the sentence to determine if it is correct rather than just listen to the way the sentence sounds.

REVIEW PRACTICE 1: Recall/Identify Underline the correct word in each of the following sentences.

1. The committee was (real, <u>very</u>) tired by the end of the day.

2. Justin walked (most, <u>more</u>) slowly than Alec.

3. *The Simpsons* has been on TV (continued, <u>continuously</u>) for years.

4. We don't have (no, <u>any</u>) candy to offer the children.

5. The golden retriever ran more (quicklier, <u>quickly</u>) than the German shepherd.

6. Of all the kings, he ruled (<u>most</u>, more) fairly.

7. Her computer crashed (<u>less</u>, least) often than mine.

8. He danced with the (<u>most</u>, more) energy of them all.

9. They haven't (no, <u>any</u>) more to give you.

10. I will love you (<u>eternally</u>, more eternally).

Practicing Adverbs

Now complete the **Recall** activities for **Adjectives and Adverbs** in the **Basic Grammar** module of **MyWritingLab.com.** If you're having a difficult time with a question, open up the video in the lower right-hand corner for some help.

REVIEW PRACTICE 2: Apply Fill in each blank in the following paragraph with an adverb that makes sense. Try not to use any adverb more than once.   *Answers will vary.*

Working as a telemarketer is much (1) _____ difficult than you might expect. It requires people to work (2) _____ long hours and to put up with rudeness. For instance, I've had to work for up to 13 hours without any more than a 10-minute break and a 30-minute lunch. The people that a telemarketer must call are not (3) _____ nice. Some are (4) _____ rude. Many people hang up (5) _____ when they learn I'm a telemarketer. They could at least say, "Thank you, but I'm (6) _____ not interested." With this job, I must (7) _____ remind myself to keep a positive attitude and (8) _____ give up. I (9) _____ want to succeed at this job, but I don't know if I am (10) _____ strong enough.

Practicing Adverbs

Next, complete the **Apply** activity for **Adjectives and Adverbs** in the **Basic Grammar** module of **MyWritingLab.com.** Pay close attention to the directions, and only click on what you're asked to.

⚙ **Complete** this **Writing Prompt** at **mywritinglab.com**

REVIEW PRACTICE 3: Write Your Own Write a paragraph explaining a favorite pastime of yours. What does the activity involve? Why do you like it? What does it do for you?   *Answers will vary.*

Practicing Adverbs

For more practice, complete the **Write** activity for **Adjectives and Adverbs** in the **Basic Grammar** module of **MyWritingLab.com.** Make sure to pay close attention to which adverbs are used incorrectly.

REVIEW PRACTICE 4: Editing Through Collaboration Exchange paragraphs from Review Practice 3 with another student, and do the following: *Answers will vary.*

1. Underline all the adverbs.

2. Circle those that are not in the correct form.

3. Put an X above any double negatives.

Then return the paper to its writer, and use the information in this chapter to correct any adverb errors in your own paragraph. Record your errors on the Error Log in Appendix 7.

32

Modifier Errors

UNIT PRE-TESTS
To check your students' abilities with the collective skills in this unit, two Unit Pre-tests are available in the *Instructor's Resource Manual.*

TEST YOURSELF

Underline the modifier problem in each sentence.

- When we arrived at the concert, Sandy told her mother that she should call home.
- Before going to the store, the car needed gas.
- The teacher told the students their grades would be posted before she dismissed them.
- To enter the contest, the application must be submitted by Friday.
- We found the magazine and put it in a safe place that had an article about saving money.

(Answers are in Appendix 3.)

As you know, a modifier describes another word or group of words. Sometimes, however, a modifier is too far from the words it refers to (*misplaced modifier*), or the word it refers to is missing altogether (*dangling modifier*). As a result, the sentence is confusing.

MyWritingLab **Understanding Modifier Errors**

To expand your understanding of modifier errors, go to **MyWritingLab. com,** and choose **Misplaced or Dangling Modifiers** in the **Sentence Skills** module. From there, watch the video called **Animation: Misplaced or Dangling Modifiers.** Then, return to this chapter, which will go into more detail about these errors and give you opportunities to practice correcting them. Finally, you will apply your understanding of modifier errors to your own writing.

MISPLACED MODIFIERS

A modifier should be placed as close as possible to the word or words it modifies, but this does not always happen. A **misplaced modifier** is too far from the word or words it refers to, making the meaning of the sentence unclear. Look at these examples.

NOT	Brad yelled at his roommate **in his underwear.**
	(Who is wearing the underwear—Brad or Brad's roommate? The modifier *in his underwear* must be moved closer to the word it modifies.)
Correct:	**In his underwear,** Brad yelled at his roommate.
Correct:	Brad yelled at his roommate, who was **in his underwear.**
NOT	The students were told to turn in their papers **after the bell.**
	(This sentence has two meanings. Were the students supposed to turn in their papers after the bell rang? Or after the bell rang, did someone tell them to turn in their papers?)
Correct:	The teacher told the students **after the bell** to turn in their papers.
Correct:	**After the bell,** the teacher told the students to turn in their papers.

Certain modifiers that limit meaning are often misplaced, causing problems. Look at how meaning changes by moving the limiting word *only* in the following sentences:

Only Laverne says that Shirley was at home in the evening.
(Laverne says this, but no one else does.)

Laverne **only** says that Shirley was at home in the evening.
(Laverne says this, but she doesn't really mean it.)

Laverne says that **only** Shirley was at home in the evening.
(Shirley—and no one else—was at home in the evening.)

Laverne says that Shirley was **only** at home in the evening.
(Shirley didn't leave the house in the evening.)

Laverne says that Shirley was at home **only** in the evening.
(Shirley was at home in the evening but out the rest of the day.)

Here is a list of common limiting words:

almost	hardly	merely	only
even just	just	nearly	scarcely

Reviewing Misplaced Modifiers

What is a misplaced modifier?

A modifier that is not as close as possible to the word it refers to

How can you correct a misplaced modifier?

Place modifiers as close as possible to the words they refer to.

PRACTICE 1A: Recall/Identify Underline the misplaced modifiers in the following sentences.

1. <u>Stolen from his car</u>, Henry saw his wallet at a pawn shop.

2. The flowers bloomed when the weather changed <u>in the front yard</u>.

3. The officers <u>quickly</u> wanted to solve the crime.

4. I went dancing with my boyfriend <u>in my new Gap jeans</u>.

5. Paul just bought the white house next to the supermarket <u>with blue trim</u>.

PRACTICE 1B: Correct Correct the misplaced modifiers in Practice 1A by rewriting the incorrect sentences.   *Answers will vary.*

PRACTICE 2: Apply Fill in each blank in the following paragraph with a modifier that makes sense.   *Answers will vary.*

    In the (1) _____ town of Salem, Sam can see himself (2) _____ walking across the stage to receive his degree. This goal was (3) _____ but he thinks now that he will make it (4) _____. He always has doubts about himself, but he is slowly learning (5) _____.

PRACTICE 3: Write Your Own Write a sentence of your own for each of the following modifiers.   *Answers will vary.*

1. since last fall _____

2. after running for 30 minutes _____

3. while taking a shower _____

4. though he was sleepy _____

5. before taking them to court (*end of sentence*) _____

DANGLING MODIFIERS

Modifiers are "dangling" when they have nothing to refer to in a sentence. **Dangling modifiers** (starting with an *-ing* word or with *to*) often appear at the beginning of a sentence. Here is an example.

NOT   Having lived in Los Angeles for 20 years, the traffic is horrible.

A modifier usually modifies the words closest to it. So the phrase *Having lived in Los Angeles* modifies *traffic*. But traffic doesn't live in Los Angeles. In fact, there is no logical word in the sentence that the phrase modifies. It is left dangling. You can correct a dangling modifier in one of two ways: by inserting the missing word being referred to or by rewriting the sentence.

Correct: **Having lived in Los Angeles for 20 years, Carrie** will tell you that the traffic is horrible.

Correct: **Carrie has lived in Los Angeles for 20 years,** and she will tell you that the traffic is horrible.

NOT   **To order more food,** the coupon must be presented in person.

Correct: **To order more food, you** must present the coupon in person.

Correct: You must present the coupon in person **to order more food.**

NOT   The refrigerator was full **after buying groceries.**

Correct: **After buying groceries, we** had a full refrigerator.

Correct: The refrigerator was full **after we bought more groceries.**

Correct: **After buying groceries, we** filled the refrigerator with them.

Reviewing Dangling Modifiers

What is a dangling modifier?

A modifier that has nothing to refer to in its sentence

How do you correct a dangling modifier?

By inserting the missing word being referred to or by rewriting the sentence

PRACTICE 4A: Recall/Identify Underline the dangling modifiers in the following sentences.

1. After price-checking for hours, the stereo at Costco was the best deal.

2. To register for the dance, the money must be paid a week in advance.

3. The restaurant was very busy <u>waiting 10 minutes for a table.</u>

4. <u>Sitting on the blanket,</u> the sun shone brightly during our family picnic.

5. <u>To meet with your counselor,</u> an appointment must be made.

PRACTICE 4B: Correct Correct the dangling modifiers in Practice 4A by rewriting the incorrect sentences.   *Answers will vary.*

PRACTICE 5: Apply Fill in the blanks with modifiers in the following paragraph.   *Answers will vary.*

(1) _____, Cheryl sets out to weed her garden and trim her bushes. Her yard has really been neglected (2) _____, because she was taking classes and had two part-time jobs. Her evenings (3) _____ are her favorite times. She knows she can rest then (4) _____. She can also dream about the future during these times (5) _____.

PRACTICE 6: Write Your Own Write a sentence of your own for each of the following phrases.   *Answers will vary.*

1. crunchy and chewy _____

2. sending an e-mail _____

3. hopping on one foot _____

4. to get up at dawn _____

5. having never been to Hawaii _____

CHAPTER REVIEW

Students often really struggle with identifying **Modifier Errors.** Have your students list words that limit meaning so they can refer to these words while they complete the exercises.

MyWritingLab   **Reviewing Modifier Errors**

To review this material before you complete the Review Practices, watch **Animation: Misplaced or Dangling Modifiers** at MyWritingLab.com one more time. This time, keep the video open as you complete the rest of the practices in this chapter. For best results, do the **MyWritingLab** exercises online as well as the Chapter Review practices in the book.

REVIEW PRACTICE 1: Recall/Identify Underline the modifier errors in the following sentences.

1. <u>Singing and cheering</u>, the van full of students pulled off.

2. <u>Broken for almost two months</u>, we finally bought a new flat screen television.

3. My parents tried <u>as a young child</u> to teach me right from <u>wrong</u>.

4. <u>To build endurance and muscle tone</u>, a health plan should be followed.

5. <u>While talking on the telephone</u>, my alarm clock went off.

6. <u>Depressed about not getting the job he applied for</u>, Deanna tried to cheer Sergio up with some ice cream.

7. Darlene said <u>at the health club</u> she would give Bert a free tennis lesson.

8. <u>To be successful in the stock market</u>, research is important.

9. <u>An overnight success story</u>, the papers followed the actor everywhere.

10. <u>Upset about losing her wallet</u>, the police officer talked to the tourist.

MyWritingLab

Practicing Modifier Errors

Now complete the **Recall** activities for **Misplaced or Dangling Modifiers** in the **Sentence Skills** module of **MyWritingLab.com.** Remember to read the answers carefully because many of them look similar.

REVIEW PRACTICE 2: Apply Rewrite the sentences in Review Practice 1 so that the phrases you underlined are as close as possible to the words they modify. *Answers will vary.*

MyWritingLab

Practicing Modifier Errors

Next, complete the **Apply** activity for **Misplaced or Dangling Modifiers** in the **Sentence Skills** module of **MyWritingLab.com.** If you're stuck, you can go to the lower right-hand corner and open up the video again, or you can click on the Hint button.

⚙️●─**Complete** this **Writing Prompt** at **mywritinglab.com**

REVIEW PRACTICE 3: Write Your Own Write a paragraph about the career you hope to have after college and your plans to begin working in this field.   *Answers will vary.*

MyWritingLab   **Practicing Modifier Errors**

For more practice, complete the **Write** activity for **Misplaced or Dangling Modifiers** in the **Sentence Skills** module of **MyWritingLab. com.** Make sure to pay close attention to any modifier errors.

REVIEW PRACTICE 4: Editing Through Collaboration Exchange paragraphs from Review Practice 3 with another student, and do the following: *Answers will vary.*

1. Underline any misplaced modifiers.

2. Put brackets around any dangling modifiers.

Then return the paper to its writer, and use the information in this chapter to correct any modifier problems in your own paragraph. Record your errors on the Error Log in Appendix 7.

Punctuation

Can you imagine streets and highways without stoplights or traffic signs? Driving would become a life-or-death adventure as motorists made risky trips with no signals to guide or protect them. Good writers, like conscientious drivers, prefer to leave little to chance. They observe the rules of punctuation to ensure that their readers arrive at their intended meaning. Without punctuation, sentences would run together, ideas would be unclear, and words would be misread. Writers need to use markers, like periods, commas, and dashes, to help them communicate as efficiently and effectively as possible.

Look at the difference punctuation makes in the meaning of the following letter.

Dear John:

I want a man who knows what love is all about. You are generous, kind, thoughtful. People who are not like you admit to being useless and inferior. You have ruined me for other men. I yearn for you. I have no feelings whatsoever when we're apart. I can be forever happy—will you let me be yours?   Susan

Dear John,

I want a man who knows what love is. All about you are generous, kind, thoughtful people, who are not like you. Admit to being useless and inferior. You have ruined me. For other men, I yearn. For you, I have no feelings whatsoever. When we're apart, I can be forever happy. Will you let me be?   Yours, Susan

This unit will help you write the love letter you actually want to write—with the punctuation that gets your message across. It will also provide you with guidelines for using the following punctuation.

End Punctuation

TEST YOURSELF

Add the appropriate end punctuation to the following sentences.

- That car almost hit us
- How can you say that
- She didn't want to go on the trip
- He asked if he could go
- I absolutely refuse to be a part of this

(Answers are in Appendix 3.)

UNIT PRE-TESTS
To check your students' abilities with the collective skills in this unit, two Unit Pre-tests are available in the *Instructor's Resource Manual.*

End punctuation signals the end of a sentence in three ways: The **period** ends a statement, the **question mark** signals a question, and the **exclamation point** marks an exclamation.

MyWritingLab

Understanding End Punctuation

To improve your understanding of these forms of punctuation, go to **MyWritingLab.com,** and choose **Final Punctuation** in the **Punctuation, Mechanics, and Spelling** module. For this topic, watch the video called **Animation: Final Punctuation.** Then, return to this chapter, which will go into more detail about these punctuation marks and give you opportunities to practice them. Finally, you will apply your understanding of end punctuation to your own writing.

Student Comment:
"**MyWritingLab** gives explanations when the answers are wrong AND when they are right."

PERIOD

1. A period is used with statements, mild commands, and indirect questions.

Statement:	Mason took his golden retriever on a walk.
Command:	Take this leash with you.
Indirect Question:	I forgot to ask him if he needed help.

TEACHING END PUNCTUATION
Distribute a lively, animated paragraph with the end punctuation taken out.

2. A period is also used with abbreviations and numbers.

Abbreviations: Dr. Finn lives at 123 Grammont St., next door to Ms. Margery Salisbury.

Numbers: $4.35   1.5 $849.50   0.033

Reviewing Periods

What are the three main uses of a period?

To mark the end of statements, mild commands, and indirect questions

What are two other uses of a period?

With abbreviations and numbers

PRACTICE 1: Recall/Identify   In the following sentences, circle the periods used incorrectly, and add those that are missing.

1. Hers was the first house on Palm Ave.south of Santa Barbara Street.

2. If you made more than $145.0 from one yard sale, you should consider it a success.

3. Mr.Woo is a nice neighbor.

4. Now that Ed Johnson has finished medical school, we call him Dr.Johnson.

5. Go with me to confront Sam.

PRACTICE 2: Apply   Add periods to the following paragraph where they are needed.

Driving a car with a stick shift is very easy once you can feel in your feet what the engine is doing. When I learned to drive a stick shift, I practiced on an old farm road called Weedpatch Hwy.because I was too nervous to practice in traffic. Mr. Turner, my driving instructor, was quite impressed when I took my final driving test in my dad's five-speed Ford Escort.

PRACTICE 3: Write Your Own   Write a sentence of your own for each of the following descriptions.   *Answers will vary.*

1. a statement about drunk driving

_____

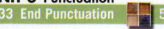
2. a statement including an address with an abbreviated street name

_____

3. an indirect question about directions

_____

4. a statement including a dollar amount

_____

5. a command to stop doing something

_____

QUESTION MARK

The **question mark** is used after a direct question.

Question Mark: Did you vote in the election today?
Question Mark: "Will Matthew turn his paper in on time?" her
                     mother asked.

Reviewing Question Marks

What is the main role of a question mark?

To indicate that a question is being asked

Give an example of a question.

Examples will vary.

PRACTICE 4: Recall/Identify In the following sentences, circle the question marks used incorrectly, and add those that are needed.

1. Is this the right way to George's house?

2. I think you have the right answer?

3. Is your grandfather Charles Curran.?

4. Susie, what time is your appointment.?

5. He asked his mother if she was still feeling ill?

PRACTICE 5: Apply Add question marks to the following paragraph where they are needed.

What makes an ideal student.❓A good student is one who studies very hard, gets to class on time with homework in hand, doesn't work too many hours, and has a limited social life. Now what makes a realistic student.❓This is one who works hard to pay for school, studies as much as possible, goes to class with homework in hand (most of the time), and doesn't party too much, right.❓Now you might ask where an ideal student comes from. Most of us are really ideal students most of the time. It's just that sometimes we need a break and might not put school first every night. But isn't that what makes school fun.❓

PRACTICE 6: Write Your Own Write a sentence of your own for each of the following descriptions.   *Answers will vary.*

1. a direct question about college requirements

   _____

2. a direct question about one of your classes

   _____

3. a direct question about the weather

   _____

4. a direct question about car maintenance

   _____

5. a direct question about dinner

   _____

EXCLAMATION POINT

The **exclamation point** indicates strong feeling.

If it is used too often, it is not as effective as it could be. You shouldn't use more than one exclamation point at a time.

Exclamation Point:	No way!
Exclamation Point:	I can't believe it!
Exclamation Point:	Stop, or I'll scream!
Exclamation Point:	"You make me so mad!" he yelled.

Reviewing Exclamation Points

What is the main use of an exclamation point?

To show strong emotion

Give an example of an exclamation.

Examples will vary.

PRACTICE 7: Recall/Identify Circle the exclamation points used incorrectly, and add those that are needed.

1. I don't think that would be possible today!

2. Are you crazy!

3. I'm not sure what you mean by that!

4. "You must be joking!" Matt screamed.

5. If we win this, we're going to the playoffs.!

PRACTICE 8: Apply Add exclamation points to the following paragraph where they are appropriate.

"Shoot, Charlie.! Shoot!" I can hear my mom in the crowd. Hearing her voice always gives me that extra push I need. I know we're down by one point. I can hear the crowd. "Shoot!" "Five more seconds!" "Shoot!" I slowly let the ball fly through the air. I watch as if time is in slow motion. *Swoosh.!* Nothing but net. As my teammates run onto the floor, I glance at the stands to find my mom. I see her beaming face looking down on me. I scream for all to hear, "Thanks, mom!"

PRACTICE 9: Write Your Own Write five sentences of your own using exclamation points correctly. *Answers will vary.*

_____

_____

_____

_____

CHAPTER REVIEW

Have students read the sentences out loud to help them decide on the correct end punctuation.

MyWritingLab **Reviewing End Punctuation**

To review this material before you complete the Review Practices, watch **Animation: Final Punctuation** at **MyWritingLab.com** one more time. This time, keep the video open as you complete the rest of the practices in this chapter. For best results, do the **MyWritingLab** exercises online as well as the Chapter Review practices in the book.

REVIEW PRACTICE 1: Recall/Identify For each sentence, add the correct end punctuation. You may also have to capitalize some letters.

1. What do you think you're doing?

2. Why you continue to smoke certainly confuses me.

3. Oh my! *C* can you believe it?

4. Take this piece of pie home with you.

5. "Where are you going?" she asked.

6. No, wait!

7. My brother wants to know who is taking us.

8. Is there a reason we have to wait?

9. You should do what you think is right.

10. I wonder if there is a way out.

MyWritingLab **Practicing End Punctuation**

Now complete the **Recall** activities for **Final Punctuation** in the **Punctuation, Mechanics, and Spelling** module of **MyWritingLab.com**. Remember to read the answers carefully because many of them look similar.

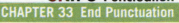
REVIEW PRACTICE 2: Apply Turn sentences 1–5 into questions and sentences 6–10 into exclamations.

1. The aerobics class is canceled.   *Is the aerobics class canceled?*

2. The Arkansas Razorbacks won.   *Did the Arkansas Razorbacks win?*

3. You will marry me.   *Will you marry me?*

4. Caroline made the final cut.   *Did Caroline make the final cut?*

5. You will save me a place.   *Will you save me a place?*

6. Please don't drive on the grass.   *Don't drive on the grass!*

7. The train is coming.*!*

8. Did you hear me?   *You heard me!*

9. You will never find out.*!*

10. No, I won't.*!*

MyWritingLab   **Practicing End Punctuation**

Next, complete the **Apply** activity for **Final Punctuation** in the **Punctuation, Mechanics, and Spelling** module of **MyWritingLab.com.** If you're stuck, go to the lower right-hand corner and open up the video again, or you can click on the Hint button.

Complete this **Writing Prompt** at **mywritinglab.com**

REVIEW PRACTICE 3: Write Your Own Write a paragraph about the house you grew up in. Try to include each type of end punctuation—the period, the question mark, and the exclamation point.   *Answers will vary.*

MyWritingLab   **Practicing End Punctuation**

For more practice, complete the **Write** activity for **Final Punctuation** in the **Punctuation, Mechanics, and Spelling** module of **MyWritingLab. com.** Make sure to pay close attention to end punctuation in your paragraph.

REVIEW PRACTICE 4: Editing Through Collaboration Exchange paragraphs from Review Practice 3 with another student, and do the following: *Answers will vary.*

1. Circle any errors in end punctuation.

2. Suggest the correct punctuation above your circle.

Then return the paragraph to its writer, and use the information in this chapter to correct any end punctuation errors in your own paragraph. Record your errors on the Error Log in Appendix 7.

Commas

UNIT PRE-TESTS
To check your students'
abilities with the collective
skills in this unit, two Unit
Pre-tests are available in
the *Instructor's Resource
Manual.*

TEST YOURSELF

Add commas to the following sentences.

- We went to the plaza and we saw a great movie.
- When we get really tired we act really silly.
- "He's taking flying lessons" said Steven.
- The job market however is starting to look better.
- On Saturday we went hiking fishing and camping.
- He was born August 5 1985 in Duluth Minnesota.

(Answers are in Appendix 3.)

The **comma** is the most frequently used punctuation mark, but it is also the most often misused. Commas make sentences easier to read by separating their parts. Following the rules in this chapter will help you write clear sentences that are easy to read.

MyWritingLab **Understanding Commas**

To find out more about commas, go to **MyWritingLab.com,** and choose **Commas** in the **Punctuation, Mechanics, and Spelling** module. From there, watch the video called **Animation: Commas.** Then, return to this chapter, which will go into more detail about this punctuation mark and give you opportunities to practice using it. Finally, you will apply your understanding of commas to your own writing.

Student Comment:
"I used to put commas just anywhere in a sentence, and now, thanks to **MyWritingLab** and *Mosaics,* I use them correctly AND I know the reason why they're there."

TEACHING COMMAS
Write 10 sentences that contain comma errors. Put each sentence on a small poster board so that you have 10 poster boards. Then create a duplicate set of poster boards. Divide the class into two teams. Place a set of 10 poster boards in front of each team, with the sentences facing down.

Begin a tag-team relay in which each team uses a marker to fix or supply the commas. When the first person finishes the first sentence, he or she hands the marker to the next person, who moves to the next sentence. The second person places commas in the second sentence and then hands the marker to the next person, and so on. Time the tag teams.

When the students have completed all the sentences, check to make sure that all the commas are correctly placed. Add five seconds to the team's time for each incorrect or missed comma. The team to finish with the lower time wins.

INSTRUCTOR'S RESOURCE MANUAL
For sample sentences, for more exercises, and for quizzes, see the *Instructor's Resource Manual,* Section II, Part IV.

UNIT POST-TESTS
To check your students' mastery of the collective skills in this unit, two Unit Post-tests are available in the *Instructor's Resource Manual.*

COMMAS WITH ITEMS IN A SERIES

Use commas to separate items in a series.
You should place commas between all items in a series.

Series: I ordered a pizza with mushrooms, sausage, and green peppers.

Series: He washed the dishes, swept the floor, and took out the garbage.

Series: Susan plans to move out when her parents give her permission, when she has enough money, and when she learns how to cook.

Sometimes this rule applies to a series of adjectives in front of a noun, but sometimes it does not. Look at these two examples.

Adjectives with Commas: The **cool, sweet** plums were delicious.

Adjectives without Commas: The **loose top** button fell off the TV.

Both of these examples are correct. So how do you know whether or not to use commas? You can use one of two tests. One test is to insert the word *and* between the adjectives. If the sentence makes sense, use a comma. Another test is to switch the order of the adjectives. If the sentence still reads clearly, use a comma between the two words.

Test 1:   The **cool and sweet** plums were delicious. **OK, so use a comma**

Test 2:   The **sweet, cool** plums were delicious. **OK, so use a comma**

Test 1:   The **loose and top** button fell off the TV. **Not OK, so no comma**

Test 2:   The **top loose** button fell off the TV. **Not OK, so no comma**

> **Reviewing Commas with Items in a Series**
>
> *Why use commas with items in a series?*
> To separate the items
> _____
>
> *Where do these commas go?*
> After all items in the series except the last
> _____

PRACTICE 1: Recall/Identify In the following sentences, circle the commas that are used incorrectly, and add any commas that are missing.

1. I need to go to the store for bread, milk, and eggs.

2. My favorite teams are the Lakers, the Spurs, and the Bulls.

3. The best things about a college education are the social aspects, the wide variety of instruction, and the career opportunities college offers.

4. Love, peace, and goodwill are my wishes for you.

5. To complete this fun exciting course successfully, you must write four papers, take two tests, and give one oral report.

PRACTICE 2: Apply Add the missing commas to the following paragraph.

When I get to the coffee house, I'm going to find a big, comfortable couch, order a latte, and read today's newspaper. I like to hang out at the coffeehouse because I see many of my friends. I usually meet Ron, Aldona, and Jennifer there. We spend our time doing homework, gossiping, or just hanging out. We tend to laugh a lot. This usually draws a lot of attention to us because Ron has a loud, hearty laugh. I love spending time with my friends at the coffeehouse. It's like spending time in a special, secret club.

PRACTICE 3: Write Your Own Write a sentence of your own for each of the following sets of items. *Answers will vary.*

1. three items on a grocery list

   _____

2. three of your favorite movies

   _____

3. three things to do at the beach

   _____

4. three kinds of sports cars

   _____

5. three cities you would like to visit

   _____

COMMAS WITH INTRODUCTORY WORDS

Use a comma to set off an introductory word, phrase, or clause from the rest of its sentence.

If you are unsure whether to add a comma, try reading the sentence with your reader in mind. If you want your reader to pause after the introductory word or phrase, you should insert a comma.

Introductory Word:	**Yes,** that would be great.
Introductory Word:	**Actually,** the plane wasn't as late as we thought it might be.
Introductory Phrase:	**In reality,** she's the best coach in town.
Introductory Phrase:	**To make the best of a bad situation,** we all went out for frozen yogurt.
Introductory Clause:	**When the band finished,** everyone clapped.
Introductory Clause:	**As the lights dimmed,** we all began screaming.

Reviewing Commas with Introductory Words

Why use commas with introductory words, phrases, and clauses?

To set them off from the rest of the sentence

How can you tell if a comma is needed?

Read the sentence to see if you want your reader to pause after the

introductory words.

PRACTICE 4: Recall/Identify In the following sentences, circle the commas that are used incorrectly, and add any commas that are missing.

1. When, he was a young boy, he lived in Texas.
2. The next time I go to the store, I will buy some snack foods.
3. Hoping to solve, the problem, Katie wrote to the school president.
4. Truly, that was the best home-cooked meal I've had in months.
5. As the band entered, the stadium, everyone stood up.

PRACTICE 5: Apply Add the missing commas to the following paragraph.

This past weekend, my sister and I took her 8-month-old daughter, Jamie, to the beach for the first time. At first, Jamie was afraid of the ocean, but she soon learned to love it. When my sister would hold Jamie in the water, Jamie would scream out loud and laugh uncontrollably. However, Jamie was still frightened when my sister wasn't holding her. Overall, we had a great time watching Jamie explore the water, sand, and seagulls for the first time. In two weeks, we are going back, and I can't wait.

PRACTICE 6: Write Your Own Write a sentence of your own for each of the following introductory words, phrases, or clauses. *Answers will vary.*

1. well

   _____

2. to make matters worse

   _____

3. when we got in the car

   _____

4. no

   _____

5. as he approached the house

   _____

COMMAS WITH INDEPENDENT CLAUSES

Use a comma before *and, but, for, nor, or, so,* and *yet* when they join two independent clauses. Remember that an independent clause must have both a subject and a verb.

Independent Clauses: Australia is a beautiful continent, **and** it holds many surprises for tourists.

Independent Clauses: Norman went to Europe, **but** he enjoyed Australia more.

Hint: Do not use a comma when a single subject has two verbs.

      s   v   **no comma**   v

Australia is a beautiful country and **has** a large tourist trade.

Adding a comma when none is needed is one of the most common errors in college writing assignments. Only if the second verb has its own subject should you add a comma.

s   v   comma   s   v

Australia is a beautiful country**,** and **it has** a large tourist trade.

Reviewing Commas with Independent Clauses

Name three coordinating conjunctions.

Answers will vary.

When should you use a comma before a coordinating conjunction?

When it joins two independent clauses

Should you use a comma before a coordinating conjunction when a single subject has two verbs?

No—only if the second verb has its own subject

PRACTICE 7: Recall/Identify Underline the subjects, and circle the coordinating conjunctions in the following sentences. Then cross out any commas used incorrectly, and add those that are missing.

1. I finished my paper tonight, (so) I will be ready for class tomorrow.

2. This gumbo smells good, (and) tastes even better.

3. Watching TV made Zack calm, (and) relaxed.

4. Mariah is going to the library today, (and) then she will go home.

5. The gardener mowed the lawn, (and) pruned the hedge in the front yard.

PRACTICE 8: Apply Add the missing commas to the following paragraph.

On Valentine's Day, my boyfriend told me we would have a special day. He would pick me up at 5:00, and he would take me to a very romantic place. He told me to dress up and look my best. I wore my new red dress and spent an hour on my hair and makeup. He picked me up promptly at 5:00. I had never been so disappointed, for he took me to the movies. We watched an action flick. I tried not to get angry, but I just couldn't help myself. After the movie, he said he needed to pick up something from his apartment, and he made me come inside. Boy, was I surprised to see the entire apartment lit up with candles and to hear music playing all around me. His table was elegantly set, and his two best friends were in tuxes waiting to serve us a five-course meal. Valentine's Day was exciting and special after all.

PRACTICE 9: Write Your Own Write a sentence of your own using each of the following coordinating conjunctions to separate two independent clauses.
Answers will vary.

1. or

_____

2. and

_____

3. so

_____

4. but

_____

5. yet

_____

COMMAS WITH INTERRUPTERS

Use a comma before and after a word or phrase that interrupts the flow of a sentence.

Most words that interrupt a sentence are not necessary for understanding the main point of a sentence. Setting them off makes it easier to recognize the main point.

Word: She called her boyfriend, **Ramon,** to pick us up.

Word: I didn't hear the buzzer, **however,** because the radio was on.

Phrase: My favorite dessert, **banana cream pie,** is on the menu.

Phrase: The governor, **running for a third term,** is very popular.

Phrase: The state with the fastest growing population, **according to government figures,** is Florida.

A very common type of interrupter is a clause that begins with *who, whose, which, when,* or *where* and is not necessary for understanding the main point of the sentence:

Clause: Rosemary Smith, **who is a travel agent,** was chosen jury foreman.

Because the information "who is a travel agent" is not necessary for understanding the main idea of the sentence, it is set off with commas.

Clause: The YMCA, **which is on Central Street,** now offers daycare.

The main point here is that the YMCA offers daycare. Since the other information isn't necessary to understanding the sentence, it can be set off with commas.

Hint: Do not use commas with *who, whose, which, when,* or *where* if the information is necessary for understanding the main point of the sentence.

My friend **who is a travel agent** was chosen as jury foreman.

Because the information in the *who* clause is necessary to understand which friend was chosen as the jury foreman, you should not set it off with commas.

Hint: Do not use commas to set off clauses beginning with *that*.

The YMCA **that is on Central Street** now offers daycare.

Reviewing Commas with Interrupters

Why should you use commas to set off words and phrases in the middle of a sentence?

To make the main point easier to recognize
_____

_____

When should you use commas with who, whose, which, when, *or* where?

When the interrupting words are not necessary for understanding the main

point

When should you not use commas before these words?

When the information is necessary to the point of the sentence

PRACTICE 10: Recall/Identify Label each sentence C if commas are used correctly with the underlined words and phrases or X if they are not.

1. ___X___ My brother, <u>trying to pass the class studied</u>, for an entire week.

2. ___X___ The dog, <u>with a bone in his mouth ran</u>, quickly down the street.

3. ___X___ The best, <u>shopping mall Fashion Plaza</u>, is not open on Sundays.

4. ___C___ The sister's baby, <u>who is asleep in the back room</u>, is my nephew.

5. ___X___ Stewart Cink, a <u>golfer played in</u>, the PGA tour.

PRACTICE 11: Apply Insert commas around the interrupting words and phrases in the following paragraph.

A rocking chair, worn by years of use, sits in a corner of my room. My grandmother used it when she had my mom, Sarah, many years ago. My mom used it with me, and I'll use it, of course, when I have children. I like looking at the rocker, which holds so many memories for so many people, because it makes me think of home. I sometimes read in the chair, however, so I can quietly sit in the most peaceful place and let my mind rest. This rocking chair, which is simply made of wood, keeps me sane while I am so far away from home.

PRACTICE 12: Write Your Own Write a sentence of your own for each of the following phrases.   *Answers will vary.*

1. the basketball player _____

2. of course _____

3. who drives recklessly _____

4. giving us his approval _____

5. which is on the kitchen counter _____

COMMAS WITH DIRECT QUOTATIONS

Use commas to mark direct quotations.

A direct quotation records a person's exact words. Commas set off the exact words from the rest of the sentence, making it easier to understand who said what.

Direct Quotation:	My friends often say, **"You are so lucky."**
Direct Quotation:	**"You are so lucky,"** my friends often say.
Direct Quotation:	**"You are so lucky,"** says my grandmother, **"to have good friends."**

Hint: If a quotation ends with a question mark or an exclamation point, do not use a comma. Only one punctuation mark is needed.

NOT	**"What did he say?,"** she asked.
Correct:	**"What did he say?"** she asked.

Reviewing Commas with Direct Quotations

Why should you use commas with a direct quotation?

To help the reader understand who said what

Should you use a comma if the quotation ends with a question mark or an exclamation point? Why or why not?

No—only one punctuation mark is needed.

PRACTICE 13: Recall/Identify In the following sentences, circle the commas that are used incorrectly, and add any commas that are missing.

1. She remarked,"My favorite food is Mexican."

2. "I don't know the answer," Mark confessed,"but I'll keep trying to figure it out."

3. "Are you out of your mind?," he asked.

4. "I remember," Ruben said, "when we all went camping in Tahoe."

5. "Get here right now!," screamed the mother.

PRACTICE 14: Apply Add the missing commas to the following passage.

Joey and Dawn decided to go to a movie. "What do you want to see?" he asked.

"Definitely the new *Harry Potter*," Dawn replied.

Joey was disappointed and responded,"But I've already seen that one."

"If you see it again," she said,"you might catch something you missed before."

"Well, I guess that's a good point," he admitted.

PRACTICE 15: Write Your Own Write five sentences of your own using commas to set off direct quotations. *Answers will vary.*

_____

_____

_____

_____

_____

OTHER USES OF COMMAS

Other commas clarify information in everyday writing.

Numbers: The answer to the third problem is **12,487.**

A comma is optional in numbers of four digits: **2000** or **2,000.**

Dates: My grandmother was born **July 12, 1942,** in Buffalo, New York.

Notice that there is a comma both before and after the year.

Addresses: Bruce's new address is **2105 Peterson Rd., Arma, KS 66712.**

Notice that there is no comma between the state and ZIP code.

States: He lives in **Monroe, Michigan,** and she lives in **Monroe, Louisiana.**

Notice that there is a comma both before and after a state.

Letters: **Dear John,**
Sincerely yours,

Reviewing Other Uses of Commas

Give one example of commas in each of the following situations:
Examples will vary.
Numbers: _____

Dates: _____

Addresses: _____

Letters: _____

Why are these commas important?
They clarify information in everyday writing.

PRACTICE 16: Recall/Identify In the following sentences, circle the commas that are used incorrectly, and add any commas that are missing.

1. I live at 4,801 Pine Street in Denver Colorado.

2. He threw 3847 pitches in his baseball career.

3. I need to deliver 14,00 mailers before the big sale this weekend.

4. There are more than 5,000 people with the last name of Martinez in the city of Los Angeles, California.

5. I think he moved to Las Vegas, Nevada.

PRACTICE 17: Apply Add the missing commas to the following paragraph.

   The world record for jump-roping is 1,200 hours. The jump-roper accomplished this feat on October 12, 1961, at his home in Biloxi, Mississippi. Another guy, who was from Ontario, Canada, tried to break the record in 1973, but he could only jump rope for 1,070 consecutive hours.

PRACTICE 18: Write Your Own Write a sentence of your own including each of the following items.   *Answers will vary.*

1. your date of birth

   _____

2. the city and state where you were born

   _____

3. your full address, including the zip code

   _____

4. the estimated number of miles between Santa Barbara, California, and New York City

   _____

5. the amount of money you would expect to pay for your dream house

   _____

CHAPTER REVIEW

Many of the questions in the Recall exercise are similar (other than the comma placement), so students need to read them carefully.

MyWritingLab   **Reviewing Commas**

To review this material before you complete the Review Practices, watch **Animation: Commas** at **MyWritingLab.com** one more time. This time, keep the video open as you complete the rest of the practices in this chapter. For best results, do the **MyWritingLab** exercises online as well as the Chapter Review practices in the book.

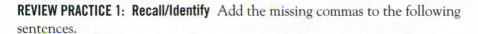
REVIEW PRACTICE 1: Recall/Identify Add the missing commas to the following sentences.

1. On the second Saturday of each month, Sensei Allen holds a Karate tournament.

2. Victor and Lou took the truck in to be fixed, but the automotive shop was closed.

3. Although Chesney had taken tap classes before, she still couldn't remember what to do.

4. The boy, however, believed that his horse would win.

5. I stood in awe as Kelsey, my beautiful golden retriever, won first place in the state dog show.

6. "Take a left at the last street on the block," said the crossing guard.

7. Downhill skiing, diving, and swimming are my favorite Olympic events.

8. The tall, lean, good-looking motorcycle cop was ticketing a speeder.

9. When the clock strikes twelve, meet me in the cemetery.

10. Saul, Tom, and Will are going to the town meeting if they get home in time.

MyWritingLab **Practicing Commas**

Now complete the **Recall** activities for **Commas** in the **Punctuation, Mechanics, and Spelling** module of **MyWritingLab.com.** If you're having a difficult time with a question, open up the video in the lower right-hand corner for some help.

REVIEW PRACTICE 2: Apply Add the missing commas to the following paragraph.

Sometimes when I walk into the library, I am immediately overwhelmed. Books, magazines, and newspapers are everywhere, and then I think to myself "This is only the first floor!" Last Friday evening, I went to the library with Ophelia, who is my science lab partner, to join a study group. We never made it to the study group, however, because we got sidetracked by the popular magazines on the first floor. Later that evening, we saw the tired, depressed faces of our study group members and were glad we had stayed in the magazine section taking magazine quizzes and reading for pleasure.

MyWritingLab   **Practicing Commas**

Next, complete the **Apply** activity for **Commas** in the **Punctuation, Mechanics, and Spelling** module of **MyWritingLab.com.** Pay close attention to the directions and only click when prompted.

⚙─**Complete** this **Writing Prompt** at **mywritinglab.com**

REVIEW PRACTICE 3: Write Your Own Write a paragraph about one of your neighbors. What are some identifying qualities of this person? Do you like him or her?   *Answers will vary.*

MyWritingLab   **Practicing Commas**

For more practice, complete the **Write** activity for **Commas** in the **Punctuation, Mechanics, and Spelling** module of **MyWritingLab.com.** Pay close attention to which sentences might contain comma errors.

REVIEW PRACTICE 4: Editing Through Collaboration Exchange paragraphs from Review Practice 3 with another student, and do the following: *Answers will vary.*

1. Circle any misplaced commas.

2. Suggest corrections for the incorrect commas.

Then return the paper to its writer, and use the information in this chapter to correct any comma errors in your own paragraph. Record your errors on the Error Log in Appendix 7.

Apostrophes

UNIT PRE-TESTS
To check your students' abilities with the collective skills in this unit, two Unit Pre-tests are available in the *Instructor's Resource Manual.*

TEST YOURSELF

Add an apostrophe or an apostrophe and *-s* where necessary in the following sentences.

- The followers went into their leaders home.
- Its not important that you understand its every function.
- Thats not a good enough reason to believe Tracys story.
- The childrens toys were scattered around the room.
- Charles party was a lot of fun.

(Answers are in Appendix 3.)

The **apostrophe** looks like a single quotation mark. Its two main purposes are to indicate where letters have been left out and to show ownership.

MyWritingLab

Understanding Apostrophes

To help you understand this form of punctuation, go to **MyWritingLab.com,** and choose **Apostrophes** in the **Punctuation, Mechanics, and Spelling** module. Next, watch the video called **Animation: Apostrophes.** Then, return to this chapter, which will go into more detail about apostrophes and give you opportunities to practice using them. Finally, you will apply your understanding of this punctuation mark to your own writing.

MARKING CONTRACTIONS

Use an apostrophe to show that letters have been omitted to form a contraction.

A **contraction** is the shortening of one or more words. Our everyday speech is filled with contractions.

TEACHING APOSTROPHES
Create a game of *Jeopardy!* with the following categories: Understanding Contractions, Forming

Contractions, Identifying Correct and Incorrect Possessives, and Forming Possessives. Write questions like the following to fit each category.

Understanding Contractions

Answer: The word that *can't* stands for

Question: What is *cannot*?

Forming Contractions

Answer: The contraction made from the words *should have*

Question: What is *should've*?

Identifying Correct and Incorrect Possessives

Answer: Of *hers*, *his*, and *it's*, the word that is an incorrect possessive pronoun

Question: What is *it's*?

Forming Possessives

Answer: Another way to write "the house of the family named Jones"

Question: What is "the Joneses' house"?

Divide the class into teams to play the game. The team to get the most correct answers wins.

INSTRUCTOR'S RESOURCE MANUAL
For directions on how to play the game and a complete set of questions and answers, for more exercises, and for quizzes, see the *Instructor's Resource Manual*, Section II, Part IV.

UNIT POST-TESTS
To check your students' mastery of the collective skills in this unit, two Unit Post-tests are available in the *Instructor's Resource Manual*.

I have	=	I've (*h* and *a* have been omitted)
you are	=	you're (*a* has been omitted)
let us	=	let's (*u* has been omitted)

Here is a list of commonly used contractions.

Some Common Contractions

I am	=	I'm		we have	=	we've
I would	=	I'd		we will	=	we'll
I will	=	I'll		they are	=	they're
you have	=	you've		they have	=	they've
you will	=	you'll		do not	=	don't
he is	=	he's		did not	=	didn't
she will	=	she'll		have not	=	haven't
it is	=	it's		could not	=	couldn't

Hint: Two words frequently misused are *it's* and *its*.

it's = contraction: it is (or it has) **It's** too late to go to the movie.

its = pronoun: belonging to it **Its** eyes are really large.

To see if you are using the correct word, say the sentence with the words *it is*. If that is what you want to say, add an apostrophe to the word.

? I think **its** boiling.

Test: I think **it is** boiling. **YES, add an apostrophe**

This sentence makes sense with *it is*, so you should write *it's*.

Correct: I think **it's** boiling.

? The kitten drank **its** milk.

Test: The kitten drank **it is** milk. **NO, so no apostrophe**

This sentence does not make sense with *it is*, so you should not use the apostrophe in *its*.

Correct: The kitten drank **its** milk.

Reviewing Contractions

What is the purpose of an apostrophe in a contraction?

To show that letters have been omitted

Write five contractions, and tell which letters have been omitted.

Answers will vary.

What is the difference between it's and its?

It's stands for it is, and its is a possessive pronoun.

PRACTICE 1: Recall/Identify In the following sentences, circle the apostrophes that are used incorrectly, and add any apostrophes that are missing.

1. It's about time to get out of bed.

2. I think Damian should'n't join us.

3. They've got a lot of nerve saying that.

4. If you're happy about it, then I'm happy for you.

5. This is the last time she'll borrow my car.

PRACTICE 2: Apply Write contractions for the following words.

1. we + would = we'd

2. they + will = they'll

3. would + not = wouldn't

4. does + not = doesn't

5. can + not = can't

PRACTICE 3: Write Your Own Write a sentence of your own for each of the contractions you wrote in Practice 2. *Answers will vary.*

SHOWING POSSESSION

Use an apostrophe to show **possession.**

1. For a singular word, use *'s* to indicate possession or ownership. You can always replace a possessive with *of* plus the noun or pronoun.

the dog**'s** collar	=	the collar **of the dog** (the dog owns the collar)
everyone**'s** opinion	=	the opinion **of everyone** (all the people possess a single opinion)
boss**'s** office	=	the office **of the boss** (the boss possesses the office)
today**'s** news	=	the news **of today** (today "owns" or "possesses" the news)

2. For plural nouns ending in *-s*, use only an apostrophe.

the dogs' collars	=	the collars **of the dogs**
the ladies' pearls	=	the pearls **of the ladies**
the owners' children	=	the children **of the owners**
the teachers' friends	=	the friends **of the teachers**
the friends' families	=	the families **of the friends**

3. For plural nouns that do not end in *-s*, add *'s*.

the men**'s** shirts	=	the shirts **of the men**
the children**'s** teachers	=	the teachers **of the children**
the women**'s** savings	=	the savings **of the women**

Reviewing Possessives

How do you mark possession or ownership for a singular word?

Add 's to the word.

How do you mark possession or ownership for a plural word that ends in -s?

Add an apostrophe after the -s ending.

> **How do you mark possession or ownership for a plural word that doesn't end in -s?**
>
> *Add 's to the word.*

PRACTICE 4: Recall/Identify In the following sentences, circle the apostrophes that are used incorrectly, and add any apostrophes that are missing.

1. The kids skateboards are in the garage.

2. Serenity had to get five shot's today in compliance with her doctor's order's.

3. The men's retreat is this weekend.

4. My boyfriends attitude is very negative today.

5. All of the babies diaper's need to be changed.

PRACTICE 5: Apply Write a possessive for each of the following phrases.

1. the parrot of Mr. Brown *Mr. Brown's parrot*

2. the shoes of Marcus *Marcus's shoes*

3. the meal of the prison inmates *the prison inmates' meal*

4. the holiday celebration of the Smith families *the Smith families' holiday celebration*

5. the water level of the lake *the lake's water level*

PRACTICE 6: Write Your Own Write a sentence of your own for each of the possessives you wrote in Practice 5. *Answers will vary.*

COMMON APOSTROPHE ERRORS

Two common errors occur with apostrophes. The following guidelines will help you avoid these errors.

No Apostrophe with Possessive Pronouns

Do not use an apostrophe with a possessive pronoun.

Possessive pronouns already show ownership, so they do not need an apostrophe.

NOT	Correct
his'	his
her's *or* hers'	hers
it's *or* its'	its
your's *or* yours'	yours
our's *or* ours'	ours
their's *or* theirs'	theirs

No Apostrophe to Form the Plural

Do not use an apostrophe to form a plural word.

This error occurs most often with plural words ending in *-s*. An apostrophe indicates possession or contraction; it does *not* indicate the plural. Therefore, a plural word never takes an apostrophe unless it is possessive.

NOT	The **shirts'** are on the hangers.
Correct:	The **shirts** are on the hangers.
NOT	She went to get the **groceries'** over an hour ago.
Correct:	She went to get the **groceries** over an hour ago.
NOT	Watching old family **movies'** is a lot of fun.
Correct:	Watching old family **movies** is a lot of fun.

Reviewing Apostrophe Errors

List three possessive pronouns.

Answers will vary. _____ _____

_____

Why don't possessive pronouns take apostrophes?

They are possessive without apostrophes.

> **What is wrong with the apostrophe in each of the following sentences?**
>
> **The last float in the parade is ours'.**
> *The pronoun ours is possessive without an apostrophe.*
>
> **There must be 100 floats' in the parade.**
> *Floats is plural only, not possessive.*

PRACTICE 7: Recall/Identify In the following sentences, circle the apostrophes that are used incorrectly, and add any apostrophes that are missing.

1. The cat licked it's paws for ten minutes after eating.

2. Why don't we go to the movie's?

3. If you join these two club's with me, we can take the members' pledge together.

4. I'm going to buy pant's just like your's.

5. That's my friend Dakota from my computer classes'.

PRACTICE 8: Apply Write a possessive for each of the following phrases.

1. the pen of him *his pen*

2. the car of her *her car*

3. the shirts of them *their shirts*

4. the sound of it *its sound*

5. a book of yours *your book*

PRACTICE 9: Write Your Own Write a sentence of your own for each of the possessives you wrote in Practice 8. *Answers will vary.*

_____

_____

_____

_____

_____

CHAPTER REVIEW

Not only do spelling and punctuation count in the Apply section, but correct spacing does as well, which makes this exercise a bit tricky for students. Make sure your students are aware of this before they complete the Apply questions.

MyWritingLab **Reviewing Apostrophes**

To review this material before you complete the Review Practices, watch **Animation: Apostrophes** at **MyWritingLab.com** one more time. This time, keep the video open as you complete the rest of the practices in this chapter. For best results, do the **MyWritingLab** exercises online as well as the Chapter Review practices in the book.

REVIEW PRACTICE 1: Recall/Identify In the following sentences, circle the apostrophes that are used incorrectly, and add any apostrophes that are missing.

1. Modern time's are difficult for many people to live in.

2. The Garners went on vacation this week.

3. Jame's dog's were jumping on the furniture.

4. I was'nt surprised that everyone admires Raymond.

5. I always have more fun on Tuesday's because Wednesday classe's are boring.

6. This pencil looks like it's mine.

7. The biochemist's could'nt figure out the error in the two formula's.

8. Eleanor's grandmother's look a lot alike.

9. The car you see sitting outside is her's.

10. Tomorrow is my grandparent's' anniversary.

MyWritingLab **Practicing Apostrophes**

Now complete the **Recall** activities for **Apostrophes** in the **Punctuation, Mechanics, and Spelling** module of **MyWritingLab.com**. Remember to read the answers carefully because many of them look similar.

REVIEW PRACTICE 2: Apply Add the missing apostrophes to the following sentences.

1. Everyone's choice is pizza, but somebody has to call in the order.

2. Women's clothing has been marked down, but all children's items are still regular price.

3. My father-in-law's job has been eliminated through downsizing.

4. The scouts admitted that the campfire was theirs.

5. There aren't any more cookies in the cupboard.

6. Ronny's apartment is located just five minutes from the beach.

7. The purse was Dana's, but the jacket belonged to someone else.

8. Don't tell me that there isn't enough; I know that the Joneses bought too much.

9. The head waiter is worried since sixteen people haven't shown up yet.

10. Tanya's mother doesn't believe the handwriting is hers.

MyWritingLab   **Practicing Apostrophes**

Next, complete the **Apply** activity for **Apostrophes** in the **Punctuation, Mechanics, and Spelling** module of **MyWritingLab.com.** If you're stuck, go to the lower right-hand corner and open up the video again, or you can click on the hint button.

⚙⊶ **Complete** this **Writing Prompt** at **mywritinglab.com**

REVIEW PRACTICE 3: Write Your Own Write a paragraph about your favorite birthday celebration in your life so far. Use at least six apostrophes correctly. *Answers will vary.*

MyWritingLab   **Practicing Apostrophes**

For more practice, complete the **Write** activity for **Apostrophes** in the **Punctuation, Mechanics, and Spelling** module of **MyWritingLab.com.** Make sure to pay close attention to which sentences might contain apostrophe errors as you revise the paragraph.

REVIEW PRACTICE 4: Editing Through Collaboration Exchange paragraphs from Review Practice 3 with another student, and do the following: *Answers will vary.*

1. Circle any misplaced or missing apostrophes.

2. Indicate whether they mark possession (P) or contraction (C).

Then return the paper to its writer, and use the information in this chapter to correct any apostrophe errors in your own paragraph. Record your errors on the Error Log in Appendix 7.

Quotation Marks

UNIT PRE-TESTS
To check your students'
abilities with the collective
skills in this unit, two Unit
Pre-tests are available in
the *Instructor's Resource
Manual.*

TEST YOURSELF

Add quotation marks where needed in the following sentences.

- Let's have a picnic, she said.
- My mom screamed, Tom! Get this spider!
- Put ice on the muscle, said Dr. Jansen, as soon as possible.
- I read three poems, including The Groundhog.
- Derek said I'll make dinner.

(Answers are in Appendix 3.)

Quotation marks are punctuation marks that work together in pairs. Their most common use is to indicate someone's exact words. They are also used to mark the title of a short piece of writing, such as a short story or a poem.

MyWritingLab   ## Understanding Quotation Marks

Student Comment:
"What I like about **MyWritingLab**
is that I can see the video again
if I need it."

To understand more about this form of punctuation, go to **MyWritingLab. com,** and choose **Quotation Marks** in the **Punctuation, Mechanics, and Spelling** module. From there, watch the video called **Animation: Quotation Marks.** Then, return to this chapter, which will go into more detail about these punctuation marks and give you opportunities to practice them. Finally, you will apply your understanding of quotation marks to your own writing.

DIRECT QUOTATIONS

Use quotation marks to indicate a **direct quotation**—someone's exact words. Here are some examples. They show the three basic forms of a direct quotation.

Direct Quotation: "I am not leaving without you," said the spy.

TEACHING QUOTATION
MARKS
Present the class with
an excerpt from a play
(one with numerous
stage directions and

comments) written as one long paragraph with no quotation marks to distinguish the spoken language from the stage directions. Have a student read the excerpt from the play. Students will see how difficult distinguishing the stage remarks from the spoken words is and will then understand the value of marking direct quotations.

Then have students work in groups of three or four to punctuate the paragraph correctly by adding quotation marks and proper spacing.

INSTRUCTOR'S RESOURCE MANUAL
For sample paragraphs, for more exercises, and for quizzes, see the *Instructor's Resource Manual*, Section II, Part IV.

UNIT POST-TESTS
To check your students' mastery of the collective skills in this unit, two Unit Post-tests are available in the *Instructor's Resource Manual*.

In this first example, the quoted words come first.

Direct Quotation: The spy said, "I am not leaving without you."

Here the quoted words come after the speaker is named.

Direct Quotation: "I am not," the spy said, "leaving without you."

In this example, the quoted words are interrupted, and the speaker is named in the middle. This form emphasizes the first few words.

INDIRECT QUOTATIONS

If you just talk about someone's words—an **indirect quotation**—you do not need quotation marks. Indirect quotations usually include the word *that*, as in *said that*. In questions, the wording is often *asked if*. Look at these examples of indirect quotations.

Direct Quotation: "I interviewed for a job at the Scott Corporation," said Bob.

These are Bob's exact words, so you must use quotation marks.

Indirect Quotation: Bob **said that** he interviewed for a job at the Scott Corporation.

This sentence explains what Bob said but does not use Bob's exact words, so quotation marks should not be used.

Direct Quotation: "We walked four miles," said Kira.

Indirect Quotation: Kira **said that** they walked four miles.

Direct Quotation: "Did you apply for a student loan?" Mom asked.

Indirect Quotation: Mom **asked if** I had applied for a student loan.

Reviewing Quotation Marks with Quotations

How do you show that you are repeating someone's exact words?

Put the words in quotation marks

What is an indirect quotation?

An explanation of someone's words but not the exact words

PRACTICE 1: Recall/Identify In the following sentences, circle the quotation marks used incorrectly, and add any quotation marks that are missing.

1. "Watch out!"screamed the police officer."

2. "I wish they'd stop throwing things" on the field,"commented the football player.

3. He asked, "How "much longer do we wait?"

4. "Go to your room,"said the father, "and clean it up."

5. Pablo said that "he enjoyed the game."

PRACTICE 2: Apply Add the missing quotation marks to the following paragraph.

    Yesterday my manager stuck up for me when a customer came in saying,"That young man sold me a defective computer."She was really mad. "Ma'am,"my manager patiently replied, "he sold you our top-of-the-line computer."She said, "But my computer still doesn't work."After a series of questions, my manager finally asked her what was wrong with her computer. "The monitor is black,"she replied. After another series of questions, my manager discovered her monitor was not plugged in, but he handled the customer as if her mistake was the most logical and frequent one ever made. The customer left happy that her system would now work. "No matter what,"my manager said, "the customer is always right . . . and smart."

PRACTICE 3: Write Your Own Write a sentence of your own for each of the following set of details.   *Answers will vary.*

1. a question asked by Natasha

_____

2. a statement spoken by the plumber

_____

3. an exclamation spoken by Thomas

_____

4. an indirect question that Ricki asked

_____

5. a statement spoken by the chemist

_____

CAPITALIZING AND USING OTHER PUNCTUATION MARKS WITH QUOTATION MARKS

When you are quoting someone's complete sentences, begin with a capital letter and use appropriate end punctuation—a period, a question mark, or an exclamation point.

Capitalize the first letter of the first word being quoted, and put a period at the end of the sentence if it is a statement. Separate the spoken words from the rest of the sentence with a comma.

"She doesn't really love me," he said.

She replied, "Tie your shoelaces."

If the quotation ends with a question mark or an exclamation point, use that punctuation instead of a comma or a period.

He yelled, "Turn off that music!"

"Why do you want to know?" she asked.

In a quotation that is interrupted, capitalize the first word being quoted, but do not capitalize words in the middle of the sentence. Use a comma both before and after the interruption. End with a period if it is a statement.

"No," said the student, "this seat isn't taken."

You do not need to capitalize the first word of a quotation that is only part of a sentence.

I don't think that he will ever "find himself."

Hint: Look at the examples again. Notice that periods and commas always go inside the quotation marks.

NOT   "Yes", she said, "please sit here".

Correct: "Yes," she said, "please sit here."

Reviewing Capitalization and Punctuation with Quotation Marks

When you quote someone's exact words, why should you begin with a capital letter?

Because the word begins a sentence

Where do commas go in relation to quotation marks? Where do periods go?

Both commas and periods go inside quotation marks.

PRACTICE 4: Recall/Identify In the following sentences, circle the quotation marks, capital letters, and other punctuation marks that are used incorrectly, and add any missing quotation marks and punctuation.

1. "How are the Broncos doing this season?" she asked her boyfriend.

2. "I need a new job," said Stan.

3. Victor wondered, "How will they ever make it without me?"

4. "If you want to meet me," he said, "just come to the concert tonight."

5. "I can't be there," Manny explained, "unless I get time off work."

PRACTICE 5: Apply Add the missing quotation marks and punctuation to the following paragraph.

I have always said that I love the snow, but I hate the cold. I'm not sure how this works actually. My best friend asked, "How can you hate the cold so much when you are constantly out skiing or making a snowman?" I replied, "I'm just weird that way, I guess." I have always been like this. My mom never had to say, "Put on your jacket." It was more like, "Why are you wearing a jacket in 80-degree weather?" No one understands this weird quirk in me. I'll say "Yes" to skiing any day. Maybe someone will invent snow skiing in Jamaica. Then I'd be set.

PRACTICE 6: Write Your Own Write a sentence of your own for each of the following direct quotations, and punctuate it correctly. *Answers will vary.*

1. "I can't believe it!"

_____

2. "What?"

_____

3. "We need to clean the garage."

_____

4. "No,"..."you are not invited."

_____

5. "I'm sorry,"..."you didn't understand what I said."

_____

QUOTATION MARKS AROUND TITLES

Put quotation marks around the titles of short works that are parts of larger works. The titles of longer works are put in italics (or underlined).

Quotation Marks	Italics/Underlining
"The Black Cat" (short story)	*Harry Potter and the Goblet of Fire* (book)
"The Emperor of Ice Cream" (poem)	*An Introduction to Literature* (book)
"Rainy Day Women" (song)	*Bob Dylan's Greatest Hits* (album)
"Florida Keys Beckon Tourists" (magazine article)	*Travel and Leisure* (magazine)
"Bush Elected President" (newspaper)	*The Washington Post* (newspaper)
"The Wedding" (episode on TV series)	*Friends* (TV series)

> ### Reviewing Quotation Marks with Titles
>
> **When do you put quotation marks around a title?**
> *When it is a short work that is part of a larger work*
>
> **When do you italicize (or underline) a title?**
> *When it is a longer work*

PRACTICE 7: Recall/Identify Put an X in front of each sentence with errors in quotation marks or italics/underlining. Add any missing quotation marks and italics or underlining.

1. __X__ I really like the song "I Will Survive" by Gloria Gaynor.

2. __X__ Did you read Keats's poem "Ode to a Nightingale?"

3. __X__ My favorite short story is Faulkner's "Barn Burning."

4. _____ The best entry in the poetry contest was "Trial" by Evelyn Main.

5. __X__ If you want to come over, we're watching the *I Love Lucy* episode called "Grape Smashing."

PRACTICE 8: Apply Place quotation marks around the titles of short works, and underline the titles of long works in the following paragraph.

When Terrance was in high school, he was in a literature club. They read the short stories "Araby," "Young Goodman Brown," and "A Dill Pickle." They also read several poems by Edward Taylor. Terrance's favorite poems were "Huswifery," "Upon Wedlock," and "Death of Children." Every week the club wrote a book review for the school newspaper, The Northbrook News. One particular article was called "Finding Bliss." It was about Edith Wharton's novel The House of Mirth. These articles really encouraged other students to read for pleasure.

PRACTICE 9: Write Your Own Write a sentence of your own for each of the following items. Make up a title if you can't think of one. *Answers will vary.*

1. a short story _____

2. a song title _____

3. a newspaper article _____

4. a poem _____

5. a magazine article _____

CHAPTER REVIEW

MyWritingLab | **Reviewing Quotation Marks**

To review this material before you complete the Review Practices, watch **Animation: Quotation Marks** at MyWritingLab.com one more time. This time, keep the video open as you complete the rest of the practices in this chapter. For best results, do the **MyWritingLab** exercises online as well as the Chapter Review practices in the book.

Let students know that many of the Recall answers for this topic look similar, so they will need to read the questions carefully. In the Apply activity, students will be asked to underline titles even though the video tells them to italicize these titles.

REVIEW PRACTICE 1: Recall/Identify Add the missing quotation marks and punctuation to the following sentences.

1. Priscilla's favorite song is "Smooth" by Carlos Santana and Rob Thomas.

2. I, on the other hand, like loud songs.

3. The short story "The Almond Tree" is my son's favorite.

4. "I hate to break the news to you," Louis said, "but I've found someone new."

5. Malik's keys are on the desk.

6. "To be, or not to be, that is the question," said Hamlet.

7. "Did you see the old-fashioned car drive by our house?" asked Paula.

8. She said, "I'm still in love with you."

9. "Did she ever answer her cell phone?" I asked.

10. The news writer titled his article "Somewhere in the Devil's Domain."

MyWritingLab | Practicing Quotation Marks

Now complete the **Recall** activities for **Quotation Marks** in the **Punctuation, Mechanics, and Spelling** module of **MyWritingLab.com**. If you're having a difficult time with a question, open up the video in the lower right hand corner for some help.

REVIEW PRACTICE 2: Apply Add the missing quotation marks, commas, and underlining for italics to the following dialogue.

"Hey, Janalee," I called, "let's go to Barnes and Noble."

"We were just there," she answered.

"Well, let's go again. I have to get a novel for English," I said.

"Which novel do you need?" asked Janalee.

"It's called Waiting by Her Jinn," I said.

"Oh, I read that. It's great. You'll love it," she said as she waved goodbye.

 **Practicing Quotation Marks**

Next, complete the **Apply** activity for **Quotation Marks** in the **Punctuation, Mechanics, and Spelling** module of **MyWritingLab. com.** Pay close attention to the directions and only click on what you're asked to.

⚙️─[**Complete** this **Writing Prompt** at **mywritinglab.com**

REVIEW PRACTICE 3: Write Your Own In paragraph form, record a conversation from your day. What did you talk about? What was the point of this conversation? What were your exact words? *Answers will vary.*

MyWritingLab **Practicing Quotation Marks**

For more practice, complete the **Write** activity for **Quotation Marks** in **Punctuation, Mechanics, and Spelling** module of **MyWritingLab. com.** Make sure to pay close attention to the use of quotation marks.

REVIEW PRACTICE 4: Editing Through Collaboration Exchange paragraphs from Review Practice 3 with another student, and do the following: *Answers will vary.*

1. Circle any incorrect or missing quotation marks.

2. Underline any faulty punctuation.

3. Put an X over any incorrect use of italics/underlining.

Then return the paper to its writer, and use the information in this chapter to correct any errors with quotation marks and italics/underlining in your own paragraph. Record your errors on the Error Log in Appendix 7.

Other Punctuation Marks

TEST YOURSELF

Add semicolons, colons, dashes, or parentheses to the following sentences.

- Matthew turned his paper in early Erica decided not to turn in a paper at all.
- Dave felt sorry for the defendant however, he had to vote for a conviction.
- Aaron needed several items for his dorm room a comforter, new sheets, a lamp, and a rug.
- Inez had only two words to say about bungee jumping "Never again."
- The recipe says to fold gently mix the berries into the batter.

(Answers are in Appendix 3.)

This chapter explains the uses of the **semicolon, colon, dash,** and **parentheses.** We'll look at these punctuation marks one by one.

MyWritingLab **Understanding Other Punctuation Marks**

To learn more about other punctuation marks, go to **MyWritingLab. com,** and choose **Semicolons, Colons, Dashes, and Parentheses** in the **Punctuation, Mechanics, and Spelling** module. For this topic, watch the video called **Animation: Semicolons, Colons, Dashes, and Parentheses.** Then, return to this chapter, which will go into more detail about these marks and give you opportunities to practice them. Finally, you will apply your understanding of semicolons, colons, dashes, and parentheses to your own writing.

SEMICOLONS

Semicolons are used to separate equal parts of a sentence. They are also used to avoid confusion when listing items in a series.

1. Use a semicolon to separate two closely related independent clauses.

    An independent clause is a group of words with a subject and a verb that can stand alone as a sentence. You might use a semicolon instead of a coordinating conjunction (*and*, *but*, *for*, *nor*, *or*, *so*, *yet*) or a period. Any one of the following three options would be correct.

	Independent	Independent
Semicolon:	Henry never took a lunch break; he was too busy at his job.	
Conjunction:	Henry never took a lunch break, **for** he was too busy at his job.	
Period:	Henry never took a lunch break. **He** was too busy at his job.	

2. Use a semicolon to join two independent clauses that are connected by such words as *however*, *therefore*, *furthermore*, *moreover*, *for example*, or *consequently*. Put a comma after the connecting word.

	Independent	Independent
Semicolon:	Shrimp is expensive; **nevertheless,** it's always worth the money.	
Semicolon:	Juanita is very talented musically; **for example,** she can play the piano and the flute.	
Semicolon:	She has always worked hard; **in fact,** she put herself through college.	

3. Use a semicolon to separate items in a series when any of the items contain commas.

NOT   At the party, Lily drank some tasty red punch, ate some delicious chicken with garlic, herbs, and lemon, and danced with several old boyfriends.

Correct: At the party, Lily drank some tasty red punch; ate some delicious chicken with garlic, herbs, and lemon; and danced with several old boyfriends.

Reviewing Semicolons

How are semicolons used between two independent clauses?

To separate the clauses

How are semicolons used with items in a series?

To separate the items when commas are included in any of the items

---

punctuation marks on small pieces of cardboard. The sentence parts should include clauses, phrases, and single parts of speech.

Assign several pieces of cardboard to each student, and have students begin by wearing one card. Then have students who are sentence parts stand in front of the class to form a sentence. For example, seven students might make the following sentence:

> *I went grocery shopping* (clause)
>
> *after school* (prep phrase)
>
> *because* (subordinating conj)
>
> *I needed food* (clause)
>
> *fruit/milk/bread* (three words)

Then have the students who are punctuation marks go to the correct places in the sentence (for example, a colon after *food* and commas after *fruit* and *milk*). By moving students around, show them how punctuation changes when certain words, phrases, and clauses are rearranged, added, or inserted.

INSTRUCTOR'S
RESOURCE MANUAL
For more words, phrases, and clauses; for more exercises; and for quizzes, see the *Instructor's Resource Manual*, Section II, Part IV.

UNIT POST-TESTS
To check your students' mastery of the collective skills in this unit, two Unit Post-tests are available in the *Instructor's Resource Manual*.

PRACTICE 1: Recall/Identify In the following sentences, circle the semicolons that are used incorrectly, and add any commas and semicolons that are missing.

1. Baking homemade bread is very easy; however, it's faster to use a bread maker.

2. I walked my dog to the park; ran into Mike, Zoe, and Christine; and invited them over for dinner.

3. She's allergic to chocolate and honey; she rarely eats other sweets either.

4. I'm a horrible cook; for example, I burned the toast at breakfast today.

5. This trip cost us a fortune; we'll be paying off the credit card for a year.

PRACTICE 2: Apply Add semicolons to the following paragraph.

One day I went fishing with Uncle Peter; it was the last day I would spend with him before he left for college. When we arrived at the lake, we realized that we forgot the bait; nevertheless, we knew where we could buy more nearby. Inside the store were racks and racks of things for sale, but we were interested in only three of them. One rack displayed bait, tackle, and fishing line; one shelved candy and snack foods; and the other held cigarettes and chewing tobacco. The bait gave us about 14 fish, and the candy gave me a cavity; however, that can of Copenhagen gave us grief from our moms every time they caught us chewing.

PRACTICE 3: Write Your Own Write five sentences of your own using semicolons correctly. *Answers will vary.*

_____

_____

_____

_____

_____

COLONS

Colons introduce a list or idea that follows them.

1. The main use of the colon is to introduce a list or thought. Here are some examples:

   Colon: Bring the following supplies to class: sketch pad, India ink, pen tips, and a charcoal pencil.

   Colon: I noticed several fire hazards: old paint cans and rags, curtains near the stove, and lit candles with no one present.

   Colon: The decision was easy: return the favor.

   The most common error with colons is using one where it isn't needed.

2. Do not use a colon after the words *such as* or *including*. A complete sentence must come before a colon.

   NOT   Use good packing materials, **such as:** bubble wrap, styro pellets, and foam.

   Correct: Use good packing materials, **such as** bubble wrap, styro pellets, and foam.

   NOT   We saw many sights, **including:** the Grand Canyon, Yosemite, and Mount Rainier.

   Correct: We saw many sights, **including** the Grand Canyon, Yosemite, and Mount Rainier.

3. In addition, you should not use a colon after a verb or after a preposition. Remember that a complete sentence must come before a colon.

   NOT   The topics to be discussed **are:** memory, hard drive, and new software.

   Correct: The topics to be discussed **are** memory, hard drive, and software.

   NOT   The program consisted **of:** a lecture, a PowerPoint presentation, and lunch.

   Correct: The program consisted **of** a lecture, a PowerPoint presentation, and lunch.

Reviewing Colons

What is the main use of a colon?

To introduce a list or thought

Why should you not use a colon after such words as is or of?

A colon must come after a complete sentence.

PRACTICE 4: Recall/Identify In the following sentences, circle the colons that are used incorrectly, and add any colons that are missing.

1. You should take: hiking boots, cotton socks, and sunscreen.

2. Mark still has to take the following classes: biology, chemistry, political science, and geometry.

3. I have a lot to do today: wash the car, pick up Theo at the airport, and finish my English paper.

4. The aerobics class consisted of: step exercises, line dancing, and the stairmaster.

5. I like: the fireplace, the gardens, and the vaulted ceilings.

6. The presentation covered many topics, including: company goals, stock options, and 401K plans.

PRACTICE 5: Apply Add colons to the following paragraph.

People can learn a lot from visiting museums: they can learn about history, psychology, and sociology for numerous cultures. Many museums have enormous collections of various types of art: ancient, Renaissance, Victorian, modern, and so on. I particularly like ancient art. Two museums have tremendous ancient art exhibits: the J. Paul Getty Museum and the San Antonio Metropolitan Museum of Art. I can spend hours looking at all the statuary and pottery. Museums are just loaded with fabulous cultural information.

PRACTICE 6: Write Your Own Write five sentences of your own using colons correctly. *Answers will vary.*

_____

_____

_____

_____

_____

DASHES AND PARENTHESES

Both **dashes** and **parentheses** mark breaks in the flow of a sentence. A dash suggests an abrupt pause in a statement, while parentheses surround words that could actually be taken out of a sentence grammatically.

Dashes

Dashes emphasize ideas.

1. Use dashes to emphasize or draw attention to a point.

   Dash: I know what I want out of life—happiness.

   In this example, the beginning of the sentence introduces an idea, and the dash then sets off the answer.

   Dash: Peace, love, and good health—these are my words for the new year.

   In this example, the key words are set off at the beginning, and the explanation follows. Beginning this way adds some suspense to the sentence.

   Dashes: I know what I want in a roommate—thoughtfulness—and I plan to get it.

   The dashes divide this sentence into three distinct parts, which makes the reader pause and think about each part.

Parentheses

Whereas dashes set off material the writer wants to emphasize, **parentheses** do just the opposite. They are always used in pairs.

2. Use parentheses to set off information that is interesting or helpful but not necessary for understanding the sentence.

   Parentheses: Their oldest son left his family at age 18 (**never to return again**).

   Parentheses: The handbook put out by the MLA (**Modern Language Association**) is the best guideline.

3. Parentheses are also used to mark a person's lifespan and to number items in a sentence. They are always used in pairs. Here are some examples:

   Parentheses: Emily Dickinson (**1830–1886**) is one of America's great poets.

   Parentheses: Follow these steps in writing a paragraph: (**1**) brainstorm for ideas, (**2**) choose a topic, and (**3**) formulate a topic sentence.

> ### Reviewing Dashes and Parentheses
>
> *What is the difference between dashes and parentheses?*
>
> *Dashes emphasize information, and parentheses set off unnecessary but helpful information.*
>
> *When do you use dashes?*
>
> *To emphasize, or draw attention to, a point*
>
> *When do you use parentheses?*
>
> *To set off information that isn't necessary to the main point of a sentence*

PRACTICE 7: Recall/Identify Use dashes or parentheses with the underlined words in the following sentences.

1. I met the new neighbors (the ones at the end of the block) and brought them cookies.

2. My wife is going out with her friends tomorrow—and taking the kids—so I can watch the big fight on TV.

3. My neighbors (the Parkers) are nice people, but they're awful housekeepers.

4. There is one kind of food that everyone likes—barbecue.

5. While you are house-sitting for us, please don't forget to (1) feed the cats, (2) check the mail, and (3) water the houseplants.

PRACTICE 8: Apply Add dashes and parentheses to the following paragraph.

Stephano and I became best friends 10 years ago in college at UCLA. Our British literature teacher (an enormously tall and bald man who enjoyed playing pranks on other faculty members) made us senior seminar partners. Ever since then, we've been best friends. We've been through a lot together—ex-wives, self-doubt, and other trying issues—but we've never abandoned each other. I hope (as I'm sure he does) that we never lose contact with one another.

PRACTICE 9: Write Your Own Write three sentences of your own using dashes and two using parentheses.   *Answers will vary.*

_____

_____

_____

_____

_____

CHAPTER REVIEW

MyWritingLab   ## Reviewing Other Punctuation Marks

Many of the answers in this topic are based on style choices, which makes it especially useful for your advanced writers.

To review this material before you complete the Review Practices, watch **Animation: Semicolons, Colons, Dashes, and Parentheses** at **MyWritingLab.com** one more time. This time, keep the video open as you complete the rest of the practices in this chapter. For best results, do the **MyWritingLab** exercises online as well as the Chapter Review practices in the book.

REVIEW PRACTICE 1: Recall/Identify Add semicolons, colons, dashes, and parentheses to the following sentences.

1. She never lost her money; she forgot to take the check out of her pocket.

2. Her competition was from three other girls: Brittany, Marci, and Desiree.

3. She never listens; she always asks questions that were already answered.

4. My favorite TV show is about to come on—*NYPD Blue*.   *(or a colon)*

5. Hand me a pencil—the yellow one—so I can make up a grocery list.
   (or parentheses)

6. We could still win if we changed the lineup; put Dave in front of Stuart.

7. There are several reasons I refuse to go out with you: You tend to ignore what I say, you treat your girlfriends disrespectfully, and I am dating your brother.

8. I'm making chocolate cake for dessert—your favorite.

9. Steve finally decided which college to attend the University of Maryland.
   (or a colon)

10. The impatient people in line at the bank (the rude ones) are usually the ones who take the longest at the counter.   *(or dashes)*

MyWritingLab | **Practicing Other Punctuation Marks**

Now complete the **Recall** activities for **Semicolons, Colons, Dashes, and Parentheses** in the **Punctuation, Mechanics, and Spelling** module of **MyWritingLab.com.** Remember to read the answers carefully because many of them look similar.

REVIEW PRACTICE 2: Apply Add semicolons, colons, dashes, and parentheses to the following paragraph.

Our house is affectionately known as the "Gibson Zoo." Outside we have two very large dogs, inside we have a smaller dog and two cats. The bird population is also recognized in our house since we have two love birds Dorris and Pierre. All of our animals (the ones we have purchased and the ones we found as strays) have been given appropriate names. Our favorite names are from literature and Greek mythology: Zeus, Apollo, Beowulf, Romeo, Juliet, and Macbeth. We're still thinking about adding one more pet; it will be either an iguana or a hamster. And we have only one requirement for the new addition it must be able to get along with the rest of the family.

MyWritingLab | **Practicing Other Punctuation Marks**

Next, complete the **Apply** activity for **Semicolons, Colons, Dashes, and Parentheses** in the **Punctuation, Mechanics, and Spelling** module of **MyWritingLab.com.** If you're stuck, you can go to the lower right-hand corner and open up the video again, or you can click on the hint button.

⚙️✎ **Complete** this **Writing Prompt** at **mywritinglab.com**

REVIEW PRACTICE 3: Write Your Own Write a paragraph explaining to someone how to do something that you do well. *Answers will vary.*

Practicing Other Punctuation Marks

For more practice, complete the **Write** activity for **Semicolons, Colons, Dashes, and Parentheses** in the **Punctuation, Mechanics, and Spelling** module of **MyWritingLab.com.** Make sure to pay close attention to which sentences might contain these types of errors as you revise the paragraph.

REVIEW PRACTICE 4: Editing Through Collaboration Exchange paragraphs from Review Practice 3 with another student, and do the following: *Answers will vary.*

1. Circle any incorrect or missing semicolons.

2. Circle any incorrect or missing colons.

3. Circle any incorrect or missing dashes.

4. Circle any incorrect or missing parentheses.

Then return the paper to its writer, and use the information in this chapter to correct any punctuation errors in your own paragraph. Record your errors on the Error Log in Appendix 7.

Mechanics

The mechanical aspects of a sentence are much like the mechanical features of a car, an appliance, or a clock. They are some of the smallest—yet most important—details in a sentence. In writing, the term *mechanics* refers to capitalization, abbreviations, and numbers. We usually take these items for granted, but when they are used incorrectly, a sentence, just like a mechanical appliance with a weak spring, starts to break down.

Following a few simple guidelines will help you keep your sentences running smoothly and efficiently. These guidelines are explained in two chapters:

Capitalization

UNIT PRE-TESTS
To check your students'
abilities with the collective
skills in this unit, two Unit
Pre-tests are available in
the *Instructor's Resource
Manual.*

TEST YOURSELF

Correct the capitalization errors in the following sentences.

- The smith family lives on washington street.
- we fly into newark airport and then get a taxi to seton hall university.
- This term I'm taking spanish, biology 200, history, and english.
- In june, I drove to california in my dodge durango.
- We read several plays by shakespeare, including *hamlet*.

(Answers are in Appendix 3.)

Because every sentence begins with a capital letter, **capitalization** is the best place to start discussing the mechanics of good writing. Capital letters signal where sentences begin. They also call attention to certain kinds of words, making sentences easier to read and understand.

Student Comment:
"When I work with **MyWriting-Lab,** I feel in control of my learning."

MyWritingLab **Understanding Capitalization**

For more information about this topic, go to **MyWritingLab.com,** and choose **Capitalization** in the **Punctuation, Mechanics, and Spelling** module. From there, watch the video called **Animation: Capitalization.** Then, return to this chapter, which will go into more detail about capitalization rules and give you opportunities to practice them. Finally, you will apply your understanding of capitalization to your own writing.

CAPITALIZATION GUIDELINES

Correct capitalization coupled with correct punctuation adds up to good, clear writing. Here are some guidelines to help you capitalize correctly.

TEACHING
CAPITALIZATION
Show students copies of
real emails that contain no

capitalization whatsoever. At the same time, show students copies of chat room conversations in which people who type in all caps are told to "stop yelling."

Have students rewrite the emails with correct capitalization.

After the exercise, talk to students about how capitalization marks sentence boundaries.

INSTRUCTOR'S RESOURCE MANUAL
For sample sentences, for more exercises, and for quizzes, see the *Instructor's Resource Manual*, Section II, Part IV.

UNIT POST-TESTS
To check your students' mastery of the collective skills in this unit, two Unit Post-tests are available in the *Instructor's Resource Manual*.

1. Capitalize the first word of every sentence, including the first word of a quotation that forms a sentence.

> The best route is down Alpine Street.
>
> "The best route is down Alpine Street," he said.
>
> He said, "The best route is down Alpine Street."

Do not capitalize the second part of a quotation that is split.

> "The best route," he said, "is down Alpine Street."

2. Do not capitalize common nouns. Capitalize all proper nouns.

Common Nouns	Proper Nouns
person	John Doe
city	Topeka
building	Sears Tower
lake	Lake Michigan
spacecraft	*Apollo 11*

Here are some examples of proper nouns:

People:	Susan, Michael Jordan, Vanna White
Groups:	Americans, Navajos, African Americans, Puerto Ricans, Japanese
Languages:	English, Spanish, French
Religions:	Protestantism, Buddhism, Judaism
Religious Books:	Koran, Bible, Book of Mormon
Holy Days:	Passover, Easter
Organizations:	New York Yankees, Republican Party, National Rifle Association, the Kiwanis Club, Alpha Kappa Delta
Places:	Yellowstone National Park, Rocky Mountains, Africa, Louisiana, Union County, Pennsylvania Avenue, Route 66, Golden Gate Bridge, La Guardia Airport
Institutions, Agencies, Businesses:	Xavier High School, Eugene Public Library, United Nations, Cook County Hospital, Ford Motor Company
Brand Names, Ships, Aircraft:	Chevy Blazer, Tide, Snickers, USS *Constitution*, Goodyear Blimp

3. Capitalize titles used with people's names or in place of their names.

    Mr. John W. Cooper, **Ms.** Gladys Reynolds, **Dr.** Kayla Robinson
    Aunt Judy, Grandpa John, Cousin Larry

    Do not capitalize words that identify family relationships.

    Not   I will ask my Mother.

    Correct   I will ask **my mother.**

    Correct   I will ask Mother.

4. Capitalize the titles of creative works.

Books:	*I Know Why the Caged Bird Sings*
Short Stories:	"The Lottery"
Plays:	*Our Town*
Poems:	"Song of Myself"
Articles:	"The Best Small Colleges in America"
Magazines:	*Sports Illustrated*
Songs:	"Jailhouse Rock"
Albums or CDs:	*Metallica Live*
Films:	*What Lies Beneath*
TV Series:	*Friends*
Works of Art:	*The Scream*
Computer Programs:	*Microsoft Word*

    Do not capitalize *a, an, the,* or short prepositions unless they are the first or last word in a title.

5. Capitalize days of the week, months, holidays, and special events.

    Friday, August, Memorial Day, Thanksgiving, Kwanzaa, Mardi Gras

    Do not capitalize the names of seasons: *summer, fall, winter, spring.*

6. Capitalize the names of historical events, periods, and documents.

    American Revolution, Stone Age, Renaissance Period, Seventies,
    Declaration of Independence, Battle of Hastings

7. Capitalize specific course titles and the names of language courses.

    History 201, Psychology 101, English 200

    Do not capitalize a course or subject you are referring to in a general way
    unless the course is a language.

my **e**conomics course, my **p**hilosophy course, my **S**panish course, my **h**istory course

8. Capitalize references to regions of the country but not words that merely indicate direction.

If you travel due south from Ohio, eventually you will end up in the South, probably in Kentucky or Tennessee.

9. Capitalize the opening of a letter and the first word of the closing.

Dear Liza, **Dear** Sir,

Best wishes, **Sincerely**,

Notice that a comma comes after the opening and closing.

Reviewing Capitalization

Why is capitalization important in your writing?

It signals the beginning of a sentence and calls attention to certain kinds of

words so that sentences are easier to read and understand.

What is the difference between a proper noun and a common noun?

Common nouns are everyday words; proper nouns name specific people and

things.

PRACTICE 1: Recall/Identify Underline and correct the capitalization errors in the following sentences.

1. My Dad bought a new ford bronco last saturday.   *(dad, Ford, Bronco, Saturday)*
2. Lake street is where the pastor of the local Church resides.   *(Street, church)*
3. Jim Morrison's Song "the End" was used as the opening music for *Apocalypse Now*, a Movie by Francis ford Coppola.   *(song, The, movie, Ford)*
4. The national association of building contractors will sponsor a trade show at the astrodome in houston, texas, next january.   *(National, Association, Building, Contractors, Astrodome, Houston, Texas, January)*
5. My family—all my brothers, sisters, cousins, Aunts, and Uncles—loves to watch the macy's Thanksgiving day parade.   *(aunts, uncles, Macy's, Day, Parade)*

PRACTICE 2: Apply Fill in each blank with words that complete the sentence. Be sure to capitalize words correctly. (You can make up titles if necessary.) *Answers will vary.*

1. Last week I went to see _____ in concert.

2. Shelley will graduate from _____ University.

3. I signed up to take _____ because _____ is such a popular teacher.

4. My favorite holiday is _____ because I get to see _____, my favorite relative.

5. The _____ is sponsoring a barbecue this weekend.

PRACTICE 3: Write Your Own Write five sentences of your own that cover at least five of the capitalization rules.   *Answers will vary.*

_____

_____

_____

_____

_____

CHAPTER REVIEW

MyWritingLab   ### Reviewing Capitalization

To review this material before you complete the Review Practices, watch **Animation: Capitalization** at **MyWritingLab.com** one more time. This time, keep the video open as you complete the rest of the practices in this chapter. For best results, do the **MyWritingLab** exercises online as well as the Chapter Review practices in the book.

Remind students that they lose points for every incorrect answer (as well as when they take hints) in the Grammar Apply.

REVIEW PRACTICE 1: Recall/Identify Underline and correct the capitalization errors in the following sentences.

1. Even though my <u>zenith</u> television has only a 13-inch screen, I still enjoy watching *<u>american idol</u>*.   *(Zenith, American Idol)*

2. According to <u>dr. phillips</u>, many Americans felt their loyalties were torn during the <u>american revolution</u>.   *(Dr. Phillips, American Revolution)*

3. Diane Glancy's *<u>pushing the bear</u>* is a retelling of the Trail of Tears.
(Pushing, Bear)

4. Didn't Hamlet say, "to be or not to be"? *(To)*

5. If you turn South at lovers' lane, you'll run directly into my Sister's Ranch, affectionately named lovers' ranch. *(south, Lovers' Lane, sister's ranch, Lovers' Ranch)*

6. My Uncle Conrad would like to hire mrs. Chandra Smith for the Department of english and communications. *(Mrs., English, Communications)*

7. My favorite Novel by Jane Austen is *emma*. *(novel, Emma)*

8. many people believe that the south is holding on to a dying concept. *(Many, South)*

9. I suppose I can always move in with mother while I attend loyola university. *(Mother, Loyola University)*

10. During Rush Week, I had tea with pi phi beta, played tennis with kappa delta, and listened to poetry with gamma phi. *(Pi Phi Beta, Kappa Delta, Gamma Phi)*

MyWritingLab **Practicing Capitalization**

Now complete the **Recall** activities for **Capitalization** in the **Punctuation, Mechanics, and Spelling** module of **MyWritingLab.com.** If you're having a difficult time with a question, open up the video in the lower right-hand corner for some help.

REVIEW PRACTICE 2: Apply Fill in each blank with words that complete the sentence. Be sure to capitalize words correctly. *Answers will vary.*

1. Over the weekend, I stayed home and reread one of my favorite books, _____.

2. Katherine hopes to obtain a degree in _____.

3. My mother joined _____, and the work she does helps save lives.

4. My friend is from _____; another friend is from _____.

5. It's possible to climb Mt. _____, but not Mt. _____.

6. My relative, _____, lives in _____.

7. We have to read _____ for my _____ literature class.

8. Travel to get to _____, and _____ to get to _____.

9. The letter opened with these words, "_____."

10. The injured man was taken to _____, where he received treatment from _____.

MyWritingLab **Practicing Capitalization**

Next, complete the **Apply** activity for **Capitalization** in the **Punctuation, Mechanics, and Spelling** module of **MyWritingLab.com**. Pay close attention to the directions, and only click on what you're asked to.

⚙— **Complete** this **Writing Prompt** at **mywritinglab.com**

REVIEW PRACTICE 3: Write Your Own Write a paragraph about a state, famous person, or course you find particularly interesting. *Answers will vary.*

MyWritingLab **Practicing Capitalizaiton**

For more practice, complete the **Write** activity for **Capitalization** in the **Punctuation, Mechanics, and Spelling** module of **MyWritingLab. com.** Make sure to pay close attention to any capitalization errors.

REVIEW PRACTICE 4: Editing Through Collaboration Exchange paragraphs from Review Practice 3 with another student, and do the following tasks: *Answers will vary.*

1. Circle any capital letters that don't follow the capitalization rules.

2. Write the rule number next to the error for the writer to refer to.

Then return the paper to its writer, and use the information in this chapter to correct any capitalization errors in your own paragraph. Record your errors on the Error Log in Appendix 7.

Abbreviations and Numbers

UNIT PRE-TESTS
To check your students'
abilities with the collective
skills in this unit, two Unit
Pre-tests are available in
the *Instructor's Resource
Manual.*

TEST YOURSELF

Underline and correct the abbreviation and number errors in these
sentences.

- Gov. Schwarzenegger is trying to protect water in this state.
- My dog had 4 puppies.
- Over one thousand two hundred and twelve people attended.
- After college, I hope to join the Cent Int Agency.
- Crystal just moved to the U.S. from Spain.

(Answers are in Appendix 3.)

Like capitalization, **abbreviations** and **numbers** are also mechanical features of writing that help us communicate what we want to say.
Following the rules that govern their use will make your writing as precise
as possible.

Student Comment:
"I thought I already knew
everything there is to know
about **Abbreviations and
Numbers,** but **MyWritingLab**
brought new information
on this topic to my
attention and clarified a
few items I was confused
about."

MyWritingLab   ## Understanding Abbreviations

To expand your understanding of this topic, go to **MyWritingLab.
com,** and choose **Abbreviations and Numbers** in the **Punctuation,
Mechanics, and Spelling** module. From there, watch the video called
Animation: Abbreviations and Numbers. Then, return to this chapter,
which will go into more detail about abbreviations and give you opportunities to practice them. Finally, you will apply your understanding of
abbreviations to your own writing.

ABBREVIATIONS

Abbreviations help us move communication along. They follow a set of rules when used in writing.

1. Abbreviate titles before proper names.

    Mr. John Davis, **Mrs.** Marschel, **Ms.** Smith, **Dr.** Poh, **Rev.** Teague, **Sen.** Martinez, **Sgt.** Marvin Taylor

    Abbreviate religious, governmental, and military titles when used with an entire name. Do not abbreviate them when used only with a last name.

NOT	We thought that **Sen.** Matthews would speak first.
Correct:	We thought that **Senator** Matthews would speak first.
Correct:	We thought that **Sen.** Dorothy Matthews would speak first.

    Professor is not usually abbreviated: Professor Sandra Cole is here.

2. Abbreviate academic degrees.

    B.S. (Bachelor of Science)
    R.N. (Registered Nurse)
    D.V.M. (Doctor of Veterinary Medicine)

3. Use the following abbreviations with numbers.

    A.M. *or* **a.m.** (ante meridiem)
    P.M. *or* **p.m.** (post meridiem)
    mph (miles per hour)

4. Abbreviate *United States* only when it is used as an adjective.

NOT	The **U.S.** is a democracy.
Correct:	The **United States** is a democracy.
Correct:	The **U.S.** Supreme Court will give its ruling today.

5. Abbreviate the names of certain government agencies, businesses, and educational institutions by using their initials without periods.

    CIA (Central Intelligence Agency)
    IRS (Internal Revenue Service)
    CBS (Columbia Broadcasting System)
    UCLA (University of California, Los Angeles)
    IBM (International Business Machines)

6. Abbreviate state names when addressing mail or writing out the postal address. Otherwise, spell out the names of states.

    Tamara's new address is 451 Kingston St., Phoenix, **AZ** 85072.
    Tamara has moved to Phoenix, **Arizona.**

TEACHING
ABBREVIATIONS AND
NUMBERS
Have students work in groups of three or four to write a paragraph filled with abbreviation and number errors. Have them be as inventive as possible yet still make the paragraph coherent.

Have the groups exchange paragraphs and try to decipher the paragraphs they now have. Point out how distracting abbreviations and numbers can be when they are not used correctly.

INSTRUCTOR'S
RESOURCE MANUAL
For a sample paragraph, for more exercises, and for quizzes, see the *Instructor's Resource Manual*, Section II, Part IV.

UNIT POST-TESTS
To check your students' mastery of the collective skills in this unit, two Unit Post-tests are available in the *Instructor's Resource Manual.*

Reviewing Abbreviations

When you write, are you free to abbreviate any words you want?

No, abbreviations in writing follow a set of rules.

PRACTICE 1: Recall/Identify Correct the underlined words in each of the following sentences.

1. The <u>Rev.</u> Jackson gave a wonderful sermon. *(Reverend)*

2. The letter was addressed to <u>Mister</u> Clark Reynolds, 758 First Avenue, Sioux Falls, <u>South Dakota</u> 57116. *(Mr., SD)*

3. Former <u>TX</u> Governor George W. Bush became a <u>United States</u> president. *(Texas, U.S.)*

4. When the police clocked Beth on Ridgeland Highway, she was going 76 <u>miles per hour</u>. *(mph)*

5. My favorite show has been picked up by <u>C.B.S.</u> *(CBS)*

PRACTICE 2: Apply In each sentence, write either an abbreviation or the complete word, whichever is correct.

1. The _____ (U.S./<u>United States</u>) will send two representatives to Paris.

2. I have _____ (Prof./<u>Professor</u>) Perry for English this term.

3. For years, J. Edgar Hoover was head of the _____ (FBI/F.B.I./ Federal Bureau of Investigation).

4. She was introduced to _____ (<u>Rev.</u>/Reverend) Barbara Shaw.

5. Matt has lived in _____ (<u>NJ</u>/New Jersey) and _____ (<u>NH</u>/New Hampshire).

PRACTICE 3: Write Your Own Write a sentence of your own for each of the following abbreviations. *Answers will vary.*

1. Mr. _____

2. mph _____

3. U.S. _____

4. CA _____

5. B.A. _____

NUMBERS

Most writers ask the same question about using **numbers:** When should a number be spelled out, and when is it all right to use numerals? The following simple rules will help you make this decision.

1. Spell out numbers from *zero* to *nine*. Use figures for numbers 10 and over.

   I have **four** brothers.

   My mom has **12** nieces and nephews and **43** cousins.

   Do not mix spelled-out numbers and figures in a sentence if they refer to the same types of items. Use numerals for all numbers in that case.

   NOT   I have **four** brothers, **12** nieces and nephews, and **43** cousins.
   Correct: I have **4** brothers, **12** nieces and nephews, and **43** cousins.

2. For very large numbers, use a combination of figures and words.

   The athletic department's yearly budget is **$4.6 million.**

   Sales last year totaled approximately **$1.2 billion.**

3. Always spell out a number that begins a sentence. If this becomes awkward, reword the sentence.

   Twenty-two people were injured in the train accident.

   Approximately **250,000** people live in Jackson.

4. Use figures for dates, addresses, ZIP codes, telephone numbers, identification numbers, and time.

   On June **1, 1985,** my parents moved to **4250** Oak St., El Dorado, AR **71730.**

   My new telephone number is **(555) 877-1420.**

   My Social Security number is **123-45-6789.**

   My alarm went off at **6:37** a.m.

5. Use figures for fractions, decimals, and percentages.

   The recipe calls for ¾ cup of milk and ½ cup of sugar.

   He registered **.03** on the Breathalyzer test.

   Almost **15** percent of the city's inhabitants are Asian American.

   Notice that *percent* is written out and is all one word.

6. Use figures for exact measurements, including amounts of money. Use a dollar sign for amounts over $1.

   The room is **16** feet wide and **20** feet, **4** inches long.

   I made **$34.60** in tips today.

7. Use figures for the parts of a book.

Chapter 10   page 20   Exercise 5   questions 4 and 6

Notice that *Chapter* and *Exercise* are capitalized when they are followed by numbers.

Reviewing Numbers

What is the general rule for spelling out numbers as opposed to using numerals?

Spell out numbers zero through nine, and use figures for 10 and higher.

PRACTICE 4: Recall/Identify Underline and correct any errors with numbers in each of the following sentences.

1. The school's 2005 budget is approximately <u>$75,000,000</u>.   *($ 75 million)*

2. The committee will choose <u>6</u> finalists for the <u>thousand-dollar</u> scholarship.
   (six, $ 1,000)

3. Nearly <u>half of a cup</u> of chocolate went into this recipe.   *(½ cup)*

4. The hotel manager agreed to give us a <u>twenty %</u> discount since we had <u>fourteen</u> people in our group.   *(20 percent, 14)*

5. <u>292</u> people voted in the school election; there were <u>fifteen</u> candidates.
   (Two hundred ninety-two or Exactly 292, 15)

PRACTICE 5: Apply Fill in each blank in the following sentences with a number in the proper form.   *Answers will vary.*

1. With _____ billion in the bank, he is the richest man I know.

2. _____ fireworks were set off for our annual charity drive.

3. Five minus two is _____.

4. To review the comma rules, do Exercise _____ on page _____.

5. You will need _____ cups of flour, _____ cup of water, and _____ eggs to make fried bread.

PRACTICE 6: Write Your Own Write a sentence demonstrating each of the following rules for numbers.   *Answers will vary.*

1. Spell out numbers from zero to nine. Use figures for number 10 and higher.

_____

2. Always spell out a number that begins a sentence.

_____

3. Use figures for amounts of money preceded by a dollar sign.

_____

4. Use figures for fractions, decimals, percentages, and amounts of money.

_____

5. For very large numbers, use a combination of figures and words.

_____

CHAPTER REVIEW

MyWritingLab **Reviewing Abbreviations**

To review this material before you complete the Review Practices, watch **Animation: Abbreviations and Numbers** at **MyWritingLab.com** one more time. This time, keep the video open as you complete the rest of the practices in this chapter. For best results, do the **MyWritingLab** exercises online as well as the Chapter Review practices in the book.

Not only does spelling count in the Apply section, but correct punctuation does as well. Make sure your students are aware of this before they complete this exercise.

REVIEW PRACTICE 1: Recall/Identify Circle the abbreviation errors and underline the number errors in each of the following sentences. Some sentences contain more than one error.

1. We must leave at ten a.m., or we will miss Sen. Breven's speech. *(10, Senator)*
2. 25 candidates showed up for the one job opening. *(Twenty-five)*
3. My address is four hundred two Park Lane Avenue, Bakersfield, California 93313. *(402, CA)*
4. The U.S. is a powerful nation. *(United States)*
5. I am going to college to receive a Registered Nurse degree. *(an R.N.)*
6. I'll need to add one-half cup of sea salt to the fish tank. *(½)*
7. Last week, Christy earned fifty-five dollars babysitting. *($55)*

8. Joanna reported the three-thousand-dollar gift to the Internal Revenue Service. *($3,000, IRS)*

9. If you had 7 puppies, and you gave away 3, then you would have 4 puppies. *(seven, three, four)*

10. The U.S. has a consumer economy. *(United States)*

MyWritingLab **Practicing Abbreviations**

Now complete the **Recall** activities for **Abbreviations and Numbers** in the **Punctuation, Mechanics, and Spelling** module of **MyWritingLab. com.** Remember to read the answers carefully because many of them look similar.

REVIEW PRACTICE 2: Apply Correct the errors in Review Practice 1 by rewriting the sentences. *See Review Practice 1.*

MyWritingLab **Practicing Abbreviations**

Next, complete the **Apply** activity for **Abbreviations and Numbers** in the **Punctuation, Mechanics, and Spelling** module of **MyWritingLab. com.** If you're stuck, go to the lower right-hand corner and open up the video again, or you can click on the hint button.

Complete this **Writing Prompt** at **mywritinglab.com**

REVIEW PRACTICE 3: Write Your Own Write a paragraph giving directions to a place near your college. Use numbers and abbreviations in your paragraph. *Answers will vary.*

MyWritingLab **Practicing Abbreviations**

For more practice, complete the **Write** activity for **Abbreviations and Numbers** in the **Punctuation, Mechanics, and Spelling** module of **MyWritingLab.com.** Make sure to pay close attention to abbreviation and number errors as you revise the paragraph.

REVIEW PRACTICE 4: Editing Through Collaboration Exchange paragraphs from Review Practice 3 with another student, and do the following: *Answers will vary.*

1. Underline all abbreviations, numbers, and figures.

2. Circle any abbreviations, numbers, or figures that are not in their correct form.

Then return the paper to its writer, and use the information in this chapter to correct any abbreviation and number errors in your own paragraph. Record your errors on the Error Log in Appendix 7.

Effective Sentences

At one time or another, you have probably been a member of a team. You may have actively participated in sports somewhere or been a part of a close-knit employee group. Or maybe you have taken part in classroom discussion groups or special projects that required your cooperation with your peers. Whatever the situation, teamwork is important in many everyday situations. To be a good team member, you must perform your individual duties with others in mind.

Sentences, too, require good teamwork to be successful. Each individual word, phrase, or clause has to express its own meaning but must also work together with other words, phrases, and clauses toward the common goal of communicating a clear message. In this unit, three chapters will help you write successful sentences that work in harmony with each other to say exactly what you want to say in the best way possible:

Chapter 40: Varying Sentence Structure
Chapter 41: Parallelism
Chapter 42: Combining Sentences

Varying Sentence Structure

UNIT PRE-TESTS
To check your students' abilities with the collective skills in this unit, two Unit Pre-tests are available in the *Instructor's Resource Manual.*

TEST YOURSELF

Turn each of the following pairs of sentences into one sentence that is more interesting.

- I live in an old house. I have lived here my whole life.
- I am too busy. I need to work less.
- I love cheeseburgers and fries. I love fast-food places.
- My dog sleeps 14 hours every day. She is overweight.
- I enjoy writing. I keep a notebook for jotting down my thoughts.

(Answers are in Appendix 3.)

Reading the same pattern—sentence after sentence—can become very monotonous for your readers. This chapter will help you solve this problem in your writing. Look at the following example.

I have never lived away from home. I am about to start my second year of college. I think I am ready to be on my own. I am excited about this new phase of my life. I have student loans and a part-time job. I can't wait to feel true independence.

This paragraph has some terrific ideas, but they are expressed in such a dull way that the readers might doze off. What this paragraph needs is variety in its sentence structure. Here are some ideas for keeping your readers awake and ready to hear your good thoughts.

MyWritingLab

Understanding Varying Sentence Structure

To find out more about this topic, go to **MyWritingLab.com,** and choose **Varying Sentence Structure** in the **Usage and Style** module. For this topic, watch the video called **Animation: Varying Sentence Structure.** Then, return to this chapter, which will go into more detail about sentence variety and give you opportunities to practice it. Finally, you will apply your understanding of sentence variety to your own writing.

ADD INTRODUCTORY WORDS

Add some introductory words to your sentences so they don't all start the same way.

In my lifetime, I have never lived away from home. **Now** I am about to start my second year of college. I think I am ready to be on my own. I am excited about this new phase of my life. **To pay for life away from home,** I have student loans and a part-time job. I can't wait to feel true independence.

PRACTICE 1: Recall/Identify Underline the sentence in each pair that could be turned into an introductory word, phrase, or clause. *Answers may vary.*

1. It was early morning. Jay had a throbbing headache. *(Early in the morning,)*

2. We stripped the paper from the walls. We started in the kitchen. *(Starting in the kitchen,)*

3. I'm shocked. The Flying Zombies Show sold out in one day. *(Shockingly,)*

4. We want fast delivery. We must place our order this week. *(If we want fast delivery,)*

5. We got center row tickets for the concert. I can't believe it. *(Unbelievably,)*

PRACTICE 2: Apply Rewrite the sentences in Practice 1 by turning each sentence you underlined into an introductory word, phrase, or clause. *See Practice 1.*

PRACTICE 3: Write Your Own Write five sentences of your own with introductory elements. *Answers will vary.*

_____

_____

_____

_____

_____

REVERSE WORDS

Reverse the order of some subjects and verbs. For example, instead of *I am so excited*, try *Am I ever excited*. You can also add or drop words and change punctuation to make the sentence read smoothly.

In my lifetime, I have never lived away from home. Now I am about to start my second year of college. I think I am ready to be on my own. **Am I ever** excited about this new phase in my life. To pay for life away from home, I have student loans and a part-time job. I can't wait to feel true independence.

PRACTICE 4: Recall/Identify Underline the words you could reverse in each of the following sentences.

1. I am glad to see you!   *(Am I glad to see you!)*

2. She is so excited about the trip.   *(Is she ever excited about the trip.)*

3. He was very scared.   *(Was he ever scared.)*

4. I am glad I studied.   *(Am I sure glad I studied.)*

5. Sue was nervous about her speech.   *(Was Sue nervous about her speech!)*

PRACTICE 5: Apply Rewrite the sentences in Practice 4 by reversing the words you underlined.   *See Practice 4.*

PRACTICE 6: Write Your Own Write five sentences of your own with subjects and verbs reversed.   *Answers will vary.*

_____

_____

_____

_____

_____

MOVE SENTENCE PARTS

Move around some parts of the sentence. Experiment to see which order works best.

> In my lifetime, I have never lived away from home. Now I am about to start my second year of college. I think I am ready to be on my own. Am I ever excited about this new phase in my life. **Student loans and a part-time job can pay for a life away from home.** I can't wait to feel true independence.

PRACTICE 7: Recall/Identify Underline any parts of the following sentences that can be moved around.

1. I was incredibly hungry <u>after breakfast</u>. *(Move to beginning of sentence.)*

2. <u>Some experts say</u> that computers increase isolation among people. *(Move to end.)*

3. Your outfit is lovely <u>today</u>. *(Move to beginning.)*

4. There is a great deal we don't know <u>about the common cold</u>. *(Move between "deal" and "we.")*

5. I absolutely love chocolate, <u>not surprisingly</u>. *(Move to beginning.)*

PRACTICE 8: Apply Rewrite the sentences in Practice 7, moving the words you underlined. *See Practice 7.*

PRACTICE 9: Write Your Own Write two sentences of your own. Then rewrite each sentence two different ways. *Answers will vary.*

_____

_____

_____

_____

_____

VARY SENTENCE TYPE

Use a question, a command, or an exclamation occasionally.

> In my lifetime, I have never lived away from home. **Have you?** Now I am about to start my second year of college. I think I am ready to be on my own. **Boy, am I ever excited about this new phase in my life!** Student loans and a part-time job can pay for a life away from home. I can't wait to feel true independence.

PRACTICE 10: Recall/Identify Identify each of the following sentences as a statement (S), a question (Q), a command (C), or an exclamation (E).

1. __C__ Look over there at the elephant

2. __Q__ How does she do that

3. __S__ My mom always asked herself why she never finished graduate school

4. __S__ Whatever you decide is fine with me

5. __E__ Look out for that falling rock

PRACTICE 11: Apply Complete the following sentences, making them into questions, commands, or exclamations. Then supply the correct punctuation. *Answers will vary.*

1. Will there ever _____

2. You should not have taken _____

3. Do you know if _____

4. At the first stop light _____

5. Don't you ever _____

PRACTICE 12: Write Your Own Write two statements, two questions, two commands, and two exclamations of your own. *Answers will vary.*

_____

_____

_____

_____

_____

_____

_____

_____

Reviewing Ways to Vary Sentence Patterns

Why is varying sentence patterns important in your writing?

Sentence variety keeps the readers interested.

Name four ways to vary your sentence patterns.

Add introductory words and phrases.

Reverse the order of some subjects and verbs.

Move some parts of your sentences around.

Use a question, command, or exclamation occasionally.

What other kinds of sentences besides statements can you use for variety?

questions _____   commands _____

exclamations _____

CHAPTER REVIEW

Many students say that the Apply exercise for this topic is one of the most difficult ones, so your students may need extra guidance when completing the Apply questions.

MyWritingLab   **Reviewing Varying Sentence Structure**

To review this material before you complete the Review Practices, watch **Animation: Varying Sentence Structure** at **MyWritingLab. com** one more time. This time, keep the video open as you complete the rest of the practices in this chapter. For best results, do the **MyWritingLab** exercises online as well as the Chapter Review practices in the book.

REVIEW PRACTICE 1: Recall/Identify Underline the words or groups of words that have been added or moved in each revised sentence. Then use the following key to tell which rule was applied to the sentence:

1. Add introductory words.
2. Reverse the order of subject and verb.
3. Move parts of the sentence around.
4. Use a question, a command, or an exclamation occasionally.

   1. She does that very well.

      ___4___ How does she do that so well?

   2. I must call Jarrett in an emergency. Can anyone tell me Jarrett's phone number?

      ___1___ In case of an emergency, can anyone tell me Jarrett's phone number?

3. Please buy some brown sugar for chocolate chip cookies <u>at the store around the corner</u>.

   ___3___ At the store around the corner, please buy some brown sugar for chocolate chip cookies.

4. I started to dance because I was so excited!

   ___3___ I was so excited <u>that I started to dance</u>!

5. I am <u>grateful to you</u>!

   ___2___ <u>Am I ever</u> grateful to you!

6. You can't play now. Finish your homework first.

   ___1___ <u>Before you can play</u>, you must finish your homework.

7. Do it quickly. Catch Dustin before he leaves.

   ___1___ <u>Quickly</u>, catch Dustin before he leaves.

8. He is an optimist. He always believes everything will turn out all right.

   ___1___ <u>An optimist</u>, he always believes everything will turn out all right.

9. Call our store, send a fax, or visit our Web site to order.

   ___3___ To order, call our store, send a fax, or visit our Web site.

10. I don't believe it. Did you really say that?

    ___1___ <u>Oh no</u>, did you really say that?

MyWritingLab **Practicing Varying Sentence Structure**

Now complete the **Recall** activities for **Varying Sentence Structure** in the **Usage and Style** module of **MyWritingLab.com**. If you're having a difficult time with a question, open up the video in the lower right-hand corner for some help.

REVIEW PRACTICE 2: Apply Vary the structure of the following sentences with at least three of the four ideas you just learned. *Answers will vary.*

   The local teen center has a problem. It cannot afford to stay open, so it might be shut down this weekend. It can't make its monthly dues any higher because most of its members cannot afford increased fees. Government funding and donations aren't enough to keep the center open. A solution has to exist.

Practicing Varying Sentence Structure

Next, complete the **Apply** activity for **Varying Sentence Structure** in the **Usage and Style** module of **MyWritingLab.com**. Pay close attention to the directions, and only click on what you're asked to.

Complete this **Writing Prompt** at **mywritinglab.com**

REVIEW PRACTICE 3: Write Your Own Write a paragraph about a historical event. Try to use each of the four ways you have learned to make sentences interesting. *Answers will vary.*

Practicing Varying Sentence Structure

For more practice, complete the **Write** activity for **Varying Sentence Structure** in the **Usage and Style** module of **MyWritingLab.com**. Pay close attention to how you vary your sentence structure.

REVIEW PRACTICE 4: Editing Through Collaboration Exchange paragraphs from Review Practice 3 with another student, and do the following: *Answers will vary.*

1. Put brackets around any sentences that sound monotonous.

2. Suggest a way to vary each of these sentences.

Then return the paper to its writer, and use the information in this chapter to vary the sentence structure in your own paragraph. Record your errors on the Error Log in Appendix 7.

Parallelism

UNIT PRE-TESTS
To check your students'
abilities with the collective
skills in this unit, two Unit
Pre-tests are available in
the *Instructor's Resource
Manual.*

TEST YOURSELF

Underline the parts in each of the following sentences that seem awkward or unbalanced.

- We decided to forget about the lawsuit and then moving on with our lives.
- Last year, I graduated from college, moved from Texas to California, and have been married.
- My sister and brother raise money to feed the homeless and for building a new shelter.
- Exercising, eating right, and water will improve a person's health.
- Jack went back to school because he wanted to get a better job and because of the girls on campus.

(Answers are in Appendix 3.)

When sentences are **parallel,** they are balanced. That is, words, phrases, or clauses in a series start with the same grammatical form. Parallel structures make your sentences interesting and clear.

MyWritingLab | **Understanding Parallelism**

To improve your understanding of this topic, go to **MyWritingLab. com,** and choose **Parallelism** in the **Sentence Skills** module. From there, watch the video called **Animation: Parallelism.** Then, return to this chapter, which will go into more detail about parallelism and give you opportunities to practice it. Finally, you will apply your understanding of parallelism to your own writing.

Student Comment
"I usually read what I'm assigned from the reading alone. However, I just didn't get **Parallelism. MyWritingLab** helped me grasp this topic."

PARALLEL STRUCTURE

Following is a paragraph that could be greatly improved with parallel structures.

> My teenaged sister, Amanda, was not thrilled when she learned the family was going to drive to San Antonio, Texas, for a spring break. She has been looking forward to her time at home. She was planning on reading romance novels, to hang out with her friends, and was going to organize her schoolwork. Instead, she will be touring the Alamo, seeing the Riverwalk, and will visit many missions.

Words and phrases in a series should be parallel, which means they should start with the same type of word. Parallelism makes your sentence structure smoother and more interesting. Look at this sentence, for example.

NOT   She was planning on **reading** romance novels,

        to hang out with her friends, and

        was going to organize her schoolwork.

Parallel: She was planning on **reading** romance novels,

        hanging out with her friends, and

        organizing her schoolwork.

Parallel: She was planning to **read** romance novels,

        hang out with her friends, and

        organize her schoolwork.

Here is another sentence that would read better if the parts were parallel:

NOT   Instead, she will be **touring** the Alamo,

        seeing the Riverwalk, and

        will visit many missions.

Parallel: Instead, she will be **touring** the Alamo,

        seeing the Riverwalk, and

        visiting many missions.

Parallel: Instead, she will tour **the Alamo,**

        the Riverwalk, and

        many missions.

Now read the paragraph with these two sentences made parallel or balanced.

> My teenaged sister, Amanda, was not thrilled when she learned the family was going to drive to San Antonio, Texas, for a spring

break. She has been looking forward to her time at home. She was planning on reading romance novels, hanging out with her friends, and organizing her schoolwork. Instead, she will be touring the Alamo, seeing the Riverwalk, and visiting many missions.

Reviewing Parallelism

What is parallelism?

Starting words, phrases, and clauses in a series with the same grammatical form

Why should you use parallelism in your writing?

To make your writing interesting and clear

PRACTICE 1: Recall/Identify Underline the parallel structures in each of the following sentences.

1. We never expected the girls to start <u>buying alcohol</u> and <u>bringing it</u> into the dorms.

2. She often prepares recipes <u>that she finds in her fancy cooking magazines</u> or <u>that she sees on the Food Network</u>.

3. He would start <u>skipping class</u> and <u>sleeping late</u>.

4. One day when I was 10 years old, my dad revealed <u>that there was no Santa Claus</u> and <u>that babies did not come from storks</u>.

5. I <u>baked cookies</u>, <u>cleaned the house</u>, and <u>paid the bills</u>.

PRACTICE 2: Apply Make the underlined elements parallel in each of the following sentences. *Answers will vary.*

1. Jessica likes <u>skiing</u>, <u>cooking</u>, and <u>to do crossword puzzles</u> in her spare time.

   _____

2. On our trip to New York City, we have many <u>things to do</u>, <u>people to visit</u>, and <u>sights that should be seen</u>.

   _____

3. Carmella went to the picnic <u>because she wanted to support her co workers</u> and <u>because of the massive fireworks show</u>.

   _____

4. In 1950, my mom and dad <u>moved out of the city</u>, <u>bought land in the high country</u>, and <u>have become self-sufficient</u>.

    _____

5. <u>Fighting</u>, <u>cheating</u>, and <u>to use drugs</u> will get you kicked out immediately.

    _____

PRACTICE 3: Write Your Own Write five sentences of your own using parallel structures in each. *Answers will vary.*

_____

_____

_____

_____

_____

CHAPTER REVIEW

Students are often wary of parallelism, mainly because they don't know what it is; however, MyWritingLab does a good job of making this complicated topic clear.

MyWritingLab   **Reviewing Parallelism**

To review this material before you complete the Review Practices, watch **Animation: Parallelism** at **MyWritingLab.com** one more time. This time, keep the video open as you complete the rest of the practices in this chapter. For best results, do the **MyWritingLab** exercises online as well as the Chapter Review practices in the book.

REVIEW PRACTICE 1: Recall/Identify Underline the parallel structures in each of the following sentences.

1. Kristi will <u>make deviled eggs</u>, <u>bring baked beans</u>, and <u>order the cake</u>.

2. In Las Vegas, you should <u>see Celine Dion</u>, <u>play blackjack</u>, and <u>ride a roller coaster</u>.

3. The house needs <u>to be painted</u>, and the grass needs <u>to be cut</u>.

4. To stay healthy, <u>do not smoke</u>, <u>stay out of the sun</u>, and <u>don't abuse alcohol</u>.

5. Students should learn to manage their time, to study efficiently, and to have a social life.

6. She bought the gift, she wrapped the gift, and she delivered the gift.

7. Biking, swimming, and hiking are all good sports to build endurance, stamina, and flexibility.

8. He can run faster than a speeding bullet, leap tall buildings in a single bound, and see through solid materials.

9. Please wake up the baby, give her a bath, and feed her.

10. Mr. Wattenbarger invests in stocks, contributes to a retirement fund, and saves a small percentage of his yearly income.

MyWritingLab   **Practicing Parallelism**

Now complete the **Recall** activities for **Parallelism** in the **Sentence Skills** module of **MyWritingLab.com.** Remember to read the answers carefully because many of them look similar.

REVIEW PRACTICE 2: Apply Complete each of the following sentences with parallel structures. *Answers will vary.*

1. My favorite hobbies are _____, _____, and _____.

2. Because _____ and because _____, I decided to stay home.

3. You will need to _____, _____, and _____ before going to your appointment.

4. Brandon _____ and _____, but he still can't fix the problem.

5. He always planned _____, _____, and _____.

6. I'm so tired of _____, _____, and _____.

7. You could have _____, _____, and _____ if you had truly wanted to pass that test.

8. _____, _____, and _____ are essential items at the beach.

9. I've already told you that _____ and that _____.

10. Sam and Tabitha enjoy _____, _____, and _____.

MyWritingLab | **Practicing Parallelism**

Next, complete the **Apply** activity for **Parallelism** in the **Sentence Skills** module of **MyWritingLab.com.** If you're stuck, you can go to the lower right-hand corner and open up the video again, or you can click on the hint button.

⚙️ **Complete** this **Writing Prompt** at **mywritinglab.com**

REVIEW PRACTICE 3: Write Your Own Write a paragraph about your favorite movie. What is the movie? Why is it your favorite? Use two examples of parallelism in your paragraph. *Answers will vary.*

MyWritingLab | **Practicing Parallelism**

For more practice, complete the **Write** activity for **Parallelism** in the **Sentence Skills** module of **MyWritingLab.com.** Pay close attention to the use of parallelism as you revise the paragraph.

REVIEW PRACTICE 4: Editing Through Collaboration Exchange paragraphs from Review Practice 3 with another student, and do the following: *Answers will vary.*

1. Underline any items in a series.

2. Put brackets around any of these items that are not grammatically parallel.

Then return the paper to its writer, and use the information in this chapter to correct any parallelism errors in your own paragraph. Record your errors on the Error Log in Appendix 7.

Combining Sentences

UNIT PRE-TESTS
To check your students' abilities with the collective skills in this unit, two Unit Pre-tests are available in the *Instructor's Resource Manual.*

TEST YOURSELF

Combine each set of sentences into one sentence.

- My mother is taking ballet lessons. She takes her lessons at the YWCA.
- We love to swim. It's just too hot to be outside.
- Robin lives in Fort Lauderdale. Jack lives in Houston.
- We lived on the beach. We were there for two weeks.
- I am going to study hard. I want to get a good grade on my final.
- I love to travel. I love the strange animals in Australia. I want to go to Australia.

(Answers are in Appendix 3.)

Still another way to add variety to your writing is to combine short, choppy sentences into longer sentences. You can combine simple sentences to make compound or complex sentences. You can also combine compound and complex sentences.

MyWritingLab **Understanding Combining**

To help you understand this subject, go to **MyWritingLab.com,** and choose **Combining Sentences** in the **Sentence Skills** module. Next, watch the video called **Animation: Combining Sentences.** Then, return to this chapter, which will go into more detail about sentence combining and give you opportunities to practice it. Finally, you will apply your understanding of combining sentences in your own writing.

Student Comment
"For this topic, I would tell fellow students to take their time, focus, and read carefully. The mistake I made was not reading each question-and-answer set word for word."

TEACHING COMBINING
SENTENCES
Have each student write a
list of 10 simple sentences
on a common subject (such
as education, war, politics,
ecology, animal rights, or
final exams). Then have
students work in pairs
to create the following
sentence patterns from the
simple sentences:

Three compound sentences
Three complex sentences
Three compound-complex
sentences

 Have the class discuss
the different effects of
these sentence types.

INSTRUCTOR'S
RESOURCE MANUAL
For more exercises and for
quizzes, see the *Instructor's
Resource Manual,*
Section II, Part IV.

UNIT POST-TESTS
To check your students'
mastery of the collective
skills in this unit, two Unit
Post-tests are available in
the *Instructor's Resource
Manual.*

SIMPLE SENTENCES

A **simple sentence** consists of one independent clause. Remember that a clause has a subject and a main verb.

In the following examples, notice that a simple sentence can have more than one subject and more than one verb. (For more on compound subjects and compound verbs, see Chapter 22.)

    s   v
I have several very good friends.

      s   s   v
Martin and Louis are good friends.

      s   s v   v
Martin and I do interesting things and go to interesting places.

Reviewing Simple Sentences

What does a simple sentence consist of?

One independent clause

Write a simple sentence.

Answers will vary.

PRACTICE 1: Recall/Identify Underline the subjects once and the verbs twice in each of the following sentences. Then label the simple sentences SS.

1. _*SS*_ Every day I went to the bagel shop and bought a newspaper.

2. _*SS*_ Sinya and I knew the answer.

3. _____ Before the last show begins, I'll get some popcorn.

4. _*SS*_ They're flying to Denver on Thursday.

5. _*SS*_ Going to the movies alone is peaceful.

PRACTICE 2: Apply Make simple sentences out of the sentences in Practice 1 that are not simple. *Answers will vary.*

PRACTICE 3: Write Your Own Write a simple sentence of your own for each of the following subjects and verbs. *Answers will vary.*

1. Carlos and Linda _____

2. routinely eats and sleeps _____

3. reading for long periods of time _____

4. Many people _____

5. The fish in the tank _____

COMPOUND SENTENCES

A **compound sentence** consists of two or more independent clauses joined by a coordinating conjunction (*and, but, for, nor, or, so,* or *yet*). In other words, you can create a compound sentence from two (or more) simple sentences.

Simple:	I can add quickly in my head.
Simple:	I am very good at math.
	s v s v
Compound:	I can add quickly in my head, **and** I am very good at math.

Simple:	He leads a very busy life.
Simple:	His family always comes first.
	s v s v
Compound:	He leads a very busy life, **but** his family always comes first.

Simple:	Bonita and Tamara are running a 5K on Saturday.
Simple:	They will not go with us Friday night.
	s s v
Compound:	Bonita and Tamara are running a 5K Saturday,
	s v v
	so they will not be going with us Friday night.

Hint: As the examples show, a comma comes before the coordinating conjunction in a compound sentence.

Reviewing Compound Sentences

What does a compound sentence consist of?

Two or more independent clauses joined by a coordinating conjunction

Write a compound sentence.

Answers will vary.

PRACTICE 4: Recall/Identify Underline the independent clauses in the following sentences, and circle the coordinating conjunctions.

1. <u>I hate to repeat myself,</u> (but) <u>I will.</u>

2. <u>Just beyond that sign is a motorcycle cop waiting to ticket someone,</u> (yet) <u>he won't catch me.</u>

3. <u>Harry began the race,</u> (and) <u>he never looked back.</u>

4. <u>She's been in these kinds of predicaments before,</u> (yet) <u>each time she's come out ahead.</u>

5. <u>You are not allowed to bring food or drinks into this room,</u> (nor) <u>are you allowed to move the desks.</u>

PRACTICE 5: Apply Combine each pair of simple sentences into a compound sentence.   *Answers will vary.*

1. Mom and Dad love to play golf. They never seem to have enough time for it.

2. Our backyard faces the highway. It's always noisy.

3. My Uncle Simon and Aunt Jean always take a month-long vacation. They are always relieved to return home.

4. Our phone rings day and night. It is very annoying.

5. My favorite meal is chicken and sausage gumbo. My favorite dessert is peach cobbler.

PRACTICE 6: Write Your Own Write five compound sentences of your own.
Answers will vary.

_____

_____

_____

_____

_____

COMPLEX SENTENCES

A **complex sentence** is composed of one independent clause and at least one dependent clause. A **dependent clause** begins with either a subordinating conjunction or a relative pronoun.

Subordinating Conjunctions

after	*because*	*since*	*until*
although	*before*	*so*	*when*
as	*even if*	*so that*	*whenever*
as if	*even though*	*than*	*where*
as long as	*how*	*that*	*wherever*
as soon as	*if*	*though*	*whether*
as though	*in order that*	*unless*	*while*

Relative Pronouns

who	*whom*	*whose*	*which*	*that*

You can use subordinating conjunctions and relative pronouns to make a simple sentence (an independent clause) into a dependent clause. Then you can add the new dependent clause to an independent clause to produce a complex sentence that adds interest and variety to your writing.

How do you know which simple sentence should be independent and which should be dependent? The idea that you think is more important should be the independent clause. The less important idea will then be the dependent clause.

Following are some examples of how to combine simple sentences to make a complex sentence.

Simple: Shawna has a big collection of video games.
Simple: Shawna plays the same games over and over.

                                        Dep
Complex: **Even though** Shawna has a big collection of video games,

                         Ind
        she plays the same ones over and over.

This complex sentence stresses that Shawna plays the same games over and over. The size of her collection is of secondary importance.

                         Ind
Complex: Shawna has a big collection of video games, **though** she

                     Dep
        plays the same ones over and over.

In this complex sentence, the size of the collection is most important, so it is the independent clause.

Simple: The winner of the 5K race was Torrie.

Simple: Torrie is my roommate.

                            Ind   Dep
Complex: The winner of the 5K race was Torrie, **who** is my roommate.

This complex sentence answers the question "Who won the 5K race?" The information about Torrie being the roommate is secondary in importance.

                        Ind   Dep
Complex: My roommate is Torrie, **who** won the 5K race.

This complex sentence answers the question "Who is your roommate?" The information that she won the race is secondary.

Reviewing Complex Sentences

What does a complex sentence consist of?

An independent clause and at least one dependent clause

Write a complex sentence.

Answers will vary.

PRACTICE 7: Recall/Identify Label the underlined part of each sentence as either an independent (Ind) or a dependent (Dep) clause.

1. ___Dep___ Although I was exhausted, I still went to work.

2. ___Ind___ If someone scores 50, the game is over.

3. ___Dep___ Trisha is majoring in marine biology because she loves working with sea life.

4. ___Dep___ Brittany, whom I've known for years, decided to move to Alaska.

5. ___Ind___ While people in third world countries starve, people in the United States eat too much and waste food.

PRACTICE 8: Apply Finish each sentence with a clause, and label the new clause either dependent (Dep) or independent (Ind).   *Answers will vary.*

1. ___Dep___ _____, call your mother.

2. ___Ind___ When you signed up for this class, _____?

3. _Dep_ Mrs. Benson, _____, won the lottery and moved to Florida.

4. _Ind_ Whenever Diane's face turns red, _____.

5. _Ind_ If Mark is cold, _____.

PRACTICE 9: Write Your Own Write five complex sentences, making sure you have one independent clause and at least one dependent clause in each. *Answers will vary.*

_____

_____

_____

_____

_____

COMPOUND-COMPLEX SENTENCES

If you combine a compound sentence with a complex sentence, you produce a **compound-complex sentence.** That means your sentence has at least two independent clauses (to make it compound) and at least one dependent clause (to make it complex). Here are some examples.

Simple:	We both love warm weather.
Simple:	We will go to Jamaica for our honeymoon.
Simple:	We plan to have a good time.

	Ind
Compound-	We will go to Jamaica for our honeymoon, **and** we plan
Complex:	Ind Dep
	to have a good time **since** we both love warm weather.

Simple:	She bought a used car.
Simple:	It has 50,000 miles on it.
Simple:	It runs like a dream.

	Ind Dep
Compound-	She bought a used car, **which** has 50,000 miles on it,
Complex:	Ind
	but it runs like a dream.

Simple:	Rush-hour traffic is very bad.
Simple:	You could miss your flight.
Simple:	You should leave soon.

                              Ind   *Ind*

Compound-   Rush-hour traffic is very bad, **and** you could miss your
Complex: *Dep*

             flight **if** you don't leave soon.

Hint: Notice in these examples that we occasionally had to change words in the combined sentences so they make sense.

Reviewing Compound-Complex Sentences

What does a compound-complex sentence consist of?

At least two independent clauses and one dependent clause

Write a compound-complex sentence.

Answers will vary.

PRACTICE 10: Recall/Identify Underline the clauses in each of the following compound-complex sentences. Then identify each clause as either independent (Ind) or dependent (Dep).

           Ind   *Ind*   *Dep*

1. We cannot host the meeting, nor can we attend because we will be out

   of town.

        Ind   *Dep*

2. Professor Shilling said that I couldn't turn in my essay late because I had

     Dep   *Ind*

   three months to write it, so I decided to turn it in on time.

         Dep   *Ind*

3. Because we were out of money, we begged our guide to take us to the

        Ind   *Dep*

   bank, yet our guide said that he didn't have enough gas in the bus.

           Dep   *Dep*

4. Even though Marcy doesn't like the water and even though she can't

        Ind   *Ind*

   swim, she should go fishing with us, for she will have a good time.

     Dep   *Ind*

5. After all the fuss died down, the boys decided to shake hands and let

                  Ind

   bygones be bygones; then, they took each other out for pizza.

PRACTICE 11: Apply Make each sentence below into a compound-complex sentence. You may have to change some of the wording.   *Answers will vary.*

1. Gina believes in ghosts.

   _____

2. Edward collects rare books.

   _____

3. The contestants were nervous.

   _____

4. Motorcycles can be dangerous.

   _____

5. Jack says that he will eat liver and onions "when pigs fly."

   _____

PRACTICE 12: Write Your Own Write five compound-complex sentences of your own.   *Answers will vary.*

_____

_____

_____

_____

_____

CHAPTER REVIEW

MyWritingLab | **Reviewing Combining Sentences**

To review this material before you complete the Review Practices, watch **Animation: Combining Sentences** at **MyWritingLab.com** one more time. This time, keep the video open as you complete the rest of the practices in this chapter. For best results, do the **MyWritingLab** exercises online as well as the Chapter Review practices in the book.

Have your students keep *Mosaics* open to the sentence types and watch the videos in MyWritingLab as they complete the Recall, Apply, and Write exercises.

REVIEW PRACTICE 1: Recall/Identify Underline the independent clauses in each sentence. Then label the sentence simple (SS), compound (C), complex (CX), or compound-complex (CCX). The following definitions might help you.

Simple (SS)	=	one independent clause
Compound (C)	=	two or more independent clauses joined by *and, but, for, nor, or, so,* or *yet*
Complex (CX)	=	one independent clause and at least one dependent clause
Compound-complex (CCX)	=	at least two independent clauses and one or more dependent clauses

1. __SS__ DVD players are becoming more popular than VCRs.

2. __SS__ Bananas are a nutritious part of Leo's breakfast each morning.

3. __CX__ The grandparents' house, which sits at the edge of the woods, was built around the turn of the century.

4. __CCX__ Sheila says that music is her passion, but she has little time to pursue her interests since she took on a part-time job.

5. __CX__ I like the feel of sand between my toes when I walk along the beach.

6. __C__ We watched the MTV awards, and then we went out for a late-night snack.

7. __C__ Last year, we scraped and saved every penny, and we took a trip during spring break.

8. __SS__ Whistling, screaming, and clapping, the fans showed their approval.

9. __SS__ Will you please help me find the top to this jar?

10. __CCX__ He sat and stared at the stars, and he decided to travel to Mexico while he wondered what adventures were ahead of him.

MyWritingLab **Practicing Combining Sentences**

Now complete the **Recall** activities for **Combining Sentences** in the **Sentence Skills** module of **MyWritingLab.com.** If you're having a difficult time with a question, open up the video in the lower right-hand corner for some help.

REVIEW PRACTICE 2: Apply Combine each set of sentences to make the sentence pattern indicated in parentheses. You may need to change some wording in the sentences so they make sense. The list of sentence types in Review Practice 1 may help you with this exercise. *Answers will vary.*

1. Please turn down the television. I can't sleep. (compound)

2. My best friend, Tina, and I always have a great time together. We share all of our secrets. (compound)

3. I have so much energy. I'm going to clean my closet. (complex)

4. You should never leave an iron on unattended. You should never use an iron on clothes you are wearing. You may be injured. (compound-complex)

5. Bob has been running marathons for many years. He trains all year. He hopes to win a marathon. (compound-complex)

6. I know you don't like pears. Try some of this pastry anyway. (complex)

7. Please take these boxes out to the curb. Don't take the boxes sitting on the stairs. (compound)

8. I'm sorry. I can't lend you any money. I am broke. (compound-complex)

9. Billy-Bob is in charge of the artwork. He is a master with colors and light. (compound)

10. The fly is annoying me. It is buzzing around my head. (complex)

MyWritingLab **Practicing Combining Sentences**

Next, complete the **Apply** activity for **Combining Sentences** in the **Sentence Skills** module of **MyWritingLab.com.** Pay close attention to the directions, and only click on what you're asked to.

Complete this **Writing Prompt** at **mywritinglab.com**

REVIEW PRACTICE 3: Write Your Own Write a paragraph about your fondest teenage memory. What are the details of this memory? Why do you remember this event? *Answers will vary.*

Practicing Combining Sentences

For more practice, complete the **Write** activity for **Combining Sentences** in the **Sentence Skills** module of **MyWritingLab.com.** Pay close attention to how you combine your sentences.

REVIEW PRACTICE 4: Editing Through Collaboration Exchange paragraphs from Review Practice 3 with another student, and do the following: *Answers will vary.*

1. Put brackets around any sentences you think should be combined.

2. Underline sentences that are incorrectly combined (for example, ones that have a weak connecting word or no connecting word).

Then return the paper to its writer, and use the information in this chapter to combine sentences in your own paragraph. Record your errors on the Error Log in Appendix 7.

Choosing the Right Word

Choosing the right word is like choosing the right snack to satisfy your appetite. If you don't select the food you are craving, your hunger does not go away. In like manner, if you do not choose the right words to say what is on your mind, your readers will not be satisfied and will not understand your message.

Choosing the right word depends on your message, your purpose, and your audience. It also involves recognizing misused, nonstandard, and misspelled words. We deal with the following topics in Unit 9:

Chapter 43: Standard and Nonstandard English
Chapter 44: Easily Confused Words
Chapter 45: Spelling

Standard and Nonstandard English

UNIT PRE-TESTS
To check your students' abilities with the collective skills in this unit, two Unit Pre-tests are available in the *Instructor's Resource Manual.*

TEST YOURSELF

Label the following sentences as correct, incorrect, or slang

- So she goes, can't I meet you at the theater?
- Julie be planning the farewell party.
- We were totally grossed out.
- They changed the tire theirselves.
- We're jamming in the morning.

(Answers are in Appendix 3.)

Choosing the right words for what you want to say is an important part of effective communication. This chapter will help you find the right words and phrases for the audience you are trying to reach.

Look, for example, at the following sentences. They all have a similar message, expressed in different words.

I want to do good in college, the reason being that I can get a good job.

I be studying hard in college, so I can get a good job.

I'm going to hit the books so I can rake in the bucks.

I want to go to college, graduate, and get a good job.

Which of these sentences would you probably say to a friend or to someone in your family? Which would you most likely say in a job interview? Which would be good for a college paper?

The first three sentences are nonstandard English. They might be said or written to a friend or family member, but they would not be appropriate in an academic setting or in a job situation. Only the fourth sentence would be appropriate in an academic paper or in a job interview.

Understanding Standard and Nonstandard English

To expand your understanding of this topic, go to **MyWritingLab. com,** and choose **Standard and Nonstandard English** in the **Usage and Style** module. From there, watch the video called **Animation: Standard and Nonstandard English.** Then, return to this chapter, which will go into more detail about levels of English and give you opportunities to practice them. Finally, you will apply your understanding of standard and nonstandard English to your own writing.

STANDARD AND NONSTANDARD ENGLISH

Most of the English language falls into one of two categories—either *standard* or *nonstandard*. **Standard English** is the language of college, business, and the media. It is used by reporters on television, by newspapers, in most magazines, and on Web sites created by schools, government agencies, businesses, and organizations. Standard English is always grammatically correct and free of slang.

Nonstandard English does not follow all the rules of grammar and often includes slang. Nonstandard English is not necessarily wrong, but it is more appropriate in some settings (with friends and family) than in others. It is not appropriate in college or business writing. To understand the difference between standard and nonstandard English, compare the following paragraphs.

Nonstandard English

My man, Max, don't understand why people go to college. He believes that college is a waste of time and the long green. He goes, my parents never gone to college, and what they be making ain't exactly chump change. But lotsa people go to college for other reasons than raising up their earning power. Irregardless of whether college be preparing you for a career or not, it helps a person find hisself and meet others who are sorta like you, I definitely be believing that a college education is worth the money and time.

Standard English

My friend, Max, can't understand why people go to college. He believes that in terms of money and time, higher education is wasteful. He likes to point out that both of his parents have high-paying jobs and never went to college. However, he doesn't realize that many people go to college for other reasons than increasing their earning power. They also hope to discover what they would enjoy doing for the rest of their lives. College not only prepares people for a career, it helps them learn more about themselves and meet others with similar interests. I strongly believe that the money and time invested in a college education are justified.

In the rest of this chapter, you will learn how to recognize and correct ungrammatical English and how to avoid slang in your writing.

> **Reviewing Standard and Nonstandard English**
>
> *Where do you hear standard English in your daily life?*
>
> On TV, in schools, in newspapers, in daily conversation
>
> *What is nonstandard English?*
>
> English that does not follow the rules of grammar and usage
>
> *Give two examples of nonstandard English.*
>
> Examples will vary.

NONSTANDARD ENGLISH

Nonstandard English is ungrammatical. It does not follow the rules of standard English that are required in college writing. The academic and business worlds expect you to be able to recognize and avoid nonstandard English. This is not always easy because some nonstandard terms are used so often in speech that many people think they are acceptable in writing. The following list might help you choose the correct words in your own writing.

ain't

NOT	Ricardo **ain't** going to school today.
CORRECT	Ricardo **is not** going to school today.

anywheres

NOT	Jake makes himself at home **anywheres** he goes.
CORRECT	Jakes makes himself at home **anywhere** he goes.

be

NOT	I **be** so tired.
CORRECT	I **am** so tired.

(For additional help with *be*, see Chapter 27, "Verb Tense.")

being as, being that

NOT	**Being as** Rhonda is late, we can't start the party.
CORRECT	**Because** Rhonda is late, we can't start the party.

coulda/could of, shoulda/should of

NOT   My brother **could of** played basketball in college. He **should of** stuck with it.

CORRECT My brother **could have** (or **could've**) played basketball in college. He **should have** (or **should've**) stuck with it.

different than

NOT   I am no **different than** all your other friends.

CORRECT I am no **different from** all your other friends.

drug

NOT   I couldn't lift the box, so I **drug** it across the room.

CORRECT I couldn't lift the box, so I **dragged** it across the room.

enthused

NOT   Jay was **enthused** about his trip to Hawaii.

CORRECT Jay was **enthusiastic** about his trip to Hawaii.

everywheres

NOT   My little sister follows me **everywheres** I go.

CORRECT My little sister follows me **everywhere** I go.

goes

NOT   Then he **goes,** I'll wait for you downstairs"

CORRECT Then he **says,** "I'll wait for you downstairs."

CORRECT Then he **said** he would wait for me downstairs.

hisself

NOT   Marshall made **hisself** a budget for the next month.

CORRECT Marshall made **himself** a budget for the next month.

in regards to

NOT   **In regards to** your proposal, we have decided to consider it

CORRECT **In regard to** your proposal, we have decided to consider it.

irregardless

NOT   **Irregardless** of how much time you spent on your paper, it still needs work.

CORRECT **Regardless** of the time you spent on your paper, it still needs work.

kinda/kind of, sorta/sort of

NOT   Abby's perfume smells **kinda** sweet, **sorta** like vanilla.

CORRECT   Abby's perfume smells **rather** sweet, **much** like vanilla.

most

NOT   **Most** everyone we invited will come to the party.

CORRECT   **Almost** everyone we invited will come to the party.

must of

NOT   I **must of** left my gloves in the car.

CORRECT   I **must have** left my gloves in the car.

off of

NOT   Jim accidentally knocked the vase **off of** the coffee table.

CORRECT   Jim accidentally knocked the vase **off** the coffee table.

oughta

NOT   Sometimes I think I **oughta** try out for the swim team.

CORRECT   Sometimes I think I **ought to** try out for the swim team.

real

NOT   My mom was **real** upset when I came in at 4 a.m.

CORRECT   My mom was **really** upset when I came in at 4 a.m.

somewheres

NOT   You must have left your notebook **somewheres** at school.

CORRECT   You must have left your notebook **somewhere** at school.

suppose to

NOT   Marc was **suppose to** meet me at the library.

CORRECT   Marc was **supposed to** meet me at the library.

theirselves

NOT   My grandfather thinks people should help **theirselves** instead of waiting for a handout.

CORRECT   My grandfather thinks people should help **themselves** instead of waiting for a handout.

use to

NOT   Nassar **use to** live in Egypt.

CORRECT   Nassar **used to** live in Egypt.

ways

NOT	Both sides say they are a long **ways** from agreement.
CORRECT	Both sides say they are a long **way** from agreement.

where...at

NOT	Do you know **where** your keys are **at**?
CORRECT	Do you know **where** your keys **are**?

Reviewing Nonstandard English

What is one reason using nonstandard English in written work is easy to do?

We hear it so often that we think it is standard.

Give four examples of nonstandard English; then correct them.

Answers will vary.

_____   _____

_____   _____

_____   _____

_____   _____

PRACTICE 1A: Recall/Identify Underline the ungrammatical words or phrases in each of the following sentences.

1. I <u>ain't</u> going to eat these turnips.   *(am not)*

2. I was <u>real</u> excited to see my new baby brother.   *(really)*

3. Sometimes people should keep their thoughts to <u>theirselves</u>.   *(themselves)*

4. <u>Being as</u> my brother has more money than I, he should pay for dinner.   *(Because)*

5. We <u>use to</u> go to the lake every summer.   *(used to)*

PRACTICE 1B: Correct Correct the ungrammatical words and expressions in Practice 1A by rewriting the incorrect sentences.   *See Practice 1A.*

PRACTICE 2: Apply Change the underlined ungrammatical words and phrases to standard English.

1. <u>where am I at</u>   *where am I*

2. Because I <u>drug</u>   *dragged*

3. She <u>goes</u>, "Sure."   *says*

4. <u>kinda</u>   *rather*

5. I <u>be</u>   *am*

PRACTICE 3: Write Your Own Write five sentences of your own using the grammatical words and phrases you chose in Practice 2. *Answers will vary.*

_____

_____

_____

_____

_____

SLANG

Another example of nonstandard English is **slang,** popular words and expressions that come and go, much like the latest fashions. For example, in the 1950s, someone might have called his or her special someone *dreamy*. In the 1960s, you might have heard a boyfriend or girlfriend described as *groovy*, and in the 1990s, *sweet* was the popular slang term. Today, your significant other might be *hot* or *dope*.

These expressions are slang because they are part of the spoken language that changes from generation to generation and from place to place. As you might suspect, slang communicates to a limited audience who share common interests and experiences. Some slang words, such as *cool* and *neat*, have become part of our language, but most slang is temporary. What's "in" today may be "out" tomorrow, so the best advice is to avoid slang in your writing.

> **Reviewing Slang**
>
> *What is slang?*
> *Popular words and expressions that come and go*
> _____
>
> _____
>
> *Give two examples of slang terms that you and your friends use today.*
> *Examples will vary.*   _____

PRACTICE 4: Recall/Identify Underline the slang words and expressions in each of the following sentences.

1. Just because she's pretty doesn't mean <u>she's all that</u>.

2. We were just <u>hangin</u> with our <u>homies</u>.

3. My sister and I are tight.

4. That guy is hot.

5. Give it up for Beyoncé.

PRACTICE 5: Apply Translate the following slang expressions into standard English.   *Answers may vary.*

1. That rocks.   *That's impressive.* _____

2. Say what?   *What did you say?* _____

3. Keep it real, man.   *Be honest.* _____

4. What up?   *What is happening?* _____

5. We're just kickin' it.   *We're just relaxing.* _____

PRACTICE 6: Write Your Own List five slang words or expressions, and use them in sentences of your own. Then rewrite each sentence using standard English to replace the slang expressions.   *Answers will vary.*

_____

_____

_____

_____

_____

CHAPTER REVIEW

MyWritingLab   ## Reviewing Standard and Nonstandard English

This topic is especially helpful to ESL students because it includes instruction on clichés, slang, and nonstandard English.

To review this material before you complete the Review Practices, watch the video called **Animation: Standard and Nonstandard English** at **MyWritingLab.com** one more time. This time, keep the video open as you complete the rest of the practices in this chapter. For best results, do the **MyWritingLab** exercises online as well as the Chapter Review practices in the book.

REVIEW PRACTICE 1: Recall/Identify Underline the ungrammatical or slang words in the following sentences.

1. <u>In regards to</u> your recent request, we are not able to give you an answer.

2. I have a shirt <u>somewheres</u> that looks just like that.

3. The music got louder and faster, and then we were really <u>rolling</u>.

4. Hey, that's <u>real cool</u>.

5. Do you know <u>where</u> my sunglasses are <u>at</u>?

6. Don't <u>be tellin'</u> me what to do.

7. My <u>bro</u> John likes to roller-blade on the boardwalk.

8. <u>Everywheres</u> I go, that dog follows.

9. She's very <u>enthused</u> about the trip.

10. Despite the snow, <u>most</u> all of the employees came to work today.

MyWritingLab

Practicing Standard and Nonstandard English

Now complete the **Recall** activities for **Standard and Nonstandard English** in the **Usage and Style** module of **MyWritingLab.com**. Remember to read the answers carefully because many of them look similar.

REVIEW PRACTICE 2: Apply Underline any nonstandard English in the following sentences, and correct the sentences by rewriting them. *Answers may vary.*

1. The girl in my economics class is <u>phat</u>. *(very good looking)*

2. You really need to <u>chill out</u>. *(calm down)*

3. Wow, I really like your new leather jacket; <u>it's bad</u>. *(it looks great)*

4. Weren't you <u>suppose to</u> go to the movie with Eddie today? *(supposed to)*

5. Timmy's brother <u>done</u> it now. *(did)*

6. I'm so sorry that I knocked your picture <u>off of</u> the wall. *(off)*

7. <u>Hey man</u>, do you think you can make room for one more person? *(Excuse me)*

8. Today, I <u>be feelin'</u> fine.   *(am feeling)*

9. You <u>could of</u> always asked for help.   *(could have/could've)*

10. <u>Whatcha doin'</u> in the basement?   *(What are you doing)*

MyWritingLab

Practicing Standard and Nonstandard English

Next, complete the **Apply** activity for **Standard and Nonstandard English** in the **Usage and Style** module of **MyWritingLab.com.** If you're stuck, you can go to the lower right-hand corner and open up the video again, or you can click on the hint button.

Complete this **Writing Prompt** at **mywritinglab.com**

REVIEW PRACTICE 3: Write Your Own Write a paragraph on a community problem. What are the details? What is the problem? What solution do you propose?   *Answers will vary.*

MyWritingLab

Practicing Standard and Nonstandard English

For more practice, complete the **Write** activity for **Standard and Nonstandard English** in the **Usage and Style** module of **MyWritingLab. com.** Make sure to pay close attention to the use of standard and nonstandard English as you revise the paragraph.

REVIEW PRACTICE 4: Editing Through Collaboration Exchange paragraphs from Review Practice 3 with another student, and do the following: *Answers will vary.*

1. Underline any ungrammatical language.

2. Circle any slang.

Then return the paper to its writer, and use the information in this chapter to correct any nonstandard or slang expressions in your own paragraph. Record your errors on the Error Log in Appendix 7.

Easily Confused Words

UNIT PRE-TESTS
To check your students' abilities with the collective skills in this unit, two Unit Pre-tests are available in the *Instructor's Resource Manual*.

TEST YOURSELF

Choose the correct word in parentheses.

- I have to (accept, except) that I won't be graduating this spring.
- (Who's, Whose) bike is this?
- I'm not saying (it's, its) Johnny's fault.
- We are going to need (their, there, they're) help.
- (Wear, where, were) did you say your parents lived?

(Answers are in Appendix 3.)

Some words are easily confused. They may look alike, sound alike, or have similar meanings. But they all play different roles in the English language. This chapter will help you choose the right words for your sentences.

Student Comment
"**Easily Confused Words** was the most helpful topic for me in **MyWritingLab** because I always get confused when to use *their, there,* or *they're.*"

MyWritingLab   ## Understanding Easily Confused Words

To find out more about this topic, go to **MyWritingLab.com,** and choose **Easily Confused Words** in the **Usage and Style** module. From there, watch the video called **Animation: Easily Confused Words.** Then, return to this chapter, which will go into more detail about word choice and give you opportunities to practice it. Finally, you will apply your understanding of word choice to your own writing.

TEACHING EASILY CONFUSED WORDS
Provide students with the following poem (author unknown), and ask them to rewrite it correctly.

EASILY CONFUSED WORDS, PART I

a/an: Use *a* before words that begin with a consonant. Use *an* before words that begin with a *vowel* (*a, e, i, o, u*).

a party, **a** dollar, **a** car

an apple, **an** elephant, **an** opportunity

accept/except: *Accept* means "receive." *Except* means "other than."

Yolanda says she will not **accept** my apology.

I answered every question **except** the last one.

advice/advise: *Advice* means "helpful information." *Advise* means "give advice or help."

Whenever I need **advice,** I call my older brother Greg.

Greg usually **advises** me to make a list before taking action.

affect/effect: *Affect* (verb) means "influence." *Effect* means "bring about" (verb) or "a result" (noun).

Omar hopes his new job won't **affect** his study time.

The governor believes higher taxes will **effect** positive economic changes.

The pill produced a calming **effect.**

already/all ready: *Already* means "in the past." *All ready* means "completely prepared."

Hope has **already** registered for the spring semester.

We were **all ready** to go when the phone rang.

among/between: Use *among* when referring to three or more people or things. Use *between* when referring to only two people or things.

Among all the students in our class, Shonda is the most mature.

I can't decide **between** cheesecake and apple pie for dessert.

bad/badly: *Bad* means "not good." *Badly* means "not well."

That milk is **bad,** so don't drink it.

The team played **badly** in the first half but came back to win.

Kiki felt **bad** that she could not go.

beside/besides: *Beside* means "next to." *Besides* means "in addition (to)."

Burt stood **beside** Kevin in the team photo.

She's a very calm person. **Besides,** she has nothing to worry about.

brake/break: *Brake* means "stop" or "the part that stops a moving vehicle." *Break* means "shatter, come apart" or "a rest between work periods."

The car behind me didn't **brake** fast enough.

My car needs new **brakes.**

Esther wants to **break** up with Stan.

They took a **break.**

ODE TO THE SPELL-CHECKER

Eye halve a spelling chequer,

It came with my pea sea.

It plainly marques for my revue

Miss steaks eye kin knot sea.

Eye strike a key and type a word

And weight four it two say

Weather eye am wrong oar write

It shows me straight a weigh.

As soon as a mist ache is maid

It nose bee fore two long,

And eye can put the error rite

Its rare lea ever wrong.

Eye have run this poem threw it;

I am shore your pleased two no.

Its letter perfect awl the weigh;

My chequer told me sew!

INSTRUCTOR'S RESOURCE MANUAL
For more exercises and for quizzes, see the *Instructor's Resource Manual,* Section II, Part IV.

UNIT POST-TESTS
To check your students' mastery of the collective skills in this unit, two Unit Post-tests are available in the *Instructor's Resource Manual.*

breath/breathe: *Breath* means "air." *Breathe* means "taking in air."

Take several big **breaths** as you cool down.
To cure hiccups, **breathe** into a paper bag.

choose/chose: *Choose* means "select." *Chose* is the past tense of *choose*.

Please **choose** something from the menu.
Andy **chose** the trip to Paris as his prize.

Reviewing Words That Are Easily Confused, Part I

Do you understand the differences in the sets of words in Part I of the list?

Answers will vary.

Have you ever confused any of these words? If so, which ones?

Answers will vary.

PRACTICE 1: Recall/Identify Underline the correct word in each of the following sentences.

1. You should try to (<u>choose</u>, chose) a computer that will meet your needs.

2. When I mixed vinegar with baking soda, the (affect, <u>effect</u>) was astounding.

3. (Beside, <u>Besides</u>) being cold, I was also hungry.

4. I'll call you when I'm on my (brake, <u>break</u>) at work.

5. Your car keys are (among, <u>between</u>) the two books on the fireplace mantel.

PRACTICE 2: Apply Complete the following sentences with correct words from Part I of this list (above).

1. I was so shocked I couldn't catch my _____*breath*_____.

2. I decided to take your _____*advice*_____.

3. Elaine will _____*accept*_____ your invitation to the prom if you will only ask her.

4. I feel _____*bad*_____ that I arrived late.

5. Thank you for the invitation to lunch, but I have _____*already*_____ eaten.

PRACTICE 3: Write Your Own Use each pair of words correctly in a sentence of your own. *Answers will vary.*

1. bad/badly _____

2. beside/besides _____

3. brake/break _____

4. choose/chose _____

5. accept/except _____

EASILY CONFUSED WORDS, PART II

coarse/course: *Coarse* refers to something that is rough. *Course* refers to a class, a path, or a part of a meal.

Sandpaper can be very fine or very **coarse.**

My computer science **course** is really interesting.

Their **course** in life was difficult.

I made a five-**course** dinner.

desert/dessert: *Desert* refers to dry, sandy land or means "abandon." *Dessert* refers to the last course of a meal.

Las Vegas was once nothing but a **desert.**

The main character in the short story **deserted** his family.

We had strawberry shortcake for **dessert.**

Hint: You can remember that *dessert* has two s's if you think of *strawberry shortcake*.

does/dose: *Does* means "performs." *Dose* refers to a specific amount of medicine.

Karla **does** whatever she wants on the weekends.

The doctor gave the child a small **dose** of penicillin.

fewer/less: *Fewer* refers to things that can be counted. *Less* refers to things that cannot be counted.

There are **fewer** cookies in the jar since Joey has been home.

Because my mom is working another job, she has **less** time to spend with us.

good/well: *Good* modifies nouns. *Well* modifies verbs, adjectives, and adverbs. *Well* also refers to a state of health.

Barbie looks **good** in her new outfit.

Dave looks as if he doesn't feel **well.**

Karen didn't do **well** on the typing test because she was nervous.

hear/here: *Hear* refers to the act of listening. *Here* means "in this place."

I can't **hear** you because the music is too loud.
You dropped some food **here** on the carpet.

it's/its: *It's* is the contraction for *it is* or *it has*. *Its* is a possessive pronoun.

The forecasters say **it's** going to snow this afternoon.
The cat ate breakfast and then washed **its** face.

knew/new: *Knew* is the past tense of *know*. *New* means "recent."

I thought you **knew** I had a **new** car.

know/no: *Know* means "understand." *No* means "not any" or is the opposite of *yes*.

We all **know** that Bart has **no** conscience.
No, I can't join you.

lay/lie: *Lay* means "set down." (Its principal parts are *lay, laid, laid*.) *Lie* means "recline." (Its principal parts are *lie, lay, lain*.)

The train crew **lays** about a mile of track a day.
He **laid** down his burden.
Morrie **lies** down and takes a short nap every afternoon.
I **lay** on the beach until the sun set.

(For additional help with *lie* and *lay*, see Chapter 26, "Regular and Irregular Verbs.")

loose/lose: *Loose* means "free" or "unattached." *Lose* means "misplace" or "not win."

I tightened the **loose** screws on the door hinge.
If the Tigers **lose** this game, they will be out of the playoffs.

passed/past: *Passed* is the past tense of *pass*. *Past* refers to an earlier time or means "beyond."

Mei **passed** the exam with an "A."
Having survived the Civil War, the mansion has an interesting **past.**
He ran **past** Ginger and into Reba's outstretched arms.

Reviewing Words That Are Easily Confused, Part II

Do you understand the differences in the sets of words in Part II of the list?

Answers will vary.

Have you ever confused any of these words? If so, which ones?

Answers will vary.

PRACTICE 4: Recall/Identify Underline the correct word in each of the following sentences.

1. Sandy, will you please come (hear, <u>here</u>) so I can show you how to set the DVR?

2. Now that I have eaten dinner, I feel (<u>good</u>, well).

3. The outdoor shutters came (<u>loose</u>, lose) during the storm.

4. (<u>It's</u>, Its) going to be a very long day.

5. My go-cart blew a tire, and so Jed (<u>passed</u>, past) me on the third lap.

PRACTICE 5: Apply Complete the following sentences with correct words from Part II of this list (above).

1. I need to take only one more _____*course*_____ to complete my degree.

2. Would you please _____*lay*_____ those clean clothes on the bed?

3. The doctor told my dad that he could _____*no*_____ longer eat salt.

4. Camels can live in the _____*desert*_____ because they store water in their humps.

5. Since Janelle has _____*fewer*_____ cookies, you should share with her.

PRACTICE 6: Write Your Own Use each pair of words correctly in a sentence of your own. *Answers will vary.*

1. loose/lose _____

2. passed/past _____

3. hear/here _____

4. good/well _____

5. knew/new _____

EASILY CONFUSED WORDS, PART III

principal/principle: *Principal* means "main, most important," "a school official," or "a sum of money." A *principle* is a rule. (Think of *principle* and *rule*—both end in -*le*.)

My **principal** reason for moving is to be nearer my family.

Mr. Reese is the **principal** of my high school.

The interest and **principal** on the loan are set.

He lives by certain **principles,** including honesty and fairness.

quiet/quite: *Quiet* means "without noise." *Quite* means "very."

It was a warm, **quiet** night.

Vanessa said she was **quite** satisfied with her grade.

raise/rise: *Raise* means "increase" or "lift up." *Rise* means "get up from a sitting or reclining position."

The governor does not plan to **raise** taxes.

Ernie **rises** at 5 a.m. every morning to go to the health club.

set/sit: *Set* means "put down." *Sit* means "take a seated position."

Mohammed, you can **set** the packages over there.

If I **sit** for a long period of time, my back starts hurting.

(For additional help with *sit* and *set,* see Chapter 26, "Regular and Irregular Verbs.")

than/then: *Than* is used in making comparisons. *Then* means "next."

Louise is younger **than** her sister Linda.

The ball rolled around the hoop, **then** dropped through the net.

their/there/they're: *Their* is possessive. *There* indicates location. *They're* is the contraction of *they are.*

Their car broke down in the middle of the freeway.

Too much trash is over **there** by the riverbank.

They're not coming to the party because **they're** tired.

threw/through: *Threw,* the past tense of *throw,* means "tossed." *Through* means "finished" or "passing from one point to another."

Beth **threw** the ball to Wes, who easily caught it.

Allen is **through** with his lunch, so he will leave soon.

Rico went **through** his closet searching for his G.I. Joes.

to/too/two: *To* means "toward" or is used with a verb. *Too* means "also" or "very." *Two* is a number.

Tori went **to** Johnny's house **to** return his ring.

Tori returned Johnny's photo albums **too**.

Mariel thinks **two** is her lucky number.

wear/were/where: *Wear* means "have on one's body." *Were* is the past tense of *be*. *Where* refers to a place.

Where were you going when I saw you?

Can you **wear** jeans to that restaurant?

weather/whether: *Weather* refers to outdoor conditions. *Whether* expresses possibility.

Whether the **weather** will improve or not is a good question.

who's/whose: *Who's* is a contraction of *who is* or *who has*. *Whose* is a possessive pronoun.

We wonder **who's** going to decide **whose** opinion is correct.

your/you're: *Your* means "belonging to you." *You're* is the contraction of *you are*.

Your appointment will be canceled if **you're** not on time.

> ### Reviewing Words That Are Easily Confused, Part III
>
> *Do you understand the differences in the sets of words in Part III of this list?*
>
> Answers will vary.
>
> *Have you ever confused any of these words? If so, which ones?*
>
> Answers will vary.

PRACTICE 7: Recall/Identify Underline the correct word in each of the following sentences.

1. There are (to, <u>too</u>, two) many swimmers in the pool.

2. (Were, Wear, <u>Where</u>) were you going in such a hurry?

3. For extra income, we (<u>raise</u>, rise) hamsters and sell them on the Internet.

4. If you don't mow the lawn, (<u>your</u>, you're) mom is going to get upset.

5. (<u>Who's</u>, Whose) that girl with Bob?

PRACTICE 8: Apply Complete the following sentences with correct words from Part III of this list (above).

1. Pedro has a better sense of humor _____*than*_____ his sister.

2. If the firefighters can't put out the blaze, _____*they're*_____ going to call for reinforcements.

3. Much to our surprise, the bird flew _____*through*_____ our car window.

4. The _____*principal*_____ of our school is very strict.

5. Could you please be _____*quiet*_____ so I can hear the speaker?

PRACTICE 9: Write Your Own Use each set of words correctly in a sentence of your own. *Answers will vary.*

1. set/sit _____

2. weather/whether _____

3. threw/through _____

4. then/than _____

5. raise/rise _____

CHAPTER REVIEW

Remind your students that spelling is calculated in their score in the Apply section.

MyWritingLab **Reviewing Easily Confused Words**

To review this material before you complete the Review Practices, watch **Animation: Easily Confused Words** at MyWritingLab.com one more time. This time, keep the video open as you complete the rest of the practices in this chapter. For best results, do the **MyWritingLab** exercises online as well as the Chapter Review practices in the book.

REVIEW PRACTICE 1: Recall/Identify Underline the correct word in each of the following sentences.

1. Simone had (fewer, less) mistakes on her quiz this time.

2. Could you please (were, wear, where) something nice for tonight's banquet?

3. I got all the answers right (accept, except) two.

4. You performed that dance very (good, well).

5. Every time Mel goes (<u>to</u>, too, two) the beach, he gets sunburned.

6. He scraped his knee (bad, <u>badly</u>) on the sidewalk.

7. The doctor recommended a small (does, <u>dose</u>) of the experimental medicine.

8. Sharla has (<u>already</u>, all ready) had her turn on the computer.

9. (Their, <u>There</u>, They're) are too many people in this room to be comfortable.

10. That smell (<u>affects</u>, effects) me in strange ways.

MyWritingLab **Practicing Easily Confused Words**

Now complete the **Recall** activities for **Easily Confused Words** in the **Usage and Style** module of **MyWritingLab.com.** If you're having a difficult time with a question, open up the video in the lower right-hand corner for some help.

REVIEW PRACTICE 2: Apply Complete the following sentences with a correct word from all three parts of the list.

1. The nurse told Wilbur to _____*lie*_____ down and try to relax.

2. The _____*weather*_____ should be just fine for our picnic today.

3. _____*Among*_____ all those thorns, I found a rose.

4. I am sure that I don't _____*know*_____ all the answers to life's questions.

5. If you need help, I can give you my _____*advice*_____ .

6. The proudest day of Ricky's life was when he _____*passed*_____ the big test.

7. Whenever you get anxious, _____*breathe*_____ deeply.

8. The group had _____*its*_____ picture taken.

9. If you have a choice, _____*choose*_____ the solution that has the fewest obstacles.

10. Yoshi should _____*set*_____ those books down before he hurts himself.

MyWritingLab Practicing Easily Confused Words

Next, complete the **Apply** activity for **Easily Confused Words** in the **Usage and Style** module of **MyWritingLab.com.** Pay close attention to the directions, and click only on what you're asked to.

Complete this **Writing Prompt** at **mywritinglab.com**

REVIEW PRACTICE 3: Write Your Own Write a paragraph about a recent decision you had to make, explaining what the problem was and why you made the decision you did. Try to use some of the easily confused words from this chapter. *Answers will vary.*

MyWritingLab Practicing Easily Confused Words

For more practice, complete the **Write** activity for **Easily Confused Words** in the **Usage and Style** module of **MyWritingLab.com.** Pay close attention to the use of any easily confused words.

REVIEW PRACTICE 4: Editing Through Collaboration Exchange paragraphs from Review Practice 3 with another student, and do the following: *Answers will vary.*

1. Circle any words used incorrectly.

2. Write the correct form of the word above the error.

Then return the paper to its writer, and use the information in this chapter to correct any confused words in your own paragraph. Record your errors on the Error Log in Appendix 7.

Spelling

UNIT PRE-TESTS
To check your students'
abilities with the collective
skills in this unit, two Unit
Pre-tests are available in
the *Instructor's Resource
Manual.*

TEST YOURSELF

Correct the misspelled words in the following sentences.

- My cousin just moved to a forign country.
- Your grandmother makes delishous chicken and dumplings.
- Dennis is trying to persuaid me to join his fraternity.
- Winning two years in a row is quite an achievment.
- Eat your vegtables.

(Answers are in Appendix 3.)

If you think back over your education, you will realize that teachers believe spelling is important. There is a good reason they feel that way: Spelling errors send negative messages. Misspellings seem to leap out at readers, creating serious doubts about the writer's abilities in general. Because you will not always have access to spell-checkers—and because spell-checkers do not catch all spelling errors—improving your spelling skills is important.

MyWritingLab **Understanding Spelling**

To improve your understanding of this topic, go to **MyWritingLab.com**, and choose **Spelling** in the **Punctuation, Mechanics, and Spelling** module. From there, watch the video called **Animation: Spelling**. Then, return to this chapter, which will go into more detail about spelling rules and give you opportunities to practice them. Finally, you will apply your understanding of these rules to your own writing.

Student Comment
"Everything's repeated in
MyWritingLab, and I need that
because my memory is short."

SPELLING HINTS

The spelling rules in this chapter will help you become a better speller. But first, here are some practical hints that will also help you improve your spelling.

1. Start a personal spelling list of your own. Use the list of commonly misspelled words on pages 652–656 as your starting point.

2. Study the lists of easily confused words in Chapter 44.

3. Avoid all nonstandard expressions (see Chapter 43).

4. Use a dictionary when you run across words you don't know.

5. Run the spell-check program if you are writing on a computer. Keep in mind, however, that spell-check cannot tell if you have incorrectly used one word in place of another (such as *to, too,* or *two*).

Reviewing Hints for Becoming a Better Speller

Name two things you can do immediately to become a better speller.
Answers will vary.

Why can't you depend on a spell-check program to find every misspelled word?
Because it won't find confused words that are spelled correctly

PRACTICE 1A: Recall/Identify Underline the misspelled words in each of the following sentences. Refer to the list of easily confused words in Chapter 44 and to the most commonly misspelled words in this chapter as necessary.

1. Maria is a beatiful person.   *(beautiful)*

2. Hugo is familar with these math formulas.   *(familiar)*

3. My mother says there are many different kinds of intelligance.   *(intelligence)*

4. Would you please acompany me to the store?   *(accompany)*

5. This is a new developement.   *(development)*

PRACTICE 1B: Correct Correct the spelling errors in Practice 1A by rewriting the incorrect sentences.   *See Practice 1A.*

PRACTICE 2: Apply Fill in each blank in the following sentences with hints that help with spelling.

1. Use a _____*dictionary*_____ to look up words you don't know.

2. Start a _____*spelling list*_____ to help you remember words you commonly misspell.

3. You can always use the *spell-check program* on your computer, but you should remember that it cannot correct easily confused words, only misspelled words.

4. Try to avoid all ___*nonstandard*___ English.

5. Study the list of ___*confused words*___ in Chapter ___*44*___.

PRACTICE 3: Write Your Own Choose the correctly spelled word in each pair, and write a sentence using it. Refer to the spelling list on pages 652–656 if necessary. *Sentences will vary.*

1. vaccum/<u>vacuum</u>

_____

2. neccessary/<u>necessary</u>

_____

3. wierd/<u>weird</u>

_____

4. <u>separate</u>/seperate

_____

5. <u>tomorrow</u>/tommorow

_____

SPELLING RULES

Four basic spelling rules can help you avoid many misspellings. It pays to spend a little time learning them now.

1. **Words that end in -e:** When adding a suffix beginning with a vowel (*a, e, i, o, u*), drop the final *-e*.

believe + -ing	=	believing
include + -ed	=	included (-e is from the -ed)
value + -able	=	valuable

When adding a suffix beginning with a consonant, keep the final *-e*.

aware + -ness	=	awareness
improve + -ment	=	improvement
leisure + -ly	=	leisurely

2. **Words with *ie* and *ei*:** Put *i* before *e* except after *c* or when sounded like *ay* as in *neighbor* and *weigh*.

c + ei	(no c) + ie	Exceptions
receive	grieve	height
conceive	niece	leisure
deceive	friend	foreign
neighbor	relief	science

3. **Words that end in -y:** When adding a suffix to a word that ends in a consonant plus -y, change the y to *i*.

funny + -er	=	funnier
try + -ed	=	tried
easy + -er	=	easier

4. **Words that double the final consonant:** When adding a suffix starting with a vowel to a one-syllable word, double the final consonant.

big + -est	=	biggest
quit + -er	=	quitter
get + -ing	=	getting

With words of more than one syllable, double the final consonant if (1) the final syllable is stressed and (2) the word ends in a single vowel plus a single consonant.

begin + -ing	=	beginning
admit + -ed	=	admitted
rebel + -ious	=	rebellious

The word *travel* has more than one syllable. Should you double the final consonant? No, you should not, because the stress is on the first syllable (**trá vel**). The word ends in a vowel and a consonant, but that is not enough. Both parts of the rule must be met.

Reviewing Four Basic Spelling Rules

What is the rule for adding a suffix to words ending in -e (such as date + -ing)?

Drop the final -e when adding a suffix that begins with a vowel, and keep the -e when adding a suffix that begins with a consonant.

What is the rule for spelling ie *and* ei *words (such as* receive, neighbor, *and* friend)?

Put i before e except after c or when sounded as ay as in neighbor or weigh.

When do you change -y *to* i *before a suffix (such as* sunny + -est)?

When the word ends in a consonant plus a -y

When do you double the final consonant of a word before adding a suffix (such as cut, begin, *or* travel + -ing)?

When a one-syllable word ends in a consonant or when words of more than one

syllable have the stress on the final syllable and end in a vowel plus a consonant

PRACTICE 4A: Recall/Identify Underline the spelling errors in each of the following sentences.

1. The <u>secretarys</u> went out to lunch together. *(secretaries)*

2. Your <u>encouragment</u> helped me get through a tough time. *(encouragement)*

3. Sarah <u>percieved</u> that Fernando was upset. *(perceived)*

4. The reason should have <u>occured</u> to you. *(occurred)*

5. In winter, Frances likes going on <u>sliegh</u> rides. *(sleigh)*

PRACTICE 4B: Correct Correct the spelling errors in Practice 4A by rewriting the incorrect sentences. *See Practice 4A.*

PRACTICE 5: Apply Complete the following spelling rules.

1. With words that end with -e, __*drop the final -e*__ when adding a suffix beginning with a vowel.

2. Put *i* before *e* except after _____*c*_____ or when sounded as _____*ay*_____ as in __*neighbor or weigh*__ .

3. With words that end in -y, change the _____*y*_____ to an _____*i*_____ when adding a suffix to a word that ends in a consonant plus -y.

4. When adding a suffix that begins with a _____vowel_____ to a one-syllable word, _____double_____ the final consonant.

5. With words that have more than one syllable, _____double_____ the final consonant if (1) the final syllable is stressed and (2) the word ends in a single vowel plus a single consonant.

PRACTICE 6: Write Your Own Make a list of words you commonly misspelled words. Then choose five of the words, and use each correctly in a sentence.
Answers will vary.

_____

_____

_____

_____

_____

COMMONLY MISSPELLED WORDS

Use the following list of commonly misspelled words for reference when you write.

abbreviate	advertisement	artificial
absence	afraid	assassin
accelerate	aggravate	athletic
accessible	aisle	attach
accidentally	although	audience
accommodate	aluminum	authority
accompany	amateur	autumn
accomplish	ambulance	auxiliary
accumulate	ancient	avenue
accurate	anonymous	awkward
ache	anxiety	baggage
achievement	anxious	balloon
acknowledgment	appreciate	banana
acre	appropriate	bankrupt
actual	approximate	banquet
address	architect	beautiful
adequate	arithmetic	beggar

beginning	collar	deceive
behavior	college	decision
benefited	column	definition
bicycle	commit	delicious
biscuit	committee	descend
bought	communicate	describe
boundary	community	description
brilliant	comparison	deteriorate
brought	competent	determine
buoyant	competition	development
bureau	complexion	dictionary
burglar	conceive	difficulty
business	concession	diploma
cabbage	concrete	disappear
cafeteria	condemn	disastrous
calendar	conference	discipline
campaign	congratulate	disease
canoe	conscience	dissatisfied
canyon	consensus	divisional
captain	continuous	dormitory
career	convenience	economy
carriage	cooperate	efficiency
cashier	corporation	eighth
catastrophe	correspond	elaborate
caterpillar	cough	electricity
ceiling	counterfeit	eligible
cemetery	courageous	embarrass
census	courteous	emphasize
certain	cozy	employee
certificate	criticize	encourage
challenge	curiosity	enormous
champion	curious	enough
character	curriculum	enthusiastic
chief	cylinder	envelope
children	dairy	environment
chimney	dangerous	equipment
coffee	dealt	equivalent

especially	grief	interrupt
essential	grocery	invitation
establish	gruesome	irrelevant
exaggerate	guarantee	irrigate
excellent	guess	issue
exceptionally	guidance	jealous
excessive	handkerchief	jewelry
exhaust	handsome	journalism
exhilarating	haphazard	judgment
existence	happiness	kindergarten
explanation	harass	knife
extinct	height	knowledge
extraordinary	hesitate	knuckles
familiar	hoping	laboratory
famous	humorous	laborious
fascinate	hygiene	language
fashion	hymn	laugh
fatigue	icicle	laundry
faucet	illustrate	league
February	imaginary	legible
fiery	immediately	legislature
financial	immortal	leisure
foreign	impossible	length
forfeit	incidentally	library
fortunate	incredible	license
forty	independence	lieutenant
freight	indispensable	lightning
friend	individual	likable
fundamental	inferior	liquid
gauge	infinite	listen
genius	influential	literature
genuine	initial	machinery
geography	initiation	magazine
gnaw	innocence	magnificent
government	installation	majority
graduation	intelligence	manufacture
grammar	interfere	marriage

material
mathematics
maximum
mayor
meant
medicine
message
mileage
miniature
minimum
minute
mirror
miscellaneous
mischievous
miserable
misspell
monotonous
mortgage
mysterious
necessary
neighborhood
niece
nineteen
ninety
noticeable
nuisance
obedience
obstacle
occasion
occurred
official
omission
omitted
opponent
opportunity
opposite
original

outrageous
pamphlet
paragraph
parallel
parentheses
partial
particular
pastime
patience
peculiar
permanent
persistent
personnel
persuade
physician
pitcher
pneumonia
politician
possess
prairie
precede
precious
preferred
prejudice
previous
privilege
procedure
proceed
pronounce
psychology
publicly
questionnaire
quotient
realize
receipt
recipe
recommend

reign
religious
representative
reservoir
responsibility
restaurant
rhyme
rhythm
salary
satisfactory
scarcity
scenery
schedule
science
scissors
secretary
seize
separate
significant
similar
skiing
soldier
souvenir
sovereign
spaghetti
squirrel
statue
stomach
strength
subtle
succeed
success
sufficient
surprise
syllable
symptom
technique

temperature	unique	Wednesday
temporary	university	weigh
terrible	usable	weird
theater	usually	whose
thief	vacuum	width
thorough	valuable	worst
tobacco	various	wreckage
tomorrow	vegetable	writing
tongue	vehicle	yacht
tournament	vicinity	yearn
tragedy	villain	yield
truly	visible	zealous
unanimous	volunteer	zoology
undoubtedly	weather	

Reviewing Commonly Misspelled Words

Why is spelling important in your writing?

Because poor spelling sends a negative message to your reader

Start a personal spelling log of your most commonly misspelled words.

Answers will vary.

_____   _____   _____

_____   _____   _____

_____   _____   _____

_____   _____   _____

PRACTICE 7A: Recall/Identify Underline any misspelled words in the following sentences.

1. My best <u>freind</u> has a tendency to <u>exagerate</u>   *(friend, exaggerate)*.

2. If Justin stays on <u>scheduele</u>, he'll be a sophomore next year.   *(schedule)*

3. My third-grader gets perfect <u>arithmatic</u> scores.   *(arithmetic)*

4. She is a very <u>sucessful</u> lawyer.   *(successful)*

5. The <u>restarant</u> is <u>undoutedly</u> the finest in town.   *(restaurant, undoubtedly)*

PRACTICE 7B: Correct Correct any spelling errors you identified in Practice 7A by rewriting the incorrect sentences.   *See Practice 7A.*

PRACTICE 8: Apply Cross out and correct the spelling errors in the following paragraph.

This past ~~Febuary~~ *February*, an ~~anonimous~~ *anonymous* tip was called into the police station. Apparently, a local ~~polition~~ *politician* was having severe ~~finantial~~ *financial* difficulties, so he started making ~~counterfit~~ *counterfeit* money. There was really no ~~noticible~~ *noticeable* difference between his funny money and real money. He passed the money through his wife's retail company. It was only when the ~~politition~~ *politician* became overly ~~enthusiastick~~ *enthusiastic* about his scam that he got caught. He revealed his scam to another ~~politition~~ *politician* one who did not want the whole ~~goverment~~ *government* to take the fall for one man. So, he called the police and left the ~~anonimous~~ *anonymous* tip. Now the only ~~londry~~ *laundry* the dirty ~~politition~~ *politician* is doing is in jail.

PRACTICE 9: Write Your Own Write a complete sentence for each word listed here.

1. laboratory _____

2. embarrass _____

3. familiar _____

4. hoping _____

5. manufacture _____

CHAPTER REVIEW

MyWritingLab   ## Reviewing Spelling

To review this material before you complete the Review Practices, watch **Animation: Spelling** at **MyWritingLab.com** one more time. This time, keep the video open as you complete the rest of the practices in this chapter. For best results, do the **MyWritingLab** exercises online as well as the Chapter Review practices in the book.

The video here focuses purely on suffix rules. Having students keep *Mosaics* open to see the other spelling rules while they work in MyWritingLab will be beneficial.

REVIEW PRACTICE 1: Recall/Identify Underline the misspelled words in each of the following sentences.

1. I always <u>mispel</u> the word "<u>mischeivous</u>." *(misspell, mischievous)*

2. I don't think Chris used good sense in <u>leting</u> his <u>lisence</u> expire. *(letting, license)*

3. My parents have <u>truely</u> had a good <u>marriege</u>. *(truly, marriage)*

4. The new <u>restraunt</u> will offer <u>incredably</u> <u>delishious</u> <u>deserts</u>. *(restaurant, ncredibly, delicious, desserts)*

5. In my <u>psichology</u> class, one guy always <u>interupts</u> the <u>profeser</u>. *(psychology, interrupts, professor)*

6. The <u>rhime</u> in that song sounds ridiculous. *(rhyme)*

7. The recommended <u>salery</u> for a <u>professer</u> is not what it should be these days. *(salary, professor)*

8. I met two <u>curagous</u> war heroes who were interesting to talk to. *(courageous)*

9. Professor Barton is an <u>extrordinary</u> teacher. *(extraordinary)*

10. Rafael's parents <u>perfered</u> that he pursue a career in <u>psycology</u>. *(preferred, psychology)*

MyWritingLab **Practicing Spelling**

Now complete the **Recall** activities for **Spelling** in the **Punctuation, Mechanics, and Spelling** module of **MyWritingLab.com.** Remember to read the answers carefully because many of them look similar.

REVIEW PRACTICE 2: Apply Correct the spelling errors in Review Practice 1 by rewriting the incorrect sentences. *See Review Practice 1.*

MyWritingLab **Practicing Spelling**

Next, complete the **Apply** activity for **Spelling** in the **Punctuation, Mechanics, and Spelling** module of **MyWritingLab.com.** If you're stuck, you can go to the lower right-hand corner and open up the video again, or you can click on the Hint button.

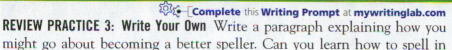
Complete this **Writing Prompt** at **mywritinglab.com**

REVIEW PRACTICE 3: Write Your Own Write a paragraph explaining how you might go about becoming a better speller. Can you learn how to spell in college? Before college? *Answers will vary.*

MyWritingLab **Practicing Spelling**

For more practice, complete the **Write** activity for **Spelling** in the **Punctuation, Mechanics, and Spelling** module of **MyWritingLab. com.** Pay close attention to the spelling of each word as you revise the paragraph.

REVIEW PRACTICE 4: Editing Through Collaboration Exchange paragraphs from Review Practice 3 with another student, and do the following: *Answers will vary.*

1. Underline any words that are used incorrectly.

2. Circle any misspelled words.

Then return the paper to its writer, and use the information in this chapter to correct any spelling errors in your own paragraph. Record your errors on the Spelling Log in Appendix 7.

Appendix 1: Critical Thinking Log

Circle the critical thinking questions you missed after each essay you read. Have your instructor explain the pattern of errors.

Reading	Content	Purpose and Audience	Essays	Number Correct
Describing				
Amy Tan	1 2 3	4 5 6	7 8 9	10
Alice Walker	1 2 3	4 5 6	7 8 9	10
Narrating				
Sandra Cisneros	1 2 3	4 5 6	7 8 9	10
Michael Arredondo	1 2 3	4 5 6	7 8 9	10
Illustrating				
Chang-Rae Lee	1 2 3	4 5 6	7 8 9	10
Brent Staples	1 2 3	4 5 6	7 8 9	10
Analyzing a Process				
Julia Bourland	1 2 3	4 5 6	7 8 9	10
Russell Freedman	1 2 3	4 5 6	7 8 9	10
Comparing and Contrasting				
Ernesto Galarza	1 2 3	4 5 6	7 8 9	10
David Brooks	1 2 3	4 5 6	7 8 9	10
Dividing and Classifying				
Camille Lavington	1 2 3	4 5 6	7 8 9	10
Stephanie Ericsson	1 2 3	4 5 6	7 8 9	10
Defining				
Gary Mack	1 2 3	4 5 6	7 8 9	10
Jo Goodwin Parker	1 2 3	4 5 6	7 8 9	10
Analyzing Causes and Effects				
Kristin Kalning	1 2 3	4 5 6	7 8 9	10
Corky Clifton	1 2 3	4 5 6	7 8 9	10
Arguing				
Alan Gomez	1 2 3	4 5 6	7 8 9	10
Tufekci and Turkle	1 2 3	4 5 6	7 8 9	10

The legend will help you identify your strengths and weaknesses in critical thinking.

Legend for Critical Thinking Log

Questions	Skill
1–2	Literal and interpretive
3–6	Critical thinking
7–9	Analyzing sentences
10	Writing paragraphs

Appendix 2A: Your EQ (Editing Quotient)

A good way to approach editing is by finding your EQ (Editing Quotient). Knowing your EQ will help you look for specific errors in your writing and make your editing more efficient.

In each of the following paragraphs, underline the errors you find, and list them on the lines below the paragraph. The number of errors corresponds to the letters in each paragraph.

The possible errors are listed here:

abbreviation	end punctuation	pronoun agreement
capitalization	fragment	run-together sentences
comma	modifier error	spelling
confused word	number	subject–verb agreement

1. A lot of teenage girls are influenced by what they see in the movies and on TV. Some of the actresses are so thin that rumors begin about their various eating disorders. [a]Which they all deny. Sometimes actresses don't get roles because they are "too heavy." [b]Even though these actresses are at their ideal weight. The message Hollywood sends is that ultra-thin is best[c] young girls take this message to heart. Hollywood provides physical role models for all of society[d] these role models are not always good to follow.

   a. _____   c. _____

   b. _____   d. _____

2. Bilingual education is a problem in California. The people have passed propositions that eliminate such programs,[a] much of the population [b]believe bilingual programs must be present in schools. [c]In order for second-language learners to learn. Surely a happy medium [d]exist somewhere between the nonfunctioning programs and total elimination. Perhaps the solution lies in finding a program. [e]To accommodate both students and taxpayers.

   a. _____   d. _____

   b. _____   e. _____

   c. _____

3. Pesticide use on fruits and vegetables [a]has ran into trouble because it is often misunderstood. The government places strict regulations on chemical use in fields,[b] each chemical must be tested and approved for each crop it is used for. Often pesticides degrade within [c]twenty-four hours when exposed to sunlight. Strict rules apply to the application of a chemical, the reentry time for workers, and the time that must lapse before harvesting the fruits and vegetables. [d]Hefty fines imposed on violators for proper pesticide use. People who [e]have swore off nonorganic foods need to become better informed about the rules and regulations regarding pesticides.

   a. _____   d. _____

   b. _____   e. _____

   c. _____

4. Political campaigns have become difficult to watch because of the constant intrusion into candidates' personal lives. What starts out as a clean campaign quickly turns dirty. [a]When one candidate exposes a secret about [b]their opponent's past. From that point on, a candidate is explaining and apologizing for [c]their past, and quite often [d]they launch an attack of [e]their own. Just once a clean political campaign would be nice to see[f] the American public would not know what to do.

a. _____   d. _____

b. _____   e. _____

c. _____   f. _____

5. Many people do not understand how severely allergies can affect someone. Most people think that a runny nose and a little sneezing are no big deal[a] allergies can cause severe headaches, asthma, rashes, and sometimes death. [b]Suffering from severe allergies, days can really be miserable. Sometimes people must take daily medications so they can live a normal life, [c]which may include steroids. But people with bad allergies live in constant fear that they'll eat, be stung by, or be prescribed something that might kill them, [d]allergies can be very hard on people.

a. _____   c. _____

b. _____   d. _____

6. Violence on television is influencing America's youth. Young children try to mimic the behavior of such characters as Bart Simpson. Teenagers whose daily lives involve watching violent [a]tv shows have killed people. Parents need to monitor what their children watch. [b]In order to guarantee the children don't see,[c] and become desensitized by too much violence. Censoring violent television shows will not help those children who are unsupervised,[d] parents must take control of what their children watch?[e]

a. _____   d. _____

b. _____   e. _____

c. _____

7. [a]17 college students were needlessly killed last Friday night because they ignored the law. A group of students held a party in an abandoned warehouse that had "CONDEMNED" signs all over the place[b] the students ignored the warnings. At about 1:00 a.m., a fire broke out,[c] because most of the exits were blocked off, some students did not get out alive. [d]Sgt. Thomas of the local fire department said that it was a horrible tragedy. Maybe now people will understand. [e]The seriousness of the signs.

a. _____   d. _____

b. _____   e. _____

c. _____

8. Genetic research has made some great, although scary, advances in the past decade. Agriculture is [a]benefitting from genetically altered crops. [b]That are comprised of insect-resistant and [c]disese-resistant plants. [d]Now that genetic research is capable of

cloning an animal. It is probably capable of cloning human life. At what point does science go [e]to far?

a. _____   d. _____

b. _____   e. _____

c. _____

9. Studies have proved that children who listen to [a]Classical music when they are young are more likely to be better students later in life. Beethoven and Mozart can stimulate young brains and open [b]there minds for further learning,[c] classical music has been proved to produce students who yearn for more knowledge. Researchers have even stated that listening to classical music while studying [d]create an environment for retaining more information. [e]Than an environment with no music. If children are brought up with classical music in their lives[f] it could become a lifelong, beneficial habit.

a. _____   d. _____

b. _____   e. _____

c. _____   f. _____

10. People who are thinking about owning a dog need to understand all that is involved in the care. [a]First of all. Dogs must be taken to the vet for a series of shots[b] the animal should also be spayed or neutered. Proper food and medicines must be purchased. [c]As well as toys and treats. People must also invest [d]alot of their time in the animal. A dog is perceptive,[e] and responds to the way [f]they are treated. Anything less than full health care and quality time is simply unfair to the dog.

a. _____   d. _____

b. _____   e. _____

c. _____   f. _____

Appendix 2B: Editing Quotient Answers

Use the answers below to score your EQ. Mark the answers that you missed.

1. a. *fragment*

b. *fragment*

c. *run-together or end punctuation*

d. *run-together or end punctuation*

2. a. *run-together or end punctuation*

b. *subject-verb agreement*

c. *fragment*

d. *subject-verb agreement*

e. *fragment*

3. a. *verb form*

b. *run-together or end punctuation*

c. *number*

d. *fragment*

e. *verb form*

4. a. fragment

b. pronoun agreement

c. pronoun agreement

d. pronoun agreement

e. pronoun agreement

f. run-together or end punctuation

5. a. run-together or end punctuation

b. modifier error

c. modifier error

d. run-together or end comm.

6. a. capitalization

b. fragment

c. comma

d. run-together or end punctuation

e. end punctuation

7. a. number

b. run-together or end punctuation

c. run-together or end punctuation

d. abbreviation

e. fragment

8. a. spelling

b. fragment

c. spelling

d. fragment

e. confused word

9. a. capitalization

b. confused word

c. run-together or end punctuation

d. subject–verb agreement

e. fragment

f. comma

10. a. fragment

b. run-together or end punctuation

c. fragment

d. spelling

e. comma

f. pronoun agreement

Appendix 2C: Editing Quotient Error Chart

Put an X in the square that corresponds to each error you made. Then record your errors in the categories below to find out where you might need help.

	a	b	c	d	e	f	g
1							
2							
3							
4							
5							
6							
7							
8							
9							
10							

Fragments   1a _____   1b _____   2c _____   2e _____   3d _____
                         4a _____   6b _____   7e _____   8b _____   8d _____
                         9e _____   10a _____ 10c _____

Run-together sentences 1c _____   1d _____   2a _____   3b _____   4f _____
                         5a _____   5d _____   6d _____   7b _____   7c _____
                         9c _____   10b _____

Subject–verb agreement 2b _____   2d _____   9d _____

Verb forms   3a _____   3e _____

Pronoun agreement   4b _____   4c _____   4d _____   4e _____   10f _____

Modifiers   5b _____   5c _____

End punctuation   1c _____   1d _____   2a _____   3b _____   4f _____
                         5a _____   5d _____   6d _____   6e _____   7b _____
                         7c _____   9c _____   10b _____

Commas   6c _____   9f _____   10e _____

Capitalization   6a _____   9a _____

Abbreviations   7d _____

Numbers   3c _____   7a _____

Confused words   8e _____   9b _____

Spelling   8a _____   8c _____   10d _____

Appendix 3: Test Yourself Answers

Here are the answers to the Test Yourself questions from the beginning of each chapter in the Handbook (Part IV). Where are your strengths? Where are your weaknesses?

Chapter 18: Parts of Speech (p. 360)

adj   n   pro pro v   adv prep   pro v pro   adj   n   prep n
The personality trait that I like best about myself is my healthy sense of humor.

adj   n   adv adj   n   v pro v   adv v   pro   adj prep pro
No matter how bad a situation is, I can usually say something funny to everyone.

 conj   adj   adj   n   v   v pro v pro pro v   n prep n   adv
When Toby's ancient car was stolen, I told him it was a piece of junk anyway,

conj pro v   adj prep   adj   n   pro   v pro int pro   v   adv adv
and I felt sorry for the foolish person who stole it. Man, we laughed so hard,

     v   adj   n   v prep   n prep   n   adv   pro n   int
imagining the car thief stalled on the side of the road somewhere in town. Oh,

   adv v adj   n   pro pro v/adv adv   v   prep prep   n   conj   n
there are some things that I don't ever joke about, like death and diseases.

    n   v v   adv   adj   prep v prep adj   n
A person would be extremely insensitive to joke about those situations.

Chapter 19: Phrases and Clauses (p. 379)

<u>After the concert</u>, [we decided <u>to get some food</u>.]

<u>To get a good grade</u> <u>on the test</u>, [I know I have <u>to study harder</u>.]

[Mallory will get] [what she wants <u>out of life</u>] [because she <u>is assertive</u>.]

[Benito lives <u>in the brick house</u> <u>at the end</u> <u>of the block</u> <u>behind the park</u>.]

[Do you <u>want</u> <u>to see</u> <u>a movie</u> <u>with us</u>?]

Chapter 20: Subjects and Verbs (p. 387)

(We) really <u>liked</u> the movie.

(Melissa) and (Giselle) <u>left</u> early.

(She) <u>is</u> in class.

<u>Clean</u> your room. (implied (You))

The (Masons) <u>have</u> never <u>remodeled</u> their kitchen.

(She) <u>checked</u> the oil and <u>put</u> air in the tires.

Chapter 21: Fragments (p. 396)

_____ We were hoping that the test would be easy.

___X___ Which he did not see at first.

_____ She wanted to become a musician.

___X___ Running to catch the plane, with her suitcase flying.

___X___ Since the newspaper had reported it.

Chapter 22: Fused Sentences and Comma Splices (p. 410)

Jennifer was elected Academic President,/I voted for her.

The beach is a great getaway/we're fortunate it's only 45 minutes away.

He wanted to participate, but he wasn't sure of the rules.

Casey is hard to get to know/she hides her thoughts and feelings well.

I hope I get into Dr. Jones's class,/I hear he's the best teacher to get.

Chapter 23: Regular and Irregular Verbs (p. 420)

_____X_____ We _brang_ our new neighbor a pizza for dinner.

_____ My brother _married_ on February 14—Valentine's Day.

_____X_____ He _drug_ the heavy suitcase down the street.

_____X_____ This CD _costed_ $15.

_____X_____ My roommate's water bed _has sprang_ a leak.

Chapter 24: Verb Tense (p. 432)

_____X_____ We _be planning_ on leaving in the morning.

_____ The team _chose_ an alligator as its mascot.

_____X_____ My sister _practice_ the flute every day.

_____X_____ He _don't look_ old enough to drive.

_____X_____ Over 1,000 students _apply_ to my college this year.

Chapter 25: Subject–Verb Agreement (p. 447)

_____X_____ _Ben_ and _Tess has_ become great friends.

_____X_____ _Each_ of the nurses _are_ with a patient.

_____X_____ _Macaroni and cheese are_ my favorite food.

_____ There _are_ two _trains_ to Baltimore in the morning.

_____X_____ _Everyone are_ ready to leave.

Chapter 26: More on Verbs (p. 461)

_____I_____ When my brother won the gold medal, my father looks very proud.

_____P_____ All new employees are trained by a professional.

_____P_____ The child was saved by the firefighters.

_____P_____ My friend got home early, so we go to the movies.

_____I_____ The student was given the answers in advance.

Chapter 27: Pronoun Problems (p. 469)

The toy was ~~hers'~~ to begin with. _(hers)_

Diego told Megan and ~~I~~ the funniest story. _(me)_

He can run a lot faster than ~~me~~. _(I)_

Those ~~there~~ ballet shoes are Laura's. _(Those)_

Ted and ~~me~~ are going to the game tonight. _(I)_

Chapter 28: Pronoun Reference and Point of View (p. 481)

Emily and Grace decided that she would try out for the team.

They say you should drink eight glasses of water a day.

I take the bus because you can save a lot of money that way.

The reporter did not check her facts or talk to the main witness, which she regretted.

It says to notify the dean if you are dropping a class.

Chapter 29: Pronoun Agreement (p. 489)

Harriett and Maureen walked their dogs in the park.

Each person is responsible for their own transportation.

Although the <u>pieces</u> of furniture were used, <u>it</u> looked new.

Someone left <u>their</u> dirty dishes in the sink.

Everyone contributed <u>his</u> work to the assignment.

Chapter 30: Adjectives (p. 498)

The <u>gray</u> stingrays were very <u>beautiful</u>.

We were <u>more happier</u> when the rain cooled the <u>hot</u> day.

This is the <u>worstest</u> cold I've ever had.

<u>This</u> textbook is <u>more better</u> than <u>that</u> one.

She is the <u>oldest</u> of the <u>two</u> sisters.

Chapter 31: Adverbs (p. 509)

We were led <u>quickly</u> out the back door.

He hugged her <u>tight</u> when he saw her.

Tina left <u>early</u> because she was<u>n't</u> feeling <u>good</u>.

She feels <u>badly</u> that she could<u>n't</u> stay.

I ca<u>n't</u> <u>never</u> meet on Tuesdays because I work that night.

Chapter 32: Modifier Errors (p. 522)

When we arrived at the concert, Sandy told her mother <u>that she should call home</u>.

<u>Before going to the store</u>, the car needed gas.

The teacher told the students their grades would be posted <u>before she dismissed them</u>.

<u>To enter the contest</u>, the application must be submitted by Friday.

We found the magazine and put it in a safe place <u>that had an article about saving money</u>.

Chapter 33: End Punctuation (p. 531)

That car almost hit us*!*

How can you say that*?*

She didn't want to go on the trip.

He asked if he could go.

I absolutely refuse to be a part of this*!*

Chapter 34: Commas (p. 539)

We went to the plaza, and we saw a great movie.

When we get really tired, we act really silly.

"He's taking flying lessons", said Steven.

The job market, however, is starting to look better.

On Saturday, we went hiking, fishing, and camping.

He was born August 5, 1985, in Duluth, Minnesota.

Chapter 35: Apostrophes (p. 553)

The followers went into their leader's home.

It's not important that you understand its every function.

That's not a good enough reason to believe Tracy's story.

The children's toys were scattered around the room.

Charles's party was a lot of fun.

Chapter 36: Quotation Marks (p. 563)

"Let's have a picnic," she said.

My mom screamed, "Tom! Get this spider!"

"Put ice on the muscle," said Dr. Jansen, "as soon as possible."

I read three poems, including "The Groundhog."

Derek said, "I'll make dinner."

Chapter 37: Other Punctuation Marks (p. 572)

Matthew turned his paper in early; Erica decided not to turn in a paper at all.

Dave felt sorry for the defendant; however he had to vote for a conviction.

Aaron needed several items for his dorm room: a comforter, new sheets, a lamp, and a rug.

Inez had only two words to say about bungee jumping —"Never again." *(or :)*

The recipe says to fold *(gently mix)* the berries into the batter. *(or —/—)*

Chapter 38: Capitalization (p. 583)

The Smith family lives on Washington Street.

We fly into Newark Airport and then get a taxi to Seton Hall University.

This term I'm taking Spanish, Biology 200, history, and English.

In June, I drove to California in my Dodge Durango.

We read several plays by Shakespeare, including *Hamlet*.

Chapter 39: Abbreviations and Numbers (p. 590)

<u>Gov.</u> Davis is trying to protect water in this state. *(Governor)*

My dog had <u>4</u> puppies. *(four)*

Over <u>one thousand two hundred and twelve</u> people attended. *(1,212)*

After college, I hope to join the <u>Central Intelligence Agency</u>. *(CIA)*

Crystal just moved to the <u>United States</u> from Spain. *(U.S.)*

Chapter 40: Varying Sentence Structure (p. 599)

Answers will vary.

Chapter 41: Parallelism (p. 607)

We decided <u>to forget about the lawsuit</u> and then <u>moving on with our lives</u>.

Last year, I <u>graduated from college</u>, <u>moved from Texas to California</u>, and <u>have been married</u>.

My sister and brother raise money <u>to feed the homeless</u> and <u>for building a new shelter</u>.

<u>Exercising</u>, <u>eating right</u>, and <u>water</u> will improve a person's health.

Jack went back to school <u>because he wanted to get a better job</u> and <u>because of the girls on campus</u>.

Chapter 42: Combining Sentences (p. 613)

Answers will vary.

Chapter 43: Standard and Nonstandard English (p. 626)

So she goes, can't I meet you at the theater? *(slang)*

Julie be planning the farewell party. *(incorrect)*

We were totally grossed out. *(slang)*

They changed the tire theirselves. *(incorrect)*

We're jamming in the morning. *(slang)*

Chapter 44: Easily Confused Words (p. 636)

I have to (<u>accept</u>, except) that I won't be graduating this spring.

(Who's, <u>Whose</u>) bike is this?

I'm not saying (<u>it's</u>, its) Johnny's fault.

We are going to need (<u>their</u>, there, they're) help.

(Wear, <u>Where</u>, Were) did you say your parents lived?

Chapter 45: Spelling (p. 647)

My cousin just moved to a <u>forign</u> country. *(foreign)*

Your grandmother makes <u>delishous</u> chicken and dumplings. *(delicious)*

Dennis is trying to <u>persuaid</u> me to join his fraternity. *(persuade)*

Winning two years in a row is quite an <u>achievment</u>. *(achievement)*

Eat your <u>vegtables</u>. *(vegetables)*

Appendix 4: Revising a Paragraph

Peer Evaluation Form A

Use the following questions to evaluate your partner's paragraph in a particular rhetorical mode. Then, continue your evaluation with the standard revision items on the following pages. Direct your comments to your partner. Explain your answers as thoroughly as possible to help your partner revise.

WRITER: _____   **PEER:** _____

Describing

1. Is the dominant impression clearly communicated? If not, how can the writer make it clearer?
2. Does the paragraph *show* rather than *tell*?

Narrating

3. What is the paragraph's main point? If you're not sure, show the writer how he or she can make the main point clearer.
4. Does the writer use the five *W*s and one *H* to construct the paragraph? Where does the paragraph need more information?
5. Does the writer use vivid descriptive details in the paragraph? Where can more details be added?

Illustrating

6. What is the paragraph's main point? If you're not sure, show the writer how he or she can make the main point clearer.
7. Did the writer choose examples that focus on the main point? If not, which examples need to be changed?
8. Does the writer use a sufficient number of examples to make his or her point? Where can more examples be added?

Analyzing a Process

9. Does the writer state in the topic sentence what the reader should be able to do or understand by the end of the paragraph? If not, what information does the topic sentence need to be clearer?
10. Does the remainder of the paragraph explain the rest of the process? If not, what seems to be missing?

Comparing and Contrasting

11. Does the paragraph state the point the writer is trying to make with a comparison in the topic sentence? If not, what part of the comparison does the writer need to focus on?
12. Does the writer choose items to compare and contrast that will make his or her point most effectively? What details need to be added to make the comparison more effective?

Dividing and Classifying

13. What is the overall purpose for the paragraph, and is it stated in the topic sentence? If not, where does the paragraph need clarification?

14. Does the writer divide the general topic into categories (division) and explain each category with details and examples (classification)? If not, where is more division or classification needed?

Defining

15. Does the paragraph have a clear audience and purpose? What are they? If you are not sure, how can the writer make them clearer?

16. Does the writer define his or her term or idea by synonym, category, or negation? Is this approach effective? Why or why not?

17. Does the writer use examples to expand on his or her definition of the term or idea? Where does the definition need more information?

Analyzing Causes and Effects

18. Does the topic sentence make a clear statement about what is being analyzed? If not, what information does it need to be clearer?

19. Does the writer use facts and details to support the topic sentence? What details need to be added?

20. Does the writer include the *real* causes and effects for his or her topic? What details are unnecessary?

Arguing

21. Does the writer state his or her opinion on the subject matter in the topic sentence? What information is missing?

22. Who is the intended audience for this paragraph? Does the writer adequately persuade this audience? Why or why not?

23. Does the writer choose appropriate evidence to support the topic sentence? What evidence is needed? What evidence is unnecessary?

Peer Evaluation Form B

After applying the specialized questions in Peer Evaluation Form A to your partner's paragraph, use the following questions to help you complete the revision process. Direct your comments to your partner. Explain your answers as thoroughly as possible to help your partner revise.

WRITER: _____ PEER: _____

Topic Sentence

1. Does the topic sentence convey the paragraph's controlling idea?

Development

2. Does the paragraph contain enough specific details to develop the topic sentence?

Unity

3. Do all the sentences in the paragraph support the topic sentence?

Organization

4. Is the paragraph organized so that readers can easily follow it?

Coherence

5. Do the sentences move smoothly and logically from one to the next?

Appendix 5: Revising an Essay

Essay Peer Evaluation Form

Use the following questions to evaluate your partner's essay. Direct your comments to your partner. Explain your answers as thoroughly as possible to help your partner revise.

WRITER: _____ PEER: _____

Thesis Statement

1. Does the thesis statement contain the paragraph's controlling idea and appear as the first or last sentence in the introduction?

Basic Elements

2. Does the writer include effective basic elements (title, introduction, single-topic paragraphs, conclusion)?

Development

3. Is the essay adequately developed (thesis, specific, and enough details)?

Unity

4. Is the essay unified (topics relate to thesis and sentences in paragraphs relate to topic sentences)?

Organization

5. Is the essay organized logically (including the paragraphs within the essay)?

Coherence

6. Do the paragraphs and sentences move smoothly and logically from one to the next?

Appendix 6: Editing

Peer Evaluation Form

Use the following questions to help you find editing errors in your partner's paragraph. Mark the errors directly on your partner's paper using the editing symbols on the inside back cover.

WRITER: _____ PEER: _____

Sentences

1. Does each sentence have a subject and verb?

   Mark any fragments you find with **frag.**

   Put a slash (/) between any fused sentences and comma splices.

2. Do all subjects and verbs agree?

   Mark any subject–verb agreement errors you find with **sv.**

3. Do all pronouns agree with their nouns?

   Mark any pronoun errors you find with **pro agr.**

4. Are all modifiers as close as possible to the words they modify?

   Mark any modifier errors you find with **ad** (adjective or adverb problem), **mm** (misplaced modifier), or **dm** (dangling modifier).

Punctuation and Mechanics

5. Are sentences punctuated correctly?

   Mark any punctuation errors you find with the appropriate symbol under Unit 5 of the editing symbols (inside back cover).

6. Are words capitalized properly?

   Mark any capitalization errors you find with **lc** (lowercase) or **cap** (capital).

Word Choice and Spelling

7. Are words used correctly?

   Mark any words that are used incorrectly with **wc** (word choice) or **ww** (wrong word).

8. Are words spelled correctly?

   Mark any misspelled words you find with **sp.**

Appendix 7: Error Log

On the following chart, list any grammar, punctuation, and mechanics errors you make in your writing. Then, to the right of this label, record (1) the actual error from your writing, (2) the rule for correcting this error, and (3) your correction.

Error		
	Example	I went to the new seafood restaurant and I ordered the shrimp.
Comma	**Rule**	Always use a comma before *and, but, for, nor, or, so,* and *yet* when joining two independent clauses.
	Correction	I went to the new seafood restaurant, and I ordered the shrimp.
Error	**Example**	
	Rule	
	Correction	
Error	**Example**	
	Rule	
	Correction	
Error	**Example**	
	Rule	
	Correction	
Error	**Example**	
	Rule	
	Correction	
Error	**Example**	
	Rule	
	Correction	
Error	**Example**	
	Rule	
	Correction	
Error	**Example**	
	Rule	
	Correction	
Error	**Example**	
	Rule	
	Correction	

Appendix 8: Spelling Log

On this chart, record any words you misspell, and write the correct spelling in the space next to the misspelled word. In the right column, write a note to yourself to help you remember the correct spelling. (See the first line for an example.) Refer to this chart as often as necessary to avoid misspelling the same words again.

Misspelled Word	Correct Spelling	Definition/Notes
there	their	there = place; their = pronoun; they're = "they are"

CREDITS

CHAPTER 2

Micanopy by Bailey White from *Mama Makes Up Her Mind,* 1993. Reproduced by permission of Perseus Books Group.

CHAPTER 3

Colin Powell, "A Promise to Our Youth."

Dave Barry, *The Ugly Truth About Beauty. The Miami Herald,* 1998.

Mario Cuomo, "Freedom of the Press Must Be Unlimited."

CHAPTER 6

Lord Acton, *The Study of History,* 1895.

Mike Rose, "Lives on the Boundary: a moving account of the struggles and achievements of America's educationally under prepared." Penguin Group (USA) Inc.

Joseph Bruchac, "Notes of a Translator's Son."

Louise Erdrich, "American Horse."

"Magpies," from *The Joy Luck Club* by Amy Tan, copyright © 1989 by Amy Tan. Used by permission of G.P. Putnam's Sons, a division of Penguin Group (USA) Inc.

"Life with Father" by Itabari Njeri from *Every Good-Bye Ain't Gone* as published in *Harper's Magazine* January 1990. Reproduced by permission of Miriam Altshuler Literary Agency.

CHAPTER 7

James Baldwin.

Russell Baker, *Growing Up,* 1982.

Brent Staples, *Parallel Time: Growing Up in Black and White,*1994.

Bernard Bragg, *Deaf in America: Voices from a Culture.* President and Fellows of Harvard College,1988.

From *Woman Hollering Creek.* Copyright © 1991 by Sandra Cisneros. Published by Vintage Books, a division of Random House, Inc., and originally in hardcover by Random House, Inc. By permission of Susan Bergholz Literary Services, New York, NY and Lamy, NM. All rights reserved.

"Choosing The Path With Honour" by Michael H Arredondo, MD, from *Native Americans,* vol. 19, no. 3–4 (Fall–Winter 2002). Reproduced by permission of Michael H Arredondo, MD.

CHAPTER 8

Wallace Terry, "It's Such a Pleasure to Learn."

Lynn Peters Alder, "A Century of Women."

William Butler Yeats

"Mute in an English-Only World" by Chang-Rae Lee from *The New York Times,* April 18, 1996. Reproduced by permission of Chang-Rae Lee.

"Walk on By" by Brent Staples from *Ms. Magazine* (1986). Reproduced by permission of Brent Staples.

CHAPTER 9

Mike Shanahan, "Playing to Win: Do You Think Like a Champ?" *Entrepreneur,* September 1999.

"Reading a Process Analysis Paragraph." eHow, Inc.

"Getting Out Of Debt (And Staying Out)," by Julia Bourland from *The Go-Girl Guide,* 2000. Reproduced by permission of McGraw Hill.

"Coming Over," from *Immigrant Kids* by Russell Freedman, copyright © 1980 by Russell Freedman. Used by permission of Dutton Children's Books, a division of Penguin Group (USA) Inc.

CHAPTER 10

F. Scott Fitzgerald

Barrio Boy by Ernesto Galarza. Copyright © 1971 by the University of Notre Dame Press. Reprinted with permission.

"Why Men Fail," by David Brooks from *New York Times,* September 10, 2012. Reproduced by permission of New York Times.

Shannon Brownlee, "Inside the Teen Brain: Behavior Can Be Baffling When Young Minds Are Taking Shape." *U.S News.com,* August 1, 1999.

Marie Winn, "Young Children," v53 n5 September, 1998.

Deborah Tannen, "You just don't understand: women and men in conversation." William Morrow & Company, Inc., 1990.

CHAPTER 11

Debra Phillips, "Tween Beat." *Entrepreneur Magazine,* September 1, 1999.

Sarah Hodgson, "Dog Perfect: The User Friendly Guide to a Well Behaved Dog." Wiley Publishing Inc, 1995.

From *You've Only Got Three Seconds* by Camille Lavington and Stephanie Losee, copyright © 1997 by Camille Lavington and Stephanie Losee. Used by permission of Doubleday, a division of Random House, Inc.

"The Ways We Lie" by Stephanie Ericsson. Copyright ©1992 by Stephanie Ericsson. Originally published by *The Utne Reader.* Reprinted by permission of Dunham Literary, Inc. as agents for the author.

CHAPTER 12

Felix Frankfurter.

"The Fire Inside" by Gary Mack and David Casstevens from *Mind Gym: An Athlete's Guide To Inner Excellence.* Copyright © 2002. Reproduced by permission of McGraw-Hill.

"What Is Poverty?" by Jo Goodwin Parker from *America's Other Children: Public Schools Outside Suburbia,* 1971. Reproduced by permission of University of Oklahoma Press.

Mary Pipher, *Writing to Change the World.* Riverhead Books, 2006.

CHAPTER 13

E. M. Forster, *Aspects of the Novel*. Literary Estates Society of Authors, 1927.

"The children became…parents' immigrant ways" from *Immigrant Kids* by Russell Freedman, copyright © 1980 by Russell Freedman. Used by permission of Dutton Children's Books, a division of Penguin Group (USA) Inc.

Robert Hine, *Second Sight*. The Regents of the University of California Press, 1993.

From MSNBC Interactive News, LLC, 2006. Reproduced by permission of MSNBC Interactive News, LLC via Copyright Clearance Center.

"Life Sentences" by Corky Clifton from *The Angolite: The Prison News Magazine*, June 1989. Reproduced by permission of *The Angolite: The Prison News Magazine*.

CHAPTER 14

From "Social Networking Benefits Validated," by Karen Goff Goldberg, *The Washington Times*, January 28, 2009. Reproduced by permission of The Washington Times.

Marie Winn, *The Plug-In Drug*. New York: Viking Press, 1977.

From "DREAM Act Would Boost Economy," by Alan Gomez. Reproduced by permission of *USA Today*, PARS International Corp.

From "The Economic Benefits of Passing the DREAM Act," by Juan Carlos Guzman and Raul Jara. Reproduced by permission of Center for American Progress.

From "The Flight From Conversation," by Sherry Turkle, *The New York Times*, Sunday Review - The Opinion Pages, April 21, 2012. Reproduced by permission of *The New York Times* via Copyright Clearance Center.

From "Social Media's Small, Positive Role in Human Relationships," by Zeynep Tufekci, *The Atlantic*, April 25, 2012. Reproduced by permission of Zeynep Tufekci.

CHAPTER 15

"Hunting for Hope" by Scott Russell Sanders from *Hunting for Hope*. Copyright © 1998 by Scott Russell Sanders. Reproduced by permission of Beacon Press, Boston.

C. H. Knoblauch.

INDEX